W9-AMY-202

THE DYNAMICS OF GLOBAL DOMINANCE

THE DYNAMICS

of GLOBAL DOMINANCE

EUROPEAN OVERSEAS EMPIRES, 1415–1980

David B. Abernethy

Yale University Press *New Haven and London*

Copyright © 2000 by Yale University.
All rights reserved.
This book may not be reproduced, in whole or in part, including
illustrations, in any form (beyond that copying permitted by Sections
107 and 108 of the U.S. Copyright Law and except by reviewers for the
public press), without written permission from the publishers.

Designed by Gregg Chase
Set in Meta and Minion typefaces
Printed in the United States of America.

Library of Congress Cataloging-in-Publication Data
Abernethy, David B.
The dynamics of global dominance : European overseas empires, 1415–
1980 / David B. Abernethy.
p.   cm.
Includes bibliographical references and index.
ISBN 0-300-07304-6 (alk. paper)
1. Europe—Territorial expansion.   2. Europe—Colonies.
3. Discoveries in geography.   I. Title.
D210 .A19 2000
940—dc21   00-033472

A catalogue record for this book is available from the
British Library.

The paper in this book meets the guidelines for permanence and
durability of the Committee on Production Guidelines for Book
Longevity of the Council on Library Resources.

10 9 8 7 6 5 4 3 2 1

(*Overleaf*) Arrival of the party led by Cortés on the Mexican
shore prior to the march to Tenochtitlán, 1519. By a sixteenth-
century Aztec artist. From Arthur Anderson and Charles
Dibble, *The War of Conquest* (Salt Lake City: University of
Utah Press, 1978), p. 1.

CONTENTS

ACKNOWLEDGMENTS

Pursuing answers to a big, important, puzzling question has been a deeply satisfying experience. I am grateful for freedom to follow where curiosity took me, for time to explore hunches as well as promising leads, and for opportunities to discuss with others what I found. Many people offered intellectual stimulation and helpful criticism along the way. I particularly thank Gabriel Almond, Alexander George, Richard Roberts, and Paul Sniderman. I learned a great deal from my fellow instructors in the topic "The World Outside the West," a two-quarter course taught at Stanford for many years and supported by the National Endowment for the Humanities. My colleagues in this venture were Harumi Befu, Joel Beinin, George Collier, Peter Duus, James Fox, John Rick, Richard Roberts, Lyman Van Slyke, and Stephano Varese. Thanks also to Robert Bates, Frederick Cooper, Mariano Cuellar, Larry Diamond, Peter Ekeh, George Fredrickson, James Gibbs, Stephen Haber, Craig Heller, Renu Heller, A. H. M. Kirk-Greene, Stephen Krasner, Ali Mazrui, John Meyer, Michel Oksenberg, John Paden, Jack Rakove, John Rickford, Oscar Rosenbloom, John Saul, the late Aaron Segal, Charles Tilly, Tetsuro Toya, Barry Weingast, and Crawford Young. Karen Fung, archivist for the Hoover Institution's Africa Collection, has been a continuing source of bibliographic leads. Yonatan Eyal, an undergraduate I quickly came to regard as a colleague, made several helpful suggestions. Research assistance was provided by Carol Rose, editorial assistance by Jennifer Daniell Bélissent. Maps for chapters 3 and 4 were prepared by Bayard Colyear III of Stanford Visual Arts Services. The map for chapter 7 was prepared by Melissa Mills.

A happy by-product of teaching students is learning from them. I benefited greatly from reactions to my undergraduate lecture course "Colonialism and Nationalism in the Third World" and from papers for research seminars entitled "Theories of European Imperialism," "Decolonization in Asia and Africa, 1940–80," and "Legacies of Empire."

A great university library is a priceless resource. An astonishingly high portion of the works I wanted to consult was accessible in Stanford's Green Library and the Hoover Institution's collections. I thank those on library staffs who make books and journals available so readers and authors can quietly converse, even when separated by centuries and continents.

I deeply appreciate the support of John Covell, senior editor at Yale University Press, and thoughtful, meticulous attention to the manuscript by Lawrence Kenney, senior manuscript editor. Critiques by several anonymous reviewers led me to recast some of my arguments, correct factual errors, and write more succinctly.

I remain responsible, of course, for errors that may remain as well as for contestable judgment calls.

My wife, Susan, has been wonderfully supportive while I worked on this project for more years than either of us anticipated. She helped me lead a more balanced life when research, writing, and editing threatened at times to unbalance it. My sons, Bruce and Brad, helped me see new things through their eyes. Brad cogently critiqued an earlier version of chapter 2.

This book is dedicated to the memory of my parents, Bradford S. Abernethy and Jean Beaven Abernethy. They introduced me early on to the world outside the United States. Their love of travel, their enthusiasm for cross-cultural encounters, their pleasure in helping others—these qualities shone through, positively affecting people around them. My parents set me on my career path in more ways than I know.

Part I

WESTERN EUROPE
AND THE WORLD

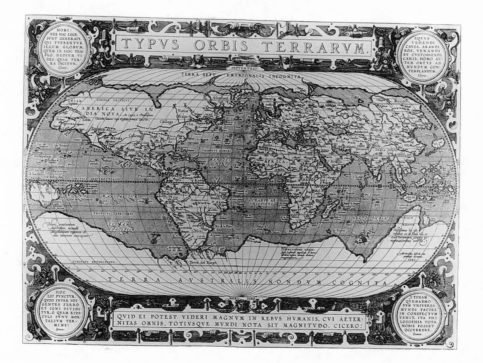

(*Overleaf*) World map from Abraham Ortelius, *Theatrum Orbis Terrarum* (Antwerp, 1570).

1
Ceuta, Bojador, and Beyond: Europeans on the Move

On a summer day in the year 1415 a fleet of Portuguese ships set off from Lisbon. On board were the king, John I, his three sons, and soldiers of noble birth from England and France, as well as Portugal. The flotilla was the largest in the country's history and among the most impressive assembled by Europeans to that date. The fleet's departure was accompanied by considerable public fanfare. Yet the event must also have been marked by confusion and uncertainty. King John had studiously avoided revealing the destination or mission of his ships. He had publicly quarreled with a ruler in the area now known as Holland, so it seemed likely that the fleet would head north. But the dispute was an elaborate ruse. The fleet took a southward course. Rounding Portugal's southwestern extremity, Cape St. Vincent, it sailed through the Strait of Gibraltar, controlled on both shores by Muslims known to Europeans as Moors. The ships dropped anchor upon reaching Ceuta, a North African port and trading center located directly across the strait from the Rock of Gibraltar. The Portuguese positioned themselves on both sides of the narrow promontory on which the town was built.

The next day they fulfilled King John's hidden objective by launching an assault on Ceuta. The town and its citadel were captured after a pitched battle. Victory was celebrated a few days later in the local mosque, hastily converted by exorcism—with salt and water—into a Christian church. Following High Mass the king knighted his sons, who, according to the royal chronicler of these events, had distinguished themselves in battle. The royal party then returned home, leaving behind twenty-seven hundred men to defend Portugal's new acquisition against expected counterattacks by the Moors.[1]

In many respects the capture of Ceuta was typical of other such episodes in the Middle Ages. The most enthusiastic advocates of the expedition were the king's sons, eager to win knighthood in battle, and attacking the Muslims carried on the tradition of the Crusades.[2] Ceuta was, furthermore, part of the Mediterranean world, with a history linking the town back to the empires of antiquity. Previous successful invaders included Carthaginians, Romans, Byzantines, Vandals, Visigoths, and—early in the eighth century—Arabs.

In other important respects, however, the Portuguese expedition and victory marked a new phase in world history, the advent of a modern era of European-centered empires that was to extend around the globe. For seven centuries prior to 1415, Muslims descended from Arabs or North African Berbers held territory in western Europe. Muslim armies advanced through the Iberian Peninsula into central France before being defeated in 732 at the Battle of Tours. Territory controlled by the Moors was much reduced by the early fifteenth century. But not until 1492, when the ruler of Granada, in southern Spain, was defeated would they lose their last west European foothold. With the capture of Ceuta, Europeans took the offensive to gain a foothold of their own in another continent.

This was not their first such foothold. Rome's troops had subdued Carthage and incorporated swaths of North Africa into the Roman empire. By the tenth century, Norse sailors founded settlements along the "New World's" northeastern reaches. Crusaders at times held portions of the Holy Land, and Venetians established trading centers along the North African coast, in the Levant, and on the shores of the Black Sea well before 1415.[3] But Ceuta became the first site since Roman times to be held by Europeans on a sustained basis and effectively administered from the capital of a European polity. The soldiers King John left behind were able to sustain Portugal's claims in the face of sieges and attacks by the Moors. In fact, Ceuta remained a Portuguese possession until 1580, when control passed to Spain, which still administers it. The little North African town whose capture marks the start of a long history of modern European imperialism is, ironically, one of the last relics of overseas empire today.

Portugal's victory at Ceuta represents a turning point in world history in other respects. The outcome was due in large measure to King John's ability to mobilize the material wealth and human energies of the first European nation-state. The domestic resources of a centralized and ethnically homogeneous polity were used to project the state's power overseas.[4] Other west European countries would follow suit as their monarchs and bureaucrats gained strength relative to the regional nobles below and Roman Catholic Church above them. Imperial expansion in turn aided European state building by placing externally generated resources at the disposal of central government authorities.

Widely held conceptions of military and political power began to shift with the Portuguese victory. The ease with which ships transported soldiers from Lisbon to North Africa showed that control of the oceans could lead to conquest of lands and peoples far from imperial capitals. A precedent was set for expansion to wherever the

Europeans' ships might take them. A state's capacity to command the high seas became an important indicator of power in its own right. Naval power could also be the means to become a great land power, for it permitted inclusion within imperial boundaries of territories on other continents.

The capture of Ceuta had the significant effect of stimulating Portuguese efforts at exploration, trade, and conquest along Africa's Atlantic coast. The youngest of King John's sons on the expedition was Prince Henry, known to English-speaking posterity as Henry the Navigator. The prince's participation in this event evidently reinforced an already strong personal interest in Africa. Ceuta was a northern terminus of trade routes bringing gold, ivory, and slaves across the Sahara. Henry knew that if Portugal could access these valuable resources at the point of origin, its gains would exceed those from controlling Ceuta.

Direct access across vast territories held by Moors was out of the question. A sea voyage was required. But before 1415 no Portuguese vessels had ventured south of Cape Bojador, a desolate headland some 850 miles southwest of the Strait of Gibraltar. Prince Henry doubtless hoped that people living beyond the cape could supply the desired commodities. He also hoped and quite possibly expected that these people would be Christians. Persistent rumors circulating in Europe told of Prester John, a Christian monarch living somewhere south of the Muslim-controlled lands. If Prester John could be found, prospects for gainful trade *and* for a grand alliance of Christian forces to defeat Islam would be greatly enhanced.

Enticed by such possibilities and encouraged by the success of the Ceuta expedition, Prince Henry was instrumental in recruiting, outfitting, financing, and motivating the men who eventually sailed beyond Cape Bojador. Not long after returning from Ceuta he established a command post of sorts at Sagres, on Cape St. Vincent. There he sought to link the basic science of astronomy with the more applied sciences of ship construction, navigational equipment design, and cartography. For many years expeditions sent out under his semiofficial aegis proved unwilling or unable to pass south of Cape Bojador. This landmark became known as the Cape of Fear, a sign that it was a psychological as well as a physical barrier to sailors. To pass beyond it a ship had to veer far out to sea to avoid mists and tricky currents near the coast. South of it lay unknown perils at sea. The cape itself offered no evidence that favorable trading prospects lay ahead, for its hinterland was a virtually uninhabited desert. Perhaps most troublesome was the challenge of returning home. Winds and currents prevented sailors from retracing the route close to the coast that took them to the cape.[5]

At last, in 1434, Henry's squire Gil Eannes broke the barrier, rounding Cape Bojador in a small *barcha*. Eannes resolved the return-voyage problem by heading seaward in a northwesterly direction toward the nearby Canary Islands, then taking the westerly winds from those islands back to Portugal. The precedent was set for a series of voyages that took Portuguese sailors as far south as Sierra Leone by the time of Henry's death in 1460. Explorers found little gold as they pushed steadily away from home base. But they did capture some of the people living along the coast, selling them for handsome profits in Portugal as slaves. No fabled Christian kingdom was found. But most inhabitants of the more verdant coastal lands south of the desert whom the sailors encountered were not Muslims. This doubtless stimulated Portuguese hopes that the Africans they met might readily be converted.[6]

Portuguese sailors set out upon the Atlantic in 1415 to enter the Mediterranean, a miniature ocean whose outlines had been known for centuries. As its name indicates, the Mediterranean occupies the center of a multicultural zone, facilitating economic and cultural exchange among the peoples of southern Europe, northern Africa, and western Asia.[7] Perhaps the most lasting effect of capturing a Mediterranean port was, ironically, to increase interest in the ocean lapping Portugal's own shores. The size and contours of this immense body of water were unknown. Yet after 1434 there was good reason to believe that ignorance of these matters would some day be dispelled. Once Gil Eannes showed that Cape Bojador need no longer be the Cape of Fear, sailors from Portugal and other west European states could set out on the Atlantic for distant lands whose inhabitants were far more culturally and physically diverse than the Mediterranean's peoples. Beyond Bojador lay the coastlines of the rest of the world.

EUROPE'S COLONIAL EMPIRES: DISTINCTIVE FEATURES

In the half millennium following Ceuta's capture, the rulers of eight countries that together account for a mere 1.6 percent of the land surface of the earth—Portugal, Spain, France, the United Kingdom, the Netherlands, Belgium, Germany, and Italy—claimed vast territories and asserted sovereign rights over hundreds of millions of human beings. It is highly unlikely that people from any part of the world should have made such audacious claims, let alone backed up their words with effective actions. Yet this is the implausible scenario that unfolded.

What occurred in the course of Europe's expansion had a profound impact on the modern history of all continents. Since the fifteenth century west Europeans have sent forth their inhabitants, their several versions of the Christian faith, their attitudes toward nature, their languages, intellectual and political controversies, consumer goods, diseases, death-dealing and life-enhancing technologies, commercial institutions, government bureaucracies, and values. Entire regions were directly incorporated, in a kind of global enclosure movement, into overseas empires.[8]

Europeans were not, of course, the only expansionist actors in the centuries following Ceuta's capture. Western Europe itself, invaded from North Africa in the eighth century and briefly threatened by Mongol forces in the thirteenth, confronted a new round of external challenges in the fifteenth. These came from the Ottoman Turks, who in 1453 captured Constantinople, the Byzantine capital and center of Eastern Orthodox Christianity. Ottoman rulers transformed the city into a center of Islamic arts and letters, went on to conquer large portions of the Balkans, and advanced as far as the outskirts of Vienna in 1529. The greatest Ottoman ruler, Suleiman I (r. 1520–66), was influential in the turbulent affairs of early-Reformation Europe.

Along the eastern edge of continental Europe, Muscovy expanded in several directions after breaking free of the Mongols in 1480. By the seventeenth century Russian czars had extended their claims thousands of miles eastward to the Pacific. During the next two centuries their immense empire was further enlarged along its southern flanks by incorporation of a number of Islamic polities. Russian trading settlements were established along the northwestern coast of North America in the late eighteenth century, providing the basis for claims to Alaska.

Elsewhere in Eurasia the Mughal dynasty, initially under the leadership of Babur (1483–1530), extended its sway over northern and central India. This empire reached its height around 1700. In China, the Ming imperial court sponsored a series of trading and diplomatic expeditions by sea at the same time as the Portuguese were commencing exploration along the African coast. Fleets of huge, heavily laden ships under the direction of Adm. Cheng Ho sailed as far west as the Red Sea and the East African coast before this ambitious initiative to reach out to other societies was halted in the 1430s. In the late seventeenth and eighteenth centuries the Chinese state under the Qing (Manchu) dynasty greatly enlarged its boundaries with campaigns of conquest in Tibet, Xinjiang, and Mongolia. In the late nineteenth and early twentieth centuries a rapidly industrializing Japan under Meiji Restoration leadership took control of portions of the Asian mainland—most notably Korea—as well as Taiwan and numerous smaller islands in the Pacific.

In Africa the Songhai Empire, centered in the Niger River valley, reached its height by the early sixteenth century. The powerful Zulu empire created by Shaka rose during the early nineteenth and had an enormous impact on neighboring southern African societies. In what Europeans termed the New World, the Aztec and Inca empires grew greatly in power and size in the fifteenth and early sixteenth centuries. Numerous other examples could be cited.

The formation of large-scale, relatively centralized polities, commanding obedience and extracting resources from physically and culturally disparate populations, is a recurring theme in human history. West Europeans were not the only peoples with expansionist agendas in the centuries following Portugal's capture of Ceuta, to say nothing of the years preceding it.

Nonetheless, the overseas empires west Europeans constructed in the past five centuries have certain distinctive and in many respects unique features. Their formation was closely associated with the most systematic, extensive exploration of the globe ever undertaken. European explorers obviously did not discover lands already inhabited by other human beings. But they did discover the seas, in that their voyages familiarized them with the huge portion of the earth's surface—some 70 percent—covered by water. Their findings enabled European cartographers to produce the first reasonably accurate images of the size, shape, and interconnectedness of the world's oceans.[9] Whether maritime explorers had imperialist designs or not, the knowledge they accumulated was essential for founding "saltwater" empires.

Because territories Europeans claimed were linked to the governing country, or metropole, by ships designed for lengthy sea voyages, colonies could be geographically dispersed in a way quite different from the empires just noted. Except for Russia (in Alaska) and Japan, the others advanced along land frontiers. The results were contiguous units, not multiple territorial fragments.[10] The first modern European empire, constructed by Portugal, is a classic illustration of dispersed power. In the century following their Ceuta expedition the Portuguese set up trading and settler enclaves along the coasts of Brazil, West Africa, East Africa, southwestern India (Malabar), China, and in the Spice Islands. They controlled two strategic ports: Hormuz, at the entrance to the Persian Gulf, and Malacca, overseeing Indian Ocean– China Sea traffic in the narrow strait between Sumatra and the Malay peninsula. The sun set only briefly on the early Portuguese empire—and not at all on the greatest one, governed by the British.

Dispersal of holdings across latitude and longitude lines gave rise to the idea that each colony should specialize in certain commodities based on its comparative economic advantage. A territory might be valued because it possessed minerals or tropical agricultural products unavailable in Europe. The tendency for metropole and colony to specialize in disparate yet complementary activities, and pressures on colonized peoples to produce designated commodities for export, were much greater when imperial possessions were distant and overseas than when polities expanded along land frontiers.

Geographic dispersal made for enormous diversity in the peoples assembled under one political authority. The differences, not only between colonizers and colonized but also among the colonized, were striking. Each European empire was the arena for an extraordinarily high level of interaction across territorial, racial, linguistic, and religious lines.

The physical space separating a metropole from its colonies meant that rulers and ruled grew up in distinct disease environments. Initial encounters between the two groups could therefore have profound demographic consequences. In the New

World and parts of Oceania, where indigenous peoples had little or no contact with humans from other continents prior to the arrival of Europeans, exposure to the invaders' diseases produced precipitous population declines. This was not the case with the non-European empires mentioned, in which newly subject populations were genetically primed, so to speak, to fight off the diseases of conquerors who were also neighbors.

The expansion of Europe is distinctive in that not one but several empires were constructed at about the same time and administered in parallel. In many respects it makes sense to consider western Europe a single category, analyzing the cumulative impact on other peoples of what is appropriately termed European imperialism. In other ways, however, it is imperative to disaggregate western Europe into its numerous states, several of them busily expanding and administering their own overseas possessions. The polities of western Europe belonged to an interstate system in which each unit was intensely aware of other units and in continual competition— sometimes peaceful, often violent—with them. The rulers of each European state lived with a pervasive sense of insecurity: the fear that neighbors would challenge the state's power and threaten its existence. Competition among these polities assumed a global dimension once the precedent for establishing overseas colonies was set and once knowledge of the possibilities for empire building was dispersed throughout the system. As I argue in part 3, a key to understanding the expansionist dynamic of western Europe is precisely the *dual* character of the region. In cultural, economic, and geographic terms it has long been relatively unified. In political terms it has been fragmented, with recurring outbreaks of bitter internecine warfare. The imperialism of western Europe is also the multiple imperialisms of the region's autonomous components.[11]

European imperialism was marked by its capacity to undermine the power and legitimacy of other expanding political systems. To take several of the post-1415 examples cited earlier, the Ottoman Turks were unable to sustain their claims to North African territory in the face of European military, diplomatic, and economic offensives in the late nineteenth and early twentieth centuries. The final collapse of Ottoman authority in the aftermath of World War I enabled the victorious British and French to become League of Nations mandatory powers, governing Arab populations in portions of the Near East formerly under Ottoman rule. In India, the century from the Battle of Plassey (1757) to the Great Mutiny (1857–58) saw gradual but steady erosion in Mughal power and a corresponding increase in British economic penetration and political influence. The mutiny in turn spurred the British Crown to assume more direct control of large portions of the old Mughal Empire than in the days of informal rule by British East India Company officials. The Qing dynasty, which extended China's territorial authority into the Central Asian interior during the seventeenth and eighteenth centuries, was humiliated in the nineteenth by European "barbarians" attacking from the sea. China lost Hong Kong to Britain in the Opium War of 1839–42, witnessed the destruction of the imperial summer palace in 1860 by a British–French punitive expedition to Beijing, and was forced to cede sovereign rights in key port cities to British, French, German (and Japanese) officials. The so-called treaty ports were foreign colonial enclaves that the Chinese were not able to reclaim until after World War I.

By the time European soldiers entered the savanna interior of West Africa the Songhai Empire had fallen. Songhai's smaller successor states, despite putting up often fierce resistance, were subdued by technically superior weaponry within two decades of the Berlin Conference in 1884–85, which set guidelines for Europe's scramble for Africa. Further south, Zulu warriors were decisively defeated by white Afrikaner (Boer) forces in the Battle of Blood River (1838). Although inflicting heavy losses on British forces at the Battle of Isandhlwana in 1879, the Zulus subsequently lost at Ulundi and could not stave off invasion of their territory by both the Afrikaners and the British. Military resistance collapsed after a brief uprising in 1906 was crushed. In the New World, the powerful Aztec and Inca empires were defeated by the cunning, tenacity, ruthlessness—and infectious diseases—of the Spanish conquistadors within a matter of months following the invaders' arrival.

The arrogant attitude Europeans displayed toward other people was due in large measure to their success at directly challenging the power and prerogatives of non-European rulers. The principal exceptions to this pattern—Japan, Thailand, Afghanistan, and Abyssinia (Ethiopia)—are interesting because the ability of these polities to remain independent in the face of external challenge was so exceptional.

A distinctive feature of the empires I will discuss was the persistent effort of Europeans to undermine and reshape the modes of production, social institutions, cultural patterns, and value systems of indigenous peoples. This transformation agenda, which in many instances proved remarkably successful, was the outward projection of tumultuous changes in the way Europeans themselves lived during the half millennium of their global dominance. At issue here is not whether Europeans were particularly cruel to other peoples in the course of subduing them. The grim truth is that all expanding polities cause loss of life and societal disruption when incorporating others into their domains. Acts of pillage, rape, and mass murder have been committed by advancing armies in diverse times and places throughout history.[12] The crucial difference lay rather in the rulers' actions following conquest. The mechanisms non-European empires devised to extract surplus from newly conquered groups typically did little to alter what these groups already produced. Neither was there substantial change in how commodities sought by new rulers were mined, grown, or fashioned by human labor.[13] In contrast, Europeans often revolutionized production in their colonies. New methods permitted extraction of minerals and metals not accessible to local people. In numerous instances animals and plants were introduced. Horses and pigs, for instance, accompanied early Spanish settlers to the New World. Settlers were responsible for "population explosions of burros in . . . the Canaries, rats in Virginia . . . and rabbits in Australia."[14] Some plants, like citrus fruits and sugarcane, were grown in the Mediterranean region and were familiar to those who transplanted them. But many others—like cassava, cocoa, coffee, groundnuts, maize, quinine, rubber, and tobacco—were not accessible until Europeans reached other world regions. These crops were transferred from one non-European continent to another, frequently through officially sponsored botanical gardens expressly established for this purpose.[15]

Having transferred commercially valuable crops, Europeans employed novel methods of mass producing them for export to the metropole. Colonial plantations may be seen as outdoor factories applying principles of industrial organization and production to tropical and semitropical agriculture well before they were applied to the indoor factories of Europe. In this respect the Industrial Revolution was given a colonial trial run. Both types of factories required large amounts of rigidly controlled human labor. In plantation colonies this typically entailed importing of slaves or indentured servants, whose presence altered a territory's racial composition and social structure as well as economic activities. Novel technologies were deployed to transport mass-produced commodities long distances over land and sea. The structure of precolonial economic life, including the largely self-reliant character of local communities, was changed after contact with a persistently intrusive western Europe.[16]

Non-European empires did not reserve large tracts of land for conquerors who had come to settle. And the number of such settlers was not substantial compared to the subjugated population. In sharp contrast, land alienation on behalf of European settlers and their descendants—with its accompanying dislocation of indigenous ways of life—was a recurring feature in many overseas possessions.[17] Colonies in the New World and the temperate zones of Africa and Oceania offered opportunities for millions of Europeans to migrate. These lands served as vents for expanding home-country populations in a way without parallel in the history of other empires.[18]

The ruling elites of non-European empires did not invariably consider themselves culturally superior to their subjects. In instances in which a group with a pastoral and nomadic tradition imposed itself upon an agricultural and urbanized population, rulers were more likely to assimilate to the culture of the ruled than the reverse. Such was the case when the Mongol Yuan dynasty ruled China (1268–1379); when the Mughals descended to the Indian plains from the mountains of Afghanistan; when the Turks progressed from Central Asia to Anatolia; and when the Aztecs

11

migrated south to the Valley of Mexico in the twelfth century.[19] Quite different were European empire builders, nomads traveling by sea, who with few exceptions showed little or no interest in adjusting to the cultures of their subjects.[20] Their challenge was rather to persuade or coerce indigenous leaders, if not the populace as a whole, to adopt what Europeans believed to be their own clearly superior religion, moral code, language, literature, artistic tradition, legal system, and technology. Adaptation was essentially a one-way process. Upon the shoulders of the colonized was placed the burden of making necessary adjustments.

Europeans were by no means the only rulers with a superiority complex vis-à-vis their subjects. But they displayed this complex in an exceptionally systematic, self-conscious way and in an unusually wide range of symbolic settings. They were ingenious in devising methods to humiliate non-Europeans and unusually skilled at encouraging those they ruled to internalize an inferiority complex. The results were often devastating for the individual and collective self-confidence of subordinate populations.[21]

A major theme of this book is that Europeans were distinctive in mounting a triple assault on other societies: on indigenous institutions of governance, on long-standing patterns of generating and distributing economic assets, and on ideas and values that gave meaning to life. When all these aspects of the old order came under direct and at times simultaneous attack, non-European societies found their ways of life imperiled as never before.

Within the genus of imperialism in human history, the west European version from the fifteenth century onward thus qualifies as a distinctive species, one deserving of study in its own right. It should be neither equated with the larger genus nor too readily broken down into the specific empires—Portuguese, Spanish, British, Dutch, and so forth—comprising its several subspecies. The history of each metropole's empire has been exhaustively recounted. This book examines broader patterns of the rise, fall, character, and impact of the empires considered collectively.

WHY STUDY EUROPE'S OVERSEAS EMPIRES?

The overseas empires deserve careful study, first, because their spatial and temporal dimensions are quite extraordinary. Two-thirds of the United Nations' member states as of January 2000—125 of 188—consisted of territories outside of Europe which at one time were governed by Europeans. Three-fifths of the world's population live in countries whose entire territory has at one time been claimed by a European state. If one includes states portions of whose current territory were under the legal jurisdiction of Europeans—notably China, with its treaty ports—then in excess of 80 percent of human beings now living inhabit states that experienced some version of formal European rule. That rule lasted for more than 250 years in 37 U.N. member states and for more than a century in 60.[22]

Second, the study of European empires raises pivotal intellectual issues. The sheer improbability of one tiny part of the world dominating so many areas for so long cries out for explanation. How and why were Europe's empires formed? How much causal weight should be placed on characteristics of the empire builders, how much on characteristics of peoples who became imperial subjects? What characteristics, whether of colonizers or colonized, are most significant? How can we account for the durability of systems of rule in which ultimate authority over a territory was lodged in a metropolitan capital thousands of miles away?

The overseas empires eventually fell, as colonial dependencies became independent, legally sovereign states. It is easier to understand why improbable political arrangements ended than why they were formed or why they lasted. But imperial collapse poses its own intriguing puzzles. Why did colonies attain independence when they did? Why was decolonization violent in some territories and relatively peaceful in others? Considering that so many colonial boundaries were artificial and externally imposed, why were new states so frequently territorial replicas of their predecessors rather than reincarnations of precolonial polities? To what extent was colonial nationalism a rejection, to what extent an affirmation, of what the imperialists accomplished?

Studying the dynamics of European global dominance enables one to pose even broader questions. What does it mean—and what would it take—to explain such large-scale phenomena as the rise and fall of empires? How does one move from describing and classifying major events and trends in this dramatic story to a theory accounting for what happened? What does the history of European empires tell us about the nature of power? about transfers of power from one group to another? about relationships across the divides of race, ethnicity, and culture? about the persistence of continuity amidst societal change and the workings of change agents amidst apparently stable societal settings? Such questions are worth asking even if the answers are more speculative and contestable than the investigator might like.

The study of European empires raises questions about the usefulness of categories used to analyze worldwide trends in the twentieth century. Social scientists have often drawn a distinction between tradition and modernity. The distinction is then harnessed to the claim that so-called Third World countries were once traditional but are now moving toward modernity, as expressed in the institutions, ideas, and living standards of advanced capitalist First World countries. Even if one sets aside problems in defining and measuring tradition and modernity, the prevalence of colonial situations in which "modern" Europeans ruled "traditional" non-Europeans through imported institutions makes the dichotomy especially problematic. Were the institutions transplanted from metropoles to colonies modern? What about the Roman Catholic Church, whose origins are deeply rooted in a world conventionally termed ancient? Was plantation slavery, introduced centuries ago to satisfy European consumer demands, traditional or modern? How should one classify current social and economic patterns inherited from plantation slavery? Are people whose racial heritage is mixed or whose culture reflects complex combinations of non-European and European practices agents of tradition or of modernity? The very existence of empires whose boundaries transgressed the line separating societies envisaged as modern and traditional and whose activities deeply implicated each type of society in the life of the other renders the distinction confusing and misleading rather than helpful. The new states emerged not from some vague traditional status, after all, but from lengthy, extensive interaction with some of the world's most economically and technologically advanced countries.

During the Cold War scholars of international relations focused on properties of the bipolar system then in place. The usual starting point for analyses of U.S.–Soviet rivalry was events in the twentieth century, notably the start of the First World War and the end of the Second. But the study of international relations in the modern world more appropriately begins in 1415 than in 1914 or 1945. European imperialism was an outward projection of the power of states. Its ultimate result was the global diffusion of the ideals and institutions of the state. Because the territorially bounded, bureaucratic state is the key unit in the study of international relations, it is surprising that so little attention has been paid to the process by which such a unit became globalized.[23] The end of the Cold War offers an opportunity to make up for this oversight. By focusing more on European imperialism, colonialism, and anticolonial nationalism, scholars can give the study of international relations the broad temporal scope it needs and deserves.

A recent attempt to shift attention from states to civilizations as essential units of identity and conflict in the post–Cold War world understates the significance of European global dominance. Had the cultural categories in Samuel Huntington's widely cited work *The Clash of Civilizations* been confined to specific regions over the past several centuries, one could plausibly imagine them functioning today as coherent expressions of radically divergent worldviews. But that is not the story of modern world history. The sustained triple assault of one of these civilizations upon others, and incorporation of the colonizers' institutions and norms into the nationalist movements that brought over a hundred colonies to independence—these realities long ago blurred civilizational boundaries. Many of the world's current conflicts are due not to fundamentally antagonistic values but to competing demands for material goods and cultural experiences whose status as good things is almost universally acknowledged. European imperialism and anti-imperial nationalism, taken together, were the driving forces in the global diffusion of ways of thinking and acting that transcend civilizational cleavage lines.[24]

Globalization is another theme in discussions of the post–Cold War world. Analysts emphasize massive, rapid flows of finance capital, technology, and labor across political boundaries, pointing out that these movements may weaken the power of governments to set and implement policy. An implication is that globalization is a historically unique phenomenon. But this is misleading. Many areas of the world were globalized long ago in the course of being incorporated into European empires. A legacy of colonial rule in many currently independent states is a high level of vulnerability to externally generated economic and technological changes. What may be different today is that the strongest, most historically insulated economies are experiencing levels of vulnerability once reserved for the world's most marginalized economies. In this situation strong, wealthy countries can learn from the more experienced weak, poor ones about the destabilizing consequences of globalization.

Implicit in these observations is a third reason for studying the rise and fall of European empires. Although the era of formal colonial rule has passed, its legacies live on, profoundly influencing the postcolonial world in ways both obvious and subtle. Chapter 16 discusses these legacies at some length. Here I want to mention a few in passing. As just noted, institutions and ideals associated with the state were passed from European metropoles to their colonies, then to successors appropriately designated new *states*. In the economic arena, production patterns introduced in the colonial era and early transport routes linking local commodities to imperially defined trade networks have in many instances shaped development options long after independence. Despite Cuba's revolutionary break with past political and diplomatic practice, its economy remains largely based on exports of sugar, an Old World crop transplanted centuries ago to the New. The economy of independent Senegal remains heavily dependent on peanuts, a New World crop transplanted long ago to Africa and developed by the French as an export commodity. Many other examples could be cited of path-dependent economic development in which the initial path was laid down at the behest of colonial rulers and for their benefit.

In the cultural arena, Christianity is in fact as well as aspiration a world religion. Its spread to many parts of the world can be traced to the initiatives of European missionaries, who aided and abetted the imperial project even when they had nonpolitical goals primarily in mind. Striking illustrations of the cultural legacy can be found in linguistics. Of 112 formerly colonized countries for which information is available, 88 (with a combined population of 2.3 billion) list a west European tongue as an official language.[25] An estimated 700 million people living outside Europe speak English, French, Portuguese, or Spanish in the home.[26]

A revealing indicator of colonialism's global impact is the names Europeans bestowed on territories they claimed. The list is especially long in what is conventionally called the New World or the Americas. (The very terms, of course, make the point. The hemisphere Columbus reached was new from the perspective of European explorers and settlers. The Americas were named in all likelihood after the Florentine explorer Amerigo Vespucci.) The New World is littered with countries, provinces, and cities named after

1. European political entities from countries to cities, for example, Hispaniola, New Spain (Mexico), New Granada (Colombia), Cartagena, New England, New Amsterdam (later New York), New Rochelle, Harlem, New Orleans, Nova Scotia, Cape Breton Island, New Hampshire, Valencia, Venezuela ("little Venice"), Guadalajara;

2. European royalty and rulers: Kingston, Montreal, Port au Prince, Louisiana, Louisbourg, Annapolis, Carolina, Georgia, Georgetown, Williamsburg, Charleston;

3. Signs, symbols, and saints of the Christian faith Europeans brought with them: Santo Domingo, Vera Cruz, Santiago, Trinidad, El Salvador, Asunción, Corpus Christi, Madre de Dios, Santa Fe, Magdalena, San Juan, San Jose, São Paulo, San Francisco, St. Louis, St. Augustine, St. Johns, and numerous Caribbean islands named for saints;

4. Prominent figures in exploration, conquest, settlement, and colonial administration: Colombia, British Columbia, De Soto, Pennsylvania, Cadillac, Hudson River and Bay, Baffin Island, Raleigh, Straits of Magellan, Delaware, Drake's Bay, James Bay, Marquette, Champlain, Humboldt Current, Grijalva River, Albuquerque, Vancouver.

Similar illustrations, though far less numerous, could be taken from Africa, Asia, and Oceania.[27] In the same categories as above, examples include the following:

1. Nova Lisboa (now Huambo), Batavia, New Holland, New South Wales, Perth, New Zealand, New Caledonia, Ile de France, East London;

2. Mauritius, Leopoldville, Philippine Islands; a lake, falls, and towns and provinces throughout the British Empire named for Queen Victoria;

3. Natal, St. Louis, São Tomé, San Salvador;

4. Southern and Northern Rhodesia, Luderitz Bay, Lourenço Marques (now Maputo), Stanleyville, Brazzaville, Tasmania (earlier called Van Diemen's Land), Livingstone, Sandwich Islands (Hawaii), Cook Bay, Pretoria, Wallis Islands, Fernando Po, Fort Lamy.

Many territories were named for a commodity highly valued by European commercial interests: Cape Cod, Minas Gerais, Argentina, Río de Oro, Walvis Bay, Gold Coast, and Côte d'Ivoire. In other cases a name bestowed by Europeans describes certain features of a territory. Nigeria, Niger, and the River Niger are derived from the Latin word for black; Cameroon is derived from the Portuguese reference to a river rich in prawns (*rio dos camarões*). As for the human beings Europeans encountered, it is ironic that because of Christopher Columbus's monumental miscalculation of the earth's circumference the New World's indigenous peoples were named after the inhabitants of the distant Indian subcontinent. The collective appellation lives on, centuries after the error was acknowledged.

Not all the names listed above were retained after colonies became independent. The two Rhodesias, for instance, became Zambia and Zimbabwe; Leopoldville and Stanleyville became Kinshasa and Kisangani. But the fact that most of the names were retained is an enduring colonial legacy, generally unnoticed because place-names are so often taken for granted.

The historian Raymond Betts sums up the legacies of colonial rule in a striking image: "The landscape of the post-colonial world resembles a beach after the tide has receded; it is still strewn with much of what the Europeans had earlier floated in."[28]

2
Why Did the Overseas Empires Rise, Persist, and Fall?

This chapter provides conceptual tools to account for the rise and decline of European global dominance. Chapters 3–7 in part 2 are largely descriptive. They discuss changes in the territorial scope of European empires in each of five phases and identify distinctive features associated with each phase. Part 3 (chapters 8–11) advances a theory of why overseas empires were formed, part 4 (chapters 12–13) an account of why they persisted, and part 5 (chapters 14 and 15) a theory of their decline and fall.

Chapter 16 identifies significant consequences of European colonialism. The final chapter addresses normative issues. Ethical judgments are scattered throughout the text, including statements reflecting biases of which I may be unaware. I have tried, however, to avoid making "too many" such judgments along the way. The aim is not to avoid considering the ethical dimension but, on the contrary, to permit thoughtful ethical reflection to take place, on its own terms and separately from the work of description, analysis, and explanation. After reflecting on how value-laden judgments might be made, chapter 17 makes them. Readers are invited to draw their own conclusions using norms, standards, and evidence that may differ substantially from mine, with correspondingly different results.

"Empire," "imperialism," "colony," "colonialism," and "decolonization" are terms one uses at considerable risk. For one thing, they have been defined in diverse ways in a vast academic and popular literature. For another, they have often been employed *without* being clearly defined, leading to confused and unproductive debates. Another problem is that they have powerful emotional and normative connotations, serving routinely as ammunition in polemic battles between defenders and critics of the European imperial project. It is difficult to "unload" loaded words and persuade readers to assign them a primarily descriptive meaning.

Abandoning these terms poses its own problems, however, not least having to locate suitable substitutes. I assign "imperialism" and "colonialism" relatively restricted meanings while stripping them, as far as possible, of nondescriptive baggage. The advantage of a narrow constructionist approach to words is that, paradoxically, it permits broader issues to be addressed than if definitions erred on the side of inclusiveness. If phenomenon A is *defined* as having features $B, C, D \ldots H$, then we have precluded by semantic fiat investigating whether A is in fact accompanied by B, $C, D \ldots H$, and whether A could be considered a cause or consequence of these features.

V. I. Lenin's enormously influential essay on imperialism, written in 1916, illustrates the problem by defining imperialism as the final stage of capitalism.[1] This permits him to count as instances of imperialism virtually everything associated with advanced capitalism, including the rise of financial institutions, the formation of industrial cartels, the scramble for unclaimed non-European territory, and the origins and early course of World War I. The concept has been stretched to cover so many things that its power to clarify and explain any one thing has been drastically compromised.[2] Lenin's usage precludes serious discussion of empire building at other periods in world history, such as precapitalist, early capitalist, or postcapitalist. Subsequent writers in this tradition have faced an even more serious explanatory problem than Lenin because they have so much more evidence—the vast and contradictory array of events occurring since the essay was written in 1916—to consign to the catchall category of advanced (final stage) capitalism.[3]

By the same token, if the phenomenon to which a word refers is defined as good or bad, claims about its moral status cannot be subjected to empirical investigation. Colonial rule might be defined as intrinsically evil. But then the question of whether colonialism was good or bad becomes moot because the answer has already been assumed. The conclusion is a tautology, there being in principle no evidence or argument that could disconfirm it. What is assumed should not also be asserted, and vice versa.

Several options are available for "empire," depending on how much one wants to concentrate on the political dimension as distinct from the economic, technological, social structural, cultural, psychological, and the like. I define "empire" in political terms as a relationship of domination and subordination between one polity (called the metropole) and one or more territories (called colonies) that lie outside the metropole's boundaries yet are claimed as its lawful possessions.[4] To be effective over the long term imperial rulers need to establish dominance in arenas outside of government. That said, the distinctive core feature is political control.

But what is political control? What indicators point to its existence and extensiveness? What does a territory need to score on these indicators to be called a colony? One way to answer these questions is to examine legal-formal aspects of unequal relationships. Does the dominant state explicitly claim authority to make binding decisions affecting the weaker territory? Does the weaker territory lack legal status as a sovereign state within the international system? An alternative approach is to examine who controls and influences whom in real-life situations. Does the dominant state control a small or large portion of the weaker territory? a small or large number of activities?

A third approach, the one I adopt, is to combine de jure and de facto considerations: a dominant state is an imperial metropole and a weaker territory a colony when

- the dominant state formally claims the right to make authoritative decisions affecting the weaker territory's domestic affairs and external relations;
- the weaker territory is not recognized as a sovereign state by major actors in the interstate system; and
- the dominant state establishes and staffs administrative structures that extract resources, allocate resources, and enforce regulations within some economically or strategically significant portion of the weaker territory. Administrative control might be exercised over a port and its hinterland, for example, or over a coastal zone or transport networks linking a port to zones of mineral and agricultural wealth.

A territory can be considered an imperial possession even if a metropole is unable effectively to govern its entire area.

This definition excludes relationships among unequally powerful entities in which

- a stronger state does not advance formal claims to control the weaker territory's domestic or foreign affairs;
- the weaker territory is widely recognized as a sovereign state; yet
- the stronger state's institutions exert marked influence over affairs in the weaker territory.

Such relationships are not only unequal; they are also conducive to exploitation of the inhabitants of the weaker territory. But these features do not by themselves make the stronger state an imperial power or the weaker territory a colony. If they did the distinction between formal power and informal influence in international relations would virtually disappear. By my definition it is misleading to speak of "informal empire" and "the imperialism of free trade," as John Gallagher and Ronald Robinson do in discussing Britain's economically dominant role in nineteenth-century Latin America and other areas the British government did not formally claim.[5] Here terms have been stretched beyond manageable limits. Winfried Baumgart puts the point well: "'Informal imperialism' creates more problems than it solves. If subjected to logic it creates no clear borderline. It is synonymous with any form of dependence and is therefore unacceptably vague."[6]

In some cases it is unclear whether a territory should be designated part of an empire. Suppose a strong state lays claim to a nonsovereign territory yet sets limits to the scope of its own authority. When Canada and Australia attained "responsible government" and their elected legislatures took control over domestic (but not foreign) affairs, did they cease to be part of the British Empire? What of Kuwait and Bahrain, protectorates in which treaties with local sheikhs confined Britain's authority to external relations? I include these territories within Britain's empire but recognize their borderline status by calling them quasi colonies.

A metropole regards components of its empire as politically subordinate and territorially distinct. The geographic difference between metropole and colony can be reinforced by racial and cultural differences when the two are not contiguous, as in the saltwater empires discussed here.

Imperialism is the process of constructing an empire. The term thus covers a period of several centuries during which west Europeans made territorial claims and regulated an increasing range of activities overseas. I am particularly interested in expansion into areas not previously claimed or effectively governed by Europeans. Of less interest are situations in which one empire grew at the expense of another. It is the *net* gain or loss in the geographic coverage of European empires, considered cumulatively, that needs to be explained, not changes in the distribution of colonies among metropoles.

A colony is a dependent territory within an empire. It has a name, specified boundaries, and an urban administrative center. Policy-making authority is exercised by a person officially designated by metropolitan rulers to hold power in their name. Typically this person is a citizen of the metropole, regards the colony as a temporary place of residence, and looks to superiors in the metropole's capital for overall guidance and direction.

A colony is a penetrated polity. Its foreign relations are monopolized and its domestic affairs strongly influenced by officials who come from outside its borders. In the modern world a colony may be seen as a protostate. That is, it is potentially a legally sovereign state like the one ruling it because many of the institutions and procedures associated with statehood have been imported and are functioning at some level. Yet the potential for sovereignty is not realized because the metropole insists on retaining ultimate authority to make critical decisions. The colony's governmental institutions are accountable outward and upward to the metropole's rulers, not downward to the territory's residents.

The residents may include settlers, emigrants from the metropole or nearby areas who came to earn their living in the colony. People tracing full genealogical descent from earlier European emigrants are counted as settlers; they are also called colonists. A territory does not need a settler community to be designated a colony. In this respect the term's original reference—to Phoenician and Greek settlements on coastal enclaves distant from the emigrants' homelands—no longer applies.[7] A defining feature of ancient colonies was the presence of settlers. But these enclaves were not necessarily subordinate to a political authority located in the settlers' homelands. In the modern world the situation is reversed: political subordination is deemed a defining feature, while the existence of a settler community is optional.

Under the colonial heading are territories assigned a wide range of administrative headings and legal statuses. These include viceroyalties, audiencias, captaincies, intendencies, protectorates, Crown colonies, overseas provinces, overseas territories and departments, League of Nations mandates, and United Nations trusteeship territories. To the extent that statuses matter—and on occasion they did, with implications for the pace and character of decolonization—the meaning of a particular status will be noted.

Colonialism is the set of formal policies, informal practices, and ideologies employed by a metropole to retain control of a colony and to benefit from control. Colonialism is the consolidation of empire, the effort to extend and deepen governance claims made in an earlier period of empire building.

Decolonization is the process by which a territory sheds colonial status and becomes a legally sovereign independent state, recognized as such by other states. Ultimate formal authority over domestic and foreign policy is removed from foreigners and placed in the hands of locally resident citizens. Decolonization reverses the flow of power that marked eras of imperial expansion. From the colony's perspective, the process is described as attainment of political independence and victory for the leading nationalist movement.

The foregoing definitions are essentially political. They focus on disparities of coercive resources and legal status that mark the formation and consolidation of empire, and on transfers of executive and legal authority that mark the end of empire. This is by no means to say that imperialism, colonialism, and decolonization are only or merely political in their nature or effects. On the contrary, it is precisely because narrow definitions are used that one can investigate the extent to which changes outside the political arena accompanied the rise and fall of European empires. And attention paid legal-formal dimensions of power does not in any way belittle the importance of informal influence in economic, technological, cultural, and psychological arenas. Europeans exerted influence in Africa and Asia long before forming empires there and in much of the New World for decades after imperial rule was ended. A definition of imperialism and colonialism that errs on the side of formalism has the advantage of permitting and indeed encouraging questions about relationships between formal power and informal influence. Under what conditions, for example, did Europeans feel they needed to create colonies in order to protect or enhance existing spheres of influence? Under what conditions was it possible to protect or enhance influence without expanding the scope of empire—or even by acquiescing to the impending loss of overseas possessions?

What to call actors in the transcontinental drama recounted here poses a semantic problem because every locution for broad categories of people is arbitrary and has its drawbacks. "Europeans" refers to people born and raised in west European countries who think of those countries as their homelands even if they reside overseas for parts of their lives. "Non-Europeans" are people born and raised outside of Europe who do not fit the above categories. This is an especially troublesome term, not only because it is an enormous residual category but also because it classifies human beings by attributes they lack rather than by ones they possess. Using it risks adding psychological insult to semantic injury because the word was employed in the past by Europeans to connote the collective inferiority and otherness of people unlike themselves. I employ it, with the historic connotation excised, for two reasons. First, it highlights a contrast with Europeans that is itself a distinctive feature of the colonial situation. The persistent tendency to classify people in terms of real or alleged blood ties to Europeans can be observed in racially, culturally, and temporally diverse settings. Second, there is no viable alternative. Eric Wolf's effort to grapple with the problem is reflected in the title of his magisterial work, *Europe and the People Without History*. But Wolf was speaking with tongue firmly implanted in cheek. He would be horrified if his residual category were put to analytic use. "Indigenous" does not work, since one consequence of Europe's global impact was the transfer of millions of human beings from one continent to colonies in other continents. Nonindigenous African slaves and Asian indentured servants and their descendants played major roles in the economic development and social/demographic evolution of lands that were initially foreign but became their homes.

"The colonized" is a composite term referring to indigenous residents of colonies, groups just mentioned, and so-called mixed blood groups tracing descent to people of diverse continental origins.

A CLASSIFICATION SCHEME: FIVE PHASES

Relations between European and non-European peoples over the past five centuries were marked by certain broad patterns. Several phases may be identified during which the predominant trend was imperial expansion or contraction. (An exception, noted below, is the period from 1914 to 1939.) These phases alternated, periods of expansion being notably lengthier than those of contraction. Cycles of expansion and contraction tended to concentrate in certain parts of the world. The initial cycle—comprising phases 1 and 2—occurred principally in the New World of the Americas. The subsequent cycle—comprising phases 3 through 5—was mainly in the Old World of Asia, Africa, the Near East, and Oceania (table 2.1).

TABLE 2.1.

IMPERIAL PHASES

Phase	Duration	Direction	Territorial Focus
1	1415–1773	Expansion	New World
2	1775–1824	Contraction	New World
3	1824–1912	Expansion	Old World
4	1914–39	Unstable equilibrium	Old World
5	1940–80	Contraction	Old World

Phase 4 was a period of equilibrium in two senses. First, metropoles experienced territorial gains *and* losses between 1914 and 1939, with limited net change in their overall position. Second, events and trends in this quarter century had contradictory effects. On the one hand, Europeans consolidated administrative control and extended economic and cultural influence within colonies. On the other hand, World War I and global economic depression undermined European power and authority. The cumulative effect of phase 4's crises was felt in phase 5, itself ushered in by another global crisis, World War II. Equilibrium in phase 4 was dynamic and unstable, a brief and only apparently stable outcome of multiple forces pressing in divergent directions.

Each phase is assigned a chapter in part 2. Given special attention are events that can be read as starting and ending points and hence set a phase apart from the others (table 2.2).

AN APPROACH TO EXPLANATION

This book links history and comparative social science in an attempt to account for broad patterns shaping the modern world. It responds to Gabriel Almond's appeal to social scientists to "take the historical cure . . . transforming historical episodes into analytical episodes," and to Charles Tilly's plea for "historically grounded analyses of big structures and large processes as alternatives to the timeless, placeless models of social organization and social change that came to us with the nineteenth century heritage."[8] A task already burdened by the subject matter's ambitious scope is made more difficult because social scientists and historians tend to pull in contrary directions: social scientists study particulars in order to advance the search for generalizations; historians emphasize what is distinctive about certain times, places, and human settings. Social scientists run the risk of advancing overstated, oversimplified, and misleading generalizations. Historians run the opposite risk, in highlighting dis-

TABLE 2.2.

CRITICAL EVENTS

Phase	Initial event	Concluding event
1	Portuguese capture of Ceuta, 1415	British Parliament's Regulating Act, 1773
2	Battle of Bunker Hill, Boston, 1775	Battle of Ayacucho, Peru, 1824
3	First Anglo-Burmese War, 1824–26	Treaty of Fez, Morocco, 1912
4	Start of World War I, 1914	Start of World War II in Europe, 1939
5	Japanese occupation of European colonies in Southeast Asia, 1940	Independence of Zimbabwe (formerly Rhodesia), 1980

tinctness, of failing to identify patterns of human behavior that recur across boundaries of time, geography, and culture. But acknowledging differences in method and purpose need not consign separate academic disciplines to separate existence and mutual isolation. A growing body of scholarship demonstrates that the social sciences are enriched when given historical depth, and that history is made more intellectually exciting when informed by social scientists' questions and approaches.[9]

A theory is a set of closely linked propositions claiming to explain a class of events.[10] Explanation is built upon foundations of description, analysis, and classification. But it is more. In searching for explanation one explores the nature and frequency of relationships among analytically separable factors, paying special attention to situations in which one or more factors appear to cause whatever it is one is trying to explain. How causation is conceptualized and identified—whether, indeed, there is such a thing in physical nature—are subjects of extended debate. For my purposes causal explanation of historical trends has three components:

1. Identifying the necessary conditions, if any, of a phenomenon. If we want to explain B, are there any factors (such as A_1) whose absence precludes the occurrence of B?
2. Identifying the sufficient conditions, if any, of a phenomenon. Are there any factors (such as A_2) whose presence ensures the occurrence of B?
3. Identifying contributing or conducive conditions. Are there factors (such as A_3) whose presence increases the likelihood that B will occur?

It takes only limited knowledge and rudimentary logic to identify necessary, or A_1, conditions for overseas empire. A colony cannot be created without the prior existence of the metropole to which it is subordinate. A metropole, in turn, cannot be a stateless society. It requires home-based governing institutions that are capable of extracting, organizing, and deploying enough material and human resources to govern territories beyond its boundaries. A metropole's ruler should command sufficient obedience from people sent out as explorers, soldiers, and overseas admin-istrators that they will not use authority delegated to them as imperial agents to seize power and govern in their own name.[11]

Over and above political and institutional prerequisites are scientific and tech-nological ones. Founders of overseas empire need ships capable of reaching distant lands and of returning home. To complete round-trip voyages, sailors require knowl-edge of the configuration of land masses and seas, the direction and intensity of winds and currents, and the movements of celestial bodies. They should be able to locate their position on at least the north-south (longitudinal) axis while out of sight of land. Creating an empire and maintaining it requires power asymmetry. Colo-nizers must be able and willing to deploy weapons more effectively against a terri-tory's population than the latter can use against them.

If necessary, or *A1*, conditions are easy to identify, the search for sufficient, or *A2*, conditions takes one into a cul-de-sac and should be abandoned. There is no factor ensuring the existence of empire, in the sense that it is found everywhere empires exist and only in such settings. This conclusion is not disheartening. If anything, it helps one avoid what Reinhard Bendix calls "the fallacy of retrospective determinism." Bendix insists that we "conceive of the future as uncertain in the past as well as the present."[12] I view history as possibilities that become probabilities under certain circumstances, including unexpected situations best described as acci-dental or random. Probabilities do not, however, become certainties; what is likely does not become inevitable. This is so because human beings possess—and con-tinually act *as if* they possessed—modest degrees of freedom to chart future courses of action. Outcomes are especially uncertain in situations considered here, in which people interact with those from other cultures who have very different understand-ings of how the world works and what norms should govern behavior. Cross-cultural interaction frequently leads to outcomes none of the participants wants or expects.

The real challenge is to identify and assign causal weight to factors whose presence, alone or in conjunction with others, substantially increases the likelihood that a pattern of events will occur. Theories advanced here to account for the rise and fall of European overseas empires focus primarily on conducive (*A3*) conditions.

Social life is extraordinarily complex, with many factors operating at any one time and place and interacting with each other in various ways. When one tries to explain not a singular event but a swath of world history encompassing multiple events, one encounters layers of interconnected complexity. It is not plausible that a broad class of events, considered as an effect, could have one and only one cause. A single-factor theory has the virtue of parsimony: a little goes a long way. But it is unlikely to account for all the events one wants to explain. If one goes to the other extreme and generates a long list of factors that each contributed in some measure to some instances of a class of events, then one abandons parsimony. Laundry lists do not manageable theories make. A good theory about social reality should steer between implausibility and unmanageability by specifying more than one yet fewer than, say, eighty-three causal factors.

But how sort through myriad candidates for inclusion in a theory, identifying some as having more explanatory weight than others and eliminating still others altogether? A sensible way to proceed is to apply the standard of appropriate comprehensiveness. A powerful theory should be neither too narrow nor too broad in scope. It should encompass the class of events it is supposed to explain. But it should not extend its reach beyond those events if in so doing it blurs or obliterates the boundary line defining what is distinctive about those events. If a theory's causal factors apply to some instances of a class of events but not to others, the theory risks mistaking a part of the whole for the whole and is insufficiently comprehensive. On the other hand, if a theory's causal factors apply to all instances of the class of events *and* to instances of a very different class with different causal properties, then the theory overshoots the mark. It is too comprehensive. A theory about world history has temporal and spatial dimensions. It gains plausibility to the extent that it passes four tests: (1) Is it sufficiently broad to cover the entire time period being examined? (2) Is it sufficiently broad to cover the entire geographical area being examined? (3) Is it sufficiently narrow to explain why events occurred in certain time periods but not in others? (4) Is it sufficiently narrow to explain why events occurred in certain geographical areas but not in others?[13]

When one applies these tests to a theory of European imperialism, the theory is strengthened if it (1) applies to the five-century period during which expansion occurred; (2) applies to more than one European empire—ideally to all; (3) helps account for why overseas empires were formed from early phase 1 onward but not before the fifteenth century; and (4) helps account for why Europeans dominated the world while others did not.

My five-phase classification scheme provides a way to assess whether explanations advanced here meet the temporal comprehensiveness test. Phases 1 and 3 share an expansionist direction. Factors clearly at work in the first phase *and* the third are candidates for inclusion in a theory of European imperialism.[14] Factors found in one phase but not the other fail the test, unless they are present in the earlier phase and can be shown to make expansion in the subsequent phase easier or more likely.[15] Phases 2 and 5 share a pattern of imperial contraction. A factor at work in the second phase *and* the fifth is a candidate for inclusion in a theory of imperial decline. A factor present in one phase but not the other fails to pass the test, unless its impact on phase 2 makes subsequent decolonization easier or more likely.

The best-known theories of European imperialism focus on scrambles for territory in Africa, Asia, and Oceania during the late nineteenth and early twentieth centuries. J. A. Hobson, Lenin, Joseph Schumpeter, Carlton Hayes, William Langer, and others identify certain features of this period, for example, advanced industrial capitalism and populist nationalism, as key contributing causes.[16] These writers explain what triggered and sustained the competitive rush for colonies over a thirty- to forty-year period. But theories this narrowly focused fail to pass the temporal comprehensiveness test. They address only the latter years of phase 3, which in turn is only one small part of a far longer process. Because Europeans constructed empires in preindustrial, prepopulist eras as well, they did not need the distinctive attributes of late phase 3 to project power outward. A theory of nineteenth-century imperialism does not account for phase 1. Indeed, to the extent that it stresses features not found earlier, a safe presumption is that it cannot.

Phases that share a direction—whether expansion or contraction—may differ in many other respects, and do. Identifying these differences is important for theoretical purposes because it enables one to rule out factors that sound plausible but fail the "both phases" test. There are so many potential candidates for inclusion in a theory of empire that any procedure eliminating candidates or casting doubt on their explanatory power makes a valuable contribution. More scrutiny can be given what remains after many alternatives have been discarded. For this reason the chapters on phases 1 and 3 take care to show how the expansionist periods are unalike; likewise the chapters on contractionist phases 2 and 5. Chapter 8 uses differences between phases 1 and 3 to discard a number of plausible sounding propositions about Europe's rise to dominance. The spatial breadth criterion can be satisfied by identifying features widely shared throughout western Europe, hence capable of influencing overseas initiatives of most—ideally all—empire-acquiring states. Chapters 8–10 focus on these features while acknowledging that variations on a theme are played by metropoles. Such variations account for dissimilarities in the size, location, demographic composition, and duration of empires.

A theory of European imperialism is strengthened if its temporal scope is not too broad. Suppose factors identified as contributing to expansion in phases 1 and 3 were prominent prior to phase 1 as well. The power of these factors to explain imperialism would be weakened because they were present when the thrust for overseas empire was absent.[17] This observation suggests the importance of the fifteenth and sixteenth centuries for theory-building purposes. To be sure, many changes in European history occurred slowly over centuries; no sharp break separates what happened before and after the conquest of Ceuta. But if patterns present in early phase 1 were less prominent or absent in preceding centuries, a theory highlighting them could explain in part why people from the same region behaved differently at various times.

A theory is likewise strengthened if its geographic scope is not too comprehensive. Suppose factors said to contribute to European expansion were prominent in societies elsewhere in the world that did not produce overseas empires. The explanatory power of these factors would be weakened because they were present in lands where the push for overseas possessions was absent. This observation suggests the importance of comparing European countries with other parts of the world. Deserving special attention would be societies that had the maritime capacity to establish overseas empires but did not use ships for that purpose. Factors prominent in Europe but absent or weakly present in such societies could help explain why overseas empires were formed by Europeans but not others.

Two societies satisfying the maritime capacity condition are the Arabs and Chinese. A question posed in chapters 8–10 is whether certain features widely found in western Europe were present in the Arab-speaking world and China, particularly in the early years of phase 1, when all three could have taken initiatives ensuring overseas dominance. The answer is that factors conducive to European expansion were not present to the same degree elsewhere. Broad observations about Europe, the Arab-speaking world, and China are reinforced by a case study of what happened when people from all three areas interacted. Malacca, a port located on the Malacca Strait in what is now Malaysia, was a leading emporium five centuries ago, linking merchant vessels plying the Indian Ocean with ships from the Spice Islands and China Sea. As such it brought together Arabs and other Muslims, Chinese merchants, and, in the early sixteenth century, the Portuguese. Having the leading candidates for global dominance present at the same time and place, Malacca comes as close as one can get to a laboratory test of why Europeans came to dominate the world while its potential rivals did not. Analysis of the resources each actor deployed when Portuguese soldiers arrived in 1511, intent on conquest, lends support to my theory.

COMPONENTS OF POWER AND UNITS OF ANALYSIS

A book about empires is a book about power. How was power over large numbers of people acquired, consolidated, used, delegated, and lost? Power is relational. It exists only when two or more parties interact. Europeans exercised power not in a vacuum but in relationship with those whom they governed. Whether the resources and techniques Europeans deployed proved effective depended to a large extent on the resources and techniques deployed by their subjects to oppose, bypass, redirect, or assist them.[18]

It follows that explanations of the exercise and transfer of power should not be restricted to one party to a relationship. Yet many well-known works on overseas empires are flawed in precisely this way, relying heavily if not exclusively on the actions of Europeans to explain their successes. Peoples who came under European rule appear as bit players in the dim recesses of a Euro-dominated stage. By implication it is the fate of the colonized not to act but to be acted upon, not to take initiative but to respond to initiatives taken by the invaders.

The classic theories of nineteenth-century imperialism take this Eurocentric form. Hobson, for instance, stresses economic inequalities within advanced industrial capitalist countries. Industrialists unable to find a sufficiently robust domestic market for mass-produced consumer and capital goods press their governments to ensure protected markets overseas. Lenin's theory is built on the same theme of growing class cleavage within European societies. Unlike the social reformer Hobson, Lenin regards this trend as an irremediable contradiction of a capitalist system painfully writhing its exit from history. From a quite opposite ideological perspective Schumpeter identifies the root cause as the "social atavism" of Europe's aristocratic, precapitalist elements. These groups, their traditional warrior function undercut by the advance of a peaceful capitalist order, seek through imperialism to carry on elsewhere a violent way of life that no longer makes sense at home.

The more recent work of Immanuel Wallerstein has the great merit of analyzing long-term historical trends in an emerging "world-system" that by definition ranges far beyond any one continent. Nonetheless, Wallerstein's model too is centered on western Europe. The explosive dynamism of mercantile and subsequent industrial capitalism in this small yet core region of the globe comes close to a sufficient condition for what occurs within the world-system as a whole.[19]

Eurocentric theories are located at many points along the ideological spectrum: on the left, among writers critical of imperialism, such as Hobson, Lenin, Wallerstein, and Andre Gunder Frank; closer to the center, as in the work of Schumpeter; and on the proimperialist right, as in the apologia for Britain's phase 3 empire by J. A. Froude, J. R. Seeley, Halford Mackinder, and Alfred Milner.[20]

I part company with these authors in emphasizing the roles non-Europeans played in Europe's global projection of power. I argue that the temporal and spatial pattern of imperial expansion was greatly influenced by successful non-European resistance, on the one hand, and by invitations to Europeans to participate in indigenous power struggles, on the other (see chapter 10). Features of non-European societies that made such invitations more likely—in effect complementing European push with indigenous pull—must be included in any theory of imperialism. The obviously crucial role non-Europeans and settlers played in decolonization is discussed in chapters 14 and 15. Throughout the book I try to avoid thinking more Eurocentrically than the evidence warrants.

Power has two components: capacity to act and will to act. Capacity is possession of the objective means to achieve a goal in a given setting. Such means include resources to coerce, threaten, or induce others to comply with one's wishes. Will is the subjective component, referring to an actor's conscious desire to achieve a goal. Typically the goal is consistent with an actor's material interests, values, and concerns over security and survival. Capacity is relatively easy for an outside analyst to measure, and it normally does not change rapidly from one time period to the next. In contrast, will is difficult for an outsider to measure, and it can change rapidly and unexpectedly. Power may be construed as the product of capacity multiplied by will. If either component is missing or present below a low threshold, not even an ample supply of the other will suffice to carry out a planned course of action. Thus, if actor X is able to act but does not wish to do so, the result is inaction. If X wishes to act but lacks means to realize a goal, its actions will not succeed. If other actors are able and willing to attain objectives they have in mind, X's inaction (or unsuccessful attempts to achieve a goal) constitutes evidence that X lacks power.

If power is relational and if its components are capacity and will, it follows that explanations for why one party (X) gains power over another (Y) should take several things into account: X's capacity to impose itself on Y, X's will to do so, and Y's capacity and will to resist, moderate, modify, deflect, or postpone X's aggressive actions. The four factors of colonizer will and capacity and colonized will and capacity are the framework for the model presented in table 2.3. Although this model applies specifically to European expansion, a modified version applies to contraction as well. Thus one can ask about the capacity and will of European metropoles to retain their colonies, as against the capacity and will of emerging colonial political elites to assert political autonomy.

For something as complex as a sustained pattern of imperial expansion it makes sense to think of power relationships as involving many types of actors whose encounters take place in a multilayered setting. Table 2.3 lists several levels of analysis that should be considered, starting with the most comprehensive and moving toward the smallest. The table suggests a way of thinking analogous to adjusting a camera's zoom lens. Imagine a photographer focusing on the broad outlines of a large object located far away in order to learn something about the object. The photographer then twists the zoom lens to obtain a more detailed, higher-resolution image of a selected part of the distant object. As a result something new is observed through greater attention to the part's details. The zoom lens may be adjusted further to permit more precise examination of an even smaller part of the object. Each adjustment permits a novel visualization of reality by enabling the observer to come closer to whatever is being observed, in a subjective if not literal sense. For this reason each twist of the zoom lens can generate a new description of reality and perhaps new ideas to account for what the lens adjustment has revealed. Yet throughout the entire operation the camera remains in the same place, pointed toward the same object.

As this analogy suggests, each shift of analytic focus contributes something of value to one's understanding—but not everything that matters. The analogy suggests that alternative hypotheses generated from the camera's multiple "insights" should be viewed as complementary rather than competitive and mutually exclusive.

CONDITIONS CONDUCIVE TO EUROPEAN GLOBAL DOMINANCE

The components of a theory of European imperialism are now ready for assembly. Causal factors listed below are considered conducive to empire formation, not its necessary or sufficient conditions. The search for explanation is not confined to Europeans. By noting how non-Europeans contributed to their own subjugation, albeit in unintended ways, one avoids the Eurocentric fallacy. The theory is designed to pass the tests of appropriate comprehensiveness discussed earlier. Table 2.3 provides the framework for arranging the principal propositions. Part 3 offers supporting evidence from the two expansionist phases.

General Characteristics of Western Europe

Geographic factors Compared with polities elsewhere in the Old World, European states with Atlantic seacoasts were in an unusually favorable location to reach other continents by sea. These states were able to take advantage of their geographical good fortune once the necessary conditions for overseas empires were met, initially by Portugal in the fifteenth century, then by other states as rulers consolidated central government power, deployed seaworthy ships, and dispatched agents with the maritime knowledge to return home from extended voyages. Arab and Chinese access to the Atlantic Ocean was both more difficult and more unlikely than west European access to the Indian and Pacific oceans. And European sailors in phase 1 were far more likely than Arab or Chinese sailors to reach the New World. That Europeans acquired and settled territories in the Americas while others did not contributed to global dominance over the long term. Resources extracted from the New World during phase 1 enhanced Europeans' capacity to expand their Old World holdings during phase 3.

West Europeans in the modern era could seriously contemplate aggressive activity in distant lands because their own region, situated at the far western edge of Eurasia, was not threatened by invaders. Arab-ruled polities and China did not enjoy this luxury because they were located closer to the Eurasian heartland. Mongol and Turkic armies posed threats that could not be ignored, contributing to a land- rather than sea-based conception of military power. Invasions by pastoralists posed cultural as well as strategic threats. Arab and Chinese elites looked inland with anxiety just when west Europeans started to dispatch ships across the oceans.

TABLE 2.3.

EXPLAINING EUROPEAN IMPERIAL EXPANSION: A MODEL

Units of Analysis	Components of Power	
Europeans	Capacity to expand	Will to expand
Western Europe: general features		
Europe as an interstate system		
Specific metropoles		
Sectors within a metropole:		
Public institutions		
Private profit institutions		
Religious institutions		
Key individuals		

Colonized Peoples	Capacity to resist	Will to resist
General features of many non-European societies		
Relations among states or societies		
Sectors within a state or society		
Public profit institutions		
Private profit institutions		
Religious institutions		
Key individuals		

Regional integration and identity   Western Europe was a homogeneous region in many respects, including a productive base in mixed agriculture, a limited influence of kinship on social structure, linguistic and legal legacies from Roman imperial rule, and a shared religious tradition of Roman Catholic Christianity. Homogeneity facilitated dense networks of economic exchange and permitted rapid diffusion of new knowledge and technologies. These shared features enhanced the capacity of several European states to project influence and power abroad. They may also have increased the will to do so by giving each metropole the sense that it was engaged in more than a self-interested national project. A nobler, more comprehensive task was involved: spreading the benefits of Christian European civilization.

An activist stance toward the natural world   Increasingly prominent in European thought from the Renaissance onward was a worldview which assumed that what was unknown could and should become known. Closely associated with the drive to uncover what had previously been hidden was the drive to classify, possess, and put to practical use whatever was found. I term this combination of restless curiosity and self-aggrandizing manipulation the explore-control-utilize syndrome. Such a worldview was directly supportive of imperialism. Its disruptive effects on other peoples and environments were especially noticeable in areas where substantial numbers of Europeans settled.

The same inquisitive, transformative stance toward the world underlies the scientific and technical breakthroughs Europeans generated throughout five centuries of overseas expansion. Imperialism and technological advance were mutually reinforcing. The capacity of explorers, overseas soldiers and administrators, scientists, and technical specialists to advance along their respective fronts was enhanced by forward movement on other fronts.

Europe as an Interstate System

Adjusting the zoom lens enables one to see western Europe not as a unit, fairly homogeneous and integrated, but as a fragmented, decentralized collection of polities. As the region emerged from feudalism a growing proportion of its political units acquired attributes of states: territorially bounded, legally sovereign units governed through centrally controlled, functionally specialized bureaucracies. The region's states constituted a system in the sense that they acknowledged each other's existence and autonomy and interacted on a sustained basis over a wide range of issues. Their relations were shaped by such shared practices as exchanges of diplomats, understandings about diplomatic immunity, limits on the scope of warfare, and international conclaves to readjust the system following major wars. Such practices were absent or far less frequently observed when states within Europe related to polities outside it.

The presence of many politically autonomous units within a culturally homogeneous, intensely interactive regional system made for high levels of insecurity and competition among the units. Insecurity was endemic because no state could ensure that its sovereign right to protect its borders against invasion would not be violated by other states exercising their sovereign right to do whatever they pleased. Insecurity led some rulers to look outside the system for resources that could reduce their vulnerability to neighbors' attacks as well as facilitate power consolidation at home. From the fifteenth century onward western Europe evolved from hundreds of tiny polities toward a far smaller number of larger, centralized states. For winners in this Darwinian process the will to reach other world regions was reinforced by an increased capacity to finance and staff overseas initiatives. The system's competitive character made it likely that successful efforts by any one state to establish itself abroad would trigger efforts by others to do the same.

The potential of such a system to explode outward is obvious. Simultaneous drives by two or more European states to project power outside the region, fueled by concerns over possible loss of power within it, figure prominently in both expansionist phases. At times these drives became frantic scrambles for available territory.

Neither Arab-ruled Muslim polities nor China were embedded in interstate systems with the cluster of characteristics—geographical compactness, coherence, integration, fragmentation, insecurity, competition—marking modern western Europe. This negative finding supports the argument that distinctive features of the European system were conducive to overseas aggression.

Sectors Within a Metropole

When one adjusts the zoom lens to examine internal characteristics of European states, a metropole ceases to appear as a unit and becomes instead a complex network of institutions, groups, and individuals.[21] Three sectors, that is, segments of a society's life in which people specialize in a certain kind of activity, figured critically in European expansion: public, private profit, and religious (fig. 2.1). The public sector refers to a country's central government: leaders and institutions charged with formulating and implementing, through laws and the legally sanctioned threat and use of force, policies affecting the country as a whole. In the private profit sector are people not directly and fully employed by government agencies who seek to enhance their income, wealth, and material well-being over and above basic subsistence needs. In the religious sector are those who direct collective rituals of worship within traditions that encompass cosmological reflection, theological claims, and ethical norms. Religious specialists pass on their tradition's rituals and beliefs to young people, often through schools and colleges that convey knowledge as well as religious instruction.

In real life, of course, people associated with a sector engage in a wider range of activities than those specific to that sector. What people do may overlap and indeed compete with what specialists in other sectors do. That said, each sector can be considered functionally distinct from others by virtue of its primary stated purpose. It may also be structurally distinct from others by virtue of the institutions performing its work.[22]

Chapter 9 argues that the public, private profit, and religious sectors of west

FIGURE 2.1

SECTORAL ACTORS IN EUROPEAN EXPANSION

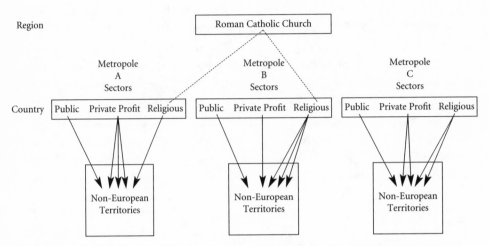

European countries have historically been highly institutionalized, autonomous, and sufficiently prestigious to recruit widely for able, suitably motivated personnel. These qualities gave each sector the capacity to reach beyond a country's borders. Monarchs, merchant companies, and missionary bodies were able to dispatch agents to distant lands while the structures controlling or supervising overseas activities remained on European soil.

To the capacity to mount overseas initiatives was added a will to do so. The primary motivation varied by sector. But whether it was power or profit or proselytization, sectoral actors believed that what their agents did abroad could complement and fulfill work done in familiar home settings.

The activities and interactions of sectoral institutions constitute the most vital factor behind European global dominance. These institutions did the real work of constructing empires. Because their specialized activities, taken together, covered many functions, they could recruit agents with a wide range of backgrounds, skills, and motivations. They sustained links between agents in distant lands and power centers in Europe. By tapping diverse sources of finance they made it easier to cover initial costs of exploratory initiatives than if only one sector were involved. Their impact derived in part from the sheer number of actors involved. When each of several European states contained institutions in several sectors with the capacity and will to operate overseas, chances that someone, sometime, would establish an effective presence abroad rose. The cumulative impact of sectoral activity was enhanced by the relative autonomy each sector enjoyed. Governmental, profit-seeking, and religious institutions had leeway to operate overseas on their own. They did not have to wait for jointly sponsored ventures that might not materialize. Autonomy in turn made possible a high degree of tactical flexibility. It is not accidental that in phase 1 missionary orders played a major role in the Americas, where indigenous opposition to Christianity was weak, while informal influence was exercised primarily by (secular) trading companies in parts of Asia like India and the East Indies, where Islam's prominence severely limited missionary prospects. Merchants and missionaries were able to carry on their work in societies whose rulers would quickly have repelled soldiers dispatched by a European government on a mission of conquest. Chapter 9 describes the range of tactical options available when several sectors were involved and shows how Europeans adjusted techniques for gaining footholds overseas depending on circumstances specific to the societies they encountered.

Sectoral institutions found they could usefully collaborate as well as operate on their own. Both expansionist phases featured more or less formal coalitions between institutions in the public and private profit sectors (chartered companies) and between governments and officially supported churches. In some instances—France in phases 1 and 3, Britain and Germany in phase 3—triple coalitions among soldier / administrators, merchants, and missionaries were formed.

When functionally specialized institutions collaborated they increased their capacity to control other people's behavior. To the extent that the public sector relied on coercion, the private profit sector on material reward, and the religious sector on normative appeals, a cross-sector alliance meant a mix of compliance mechanisms likely to have far greater impact than if only one mechanism were at work. The cumulative effect of organized, deliberately coordinated attacks on the political structures *and* modes of production *and* religious beliefs of non-European societies made it difficult to mobilize effective popular resistance. Repelling a triple assault posed a difficult and frequently insuperable challenge.

Portugal's conquest of Malacca illustrates the empowering effect of cross-sector coalitions. Portuguese initiatives featured close collaboration between merchants and agents of the Crown, with strong support from the Catholic Church. The city's Chinese and Arab residents, for their part, were unable or unwilling to assemble equivalent coalitions to defeat the invader. What happened in Malacca in 1511 cannot prove that the sectoral component of my theory of imperialism is valid. But because this place and time provide such a significant "laboratory" test of the theory's spatial comprehensiveness, findings from those events offer valuable supporting evidence.

By combining levels of analysis in table 2.3 one can see the dynamic, synergistic character of Europe's presence overseas. For instance, it is easy to see how formation of a cross-sector coalition in one expanding state could trigger formation of similar coalitions in others. Proliferation of chartered companies among several metropoles in the seventeenth century may be due to this sort of dynamic. Replication of coalitional patterns within several states increased the likelihood of struggle among them for available overseas possessions. When entrepreneurs or missionaries from one state found themselves competing with counterparts from another state for predominance in an area, an obvious response was to seek assistance from their respective home governments. Chances of a turf war between two metropoles were increased when nongovernmental actors from the two countries were waging trade wars and conversion wars on that same turf.

Colonized Peoples: General Features

The enormous diversity among peoples incorporated into overseas empires precludes generalizing about them the way one can about west Europeans. For example, many non-Europeans lived in stateless societies, others in states. It is less inaccurate to refer to them by nonpolitical expressions like "peoples" or "societies" than to employ a term like "state," which does in fact apply to all European metropoles. Chapter 10 trains the zoom lens on colonized peoples. It notes many situations in which non-Europeans' actions had the effect though not the intent of facilitating political subordination. Chapter 10 does not advance the obviously false claim that non-European societies were alike in all or even many respects when they encountered Europeans. The argument is rather that some attributes were present in many non-European societies at the moment of contact, and that where a specific feature was present it increased the likelihood of subordination.

Several recurring patterns are noteworthy:

- States capable of defeating the first European arrivals were generally land-based and had limited control over coastal zones and little interest in defending against maritime invasion. Europeans took advantage of the surprise factor when they landed, quickly setting up fortified coastal enclaves. The physical base was thereby established for penetration inland. This could take place later when the enclave was strengthened by ships bringing the latest round of men, weapons, transport equipment, medicine, and the like. Hinterland polities were at a strategic disadvantage when confronted by aggressive seafarers.
- Initial encounters with Europeans were persistently based on misunderstandings of what the newcomers wanted. Europeans were often treated hospitably as visitors when in fact they had a permanent stay in mind. When land first exchanged hands non-Europeans interpreted the transaction as a temporary, carefully qualified loan of use rights, whereas Europeans saw it as a permanent, unqualified, and full transfer of ownership rights. Such misunderstandings enabled land-hungry settlers and others to entrench themselves on foreign soil. When indigenous people realized that

they had misinterpreted what was happening, it was usually too late to take back alienated land. At the moment of contact non-Europeans were able to resist Europeans but were frequently unwilling to do so because they did not believe newcomers posed a serious threat. When at a later point non-Europeans did have the will to resist they lacked the capacity to expel or exterminate outsiders who by then had become entrenched. In both situations non-Europeans lacked power, though for opposite reasons in each case.

- To the extent that non-European societies did not possess or value the explore-control-utilize syndrome, they were at a power disadvantage when encountering people who did. Where institutions and norms did not support scientific investigation and technological development, it was practically impossible to resist invaders who could call upon the latest round of advances generated by their home societies.

Relations among Societies

Empire building in both expansionist phases was made easier by competition among non-European societies. Indigenous political elites often requested Europeans to ally with them against a rival neighbor. A local pull factor thus reinforced external push factors discussed earlier. At work here was not a misreading of European capacity but, on the contrary, intense awareness of the strategic value of having well-armed foreigners on one's side. The initiatives indigenous elites took to solicit European support were motivated more by the current threat posed by nearby enemies well known to them than by threats a few poorly understood strangers might pose in a dimly imagined future. Elites had a firm grasp of their societies' interests. They could not have known when they tried to advance those interests by forging an alliance that Europeans would use it to advance European interests at the expense of indigenous clients. Each side attempted to use the other for its own ends. Non-Europeans understood their current condition but seriously miscalculated how they would ultimately fare in the high-stakes game of mutual manipulation.

Europeans were often asked to take sides in disputes within other societies, with similar results. To take a recurring pattern, a state lacking rules for succession to the monarchy was thrown into crisis when its ruler died. An aspirant to the throne sought support from a European to strengthen his hand against other contenders. The outsider was only too happy to oblige, using the invitation as an opportunity to play off rival parties against each other (see chapter 10).

Invitations to intervene in peoples' affairs enabled Europeans to establish beachheads of influence and power at little expense to themselves. Their initially limited capacity to control people in distant lands was offset by unusually low costs of entry to non-European public sectors.

Sectors

Did sectoral institutions equivalent to those in Europe exist in other continents? If so, were they able to block agents of European governments, companies, and missionary agencies from penetrating their societies? Degrees of success in countering the triple assault varied greatly from one society and time period to another. What explains these variations is not clear. Fragmentary evidence suggests that a society was especially vulnerable to takeover when its sectoral activities were assigned unequal statuses. If indigenous government officials looked down on artisans and traders, for example, it would be difficult to link public and private profit sectors to resist an equivalent cross-sector coalition fashioned by European invaders. Or if political, economic, and religious tasks were assigned to castes occupying very different positions on the status hierarchy, a society was weakened because of self-imposed restrictions on recruiting people most qualified to fill various tasks.

FACTORS ACCOUNTING FOR DECOLONIZATION

Any historical survey of European empires must address their decline and fall as well as their rise. Decolonization was concentrated in two periods—phases 2 and 5—each lasting for roughly half a century. Chapters 4 and 7 describe major features of these phases and show how they differed. These differences are important for theoretical purposes because they enable us to eliminate or discount explanations that sound plausible but fail the temporal comprehensiveness test. Features prominent in one contraction phase but absent in the other cannot figure in a theory of decolonization unless it can be shown that events in the earlier phase made decolonization in the later one easier or more likely. The underlying reasoning is the same whether one is trying to explain two phases of imperial expansion or two phases of decline. The decolonization phases also have certain features in common. Chapters 14 and 15 argue that the similarities were not accidentally associated with successful independence movements but directly contributed to them.

Prospects for independence were slim until leaders in the colonies wanted to become politically autonomous and had the capacity to take over central administrative posts in the colonial public sector. Chapter 14 argues that for the most part settlers in phase 1 New World colonies scored low on the first score and high on the second, while non-Europeans in phase 3 and 4 Old World colonies scored high on the first and low on the second. With the passage of time New World settler elites came to identify more with the colony and continent they inhabited than with the European country from which they or their ancestors had migrated. The identity shift made it increasingly possible for settlers to imagine a future politically separate from the metropole. With the spread of Western education growing numbers of indigenous people in Old World colonies acquired skills, attitudes, and diplomas

qualifying them for posts in the middle and upper ranks of public sector institutions. Settler elites satisfied the missing will for autonomy condition long before
non-European elites satisfied the missing administrative capacity condition. Consequently settlers led the initial round of independence movements in phase 2, several
decades before non-Europeans led the final round in phase 5. But neither phase
could begin or develop momentum until a sizable number of colonial residents
satisfied both conditions. A convergence process was at work here: the stage was set
for independence when phase 2 elites became more like phase 5 elites in desiring
autonomy and when phase 5 elites became more like phase 2 elites in their capacity to
administer the colonial state.

That a stage is set does not guarantee that something will happen on it. The
timing of a wave of independence movements depended on major crises that led colonial elites to reassess long-standing dependency ties. Institutions based in Europe
created empires; worldwide events dismantled them. Wars among major powers for
global hegemony triggered imperial dissolution in both decolonization phases (see
chapter 15). Hegemonic wars fostered widely diverging expectations in colonies and
metropoles over the nature of their relationship once the conflicts were over. Colonial elites, anticipating greater leeway to chart their territory's future, were shocked
when metropoles used the return to peace to return as well to the status quo ante
bellum. Political crises in the aftermath of war revealed and in turn accentuated
diverging expectations about who held power and legitimate authority. Postwar
crises not only intensified the will but also increased the organizational capacity of
colonial elites to press for autonomy. This point becomes clear when one compares
the remarkably similar dynamics of otherwise vastly different scenarios:

- Britain and the thirteen North American colonies following the Seven Years' War;
- France and Saint Domingue (Haiti) during a lull in the Napoleonic Wars;
- Spain and its New World mainland possessions following the Napoleonic Wars;
- Britain and India after World War I; and
- France and Vietnam and Algeria after World War II.

Being on the winning side of hegemonic wars contributed, paradoxically, to
imperial decline by giving metropoles confidence they could dictate terms to their
possessions.[23] Policies based on this attitude set off rounds of conflict with key
colonies that resulted in successful breakaway movements.

Once early independence precedents were set, the momentum of imperial
decline was accelerated by interactions among a growing number of new states.
Observation and demonstration effects from one territory's independence made it
likely that others would soon follow the same path. The dynamic at work after phases
2 and 5 began was similar in kind, albeit opposite in direction, to the expansionist
scrambles marking phases 1 and 3.

The theory of decolonization advanced here contrasts in interesting ways with the theory of imperialism. Whereas the starting point for understanding expansion of European power was developments in Europe, the starting point for understanding imperial contraction was developments in the colonies. To explain expansion one must examine several sectors embedded in several metropoles; to explain contraction one can concentrate on struggles to control one sector: colonial government. For overseas expansion to succeed, actors needed both a high capacity and a strong will to assert themselves. A striking trait of successful independence movements is not so much their increased capacity to challenge the metropole as the change in will to do so. True, changes in will led in time to changes in capacity to act. But this sequence distinguishes political change in the colonies from the dynamics of European expansion, in which the two components of power were present in more balanced, mutually reinforcing ways.

In one respect expansionist and contractionist phases were similar. The will of Europeans to create empire stemmed in large measure from features peculiar to their home region. The will of colonial nationalists to organize for independence also stemmed in large measure from developments in Europe. The rise of representative democracy and the growing appeal of nationalism in Europe led politically aware groups overseas to perceive colonialism as morally flawed and self-contradictory. This perception gave colonial nationalists ethical and empirical grounds for organizing to challenge an untenably unequal status quo. Characteristics of the region that dominated the world for centuries contributed, eventually, to the end of dominance.

Part II

PHASES OF IMPERIAL EXPANSION
AND CONTRACTION

(*Overleaf*) Land wars between Maoris and British settlers and soldiers, New Zealand. From *Illustrated London News*, August 29, 1863.

3
Phase 1: Expansion, 1415–1773

The first of the five phases was by far the longest, lasting roughly three and a half centuries. This was a period of unprecedented growth in western Europe's formal power and informal influence overseas. Expansion did not proceed evenly throughout phase 1 but rather in spurts, the most notable being the early sixteenth century in the Indian Ocean basin, 1520s through 1650s in the New World, and 1750s–1760s on the Indian subcontinent.

As noted in chapter 1, the phase began with the Portuguese capture of Ceuta, followed two decades later by Gil Eannes's voyage past Cape Bojador. An event marking the phase's end was the British Parliament's Regulating Act of 1773. This was a response to the substantial increase in administrative responsibilities assumed by the royally chartered English East India Company following the victory of its troops over a local ruler's forces at Plassey (Bengal) in 1757. The Regulating Act broke new ground by asserting some parliamentary authority over company employees. In authorizing appointment of the first governor-general of the company's possessions, the act showed greater metropolitan commitment to political control in an important Old World region.

The century and a half following Eannes's voyage was a period of recorded maritime exploration unequalled before or since. Fifteenth-century explorers sailing south so as to sail east—among them Eannes, Diogo Cão, Bartolomeu Dias, and Vasco da Gama—produced maps outlining the shape of Africa and the western Indian Ocean. These explorers also charted the direction of winds and currents. While sailing the Atlantic they had to rely on their experience. In the Indian Ocean they could rely on others': Da Gama drew upon Arab knowledge of winds and currents to make the final Mombasa–Calicut leg of his voyage to India in 1497–98. Knowledge the early explorers accumulated was passed on to fellow Europeans, making it vastly easier for later generations to make long-distance voyages.

An alternative route to the east—by sailing westward—was first attempted by

Christopher Columbus and shortly afterward by John Cabot. Both men believed they had reached Asia. Successors like Amerigo Vespucci, Giovanni da Verrazzano, Juan Díaz de Solís, Sebastian Cabot, Jacques Cartier, Martin Frobisher, and Henry Hudson realized that a "new world" intervened between Europe and Asia. These men combined in varying degrees the original European search for a sea passage to Asia with the search for greater knowledge of the Americas, whose minerals, lands, and plants were increasingly valued for their own sake. The first circumnavigation of the globe by Ferdinand Magellan and Juan Sebastián de Elcano (1519–22) and the subsequent globe-circling expedition led by Sir Francis Drake (1577–80) gave Europeans a relatively accurate sense of the westward edge of the Americas, the vastness of the Pacific, and island chains off the southeast Asian mainland.

An ambitious new phase of maritime exploration was launched in 1768, at the very end of phase 1, with the first of Capt. James Cook's three voyages to locate what was believed to be a large continent (*Terra Australis*) in the Pacific's far southern reaches.

With new knowledge came new power. The early explorers' reports stimulated initiatives to gain military and commercial supremacy on the high seas. West European dominance was never contested in the Atlantic, Caribbean, and Pacific. The Indian Ocean and waters off the eastern and southeastern Asian coast, however, were different. The Portuguese quickly became the single most important maritime power in this huge region with their victory over a much larger Egyptian-Gujarati flotilla off Diu (1509), seizure of the strategically key ports of Malacca (1511) and Hormuz (1515), and establishment of trading enclaves in the Spice Islands. But neither the Portuguese nor agents of other European trading states arriving later could stamp out competition from Asian merchants along the lucrative routes linking East Africa, the Arabian peninsula, India, the southeast Asian islands, and the China coast.

Exploration of continental interiors was uneven during phase 1, most of it taking place in the New World. Spaniards and others searching for gold and silver mapped much of present-day Mexico, the southern United States, Colombia, Venezuela, Peru, and Bolivia within fifty years of Hernán Cortés's arrival (1519) on the American mainland. Further to the north fur trappers, traders, and missionaries, mostly of French origin, penetrated deep into what is now the Canadian and midwest U.S. hinterland by the seventeenth century. Of enormous help to early explorers of North America was ready waterborne access to inland areas. The Gulf of Mexico, Hudson's Bay, the St. Lawrence and Mississippi rivers, and the Great Lakes facilitated travel to the interior. The absence of Old World equivalents to these features of North American geography contributed to a very different outcome in Asia and Africa: there, Europeans were virtually confined to coastal zones.

The geographic distribution of territorial claims paralleled that of inland exploration. From the start of Europe's relationship with the Americas a pattern was established by which newly found lands were quickly (and unilaterally) declared under the authority of the monarch sponsoring an explorer's voyage. Columbus's first action after landing on the island of Guanahani on October 12, 1492, was to claim it for Queen Isabella and King Ferdinand. Three days later he wrote in his journal, "It was . . . my wish not to pass any island without taking possession of it," adding the comforting thought that "when one had been annexed, all might be said to have been."[1] The royal standard Columbus planted on Guanahani was only the first of a series of flags thrust boldly into the soil by explorers and conquerors in the Americas.

Europeans had a special sense of possessiveness about the New World. Their characterization of the hemisphere as new suggests they considered it untouched land whose destiny went unfulfilled until Europeans reached it and transformed a vast, hitherto unowned territory into productive, commercially valuable property. A corollary to this view was that the New World's indigenous inhabitants were interlopers on land they occupied. Such people could have no claim to control their own labor, much less a right to the land sustaining them, that might take precedence over Europeans' economic interests. This possessive attitude is shown by the explorers' propensity from Columbus onward to name New World towns and administrative regions after European places and prominent rulers. Europeans never doubted their right to assign names they chose to places they claimed. To call a territory New Spain or New Amsterdam conveyed conflicting messages. On the one hand, replication of Europe overseas was desirable and possible; fortunately, the New World was sufficiently malleable to be made over to resemble the Old. On the other hand, an Old World in need of improvement was being given a chance at revitalization in an unfamiliar setting. Here was a marvelous, divinely offered opportunity to compile a better record the second time around.

Initially, of course, the new arrivals could not match their grandiose political claims with comparably effective action on the ground. Still, it is striking how rapidly European power was projected over large areas of the New World. In 1519 Cortés and his men marched two hundred miles from the tropical lowlands of Vera Cruz over lofty mountain passes to the Aztec capital at Tenochtitlán, in the heart of what is now Mexico. Francisco Pizarro and his men set out in 1531 from Panama on a venture that took them hundreds of miles along the spine of the Andes to the mountain fastness of Cuzco, capital of the Inca Empire. The remarkably swift conquest of these two extensive, populous, land-based empires, coupled with an ongoing search for sources of the mineral wealth so abundantly evident in Tenochtitlán and Cuzco, brought large numbers of Spanish fortune seekers deep into the interior of Central and South America within a few decades of Cortés's landing at Vera Cruz. An estimated quarter million Europeans emigrated to Spain's American possessions between 1493 and 1579.[2] Once arrived, they moved off in many directions, establishing not one but several frontiers depending on their primary activity. Alistair Hennessy refers to the gold, silver, cattle, agricultural, political / administrative, and mission frontiers of colonial Latin America.[3]

Occupation of the North American interior did not occur to any substantial degree until the end of phase 1. Still, from the early sixteenth century indigenous peoples could not ignore the presence of European traders, missionaries, and soldiers on or near the continent's major waterways.

In the Old World, Europeans exerted influence and some degree of territorial control back of the coastline: the Spanish in Luzon Island (Philippines), the Dutch around Batavia in Java (Dutch East Indies), Portuguese *prazeros* in the Zambezi Valley (Mozambique), farmers and herders descended from Dutch and French Huguenot settlers who migrated inland from Cape Town (South Africa), and agents of the English East India Company who controlled tax collection in Bengal by the 1760s. But the far more common pattern was small coastal enclaves whose principal purpose was commerce with peoples living outside the enclaves' borders. Trading ports in Africa included St. Louis, Gorée, Elmina, São Tomé, Luanda, Sofala, Mombasa, and Malindi. Asian examples included Hormuz, Diu, Goa, Colombo, Pondicherry, Madras, Calcutta, Malacca, Macao, and Deshima Island in Nagasaki harbor. In contrast to the New World pattern, Europeans did not typically claim large swaths of inland territory when they arrived. Indeed, in many cases they did not even pretend to rule enclaves where their traders were active. For it was clear, at least at the outset, that many ports were governed by local rulers and that Europeans were there by permission.

In North Africa and in South and East Asia Europeans encountered highly organized polities which they were unable to conquer. Perhaps the most dramatic setback occurred in 1578, when King Sebastian of Portugal led a large army into the Moroccan interior in a holy war against the infidels. The ensuing Battle of El Ksar-el-Kabir was a disaster for Portugal. Eight thousand soldiers were killed, including the king, and another fifteen thousand captured. The part of Africa closest to an expanding European power was to remain off limits—aside from Ceuta and a few other coastal ports—for another three centuries. The Moors' victory had far-reaching effects on Iberian politics. Portugal was so weakened that Spain's Habsburg monarch Philip II was able to occupy its vacant throne (1581). For the next eighty years Portugal and its overseas possessions were incorporated into the Habsburgs' domains.

Japan's rulers imposed severe limits on European activities. The strong reaction against missionaries, traders, and diplomats that informed official policy in the early seventeenth century was to remain in effect, self-consciously isolating Japan from the West, for almost 250 years. Catholic missionaries were expelled and Japanese converts persecuted. European traders were confined to a small, artificial island in Nagasaki Bay. Among Europeans the Japanese preferred to deal with the Dutch, who were believed incapable of mounting a military threat. Holland posed no religious threat either, as its Protestants, unlike Catholic missionaries from Spain and Portugal, were not active proselytizers.

Morocco and Japan are extreme examples. But many other Old World polities were able and willing to rebuff European advances during phase 1. Whereas in the New World only a few months or years typically elapsed between initial culture contact and a decisive display of the invader's military superiority, in many parts of the Old World these two events were separated by centuries. Large portions of the Old World succumbed only after the Industrial Revolution's technological breakthroughs gave outsiders a new power edge.

COMPETITION AMONG WEST EUROPEAN STATES

One cannot understand western Europe's expansionist drives without seeing the region as a system of separate political units interacting intensively and competitively with each other (see chapter 2). Phase 1 was the great era of European state building. Because polities constructing empires overseas were simultaneously becoming more cohesive and centralized at home, it is reasonable to assume that the two processes were intertwined. Mutual reinforcement was most evident in the reigns of Ferdinand and Isabella and the early monarchs of centralizing dynasties: Aviz in Portugal, Tudor in England, Bourbon in France. The fact that not one but several empires were constructed during phase 1 strongly suggests that competition among west European states encouraged many of them to reduce their insecurity within the region by advancing ambitious claims outside it.

Five states embarked upon serious empire building during phase 1, shifts in their relative power occurring over time. The Portuguese attained prominence in the century following victory at Ceuta, the Spanish made their greatest advances in the sixteenth century, while the Netherlands reached its height as a mercantile power in the seventeenth. The English, resolutely challenged by the Spanish and then by the Dutch and French, gradually rose to become the world's most powerful and economically dynamic state by the mid–eighteenth century.[4] England's dominance was reinforced by the successful outcome of its worldwide struggle with France during the Seven Years' War (1756–63).

Portugal's principal possessions were widely dispersed across three continents, from Brazil to enclaves along the southern African coast to Goa in India and Macao in China. The empire of Spain (or more accurately of the Castilian monarchy) was concentrated in the Caribbean and Central and South America, with a distant

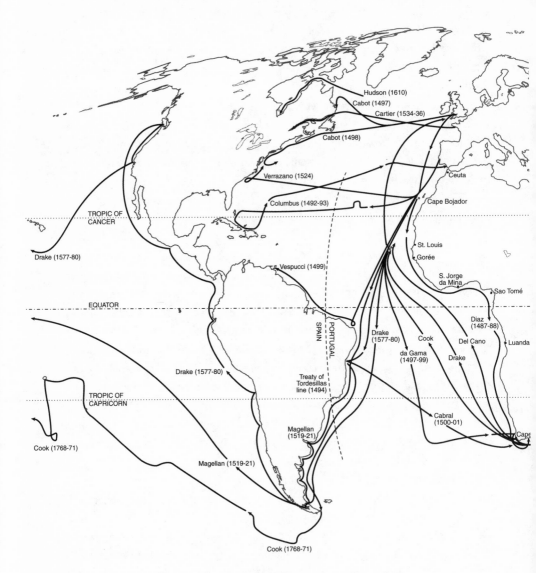

Major phase 1 maritime exploration routes and Old World maritime trading enclaves.

The following labels appear on the map:

Hudson (1610)
Cabot (1497)
Cartier (1534-36)
Cabot (1498)
Verrazano (1524)
Ceuta
Cape Bojador
Columbus (1492-93)
Drake (1577-80)
TROPIC OF CANCER
St. Louis
Gorée
S. Jorge da Mina
Sao Tomé
Vespucci (1499)
EQUATOR
SPAIN
PORTUGAL
Diaz (1487-88)
Drake (1577-80)
Cook
Del Cano
Luanda
da Gama (1497-99)
Drake
Drake (1577-80)
Treaty of Tordesillas line (1494)
TROPIC OF CAPRICORN
Cabral (1500-01)
Cape
Magellan (1519-21)
Cook (1768-71)
Magellan (1519-21)
Cook (1768-71)

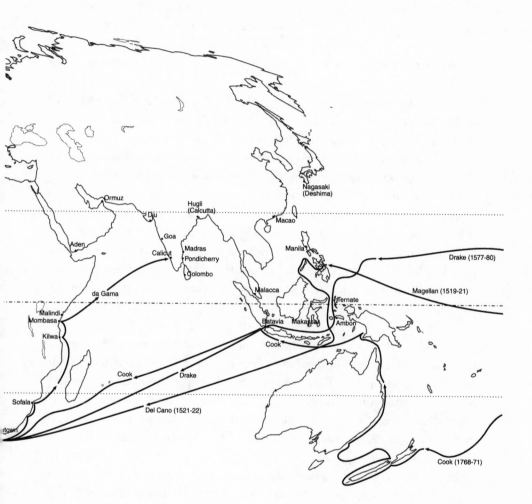

Ormuz
Diu
Hugli
(Calcutta)
Macao
Nagasaki
(Deshima)
Aden
Goa
Madras
Manila
Drake (1577-80)
Calicut
Pondicherry
Colombo
Magellan (1519-21)
da Gama
Malacca
Malindi
Ternate
Mombasa
Batavia
Makassar
Ambon
Kilwa
Cook
Cook
Drake
Sofala
Del Cano (1521-22)
town
Cook (1768-71)

complement in the Philippine Islands. Each Iberian power concentrated on the hemisphere allotted to it by Pope Alexander VI following news of Columbus's first voyage. This conveniently dual division of earthly spoils was confirmed in revised form by the Spanish-Portuguese Treaty of Tordesillas (1494). Neither the papal bull nor the treaty was considered binding by other contestants for overseas territory. The Dutch controlled small settlements in North America, South America, and South Africa. But their principal interest was the islands off southeast Asia's mainland that became known as the Dutch East Indies. The English and French concentrated on North America and the Indian subcontinent.

People living in the metropoles were generally uninformed about and uninterested in overseas expansion during this phase. Important decisions were made by leaders of sectoral institutions: monarchs, officials in the royal court, directors of government-chartered companies, heads of Roman Catholic missionary orders. Decisions were also made by agents of sectoral institutions in far-off regions, men who had to rely on their own resources and judgment as to what was appropriate under a given set of circumstances. Monarchs, merchants, and missionaries were not pressed by metropolitan public opinion to act in certain ways abroad. Neither, in a prepopulist era, did sectoral leaders attempt systematically to mobilize and shape public opinion to support imperial ventures.

Rivalry among metropoles frequently took a violent turn. Some of the wars that took place during phase 1 involved coalitions of states. Thus, England and Holland were allied against Spain and France in the War of the Spanish Succession (1701–14). Many wars pitted two metropoles against each other. Examples include Portugal against Spain (1581–89; 1641–44); the protracted Dutch struggle for independence from Spain (1568–1648); Spain against France (1547–49; 1648–59); England against Spain (1587–1604; 1655–59; 1739–42); Holland against England (intermittently between 1652 and 1678); and England against France (1488–92; intermittently between 1542 and 1560; 1627–28; 1756–63).[5] Conflict was particularly intense when nationality differences were reinforced by differences of official religious preference. Thus, Protestant England and Holland were often locked in bitter struggle with Catholic Spain or France or both.

In some cases, such as the War of Spanish Succession, violent struggles commencing in the European theater set off conflict in colonial peripheries. In other cases conflict in the periphery triggered warfare in Europe. The skirmish between English and French colonial troops and their respective Amerindian allies over Fort Duquesne (present-day Pittsburgh) in 1754–55 helped precipitate the Seven Years' War. This conflict eventually became globalized as battles between the two metropoles and their allies were waged on the European mainland, in Canada, the Caribbean, Senegambia (West Africa), and India's Carnatic (southeastern) coast. In other instances violent competition was largely confined to non-European regions. Examples include Portuguese-Spanish conflicts over Ternate in the Moluccas (1550–88); the murder of English and Portuguese traders in 1623 by Dutch East India Company officials on the East Indian island of Amboina; Portuguese versus Dutch in West Africa (1620–55), Brazil (1624–29; 1640–54), and Malacca (1640–41); and England versus France in India (Carnatic Wars of 1744–48 and 1749–54) and North America (King George's War, 1744–48).[6] In the Caribbean basin, where the Spanish, English, French, and Dutch all held territories, raids by privateers loosely aligned with one metropole against a rival's ships or major towns were so frequent as to become virtually a way of life.

DEMOGRAPHIC AND SOCIAL DIMENSIONS OF EXPANSION

The New World's indigenous (Amerindian) inhabitants were extremely vulnerable to European diseases and hence suffered catastrophic losses, above all in the century following Columbus's arrival. Ralph Davis estimates that the indigenous population of the Americas equalled Europe's in 1500 but was probably under one-tenth of it by 1600. The greatest devastation occurred in the Caribbean. The estimated three to four million Amerindians who inhabited Hispaniola as of 1492 numbered about fifteen thousand by 1518 and essentially disappeared by 1570. The heaviest preconquest concentration of population, an estimated twenty-five million, lay in the heartland of what became known as New Spain. By 1548 the area's Amerindians had declined to about a quarter of this figure. Subsequent smallpox and influenza epidemics further reduced it to a little over a million by century's end. "Spain's principal gift to the Americas," writes Davis, "was the destruction of its people."[7] Lyle McAlister concludes that "a demographic disaster of continental proportions occurred in the New World in the sixteenth century. . . . The quantitative and qualitative devastation of the indigenous population far exceeded anything accomplished by the Black Death in Europe."[8]

Disease had the opposite effect along the African coastline. Malaria and other tropical illnesses to which Africans had developed some immunity gave the West African coast a well-deserved reputation as "the white man's grave" until Europeans learned of quinine's prophylactic powers in the nineteenth century.[9] Ghana's first president, Kwame Nkrumah, only half-jokingly proposed erecting a monument to the anopheles mosquito to acknowledge its contribution in keeping settlers out of his country. Tropical diseases performed a similar deflective role in many parts of Asia.

The result is that European settlers in phase 1 were concentrated overwhelmingly in the New World, the hemisphere in which disease was their ally rather than their foe.

The Americas were demographically rearranged in phase 1, the implosion of indigenous population being accompanied by an explosion of newcomers who constituted racially distinct groups.[10] Millions of Europeans arrived as settlers, drawn by many lures: hopes for vast and easily accessible mineral wealth, plentiful and bountiful land, adventure, power, prospects (for men) of sex with non-European women, higher social status, and avoidance of religious persecution. A much larger number came involuntarily as slaves from Africa, responding not to their aspirations but to the demands of European settlers for accessible, low-cost labor in agriculture, mining, and domestic service. In another category were the offspring of sexual unions across racial lines. To use the Spanish terms, unions between Europeans and Amerindians produced mestizos; between Europeans and Africans, mulattoes; between Amerindians and Africans, zambos. The literal embodiment of racial pluralism, these people added further to the complex layering of castelike structures in which status was allocated largely along lines of continental origin and skin color.

Despite their severe early losses, Amerindians remained the largest single racial category in the population of many New World colonies throughout phase 1. By one estimate, in 1570 they made up 96 percent and 94 percent of the population in Spain's and Portugal's New World empires, respectively. Comparable figures for 1650 were 81 percent and 74 percent. Some 60 percent of Peru's population as of 1795 was Amerindian.[11] A quite dissimilar distribution emerged in the British North American (BNA) colonies that eventually formed the nucleus of the United States. Along the coastal zone east of the Appalachians settlers quickly became numerically dominant because of initially small and dispersed indigenous population, the effects of disease and settler attacks upon Amerindians, their withdrawal to lands back of the settler frontier, and a steady stream of new immigrants from the British Isles. By 1700 a quarter million white settlers lived in the thirteen BNA colonies, a figure roughly equalling the indigenous population east of the Mississippi at that time. By 1776 settlers constituted three-quarters of the BNA colonies' population of two and a half million, Amerindians about 4 percent. Black slaves accounted for the remaining 20 percent.[12]

On Caribbean islands and along coastal zones from the southern BNA colonies to Brazil, the influx of forcibly transplanted Africans that began early in the 1500s continued unabated through the rest of phase 1. Indeed, more Africans made the dreaded Middle Passage in the 1700s than in either of the preceding centuries. The transatlantic slave trade profoundly affected the racial demographics of Africans' destination points. By 1650 the black slave population outnumbered whites in Brazil and was five times greater than whites in the Spanish Antilles. The British West Indies' black population rose from 25 percent of the total in 1650 to 83 percent in 1710 and 90 percent in 1770. For the same years it rose from 3 percent to 24 percent to 39 percent in the southern BNA colonies.[13]

In many New World colonies the percentage of the population that was racially mixed rose steadily over time. And time there was, considering that from the six-teenth century onward, in the Caribbean region and outlying coastal zones, substan-tial numbers from the Americas, Europe, and Africa lived in close proximity. That the colonial era began so much earlier and lasted so much longer in the Americas than in virtually all parts of the Old World accounts for the growing numerical and social influence of racial categories that were literally new under the sun. By one estimate mestizos composed 3 percent of the Spanish American and 5 percent of the Brazilian population in 1650, with somewhat smaller percentages for mulattoes. In the eighteenth century the mestizo proportion rose rapidly in Brazil and in the principal Spanish territories, New Spain and Peru. By the 1790s mestizos accounted for 22 percent of Peru's population and perhaps 40–50 percent of New Spain's. Mulattoes formed a small but socially influential intermediary group in France's most economically important New World colony, Saint Domingue (Haiti).[14]

In the Old World the major demographic effect of Europe's presence was the removal of tens of millions of Africans from their continent of birth. This process, lasting for more than four centuries, was both cause and consequence of slave-raiding activities among Africans that severely disrupted sub-Saharan economies and social relations. But the transatlantic slave trade did little to change the racial composition of Africa's inhabitants. Apart from southern Africa's Khoikhoi and San peoples there was no African equivalent of the decimation of New World popula-tions from disease. Neither did millions of people come from other continents as permanent settlers. In only a few places, such as Cape Town and Luanda, did a mixed-race population of any size arise.

In Asia the demographic impact of Europe's presence was even less significant. Some people were taken from the Dutch East Indies and the Malay peninsula to South Africa as slaves. On Java and in trading enclaves like Goa, Colombo, and Macao a small mixed-race group emerged. But otherwise little change from precon-tact days took place, in striking contrast to the Americas.

TYPES OF COLONIES

D. K. Fieldhouse has proposed a helpful classification of European colonies based on the numbers, population ratios, and economic functions of groups not indigenous to a given territory.[15] His five types, slightly modified for purposes of my analysis, are as follows:

1. Pure settlement colonies, in which European immigrants and their descendants be-came a substantial majority of the population. These colonies began as small, com-pact territories and gradually but steadily expanded along a frontier separating lands occupied by settlers from lands occupied by indigenous peoples. Settlers wanted land but did not need indigenous labor to work it. Labor was supplied by the settlers

themselves or by imported slaves. Colonial boundaries generally marked a racial and cultural "frontier of exclusion"[16] between settlers and indigenous people. As boundaries pushed steadily back from coast to interior, the area's original inhabitants experienced land dispossession and massive psychological as well as physical dislocation.

2. Mixed colonies, in which a substantial number of settlers lived in the same territory as a larger indigenous population. Settler well-being depended upon ready access to—and a high degree of control over—indigenous labor. Physical proximity of the two groups meant that a mixed colony featured a "frontier of inclusion."[17] Over time the colony became mixed in a second sense, as the sexual unions of settlers and indigenous peoples produced a group classified as racially hybrid.

3. Plantation colonies, in which a small settler minority owned and managed plantations producing agricultural commodities for export. Labor on the plantation and in the settler household was performed by slaves. The first slave generation was imported from another area and was unfamiliar with the colony's terrain, hence amenable to close control by slaveholders. Over time a separate racial category emerged from the sexual unions of settlers and slaves.

4. Colonies of occupation, in which few if any settlers were present. The vast majority of the population was indigenous to the territory. The most visible European presence was that of military personnel and civilian administrators sent out by the metropole; a few traders and missionaries might also be present. These individuals were only temporarily stationed in the colony and eventually returned to the metropole, which they considered their homeland.

5. Trading settlements or naval bases comprising tiny parcels of coastal or riverine land. Few Europeans lived in these enclaves. Those who did were typically temporary residents whose main function was to foster commercial relations with people living outside the settlements.

   The European presence in the New World quickly became a settler presence. Hence the most economically viable and strategically important colonies in the Americas were of the first three types: BNA (pure settlement), New Spain and Peru (mixed), Brazil and islands in the Caribbean (plantation). The more peripheral mainland colonies of Spain could be classified as colonies of occupation. Settlements that began as trading enclaves or naval bases rapidly evolved into the other types.

   In phase 1 Old World colonies, in sharp contrast, nonindigenous groups played a minimal role. The coastal enclaves dotting African and Asian coastlines are examples of Fieldhouse's fifth type. Areas of more extensive inland influence like Luzon and the Zambezi valley come closest to mixed colonies. But even these are better classified as colonies of occupation.

   The sole Old World candidate for any of Fieldhouse's first three types was South Africa. There the Dutch East India Company and French Huguenot immi-

grants and their Boer ("farmer") descendants exterminated or enslaved the indigenous Khoikhoi and San peoples and imported slaves from Madagascar and the East
Indies. Accompanied by their slaves, they migrated inland to pursue farming and
herding activities. By the eighteenth century Boers were pushing eastward into an
increasingly contested frontier on the other side of which were Bantu-speaking
Africans, whose large numbers and ability to resist European diseases made extermination impossible. South Africa resembled a pure settlement colony with respect
to the settlers' behavior toward Khoikhoi and San, their efforts to extend an inland
frontier, and their obsessive concern with maintaining racial purity. In areas controlled by settlers could be found elements of a mixed colony, in that whites constituted a minority of the total population and a mixed-blood, or "colored," community soon emerged. Traces of a plantation colony could also be found, to the extent
that settlers relied heavily upon slaves to perform manual labor and domestic service.
South Africa's historical path thus parallels settler-dominated societies in the New
World.[18] South African settlers set the stage for interracial conflict on a grand scale by
attempting to apply the methods and worldviews of New World settlers to an Old
World land whose demographic and epidemiological features were quite different.

ECONOMIC DIMENSIONS OF EXPANSION

Hope of economic gain was the principal motivator behind exploration and the
formation of overseas enclaves and settlements. Profits could be realized by obtaining, at minimal production or purchase cost, commodities highly valued in Europe
that mostly were available only outside it. European ships unwound off their sterns,
as it were, the lengthy threads of commerce that for the first time stitched together
the world's continents. Production and trade patterns originating in phase 1 profoundly shaped economic development prospects of metropoles and colonies alike
in subsequent phases.

Oceanic trade developed along two axes, the first linking metropoles vertically
with their colonies, the second linking non-European areas laterally with each other.
Trade of the first kind brought commodities a metropole's consumers valued. These
included raw and semiprocessed primary products: gold, silver, and precious stones;
spices, dyewoods, sugar, tobacco, indigo, beaver furs, and cattle hides. Also shipped
to Europe were such handcrafted luxury goods from Asia and the Near East as silk
brocades, cotton cloth and piece goods, porcelains and chinaware, lacquerware, fine-
tempered steel, and ivory and wood carvings. Early contacts with the New World
generated vertical trade of another sort that Alfred Crosby has called "the Columbian
exchange." An astonishing variety of flora and fauna moved in both directions across
the Atlantic, in many instances becoming commercially valuable in their new environments. Europe sent to the Americas sugar, citrus fruits, horses, cows, and pigs

while importing maize and potatoes.[19] Successful propagation of these plants and animals in their new settings enabled both hemispheres to become more nutritionally self-sufficient.

The doctrine of mercantilism, which originated during phase 1 and became the dominant way of thinking about imperial economic relations, stressed vertical trade. In the ideal mercantilist system a metropole maximized gain by ensuring that its colonies imported goods only from itself, that colonial exports were sent only to its ports, and that all transactions occurred on ships flying the metropole's flag.

Yet the most significant trade patterns in phase 1 violated the mercantilist ideal by being lateral, not vertical. In the course of creating what Wallerstein termed the first genuine "world-economy," Europeans found they could profit by connecting non-European regions with each other. Africa was linked to the Americas through the transatlantic slave trade. Slave ships also transferred staple crops (notably cassava and maize) from the New World to Africa, and peanuts and bananas in the reverse direction. The staple crops, initially planted to feed Africans held in coastal "factories" pending the ocean voyage, spread inland and probably increased population densities in areas heavily hit by slave raiding. East Asia and the New World were connected by "Manila galleons" that exchanged bullion from the mines of New Spain and Peru for silks, tea, chinaware, and other Asian luxury goods.[20] Coffee, initially grown in the Middle East, became a commercial tree crop in the Dutch East Indies and the Americas. Indian textiles and Indian Ocean cowries were exchanged for slaves along the West African coast. Indeed, Indian textiles were for a considerable time the most important and expensive category of European trade with Africa.[21] In the eastern Indian Ocean, among the Moluccas and other Spice Islands, and along the Chinese and Japanese coasts chartered companies amassed trade goods and profits by exchanging raw materials and manufactured goods. Bengal cloth, for example, was traded for Amboina spices, which were then sold for Chinese teas and silks. Opium from India, whose production was strongly encouraged by the English East India Company, bought access to the Chinese market. European merchants sometimes purchased Asian commodities with gold from southern Africa.

Paradoxically, the dominant theory of intercontinental trade in phase 1 emphasized the vertical, north-south component. But the dominant practice was a complex series of lateral, south-south links.

The volume of transactions in phase 1, whether vertical or horizontal, was limited by the technology of maritime transport. Obvious constraints were the size, speed, and safety of wooden ships utterly dependent on ocean winds and currents. These limits affected the composition of trade, which consisted principally of commodities with high ratios of value to bulk. Most trade goods were destined for consumption by economic elites, above all those in metropoles and New World settler communities.[22]

Existing production technologies set another constraint. What western Europe exported during phase 1 it produced in modest amounts, at least in comparison with its performance in later centuries. The astounding advances marking the early Industrial Revolution—notably the substitution of inanimate for human energy and economies of scale from factory production—had yet to take place.[23] Europe enjoyed no decided technological edge over many of the societies its explorers encountered. If anything, it lagged behind some trading partners in certain respects, including the production of silk, cotton cloth, and tempered steel.

Moreover, the first round of the Industrial Revolution may be said to have occurred not in Europe but in New World plantation colonies, with greater effects on the composition of Europe's imports than of its exports. Sugar plantations were in effect huge outdoor factories. They employed advanced techniques of mass production and processing, involved a landless labor force whose work patterns were monitored and controlled, and enabled plantation owners to amass great fortunes. C. L. R. James writes of the slaves in Saint Domingue, "Working and living together in gangs of hundreds on the huge sugar-factories that covered the North Plain, they were closer to a modern proletariat than any group of workers at the time."[24]

Limits on the volume of exports were sometimes set by indigenous elites. When Vasco da Gama reached India in 1498 after sailing thousands of miles to reach this land of fabled wealth, the first ruler he met was the Zamorin of Calicut. After a ritual exchange of greetings the Zamorin ordered the Portuguese to land their merchandise and offer it for sale. J. H. Parry writes, "The goods were duly landed; they were shoddy and unsuitable, and no one would buy them. . . . When reminded that usage demanded a diplomatic gift for the Zamorin, [da Gama] produced the usual collection of hats, basins, and pieces of trade cloth; and when the officials refused to deliver a gift they thought derisory, and the Zamorin himself complained of a show of disrespect, da Gama virtually forced his way into the [ruler's] presence in order to make lame and lying excuses."[25] A few years later the Portuguese started to trade in Sofala (Mozambique). They "awaited the arrival of quantities of gold bullion [from the interior], but found that their offers of woolen caps, table cloths, and brass chamber pots attracted few African traders."[26]

Writing of the English East India Company, chartered in 1600, the Indian historian and diplomat K. M. Panikkar notes that during the first few years "the company's affairs did not progress very satisfactorily, for nothing was available in England to sell in exchange" for the spices and gems English merchants desired.[27] Not until the company carved out a share of the inter-Asian carrying trade did it start to earn sizable profits. Until well into the nineteenth century the Chinese imperial court actively discouraged trade with Europeans. The famous edict in 1793 of the Ch'ien-lung emperor to Britain's King George III noted that of material goods "there is nothing we lack, as your principal envoy and others have themselves observed. We have never set much store on strange or ingenious objects, nor do we need any more of your country's manufactures."[28] What rulers of the great Asian polities wanted more than Europe's luxury goods were gold and silver from the Americas and Africa that foreign traders had on board.

In the Americas and along Africa's west coast, where material culture was generally not as technologically advanced as in Asia, European trade goods found a decidedly more favorable reception. "Weapons were of paramount importance to the feudal native polities of North America," writes James Axtell, "but metal objects of any kind, cloth goods, and cleverly designed or sizable wooden objects also drew their admiration."[29] Even here, however, the impact of foreign commodities on indigenous economies was limited. (The effect of guns on political life was another matter.) Many societies remained self-sufficient, minimally altering familiar production patterns to gain access to the new goods. Frequently, however, indigenous people became more aggressive outside their community boundaries, searching for resources to exchange for metal goods, cloth, alcohol, and the like. Slave raiding was hugely disruptive in many parts of Africa. In North America a vast increase in trapping visibly impacted the physical environment that beavers had done so much to shape.

Europeans in phase 1 had a long list of raw materials and manufactured goods they wanted from other parts of the world. But in general they were unable or unwilling to provide goods from their home economies to purchase what they wanted in free market settings. The simplest way to get something without exchanging it for what others are prepared to offer is to use force. A striking feature of phase 1 was the extensive European reliance upon coercion to satisfy economic demands. This was most evident in the New World. The Spanish colonial state used a variety of mechanisms—encomienda and corregimiento, mita (Peru) and repartimiento (New Spain)—to force Amerindians to work at minimal expense on large agricultural and mining operations.[30] The profitability of New World plantation economies depended upon efficient, coercion-intensive exploitation of black slaves, who had to work long hours in exchange for derisory material comforts and little or no acknowledgment of their humanity. Plantation owners had no compunctions about using torture and terror to put down the slave revolts that repeatedly erupted in the Caribbean basin.[31] Europeans routinely employed force to extract profits from Old World trading enclaves. Weapons supplied to indigenous agents to mount slave raids or collect spices imposed heavy burdens upon people living far from the coastal zones where these operations were planned.

EUROPEAN SECTORAL INSTITUTIONS: ROLES AND INTERACTIONS

When Europeans emigrated to the New World in phase 1 they were typically motivated by a desire to generate economic gains over and above subsistence. They wanted consumer and luxury goods from Europe and were prepared to devote some or all of their labor to producing export commodities whose sale paid for imported goods. In these respects the original settlers and their descendants comprised a transplanted private profit sector. To the extent that the basic unit of economic activity was the family, settlers were a noninstitutionalized component of a colony's private profit sector. But settlers also founded, managed, and owned their own profit-oriented institutions. Examples were large-scale haciendas and ranches, plantations, and—most notably in the BNA colonies—a wide range of small-scale manufacturing, commercial, and shipping enterprises.

Even in pure settlement, mixed, and plantation colonies, however, metropole-based private profit institutions played major roles. Whether operating on their own or in conjunction with the metropolitan state, European companies controlled trade between a metropole and its colonies. They were particularly well positioned to reap handsome profits if they monopolized trade with colonies exporting highly valued commodities like spices and sugar. Banking houses extended credit to overseas ventures. European companies handled the vast bulk of the transatlantic slave trade. Many plantation owners lived lavishly in the metropole thanks to profits from their outdoor factories.

A recurring pattern in phase 1 was the formalization of cooperative arrangements between a metropole's public and private profit sectors. A common Iberian pattern was for a monarch to authorize a ship's captain to trade on condition that a fifth of the proceeds was handed over to the royal exchequer. A mechanism popular in seventeenth- and eighteenth-century England, Holland, and France was the chartered company, a corporate body authorized by royal or legislative charter to operate overseas for profit and to carry out quasi-governmental functions in territories assigned to it. Nonreinvested gains from a chartered company's activities were frequently divided between government officials and agencies, on the one hand, and private investors on the other. Prominent actors in both sectors thus had a shared interest in the venture's success. Some enterprises, such as the Virginia Company and Dutch West India Company, sponsored initial rounds of settlement in new colonies and laid out the basic policies of colonial governance. Others were primarily trading operations, formally authorized to use force as need be to ensure access to desired commodities, keep purchase prices low, and protect company property and personnel. Among the best known trading ventures were the English East India Company (1600); the Dutch East India Company (1602); the French East India Company (1664); and the Hudson's Bay Company (1670).[32]

Christian missionary activity was most evident in the New World colonies of Catholic countries. Among Catholic orders sending priests to Iberian colonies to observe, convert, and teach indigenous peoples were the Dominicans, Franciscans, Augustinians, Mercedarians, and Jesuits. More than a hundred houses and mission centers belonging to various orders were at work in Spanish America by 1600. The leading religious congregations in French North America were the Jesuits, Recollects, Capuchins, and Sulpicians.[33] Missionaries often operated far outside areas effectively controlled by a colonial administration. In Japan and China they worked in lands never taken over.[34] In effect they created their own religious and cultural frontiers.

Cooperative links between public and religious sectors were most evident in the Spanish and Portuguese empires. Papal bulls authorizing these countries' monarchs to claim overseas possessions made it clear that propagation of the Catholic faith was a precondition and principal purpose of the entire operation. From the start close ties were maintained between secular governing structures and the Roman Catholic hierarchy. Even when monarchs exercised veto power over the hierarchy's choice of personnel to be sent abroad, the state never completely controlled the church's work at home or in the colonies. Neither was there a fusion of sectoral institutions at home or abroad. Rather, each found it in its own interest to form an ongoing coalition with the other. The colonial state's coercive and financial resources supported the work of religious conversion. The church in turn preached that indigenous peoples and settlers should obey constituted authority.

A different pattern obtained in England and Holland after Catholicism ceased to be the official religion. Protestant denominations, whether accorded official status or not, showed little interest in converting indigenous people to Christianity. Not until phase 3 did Protestants become seriously involved in missionary work. Rather, phase 1 Protestantism was the more or less exclusive possession of settler communities. Indeed, it was precisely the "heathen" character of non-Europeans that enabled settlers to justify exterminating them and taking their land. To the extent that a church–state alliance obtained in English and Dutch settler colonies, the decentralized nature of Protestant denominational governance gave settlers a degree of control over the religious sector that was not possible in officially Catholic colonies.

The kinds of cross-sector coalitions forged in the metropoles affected the ways in which overseas empires were governed. The nature of these coalitions and the degree to which decision-making authority in each sector was retained in metropolitan hands influenced the degree of leverage settler communities could exert on sectoral institutions at the point when political leaders in the colonies considered breaking with the metropole. But such observations run well ahead of the story. The point here is that during phase 1 Europeans experimented with a variety of ways in which public sector institutions could collaborate with institutions from other metropolitan sectors to advance their interests overseas.

4

Phase 2: Contraction, 1775–1824

For three and a half centuries Europeans extended the bounds of their overseas possessions. In the half century that commenced in the 1770s the scope of imperial holdings shrank dramatically. Twenty countries recognized today as sovereign states gained independence as a direct or indirect result of political upheavals in phase 2.[1] Decolonization was confined to the Americas. Virtually unaffected by demands for independence were the islands and coastal enclaves Europeans had acquired throughout the Old World.

Phase 2 began in British North America (BNA) with the outbreak in 1775 of armed conflict between colonists and troops loyal to the British monarchy and to the monarch's local agents. In the background was a decade of tension between the metropole and residents of several colonies, notably Massachusetts, Pennsylvania, and Virginia. Disputes initially arose from parliamentary decisions following successful prosecution of the Seven Years' War (1756–63) to impose new taxes on the colonists and station troops among them. The American Duties ("Sugar") Act of 1764 and the Stamp Act the following year came as a shock to colonists, many of whom had fought on Britain's side and expected to be treated more rather than less favorably now that France's loss of North American mainland possessions ended the most serious threat to BNA security. A hastily gathered assembly of prominent figures from several colonies, the Stamp Act Congress, objected in principle to taxation by a distant legislature in which colonists were not represented. The scope of disagreement widened from political theory to political activism with the Boston Massacre (1770) and Tea Party (1773), British closure of the port, and formation of local militias to defend colonists against British troops.

The first major armed confrontation, the Battle of Bunker Hill, took place in June 1775 on a peninsula opposite Boston harbor.[2] In a dramatic escalation from skirmishes with local residents at Lexington and Concord two months earlier, the battle involved volunteer units drawn widely from the New England colonies, engaged thousands of troops on both sides, led to extensive property damage (much of Charlestown was leveled by fire from naval bombardment), and ended with substantial casualties: 268 dead on the British side, 115 on the colonists'. There was no going back from violence on this scale. Three weeks later George Washington assumed command of the new Continental Army, and an eastern Massachusetts revolt was a step closer to becoming an American revolution. A year later the revolution's leaders took the momentous step of declaring independence from Great Britain.

The concluding event of phase 2 was another major battle, fought in 1824 on the outskirts of Ayacucho in the Peruvian highlands. The town, known earlier as Huamanga, had been founded in 1539 by Francisco Pizarro. The battle pitted the conquistador's successors—the Spanish viceroy of Peru and royalist forces—against Colombian and Peruvian troops seeking independence. The royalist side was defeated and the viceroy captured in the decisive, and final, effort by Spain to retain a hold on the New World mainland. By 1825, when the independence of Charcas (Bolivia) was proclaimed, the imperial edifice constructed by Spain on the mainland had collapsed.

In the years between the battles of Bunker Hill and Ayacucho, every European state with significant New World colonies lost its most economically and strategically valuable New World territory. The British were the first to undergo major loss. Thirteen North American colonies fought from 1775 to 1781, achieving a decisive military victory at Yorktown, then engaged in intense diplomacy to form one polity out of many. The independent status of the "first new nation" was formally acknowledged by Britain in 1783.[3] The French came next. A massive slave revolt broke out in 1791 in their most lucrative colony, Saint Domingue. This led to de facto control of the entire island of Hispaniola a decade later by forces commanded by the ex-slave general François Toussaint L'Ouverture. In 1802 Napoleon Bonaparte sent twenty thousand soldiers across the Atlantic to restore French control and reimpose slavery. Toussaint was captured and exiled to France, where he died in captivity. But his associates waged a successful guerrilla campaign against French troops and in 1804 proclaimed the independence of Saint Domingue, renamed Hayti or Haiti. French officials were unwilling to admit that they were no longer in control, but in 1825 France's monarch, Charles X, formally acknowledged Haiti's independence.

The initial challenges to Spanish rule came not from its most important New World colonies, as in the British and French cases, but from its peripheral ones. The ideological foundations of independence from Spain were distinctly more conservative than those in the BNA colonies and Haiti. The financial and administrative nerve centers of Spain's mainland empire were New Spain and Peru. But it was from Venezuela and New Granada (Colombia) that Simón Bolívar led his protracted armed struggle against the metropole, beginning in 1810. In Argentina that same year selection by settlers (criollos) of a provisional junta marked a de facto break with Spain that was formalized six years later. It was from Argentina that Gen. José de San Martín and his troops set out in 1817 on their epic march over the Andes to fight royalist forces in Chile and later in Peru.

The transition from colonial New Spain to independent Mexico came relatively late, in 1821. Moreover, Mexican independence was a conservative reaction against the unsuccessful grassroots revolts led earlier by the populist priests Miguel Hidalgo y Costilla (in 1810–11) and José María Morelos (1810–15). Peru's criollo elites were likewise cautious about breaking with Spain. They feared that independence might trigger Amerindian revolts in the interior and slave revolts along the coast that could undercut their privileged position. If change was to occur it required outside intervention. This took the form of San Martín's forces from the south and Bolívar's and Antonio José de Sucre's forces from the north converging on Lima. These maneuvers culminated in defeat of royalist forces at Ayacucho. The two bastions of Spanish authority were thus reluctant to assert independence. But once it was declared, Mexico and Peru experienced no serious domestic pressures to return to colonial status.

Portugal's immense New World colony, Brazil, gained independence in 1822 under unusual circumstances. The Portuguese regent, Joao VI, and most of his court fled Portugal for Brazil in 1808, just before invading forces loyal to Napoleon reached Lisbon. During the regent's years in Brazil (1808–21) the roles of metropole and colony were in effect reversed. With Joao's return to Portugal as king, Portuguese interests attempted to reassert the dominant position they had once held over Brazilian affairs. This triggered a negative reaction from Brazil's landholding elites. Joao's son Dom Pedro, who had remained in Brazil as his father's appointed agent, took up the nationalist cause. Rejecting orders to return to Lisbon in 1822, he instead proclaimed himself emperor of Brazil. Though at one level Dom Pedro clearly disobeyed Joao, at another the son simply followed advice offered earlier by his departing father: "If the worst comes to the worst and Brazil demands independence, proclaim it yourself and put the crown on your own head."[4] The transition to independence in Brazil was incremental, in the sense that the monarchical principle was retained, as was the authority of Portugal's ruling House of Braganza. Transition was also quite peaceful, in contrast with the other cases noted.

A distinctive feature of phase 2 is its short duration. The decolonization of most of the New World mainland and the island of Hispaniola (Haiti and the Dominican Republic) was compressed into five decades. The rapidity of imperial decline becomes even more striking if one examines independence dates within phase 2. In many cases there was a lag between the year independence was proclaimed and when it was acknowledged by the metropole; the extreme example was

Haiti at twenty-one years. If the event that counts is the declaration of independence by individuals or groups able to sustain that claim, the first two cases stand alone: the United States in 1776 and Haiti in 1804. Independence for the Spanish colonies and Brazil took place within a mere fifteen years, if one considers 1810 the start of serious struggles for autonomy in Venezuela and Argentina. Formal declarations of independence for many territories were clustered in an even smaller time period, between 1816 and 1822. Thus, after a slow start the number of new states escalated sharply toward the end of phase 2. Another distinctive feature is that decolonization was largely confined to the mainland. Except for Hispaniola the Caribbean islands remained in the hands of west European powers. In Cuba, for example, an independence movement with popular support and a chance of success did not develop until the late nineteenth century. Independence for the Caribbean region, the first part of the Americas extensively explored and settled by Europeans in phase 1, was by and large postponed to phase 5. Some Caribbean islands did, however, change metropolitan rulers. The British captured numerous islands, among them Martinique and Guadeloupe from France in 1794, Trinidad from Spain in 1797, and Curaçao from the Dutch in 1807. Several territories returned to their former rulers in the general settlement of international accounts that followed Napoleon's final defeat in 1815.

As noted, inhabitants of small islands and mainland enclaves held by European powers in the Old World did not break from colonial status in phase 2. Where change did occur it involved redistribution among imperial powers of previously acquired territories. These were a direct consequence of France's drive for hegemony in Europe, initially through armies mobilized in the Revolution's early years, then (1803–15) through armies directed by Napoleon. The more the French extended their power on the mainland, the more they ceded control of the high seas by default to their archenemies the British. Britain's naval victory over a French–Spanish armada off Trafalgar in 1805 was in both real and symbolic terms the proclamation of its dominance over the world's oceans. Britain retained this position for the rest of the century.[5] Not surprisingly, during phase 2 British naval forces captured French enclaves along the coast of Senegal and the French-held Indian Ocean islands of Mauritius, Réunion, and the Seychelles.

France's takeover of the Netherlands and Napoleon's invasion of the Iberian Peninsula in 1808, moreover, prevented other imperial powers from defending their possessions against the British. Particularly weakened were the Dutch, the only phase 1 power with more substantial economic interests in the Old World than the New. French revolutionary forces established the Batavian Republic (1795–1806) in Holland, and by 1810 the Netherlands was ruled directly from Paris. The Dutch were thus isolated for many years from their settlement colony at the Cape of Good Hope and trade centers administered by the Dutch East India Company in Ceylon, Java,

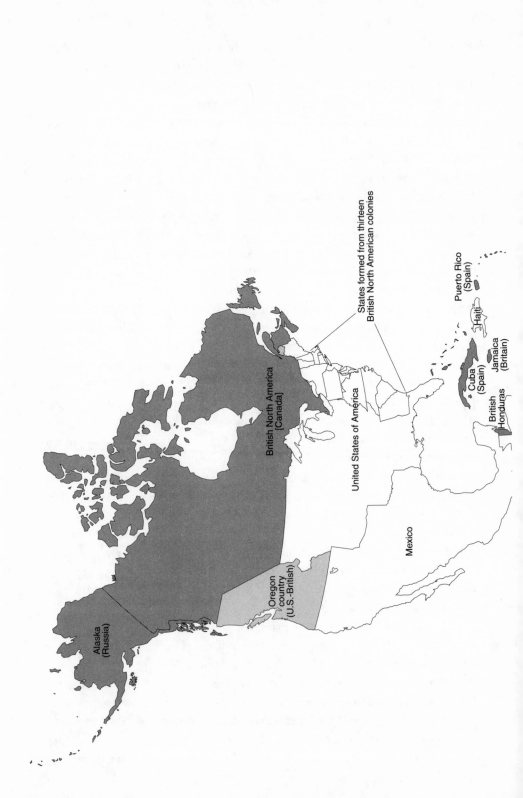

Alaska
(Russia)

British North America
[Canada]

Oregon
country
(U.S.-British)

United States of America

States formed from thirteen
British North American colonies

Mexico

Cuba
(Spain)

Haiti

Puerto Rico
(Spain)

Jamaica
(Britain)

British
Honduras

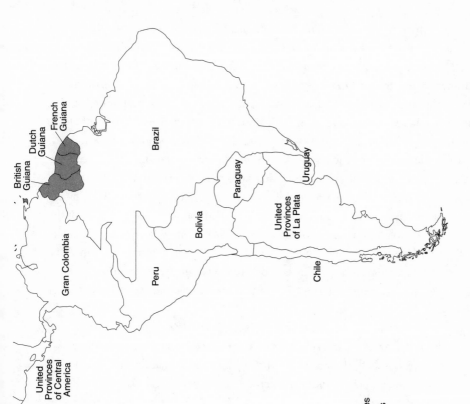

United Provinces of Central America

Gran Colombia

British Guiana

Dutch Guiana

French Guiana

Brazil

Peru

Bolivia

Paraguay

Uruguay

United Provinces of La Plata

Chile

Independent countries

Colonial possessions

New World political boundaries, ca. 1830.

Amboina, and elsewhere. This isolation offered the British an ideal opportunity to occupy the Cape, Ceylon, Java, and several Spice Islands. Following Napoleon's defeat and formation of a new diplomatic Concert of Europe, Holland regained control of its East Indian islands. But the Cape and Ceylon remained in British hands.

By the end of phase 2 Britain held strategic outposts at the southwestern entrance to the Indian Ocean (Cape Town) and along a major southeastern entryway, the Strait of Malacca.[6] The British could have used these enclaves to expand inland had they wished to do so, but during phase 2 they regarded them essentially as components of sea power. English-speaking settlers arriving at Grahamstown, South Africa, in 1820 were not encouraged to press into the interior. Expansion into the Malayan interior from the Straits Settlements did not take place until the 1870s.

There were two exceptions to this Old World pattern. Following the exploratory South Pacific voyages of Captain Cook, the British gained a foothold in Australia when they established a penal colony at Fort Jackson, now Sydney, in 1788. The settlement's frontiers gradually shifted inland during the next thirty years, the Blue Mountains back of Sydney being crossed by sheep-breeding settlers in 1813. Penetration of the vast Australian interior by a wave of settlers awaited the early decades of phase 3.

A far more significant exception was British activity on the Indian subcontinent. The India Act of 1784 declared Parliament's view that expansion there was "repugnant to the wish, the honour and the policy of this nation." Nonetheless, a series of military campaigns under two activist governor-generals, Lords Cornwallis (1786–98) and Wellesley (1798–1805), extended British power in areas surrounding the Madras and Bombay enclaves and in the Mughal Empire's northern heartland. Cornwallis's career nicely summarized Britain's diverging fortunes in New World and Old. After signing the instrument of surrender at Yorktown in 1781, he went on to extend British holdings in India. Military campaigns in Nepal in 1813 and the last Maratha War of 1817–19 augmented territory administered directly by British East India Company officials or ruled indirectly through the so-called subsidiary system. The British in India proceeded on their steady expansionist course from late phase 1 through phases 2 and 3. The timing of their takeover differed from that found in any other world region, and in this respect generalizations about phase 2 do not fit Indian history.

DECOLONIZATION AND VIOLENCE

Decolonization took place in a context of protracted and often intensely violent conflict. Violence was of three sorts:

1. Wars among European states, which affected both the European theater and colonies of contending metropoles;

2. Warfare in which a metropole attempted to prevent a colony from gaining independence;
3. Conflict within a colony pitting some of its residents against others. Contentious issues included the advisability of seeking independence, what kind of postindependence regime should be established, and who should lead the new state.

Warfare among west European powers was if anything more intense and protracted in this period than in phase 1. In particular, the English–French rivalry that erupted into war on several occasions earlier in the eighteenth century took new forms in phase 2. The British found themselves engaged ideologically against French revolutionary populist doctrines and militarily against Napoleon's armies. Between 1775 and 1824 the two countries and their respective European allies were at war more often than at peace.[7] Although the principal staging areas were Europe's mainland and its coastal waters, the struggle affected many other parts of the world as well. The Caribbean islands (especially between 1793 and 1796), the Nile Delta (1798–1801), and the Indian subcontinent all experienced the outward projection of European fratricide.[8] Only historical myopia permits us to call the terrible events of 1914–18 the *First World War*. Phase 2 struggles for hegemony on four continents, in the Atlantic and Indian oceans, and in the Mediterranean had global dimensions.

A second type of conflict pitted metropoles against independence movements. No European state was prepared to concede that its possessions had the right to rebel, much less unilaterally to proclaim sovereignty. The British, French, and Spanish sent sizable contingents of troops across the Atlantic to reinforce loyalist forces on the ground in crushing insurrection. Napoleon sent thirty thousand troops to Saint Domingue in 1802; Ferdinand VII deployed ten thousand to Venezuela and New Granada in 1815 shortly after being restored to the Spanish throne. Wars for independence normally lasted several years, included guerrilla attacks as well as conventional battles, and generated serious casualties among opposing forces and civilian populations. Of twenty countries tracing independence to phase 2, nine experienced violent outbreaks between proindependence and prometropolitan forces. In a tenth, New Spain, protoindependence movements led by Hidalgo and Morelos were brutally suppressed by royalist troops.[9]

Often the first and second types of conflict were linked, one European state supporting the breakup of a rival's empire. France assisted the American colonists by providing the critical support on land (Lafayette) and sea (de Grasse) to force Cornwallis's surrender at Yorktown. In fact, over twice as many French soldiers as American were killed and wounded in the Yorktown campaign. For their part the British, having failed to conquer Toussaint's Saint Domingue in the 1790s, gave naval support to Jean Jacques Dessalines against the French when he became Haiti's first head of state in 1804. In 1823, the prospect that Bourbon France might invade Spain and then try to reconquer Spain's former colonies led British Foreign Secretary George Canning to issue his famous declaration recognizing the sovereignty of these New World countries and placing British naval power on the side of their continued independence.[10]

A third type of violence, that among a territory's residents, figured in about a third of the independence struggles of phase 2. Most dramatic was Haiti, where, beginning in 1791, a struggle among black ex-slaves, mulattoes, and white plantation owners had devastating effects on lives and property. In 1804 virtually all whites were expelled or massacred. The American Revolution, too, had a civil war dimension. About a fifth of the thirteen colonies' residents remained loyal to the British Crown, and some fought on the British side. Most of the eighty thousand Loyalists forced into permanent exile after the war had property confiscated by revolutionary forces. Indeed, on a per capita basis the American Revolution produced as much property confiscation as the French. Far more political émigrés left America than France.[11] In New Spain, suppression of the Hidalgo and Morelos uprisings was undertaken primarily by locally born criollos or mestizos. The decade of violence that wracked Venezuela and New Granada (Colombia) after 1810 was in large measure a civil war, as many of the soldiers and civilians loyal to the Spanish Crown were born and raised in those territories. The briefer but still contentious drive for independence in Peru and Upper Peru (Bolivia) likewise involved locally born partisans on both sides.

Brazil's political transition was remarkably peaceful. Portugal did not seriously contest Dom Pedro's Cry of Ypiranga asserting independence. And his declaration did not trigger the conflicts among regions, racial groups, and classes that might have been expected given the country's size, ecological and social diversity, and pronounced economic inequalities. The contrast with phase 5 is striking. For after World War II it was the Portuguese who fought most stubbornly of all the metropoles to retain their empire. And it was in Portugal's principal colony, Angola, that one of the most devastating and prolonged postindependence civil wars of phase 5 took place. On the other hand, the British, Belgians, and, after 1958, the French generally avoided resorting to force when dealing with nationalist movements. It was as if Portugal's leaders had forgotten or repressed a chapter from their country's history, leaving it to other metropoles to follow its own earlier precedent.

ELITES IN THE NEW STATES: BACKGROUNDS, IDENTITIES, OBJECTIVES

The sweeping demographic changes the Americas experienced in phase 1 had differing impacts on the territories that gained independence in phase 2. As of the 1770s indigenous Amerindians comprised the substantial majority in Spain's Central and South American possessions. People of African descent predominated in the Caribbean basin plantation colonies. People of European descent were the majority only in the thirteen BNA colonies. In New Spain and Brazil it is likely that none of the three racial/continental categories formed a majority, in large part because sizable numbers were of mixed racial ancestry and socially defined as such.

Given the demographic diversity and complexity of these New World colonies, the most striking feature of the political elites who led phase 2's independence movements is their racial homogeneity. Except for Haiti, nationalist leaders were all from the European settler community. Only in the United States and Haiti did the first generation of powerholders come from a group constituting a majority of the population. In the other cases political power was captured and effectively monopolized by members of racial minority groups.

By the standards of the time the objectives of settler nationalists were quite ambitious and radical: widespread rejection of the monarchical principle that for centuries had been the basis of political legitimacy in Europe; rejection of titled aristocracies with inherited privileges; creation of republican forms of government based, at least in theory, on expressions of popular will; and formation of large political units from separate components of a former empire. The thirteen English-speaking states were able in the 1780s to shift from a loose confederation to a more centrally structured federal system. Composite polities in Spanish-speaking territories were less successful: Gran Colombia lasted from 1819 to 1830, the United Provinces of Central America from 1823 to 1838.

In the one movement not led by settlers, goals and outcomes went far beyond politics. The slave uprising of 1791 in Saint Domingue wrought a social revolution, one of the first in the modern world and arguably one of the most profound in history. Slavery was abolished in practice as well as in law, and the plantation basis of economic production was undermined. The old caste system with whites on top and blacks at the bottom was challenged in the decade following the uprising, then permanently destroyed with the expulsion and massacre of whites shortly after independence. The most far-reaching challenge to the colonial order in the Americas was led by people of African descent.

Perhaps more striking than the political innovations was the limited scope of phase 2 nationalist goals. Even the innovations were hedged about with exceptions and qualifications. The monarchical principle was not universally rejected. Haiti's first head of state elevated his title from governor to emperor. Between 1811 and 1820 the self-styled King Henri Christophe ruled the northern part of Haiti. Brazil entered the family of nations under an emperor tracing descent to Portugal's House of Braganza, while the arbiter of Mexico's independence, Gen. Agustín Iturbide, was formally declared Emperor Agustín I in 1822.

Moreover, settler-led polities calling themselves republics were by no means democracies. In the vast majority of phase 2 cases independence movements were restricted to men of pure European descent. If one goal was to mobilize settler support, another was to keep indigenous, slave, and mixed-blood populations politically demobilized. After independence the franchise was effectively limited to the small portion of the adult population that was male, property-owning, and descended from Europeans. Fear of popular participation in politics figured in Dom Pedro's decision to proclaim Brazilian independence. A similar motive lay behind independence proclamations in New Spain and the United Provinces of Central America. A popular revolution in Spain in 1820 had established a liberal constitutional order, raising the prospect of a broadened political base within the colonies and restricted privileges for colonial landowners and Roman Catholic clergy. Declaring independence was a way of preventing imposition of populist reforms from abroad. General Iturbide, the soldier who mercilessly hounded the remnants of Hidalgo's revolutionary forces, broke ties with Spain in 1821 in order to preserve the societal status quo at home. The junta which in that same year declared independence for Central America openly expressed its fear of the very people on whose behalf it claimed to act: "It was agreed by the Deputation and the members of the honorable cabildo that independence from Spain being the general will of the people, and without prejudice to what the future Congress may decide in regard to independence, the Jefe Político orders that it be published in order to preclude the dreadful consequences should the general public take this matter in their hands and proclaim it *de facto*."[12]

Independence was generally perceived by settler elements as a way of *preventing* major social and economic changes from taking place. Although slavery was formally abolished in several Spanish-speaking territories shortly after independence, the peculiar institution continued to function with full vigor in the two largest and most populous new states, the United States and Brazil. Slave status precluded citizenship status. Amerindians were effectively if not always formally deprived of citizenship. Among numerous reasons advanced for excluding them were their ignorance of the official language (that is, the language of the ex-metropole); their unwillingness to abandon communal land tenure; and aspects of indigenous culture deemed uncivilized. Denial of citizenship rights to blacks and Amerindians, the very categories most marginalized in colonial society, prevented these groups from gaining access to benefits the new governments offered the white population, benefits such as modest social services and legally secured land titles. Haiti excepted, the only people who really mattered in polities that broke with Europe in phase 2 were persons tracing descent to that very continent.

If anything, independence had the effect of reinforcing race-based social and economic inequalities inherited from the colonial era. In mainland plantation economies dependent upon slave labor, separation from the metropole offered protection from the critiques of an abolitionist movement initially more powerful in Europe than in the Americas. In the United States, southern states retained slavery for eight decades after independence, and for almost three decades after Great Britain abolished the institution throughout the empire (between 1834 and 1838). In Brazil, about half of whose population was enslaved, a serious abolitionist movement developed only in the 1870s. Slavery was not abolished until 1888.[13]

In territories that had been mixed or occupation colonies, independence ensured continuation of earlier patterns of mobilizing and exploiting indigenous labor. This was the predominant pattern in the Spanish-speaking New World. Criollos who in the colonial era dominated the private profit sector, primarily through titles to land and rights to Amerindian labor, were able by leading independence movements to wrest control of the public sector as well. The legal and coercive mechanisms of government were then used to protect the unequal distribution of private property inherited from colonial days. The next step, which took place during phase 3, was to accentuate inherited inequalities. This was done by undermining legal protection for Amerindian communal property rights while affirming as modern and progressive the property rights of individuals, who in the vast majority of cases were of European descent.[14]

In the pure settlement colonies that evolved into the United States, a festering grievance since the end of what colonists revealingly termed the French and Indian War (1754–63) was British opposition to settlement west of the Appalachians. The war succeeded in evicting the French and their thin line of fortifications from the vast territory between Appalachia and the Mississippi. What could be more unacceptable from the colonists' perspective than Britain's assignment of those lands to the other enemy, the Indians? Yet this is what occurred in 1763 when King George III issued a proclamation setting the Appalachian ridgeline as a fixed boundary between English settlers and Indians. The king acted to honor commitments made earlier to Indian leaders in exchange for their help against the French. But legally binding agreements rooted in the past were of scant consequence to thousands of forward-looking settlers hungry for land, who after 1763 could take the war's favorable outcome for granted. It is not by accident that Virginia and Pennsylvania, two colonies with extensive western frontiers and the most accessible routes over the mountains, were prominent opponents of British policies. Such leaders as Patrick Henry, Benjamin Franklin, and Washington were upset over restrictions on settler access to western lands, which in turn limited profits from land speculation in which many prominent settlers were involved.

Independence meant rejection of the letter and spirit of these restrictions. The metropole had tried to balance the interests of colonists and indigenous peoples. The new government reflected the colonists' interests and ensured the Indians' exclusion.

In a sense independence permitted settlers to apply west of the Appalachians land alienation policies and practices developed from the earliest years of English settlement along the coast. From the early seventeenth century through Daniel Boone's pioneering activities in the 1770s to Andrew Jackson's relocation policies in the 1820s, the most striking feature of settler attitudes and actions toward Amerindians is its consistency.[15]

In other respects the goals of new-state elites reflected continuity with the colonial past. While valuing economic prosperity, phase 2 elites did not perceive independence as a way to bring about sustained, dramatic increases in a country's productive base or greatly to increase consumer goods and social services. This attitude is not surprising. Only a few parts of western Europe were beginning to experience the burst of economic development and technological change associated with the Industrial Revolution. To the extent that European countries served as developmental role models, as of phase 2 they had not yet modeled for themselves, much less for others, how to transform economic life. Neither had their governments developed the array of services associated with the welfare state. And European governments were not as democratic and responsive to societal pressures as they became in phase 3.

To the extent that increased national prosperity was a goal, the intellectual trend of the time in the Americas, as in Europe, was to favor initiatives financed and managed by the private profit sector. The doctrine of mercantilism was moving out of favor, laissez-faire and free trade were gaining favor, and Keynesian and socialist ideas favoring a prominent economic role for the state had not yet been articulated. During the colonial period settlers acquired legal title to land. They owned and managed small enterprises servicing the domestic economy. Many nationalist leaders were personally well off before taking leading positions in the public sector. Understandably, they encouraged people of European descent to carry on a long tradition of private entrepreneurship. They did not feel the enormous pressures exerted on leaders of phase 5 new states to use public sector institutions for developmental ends. Nor was failure to preside over a growing economy as likely to count as a reason for forcibly removing political elites from power as it became in countries attaining independence after 1945.

The most innovative New World political system, that of the United States, was an experiment not in expanding and centralizing the public sector but in limiting its scope and diffusing its responsibilities. The architects of the Articles of Confederation and then of the Constitution of 1789, motivated by fear that concentrated political power would be misused, created an elaborate set of checks and balances on the institutions they constructed. Underlying the American Constitution was a high degree of skepticism about what could and should be done to improve human nature. The underlying assumption was that self-interest would continue to motivate citizens, not only in their private lives but also in their involvement in public affairs. Trying to transform citizens into thinking primarily about the general good was deemed inappropriate and too daunting a task for government to undertake beyond providing some public education.

RELATIONS AMONG INDEPENDENCE MOVEMENTS

Termination of formal rule within the vertical structures of empire was accompanied by a rise in horizontal contacts among the new states. In the vast majority of cases these contacts had the intent and effect of accelerating the drive for independence in territories still under metropolitan rule. Horizontal interactions took two forms. In the first, which I call the *observation effect,* the independence of country *A* was noted with interest and approval by people in country *B*. *B*'s nationalists were emboldened by *A*'s example to intensify their efforts, using ideas and mobilizing techniques that worked in *A*. In the second, called the *direct influence effect, A* used its material and human resources to increase the capacity of groups in *B* to press for *B*'s independence.

Phase 2 offers many instances of the observation effect. The American Declaration of Independence, the Continental Army's defeat of a European great power, and formation of a federal government based on a carefully crafted written constitution were noted with great interest elsewhere in the New World. Among the troops sent by France to fight for American independence were mulattoes from Saint Domingue, who later took part in overthrowing that colony's slaveholding aristocracy. The Venezuelan Francisco de Miranda, known to posterity as "the morning star of the Spanish American Revolution," also fought in the American Revolution. Miranda's visit to the United States in 1783–84 and Bolívar's travels there almost a quarter century later only intensified each man's desire to liberate Spain's colonies. "In the years before and after 1810," writes John Lynch, "the very existence of the United States excited the imagination of Spanish Americans, and its embodiment of liberty and republicanism placed a powerful example before their eyes."[16] Manuel García de Sena of Venezuela and Miguel de Pombo of Colombia circulated translations of Thomas Paine's writings, the Articles of Confederation, and the U.S. Constitution to fellow nationalists during the formative 1810–12 years. Pombo told authors of Colombia's Charter of 1811 that the U.S. Constitution "has promoted the happiness of our brothers of the North and will promote our happiness also, if we imitate their virtues and adopt their principles."[17] In 1810 the *Gazeta de Buenos Aires* printed the following verse:

If there was a Washington in the North land,
We have many Washingtons in the South;
If arts and commerce have prospered there—
Courage, fellow countrymen:
Let us follow their example.[18]

As the drive for liberation from Spain gathered momentum, developments in one part of its far-flung empire influenced other parts. In the impassioned prose of the Dominican Republic's Declaration of Independence of 1821,

From Cape Horn to the Californias the contest rages ardently and fiercely, for the incomparable blessing of Independence: everywhere does the decrepit Lion of Spain fly terrified, leaving the land unoccupied, to the vigorous prowess of the youthful Lion of America. The political horizon now exhibits the dawn of a great day for the Sons of Columbus; which will shine forth by degrees, as the smiling Aurora of Independence, to all America. . . . When the most remote and obscure People unite with one accord, to secure the incalculable advantages of this new life, would it become the first Colony of the New World to stand aloof in this heroic struggle?[19]

Phase 2 furnishes ample evidence of the direct influence effect, stemming from actions by government officials and by individuals operating largely on their own. American ships aided Toussaint during his undeclared war with France in the 1790s. "It is doubtful," writes David Brion Davis, "whether Haitian independence could have been achieved without American arms and recognition."[20] Haiti in turn gave refuge to Bolívar on two occasions when his prospects were at their lowest ebb. Haitian president Alexandre Petion supplied the South American liberator with arms, munitions, men, and printing supplies to carry on his struggle in Venezuela. Lynch notes that "copies of the [U.S.] Constitution and the Declaration of Independence, conveniently translated into Spanish, were carried into the area by United States traders whose liberal views coincided with their interest in developing a market free of the Spanish monopoly."[21]

Most significantly, the military campaigns that ended Spain's mainland rule repeatedly cut across colonial boundaries. In Peru, San Martín's forces from the south evicted the viceroy's troops from Lima, while troops from the north led by Sucre fought victoriously at Ayacucho. South America's wars of national liberation were fought by a truly transcolonial cast of characters. General Sucre's career is revealing. Born in Venezuela, he fought in what became Venezuela, Colombia, Ecuador, and Peru, then became Bolivia's first president.

Horizontal influences can have the reverse effect, independence in country *A* inhibiting or blocking movement toward a similar result in country *B*. This pattern characterizes the first two instances of decolonization: the United States in relation to Canada and Haiti in relation to other Caribbean islands.

Several events during and after the American Revolution gave inhabitants of Britain's provinces to the north cause for alarm. In the revolution's first year the Continental Congress dispatched troops to conquer Canada. The invaders captured Montreal and tried unsuccessfully to take Quebec City. As expected, they were opposed by troops and civilians loyal to the British Crown. Unexpectedly, the Americans failed to win support from the francophone population, which only a few years earlier had been conquered by the British. A plausible explanation is that British governors had taken care not to interfere with the language, religious practices, and property rights of their French-speaking subjects. The invaders seemed far more likely to insist on spreading their alien Anglo culture throughout Canada.

At war's end between forty thousand and sixty thousand Loyalists, expelled from the thirteen states, moved north. They brought with them a strong emotional attachment to the British monarchy, for whose sake they had suffered loss of life, property, and dignity. They also carried a strong antipathy to the republic the revolution produced. Their presence reinforced existing sentiments unsympathetic to the idea of independence. As the Canadian scholar S. D. Clark puts it, "Whereas the American nation was a product of the revolutionary spirit, the Canadian nation grew mainly out of forces of a counter-revolutionary character."[22] Fears that Americans might forcibly incorporate Canada into the United States were heightened by the War of 1812. Anglophone and francophone Canadians alike fought spiritedly against troops who once again invaded their land.

Events in phase 2 led many Canadians to conclude that their southern neighbor posed a security threat. If Canadians could assert political and cultural claims within the British Empire, they could satisfy their goals while retaining external protection from the neighbor's expansionist ambitions. Thus the war that separated Britain from its thirteen colonies helped strengthen its ties with bicultural Canada.[23]

The prolonged, bloody slave uprising in Saint Domingue, culminating in the slaughter of whites remaining after independence, profoundly affected political evolution in the Caribbean. Slaveholders elsewhere were obsessed with fear that slaves working for them would follow Haiti's example. Any constraints a metropole might impose on dominant economic interests in its plantation colonies were minor compared to the populist danger from below.[24] Colonists therefore preferred to maintain the colonial status quo. The metropole, they reasoned, could supply troops to repress serious uprisings while offering a safe haven for whites returning home should uprisings succeed. The observation effect of developments in Haiti is probably the principal explanation for delayed decolonization in the part of the Americas with the longest European presence.

By an unintended irony of history the negative observation effects of the first and second anticolonial revolutions in phase 2 contributed to peaceful decolonization in phase 5. For reasons just noted, Great Britain was able to retain control of Canada and numerous Caribbean islands. People from the British Isles inhabited these territories. Their presence abroad posed delicate questions for nineteenth-century imperial policy makers. What could be learned from the thirteen North American colonies that might prevent loss of other New World possessions? When kith and kin in Canada and the Caribbean demanded political rights, could their demands be accommodated in such a way that the British tradition of settler self-government was compatible with imperial rule? When people in Canada and the Caribbean who were not of British descent wished to participate in political life, could their demands be accommodated in such a way that civil war based on language, religion, or race was avoided, while at the same time the metropole's economic and strategic interests were safeguarded?

The first, tentative answers to these questions awaited developments in phase 3. Such documents as the Durham Report (1839) provided both the constitutional and the moral-philosophical basis for the British Empire's evolution toward the British Commonwealth. The latter contained institutions, procedures, and values that could be reshaped to form the Commonwealth, an organization of sovereign English-speaking states that by phase 5 was spread throughout the globe.

New World colonies retained by Britain—in large measure because of the negative observation effects of the American and Haitian revolutions—constituted the testing grounds for experiments in peaceful, evolutionary, pragmatic transfers of power from metropole to colony in the twentieth century. Decades after precedent-setting experiments with settler self-government were launched, experiments patterned on these precedents would be carried out in Asian and African colonies of occupation. There the beneficiaries of transferred power would be not kith and kin but indigenous people of color.

5
Phase 3: Expansion, 1824–1912

The era of European losses in the Americas was followed by a significant expansion of holdings in Asia, Africa, and Oceania, most visibly and highly publicized from the 1870s onward, when a scramble for still-unclaimed territories took place. Between 1878 and 1913 European countries claimed 8.6 million square miles, roughly one-sixth of the earth's land surface.[1] But it would be a mistake to ignore developments during the first half century of phase 3. Between 1824 and 1870 Europeans acquired roughly 5 million square miles, with notable advances in Africa's southern, northern, and western extremities (South Africa, Algeria, Senegal), in India (Punjab, for example), Australia and New Zealand, and Cochinchina (southern Vietnam). Prior to 1870, moreover, Britain and France sent military expeditions to China that resulted in numerous foreign-controlled enclaves, the so-called treaty ports, within that vast independent empire. Phase 3 lasted for a full nine decades, not four.

Though phases 1 and 3 are similar in their expansionist direction, they differ in the way Europe's presence was felt abroad. During the earlier phase Europeans created formal empires in the New World while exerting influence informally and indirectly on Old World hinterlands through trading enclaves. During phase 3 the pattern was reversed. In the Old World Europeans used coastal enclaves as staging areas to penetrate continental interiors. Informal economic and cultural influence in the hinterland was no longer deemed sufficient; it had to be reinforced by political control. Meanwhile, in the New World Europeans seemed content to accept loss of control. France's halfhearted, hapless effort to conquer Mexico in the early 1860s, with an army loyal to Austria's Emperor Maximilian, is notable not only because it failed but also because the attempt was so unusual. The challenge in the Americas was not to resurrect colonialism but to devise new techniques of postcolonial influence. Europeans came to value influence in the New World at the very time they found it inadequate in the Old.

The event marking the start of phase 3 was the first Anglo-Burmese War, begun in 1824 and concluded two years later. The war pitted British East India Company forces against the army of the Burmese king, Bagyidaw. In some respects it was simply the latest in a series of conflicts between the chartered company and indigenous rulers threatened by the company's political and economic ambitions. But its location and the manner in which it was fought pointed toward a new era in relations between Europeans and peoples in other continents.

The Treaty of Yandibaw that concluded the war ceded to the British victors Assam, Manipur, Arakan, and Tenasserim. By acquiring the first two Britain extended its hold from the coastal and Gangetic delta areas of Bengal deep into the mountainous interior of Asia. By acquiring the latter two Britain advanced into Southeast Asia.[2] The war thus set the leading metropole on an expansionist path well outside its traditional South Asian domain. During the next nine decades other Old World areas previously thought of as being off-limits would likewise become takeover targets.

The Anglo-Burmese War was also the first in which a technology linked to the Industrial Revolution decisively influenced distant events. King Bagyidaw initiated hostilities, confident his army would overwhelm the company's British officers and Indian troops. At first the British seemed to do their best to oblige the king. In one of the worst-managed wars in British history, fifteen thousand of the forty thousand troops were lost, mostly to diseases contracted while soldiers were quartered for months in Rangoon with nothing to do. What transformed an otherwise costly defeat into victory was the arrival of three steamships. One of these, the *Diana*, was initially assigned by the East India Company as a tugboat in Calcutta harbor but then pressed into service on Burma's Irrawaddy River. There, as Daniel Headrick notes, it "towed sailing ships into position, transported troops, reconnoitered advance positions, and bombarded Burmese fortifications with her swivel guns and Congreve rockets. The most important contribution of the *Diana* was to capture the Burmese praus, or war boats. . . . By February 1826 the *Diana*, which the Burmese called 'fire devil,' had pushed with the British fleet up to Amarapura, over 400 miles upriver. The King of Burma, seeing his capital [at Ava] threatened, sued for peace."[3]

The *Diana* was more than a tugboat. It was also a gunboat. The ship's speed, its reliance on steam engines to advance steadily against unfavorable currents, and the destruction its guns wreaked on both sides of the river gave the East India Company a decisive advantage over Bagyidaw's army. The Burmese were perhaps the first non-Europeans—but certainly not the last—to experience the political implications of the Industrial Revolution's technological advances.

An event marking the end of phase 3 was the Treaty of Fez (1912) between France and Abdul-Hafiz, sultan of Morocco, declaring a French protectorate over the territory. The Sherifian dynasty was retained, but France took control of Morocco's domestic and foreign affairs. The treaty capped lengthy efforts by France to control the northwest African territory, thereby reinforcing its rule in neighboring Algeria and West Africa.[4] Morocco was the last sizable European acquisition before World War I. Creation of the protectorate brings the story of overseas empires full circle. Phase 3 concluded where phase 1 began. Ceuta and Fez are separated by almost five hundred years—but only one hundred fifty miles.

The complex diplomatic maneuvers preceding Morocco's takeover constituted the final round of Europe's scramble for what remained of independent Africa. The scramble had its parallels with phase 1, in particular the way intense competition among several metropoles stimulated each of them to claim more territory. But events leading up to the Treaty of Fez also showed how phase 3 differed from phase 1. Novel features included concentration on empire building in the Old World; entry of new powers with imperial ambitions (Germany and Italy); the prominence of diplomatic bargaining and the greatly reduced role of warfare as methods of resolving disputes among metropoles; and the considerable part that financial credit—extended by European banks in this case to the heavily indebted sultan—played in extending Europe's reach.

To these and other features of phase 3 I now turn. The chapter's structure parallels the discussion of phase 1 in order to highlight similarities and differences between the expansionist phases. As noted in chapter 2, one can use the similarities to construct a temporally comprehensive theory of European imperialism, while one can use differences to discard insufficiently comprehensive explanations.

Phase 3 was not an era of maritime exploration, if only because the discovery of the seas had already taken place. Europeans were less interested in finding new routes across oceans than in traveling more rapidly, safely, and predictably over familiar sea routes. The steam engine replaced the sail; iron and then steel replaced wood as the basic material in ship construction. Carrying capacity was enormously expanded, while refrigeration and canning increased the variety of transportable goods. Innovations in ocean transportation had the figurative if not literal effect of shrinking the globe.

Exploration in phase 3 was directed primarily at the poorly charted interiors of known continents. Heinrich Barth, Richard Burton, René Caillié, Mary Kingsley, David Livingstone, Jean-Baptiste Marchand, Gustav Nachtigal, Serpa Pinto, John Hanning Speke, Henry Morton Stanley, and Joseph Thomson in Africa, François Garnier and Francis Younghusband in Asia, Charles Sturt and Thomas Mitchell in Australia did for inland geography what Columbus, da Gama, Magellan, Drake, and Cook had done earlier in mapping the oceans and continental coastlines. Of special interest to many explorers were the origin and course of rivers that might facilitate inland penetration by European traders, missionaries, and soldiers. Among these were the White and Blue Nile, Congo, Zambezi, Niger, Salween, and Mekong.

Phase 3 was marked by a railway construction boom that spread rapidly from Europe to other continents. Railroads pushed inland from coastal ports, opening up areas hitherto unconnected to the world market and making it easier for outsiders to govern hinterlands back of phase 1 Old World enclaves. In Jan Morris's evocative words, "The spectacle of the steam locomotive puffing brass-bound and aglow across steppe, prairie or scorched veld was to remain one of the perennial inspirations of the imperial mission."[5]

BUILDERS OF EMPIRE: OLD ACTORS AND NEW

The number of expansionist states was greater and the territorial spread of empire builders wider now than in phase 1. The five states active earlier remained so in the nineteenth century. Each gained Old World territories not previously held. Spain grew the least, acquiring minor holdings in northwest and equatorial Africa, while it lost the island remnants of its old empire at the turn of the century: the Philippines, Cuba, and Puerto Rico. Holland extended effective control of the East Indies from its base in Java to the interior of Sumatra and other islands. Portugal moved inland from enclaves in Angola and Mozambique to claim large swaths of southern Africa. France constructed an immense empire in north, west, and equatorial Africa, Madagascar, Indochina, and the Pacific.

Great Britain began phase 3 with the largest empire retained from phase 1—notably Canada, numerous Caribbean islands, and parts of India—supplemented by territories acquired in the wars of phase 2. It proceeded to build on this formidable foundation by gaining direct or indirect control of all South Asia, acquiring portions of mainland and insular Southeast Asia, an almost uninterrupted line of territory from Egypt south to the Cape of Good Hope, four colonies in West Africa, and numerous Pacific Islands. Extensive emigration from the British Isles transformed Australia and New Zealand into virtually pure settlement colonies. First in Canada, then in Australia and New Zealand, control over domestic affairs was transferred to locally elected officials from the numerically dominant settler community, while London retained control of monetary and foreign policy. Britain called these quasi colonies dominions. As of 1912 its empire, including the so-called white dominions, covered almost a quarter of the earth's land surface.[6]

To the five old imperial powers were added three west European countries which, as a result of the merger of many small, previously autonomous political entities, became new states during phase 3. Belgium, Italy, and Germany celebrated statehood by promptly entering the imperial sweepstakes. Belgium gained a large, strategically valuable colony in the heart of Africa, the so-called Congo Free State.[7] Italy gained coastal footholds in the Horn of Africa. Its attempt to advance inland into Abyssinia, however, led, at the Battle of Adowa (1896), to the most dramatic phase 3 defeat of a European power by an indigenous army. In 1911 Italian troops successfully attacked Tripoli. From there, in the face of intense resistance, they gradually consolidated their hold over Libya.

The most noteworthy new European candidate for great-power status was Germany, after it became unified politically under Prussian leadership and demonstrated its military prowess by defeating Denmark (1864), Austria (1866), and France (1870–71). To its size and strategic location in Europe should be added the crucial asset of skilled diplomatic leadership, at least during the chancellorship of Otto von Bismarck (1871–90). By the late nineteenth century, moreover, Germany took the lead in what Geoffrey Barraclough terms the Second Industrial Revolution, based on steel, electricity, and chemicals.[8] It was thus in a position to challenge British preeminence on several fronts. The empire Germany acquired in the 1880s and 1890s consisted of widely dispersed territories in west, southern, and east Africa and minor island chains in the Pacific.

To five old and three new west European empire builders should be added two countries outside the region but in many respects intimately linked with it. The United States, a new state derivatively European by virtue of former colonial status and emigration, and Russia, an old state peripherally and ambiguously European by virtue of location, both accelerated the pace of territorial growth. This was an overland process, each country advancing rapidly along a frontier of thinly populated territory. In both cases non-European peoples were subdued. Americans "won the West" from the Sioux, Nez Perces, Apaches, and Modoc. Russians "won the South" from the Kazakhs, Uzbeks, and Turkmen and the east from the Yakut and Koryak. The United States and Russia hastily constructed railroads to facilitate imposition of political control over newly acquired lands and pushed their frontiers steadily away from Europe, until by the early twentieth century the two countries were recognized as Pacific Ocean powers. In expanding in opposite directions from Europe the two moved closer to each other. These phase 3 initiatives set the stage for both states to ascend to global superpower status in phase 5.

The American and Russian pattern of overland expansion resembles the usual manner of constructing large multicultural empires. The two rising world powers may thus be distinguished from west European states, which deviated from the norm by establishing empires overseas. The United States and Russia, however, sanctioned the European scramble for territory by attending the Conference of Berlin in 1884–85 and signing the Berlin Act. This act codified procedures for acquiring territory with minimal risk that contestants would fight over the spoils. More significant, the

United States temporarily abandoned its anticolonial heritage to construct an overseas empire of its own, wresting the island remnants of Spain's empire in the Pacific and Caribbean. The country that had proclaimed the Monroe Doctrine to protect the independence of Spanish-speaking countries on the New World mainland now found itself in the anomalous position of replacing Spain as a colonial ruler and repressing national independence movements.[9] The United States also took the Hawaiian islands, which until the 1890s were nominally ruled by indigenous monarchs. The Russians were not comparably aggressive overseas. Indeed, with the sale of Alaska to the United States in 1867 they ended an earlier experiment in saltwater colonialism. But their expansion on the Asian mainland markedly affected the foreign policies of other major actors, notably Great Britain and Japan.

Japan was the first non-European state to create a saltwater empire through the use of Industrial Revolution technologies. Having insulated itself from non-Asian influences since the early seventeenth century, Japan made an abrupt about-face in the latter half of the nineteenth when its rulers realized that insulation was no longer viable. In 1853 four U.S. warships commanded by Comdr. Matthew Perry sailed into Edo (Tokyo) Bay. Perry demanded permission for American ships to enter Japanese ports for coal and supplies. More generally, he wanted Japan to establish regular trade relations with the United States. The Treaty of Kanagawa, signed the next year after Perry returned with a larger contingent of warships, imposed humiliating concessions on the shogun's government, the Bakufu. Similar concessions to European countries followed. Reacting against these moves, a revolution-from-above in 1868 known as the Meiji Restoration destroyed the shogun's power, enhanced the emperor's symbolic status, and launched Japan on an extremely rapid course of what C. E. Black has called "defensive modernization." The latest technology and bureaucratic institutions were borrowed from the West to enable Japan to resist the power of the West.[10] The change of direction was strikingly demonstrated in the military arena. Whereas in phase 1 Japan's rulers abandoned domestic production and importation of guns in order to rely upon the samurai sword, Meiji Restoration elites abandoned the sword to mass-produce the most advanced weapons available anywhere.

Literally armed with the latest technology, Japan set about creating an empire. Initially the island state claimed and occupied other islands: the Ryukyus in the 1870s, Taiwan (Formosa) and the Pescadores following victory over China in 1894–95. But it was Asian mainland territory Japan most fervently desired. By defeating Russian land and naval forces in 1904–05 the Japanese took over rights and privileges Russia had recently acquired in southern Manchuria. Korea was declared a protectorate in 1905 and formally annexed as a colony (Chosen) in 1910. In creating an empire, Japan modeled its foreign policy on that of the West—though Japan was physically closer to its colonies than European powers were to the vast majority of theirs.[11]

How large were the saltwater empires when phase 3 ended? In his study *The Balance Sheets of Empire* (1936) Grover Clark gave the following figures for 1913 in thousands of square kilometers:[12]

Great Britain	31,692
France	10,942
Germany	2,982
Belgium	2,385
Italy	2,239
Portugal	2,091
The Netherlands	2,055
Spain	334
United States	325
Japan	297

West European countries on the list occupied only 1.6 percent of the world's land area but controlled an additional 41.3 percent. Roughly nine-tenths of the latter was territory acquired or effectively occupied by Europeans since the start of phase 3.

RELATIONS AMONG IMPERIAL POWERS

Phase 3 thus experienced more empire builders, more widely dispersed, than phase 1. One might infer that interstate competition became more intense, hence more liable to erupt into warfare. But such an inference would be off the mark. To be sure, competition was often vigorous, especially after 1870. The two most important actors, Britain and France, vied for control of the Suez Canal, Egypt, and Morocco, for territory in West Africa's interior, and for influence at royal courts in Siam and Madagascar. Their most serious crisis, at Fashoda on the upper Nile in 1898, threatened for a time to become a *casus belli*. It is also true that newspapers and journals reached large audiences with unabashed jingoistic appeals, giving late nineteenth-century imperialism an unprecedented degree of popular involvement and appeal. This made it difficult for political leaders to moderate aggressive stands once their commitments became matters of public record. All the more surprising, then, that rivalry among imperial powers so seldom took a violent turn.

The century between the end of the Napoleonic Wars and the start of World War I was by far the most peaceful in European history. Not a single war was fought among the five original imperial powers, and only one—the Franco-Prussian War of 1870–71—between one of the original five and a new state. This conflict was not over the disposition of overseas territory. Indeed, after the war the victorious Germans encouraged France to intensify empire-building activities abroad to compensate for losing Alsace and Lorraine at home.

In phase 3 west European metropoles devised workable diplomatic mecha-

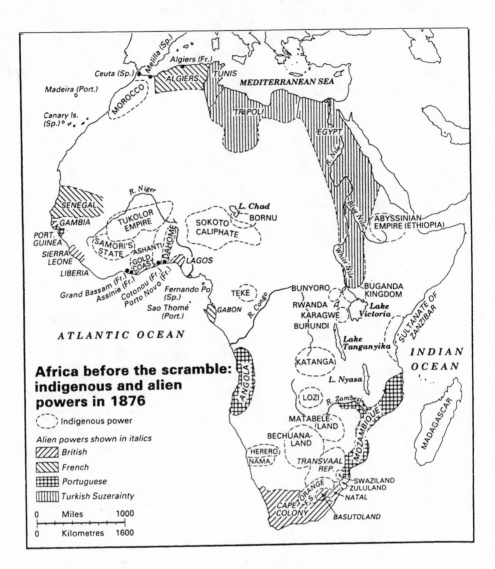

Africa before the scramble: indigenous and alien powers in 1876

- Indigenous power

Alien powers shown in italics

British
French
Portuguese
Turkish Suzerainty

| 0 | Miles | 1000 |
| 0 | Kilometres | 1600 |

nisms to resolve disputes about overseas claims. The most prominent instances of the new "international regime"[13] were the Berlin Conference of 1884–85, the Entente Cordiale of 1904, which settled a wide range of issues between Britain and France, and the Algeciras Conference of 1906 on Morocco. Imperialism appears to have functioned as a substitute for intra-European war in this period, instead of being the cause or consequence of war, as in phase 1. The connection Lenin drew between imperialism and war in *Imperialism, the Highest State of Capitalism* was more applicable to the early years of capitalist development than to the finance-capital stage about which he wrote. It was only after imperial powers had virtually run out of

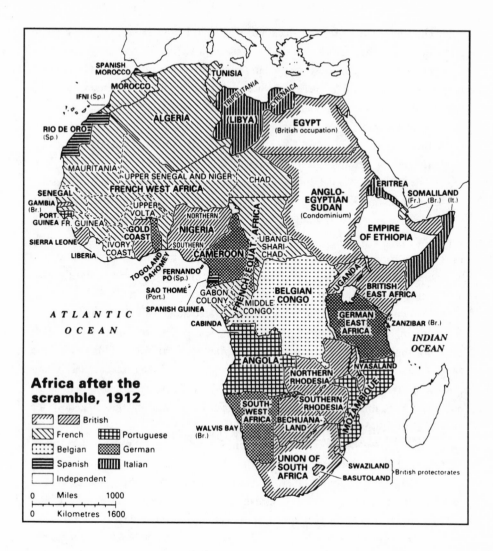

Africa after the scramble, 1912

British
French
Belgian
Spanish
Independent

Portuguese
German
Italian

0   Miles   1000
0   Kilometres   1600

territory abroad that new international tensions unconnected with overseas scrambles set off World War I.

Diplomatic mechanisms were less operative or effective, however, where the expansionist powers *not* in western Europe were involved. They were more inclined to follow the long-standing practice of settling conflicting claims by resort to war. The United States fought Spain in 1898; Japan fought Russia in 1904–05. A third war reflected west European concern over Russian territorial aspirations. As Russia's presence in the Black Sea area increased, British diplomats and military strategists grew alarmed that the tsar's navy might gain access to the Mediterranean, where it could challenge British preeminence. In the Crimean War (1854–56), British, French, and Ottoman forces combined to deal a severe blow to Russian naval capabilities.

Once the Suez Canal was opened in 1869, control of the eastern Mediterranean became even more vital to the British. Suez was the strategic and commercial lifeline between the metropole and a large number of possessions stretched along the Indian Ocean's shores. Still concerned about a possible resurgence of Russian naval power, Great Britain and several other European powers tried to contain tsarist ambitions by shoring up the Ottoman Empire. This was most vividly demonstrated at the Congress of Berlin in 1878, which in essence annulled a Russian victory over the Turks.

Queen Victoria expressed what British officials were thinking when she wrote, "It is not a question of upholding Turkey; it is a question of Russian or British supremacy in the world."[14] Several European states acquired portions of the Ottoman Empire most distant from Moscow. But they made sure that equivalent Russian acquisitions were thwarted by prescribing just enough diplomatic medication for Turkey that the "sick man of Europe" retained a tenuous hold on life.[15]

Russian expansion into Central Asia generated an equally concerned response from Britain, but one with very different consequences. The containment policy that called for shoring up the Ottoman Empire argued for weakening and bypassing the Mughal Empire. The British countered what they perceived as a threat to their Indian possessions by more directly controlling affairs in the Mughal domains. They also attempted, with mixed results, to control the small states and stateless societies lying athwart Himalayan mountain passes.

Much further east, Russian acquisition of territory and of railroad and Pacific port rights from China may have predisposed European powers to employ what might be called an Ottoman strategy toward the Ch'ing dynasty. Europeans preferred to administer medication to the "sick man of East Asia"—even if it was on occasion the bitter medicine of military expeditions to Peking (in 1860 and 1900)—rather than formally challenge the Beijing court's authority over a vast land. A China that did not have to mobilize against the threat of European invasion by sea was presumably better able to halt Russian advances in northeast Asia by land.[16]

Japanese officials felt directly threatened as Russia moved into what they regarded as their country's sphere of influence. The response was to intervene directly on the Asian mainland, somewhat as the British had done in India. Japan's defeat of China (1895) gave it treaty-port rights there and enabled it to assert growing influence in Korea. Scarcely had the Russians completed the Trans-Siberian Railroad than the Japanese challenged them head-on. The result was a resounding defeat of a peripherally European power by a purely Asian power. The war's outcome caught European diplomats by surprise. It was an unmistakable sign that the era of European global hegemony was drawing to a close.

The policies of west European metropoles toward the three great mainland Asian empires of the nineteenth century—Ottoman, Mughal, Ch'ing—were driven in large measure by a consistent strategy on the part of the world's leading maritime powers to counter the world's leading land-based power. Similarly, Japan's behavior during the last two decades of phase 3 was the nervous response of a maritime state on the periphery of Eurasia to Russian consolidation of control over the Eurasian heartland. The containment policy the United States adopted toward the Soviet Union in phase 5 is a direct descendant of strategies Europeans and Japanese developed in phase 3 to counter tsarist ambitions.

DEMOGRAPHIC AND SOCIAL ASPECTS OF EUROPEAN EXPANSION

The devastating impact on indigenous peoples of the Europeans' arrival in the New World continued to be felt long after phase 1. As descendants of the early settlers, reinforced by millions of new immigrants from Europe, pushed back frontiers they interacted for the first time with new groups of Amerindians. To death from imported diseases was added expulsion from ancestral lands by settlers intent on occupying the allegedly open spaces of temperate-zone North and South America. When settlers did not need indigenous labor, the maxim "The only good Indian is a dead Indian" was put into practice. Araucanian speakers in southern Argentina and Chile and horse-riding tribes on the U.S. plains felt the full force of this maxim. The typical nineteenth-century settler on the great plains of the Americas doubtless viewed Amerindians much as the first governor of Massachusetts did. "For the natives," John Winthrop wrote triumphantly in 1634, "they are neere all dead of small Poxe, so as the Lord hath cleared our title to what we possess."[17] Severe demographic and territorial losses lowered the capacity and often the will of Amerindians to resist further rounds of physical, cultural, and spiritual dislocation.

These patterns were replicated in many parts of Oceania in phase 3. Measles, smallpox, dysentery, diphtheria, and tuberculosis ravaged Melanesian and Polynesian islands, whose isolation had prevented their inhabitants from building up the necessary immunities. Land-hungry settlers in Tasmania and the Australian outback organized officially sanctioned hunting parties in the 1830s and 1840s to exterminate the original inhabitants. Visiting Tasmania in 1836, when genocide was proceeding full tilt, Charles Darwin lamented, "Wherever the European has trod death seems to pursue the aboriginal. We may look to the wide extent of the Americas, Polynesia, the Cape of Good Hope and Australia, and we find the same result."[18]

Yet Oceania was peripheral, not central, to the phase 3 imperial enterprise. Mainland Asia and Africa were central. Here the striking fact is that, with few exceptions, indigenous populations did not decline following initial contact with outsiders. If anything, Asians and Africans held an edge over Europeans, who initially could not cope with such unfamiliar tropical maladies as malaria and yellow fever. Nineteenth-century European medical advances, however, undercut that advantage. Whereas thirty-nine of forty-eight Europeans died of malaria on Macgregor Laird's expedition up the Niger River in 1832, not a single fatality occurred among the dozen Europeans who spent three months with Laird on the same river in 1854: on the second trip each crew member took six to eight grains of quinine daily. In the 1850s seedlings of the cinchona tree, from whose bark quinine is derived, were taken surreptitiously from the tree's Andean habitat and transferred to botanical gardens in India, Ceylon, and the Dutch East Indies. Mass production via cinchona plantations was the next step. A readily available antimalarial medication in Asia was crucial to the penetration of tropical Africa. Europe's head start in technology and organization eventually overcame the disease advantage held by Asians and Africans.[19]

European settlers and their descendants played key roles in the major New World colonies of phase 1, most obviously in pure settlement colonies, but also in mixed settlement and plantation colonies, whose economies and social structures were shaped by settler control of land and labor. The typical phase 3 territory, by contrast, was the colony of occupation. There, few if any Europeans were present other than administrators, soldiers, traders, and missionaries—people, that is, for whom the metropole rather than the colony was the psychological reference point and legal domicile. In the great majority of Asian and African colonies more than 98 percent of the population was indigenous. Public health advances that permitted Europeans to survive in Old World colonies were insufficiently effective or comprehensive to encourage large-scale settlement there. Additional barriers to settlement included a hot, damp climate, poor soil quality, and the ever-present possibility of indigenous uprisings.

To be sure, Europeans did migrate in phase 3 to Old World zones where latitude or altitude produced congenial climatic conditions. The most prominent examples were Australia, New Zealand, New Caledonia, South Africa, Southern Rhodesia, the highlands of central Kenya, Eritrea, and the Mediterranean coast of Algeria. But the numbers involved were small compared to the simultaneous flood of emigrants to the Americas. Of the estimated 22.7 million people migrating from Britain between 1815 and 1915, only 10 percent went to Australia and New Zealand, 4 percent to South Africa, and 1 percent to India. Nineteen percent migrated to Canada, 62 percent to the United States.[20]

Of those who did leave Europe for Old World colonies, the vast majority settled in lands ruled by Great Britain. There, as in Canada and Britain's Caribbean possessions, settlers pressed for an increasing share of political power, at least over internal matters. Canada set the crucial precedent with publication in 1839 of the *Report on the Affairs of British North America* by Gov.-Gen. John George Lambton,

Earl of Durham. The Durham Report proposed a system known as "responsible government" under which the monarch's representative was expected to endorse domestic policies approved by the majority party in a locally elected, territorially based legislature. The report's recommendations led to the Union Act of 1840, then to the British North America Act of 1867 authorizing complete self-government in Canada's internal affairs. Australia and New Zealand followed Canada in obtaining responsible government in incremental steps from the 1840s onward. Starting in 1902 parliamentary leaders from the white dominions of Canada, Australia, and New Zealand could express advisory opinions on imperial defense, tariffs, and other foreign affairs through Colonial (renamed Imperial) Conferences held periodically in London.[21]

At the other end of the spectrum of local political participation were colonies of occupation. There, European energies were directed toward gaining control of formerly independent societies. Pacification campaigns and creation of colonywide administrative structures required a government apparatus firmly in the hands of metropolitan officials. Institutions representing indigenous interests were either rudimentary and ineffective—as in British India and the four French communes of Senegal—or nonexistent. The idea that colonies of occupation might follow the model of the white dominions toward responsible government was not seriously contemplated by officials in London, to say nothing of policy makers in other metropolitan capitals who ruled out devolution of responsibility even to settlers.

South Africa, which in phase 1 combined features of a mixed settlement colony, a plantation colony, and a colony of occupation, experienced developments in phase 3 that underlined its uniqueness. The population of European origin became more complex as the initial settler wave from Holland and France was supplemented by a nineteenth-century influx from Great Britain. English-speaking immigrants were initially drawn to South Africa's coastal areas as farmers and merchants. Others came later in response to the discovery of diamonds (1867) and gold (1886) in the interior.

Descendants of phase 1 settlers increasingly identified themselves not as Europeans but as indigenous people (Afrikaners), paralleling the tendency of descendants of Europeans in the New World to redefine themselves in phase 2 as indigenous to America. In contrast, phase 3 emigrants from the British Isles saw themselves as settlers and retained economic and cultural ties to the metropole. Ethnic differences were reinforced politically by formation of two independent Boer (Afrikaner) republics, whose domestic and foreign policies were at odds with British imperial interests and values. The Anglo-Boer War of 1899–1902 pitted the British government and its settler allies against the Boer republics. Britain's victory incorporated them into a new Union of South Africa. A constitutional settlement devised by leaders of the two white ethnic groups permitted the country to become a self-governing dominion in 1910.

Underlying the willingness of the recently warring white parties to resolve their antagonism through constitutional compromise was recognition that their shared interest lay in excluding the country's nonwhite population from political power and economic privilege. The basis for domestic self-government in South Africa was a pact explicitly rejecting all political rights for nonwhites in the two former Boer republics and offering severely limited participation rights for nonwhites in the two British-ruled provinces. For South Africa's English-speaking whites the reference group was the United States, Canada, Australia, and New Zealand, where indigenous people were also effectively excluded from the political system. The difference was that whites formed the majority in these other countries, whereas Africans constituted the overwhelming majority in South Africa. In the United States and the white dominions electoral democracy was consistent with racially exclusionary public policies. In South Africa the racist ideological foundations of a minority-ruled polity precluded evolution toward democracy.

Plantation colonies in the Caribbean experienced social and economic changes in phase 3 when the Atlantic slave trade and the institution of slavery built upon it were abolished. Meanwhile, a variant of the plantation colony model emerged in several Indian and Pacific Ocean islands and in South Africa's Natal Province. This time it was indentured servants from India who constituted the labor force for plantations producing sugar (in Mauritius, Réunion, the Fiji Islands, Natal), copra (Fiji), and tea (Ceylon). Many Old World islands acquired characteristics found earlier in the Caribbean: racially plural societies, rigid race-based caste systems, and economies extraordinarily dependent on export of a limited range of commodities grown by the most advanced mass-production methods.[22]

The social structure of colonies of occupation acquired in phase 3 was dichotomized along racial lines. On one side were the few rulers, who were white; on the other the vast majority classified as native, nonwhite, or in subcategories based on shade of skin, religion, language, and social custom. In many instances colonial societies were trichotomized, so to speak, by the officially sanctioned entry of a non-European group to perform intermediate economic functions. Examples were Indians in East Africa, Burma, and Malaya; Chinese in Indochina, the Dutch East Indies, and Malaya; and Lebanese in French West Africa. Such third parties were separate in continental origin and culture from both the colonizers and the indigenous populace.

Whether a society was divided into two or three racial castes, opportunities for informal interaction across caste lines were severely reduced in phase 3 as compared to phase 1. This was consistent with a growing European preoccupation with race,

94

seen not simply as the principal means of identifying and classifying people but also as a way of placing them in a hierarchy of more or less civilized societies. Sexual intercourse across racial lines was increasingly frowned upon, interracial marriage even more so. The more rigid sexual code was part of an increasingly dominant ideology asserting white (Caucasian) superiority and insisting that "pure" white descent lines be maintained.[23]

The use of race to differentiate, stigmatize, and physically isolate groups of people meant that phase 3 colonies of occupation had sharply polarized social structures. People of mixed racial ancestry composed a small fraction of the population, at least compared to New World countries that in phase 1 had been mixed or plantation colonies. A more prominent role for mixed-blood groups might have reduced racial polarization by raising the number of socially recognized racial categories, complicating the process of classifying human beings along color lines and dramatizing how arbitrary the process was.[24]

THE ECONOMIC DIMENSION: INDUSTRIALIZATION AND ITS EFFECTS

The direction, composition, and volume of trade in phase 3 empires hinged upon the Industrial Revolution, which by this time was reshaping the economies and social structures of northwestern Europe. Industrialization involved several breaks with the past:

- increased use of inanimate sources of energy, including compressed steam and electricity;
- machine-based technologies permitting mass production of virtually identical items;
- a shift of production sites from scattered rural households to large factories in urban centers;
- production of a vast array of consumer goods, complemented by capital goods (machinery of all types, railroads, steamships);
- economies of scale in production, leading to low unit costs;
- generation of a steady stream of new products and productive techniques with practical uses;
- greater reliance on scientific enquiry into underlying natural laws as the basis for technological innovation;
- a growing tendency to view the natural world and human relationships in economic terms: land, other natural resources, and labor were commodified and assigned monetary value as factors of production.

The planning, management, and finance of industrialization in northwestern Europe was mainly in private hands. Capitalist entrepreneurs and financiers found they could amass profits by controlling critical factors of production and combining them in new ways; reducing unit costs of production by increasing the scale of operations, repressing workers' demands for higher wages, and introducing effi-cient, labor-saving new techniques; stimulating demand for their goods and services through advertising; and reinvesting profits from past activities to extend the scope of profitable future operations. A steadily increasing scale of operations entailed major changes on both the input and output sides of the productive process. Indus-trialists needed assured access to a greater volume and variety of raw materials used in their factories. At the same time they needed people able and willing to buy what factories turned out.

These characteristics of the productive and technological revolution north-western Europe experienced in phase 3 radically altered economic relations with the rest of the world. Changes from phase 1 include the following:

The kinds of commodities Europeans imported   Imports in the preindustrial era consisted largely of items requiring little or no processing in Europe before being marketed, for example, bullion and cane sugar from the New World and spices, precious stones, and handcrafted luxury goods from Asia. Industrialization raised demand for primary products that had to be processed and combined with other imported inputs before being sold. These included long- and short-staple cotton, vegetable oils, natural rubber, sisal, tin, sodium nitrates, phosphates, and copper. Late nineteenth-century advances in metallurgy created a demand for such rare metals as tungsten, manganese, chromium, and nickel. Many of these were available only (or at lowest cost) outside of Europe. An assured supply of the new imports was more critical to the European economy in phase 3 than before industrialization began.

Earlier imports were geared to economic elites and their desire for luxury goods. New imports reached a far larger, middle-class market and were made into what purchasers increasingly saw as ordinary consumption items. The range of foodstuffs and beverages imported in phase 1 was limited, the main items being sugar, sugar's alcoholic by-products, tea, and coffee. The range expanded enor-mously in phase 3 to include wheat and wheat products, butter and cheese, canned and frozen meat, vegetable oils, citrus fruits, bananas, coconuts, and cocoa.[25]

The volume and value of European imports   To exponential increases in the scale of European production during phase 3 should be added technological ad-vances that increased the size, speed, and carrying capacity of commercial ships. The greater volume of inputs needed by Europe's factories could thus be brought from overseas without encountering a transport bottleneck.

The economic gap between the world's first industrializers and nonindustrial societies became a yawning chasm in phase 3. Paul Bairoch estimates that between 1800 and 1913 real per capita income rose 458 percent in North America, 222 percent in western Europe, 77 percent in Latin America, 9 percent in Africa, and 1 percent in

Asia.[26] Commodities that wealthy regions wanted to import were readily affordable. The volume of imports into North America rose much less than its rapidly rising income level would suggest. This is because the raw materials used as the United States and Canada industrialized were in general domestically available and because North America's population was still relatively small. Western Europe's growing prosperity was more directly reflected in the rising volume of commodities imported from abroad.

The regional source of exports to Europe.   In phase 1 each non-European continent tended to specialize in certain exports to the metropoles. The Americas focused on raw materials or semiprocessed commodities from its mines, plantations, and ranches. Asia sent handcrafted luxury goods in addition to primary products. Africa exported little directly to Europe, though a substantial amount indirectly when one takes into account the vital role African slaves played in producing New World plantation crops.

In phase 3 the composition of exports to Europe from other regions began to converge. The Americas continued as before to export agricultural and mineral primary products, though the nature of these products changed over time. Newly formed African colonies began to send agricultural commodities and minerals directly to their metropoles. Perhaps the most significant transformation occurred in Asia, the region least affected in phase 1 by changes in the world economy. Europe's demand for Asia's handcrafted goods fell while demand for its raw materials rose, pushing it in this respect closer to other non-European regions. The change was most conspicuous in trade between Great Britain and India. Prior to the Napoleonic Wars one of the East India Company's specialties was cotton textiles shipped from India to the British Isles and European mainland. Following the wars, Britain reversed the pattern by exporting its inexpensive factory-woven cotton cloth to India. At the same time British officials and merchants did what they could to stimulate Indian production of raw cotton and indigo to supply the Lancashire mills. The effect was to undercut employment in the high-skill handloom weaving industry in places like Bengal and Bihar, while probably increasing employment in the export crop sector. Britain's industrialization went hand in hand with a decline of manufacturing—in the original and literal sense of products made by skilled hands—in its principal Asian colony.[27]

The composition of European exports   As noted in chapter 3, Europeans in the preindustrial era produced a limited range of consumer goods for overseas markets. What they did sell or barter was targeted at a society's wealthiest and most powerful elements, whether settlers or indigenous elites. In contrast, by phase 3 Europeans had an enormously wide range of consumer goods to sell, many designed for everyday use by people of limited means. Writing in 1862, the explorer W. B. Baikie listed the

British-made goods traded on the Niger and Benue rivers in West Africa's impoverished interior: tin dishes and pans, white calico cloth, cotton blankets, scissors, razors, fishhooks, padlocks, zinc mirrors, sewing thread and needles, pistols, machetes, and iron spoons.[28] At the other end of the spectrum, Europeans began for the first time to export capital goods. Railway ties, railroad cars and engines, steel girders for bridges and docks, tugboats, and eventually factory machinery were sent to destinations around the globe. Many capital goods were so expensive that they were purchased by governments overseas, the necessary financing being furnished by private European banks.

The volume and value of European exports　Europe absorbed the bulk of the region's industrial output in phase 3. But the existence of a market elsewhere for its consumer and capital goods was significant, both as a stimulus to expand the scale and cost-effectiveness of industrial operations and as a supplementary source of demand should the European business cycle turn downward. Export of machine-made goods was greatly aided by the cost-reducing effects of new technology. David Landes notes that in Britain around 1810 "the price of yarn had fallen to perhaps one-twentieth of what it had been [fifty years earlier], and the cheapest Hindu labour could not compete in either quality or quantity with Lancashire's mules and throstles."[29] This trend helps explain the rise of cotton fabric exports to India from a negligible amount in 1813 to 51 million yards in 1830 and more than 2 billion yards by 1890. Bairoch estimates that about a tenth of western Europe's and North America's manufactures was exported to South and Central America, Africa, and Asia in the nineteenth century.[30] As Europe's industrial output exploded, so did its exports.

The cumulative effect of these trends was emergence of a global economy marked by a distinctive territorial division of labor. Broadly, regions outside Europe specialized in exporting raw and semiprocessed goods to Europe, which in turn exported factory-manufactured goods to them. Bairoch estimates that in 1830 Latin America, Asia, and Africa generated 60.5 percent of the world's goods made by hand or machine. By 1860 the figure had fallen to 36.6 percent. By 1913 it had plummeted to 7.5 percent.[31] Such an astonishingly rapid change could not have taken place had western Europe not transformed itself through industrialization.

World trade flows: theory and practice　As noted earlier, there was a discrepancy in phase 1 between the way Europeans thought imperial trade should flow and the kind of trade that actually took place. While mercantilist doctrine stressed the importance of confining a colony's trade to its metropole, European merchants complemented this vertical pattern by carrying on an extensive lateral trade linking colonies and enclaves in the Americas, Africa, and Asia directly with one another. Control of this South-South trade was highly profitable, particularly in the transatlantic slave trade and exchanges of goods among Asian ports.

In phase 3 the relationship between dominant ideology and actual trade practices was in effect reversed. The doctrine of free trade—most persuasively articulated by political economists in the United Kingdom, more reluctantly accepted in other metropoles—opposed imposition of formal restrictions on colonial exports or imports. Free trade theory was noncommittal on the relative merits of vertical and lateral trade. Presumably if lateral trade made economic sense it should be allowed to flourish. But industrial Europe's capacity to direct global production and trade toward itself was so great that vertical patterns increasingly dominated lateral ones. As Europe's comparative advantage in generating consumer and capital goods grew over time, people elsewhere who wanted these goods looked to the source to provide them. Moreover, rulers of newly acquired Asian and African colonies used the coercive and fiscal policy levers at their disposal to push each colony toward specializing in a few commodities the metropole needed. Nonmarket public policies reinforced market forces in verticalizing world trade.

Meanwhile south-south economic ties atrophied. Abolition of the transatlantic slave trade ended the old link between Africa and the New World, with little to take its place. There was no phase 3 equivalent of the old transpacific trade in which Spanish galleons exchanged New World bullion for the East Asian silks and chinaware that criollo elites in New Spain and Peru desired. African gold was no longer shipped east to pay for Asian luxury goods. Intra-Asian maritime trade did, however, continue. While the older exchanges of local handcrafted goods declined in relative importance, new commodities emerged. Indian opium was exchanged for Chinese silver and tea despite strong objections by the Chinese government. Rice grown on the Asian mainland was exported to plantation colonies in the Indian Ocean. Movements of Indian and Chinese laborers to other parts of Asia—and to eastern and southern Africa and even the Caribbean—represented a new human dimension of lateralization.

Even taking the Asian experience into account, the overriding reality is that Europe's industrialization channeled world trade along north-south lines to a far greater extent than in the preindustrial era. Mercantilist theory could afford to lose favor in Europe because mercantilist practice, driven largely by technological change, was coming into its own.[32]

COMPLIANCE MECHANISMS

Europeans used a wider range of mechanisms in phase 3 than in phase 1 to gain compliance with their demands. In the earlier era their capacity to reward others for cooperation was limited by a small volume and variety of trade goods. But they did enjoy a comparative advantage from the start in the means of dispensing death. Coercion consequently took precedence over inducement. By seizing valuable commodities from conquered kingdoms and using forced labor on a massive scale to extract precious metals and grow export crops, Europeans acquired the wealth that made their initial round of empire building a paying proposition.

Their coercive capacity increased exponentially in phase 3. When the phase began, soldiers placed cartridges one by one into a gun's muzzle. When it ended, multiple cartridges were automatically loaded through the breech, then fired with unprecedented speed and accuracy over far greater distances. The military virtues of the Maxim machine gun, employed on colonial battlefields from the 1890s onward, were summarized by Daniel Headrick: "The Maxim was light enough for infantry to carry, it could be set up inconspicuously, and it spat out eleven bullets per second."[33] Any conflict pitting a Maxim against a muzzle-loader—to say nothing of spears, swords, and poisoned arrows—was not really a battle. It was a slaughter.

The classic confrontation took place in 1898 at Omdurman in the Sudan, where British and Egyptian forces met the Mahdi's army of forty thousand. The encounter was brief, intense, and decisive: the British lost twenty soldiers, the Egyptians twenty, the Mahdi eleven thousand. A young correspondent named Winston Churchill was present and wrote that the Battle of Omdurman was "the most signal triumph ever gained by the arms of science over barbarians. Within the space of five hours the strongest and best-armed savage army yet arrayed against a modern European Power had been destroyed and dispersed, with hardly any difficulty, comparatively small risk, and insignificant loss to the victors."[34]

News of unequal encounters like these traveled fast. The new weapons intimidated people who might otherwise have fought to retain, or try to reclaim, their freedom.[35] It is precisely because machine guns were so effortlessly lethal that they were infrequently used. The mere presence of a few Maxims or Lebels in colonial armories usually sufficed.

But the mechanized factories and workshops of nineteenth-century western Europe mass-produced what people in other continents desired as well as what they feared. Consumer goods were increasingly available abroad as networks of long-distance transport, communication, and trade expanded. To the extent that these goods outcompeted locally made products in price, quality, and convenience, Europe had what indigenous peoples valued. Hence Europeans could rely far more than in the past on rewarding compliant behavior by providing or promising manufactured articles. Peasants could be persuaded to abandon traditionally self-reliant, localized systems of production and consumption for participation in a globalized economy. Only by producing for export could they earn the cash to purchase imported kerosene lamps, cotton piece goods, corrugated iron roofing, fishnets, cutlery, bicycles, medicines, and bottled liquor.

Europeans in phase 3 were able to deploy high levels of coercion *and* high levels of economic inducement to get what they wanted. The threat of a Maxim gun if a colonial subject joined a revolt was reinforced by the enticing prospect of a cement floor and tin roof if the same person paid hut taxes and diligently tended coffee trees. The coercive threat was blunt and externally imposed. The material reward was more subtle and entailed an internalization of consumption norms by the colonized.

The mix of compliance mechanisms varied by time, place, and circumstance. The ratio of coercion to inducement, for example, was generally higher in the early pacification and railroad construction phases than in a colony's later years. Reliance on force to repress indigenous groups was more pervasive in lands with European settlers than in colonies of occupation. Whatever the combination in particular circumstances, however, the mere fact that foreign rulers could simultaneously display terrorizing power on the battlefield and exert attractive power in the marketplace gave them an unprecedented degree of flexibility in choosing the most cost-effective and persuasive ways to achieve their goals.

SECTORAL INSTITUTIONS: ROLES AND INTERRELATIONSHIPS

Europeans impacted other regions in phase 3 through a wide range of specialized institutions. Soldiers and administrators accountable to metropolitan governments were essential to empire building. But they were not alone. Agents of private profit and religious sectors also played central roles. At times nongovernmental actors contributed directly and deliberately to the extension of metropolitan power. At times they contributed indirectly through the unintended and largely uncoordinated consequences of their overseas activities. A comparison of nongovernmental actors in phases 3 and 1 illustrates underlying similarities as well as clear disparities.

Both expansionist phases saw extensive immigration to distant colonies. Each settler fragment—to use Louis Hartz's word—struck off from European society carried features of the society it left at the time of departure. In this respect emigrants from nineteenth-century Britain to Australia differed from, say, those who left seventeenth-century Spain for Peru.[36] But the contrast should not be overdrawn. Settlers in both phases wanted to acquire land and profit by transforming available natural resources into marketable commodities. Whether in Australia or Peru they looked down on indigenous people for having failed to develop land for commercial purposes. They were prepared to use force to seize land from such people. In both phases settlers constituted elements of a private profit sector, which quickly took root after being transplanted from the homeland. The private search for economic gain took noninstitutional form in the family homesteads established as frontiers were pushed back from the coast. But settlers also set up local institutions to stimulate economic development directly benefiting themselves.

Given the nature of the Industrial Revolution and the prosperity it generated in Europe, phase 3 settlers were more focused on producing for metropolitan markets than many of their phase 1 predecessors. They exported wheat from Canada, gold and diamonds from South Africa, mutton and butter from Australia and New Zealand, and wine from Algeria. The vast bulk of trade in these commodities was controlled by firms headquartered in Europe: shipyard owners, steamship lines, wholesale commercial companies, banks and insurance brokerage houses. European manufacturing firms gained valuable market niches among settler communities, whose members were more affluent and better informed about the latest consumption goods than indigenous populations. In these respects European sectoral institutions stretched outward to shape settler economies. In colonies of occupation metropolitan enterprises played even more dominant economic roles. Private firms handled wholesale and retail trade, ran shipping lines, and invested in plantations, ranches, and mines.

European traders, manufacturers, and financiers did not have identical economic interests or political preferences. But in the latter half of phase 3 many prominent capitalists agreed that having an empire was good for business. French enterprises were active in lobby groups like the Union Coloniale Française, the Comité de l'Afrique Française, the Comité de l'Asie Française, and the Comité du Maroc.[37] Merchants like Adolf Luderitz from Bremen and Adolf Woerman from Hamburg urged Germany to enter the imperial sweepstakes. Luderitz bought long stretches of the southwest African coast, then asked his government to intervene to protect what he had just purchased. In 1885 the London Chamber of Commerce urged the British government to annex Upper Burma to secure the area's forest and mineral resources for British rather than French companies and to gain overland access to the China market.[38] The British turned to the chartered company mechanism to sponsor ventures into the African interior. Best known was the British South Africa Company, Cecil Rhodes's ingenious instrument for enlarging the empire while simultaneously amassing a personal fortune. Other examples were the Imperial British East Africa Company and Royal Niger Company. The latter's leading figure, Sir George Taubman Goldie, was an unofficial adviser to the British delegation attending the Berlin Conference of 1884–85.

A comparable proliferation of institutions can be seen in the religious sectors of major metropoles. Whereas the Roman Catholic Church virtually monopolized mission work in phase 1, by phase 3 Catholics shared the field with numerous Protestant agencies. Between the late 1840s and World War I six Catholic orders, nine Protestant denominational agencies, and two Protestant interdenominational agencies began work in East Africa.[39] Prominent there and in the rest of Africa were the Holy Ghost Fathers and White Fathers for the Catholics, the Church Missionary Society (Anglican), London Missionary Society (primarily Congregational), Church of Scotland Mission, United Methodist Mission, and Lutherans and Moravians from Germany. Missionaries often set up their first churches, schools, and medical clinics outside zones of European control. But they generally welcomed inclusion of their stations within an expanding colonial frontier. Some religious leaders preached the gospel of imperialism. Cardinal Charles Lavigerie, founder of the White Fathers, was among the most fervent lobbyists for French expansion in North Africa. Friedrich Fabri, supervisor of the Rhenish Missionary Society, published an influential pro-imperial pamphlet in 1879, "Does Germany Need Colonies?" The widely read *Narrative of an Expedition to the Zambesi* (1866), by the Scottish missionary-explorer David Livingstone concluded with a plea that British officials extend to eastern and central Africa the authority they exercised on the West African coast.[40]

Phase 3 thus saw the rise to prominence of nongovernmental actors—notably industrialists and Protestant missionaries—who were absent or minimally present in phase 1. The goals, interests, and concerns of these new actors set them apart from their sectoral predecessors. Industrialists wanted to sell factory-made goods abroad and import unprecedented amounts of raw materials as inputs for mass-production processes. The Industrial Revolution raised for the first time the specter that diffusion of mass-production methods to several European countries and North America might place far more commodities on the market than consumers could purchase. From the early 1870s to the mid-1890s western Europe's economy did in fact stagnate, largely as a consequence of industrial overproduction. Industrialists had special reason to favor imperial expansion as a way to stimulate overseas demand for unsold products. New kinds of motives were also at work in the mission field as Christian agencies competed with each other for adherents. Competition was most obvious between Catholic and non-Catholic agencies. But Protestant groups had their own internecine rivalries. In some parts of Asia and Africa the missionary scramble for converts resembled the governmental scramble for territory.

These differences should not, however, deflect attention from underlying similarities between the two expansionist phases. Settlers transplanted to the colonies important aspects of their metropole's private profit sector. Institutions specializing in profit and proselytization dispatched agents from Europe to distant lands. In following their agendas, these institutions showed they could operate outside the formal jurisdiction of European administrators. But they were amenable to the extension of colonial rule and in many instances actively campaigned for it, both in the metropole and overseas.

6
Phase 4: Unstable Equilibrium, 1914–39

The fourth phase in the history of overseas empires encompassed two world wars and global economic depression. Western Europe was profoundly shaken by the unexpectedly long, bloody conflict of 1914–18, fought on its own soil, that terminated a century of relatively peaceful relations among its major states. Scarcely more than a decade after war's end the region's industrialized economies were battered by an unexpectedly severe fall in production, consumption, investment, and trade. Economic revival in the late 1930s was linked to preparations for another war.

The colonies, by this time closely linked to their metropoles' economies, could not avoid being affected by these traumatic events. They found themselves on a roller coaster ride, their human and material resources alternately mobilized and demobilized, their people's expectations for change raised and then disappointed. The ups and downs of the ride deserve attention even if the political consequences of this dizzying experience were delayed for the most part until yet another global crisis, World War II, set off the final contractionist phase.

Phase 4 was a period of equilibrium in two senses. First, the net territorial dimensions of empire changed little, for imperial losses and gains were to some extent self-canceling. Second, powerful forces worked to consolidate European rule *and* to undermine it, thereby countering or neutralizing each other. Phase 4 was connected to the phases preceding and following it: to phase 3 because Europeans were able to act on territorial claims made earlier, turning the governance of vast areas from ambitious aspiration to institutionalized practice; and to phase 5 through the powerful stimulus war and depression gave indigenous forces challenging external rule. In this respect the equilibrium was unstable, a moment of apparent stasis at a time of transition between the rise and decline of European dominance.

CHANGES IN THE SCOPE OF EMPIRE

West European countries added a little more than half a million square miles to their empires during phase 4: 104,000 in the Middle East in the early 1920s and 460,000 in the Horn of Africa as a result of Italy's invasion of Ethiopia (Abyssinia) in 1935–36. This stands in striking contrast to the 8.6 million square miles acquired between 1878 and 1913. Territories taken in the Middle East, under Ottoman rule prior to 1914, were awarded to the leading imperial powers, Britain and France, by the League of Nations, the international organization that emerged from the postwar conference at Versailles. Britain and France were leading partners in the winning Entente alliance, while the Ottoman Turks made the mistake of joining Germany and Austro-Hungary. Ethiopia was conquered by a relatively weak power, Italy, in the face of vigorous but ineffective protest by the league. By solidifying ties between Mussolini's and Hitler's regimes and further alienating west European democracies from these fascist states, the takeover was a grim precursor of World War II and its pattern of alliances.

The acquisitions by Britain and France were most significant politically. The rise of the Ottoman Empire five centuries earlier severely reduced European influence in the eastern Mediterranean, stimulating the Atlantic explorations that were so crucial to phase 1 expansion. Collapse of the Ottoman Empire in the wake of World War I produced the opposite result: a power vacuum in the eastern Mediterranean which leading European states moved swiftly to fill. The area was vital to the British, who considered control of the Suez Canal essential for ruling and trading with colonies in the Indian Ocean basin. Late in phase 3 they took de facto control of two territories nominally under Ottoman rule: Cyprus (1878) and Egypt (1881–82). After the Ottoman Sublime Porte allied with Germany in late 1914, Britain abandoned the legal fiction, unilaterally annexing Cyprus and declaring a protectorate over Egypt. British and French diplomats held secret wartime negotiations to carve up the predominantly Arab parts of the Ottoman Empire that became Syria, Lebanon, Palestine, Trans-Jordan, and Iraq.[1] Following the war the League of Nations assigned the first two to France, the others to Great Britain.

The form this award took limited it in novel respects. The league set up what it termed a mandate system to govern non-Turkish parts of the former Ottoman Empire and Germany's ex-colonies. Administrative authority over these territories was granted from above by the league, not simply asserted by a metropole on its own behalf as in the past. Moreover, the grant of authority was conditional. Mandatory powers had to agree to exercise "tutelage . . . on behalf of the League [over] peoples not yet able to stand by themselves under the strenuous conditions of the modern world." Tutelage was based on the principle that "the well-being and development of such peoples form a sacred trust of civilization."[2]

Granted, the mandate system was premised on the idea of a hierarchy of races that Europeans used to explain and justify imperialism in phase 3. That the league's paternalism was benevolent could not disguise the fact that its benevolence was deeply paternalistic. Its ability to monitor and change the behavior of mandatory powers was also limited, both in theory and practice. Nonetheless, acknowledgment by colonial powers that they had a moral and legal responsibility to foster the well-being of colonized peoples on behalf of the larger international community was an important break from the past.

Assignment of responsibility for administering Germany's former colonies was another indication that the world was less Eurocentric than in previous phases. Several territories were handed over by the league to Britain, France, and Belgium, in a reshuffle reminiscent of the aftermath of the Seven Years' and Napoleonic wars. But non-European actors also received mandates. Japan extended its empire by taking over ex-German island possessions in the Pacific north of the equator. Australia, New Zealand, and South Africa, exhibiting a surge of what D. K. Fieldhouse has aptly termed "subimperial" sentiment, pressed successfully to administer neighboring territories their troops had helped wrest from German control. These included New Guinea (to Australia), Western Samoa and Nauru (to New Zealand), and Southwest Africa, later known as Namibia (to South Africa).

The only instance of outright seizure of overseas territory in phase 4 unconnected with World War I and unsanctioned by the League of Nations was Italy's conquest of Ethiopia. Protests over this action by the league, including its west European members, went for nought. Yet the fact that other metropoles protested at all over the kind of behavior they themselves had engaged in a few decades before is significant in its own right. One explanation is that formation of the league represented a broadening of earlier conceptions of the international political system. Whereas in phase 3 uncolonized areas of Asia, Africa, and Oceania were regarded by Europeans as residual space lacking clear legal status, by phase 4 territories unincorporated into European empires were more widely acknowledged as having legal and political rights of their own.

The astute diplomacy and military skill of Emperor Menelik II having enabled Ethiopia to retain independence throughout the scramble for Africa, the country was accorded regular membership in the League of Nations. Invasion of Ethiopian soil was deemed just as unacceptable as violation of any other sovereign state's boundaries. If Italy's temporarily successful aggression harkened back to phase 3, the league's hostile reaction anticipated a phase 5 view of international relations that rejected earlier European assumptions about who mattered and who did not.[3]

PRESSURES FOR CHANGE IN THE BRITISH EMPIRE

For Britain, the leading imperial state, phase 4 was marked by losses as well as gains in power. Following World War I, leaders in the quasi colonies of Canada, Australia, New Zealand, and South Africa were eager to take the next step after responsible government: greater control over foreign policy. Imperial Conferences in 1926 and 1930 devised artfully crafted verbal formulae to try to square the circle: recognizing the de facto equality and sovereignty of each dominion while affirming the empire's unity as symbolized by common allegiance to the British Crown. Parliament's Statute of Westminster (1931) granted independence in all but name to the dominions. Increasingly, the term "British Commonwealth of Nations" was used instead of "British Empire" to refer to Great Britain and the dominions. Here was a new kind of international organization, one held together by voluntary bonds of friendship and ties of race and culture rather than by the metropole's power and historically preeminent role.[4]

It was one thing for the British government to accept devolution of political authority to people of European descent in pure settlement or mixed settlement/ occupation colonies. It was quite another to accept, either in principle or in practice, a similar evolution for colonies of occupation whose political leaders emerged from an overwhelmingly non-European population. The white dominions were not supposed to set precedents for the rest of the empire. Yet it was in colonies of occupation that popular pressures for domestic self-rule, and even full independence, began to build in phase 4. Officials in London had to decide whether, when, and how to respond to nationalist demands that increasingly questioned the basic premises of the imperial project.

The observation effect was at work here, as in phase 2. Nationalists in colonies of occupation asked, initially in indignation and then in anger, why full self-government should be extended to white settlers in the dominions while people of color elsewhere were denied far more modest forms of autonomy. Was this not evidence of racial and cultural discrimination?

British policy toward occupation colonies further fueled nationalist resentment. The critical period was the years during and immediately after World War I. What triggered anger was the willingness of British officials, savoring victory at war's end, to renege on commitments given non-Europeans during wartime when victory was by no means assured and colonial support was deemed vital. This pattern of concessions offered and withdrawn could be most noticeably observed in the Middle East. A key wartime goal was to weaken the Ottoman Empire by encouraging Arabs living under Ottoman rule to revolt. In 1915 the high commissioner in Egypt, Sir Henry McMahon, privately assured Mecca's Sharif Husayn that Arabs could obtain some form of independence if they took up arms against the Turks. The impact of Arab revolts that subsequently broke out was magnified by British tactical support. Only days before the Armistice was signed in 1918 Britain and France stated their goal as "the complete and definitive liberation of the peoples so long oppressed by the Turks and the establishment of national Governments and Administrations drawing their authority from the initiative and free choice of indigenous populations."[5] The two countries did not disclose earlier Sykes-Picot negotiations to share Ottoman territory among themselves.

When Arabs realized that Britain wanted to take what it had promised them, their positive sentiments quickly turned to suspicion and anger. Hostility intensified as the implications of a statement by Britain's minister of foreign affairs, Lord Balfour, supporting "the establishment in Palestine of a national home for the Jewish people" became clearer. The Balfour Declaration (1917) was seen as contradicting commitments Britain subsequently made as a mandatory power to protect the interests of Palestine's overwhelmingly Arab population.[6]

In Egypt, demands that Britain terminate its recently imposed protectorate, coupled with war-related economic grievances among the populace, led to an uprising in March 1919 and to mass demonstrations under the leadership of Saad Zaghlul. Following prolonged cabinet-level discussion, the British government decided to grant independence to Egypt in 1922. Politically conscious Egyptians had good reason to question this decision and the motives behind it. For one thing, independence was unilaterally accorded rather than negotiated with Zaghlul and other Wafd Party nationalists. For another, the Egyptian government's freedom to act in both domestic and foreign policy matters was circumscribed by treaty arrangements formalizing the change in status. Elizabeth Monroe observes that "the independence [the Egyptians] were given amounted to independence to do right, but not independence to do wrong, in situations in which the sole arbiter of right and wrong was Great Britain."[7] Nonetheless, the critical precedent was set that a colony of occupation could become an independent state. This was followed in 1932 by another: the first termination of a mandate, when Britain sponsored Iraq (then known as Mesopotamia) for membership in the League of Nations. As in the Egyptian case, Iraqi independence was circumscribed and conditional. Power passed to King Faisal, whom the British had virtually placed upon the Iraqi throne. Britain retained substantial military and economic presence in the oil-producing kingdom as its price for relinquishing formal control. Still, a territory the Colonial Office had begun to administer in 1921 was no longer part of the British Empire a dozen years later.

Though formal control over India in phase 4 was not relinquished as much as in the white dominions or Egypt and Iraq, it was seriously challenged by a mass political party, the Indian National Congress (INC). Cautious concessions to the demands of INC nationalists produced the Government of India Act in 1935, permitting provincial assemblies led by elected politicians to set their budgets and control important aspects of provincial life. Elected representatives from the eleven provinces were to sit in a Central Legislative Assembly along with delegates from the indirectly ruled princely states. British officials retained control, however, of policy areas affecting India as a whole, such as defense, communications, and monetary matters. Leaders of the INC were dissatisfied with many provisions of the act. But they decided to participate in the elections of 1937, which ushered in provincial self-rule, and the INC won control of seven of the eleven provincial legislatures. For various reasons the Central Legislative Assembly never functioned.

During phase 4 the INC progressively radicalized its goals and tactics. From its founding in 1885 through the early years of World War I the movement consisted largely of Western-educated urban professionals who communicated directly to the British their desire for modest reforms within the framework of foreign rule. But a series of fast-paced events between 1917 and 1920 transformed the INC and hence the political life of British India. More than 1.4 million Indians were mobilized to serve on the battlefields of France, the Middle East, and East Africa. In recognition of their invaluable contributions and in order to generate additional support at a critical juncture of the war, the secretary of state for India, Edwin Montagu, issued a public statement in August 1917. Montagu committed his government to "the increasing association of Indians in every branch of government, and the gradual development of self-governing institutions, with a view to the progressive realization of responsible government in India as an integral part of the Empire."[8] His statement marked the first time that any metropole had committed itself in advance to alter a colony of occupation's political status.

Having raised expectations during the war, Britain did little to satisfy them at war's end with its modest Montagu-Chelmsford constitutional proposals of 1919. They had in mind a power-sharing arrangement in the provinces but not at the center, in New Delhi, where real power lay. At the proposed rate of progress, many disappointed Indians asked themselves, would not dominion status be decades rather than years away? Further alienating Indian opinion leaders was the decision by authorities in New Delhi—known collectively as the *raj*—to replace wartime internal security arrangements with the harshly repressive Rowlatt Acts in order to quash possible outbreaks of sedition and terrorism. Indians perceived the Rowlatt Acts as a regressive move, an official vote of no confidence in their ability and will to win self-government by peaceful means. Adding insult to injury, the laws were passed by the British official majority in the central legislature despite the unanimous opposition of its few Indian members. On both substantive and procedural grounds the raj was dramatizing, for all to see, the extent of its subjects' powerlessness.

Anti-Rowlatt demonstrations in the Punjab capital of Amritsar resulted in the death and injury of several Europeans. In response, on April 19, 1919, Brig. Gen. Reginald Dyer led his Gurkha troops to the Jallianwala Bagh, a large but virtually enclosed open area in the center of Amritsar where a crowd had peacefully gathered to protest the new regulations. Dyer ordered his troops to fire repeated rounds, without warning, into the crowd. By the time his soldiers ran out of ammunition more than 370 Indians lay dead, about 1,100 injured. Almost every bullet found a human target.[9]

News of the Amritsar massacre hit politically aware Indians like a seismic shock. Almost overnight formerly moderate leaders of the INC were transformed into committed activists for Indian self-rule. Compounding the shock was realization that General Dyer's actions were supported by many British in India and conservative politicians and newspapers in the United Kingdom. Among those radicalized by the massacre were Mohandas K. Gandhi and Jawaharlal Nehru, two English-trained lawyers who were to play leading roles during the next three decades in mobilizing mass support for the INC's agenda. Gandhi had lived in South Africa from 1893 to 1914 and while there, as an activist lawyer, had devised innovative methods of nonviolent resistance to laws discriminating against Indian residents. His South African experience strongly influenced the *satyagraha* ("soul-force" or "truth-force") campaigns he later led in India, which began in 1920 and were employed intermittently into the 1930s. Through them Gandhi used his extraordinary gift for symbolic dramatization of the anticolonial struggle to change the behavior and worldview of millions of fellow Indians.

Until 1929 INC leaders demanded dominion status for India, comparable to the constitutional position held by the white dominions. But authorities in London and New Delhi were unwilling to go along. At issue was not only continued control of domestic policy in Britain's most important possession but also foreign policy, since dominion status was redefined in the 1920s to include greater control over foreign affairs. Indian troops and infantry battalions of British troops stationed in the subcontinent were responsible for defending other parts of the empire. London feared that an Indian dominion able to chart its own foreign course might not act in accord with Britain's geostrategic interests. If anything, fears about imperial defense grew as the 1930s progressed, with the increasingly likely prospect of a Japanese attack on Britain's southeast Asian colonies.

Leaders of the INC for their part grew less interested in dominion status as the struggle against foreign rule wore on. In 1929 they declared that their goal was *purna swaraj*, "complete freedom." This raised the possibility of exit from the British Commonwealth once independence was attained. A new round of mass-based civil disobedience campaigns followed the *purna swaraj* declaration. That Indians remained powerless to set foreign policy was dramatically underscored in 1939 when the viceroy, Lord Linlithgow, committed India to war against the Axis powers without bothering to consult INC leaders. Though hostile to the Axis cause, Gandhi and others demanded in 1942 that Britain quit India so the country's leaders could decide whether to participate in the war. The British responded by placing leading INC figures under house arrest and swiftly crushing all signs of insurrection.[10]

The principal reason India (and Pakistan) won independence in 1947, earlier than the vast majority of phase 5 new states, was because of the INC's success in mobilizing mass support during phase 4. The raj found itself on the defensive in the interwar years, compelled to respond in largely ad hoc fashion to initiatives taken— and issues and tactics selected--by leaders from the colonized population.

Another sign of the decline of European power in phase 4 was the termination of special privileges Europeans and other foreigners extracted earlier from Ottoman and Chinese authorities. Financial and diplomatic concessions known as capitulations were abrogated by the Ottoman Porte when it entered World War I but were in effect reimposed in 1920 by the victorious Allies. By mobilizing Turkish armed forces and nationalist sentiment against the threatened dismemberment of Turkey by Allied powers, the military leader Mustapha Kemal (Ataturk) managed to have the capitulations abolished in 1923 in the Treaty of Lausanne. Five years later the Turkish Republic gained full control over tariff-setting policy. In China, collapse of the Ch'ing dynasty in 1911–12 did not immediately lead to renunciation of the humiliating "unequal treaties" Ch'ing rulers had signed with the European powers, the United States, and Japan over the preceding seven decades. But Chinese nationalist sentiment ran strongly in favor of "rights recovery." At the Washington Conference of 1922 the Chinese were able to restrict the right of foreign governments to exercise jurisdiction over foreign nationals residing in China. By 1930 the Nationalist government in Nanking had gained effective control over tariff policy. In 1943 it abolished the last vestiges of the unequal treaty regime.[11]

UNDERLYING CHANGES: CONSOLIDATION OF EUROPEAN RULE

A survey of formal responsibilities Europeans exercised overseas during phase 4 thus shows modest gains as well as modest losses, with little overall change in the number or size of holdings. If one delves below the legal-formal level, one can likewise identify events and trends on both sides of the ledger. Europeans gained power by consolidating economic and bureaucratic control over territories that in many cases were only nominally ruled by them prior to World War I. Evidence for the view that phase 4 was the high-water mark of colonialism will be presented first. But Europeans also lost power through global crises that reduced their capacity and will to maintain the status quo while simultaneously increasing the capacity and will of colonized peoples to challenge it. Many changes in power relationships within empires, though not easily measurable or perceptible, set the stage for the readily measurable, dramatic decolonization events of phase 5.

Among the most persuasive arguments for empire is that colonies' human and material resources can be called upon when a metropole is in trouble. All the European metropoles save Spain and Portugal were deeply engaged in World War I. They found themselves in unexpectedly serious trouble as the conflict dragged on, year after year, inflicting staggering losses of life and property on both sides. World War I gave metropoles urgent reason to extract more from their dependencies and showed how valuable dependencies could be in time of crisis. This was especially true of the Entente alliance. Indeed, Britain's and France's colonies were major players contributing to Entente victory. Supplementing 5.7 million men recruited from the British Isles for the war effort were 1.4 million from India, 1.3 million from the white dominions, and 134,000 from other British colonies. From France's colonies came 600,000 soldiers and 200,000 workers employed in the metropole's factories.[12] The government of India contributed £100 million in 1917 to pay off the British government's war debt and spent £20–30 million annually on war-related expenses.[13] Strategically valuable materials sent from the colonies included cotton, rubber, tin, leather, and jute, this last being used to make the ubiquitous sandbags of trench warfare. Soldiers from Nigeria, Kenya, and South Africa were instrumental in capturing German colonies, thereby depriving Germany of the potential for overseas extraction that Entente powers utilized for themselves.

These wartime contributions influenced metropolitan policy makers' postwar thinking about empire. Colonies could become even more valuable in the future, so the thinking went, if their economic potential were further realized. This should be brought about by increasing public expenditure on economic infrastructure and by encouraging greater investment in the directly productive activities of private profit sectors. The new emphasis on economic development could be seen in two influential books published in the early 1920s by leading practitioner-theorists of empire: France's Albert Sarraut and Britain's Sir (later Lord) Frederick Lugard. In *La Mise en Valeur des Colonies Françaises,* Sarraut wrote, "It is not by wearing out its colonies that a nation acquires power, wealth, and influence; the past has already shown that development, prosperity, consistent growth and vitality in the colonies are the prime conditions for the economic power and external influence of a colonial metropolis." In *The Dual Mandate in Tropical Africa* Lugard argued that colonialism should be judged—and in the British case judged favorably—by the ability to satisfy two obligations: providing tangible benefits to rulers *and* to the colonized population.[14]

New ideas about development were accompanied by new levels of activity. Government-financed railways probed deeply into continental interiors. Examples were the Benguela-Katanga and Dakar-Bamako routes. The advent of automobiles and trucks stimulated a tremendous increase in road construction. The colonial state became directly involved in large-scale agricultural enterprises in the valleys of the Nile (Gezira Scheme) and Niger (Office du Niger). Agricultural research stations generated information about yield-increasing techniques that was then passed on to farmers by a growing cadre of extension agents. A remarkably ambitious program to build physical infrastructure and expand social services was the long-term (1919–28) development plan for Britain's Gold Coast, announced by its governor, Sir F. G. Guggisberg. Malaya's governor, Sir Frank Swettenham, was another outspoken advocate of rapid economic and social development. In general the scope of colonial public sector responsibilities was greater after World War I than before it.

During this same period European business enterprises substantially expanded trading, agricultural, and mining activities in the colonies. Examples were Lever Brothers (renamed Unilever), which operated throughout the British Empire and in the Dutch and Belgian possessions; S.C.O.A. in French West Africa; Société Général and Union Minière in the Congo; Tanganyika Concessions; Royal Dutch Shell in the Netherlands Indies; powerful banks like the Nederlandsche Handel-Maatschappij and the Banque de l'Indochine; and numerous shipping firms.[15] With large trading companies acting as wholesalers, European consumer goods reached previously inaccessible hinterland markets. Advertisements touting the high status, convenience, and reliability of these goods helped shift colonial consumer tastes from local to imported products. The plantation model of production for export was widely diffused throughout Asia, Africa, and Oceania. For the most part plantations were owned and managed by settlers or large Europe-based enterprises. Among commodities grown for export were cane sugar, sisal, and a wide array of tree crops: rubber, tea, coffee, cocoa, cloves, coconuts, cinchona bark, kapok, and palm oil.[16]

These public and private profit sector initiatives were designed to link colonial economies more tightly than ever to metropoles. Vertical economic ties were further strengthened during the Great Depression, when metropolitan governments concerned by declining trade with other developed countries adopted protectionist (in the British case, "imperial preference") policies directing colonial trade toward themselves. The global division of labor became more pronounced in phase 4, colonies accounting for a growing portion of the world's primary product exports.[17] Western Europe still dominated in exports of factory-made goods, though market shares held by the United States and Japan were rapidly rising.

Along with the outward orientation of colonial economies went a tendency for each colony to specialize in a few commodities for export. This resulted not simply from comparative advantage in a particular commodity but also from policies set by imperial officials with the empire's interests primarily in mind. A metropole might have a greater volume and variety of resources at its disposal if each possession concentrated on certain items. The assumption was that the sum total of multiple specializations was a more diversified and viable resource base for the empire as a whole. Government decisions on trade, infrastructure, and research priorities pushed colonies—above all, smaller ones—toward specialization.

Because of such policies, the typical colony's economic prospects were unusually dependent on forces operating outside its boundaries and beyond its control. These included investment decisions of foreign companies and banks, export strategies of other primary-producing areas, international demand for commodities in which a colony specialized, and terms of trade between colonial exports and manufactured imports. In a time of global economic growth, as in the 1920s, these vulnerabilities benefited some segments of the colonized population. But in the global economic crisis of the 1930s the same vulnerabilities produced tremendous hardships, widely shared. Between 1925–29 and 1930–34 the value of traded goods fell 28 percent in the Netherlands Indies, 46 percent in Malaya, and over 50 percent in India, Ceylon, and Nigeria.[18] These declines hit the export-oriented labor force hard. In the Netherlands Indies, for example, plantation employment fell from 1.2 million to half that figure between 1929 and 1933. Smallholders in Burma growing rice for export were devastated.[19]

Expansion of European economic activity in the public and private profit sectors was more marked in the 1920s than in the 1930s, as the Great Depression curtailed funds to finance development projects officials and private employers had in mind. Still, taking the interwar period as a whole, the assessment of the colonial historian Raymond Betts seems valid: "Most of the physical changes and development in the colonial territories were initiated and, in large measure, executed during the interwar period. In these days the structure of modern empire was established, what was good and bad about it was institutionally fixed."[20]

Accompanying increased metropolitan economic influence was a consolidation of administrative control. In much of rural Asia and Africa the impact of European rule had scarcely been felt when World War I broke out, if only because rule existed primarily in the colonizer's imagination. The situation changed after war's end. In many territories European soldiers and bureaucrats assigned high priority to pacifying outlying areas and subordinating them to directives from the colonial capital city.[21] Administrative staffs expanded, particularly in such technical fields as botany, agricultural extension, forestry, public health, civil engineering, and vocational education. Even when local administration was handled by indigenous rulers acceptable to colonial authorities, European officials spent a great deal of time traveling "in the bush" to settle disputes and enforce their version of law and order. The interwar period was the era par excellence of the British district officer, French commandant de cercle, Belgian administrateur de territoire, and Portuguese chefe do posto. Acting largely on their own, these men often became undisputed "rois de la brousse" (monarchs of the bush).[22]

Norms prohibiting interracial sexual relations and severely restricting interracial social relations became more explicit and were more rigidly enforced. As pacification campaigns wound down and public health facilities improved, European women arrived in greater numbers to join their husbands or meet prospective partners. European men who had previously been on their own, with ample time to interact informally with those they ruled, now spent more of their off-duty time with men and women of their own kind. The administrator's social life came to revolve around the athletic and alcohol-intensive activities of racially exclusive social clubs— a situation evocatively portrayed in George Orwell's *Burmese Days* and W. Somerset Maugham's short stories about the British in Malaya.

Perhaps because informal links across racial lines declined in the interwar years, administrators tried to compensate for lack of knowledge of what the colonized were thinking by designing systematic methods of learning about their subjects. Findings from fieldwork by anthropologists helped them understand better why local revolts and work stoppages had occurred. Fieldwork studies helped officials avoid egregious mistakes when selecting the "traditional" authorities of indirect rule systems.[23] Anthropologists tended to see themselves as students of small-scale, autonomous non-European societies minimally affected by the outside world. Yet their own activities belied these assumptions. Fieldworkers in colonies operated under the protective shield of an externally imposed government. The societies they studied were no longer autonomous: the ultimate sanction of capital punishment, for example, had been removed from indigenous institutions and placed in foreign hands. The anthropologist's presence in an out-of-the-way village was itself testimony to the penetrative capacity of outside forces.[24]

As in earlier phases, settlers emigrating from Europe threatened indigenous peoples' claims to land. Ex-servicemen from Great Britain were officially encouraged to settle in Kenya. Their numbers made it more possible and more necessary to dispossess Africans from what became known as the White Highlands. An extraordinarily complex and controversial case of settlement involved Jews in Palestine, as Britain attempted to work out the mutually incompatible implications of its Balfour Declaration and the League of Nations mandate. From the outset the mandatory power found itself not only presiding over but also actively encouraging a head-on collision over land and legal rights between the immigrant population and resident Palestinians. Conflict was intensified because these immigrants, unlike others noted in this book, did not consider themselves settlers in a foreign territory, but rather returnees to land from which their ancestors had been forcibly driven centuries earlier. Even more important to Zionists, this was the land promised the Jewish people by God.

Tensions between Jews and Palestinians intensified in the 1930s as Nazism's spread in central Europe swelled the number of Jews who saw a Palestinian homeland as their only means of personal and collective survival. On the other side, many Arab residents of Palestine felt their community's future was in danger unless Britain respected its mandate to protect the territory's overwhelming majority. As Palestinian leaders saw it, encouraging Jewish immigration was yet another instance of what European powers had unjustly done in so many parts of the world: sponsor settlement by fellow Europeans with scant regard for the rights of non-Europeans already living there.

Phase 4 witnessed an unprecedented degree of cultural penetration by European and North American religious sectors. Catholic and Protestant missionaries working in sub-Saharan Africa increased from 12,500 in 1924 to 17,900 twelve years later; Catholic missionary orders had 20 percent more foreigners in India in 1933 than in 1912. As of the late 1930s England and Scotland were headquarters for 140 Protestant mission agencies, many formed since the start of World War I. Thirty-two agencies based in the Netherlands worked overseas, mostly in East Indies outer islands. Efforts to coordinate the work of major Protestant denominations resulted in formation of the International Missionary Council in 1921. Christian adherents in India rose from 2.7 million in 1911 to 6 million in 1936, in sub-Saharan Africa from 1.3 million in 1911 to 6.7 million in 1936, in French Indochina from fewer than 1 million in 1912 to 1.4 million in 1935.[25] Mission schools and health clinics in remote rural areas as well as cities exposed an ever-growing number of colonial subjects to Western ideas, values, and lifestyles.[26]

Marking the apex of European power and self-confidence was the International Colonial Exposition held in Vincennes, outside Paris, in 1931. Its commissioner-general and guiding spirit was Marshall Louis Hubert Lyautey, the legendary soldier and administrator who had brought Morocco under French control. The exposition was enormously popular, attracting 3.5 million visitors in its first month. An International City of Information dispensed handouts on the possessions of France, Great Britain, Belgium, Holland, Portugal, Italy, Denmark (Greenland), and the United States. Many colonies had their own pavilions, designed to portray distinctive cultural features. Inside were elaborate dioramas of village scenes, replete with indigenous inhabitants brought to France for the occasion. Other pavilions focused on the French army, European private enterprises, and Christian missionaries. The exposition conveyed an image of peaceful, economically progressing societies whose diverse peoples were grateful to be living under benevolent tutelage.[27]

Carrying such images in their heads, Europeans could comfort themselves, at least until the outbreak of World War II, that the colonial enterprise was firmly in their hands. They and doubtless many of their subjects as well took the status quo as a reliable predictor of the future.

UNDERLYING CHANGES: THE EROSION OF EUROPEAN POWER

Counteracting these trends and events were changes eroding European capacity and will to control far-flung empires. Capacity was lowered in several respects. Perhaps most important, World War I had a devastating impact upon lives, property, and the fabric of society in western Europe. From 1914 to 1918 contending armies inflicted on one another the destructive power of repeating-rifle technologies used with such lethal effectiveness against non-Europeans in phase 3. European powers consumed, for unproductive military purposes, financial and material resources accumulated from productive activities elsewhere. By one estimate Britain's prewar foreign investments were diminished by a quarter, France's by over half, and Germany's by over 90 percent as a result of war and the forced sale of securities.[28] American corporations and banks purchased many of these assets, especially investments in Canada and South and Central America, thereby replacing European private profit sectors with their own as an influential force in New World economic and political affairs.

With reduced public and private capital, and with France and Belgium facing a major task of postwar reconstruction at home, imperial powers had limited amounts to invest abroad in the 1920s. Ironically, the war that convinced Europeans that accelerated colonial development would benefit all parties also severely constrained capacity to carry out projects consistent with that goal. And, of course, after 1929 the global depression made it hard for financially strapped metropolitan governments to implement even their most modest overseas development schemes.

The crises of phase 4 dramatized the limited ability of Europeans to control world events. In phase 3 imperial powers prided themselves on their "civilized" avoidance of fratricidal war. Yet in 1914 they embarked upon a round of fratricide costing the lives of at least eight million combatants. On the Middle East front in 1915–16 British, French, Australian, and New Zealand forces failed in the Gallipoli offensive against Ottoman forces, while Anglo-Indian troops marching into Mesopotamia were forced to surrender at Kut in 1916. Following the war, Britain proved unable to channel the course of events in Egypt and Iraq, as witnessed by unanticipated grants of independence. Britain's contradictory policies in Palestine created a situation which by the late 1930s threatened to explode. For decades Europeans boasted of industrial capitalism's power to generate economic and technological progress. Yet they were obviously unable to insulate themselves from an economic depression their finest forecasters had failed to predict. As crises engulfed Europe, the image of its omnipotence lost all credibility.

World War I undercut Europe's global dominance by accelerating the rise to great-power status of a few countries outside the region. Far from being weakened by participation in the war, the United States and Japan emerged from it economically and militarily strengthened. Their industrial base benefited from the spread of productive technologies initially concentrated in Europe. Between 1913 and 1920 manufacturing production rose 22 percent in the United States, 76 percent in Japan.[29] The two countries gained geostrategically as global attention shifted from the Atlantic to the Pacific, where both powers maintained a strong naval and commercial presence. The end of British preeminence at sea was signaled by the Washington Naval Disarmament Conference of 1921–22, which set ratios of 5:5:3 for battleships of the British, American, and Japanese navies, respectively.

The rise of the United States and Japan did not initially challenge the European empires. The United States focused on consolidating informal influence within its own hemisphere, occasionally intervening militarily in the affairs of recalcitrant New World states. In 1934 Congress set a target date of July 4, 1946, for Philippine independence, reflecting the anticolonial tradition that antedated America's brief fling with overseas empire. But the United States did not press other imperial powers to follow suit. The Japanese tried to enhance the economic performance of their existing empire. By the early 1930s they had begun to expand into northeast Asian mainland areas never claimed by Europeans. European powers could hardly ignore the growing challenge posed by the United States and Japan as centers of trade and investment. Neither could the possibility be foreclosed that Japan would one day look to Southeast Asia to satisfy a growing appetite for raw materials.

Another candidate for great-power status was the world's largest polity, which entered World War I as tsarist Russia and emerged at war's end as the Soviet Union under Bolshevik leadership. From the start official Soviet ideology posed a more direct and fundamental threat to European colonialism than the official stance of the United States or Japan. But the Soviet Union's anticolonial role was quite limited in phase 4. Placed on the defensive, its military forces were in no position to mount offensives elsewhere. First things came first: protecting the new regime against invading foreign armies and domestic anticommunist forces while trying to hold together the vast, restive, multiethnic overland empire bequeathed by the Romanov tsars. Moreover, the Stalinist option for "socialism in one country" entailed economic modernization through economic autarchy. Only after the Soviet leadership had consolidated and centralized domestic power during phase 4 and managed to pull the country through the devastating experience of World War II was the regime in a position to conduct an aggressive foreign policy in line with its anticolonial ideology.

Accompanying the erosion of Europe's capacity to dominate the world in phase 4 were signs of a less resolute and more ambivalent will to do so. The war led

done to their subjects' psyches and social relationships. Inevitably, belief in the revised colonial mission entailed a searching critique of the intended purposes as well as actual results of the earlier mission. Self-criticism was in order even though its announced aim was to enhance empire's long-term prospects.

UNDERLYING CHANGES: EMPOWERMENT OF THE COLONIZED

Accompanying these changes on the European side was an increased capacity and will on the part of colonized people to assert their own interests and move toward political autonomy. Paradoxically, the success of dominant sectoral institutions in incorporating subject populations into a Eurocentric world facilitated formation and spread of institutions expressing the views of the colonized in ways authorities could not ignore. Consolidation of European power after World War I helped create the organizational bases for transfer of power after World War II.

Several complementary, converging processes were at work. As the years went by, the colonial situation became less a distant abstraction and more a lived experience for hundreds of millions of people. As the coercive, extractive, culturally disruptive presence of foreign rulers became increasingly obvious to ever-larger numbers, the grounds for widespread disaffection grew. Most unpopular were government initiatives spurred by global crises: recruitment of young men for military service, forced labor in war-related road maintenance, cotton, and rubber production schemes, price cutbacks for colonial exports as the depression took hold, higher head and hut taxes to cover development projects metropoles were unable or unwilling to finance. Growing awareness of government's impact meant that people were more likely to attribute problems they faced to the malevolent intentions and actions of their rulers. The idea that a colony's residents had common grievances and interests became more plausible and more attractive. The basis was laid for the spread of corollary ideas: that these shared features entitled colonized subjects to be considered a nation, and that the nation deserved one day to become an independent state.

Changes in the way the colonized perceived themselves and defined their situation were due in part to new experiences affecting individuals: enrollment in Western-style schools, migration to urban centers, and recruitment to jobs involving sustained contact with Europeans. These processes were accelerated in phase 4 by official efforts to stimulate economic development and by expanded missionary conversion and educational activities. As more people found precolonial patterns of thought and action irrelevant or unattractive, and as they gained familiarity with patterns imported from Europe, they joined the ranks of what Karl Deutsch has called the "socially mobilized."[36] Changes they experienced brought them closer in many ways to their rulers. There was a far greater likelihood of physical proximity and personal interaction across the boundary lines of race and power if a non-European were a junior civil servant, army conscript, mine worker, trading company employee, domestic servant, pupil, catechist, or mission teacher than if one were a peasant. Young people attending mission or government schools came close to their rulers by being exposed—and often powerfully attracted—to European culture. The socially mobilized held occupations patterned after those in the metropole. They began to think of their material and workplace interests much as manual and service workers in Europe did, using metropolitan workers' living standards and demands for a better life as reference points for their own lives.

Physical and psychological proximity to colonizers produced a range of responses. One was resentment. Seen up close, Europeans were not the superior and invulnerable creatures they took such pains to represent themselves as being. It became obvious that they persistently failed to behave according to their own so-called civilized standards. Colonized peoples closest to them were the most likely to be on the receiving end of racially offensive words and actions. The more culturally assimilated to European ways a colonized person became, the more galling were expressions of white racial superiority, since racism was more manifest when it lacked the supportive shield of cultural difference to protect it. The irrational, hurtful nature of racism was further reinforced when non-Europeans who had obtained the educational qualifications to move up sectoral institutional hierarchies found their advance blocked. Individual merit, it turned out, was overridden by the collective interests of Europeans fearing loss of control of key institutions. The crowning hypocrisy was European insistence that one reason for their civilization's superiority over others was its respect for the individual.

Mobilization into foreign-dominated sectoral activity made it easier than before to channel resentments through organizations the colonized controlled. A shared Western language, physical proximity in growing urban centers, common occupational outlooks—these factors converged to produce a veritable organizational explosion in phase 4. In the public sector were junior civil servants, soldiers, and ex-servicemen. In the private profit sector were workers in mines, plantations, and trading firms as well as peasants growing export crops. In the religious sector were preachers and mission teachers. Not readily identifiable by sector were groups organized around gender, kinship, linguistic, and local or regional territorial affiliations. The success of efforts to organize such groups varied greatly, depending for example on whether a colonial government was willing to recognize organizations and negotiate with their leaders. Many were illegal or operated uneasily on the margins of legal status. Still, the sheer scope and variety of their activities evidenced new forms of empowerment.

Involvement in European-directed sectors permitted socially mobilized colonial subjects to choose among a wide range of tactics to express their interests. One option was to withdraw from participation in the colonial economy by going on strike, not supplying primary products for export, or boycotting imported consumer goods. Examples were copper miners' strikes in Northern Rhodesia, holdups of cocoa sales by Gold Coast farmers, and the boycott of British cloth organized by INC activists. These tactics could succeed only in arenas in which colonized people had become essential to the smooth functioning of the economy, to the point that even a temporary withdrawal interrupted the flow of income their rulers had come to expect and caused metropolitan officials great anxiety.

Another option was infiltration: upward movement of individuals within institutions, whether by promotion from below or by securing educational qualifications to enter hierarchies at more responsible middle levels. In general, infiltration was least rapid in the large-scale private profit sector, somewhat more so in the public sector, and most successful in the religious sector. Upward mobility in the civil service varied by metropole, being more pronounced in British and French colonies of occupation than in Dutch, Belgian, and Portuguese possessions. Especially noteworthy were developments in India. In 1919 Indians constituted 12.4 percent of the Indian Civil Service (ICS), the elite corps of about twelve hundred men described by Prime Minister David Lloyd George as "the steel frame of the whole structure" of imperial rule. The figure rose to 15 percent in 1922, helped by that year's decision to hold ICS entrance examinations for the first time in India instead of only in Great Britain. Two years later an official commission recommended that Indians attain parity with British citizens by the late 1930s. This ambitious goal was achieved, the indigenous proportion reaching 49.5 percent in 1939. By the end of phase 4 the ICS had not only taken root as a foreign import in Indian soil. It also increasingly resembled the vast land it governed.[37]

As for the religious sector, many Christian churches indigenized rapidly, even in territories where the subject population enjoyed virtually no opportunities for political expression or bureaucratic advancement. In the Belgian Congo the number of Catholic priests who were African rose from 0 to 43 between 1912 and 1935, with over 18,000 catechists by 1935. Five Congolese served as ordained Protestant pastors in 1923, 336 by 1936. In French Indochina by the mid-1930s there were four times as many indigenous Catholic priests and fourteen times as many indigenous sisters as foreign missionaries. In the Dutch East Indies the (Reformed) Church of Eastern Java was founded in 1931 with Europeans constituting only 10 percent of the governing synod. By one estimate over a quarter of India's Roman Catholics were in churches entirely staffed by Indians. In 1923 the (Protestant) National Missionary Council was renamed the National Christian Council of India, Burma, and Ceylon. K. S. Latourette observes that "the change in the name from 'missionary' to 'Christian' was significant, for it indicated that the body was not to be a foreign importation but in the hands of nationals."[38] Speaking more generally, Latourette says of the interwar years that "for the first time in its history Christianity was becoming really worldwide and not a colonial or imperial extension, ecclesiastically speaking, of an Occidental faith. . . . No other set of ideas, not even the widely propagated Communism of the period, had ever been so extensively represented by organized groups or so rooted among so many different peoples."[39]

Infiltration of sectoral institutions from below raises an intriguing question: who was using whom in this situation? On the one hand, the penetration of colonial society by sectoral institutions, described earlier as the basis for consolidation of European rule, depended on recruiting colonized people as employees. On the other hand, as recruits moved up in government, business, and religious agencies, they were able to use their positions to further their own goals as well as gain administrative experience that could be called upon later when the transfer of power took place. In effect two penetrative processes were simultaneously at work: downward by imported institutions into indigenous society, upward within these same institutions by selected indigenous individuals. Were these individuals collaborators or infiltrators, agents or subverters of colonial consolidation? The answer depended on the motivations of the individuals concerned, the level of administrative responsibility they attained, and the leeway for autonomous action in the territory where they worked. In general, the upward penetrative process may have had the effect of moderating and blurring, if not halting, the power-enhancing effects of the downward penetration described earlier in this chapter. The complexities and ambiguities of institutional life in phase 4 are additional reasons for not fitting it into the expansion-contraction framework employed for other time periods.

Another option was to set up or expand organizations that were separate from ones Europeans controlled yet in a position to challenge assertions of European authority. Such organizations both expressed the interests of colonized peoples and gave practical expression to the ideal of self-government. In the public sector were nationalist movements calling colonial rule into question. Operating in some cases as legally recognized political parties and in others as clandestine operations, these movements increasingly functioned as alternatives to the colonial regime. Prominent examples were the INC, Wafd Party in Egypt, Neo-Destour Party in Tunisia, Indonesian National Party, the Thakins of Burma, the Viet Nam Quoc Dan Dang, and in Jamaica the People's National Party.

In the private profit sector were unions, whose demands to redistribute gains from European capitalist enterprise were at times backed up by strikes. Examples were the Industrial and Commercial Workers' Union in South Africa, les Employées de Commerce de l'Industrie et des Banques (Senegal), and the British Empire Workers' and Citizens' Home Rule Party led by "Buzz" Butler (Trinidad).[40]

India was unique in having an indigenous business class that played a large role in financing, managing, and owning industrial enterprises. Indians were prominent in the manufacture of cotton yarn and cloth for the domestic market and in iron and steel production. They were aided by import-substitution policies the raj adopted in World War I, when access to the metropole was virtually cut off, and retained after the war ended. The Tata Iron and Steel Company, founded by sons of the great Parsi entrepreneur J. N. Tata (1839–1904), began production in 1911 and benefited from wartime sales to government agencies. The House of Tata was instrumental in developing hydroelectric power for Bombay from monsoon-fed lakes in mountains east of the city. It also supported technical education by founding the Institute of Science at Bangalore. Members of commercially oriented groups like the Parsis, Bhatias, and Marwaris became successful bankers by tapping savings of middle-income people as well as rulers of princely states. The existence of indigenous banking institutions made it possible to transfer local funds to industrial purposes in the 1930s, when a slump in agricultural production made it more profitable to invest in factory-based enterprises than in land. The Federation of Indian Chambers of Commerce and Industry, formed in 1927, coordinated indigenous business interests throughout India.[41] In these respects India gained greater control of its private profit sector than did other colonies in phase 4.

In the religious sector were organizations that broke with European-controlled agencies over a variety of issues: theology, liturgy and ritual, the acceptability of indigenous social practices, and the unwillingness of missionaries to share control. In French Indochina the Caodai movement, a compound of Roman Catholicism, Buddhism, and Taoism, was founded in the 1920s. In Borneo the Dayak Church was established. Many Kikuyu in Kenya formed their own churches and schools in reaction to missionary attacks on female circumcision. A movement led by Simon Kimbangu spread in the Belgian Congo, as did the millennial Kitawala movement in the Rhodesias and hundreds of independent churches in South Africa.

Organized expressions of autonomy in the private profit and religious sectors were not necessarily intended as challenges to European control of the public sector. But colonial officials were prone to interpret activities of unions and independent religious movements as political threats. Efforts to suppress these activities often backfired, broadening the scope of popular protest to include the political arena. As Karl Deutsch notes, social mobilization makes people readily available for political participation. Proliferation of all types of organizations among the colonized in phase 4 increased opportunities for political leaders to use them as building blocks for anticolonial movements.

Mobilization of non-Europeans for political purposes was made easier by the transport and communications networks devised by colonial rulers for their own ends. The railroads Britain built in India to permit rapid troop movements should another Great Mutiny break out were the same ones Gandhi, Nehru, and Vallabhbhai Patel used to travel about the country seeking mass support for the INC. Over time the primary mode of transport shifted from expensive locomotives owned by European public or private agencies to far less costly automobiles, trucks, and buses that at least a few non-Europeans could afford. The result was greatly expanded possibilities for autonomous movement to places distant from existing rail lines. Telephones and telegraphs could be used not only by rulers to assert authority but also by some of their subjects, some of the time, to convey messages challenging it.

The technological edge Europeans enjoyed over the rest of the world in phase 3 was diminished in phase 4 by the diffusion of technology to other areas. Colonial rulers made every effort, of course, to monopolize access to the most advanced means of waging war. But they were not always successful. In 1921 a rebellion broke out in the Rif mountains of Spanish Morocco. Using smuggled French rifles and Mausers illegally acquired from Moroccan troops employed by Spain, about four thousand fighters under the skilled leadership of Abd el Krim attacked a number of Spanish outposts. Carefully coordinated surprise attacks netted the rebels an estimated 20,000 rifles, 400 machine guns, and 129 cannon.[42] By 1925 Abd el Krim had expanded the rebellion and begun to attack outposts on the French Moroccan side of the Rif. His forces excelled at guerrilla tactics in the harsh mountain setting they knew so well. But they also had at their disposal rockets and other modern weapons captured from their enemies. The French and Spanish countered with even more modern military technology: aerial bombing of mountain villages and generous applications of poison gas. By 1926 the combined efforts of the two metropoles brought the rebellion to an end. Nonetheless, the ability of Abd el Krim's forces to acquire and use modern weapons in a sustained guerrilla struggle was a portent of events in phase 5, most notably in French Indochina, the Dutch East Indies, and Algeria.

COLONIZED VERSUS COLONIZERS

Expressions of popular discontent were not evenly distributed across time and space. Much depended on the policies of individual metropoles—in particular, their attitudes toward dissidence and their willingness to set up legislative bodies in which indigenous interests were represented. Britain was at one end of the spectrum in these respects, Belgium and Portugal at the other. Much also depended on the way leaders articulated, interpreted, and channeled popular sentiments. The general pattern was for protest to come in waves whose crests—1919–22, 1929–32, and 1937–39—coincided with turning points in global crises.

The parallel between localized discontent and global crisis was not coincidental. Just as World War I and the Great Depression led Europeans to reconsider whether they were as superior to others as they had assumed, so these same crises led many colonial subjects who had internalized the idea of European superiority to call it into question. The colonized observed an international system that could not maintain the peace, a war that in pitting Europeans against each other destroyed the myth of white racial solidarity, and a capitalist system that could not prevent precipitous worldwide declines in employment and production. In justifying colonialism, Europeans argued that they dominated the world because they were morally, intellectually, and culturally as well as materially and technologically more advanced than others. They interpreted political dominance as both the symbol and the practical outcome of civilizational superiority. The more their performance contradicted their claims, the less credible and the more hypocritical and narrowly self-serving appeals to civilizational superiority became. It was but a short step for many in the colonies to challenge European rule as resting on premises that were morally flawed and empirically invalid.

The growing tendency to question the status quo was not simply a response to global crises. It was also a reaction to the nature and timing of Europe's actions as metropoles tried to respond to crises they too could not control. As noted earlier, the strains of fighting the war of 1914–18 led Britain to make political concessions to non-Europeans in hopes of mobilizing all available imperial resources. Among the notable instances were Sir Henry McMahon's private commitment to Sharif Husayn regarding the Arabs and Sir Edwin Montagu's public commitment to the people of India.

Britain was not alone in this respect. In late 1916 the Dutch government voted to break with authoritarian tradition by establishing a Netherlands Indies Volksrad, an advisory body that would include indigenous members as well as Dutch settlers. The Volksrad held its first meeting in May 1918, when war was still raging. In November the Dutch governor-general spoke of giving it progressively greater powers. France recruited nearly three hundred thousand Algerian Muslims to fight in the trenches and work in its factories. Many joined the war effort with the understanding—encouraged by Prime Minister Georges Clemenceau's comments in 1914, 1917, and again in 1919—that the Muslim majority would participate more actively in Algerian and French electoral politics after the war. France's earlier insistence that Muslims choose between political status as naturalized French citizens and personal status as Muslims had effectively disenfranchised the vast majority of Algerians, who were unwilling to win the right to vote for representatives in Paris if it meant abandoning application of Islamic *sharia* law to their lives. Clemenceau strongly implied that French citizenship would soon be granted without altering the Muslims' personal status. In Vietnam, Governor-General Sarraut justified the forcible roundup of some one hundred thousand peasants and artisans to be shipped off to

France to serve in labor battalions "by painting a vision of Franco-Vietnamese collaboration, complete with references to Liberty, Equality, and Fraternity. France, he said, was willing to act as 'elder brother' in transmitting the full benefits of modern civilization, and to consider the possibility of native self-rule at some unspecified point in the future."[43]

After the war ended, however, metropolitan politicians played down or ignored altogether promises made months earlier when victory was by no means assured. Britain and France took over Middle East territories that they had solemnly declared deserved independence. In India, the Armistice of November 1918 was followed by disappointingly modest constitutional reforms, the Rowlatt Acts, and the Amritsar massacre. In the Dutch East Indies the Volksrad quickly became little more than a government mouthpiece. Any illusions that it might set policy were dashed by the Dutch constitution of 1922, which declared that the East Indies were not a colony but integral parts of the Dutch Kingdom. Relatively liberal wartime governors there and in French Indochina were replaced in the 1920s by more conservative, repressive officials. Sarraut's vision of eventual self-rule disappeared from view. A French reform plan for Algeria in 1919, while making naturalization somewhat easier, insisted upon abandonment of Muslim personal status as a condition for the franchise.

A similar pattern of raising and then lowering expectations can be seen in U.S. President Woodrow Wilson's Fourteen Points. Proclaimed in January 1918 as the rationale for American participation in the war, they included a call for national self-determination against the supranational claims of the Austro-Hungarian and Ottoman empires. Wilson's appeal to the moral value of self-determination encouraged some colonial subjects to believe that this principle would some day be applied to them, not simply to inhabitants of polities against which America's allies were fighting. M. M. Malaviya in India and Saad Zaghlul in Egypt referred to the Fourteen Points when pressing their nationalist demands. But this hopeful prospect was dashed at the Versailles Peace Conference of 1919–20. Several would-be spokesmen for colonized peoples assembled in Paris and tried to influence conference decisions. They included Ho Chi Minh of Vietnam, Blaise Diagne of Senegal, and W. E. B. Du Bois, the black American organizer of the Pan-African Congress held in Paris in 1919.[44] But they were given short shrift by victorious Allied delegations. The winners were too busy negotiating terms of a postwar settlement that envisaged no fundamental change in Europe's world role.

The roller-coaster pattern of raised and dashed expectations held in the economic arena. The heavy exactions and enforced austerities of 1914–18 gave rise to hope that economic conditions in the colonies would improve at war's end. But inflationary pressures that built up during the war years could not be promptly relieved. If anything, prices rose after the Armistice as formerly repressed demands were at last openly expressed. And the faltering performance of European economies in 1919–22 failed to stimulate new investment and production overseas. Then came years of economic growth, inducing millions of colonial subjects to enter production for export. Following this came the disastrous downturn of 1929–34. The depression hurt most the very people who had abandoned older localized, self-reliant economic patterns for the international market. Writing in 1934, a French scholar described the plight of Tunisian grape growers: "The native, bewildered at having first been encouraged to get the most out of his land and then discouraged by a refusal to receive his crop, is at once discontented and . . . reduced to poverty."[45] Similar comments could be made about rice-growing peasants in Lower Burma and Vietnam, palm oil collectors in the Niger delta, rubber plantation workers in West Africa and Southeast Asia, sugar harvesters in Caribbean, Indian Ocean, and Pacific Ocean islands, and copper miners in Northern Rhodesia.

Such seesawing experiences caused many colonized peoples to lose whatever confidence they may have placed in their rulers' ability or desire to improve their lives. The belief that colonies were being politically betrayed and economically exploited spread. Waves of protest just after World War I and at the start of the depression ensued. Examples from 1919 to 1922 include events in India leading up to and following the Amritsar massacre and Gandhi's first intensive *satyagraha* campaigns; the nationalist uprising in Egypt; a revolt in Iraq against British rule; anti-inflation riots in Freetown, Sierra Leone, and Saigon, Vietnam; the start of the Rif rebellion; anti-Belgian unrest in the Congo triggered by arrest of the prophet Simon Kimbangu; formation of the first mass-based black union in South Africa, the Industrial and Commercial Union; protests in Kenya led by Harry Thuku against higher taxes and harsh labor recruitment policies affecting Africans; and the cocoa holdup by Gold Coast producers in 1921. The immediate postwar years were also the high point for Marcus Garvey, a Jamaican who developed a mass following among blacks in the Caribbean and the United States. Garvey's rallying cry, "Africa for the Africans," was increasingly heard in Africa and caused extreme anxiety among British, French, and Belgian colonial administrators.

Anticolonial activity between 1929 and 1932 included Gandhi's second intensive *satyagraha* campaign in India; the rebellion in Lower Burma led by Saya San; the Aba Women's War in southeastern Nigeria; the Gold Coast cocoa holdup of 1930–31; a series of uprisings by peasants, indigenous troops, and intellectuals in Vietnam, brutally repressed by the French; formation in Algeria of the Association des Ulema by the nationalist cleric Sheikh Abdul-hamid Ben Badis; and in the Dutch East Indies a call for independence from Dutch rule by Mohammad Hatta and Sukarno, resulting in the highly publicized trial and imprisonment of these prominent nationalists.

A third round of concentrated protest activity occurred in 1936–38. Its timing calls into question the roller-coaster hypothesis. Yet one factor in the numerous strikes in Africa and the Caribbean during this period was anger and disillusionment over the League of Nations' pitiful response to Italy's invasion of Ethiopia. The league's high-minded commitment to protect the sovereignty of member states evaporated when survival of an African state was at stake. Also fueling anger was maintenance of colonial export prices at depression levels when metropolitan econo-mies were picking up. There was a sense in many colonies that while Europe could expect to recover, its colonies were being deliberately left behind.

India in phase 4 was in a class by itself in terms of the range and depth of autonomous activity. In the public sector was the INC, which by the late 1930s was the governing party in a majority of the territory's provincial legislatures. The ICS was quietly being captured from within. Gandhi's innovative experiments in peaceful mass political mobilization, which challenged and embarrassed the raj while de-manding a high level of self-discipline among *satyagraha*'s adherents, had some positive results. His highly publicized Salt March in 1930 was carefully noted in colonies elsewhere—a sign that political developments in India were having observa-tion effects. In other sectors, indigenous entrepreneurs held important positions in industrial and financial life. Indians removed the word "missionary" from the work of Christian churches, and of course the religious sector remained overwhelmingly in the hands of Hindus and Muslims. The sectoral basis for self-government was in place. I elaborate on this point in part 5 in drawing a parallel with the thirteen BNA colonies at the end of phase 1.

NATIONALISM AND ITS ALTERNATIVES

Knowing that decolonization occurred on a massive scale after 1945, one should not misuse hindsight by assuming that everything the colonized did in phase 4 was deliberately directed toward this end. There were, to be sure, movements that were clearly nationalist, in the sense that they took a colony as their primary unit of analysis, emphasized shared features entitling its inhabitants to be called a nation, and made the case for the nation's independence.

But many organizations formed in phase 4 did not have all or even any of these characteristics. The primary unit of identity and loyalty often was not the colony but a group within it. This might be

- an existing religious community (Sarekat Islam in the Netherlands Indies and the Muslim League in India);
- a religious community in process of formation (the Kimbanguist movement in the Belgian Congo; Rastafarians in Jamaica);
- an ethnic group (Kikuyu Central Association in Kenya; Ibibio State Union in Nigeria);
- a local community (community improvement associations);

- a group defined by gender (participants in the Aba Women's War) or age (youth leagues, student associations);
- a group defined by occupation and economic interest (farmers' associations, trade unions of teachers or dockworkers).

For many organizations the primary unit was a category far more comprehensive than any one colony. The transcendent tie might be race, as in the "Africa for the Africans" appeal of the Garveyites, the pan-African congresses organized by Du Bois, and the *négritude* literary movement of Aimé Césaire, Léopold Senghor, and other francophone intellectuals. The tie might be religion, as in the pan-Islamic movement of the early 1920s that temporarily united Muslims from the Middle East, India, and Southeast Asia. The tie might be a larger territory, as in the National Congress of British West Africa. Or it might be class, notably shared working-class interests. In some cases appeals to class loyalty were expressed through the Communist movement, with its strong emphasis on solidarity within an international proletariat. Vietnam's Ho Chi Minh and, for a time, Trinidad's George Padmore were active in the Communist International. In other instances working-class identity was encouraged by noncommunist trade union movements, as in the British Guiana and West Indian Labour Congress.

The experience of being a colonial subject was itself the basis for a newly emerging sense of identity. A novel by the Barbadian writer George Lamming, *In the Castle of My Skin*, describes a shoemaker who, after being exposed in the 1930s to new ideas and to word of protest activities elsewhere in the Caribbean, "starts to think of Little England [Barbados] as a part of some gigantic thing called colonial."[46]

Organizations emphasizing interests and identities of specific groups within a colony or appealing to larger social categories transcending its borders were not inclined to stress characteristics residents of a given territory had—or allegedly had— in common. In this sense they could be termed sub- or supranationalist. As such they existed in a state of tension with nationalist organizations whose imagined community was a colony's population or at least its non-European majority.[47] The most explicit and historically momentous instance of tension was in India. There, by the late 1930s, the Muslim League, led by M. A. Jinnah, was challenging the INC's claim to speak for India's Muslims and increasingly threatening to form a separate state for the subcontinent's Muslims.

But this tension was not irresolvable. Nationalist movements had the potential to absorb or coopt subnational and supranational organizations. Much depended on who the nationalist leaders were, what they said, how they said it, and their ability to form coalitions of diverse communities and interests. Nationalist movements were most likely to succeed when their leaders were widely regarded as articulating a territory's general interests rather than the goals of particular groups. It helped, too, when leaders could convincingly argue that independence was the most effective way to achieve goals other groups wished to advance. It certainly helped when leaders could show that independence was more likely if people emphasized what united them and downplayed differences and rivalries.

Many colonial organizations phrased their grievances in specific rather than general terms. The goal might be to end official discrimination against indigenous civil servants, to extend the franchise, or to spend more government funds on a local community. It might be to increase representation in a legislature, abolish forced labor, establish a publicly funded university, or guarantee higher prices for a territory's major exports. If attained, such goals would reform colonialism in a direction more responsive to demands from below. But these changes would not necessarily bring colonial rule to an end. Indeed, a prerequisite for attaining reformist goals was a colonial regime sufficiently effective to carry out the desired improvements. Organizations pressing these kinds of demands could be deemed protonationalist. But they were not nationalist, if one defines "nationalism" as identifying colonial rule itself, not specific metropolitan policies, as the fundamental problem. Over time protonationalist organizations tended to convert to nationalism, above all when their reformist demands were not met. But in many parts of the colonial world as of the late 1930s that time had not yet arrived.

Phase 4 offers several examples of nationalist movements with a broad popular following—but far more examples of organizations that, while not nationalist in composition or goals, were available for mobilization into comprehensive movements for independence. This potential was to be more fully realized in the wake of yet another twentieth-century global crisis, the war that commenced phase 5.

7
Phase 5: Contraction, 1940–80

The end of empire came swiftly. Between 1940 and 1980, eighty-one colonies and four quasi-colonies gained independence from a European metropole and were recognized as sovereign states. The story of decolonization in phase 5 is immensely complex, not least because so many territories in so many parts of the world were involved. Each differed in some respects from all others in the path it took to independence and in the kind of state it became. Hence there are exceptions to many of the generalizations in this chapter's survey of major trends.

The sheer scope of imperial collapse and new-state formation has no precedent in history. Every metropole lost possessions. Between 1940 and 1980, forty-three colonies and four quasi-colonies of Britain became independent, as did twenty-five colonies of France, five of Portugal, three of Belgium, two each of Italy and Holland, and one of Spain.[1] Four territories that were European colonies in phase 3—the Philippines, Papua New Guinea, Western Samoa, and Nauru—attained independence from non-European metropoles. Almost 40 percent of the world's population—2.2 billion people in the year 2000—inhabits states that made the transition from colonial to independent status between 1940 and 1980. Decolonization took a different course for a half dozen colonies absorbed, by force or through diplomatic negotiation, into larger contiguous states.[2]

Decolonization had largely run its course by 1980. Of the remaining possessions most were small island chains in the Pacific. Between 1981 and 1999 five European colonies and five former colonies administered by non-European powers became independent. Control over Britain's Hong Kong and Portugal's Macao passed to the People's Republic of China. When the twentieth century ended only a few scattered territories, with minimal economic or strategic significance, were in European hands.

From European colony to independent state, 1946–80.

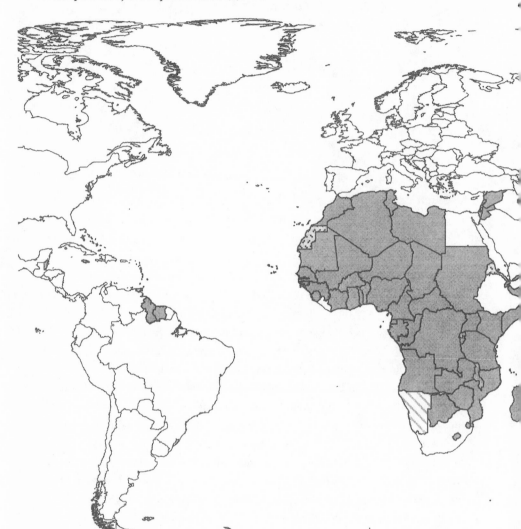

◼ Independence From a European State
▨ Independence From a Former European Colony
▦ Claimed By a Neighboring State

0   3000 Miles

0   3000 Kilometers

CRITICAL EVENTS

Phase 5 began in 1940, when the major colonial powers faced a two-pronged military assault. One part was directed at the metropoles themselves, the other against their colonies in Southeast Asia and Oceania. Attacks on the European front were mounted by Germany, whose overseas empire had been dismantled following defeat of the Second Reich in 1918. The assault in Asia and Oceania was led by Japan, whose overseas empire had steadily grown since the 1890s. In the wake of conquests on the Asian mainland in areas not formally controlled by Europeans (Manchuria, 1931, and China, beginning in 1937), Japan's military leadership increasingly focused on Southeast Asia, where European powers and the United States were entrenched. The region's major exports—petroleum, rubber, tin, and rice—were assets Japan's rulers reckoned were essential to their country's rise to great-power status.

The double assault on the colonial status quo was dramatized when France fell to the Germans in June 1940 and Japanese troops entered Indochina three months later, under terms approved by the collaborationist Vichy regime. Indochina was nominally ruled by French administrators until the Japanese formally took control in March 1945. But it was clear to everyone from late 1940 onward who was in charge. Holland was likewise subjected to two-pronged attack. It fell to the Germans in mid-1940, and by early 1942 the Dutch East Indies were conquered by Japanese troops. The British, their homeland under German siege by air and sea, could do little to stop Japanese forces from landing in Malaya (December 1941), capturing the strategically vital naval base and port of Singapore (February 1942), and overrunning Burma the following month. Japan took the Philippines following its attack on Pearl Harbor as well as Allied island possessions dispersed throughout Melanesia and Micronesia.

Japan's conquests did not, of course, liberate the territories it occupied. One set of externally imposed rulers was replaced by another. Many indigenous peoples suffered harsher treatment during the short period of Japanese rule than under the Europeans. Nonetheless, the fast-paced events of 1940–42 markedly reduced the scope of Europe's colonial possessions and contributed directly to the end of empire in Asia. Any lingering myth of European or white invincibility was destroyed by Japan's stunningly rapid, decisive triumphs. The Japanese slogan "Asia for Asians" had wide appeal even if the reality behind the slogan—"Asia for the Japanese"—did not. In Indonesia and Burma the new rulers attempted to work through nationalist movements suppressed by Dutch and British authorities. Sukarno and Hatta in Indonesia, Ba Maw and Ne Win in Burma, and other less prominent nationalists were released from detention and allowed to carry out modest organizing activities. Japanese officers trained tens of thousands of Javanese youth in an auxiliary guerrilla army called Peta. The young soldiers were able to put their training to practical use, first against those who had trained them and later against the Dutch. The ground-work was laid for movements capable of mobilizing effectively for freedom against *all* outsiders, whether Asian or European.

Japan's conquests in Southeast Asia meant that if Europeans wished to return to the prewar state of affairs they would have to reoccupy territory temporarily lost to them. Recolonization was a formidable task, for it meant starting another round of imperial expansion almost from scratch.[3] Prospects of success in this venture were further lowered in situations in which a chaotic period between the collapse of Japanese rule and the arrival of Allied forces permitted nationalists to announce formation of independent states: the Republic of Indonesia (August 17, 1945) and the Democratic Republic of Vietnam (September 2, 1945). As the Dutch in Indonesia and the French in Vietnam quickly discovered, reoccupation entailed a major pacifica-tion drive against well-entrenched, relatively well armed, widely popular nationalist movements. In both cases the pacification campaign failed. Holland departed in 1949 after two years of intermittent fighting, France in 1954 after eight years of increasingly intense warfare. In retrospect it can be said that the European hold on these two important territories was terminated in the early years of World War II.

The end of phase 5 was marked by the independence of Zimbabwe in 1980. This was not the last territory to make the transition from colonial rule to statehood. But those that followed it, and the few remaining colonies likely to do so, are microstates that cannot rival it in population, economic resources, or diplomatic influence. The story of Zimbabwe's decolonization is complicated by the presence of a powerful European settler community. In 1923 Great Britain replaced the British South Africa Company as formal ruler of what was then called Southern Rhodesia. But officials in London permitted settlers to exercise de facto control over the terri-tory's domestic affairs. The settler community enjoyed the privileges of the responsi-ble government system first devised in Canada and later applied to the other white dominions. The key to settler power lay in a racially discriminatory electoral system weighted so that whites, who never constituted more than 5 percent of the popula-tion, came close to monopolizing the electoral rolls and hence controlled the legisla-ture. By the early 1960s an arrangement so manifestly racist was unacceptable not only to Southern Rhodesia's Africans but also to the British government. London insisted that it would not negotiate independence until the franchise was extended to the African majority. A universal adult franchise was the last thing politicians repre-senting a tiny racial minority were willing to accept. In 1965, faced with opposition to continued minority rule from the territory's majority population and from the metropole, the settler-led Rhodesian Front government took matters into its own hands and issued a unilateral declaration of independence from Great Britain.

The new regime faced diplomatic isolation and economic sanctions imposed by many countries, including Great Britain. By the early 1970s armed attacks against the settlers and their government by two competing African nationalist movements began in earnest. By decade's end these attacks, in combination with sanctions, had effectively undermined the secessionist regime's military and economic position.

Under pressure from newly independent members of the Commonwealth to intervene on behalf of a majority rule solution, Britain in 1979 convened a conference of the contending parties at London's Lancaster House. The conference produced formulae for a cease-fire, arrangements for a British-supervised election based on a universal adult franchise, and the outline of a postindependence constitution. Upon conclusion of the Lancaster House conference Britain formally reasserted authority as the colonial power. It did so not, as in Vietnam and Indonesia, to reclaim power in autocratic fashion but rather to turn over power to a democratically chosen successor. Winner of the election was Robert Mugabe, leader of the Zimbabwe African National Union (ZANU), which had led the guerrilla struggle against the minority regime. Mugabe was prime minister when independence was celebrated at midnight on April 17, 1980.[4]

SPATIAL AND TEMPORAL ASPECTS OF DECOLONIZATION

The pattern of phase 5 decolonization, as it unfolded across space and over time, is shown in table 7.1. Whereas phase 2 was confined to the New World, phase 5 occurred primarily in the Old. Also affected were Caribbean basin territories insulated from the independence movements of phase 2. The territorial scope of phase 5 was thus far more comprehensive than in the earlier period. States emerging from phase 2 were predominantly on the New World mainland. In contrast, approximately 30 percent of phase 5 new states were islands.

Space and time were linked in new-state formation (see table 7.1). The first wave was in South Asia and the Near East. Southeast Asia followed, then North Africa, then sub-Saharan Africa, with a general shift from western to eastern to southern Africa. Independence for island territories was achieved over a relatively protracted period, most of the transfers of power occurring relatively late, after 1970.

It took far less time to dismantle European empires than to construct them. Phases 2 and 5 lasted for about five and four decades, respectively, in contrast to more than three centuries for phase 1 and almost a century for phase 3. The historical depth of colonial ties varied enormously for the new states of phase 5. At the low end were Syria and Lebanon, acquired as mandates in the 1920s and declared independent in the 1940s. Libya was a colony for four decades, most of Africa and Oceania for six to eight. At the upper end were Caribbean islands like the Bahamas, Jamaica, and Trinidad-Tobago (more than 450 years) and islands off the African coast like the Cape Verdes and São Tomé and Príncipe, where Portuguese trading enclaves were established more than 500 years ago. Phase 2 new states lay within these extremes, the colonial experience for the great majority lasting between 150 and 300 years.

For European powers phase 5 marked the end of empire. By contrast, at the end of phase 2, all the imperial powers had managed, despite permanent losses in every case except Holland, to retain a portion of their original possessions. The two largest empires as of 1940—those of Great Britain and France—were the most drastically reduced in size by 1980. The two largest as of 1773—Spain and Great Britain— followed divergent paths during phase 2. Spain ceased to count as a major international actor following loss of its New World mainland territories, while Britain compensated for losing the BNA colonies by expanding in South Asia and the Indian Ocean basin. The British were well positioned by the end of phase 2 to start a new phase of empire building in Asia and Africa, which they proceeded to do. In contrast, by the end of phase 5 neither they nor any other world powers were about to create new overseas empires. Britain and France did assert themselves in the old style in 1956, when they and Israel invaded the Suez Canal Zone following nationalization of the canal's assets by President Gamal Abdel Nasser of Egypt. But their attempt to apply nineteenth-century gunboat diplomacy to the very different conditions of the mid–twentieth century generated a universal outcry of protest. Britain and France had to withdraw, under humiliating circumstances, the troops they had landed. The fiasco cost Prime Minister Anthony Eden of Britain his job.

This is by no means to say that power ceased to matter in international affairs after 1945. Rather, pressures grew to exercise it in more subtle, indirect, and informal ways than in the past. There have always been inequalities in economic and military resources among states and world regions. Prior to World War II Europeans felt few compunctions about expressing and reinforcing these inequalities in the legal/political sphere by establishing colonies in which the powerful openly dominated the weak. Indeed, having colonial possessions was a classic indicator of a metropole's great-power status. After 1945 interstate inequalities remained. If anything, gaps between richest and poorest and between militarily strongest and weakest grew steadily wider over time. But it was no longer acceptable to express inequalities overtly in legal and political terms. Would-be great powers no longer had the option to create new empires because colonialism violated norms of national self-determination and state sovereignty that now applied not just in Europe but throughout the globe. Decolonization placed ex-colonized and ex-metropolitan states on a footing of legal and political parity. That kind of equality could not be dismissed as insignificant or rhetorical no matter how unequal the units might be in other respects.[5]

TABLE 7.1.

FROM EUROPEAN COLONY TO INDEPENDENT STATE, 1946–80

Year of Independence*	South Asia	Southeast Asia	North Africa/ Middle East/ Mediterranean	Sub-Saharan Africa	New World (Caribbean)	Oceania (Pacific, Indian Oceans)
1946			Jordan Lebanon[1] Syria[1]			
1947	India Pakistan[2]					
1948	Ceylon	Burma[3]	Israel			
1949		Indonesia[4]				
1950						
1951			Libya			
1952						
1953		Cambodia Laos				
1954		Vietnam[5]				
1955						
1956			Morocco Tunisia	Sudan		
1957		Malaya		Ghana		
1958				Guinea		
1959						
1960			Cyprus	Cameroon Central African Republic Chad Congo-Brazzaville Congo-Leopoldville Dahomey Gabon Ivory Coast Malagasy Republic Mali Mauritania		

TABLE 7.1.

CONTINUED

Year of Independence*	South Asia	Southeast Asia	North Africa/ Middle East/ Mediterranean	Sub-Saharan Africa	New World (Caribbean)	Oceania (Pacific, Indian Oceans)
				Niger		
				Nigeria		
				Senegal		
				Somalia		
				Togo		
				Upper Volta		
1961			Kuwait[6]	Sierra Leone		
				Tanganyika		
				Burundi		
1962			Algeria	Rwanda	Jamaica	
				Uganda	Trinidad & Tobago	
1963		Malaysia[7]		Kenya		
				Zanzibar[8]		
1964			Malta	Malawi		
				Zambia		
1965				Gambia		Maldives
1966				Botswana	Barbados	
				Lesotho	Guyana	
1967			Yemen (South)			
1968				Equatorial Guinea		Mauritius
				Swaziland		
1969						
1970						Fiji
						Tonga
1971			Bahrain			
			Qatar			
			United Arab Emirates			
1972						
1973					Bahamas	
1974				Guinea-Bissau	Grenada	

TABLE 7.1.

CONTINUED

Year of Independence*	South Asia	Southeast Asia	North Africa/ Middle East/ Mediterranean	Sub-Saharan Africa	New World (Caribbean)	Oceania (Pacific, Indian Oceans)
1975				Angola Cape Verde Comoros Mozambique São Tomé & Príncipe	Suriname	
1976						Seychelles
1977				Djibouti		
1978					Dominica	Solomon Islands Tuvalu
1979					St. Lucia St. Vincent & Grenadines	Kiribati
1980				Zimbabwe		Vanuatu

* Date of independence is the year in which leaders of the metropole and leaders of the colony mutually agree that the territory is independent. Exceptions and special cases are noted below. The country's name is as formally listed or commonly called at the time of independence.

[1] Lebanon and Syria were declared independent by the Free French in 1941. But they did not consider themselves independent until French troops departed in 1946, following a formal request that the French evacuate their former mandates.

[2] At independence Pakistan consisted of two noncontiguous areas, West and East. The East broke away in 1971, and West Pakistan forces were unable to prevent secession. The former East Pakistan was internationally recognized in 1972 as Bangladesh. (West) Pakistan acknowledged the independence of Bangladesh in 1974.

[3] The Japanese proclaimed the independence of Burma in August 1943. But even the Burmese nationalists who collaborated with them did not regard this gesture as genuine.

[4] Indonesian nationalists proclaimed the independent Republic of Indonesia in August 1945. In 1946 the Dutch recognized the Republic but not its claim to represent the entire Netherlands Indies. Dutch recognition of the sovereignty of a federal United States of Indonesia came in 1949.

TABLE 7.1.

CONTINUED

[5] Vietminh nationalists led by Ho Chi Minh declared Vietnam's independence in September 1945. War between Vietminh and French forces raged almost continuously until 1954, when at the Geneva Convention France recognized the independence of Vietnam. The Geneva Convention also "temporarily" divided Vietnam into a northern and southern half. After more than two decades of intense armed conflict between these two entities and their respective outside supporters, North Vietnamese forces brought the South under their control and unified Vietnam politically in 1975.

[6] Kuwait, Bahrain, Qatar, and the United Arab Emirates are classified in the Appendix as quasi colonies.

[7] The Federation of Malaysia linked Malaya (already independent) with three former British colonies: Singapore, Sarawak, and Sabah. In 1965 Singapore left the Federation—or, more accurately, was expelled from it by Malayan leaders—and became an independent state.

[8] In the wake of a social and political revolution in Zanzibar in January 1964, a few weeks after its independence, the island state merged with mainland Tanganyika in April 1964. The new entity was known as the United Republic of Tanzania.

THE IMPERIAL DESTABILIZER: WORLD WAR II

The three kinds of violence described in phase 2 figured in phase 5 as well. In general, however, phase 5 involved less pervasive hegemonic conflict and less extensive vertical and horizontal violence than phase 2.

Several metropoles were invaded in the wars of each phase: Holland, Spain, and Portugal by French revolutionary or Napoleonic armies; Holland, Belgium, and France more than a century later by the Germans. Countries whose territory was invaded and whose leaders were muzzled or forced into exile were obviously unable to control what happened in their overseas holdings. Interestingly, however, in both phases it was not during wartime, when metropolitan capacity was at low ebb, but in the immediate postwar period that the major movements for independence took shape and asserted themselves. In several cases the trigger was the metropole's effort to reassert prerogatives it enjoyed before the war. The dynamics of this pattern are explored at greater length in part 5.

World War II occupied only the first few years of 1940–80, whereas European great powers fought intermittently for more than half the length of phase 2. World War II did not pit the major metropoles against each other. In contrast, wars connected with the French Revolution and the rise of Napoleon involved struggles at home and abroad among the three leading imperial states: Britain, France, and

Spain. World War II thus saw to a far lesser degree than the earlier period situations in which metropoles encouraged their enemies' colonies to break away. On the other hand, Japan's role in World War II posed a more serious non-European threat to the global status quo than anything experienced in phase 2.

World War II had a much greater impact on overseas possessions than the hegemonic wars of phase 2. Intense fighting raged in Southeast Asia, North Africa, and Oceania. Hundreds of thousands of young Asians and Africans were recruited and trained to take part in battle. Sometimes recruits fought on home ground—for example, Japanese-trained armies and paramilitary organizations in Burma and the Dutch East Indies. Sometimes soldiers fought far from home. The Gold Coast in British West Africa dispatched more than thirty thousand young men to Burma, eleven thousand to East Africa and the Middle East.[6] The Japanese and Allied powers alike, desperate to secure access to petroleum, rubber, tin, cotton, and other strategically vital raw materials, relied heavily on forced labor to extract them. The frenzied construction of ports, airstrips, railways, roads, and bridges to support the war effort accelerated social mobilization in the colonies by enlarging the technically trained labor force and stimulating rapid growth of urban centers.

World War II mobilized bodies. It also changed minds. Far more than any previous global conflict, this war had an ideological dimension, one directly relevant to colonialism. To be sure, President Wilson's Fourteen Points were potentially applicable. But Wilson's speech was delivered in the final year of World War I, and it did not pretend to articulate the war aims of countries other than the United States. In contrast, the Atlantic Charter of Prime Minister Winston Churchill and President Franklin Roosevelt was issued at an early stage in the war (August 1941, before the United States had formally entered), and it signaled the shared objectives of the "first new nation" and the world's greatest imperial power. The charter's third point stated that the signatories "respect the right of all peoples to choose the form of government under which they will live; and they wish to see sovereign rights and self-government restored to those who have been forcibly deprived of them." Churchill, a lifelong defender of empire, made it clear in a parliamentary speech a few weeks later that these words applied only to territories forcibly conquered by the Axis powers. He insisted that the charter had no bearing on Britain's overseas possessions. But it was equally evident that the American president, long a critic of European imperialism, believed the charter to have wide application.[7] The language was universal in scope, without the restrictions and qualifications Churchill claimed were embedded in it.

Opinion leaders in the colonies readily perceived the broader import of the Atlantic Charter and repeatedly referred to it when prodding metropoles to accelerate the transfer of power. In October 1941, for example, the London-based West

African Students Union sent a memorandum to Deputy Prime Minister Clement Attlee noting that "Great Britain has proclaimed her determination to re-establish and support the national independence of the countries of Europe, of Ethiopia, and of Syria, but what of West Africa?"[8] India's Legislative Assembly discussed and passed without dissent a resolution that the Atlantic Charter should apply to India.

Churchill's clarification only fanned the flames of discontent. Reginald Coupland, a professor who lived in India during 1941 and 1942, wrote, "It is difficult to exaggerate the disquieting effect of [this statement] . . . a feeling, if not of distrust, at least of a new and uncomfortable suspicion, began to spread beyond nationalist circles. Moderate-minded Indians, who still valued the British connexion . . . were shaken, for the moment, at any rate, in their faith." The Burmese nationalist leader Ba Maw referred bitterly to this episode in his memoirs: "To all for whom words, honestly used, must mean what they say, the words of the Atlantic Charter were clear. The Burmese believed that they meant what they said. Churchill, however, did not." Speaking to the Burmese legislature in February 1940 when it debated a resolution declaring war, Ba Maw asserted, "West of Suez freedom is an unqualified war aim, but east of Suez it is not so."[9]

Complementing the anti-imperial element in Allied war aims was the anti-racist element. Nazism was not simply the aggressive expression of German communal ardor. Behind the nationalist rhetoric was a doctrine asserting Teutonic superiority and calling for extermination of allegedly inferior racial stocks. In order to attack the moral and intellectual foundations of Nazism its enemies had to critique the Nazi assumption that people are first and foremost members of racial groups and its claim that some groups are incapable of leading a civilized existence. The Allied powers were placed in a self-contradictory position. People of color in their overseas possessions were asked to support a struggle against the very doctrine which, in more benevolently paternalist form, underlay the European colonial enterprise. Gandhi wrote in 1941 that there were "powerful elements of Fascism in British rule. Both America and Great Britain lack the moral basis for engaging in this war unless they put their own houses in order. . . . They have no right to talk about protecting democracies and protecting civilization and human freedom, until the canker of white superiority is destroyed in its entirety."[10] Writing a decade after the war's end, the Martiniquan poet and politician Aimé Césaire caustically noted this contradiction: "At bottom, what . . . the very distinguished, very humanistic, very Christian bourgeois of the twentieth century . . . cannot forgive Hitler is not crime in itself, the crime against man, it is not the humiliation of man as such, it is the crime against the white man, the humiliation of the white man, and the fact that [Hitler] applied to Europe colonialist procedures which until then had been reserved exclusively for the Arabs of Algeria, the coolies of India, and the blacks of Africa."[11]

Just as Europeans were shocked in World War I to discover that weapons of destruction they had earlier aimed at Asians and Africans were being turned upon themselves, so they were dismayed in World War II to discover that the ideas they employed to justify conquering Asians and Africans were being turned against themselves.

The hypocrisy of the Allies' stance on race was not lost on politically aware individuals in the colonies. The response in most cases was to support the Allies, since the struggle was against an unambiguously evil doctrine. But support came with one qualification: that metropoles dismantle or democratize their empires after the war to put into practice the admirable values for which they claimed to be fighting. The war thus induced a climate of expectation that self-determination would soon be universally applied. The failure of imperial powers to move quickly after 1945 to satisfy this expectation generated a volatile mix of frustration, anger, and sense of betrayal that fueled nationalist movements worldwide.

World War II fundamentally altered the distribution of global power. By war's end Western Europe lay in self-inflicted ruin, many areas reduced to rubble for the second time in thirty years. Troops from two countries outside the region—the United States and the Soviet Union—had played decisive roles in defeating the Nazis and were quartered on European soil. By taking the lead in developing nuclear weapons and the airborne means to deliver them, the United States and the Soviet Union rose to transcontinental superpower status. As their relations deteriorated from wartime alliance to ideological and geostrategic rivalry, Europe became one of the principal arenas in the Cold War between the alliance systems they led. Not only was the world no longer dominated by Europe; a region that had penetrated the rest of the world for centuries now found itself penetrated by outside forces.

Metropoles found it increasingly difficult in this setting to retain possessions that were, after all, both cause and consequence of an earlier hegemony. Colonial rulers shifted to defensive mode as they came under mounting criticism from several quarters at once. From the colonies came organized opposition by nationalist movements whose morale had been raised and whose base of popular support expanded by the war. From outside came challenges by the newly ascendant superpowers, each anxious to undermine the old Eurocentric order. These assaults had ideological and normative dimensions that metropoles could not ignore. Nationalists demanded that self-determination principles apply to colonies and that representative institutions the metropoles had designed for home use be transplanted abroad. Americans approached the world with an anti-imperial ideology that was a direct legacy of their earlier colonial experience. Soviet leaders saw the world through anticapitalist, anti-imperialist lenses, in large part because of Russia's long experience with a far more powerful, technologically advanced, arrogant western Europe. Critics from these diverse quarters converged on the idea that colonialism was morally indefensible and should be quickly phased out.

Superpower involvement in decolonization added a layer of complexity not present in phase 2. The outcome of independence struggles depended not only on relations between colonizer and colonized but also on the stance one or both superpowers adopted toward these struggles. Whether a superpower became involved, and on whose side, depended on whether a nationalist movement was perceived to be friendly or hostile to its geostrategic interests and ideology. Phase 5 decolonization was the quintessential North-South issue. But it took place in the context of an East-West struggle pitting capitalist, liberal-democratic countries against communist, one-party states. One could not understand the process without referring to all four cardinal points of the compass.

That East-West rivalry could affect decolonization struggles in far-reaching and tragic ways was most clearly shown in Vietnam from the late 1940s to 1975 and in Angola from the early 1960s to the late 1980s.[12] The Cold War also meant that newly independent states had to develop, at short notice, a position on the American–Soviet rivalry. Should a country that had just decoupled from western Europe align itself with the power to the west or east of Europe? Or could a neutral, nonaligned policy, a third way for a Third World, be staked out? Such questions made no sense and were therefore not posed in phase 2. But they could not be avoided after 1945.

Placed collectively on the defensive by the sheer fact of having empires, metropoles played down old rivalries and emphasized shared interests in preserving what they could of the pre-1940 world order. Britain and France, bitter enemies in phases 1 and 2, ardent rivals for most of phase 3, found themselves in the same camp in phase 5, defending their colonial records against critics in the United Nations and other international agencies.[13] In 1956 the two countries formed a military alliance in the invasion of the Suez Canal Zone, the very area they had so fervently contested less than a century earlier.

VERTICAL VIOLENCE: DIFFERENCES IN METROPOLES' POLICIES

The typical path to independence in phase 5 did not involve vertical violence. Of the roughly one hundred countries listed in table 7.1, in fewer than a dozen was there a sustained indigenous uprising forcefully opposed by local or imported troops acting under orders from a metropole. These include Madagascar, Vietnam, Palestine (Israel), Kenya, Malaya, Indonesia, Algeria, Cameroon, Angola, Guinea Bissau, and Mozambique. The ratio of major vertically violent conflicts to new states, 1 : 2 in phase 2, was about 1 : 9 in phase 5.

Why the later decolonization phase was relatively peaceful will be explored in part 5. I note here that the incidence of vertical violence varied greatly from one empire to another. How a territory achieved independence was closely related to which European country ruled it. At one end of the spectrum was Portugal, whose rulers considered independence an unacceptable option. The one metropole that quietly accepted the loss of its major colony in phase 2 was the most adamant in refusing to accommodate pressures for change in phase 5. In 1951 the dictator Antonio Salazar declared that his country's overseas possessions were integral parts of Portugal. He took this move to avoid reporting to the United Nations on developments in overseas territories. For if by a wave of the semantic wand the Portuguese empire no longer existed, there would be nothing to report to anyone. By "domesticating" the colonies and repressing all attempts peacefully to organize against Portuguese rule, Salazar and his successor, Marcello Caetano, virtually guaranteed that nationalist movements would turn to violence as the only way to assert their political claims. Through most of the 1960s and into the early 1970s the Portuguese fought three simultaneous wars—in Guinea-Bissau, Angola, and Mozambique—against nationalist movements.

The persistence, broad popular support, and guerrilla tactics of these movements ultimately proved decisive, not only in the field but also in Lisbon. A coup led by soldiers anxious to extricate Portugal from unwinnable wars overthrew the Caetano dictatorship in April 1974. The regime change at home was prelude to hastily arranged departures overseas. In Guinea-Bissau and Mozambique power was transferred directly to the preeminent nationalist movements, Partido Africano de Independência de Guiné e Cabo Verde (PAIGC) and Frente de Libertação de Moçambique (FRELIMO). No national election was held, as neither the Portuguese nor their successors felt one was needed to legitimate the transition. In Angola, where the anticolonial struggle was deeply split among regionally based movements, civil war continued long after independence. Violence was intensified and prolonged by outside actors—South Africa and non-African rivals in the East-West contest—who supported movements aligned with them.[14]

At the spectrum's other end was Great Britain. Its experience with the white dominions set precedents for the gradual, peaceful devolution of power from London to settler communities. By the 1930s Canada, Australia, New Zealand, South Africa, and the Republic of Ireland were internationally regarded as sovereign states, though all except Ireland retained Commonwealth ties with the former ruler. The crucial test of whether the dominion precedent applied to non-Europeans was India. The British managed to govern the subcontinent with a firm hand during World War II, locking up INC leaders who in 1942 demanded their departure. But whether Britain was prepared at war's end to hold on indefinitely, employing armed force if need be, was another matter altogether.

Three factors converged to push Britain toward rapid, negotiated withdrawal.

The first was the popularity and organizational resources of Indian nationalism. Nationalists greatly expanded their support base in phase 4 by arguing that Britain, having promised political advance during World War I, abandoned its commitments as soon as the war was won. Leaders of the INC were privately assured by a top British emissary in 1942 that India would move rapidly to self-government after the Axis powers were defeated. Having been misled once, the INC was not going to tolerate a repeat performance. Failure to turn over the central government to Indians would set off massive protests. Gandhi's preference for nonviolent resistance notwithstanding, the result might resemble the Great Mutiny of 1857–58 more than the *satyagraha* campaigns of phase 4.

Added to the prospect of vertical violence was the actual experience of horizontal violence. In 1945 and 1946 a rising tide of conflict between Hindu and Muslim communities engulfed many parts of the subcontinent. The Muslim League, led by a single-minded and tactically gifted lawyer, M. A. Jinnah, asserted that it represented all Muslims in India and was the only party speaking for their interests. This position directly challenged the INC's claim to represent all the people regardless of religious affiliation. In 1940 the league called for a separate Islamic state to be carved out of British India. The league gained support among Muslims during the war years, for its leaders traveled about proclaiming the gospel of Pakistan. The INC, meanwhile, was ill-prepared to respond as its leaders were in detention for demanding Britain's immediate departure. When communal violence broke out politicians in both parties were helpless to stop it. Even Gandhi's desperate appeals for peace and tolerance went unheeded. British officials saw no reason they should be more successful than Indian leaders in resolving conflicts rooted in the subcontinent's history, culture, and social structure and exacerbated by party competition. Did it not make sense to leave quickly, before more strife erupted for which raj officials would be blamed even if there was little or nothing they could do?

The third factor was British domestic politics. The Labour Party government that was elected shortly after Nazi Germany's surrender was committed not only to rebuild a war-damaged economy but also to construct a welfare state. Labour's electoral platform focused popular expectations and public finances on the home front. The government's future was staked not on what it did in far-off colonies but on what it could deliver to the voters by way of insured medical care, mass education, town council housing, employment in nationalized heavy industries, and the like. Moreover, Labour had historically been more critical of Britain's imperial role than the Conservatives. Loss of India need not badly damage Prime Minister Attlee's government. In fact, any attempt to hold on would require more troops to repress rebellion or more funds to placate Indians through new social welfare programs—or both. Any imagined scenario was bound to be expensive, leaving fewer resources for

Labour's ambitious domestic programs. On strictly pragmatic political and economic grounds it was preferable to leave than stay.

On August 15, 1947, following months of negotiations among British officials, INC, and Muslim League leaders, the world's most populous overseas colony became independent as a secular India and an officially Islamic Pakistan.[15] The diplomatic adroitness and personal warmth of the last viceregal couple, Lord and Lady Mountbatten, greatly facilitated the transfer process.

Peaceful decolonization of the white dominions in phase 4 set precedents for Britain's negotiated withdrawal from its principal colony of occupation. India's example, in turn, set a precedent for peacefully negotiated independence in other parts of the empire. The observation effect was powerfully at work here. Nationalists in Burma, the Gold Coast, Uganda, Jamaica, Fiji, and elsewhere learned that they would not have to threaten a war of national liberation to win sovereignty. British diplomats and colonial administrators learned that a negotiated departure was the best way to form positive relations with leaders and citizens of newly independent regimes.

That positive relations were possible after independence was shown when India, Pakistan, and Ceylon decided to seek membership in the Commonwealth.[16] Almost all Britain's ex-colonies subsequently took the same course. In so doing they transformed the Commonwealth from a racially exclusive club to a multiracial collection of sovereign states. Regular heads-of-government meetings from 1948 onward gave leaders of former colonies opportunities to prod the British to move more rapidly and decisively to dismantle what remained of the old empire. That these occasions could be fruitful was shown by the meeting in Lusaka, Zambia, in 1979, which successfully pressed a reluctant Prime Minister Margaret Thatcher to intervene in Rhodesia's civil war.

More than forty British colonies attained independence in phase 5, the vast majority by peaceful negotiation. Violence did occur, however, in three territories. In Malaya and Kenya the British suppressed rural uprisings that were pushing not so much for national independence as for a more equitable domestic distribution of political rights and economic resources. Efforts to address grievances of the Chinese minority in Malaya and of the Kikuyu and other groups hurt by the land-alienation practices of Kenya's white settlers substantially reduced rural unrest by the time colonial rule ended.

In Palestine the predictable outcome of the mandatory power's contradictory policies in phase 4 was bitter conflict between resident Arabs and Jewish immigrants committed to making the Balfour Declaration's "national home" for Jews a sovereign state. Horizontal violence became vertical as well when fighters from both sides attacked British administrators and soldiers for not acceding to their demands. Faced with a dilemma even more intractable and explosive than that in India, the Labour government referred the matter to the United Nations in 1947, then withdrew its forces early the next year. An impotent United Nations was handed responsibility for implementing a controversial partition plan. In the meantime Arabs and Jews waged war over a tiny, densely populated territory with immense religious meaning to both sides. Out of the war emerged the state of Israel, fulfilling the Zionist movement's dream. But the hostility of displaced Palestinians living within the new state and outside its borders, reinforced by the implacable enmity of neighboring Arab states, gave a nightmarish aspect to the dream.[17]

With respect to vertical violence Holland, France, and Belgium lay between Portugal and Britain. The Dutch were closer to the Portuguese end of the spectrum. The French experienced first the trauma of prolonged colonial warfare and then a series of peacefully negotiated transfers of power. The Belgian experience was closer to the British, though for reasons unlike those at work in Britain's colonies.

Holland neither prepared for nor anticipated the independence of the Dutch East Indies. The official position in the 1930s was bluntly stated by one governor-general: "We have ruled here for three hundred years with the whip and the club, and we shall still be doing it in another three hundred years."[18] With the departure of Japanese forces in 1945, the Dutch were anxious to regain control of Java and the resource-rich outer islands. But they had not counted on the declaration of an independent Republic of Indonesia in August 1945 by Sukarno and Mohammad Hatta, nationalists they had jailed for sedition in the 1930s. Dutch officials negotiated when necessary with republican leaders, in late 1946 reluctantly acknowledging nationalist claims to control sizable portions of Java and Sumatra. At the same time they did everything they could to return to the prewar dispensation. In two separate police actions between 1947 and 1949 Dutch forces seized many of the outer islands and captured most of the Javanese territory held by nationalist troops. In response, Indonesian guerrillas escalated attacks on government installations and Dutch-owned plantations.

The bitter struggle came to an end in 1949, largely through intervention by the United Nations and the United States. The United Nations provided a public forum which India and the Soviet bloc used to attack Holland for imperialist aggression. The Americans, after being assured that Indonesian nationalists were not procommunist, privately threatened Holland with loss of Marshall Plan funds if it did not withdraw. A compromise agreement in November 1949 transferred sovereignty to a federal United States of Indonesia, designated a partner in a vaguely defined Dutch-Indonesia Union. But such was the ill will and suspicion Indonesian leaders harbored toward Holland that they withdrew from the union five years later and in 1957 expropriated Dutch business assets.[19]

In the decade following World War II the French were no more prepared than the Portuguese or Dutch to preside peacefully over the dissolution of empire. French citizens were acutely aware how easily their homeland had recently been subjugated. Politicians who founded the Fourth Republic in 1946 were upset over the limited role Free French forces played in designing Allied war strategy, to say nothing of the absence of French participation in the American–Soviet–British conferences at Yalta and Potsdam that shaped the postwar world. France's wartime experiences offered abundant evidence of its loss of great-power status. Why should it tolerate further debasement by giving up territories that were still symbols of greatness?

Unlike the British, the French did not experiment during phases 3 and 4 with devolution of power to settler communities. The closest analogue to the white dominions, Algeria, was not defined as a colony. Legally its populated coastal zones were *départements* of France, as integral to the metropole as Savoie, Seine-Maritime, or Pas-de-Calais, and as off-limits as they to secessionist appeals. Fourth Republic politicians had no precedent to call upon that might have made decolonization, with or without a settler presence, appear other than defeat. There was no Commonwealth to cushion the fall psychologically. Neither were arrangements in place for terminal colonial elections whose results could be interpreted, as they were by London officials, as fulfilling the imperial mission.

An additional contrast stemmed from the political upheaval France experienced and Britain avoided in phase 2. The French revolutionary tradition spoke of liberty, equality, and fraternity as universal values. Events after 1789 gave these values concrete form by planting republican institutions in French soil. The revolutionary tradition enabled overseas expansion to be justified not only as the expression of a nation-state's interests, but also as an effective way to diffuse universally valid norms and institutions. From this perspective, colonized peoples experienced true liberty when they were incorporated within Greater France. To desire liberty *from* France was a contradiction in terms, an irrational rejection of the noblest of human ideals.

Such arguments were advanced throughout the life of the Fourth Republic (1946–58). They resonated with leaders on the right, for whom appeals to universalism were convenient rhetorical cover for retaining national power and prestige. But the same arguments also appealed to many on the left, for whom French global prominence was a means to advance the old revolutionary ideals. Except for the French Communist Party, which after 1947 was excluded from ruling parliamentary coalitions, a consensus developed across party lines that France should oppose movements calling for independence. French left-wing politics lacked an equivalent to the moderately anti-imperial stance of Britain's Labour Party. Whereas Prime Minister Attlee considered Indian independence compatible with socialism's domestic and foreign policy goals, Prime Minister Guy Mollet of France, also a socialist, vehemently opposed the struggle for Algerian independence as an affront to the left's ideals.[20]

These factors explain in part why the French were willing and able to deploy force to retain their empire. Factors specific to Vietnam and Algeria help account for the extensive vertical violence that occurred during 1946–54 in Vietnam and 1954–62 in Algeria. Vietnamese nationalism was linked to communism in the person of Ho Chi Minh and in the tightly disciplined Vietminh organization he led. Ho's lifetime goal was to liberate Vietnam from the control of foreigners, whether French, Japanese, or American. One of his early aliases was Nguyen ai Quoc, Nguyen the Patriot. "Vietminh" translates as "league for the independence of Vietnam." Ho was also a communist of long standing. A founding member of the French Communist Party who lived in Moscow intermittently during the interwar years, he was also the leading founder of the Indochinese Communist Party in 1930. Far from thinking national liberation to be at odds with international communism, he regarded the two as compatible and ultimately complementary.

Others did not see it that way. Or rather, others perceived Ho and the Vietminh as partisans of one cause or the other but not both. The source of Ho's popular appeal within Vietnam was his fierce nationalism. The source of the fear and loathing he generated among French decision makers was his identity as a dedicated communist. The selective misperceptions of Vietnamese peasants gave them a communist government far more manipulative and repressive than they had had in mind when supporting their nationalist hero. The selective misperceptions of the French— and of the Americans after them—meant that in fighting to keep Indochina free of communism foreigners found themselves battling Vietnamese nationalism. In the postwar era of awakened anticolonial fervor this task proved too formidable even for great powers.

Communist Viet Cong forces, under the tactically brilliant leadership of Vo Nguyen Giap, carried out protracted guerrilla attacks on French military outposts. From March to May 1954 the Viet Cong besieged heavily fortified French positions in Dien Bien Phu, a remote site close to the Laotian border.[21] The decisive Viet Cong victory there led to a government crisis in France, departure from Vietnam of a humiliated French army, and international negotiations in Geneva. The ambiguous outcome of the Geneva conference was de jure recognition of Vietnam's independence and the country's de facto partition into communist and noncommunist segments. The stage was set for two decades of postcolonial violence that combined in one mighty conflagration a civil war, an international war, north-south issues of autonomy versus neocolonialism, and east-west issues of communism versus capitalism.

In Algeria the special circumstance was not the ideology of nationalist leaders but the territory's status as part of France and the presence of a vociferous settler community. Settlers from France, supplemented by others from Spain and Italy, took the best land for their wheat farms, vineyards, and olive orchards. By the 1940s they were also a sizable working class and small-business element in the coastal cities. *Colons,* as they were called, enjoyed the rights of French citizens. Their interests were effectively expressed in Paris by representatives to the National Assembly and well-organized lobbies. Colons adamantly opposed anything that might enhance the economic or political status of the vast majority, of Arab or Berber descent, who were Muslim. With few exceptions Muslims were disenfranchised prior to World War II, hence unable to exercise the rights to which Algeria's incorporation into the metropole presumably entitled them.

The war stimulated nationalist sentiment among Muslims and gave rise to hope that things would soon change for the better. The successful British–American invasion of North Africa in 1942 dislodged Nazi collaborators and enabled Free French forces led by Gen. Charles de Gaulle to wrest control of Algiers. The presence of British and American forces highlighted the Atlantic Charter their leaders had signed earlier. Did not the charter's words describe the Algerian people, "forcibly deprived of sovereign rights and self-determination" for more than a century? President Roosevelt's personal envoy in Algiers, Robert Murphy, met on at least one occasion with the prominent Muslim leader Ferhat Abbas. Their discussions may have encouraged Abbas to abandon an earlier stance favoring reform within the colonial system and to issue, in February 1943, his "Manifesto of the Algerian People" demanding a majority-ruled Algerian state free of French control.[22] British officials, their own imperial interests firmly in mind, backed away from the radical implications of what Churchill had signed. A directive to the Arabic-language service of the British Broadcasting Corporation in August 1943 stated, "All references to the Atlantic Charter, other than hard news, must be avoided, since its application to French North Africa raises controversial questions."[23]

France fought to free itself from German rule *and* to deny freedom to others. The paradox was highlighted by events in Sétif, a town about 150 miles east of Algiers. On May 8, 1945, the day the world celebrated the surrender of Nazi Germany, about eight thousand Muslims converged on Sétif for a victory march of their own. They carried nationalist banners, one with the slogan, "For the Liberation of the People, Long Live Free and Independent Algeria." Some marchers displayed the green and white flag of Abd-el-Kadir, redoubtable leader of armed resistance to French invaders in the 1830s and 1840s. The subprefect, insulted and terrified by the message these symbols conveyed, tried to have the banners seized. The ensuing fracas triggered an angry outburst in which Muslims massacred almost two hundred colons in Sétif and surrounding areas. The French retaliated with dive-bombers and offshore cruiser guns against more than forty Muslim villages, while the enraged colons went on unimpeded lynching expeditions throughout the countryside. By the most conservative estimate a thousand Muslims were killed following the Sétif massacre. The least conservative estimate, widely believed in the Muslim community, was between forty-five and fifty thousand.[24]

It was now the Muslims' turn to be enraged. The massive scope and indiscriminate character of the slaughter radicalized the populace in much the same way the Amritsar massacre transformed Indian political attitudes a quarter century earlier. Repression by the army and by colons had the intended effect of crushing armed resistance—but only for a few years. In 1954 a group of young Algerians, meeting clandestinely on the day the fall of Dien Bien Phu was announced, formed an organization later known as the Front de Libération Nationale (FLN). On November 1 the FLN launched coordinated attacks against targets throughout the country. Thus began a war that lasted until 1962, when an accord reached at Evian, Switzerland, affirmed Algeria's independence and turned power over to the FLN.

The conflict was marked by horrific brutality on both sides against civilians as well as soldiers. Its intensity signaled the clash of powerful interests and values. Yet, ironically, the Algerian war made possible a new and dramatically different pattern of peacefully negotiated decolonization. The first signs of change were seen in France's other North African territories, Morocco and Tunisia. There too nationalism had been stimulated by World War II. Prominent leaders in Fez and Tunis opposed France's resort to force against fellow North Africans. They knew that the campaign against the FLN deprived Paris of resources to launch similar attacks against them. In 1956 French authorities, confronted by capably led mass movements in both territories, reluctantly consented to Moroccan and Tunisian independence.

The second change occurred in the metropole. In military terms the French army was more successful in Algeria than in Vietnam. But its successes did not translate into defeat of elusive yet ever-present FLN guerrillas. Moreover, Fourth Republic leaders found themselves increasingly criticized at home and abroad, on the left for brutally prosecuting the war, on the right for not fighting more vigorously. In May 1958 colons in Algiers took to the barricades to overturn a metropolitan government they considered hopelessly effete. When they were supported by key military officers stationed in Algeria, civilian authority in Paris collapsed. The Fourth Republic's demise brought World War II war hero General de Gaulle out of self-imposed retirement and into national life. A Fifth Republic was formed with power concentrated in the hands of de Gaulle as its first president.

Because of the general's lifelong record as an outspoken proponent of French global greatness, the army and colons were confident he would intensify the struggle against the FLN. But de Gaulle had come to believe that the Algerian war, while not lost, could not be won. Slowly, carefully employing for public consumption the grandiose but delphic phrases of which he was a master, he set himself on the path of negotiation that would lead to the end of "Algérie française." Remarkably, he survived the numerous attempts on his life by colons and soldiers convinced he had betrayed them.

President de Gaulle quickly seized the initiative to redefine France's relations with its remaining colonies, most of them in sub-Saharan Africa. He announced that a referendum would be held in September 1958 posing for voters in each territory the choice between association with a vaguely defined French Community and full political independence. He strongly favored the first option and campaigned hard for the community in highly publicized visits to Africa in the summer of 1958. The fact remained, however, that for the first time a French leader had spoken of independence as a possibility. And, for the first time, voters in each colony could express their views on future relations with the metropole.

The leading party in several French African territories, the Rassemblement Démocratique Africain (RDA), did not demand independence during the Fourth Republic era. Many leaders, after election to the National Assembly in Paris, secured high positions within the French political system and negotiated successfully from within for policy reforms.[25] To critics arguing that African politicians had been coopted by France's strategy of politically assimilating its colonies, the response was that leaders were coopting the French system to serve African interests. Most RDA leaders were not disposed to break with France after hearing de Gaulle's description of referendum options. Clearly, a vote for independence would be costly, with France withdrawing administrators, technical personnel, and financial support from the offending territory. The impact of such moves on the small, impoverished, vulnerable economies of French Africa could be disastrous.

Primarily for these reasons, leaders in all territories save one recommended— and received from their electorates—a mandate for membership in the French Community. In the remaining colony, Guinea, a popular and articulate leader named Sékou Touré asserted, "Liberty in poverty is preferable to slavery in affluence" and took a strong stand for autonomy. Guinea's voters followed Touré's recommendation, with the result that independence was declared following the referendum. The French retaliated as expected. But having a tightly organized political party at home and taking adroit diplomatic initiatives to locate alternative sources of support, Guinea managed to survive de Gaulle's campaign to prove that independence could not work.[26]

Leaders whose territories opted for the community were impressed by—and envious of—Guinea's new status in world affairs. They intensified their efforts to negotiate for independence without the heavy costs de Gaulle had threatened to attach to it. Negotiations proceeded rapidly. In 1960 fourteen French African territories gained independence and joined the United Nations.[27] In exchange for abandoning formal control French authorities extracted policies favoring their country's interests. Agreements signed at the time—many not publicly revealed until later—kept the new states in the franc zone, maintained colonial-style banking and educational systems, and in some countries assured a continuing French military presence.[28]

The violent struggle in Algeria thus had the unexpected effect—mediated through political crisis and regime change in the metropole—of transforming France's colonial policy. The new policy, coupled with initiatives by Guinea's leader, opened up possibilities for negotiated transfers of power elsewhere. The vast majority of France's colonies gained sovereignty peacefully, in large measure because France learned from bitter experience in Vietnam and Algeria that fighting to retain an old empire in the new international setting was futile and counterproductive.

Belgium's huge African colony, the Congo, also gained independence in 1960. The change involved minor levels of vertical violence. But this was not due to advance planning for evolutionary change of the sort that marked British policy. On the contrary, a near-complete absence of planning for any kind of change led to panicked departure at the first serious signs of Congolese nationalism. Prior to 1959 a tight administrative grip on the populace, combined with minimal communication links among a multitude of widely dispersed ethnic groups, restricted organized expressions of anti-Belgian sentiment. Pent-up feelings were powerfully expressed, however, by riots in the capital city, Leopoldville, in January 1959. The timing was influenced by the referendum held a few months earlier in French territories. Leopoldville was across the river from Brazzaville, capital of the French Congo and one of the cities visited by de Gaulle during the referendum campaign. If the French Congo could choose independence, many of Leopoldville's residents wondered why the far larger, wealthier, and more strategically located Belgian Congo should not do the same.

Belgium's policy was to provide primary education and health care for the population in hopes that these rudiments of a welfare state would create an economically productive and politically contented work force. Shocked that Leopoldville's Africans, who should have been grateful for benefits conferred upon them, were instead looting European private property and attacking the symbols of Belgian rule, the colonizers reacted forcefully. Colonial troops killed about fifty Leopoldville residents, these deaths mobilizing still more Africans into the political arena. In the aftermath of the riots, new political parties proliferated throughout the colony. The one thing on which party leaders agreed was that the Belgians should leave. Beyond that was profound disagreement over who should replace them and whether power should be centralized or shared with provinces and local districts. The government, aware that the situation was fast moving beyond its control, shifted from repression to bargaining. Congolese party leaders and Belgian officials met in January 1960 and agreed to hold elections for a national legislature in May. Independence was set for June. The Congo, it seemed, was aiming to set a world record for compressed political change.

On schedule, the Belgian king, Baudouin, flew to Leopoldville for the independence ceremonies. The two most important Congolese party leaders had radically opposed visions for the Congo: Prime Minister Patrice Lumumba was an ardent nationalist and President Joseph Kasavubu, an ethnically oriented federalist. The self-congratulatory, paternalistic tone of Baudouin's remarks drew an eloquently bitter retort from Lumumba. In the days following independence it became clear that the Belgians, while willing to turn over formal responsibility for central government affairs to elected Congolese, did not intend to give up de facto control of the country's armed forces or its vast mineral resources. Within two weeks of independence Belgian paratroopers landed in the Congo. One goal was to suppress a mutiny of Congolese soldiers against Belgian officers in the Force Publique. The other was to lend logistical support to a secessionist movement in mineral-rich Katanga Province. From the outset the new Congolese regime faced formidable external and internal opposition from the very country that had created the Congo.

Civil war, government instability, and widespread anarchy marked the first three years of Congolese independence. Belgium's armed intervention contributed to the assassination of Patrice Lumumba, weakened the central government, and brightened Katanga's prospects for secession. In these respects there was a strong vertical component to the postcolonial horizontal violence wracking the huge country.[29]

In summary, the extent of vertical violence varied greatly from one empire to another. Metropolitan leaders' attitudes toward the loss of overseas territory strongly influenced whether nationalist movements resorted to force or went to the bargaining table. Because the metropole with the most colonies was willing to tolerate losing them, and because the second largest empire eventually learned from bitter experience the value of negotiating with nationalists, the overall pattern of phase 5 decolonization was remarkably peaceful. Of the wars for independence that did take place, a high proportion was fought against metropoles with few colonies.

Several factors explain why European countries varied so widely in responding to colonial nationalism. At the symbolic as well as material level, overseas territories helped Portugal to compensate for its small size and economic backwardness. Losing an empire was intolerable to the Salazar/Caetano regime, for it would dramatize how insignificant a player on the world scene Portugal had become. The regime was able to sustain a war strategy for years because it was authoritarian, more adept at repressing and dismissing critics than a democratic regime would have been. France's history of military defeat in Europe from 1870 through 1940 and its demotion from great-power status at Allied conferences held in 1945 may have led it to value colonies highly on compensatory grounds, hence to fight to retain them. At the other end of the scale, Britain's confidence that its high international standing did not rest solely on having an empire, its close relationship with the United States, its long record of accommo-dating settler demands for autonomy, its tradition of exporting parliamentary in-stitutions to the colonies, the relative ease with which these parliaments could be peacefully captured by nationalist movements, the Commonwealth as a mechanism for regular postcolonial interaction, Labour Party qualms about imperialism—all these predisposed the greatest metropole to treat decolonization as unfortunate but not calamitous. Features specific to the geography, political history, economics, and culture of each metropole shaped its response to the prospect and reality of decline.

HORIZONTAL VIOLENCE

In fewer than fifteen of the one hundred states formed after 1940 was there domestic conflict before or shortly after independence that involved substantial loss of life or forcible exchanges of property. Considering the social pluralism and interethnic inequalities marking these states, the limited extent of horizontal violence was a surprising and impressive achievement. As noted earlier, in phase 2 about a third of the new states experienced serious civil strife.

Instances of horizontal violence in phase 5 should nonetheless be noted. They were more publicized and required greater attention from metropolitan officials than peaceful transitions. The process and results of civil strife influenced decolo-nization in surrounding territories. The underlying tensions and cleavages they reflected illustrate a broader set of problems faced by newly independent states.

In several territories horizontal and vertical violence occurred simultaneously, often in mutually reinforcing ways. Examples are Palestine/Israel, Vietnam, Kenya, Malaya, Algeria, and Angola. The former Belgian Congo could also be listed if one counts Belgian intervention and attempted Katangan secession immediately follow-ing independence. A wide range of groups was embroiled in the civil wars accom-panying national liberation wars. Rebellions in Kenya and Malaya were waged pri-marily by members of specific ethnic groups—Kikuyu in the first instance, Chinese in the second—who wanted their colony's economic assets radically redistributed. Ranged against them were people from the same communities who opposed the rebellion's goals, leaders, or methods and groups with less intensely felt grievances against the government. Struggles in Palestine/Israel, Vietnam, and Angola drew in virtually the entire society. Fault lines included religion (Palestine/Israel, Viet-nam), East-West ideology (Vietnam, Angola), and ethnolinguistic identity (all three cases). The Algerian war pitted FLN supporters against colons, FLN guerrillas against

Algerian "harkeys" fighting under French command, Arabs against Berbers, and FLN factions against each other.

Britain, France, Portugal, and Belgium presided over at least one territory in which horizontal and vertical conflicts were intertwined. Most instances of substantial horizontal violence in which vertical violence was absent or minimal were in the British empire.[30] By far the most significant were the mass killings preceding and following partition of British India. An estimated five hundred thousand Hindus and Muslims lost their lives in the riots and massacres of 1946 and 1947. More than ten million fled their homes, hoping for safety on the other side of hastily and arbitrarily drawn lines between a diminished India and the two noncontiguous components of newly created Pakistan.[31] In the Sudan, Nigeria, and Cyprus peacefully negotiated transfers of power were accompanied by intense domestic conflict shortly after independence. The principal bases for conflict were religion (in all three), ethnolinguistic identity (all three), and varying rates of economic and political development among regions within a territory (Sudan, Nigeria). In British Guyana, where the leading parties appealed primarily to racially distinct communities—those of African descent versus more recent immigrants from India—arson and looting marred the elections of 1961 and 1963. In Burma independence was followed by the enforced departure of many Indians, who had become unpopular for acquiring wealth in the colonial era and had to leave much of it behind. In newly independent Malaya and Pakistan, violent disputes precipitated the breakaway of units—Singapore and Bangladesh—that were then recognized as separate states.

In these instances violence occurred among non-Europeans. The Rhodesian civil war, as noted earlier, pitted indigenous peoples against European settlers. The toll on both sides was high: an estimated thirty to forty thousand deaths before ballots replaced bullets in the transitional election of 1980.

Why Britain presided over so many episodes of horizontal violence is an interesting question. More than other imperial powers, Britain formally acknowledged differences of religion, language, continental origin, culture, and political tradition among its non-European subjects. It did so by creating local administrative units for specific groups; by governing a colony's regions as if they were separate entities; by ruling the populace indirectly through traditional rulers; by encouraging some groups to specialize in certain occupations, such as commerce and military service; and by creating separate voting rolls for groups in response to demands for representation in local legislatures. Policies *reflecting* a colony's social diversity often *reinforced* diversity, as groups became more conscious of their separate identities and interests by the recognition accorded them. Britain's willingness to permit representation from below increased the likelihood that identities initially defined in cultural or racial terms would become politicized in competition for legislative seats, government posts, and public sector goods and services. In these settings it was not easy for nationalists to persuade the colonized that they belonged to a single national community. Group-based political competition took highly divisive, ultimately violent forms in India, Nigeria, the Sudan, Uganda, and British Guyana.

Britain's long-standing policy of encouraging its people to settle overseas created, in Rhodesia as in other colonies where settlers were present, a deep societal cleavage. Racial differences were politicized and systematically turned into economic inequalities by the Rhodesian whites' control of public sector institutions. Not until the late 1950s did officials in London question the metropole's lengthy acquiescence in policy decisions made by the white minority. The settlers' declaration of independence in 1965, being unilateral and strongly opposed by London, was the most radical break with the metropole since the unilateral declaration of independence of 1776. But British authorities were unwilling to use force to reclaim Rhodesia because the rebels were racially, nationally, and in some instances literally kith and kin. Racial homogeneity trumped political unacceptability. As it became clear to Rhodesia's Africans that Britain would not fight, it became equally clear that the only way to liberate the country was to take up arms themselves. In this respect the Indian and Rhodesian situations were opposites. In India the specter of ever-widening domestic violence encouraged the British to leave quietly; in Rhodesia their unwillingness to employ force was a virtual invitation to civil war.

These aspects of British policy help explain the paradox that English-speaking colonies attained independence in phase 5 with a minimum of violent opposition from the metropole, yet experienced a high proportion of serious outbreaks of pre- and postindependence domestic violence.

POLITICAL ELITES IN THE NEW STATES

The parties and movements that took control of a hundred new states varied enormously in internal cohesion, depth and breadth of popular support, ideological orientation, and the personalities, values, and roles of their leaders. Generalizing about the political elites of phase 5[32] is thus a hazardous business. In three respects, however, these elites differed markedly from leaders of new states in phase 2.

First, phase 5 elites were non-Europeans. Power transfers took place across racial lines, in contrast to those of phase 2, in which the same racial category dominated after independence as before (Haiti excepted). Phase 5 nationalism had a racial edge to it, a principal goal being to attack assumptions of European biological and cultural superiority that underlay the colonial enterprise. Nationalists demanded more than political change. They insisted on their people's humanity and right to dignity in the face of repeated messages that non-Europeans were not civilized— perhaps not fully human. Phase 5 decolonization entailed a frontal challenge to the way racial groups thought about and behaved toward each other. The unilateral declaration of independence by Rhodesia's whites was the closest parallel to phase 2 in its commitment to maintain race relations patterns developed during the colonial era. But the Rhodesian settler revolution failed, in sharp contrast to its predecessors in the Americas. It took place in the wrong century, on the wrong continent, and for reasons the world's states found morally unacceptable.

Second, phase 5 elites came to power by mobilizing support from broad segments of the population. One reason they could do this is that world depression and world war had produced a huge audience ready to participate in politics and highly receptive to anticolonial messages. Another reason is that politicians knew they could not capture the public sector unless they gained popular support. By mid–twentieth century the belief that political legitimacy derived from popular consent was widely accepted. Colonialism, being inherently antidemocratic, was open to ideological attack by movements with a broader following and more populist ideology than foreign rulers could possibly muster. Mass mobilization enabled nationalists to make good use of a political resource in which colonized peoples held a distinct comparative advantage: numbers.

The cultural formation of phase 5 nationalists led them to reach out for popular support. Virtually all of them attended Western-style educational institutions; many enrolled in prestigious metropolitan universities. Through formal schooling they became fluent in the colonizer's language, familiar with European intellectual debates and political trends, and attracted to a high-consumption lifestyle. Many became Christians in the course of attending mission schools. The more assimilated the educated elite became, the more vulnerable they were to the colonizer's taunt that they did not represent the masses in whose name they claimed to speak. How could a small group alienated from its own culture know the wants and needs of ordinary people who were not alienated?[33] Nationalists were stung by this taunt, many privately admitting that it hit the mark. The only way to convince themselves as well as their rulers that Western-style education did not disqualify them from leadership was to go out to the uneducated masses and recruit supporters.

Effective mobilization required a link between aspiring leaders and potential followers. Where elections were allowed this link was the political party. Where evolutionary change was not permitted the typical linking structure was what might be termed the movement/army. Examples of parties with a mass support base were the INC (India), Muslim League (India, Pakistan), Neo-Destour (Tunisia), Istaqlal (Morocco), Convention People's Party (Gold Coast/Ghana), RDA/Parti Démocratique du Côte d'Ivoire (Ivory Coast), Parti Démocratique de Guinée (Guinea), Tanganyika African National Union (TANU) (Tanganyika/Tanzania), and People's National Movement (Trinidad and Tobago). Movement/armies included the Viet

Minh and Viet Cong (Vietnam), the pemuda movement (Indonesia), FLN (Algeria), FRELIMO (Mozambique), and PAIGC (Guinea-Bissau, Cape Verde Islands). Eventually these homegrown institutions became part of the territory's public sector, simultaneously supplementing and challenging bureaucratic structures imported from abroad.

In phase 2, settler nationalists mobilized varying degrees of support from within their communities but generally took care not to reach out to indigenous, slave, or mixed-blood populations.[34] The economic viability of most New World colonies depended on efficient exploitation of non-European labor. Political stability depended on excluding the exploited labor force from participation in public affairs. For independence to succeed, non-Europeans had to be kept, as in the colonial era, economically mobilized and politically unmobilized. A major reason so many Caribbean basin colonies did not become independent in phase 2 was that slaveholders feared the destabilizing effects a drive for colonial freedom might have on the vast majority of the population whose freedom their owners had powerful incentives to oppose. Phase 2 settler elites did not need or want populist political parties and movement/armies.

The contrast can be made in reverse by comparing the deviant cases of phases 2 and 5: Haiti and Rhodesia. Haiti experienced the most profound social and political transformation of any colony on its way to independence, with a successful revolt against slavery followed by sustained guerrilla warfare against invading French troops. Because invasion was seen as a prelude to reimposition of slavery, ordinary Haitians had an enormous personal stake in the collective struggle against Napoleon's army. In Rhodesia a small settler minority declared independence in order to deny the vast bulk of the African population voting privileges that whites enjoyed as a matter of racial right. The two colonies stand out as dramatic exceptions to political mobilization patterns in their respective phases.

Third, phase 5 elites set ambitious goals for their countries. They wanted citizenship to be an inclusive category, based in most instances on birth or residence in a territory without regard to racial/ethnic identity. Elites wanted the meaning of citizenship broadly construed to include rights to education, health, and other social services. Independence was valued not only for its own sake but also as a means to accelerate economic growth and catch up to the world's advanced economies. For many new states the goal was rapid growth combined with structural change: creating an industrial base in economies that had specialized for too long in exporting primary products. The public sector was to play the leading role in stimulating and directing development, the nationalists themselves being in charge of the planning effort.

The contrast with phase 2 in these respects is striking. Citizenship in states the earlier settler elites took over was defined, in practice if not always in law, along racially exclusionary lines. That citizens possessed rights to extensive social services provided by government was an idea whose time had not yet come. Similarly premature was the idea of accelerated economic development, whether as an intrinsically desirable goal or as a way to emulate advanced countries. Settler elites would have regarded statist solutions to economic and social problems with mistrust, preferring the lead be taken by the private profit sector, in which they played a key role. In their view government should assist the private sector but not carefully regulate its activities, much less compete with or replace private initiatives.

Why new-state elite goals were more ambitious in phase 5 than phase 2 is largely explained by developments in western Europe following the initial decolonization wave. Most west European countries substantially broadened their conceptions of citizenship. In T. H. Marshall's terms, civil rights of personal liberty asserted in eighteenth-century Britain and France were complemented in the nineteenth and early twentieth centuries by political rights (extension of the franchise, eventually to cover all adults), then in the mid-twentieth by social rights. By social rights Marshall meant equal access to a wide range of services normally provided free or on a subsidized basis by government. These included primary education, protection against infectious diseases, unemployment insurance, coverage for on-the-job injuries, and retirement benefits.[35] By phase 5 citizenship in metropoles included participation in selecting rulers *and* in receiving services from them. Democracy and the welfare state had come into their own. In the economic arena, many parts of western Europe became industrialized, generating a hitherto unimagined volume and range of consumer and capital goods. Industrialization was the material base for financing the welfare state. (Portugal was a notable exception to these trends.)

What colonial elites in phases 2 and 5 had in common across the dividing lines of time, race, and culture was an educational formation that made them intensely aware of what Europeans were thinking and doing. In each phase western Europe was a role model for those struggling to wrest their territories from metropolitan control. But because western Europe changed, the role models changed. Predemocratic metropoles barely beginning to industrialize did not constitute especially challenging reference points for phase 2 elites. More than a century later, democratic, industrialized welfare states set high performance standards that new-state elites wanted very much to emulate.

In 1800, by one estimate, per capita income in North America and Latin America was slightly higher than in western Europe. There was no reason for phase 2 elites to drive their countries to catch up to economies performing about as well as their own. In 1950 western Europe's real product per capita was five times greater than that for Africa and Asia. By 1970 the gap had grown to about 8:1 for Africa and 8.5:1 for Asia. And development models were no longer confined to Europe: the gap between North America and Africa and Asia was 13:1 in 1950, slightly higher in 1970.[36] Phase 5 nationalists had objective grounds for believing their countries were far behind world economic leaders—and that time was not on their side. A pervasive, at times obsessive theme was the necessity to catch up. Jawaharlal Nehru wrote in 1946, "It must be remembered that the peoples of Asia and Africa have been exploited and deprived of their natural riches and resources for many generations, and others have profited enormously from these one-sided transactions. . . . This has resulted in terrible poverty and backward conditions. The balance has to be righted."[37] Stephen Awokoya, the first minister of education in Nigeria's Western Region and architect of the region's ambitious Universal Primary Education scheme, wrote in 1952, "We are gradually coming into the world heritage of knowledge. It is a legacy which we have missed for ever so long. We must therefore acquire our rightful portion of this heritage with great avidity."[38] A biography of President Julius Nyerere of Tanzania entitled *We Must Run While They Walk* puts the challenge most succinctly.[39]

In the eyes of phase 5 nationalists, colonial rulers were indifferent or actively opposed to the necessity of accelerated development. Foreign rulers should step aside and let nationalists get the modernization job done. The case for independence was based on a paradox: political separation from the metropole was a necessary condition for the "radical" goal of becoming more like the metropole.

Nationalists quickly discovered that they could win popular support by promising the rudiments of a welfare state after they came to power. Before becoming the first prime minister of the Gold Coast (Ghana), Kwame Nkrumah urged audiences as he traveled about the country to "seek ye first the political kingdom, and all else shall be added unto you." Nkrumah's listeners knew that "all else" included such amenities as primary and secondary education, clean piped water, electric lighting, tarred roads, employment in new industries, and the like. A vote for Nkrumah's Convention Peoples Party was a vote for access to a modern way of life.

When nationalists took power they came under intense pressure to make good on preindependence commitments. But delivering on their pledges was difficult and in many situations impossible. Promises of future performance are free. Actual performance takes money and professionally qualified personnel, and these were precisely what poor, technologically backward countries lacked. Borrowing from abroad to finance welfare state services and industrial development was one option. But this could only go so far before debt repayment became a burden in its own right and before repayment conditions set by lenders threatened policy-setting prerogatives normally associated with sovereign status.

Performance pressures on phase 5 political elites were intensified by widespread expectations that central governments would take the lead in accelerating economic growth and structural change. Nationalists generally preferred a statist or socialist over a capitalist development path. They felt more secure working through the public sector they had just captured than through a private profit sector they had not. The private sector's commanding heights typically remained under foreign control after independence, embarrassing if not painful evidence that it was harder to capture the economic than the political kingdom. Hence capitalism was associated with forces different from the nation and potentially hostile to its interests. Socialism's appeals to the masses' shared collective interests had more in common with nationalist rhetoric than capitalism's appeals to individual self-interest. An important pragmatic consideration was that the easiest, most direct way to reward a nationalist movement's supporters was to expand the size and scope of government. A bureaucratic post was the ideal form of patronage.

Phase 5 elites were influenced by a climate of opinion in European political and intellectual circles much more favorably inclined toward government economic initiatives than in phase 2. As of the early nineteenth century the dominant world power, Great Britain, possessed a small, functionally limited central government. Laissez-faire doctrines espoused by Adam Smith and Manchester School theorists were ascendant, critiquing what remained of the country's mercantilist (that is, state-directed) policies. In sharp contrast, in 1945 the socialist Labour Party took over a substantially larger central government and, influenced by the ideas of John Maynard Keynes, Harold Laski, and William Beveridge, undertook a major expansion of functions. Indeed, by the start of phase 5 central governments played extensive economic roles in all major countries. The Soviet Union was the most extreme example of state-directed development. But even the self-proclaimed bastion of free enterprise, the United States, possessed a large and activist public sector as the legacy of President Roosevelt's New Deal. U.S. aid programs funneled loans to Third World countries to support their governments' dam construction, electrification, port development, and industrialization projects. The critical stance toward government's economic role associated with Prime Minister Thatcher and President Ronald Reagan did not become politically significant until many years after the initial development agendas of most Afro-Asian countries were set.

The socioeconomic background of phase 5 nationalists may also have led them to rely on the public sector as the motor for development. Few of them were privately wealthy before entering politics. Most got their start not by skillfully managing productive assets but by skillfully utilizing Western learning. Employment in government service—or in professions closely associated with government like law, teaching, and journalism—was their principal source of income. Capturing the public sector was the only way to regulate and eventually capture private profit institutions from which nationalists felt they and their followers had been excluded. Government jobs, moreover, offered alluring personal enrichment opportunities to individuals who had begun life in poverty. In the words of the Nigerian novelist Chinua Achebe, "A man who has just come in from the rain and dried his body and put on dry clothes is more reluctant to go out again than another who has been indoors all the time. We [in our new nation] had all been in the rain together until yesterday."[40] Government, the shelter colonialists built, was for the first time available for new occupants.

Many phase 2 leaders, by contrast, belonged to a property-owning elite before gaining political power. Having private sources of wealth, these leaders did not feel pressing economic incentives to expand the public sector's size or functional scope. Indeed, a principal goal of government was to protect an inherited system of private property rights from which the settler community benefited. The phase 2 ideal was a complementary relationship between state and market, not the competitive relationship so often emphasized by phase 5 leaders. In phase 5 one must study political life to understand the origins and content of economic policies adopted by the new states. In phase 2 one must study the economic and social bases of settler life to understand who gained political power after independence and how that power was used. To understand the political economy of phase 5 it may be most useful to start with politics and conclude with economics, while for phase 2 it may be most useful to reverse the sequence.

In the short term phase 5 elites gained power and legitimacy through the popular appeal of their ambitious development agendas. But if they failed to perform as expected they faced greater political challenges from disillusioned supporters than did the far more cautious state builders of phase 2. Reliance on government to carry the development burden raised the likelihood that phase 5 political leaders would be credited when programs worked—but also blamed when they did not. The reality was that poor countries lacked the financial resources and trained personnel to finance modern welfare states and industrialize agrarian economies. And, too often, government-led development meant that the public sector grew while the economy stagnated, the cost and inefficiencies of large government bureaucracies contributing directly to poor performance. The nationalists' goals were too expensive, and the socialist means chosen to attain the goals ineffective and often counterproductive. Popular disillusionment with the new elites' performance in office was bound to grow.

Phase 5 leaders confronted a dilemma. In most territories political mobilization of the masses was a necessary condition for ending European rule. And it was the leaders' own mobilizational skills that set them on the path to power. After independence, however, many leaders feared that mass participation in politics might generate challenges to their power. Unleashed energies attached to disappointed expectations could topple the regimes that had toppled the colonialists. There was an ironic parallel here to the widespread disillusionment over unmet metropolitan promises that so strengthened nationalist movements after World Wars I and II.

THE INTERNATIONAL DEMONSTRATION EFFECT

Phases of imperial contraction were briefer than expansionist phases. If anything, assigning four decades to phase 5 underestimates the speed with which empires collapsed. The vast bulk of colonized peoples and more than forty territories gained independence between 1947 and 1962. Successful movements for change in some colonies accelerated similar processes elsewhere. Nationalism's appeal was contagious—a major reason decolonization was so compressed in phase 5 (as in phase 2).

The two types of international demonstration effects, observation and direct influence, were present in phase 5. A distinctive feature of 1940–80 is a third factor, termed the indirect influence effect. In this situation a new state worked within an international organization to shape the organization's agenda. The policies and initiatives of the organization in turn strengthened independence movements in other territories or reduced a metropole's capacity and will to retain power. All three processes are illustrated in the examples that follow.

The independence of India/Pakistan in 1947 had an enormous observation effect. Here was a subcontinent containing hundreds of millions of people, the most important possession of the most important imperial power, and a focus of world attention as the dramatic events of 1946–47 unfolded. Independence for such a key territory so soon after World War II ended signaled that the postwar era would be unlike any that had gone before. The techniques Indian nationalists employed to mobilize popular support inspired leaders elsewhere, particularly in English-speaking colonies. Nkrumah's "positive action" campaigns in the Gold Coast and Kenneth Kaunda's organizing efforts in Northern Rhodesia against the settler-backed Central African Federation were inspired by Gandhi's *satyagraha* campaigns.[41] That Asia affected Africa in this way seems fitting compensation, for Gandhi's techniques were developed in South Africa.

Another widely observed event was Ghana's independence in 1957. The first territory in sub-Saharan Africa in which sovereignty was won by indigenous leaders, Ghana under its dynamic prime minister Nkrumah was seen throughout the continent and the New World diaspora as heralding a new day for black people everywhere. British-supervised elections preceding the formal transfer of power there became the model for decolonization in other territories. Ghana's neighbors were all French colonies. Its example emboldened francophone activists to criticize France for not permitting a comparable devolution of power.[42]

As noted earlier, the outbreak of war in Algeria accelerated pressures for independence in neighboring Morocco and Tunisia. President de Gaulle's visit to the French Congo in 1958 had unintended effects in the Belgian Congo. Guinea's ability to survive the cutoff of French financial and technical assistance emboldened African leaders to abandon the French Community and press for independence.

Numerous instances of the direct influence effect may be cited. From the outset, a central theme in India's foreign policy was an attack on colonialism as an evil that must go. India was an outspoken critic of French and Dutch military action in Indochina and Indonesia, respectively. In a press release a few weeks after independence Prime Minister Nehru stated that "no European country, whatever it might be, has any business to use its army in Asia. The fact that foreign armies are functioning on Asian soil is itself an outrage against Asian sentiment."[43] Nehru convened a meeting of independent Asian states in early 1949 to organize support for Indonesian independence. Indonesia in turn hosted the Bandung Conference in 1955. High on the agenda when Sukarno, Nehru, Nasser, Chou En-lai, and other Afro-Asian leaders met was the design of workable anticolonial strategies. The Bandung Conference marks the start of what one analyst called "the Third World coalition in international politics."[44]

Ghana's direct influence in Africa was even more substantial than India's or Indonesia's in Asia. Nkrumah often said that no part of Africa would be truly free until all of Africa was free. Acting on this belief, he hosted the first Conference of Independent African States in April 1958 and an All-African People's Conference in December of that year. The All-African People's meeting convened activists from many colonies, among them leaders in the struggle against three metropoles: Tom Mboya (Kenya), Holden Roberto (Angola), and Lumumba (Belgian Congo). The conferees returned home with renewed resolve to organize for independence and with a strong sense that they were all taking part in the larger enterprise of continental liberation.[45] Speaking in Leopoldville shortly after his return, Lumumba announced formation of the party he was to lead, the Mouvement National Congolais. This speech may have been an even more direct precipitant of the riots of January 1959 than de Gaulle's presence across the river a few months earlier.

Several newly independent African countries gave crucial logistical support to movement/armies struggling against Portuguese and settler regimes. Congo-Leopoldville was a training and recruitment ground for Roberto's União des Populações de Angola (UPA), renamed Frente Nacional de Libertação de Angola (FNLA) in 1961. Tanzania offered bases for FRELIMO fighters and community organizers preparing to cross the Ruvuma River to northern Mozambique. When FRELIMO took power in 1975 it permitted ZANU's military wing to open up a war front along Mozambique's border with Rhodesia. Algerians passed lessons about guerrilla warfare to southern African movement/armies.

The third external impact—indirect influence—was made possible by international organizations, whose presence was a distinctive feature of postwar global politics. There was no equivalent in phase 2 of the United Nations, the complex of specialized agencies affiliated with it, or the Commonwealth. New states in phase 5 had opportunities unavailable to their New World predecessors to shape the agenda of international organizations, and they used their large and steadily growing numbers to take advantage of them.

Terminating overseas empires was not a goal of the United Nations at its founding. Indeed, because metropoles figured prominently among the charter's fifty-one signatories and because Britain and France exercised veto power as permanent members of the Security Council, an important bloc favoring the imperial status quo was in place at the outset. But the United Nations was amenable, both ideologically and structurally, to pressures from the opposite direction. Article I of the charter urged "respect for the principle of equal rights and self-determination of peoples." The General Assembly operated on a one-country one-vote basis, and its annual opening ceremonies enabled leaders of all member states to speak in a globally publicized setting. With every new entry the balance of opinion shifted in a more anticolonial direction. By the late 1960s the United Nations' founding member-states were outnumbered by those that had been colonies in 1945.

India skillfully employed U.N. membership to pressure the Dutch to leave Indonesia. From 1947 through 1949 Indian diplomats urged the Security Council to label Dutch military actions a threat to the peace. Although the Security Council was unable to take decisive action, India's initiatives placed the United States in an awkward position. Support for Indonesia's republicans in Security Council resolutions was consistent with the U.S. self-image as the first new nation and might win friends for America in other parts of Asia likely to become independent. But the United States did not want to break with the Netherlands, particularly in the late 1940s, when western Europe's future hung in the balance. The Dutch needed Marshall Plan aid for their war-ravaged economy, and the Americans desired Dutch support in the drive to halt the spread of Soviet-assisted communism in Europe. The Americans tried to resolve their dilemma by quietly but firmly urging the Dutch to leave Indonesia while restraining the anti-Dutch tone of U.N. resolutions. In this case, one new state prodded an international organization to put sufficient pressure on its most important member to bring another new state into being. The Indian diplomat V. K. Krishna Menon mediated among the bitterly divided parties at the Geneva conference on Indochina in 1954. He helped negotiate independence for Laos and Cambodia, where east-west rivalries were less acute than in Vietnam.[46]

As the independence wave swept west from Asia to Africa, new states further increased their influence over United Nations decision making. In 1963 the Security Council was expanded from eleven to fifteen members on the understanding that at least five seats would be held by Afro-Asian countries. African states did everything they could to focus attention on Portugal's refusal to leave Mozambique, Angola, and Guinea-Bissau, South Africa's occupation of Namibia, and the "internal colonialism" of white-minority regimes in Rhodesia and South Africa.[47] Western countries that for strategic or economic reasons preferred not to press for changes in southern Africa found themselves on the defensive and had to adjust policies as well as rhetoric in response to sustained criticism directed their way in various U.N. settings.

The United Nations not only reflected changes in the international system; it was also an agent of change. The Trusteeship Council, established by chapter XIII of the charter, was not dominated by administering powers, as was the League of Nations' Mandates Commission which it replaced. Half the council's members were countries not administering overseas territories. This arrangement permitted new states to join the council and shape its goals, timetables, and procedures in accord with their preferences. League mandates were justified on benevolent paternalist grounds as protection for peoples not considered fully civilized by European standards. No time limit was set for terminating mandates. In practice the mandatory power was unaccountable to those under its charge or to the league. In sharp contrast, the U.N. Charter stated that countries administering trust territories were "to promote the political, economic, social, and educational advancement of [their] inhabitants . . . and their progressive development toward self-government or independence as may be appropriate to the particular circumstances of each territory and its peoples and the freely expressed wishes of the people concerned."[48] Trusteeship Council committees visited trust territories; assessed political, economic, and social progress; met representatives of the population; and supervised elections and plebiscites to determine what people wanted. Individuals and organizations within a trust territory could write to the council or send delegations to New York if they felt the administering power was not adequately preparing them for self-government. Accountability was thus ensured.

Events in Tanganyika illustrate the system in operation. A U.N. visiting mission traveled throughout the territory in 1954 and issued a report critical of Britain's performance. The mission included an American and an Indian, representatives of phase 2's first state and phase 5's first major state. Nyerere, leader of TANU, visited U.N. headquarters in 1955 and pleaded eloquently for more rapid African political advance than London wanted to concede. Publicity attending Nyerere's visit pressured the British from above, as it were, as well as from below to speed up the pace of change.[49]

Participation in the trusteeship system was not a serious challenge for Britain, as the United Nations' goals did not deviate fundamentally from those articulated in London from 1945 onward. But accepting trusteeship responsibilities proved burdensome for France and Belgium, which neither envisaged nor actively prepared for colonial independence. Yet this is precisely what they were expected to do in territories administered on the Trusteeship Council's behalf: portions of Togoland and the

Cameroun (France) and Ruanda-Urundi (Belgium). Once France and Belgium undertook these responsibilities it was far less tenable to argue that self-government in other colonies was out of the question.[50]

South Africa, the league's designated mandatory power for neighboring South-West Africa (Namibia), foresaw the domestic as well as regional problems it would confront if it operated under trusteeship system rules. The South African government therefore refused to report to the United Nations, arguing that the mandate lapsed when the league died. A lengthy legal dispute ensued, the International Court of Justice ruling in 1971 that South Africa lacked the right to administer Namibia and that the United Nations itself was the legitimate agent to arrange the transition to independence. Until the late 1980s the apartheid regime paid scant attention to this ruling. Indeed, its obduracy at home and in Namibia in response to decolonization elsewhere in Africa may qualify as a phase 5 instance of the negative demonstration effect noted in phase 2. By 1989 and 1990, however, the cumulative effect of changes in southern Africa and in U.S.–Soviet relations led South Africa to agree to turn over power. Jointly with the United Nations, it administered an election open to all adults without regard to race. The result was victory for the South West African People's Organization (SWAPO), the movement/army that had led the struggle against South Africa. In Namibia the United Nations was not simply the vehicle through which new members expressed their concerns; it was itself the agent of political transformation.

Indirect influence may be observed in the Commonwealth's evolution from an instrument of imperial power to its opposite. Britain's ex-colonies in Africa were too weak to challenge white-minority governments in South Africa and Rhodesia. Recognizing their limits, they employed the Commonwealth to pressure officials in London to take stronger punitive action than officials would have preferred. It is no coincidence that South Africa left the organization in 1961, the year after more than a dozen African countries gained independence, with many more expected soon. African leaders presented Britain with a stark choice: either South Africa leaves or they do. An old white dominion departed in time to avoid being expelled. Its isolation was not merely symbolic. The cumulative effect of being excluded from practically all international events doubtless figured in the 1990 decision by President F. W. de Klerk to abandon decades of racially restrictive policies. As noted earlier, Commonwealth members successfully pressed Britain in the late 1970s to intervene in Rhodesia.

The international demonstration effect thus operated at several levels in phase 5. Observation and direct influence effects, which have their parallels in phase 2, were supplemented by the indirect influence effect, which has no phase 2 parallel. International organizations were not simply responsive to the concerns of new members but also took initiatives of their own to hasten the demise of the old order.

Part III

ACCOUNTING FOR
IMPERIAL EXPANSION

(*Overleaf*) Fort Batavia (Java), administrative headquarters of the Verenigde Oost-Indische Compagnie in Asia. Painting by A. Beeckman, 1656. Tropenmuseum, Amsterdam

8
Western Europe as a Region: Shared Features

I now turn from describing and analyzing events to the more challenging task of interpreting and explaining them. Part 3 addresses expansion. The central question is why, from the fifteenth century onward, a few west European states governed so many lands and peoples in so many parts of the world. A secondary question concerns the timing and geography of initiatives. Why was the predominant pattern in phase 1 formal empire in the New World and informal influence in the Old, while phase 3 featured the reverse?

The subject's vast scope and complexity and the variety of forms expansion took in specific situations pose formidable obstacles to efforts to devise a theory of European imperialism. Such a theory cannot be simultaneously comprehensive in scope, accurate in accounting for all the story's details, and parsimonious in identifying causal factors. My task is not to account for every event described in the preceding chapters but rather to make sense of broad historical patterns. It is not to search for one factor explaining everything but to identify several factors whose interaction and cumulative impact go a long way toward making broad patterns comprehensible. For reasons given earlier, the search is for conditions conducive to overseas expansion, since sufficient conditions cannot be found.

A theory of European imperialism is strengthened by being neither too restricted nor too broad in temporal and spatial coverage. Is its time span sufficiently broad to account for several centuries of overseas rule? Answering this question entails a search for factors prominent in both expansionist phases, not just one. Is spatial coverage sufficiently comprehensive to account for parallel empire building by several European states? Answering this question entails a search for features widely shared throughout western Europe, not features prominent in a few metropoles but absent in others.

Does the theory avoid covering too long a span? Specifically, does it help explain not only why Europeans formed overseas empires from phase 1 onward but also why they did not do so in earlier centuries? The best way to answer this question is to focus on early phase 1 to see if changes in the fifteenth and sixteenth centuries significantly increased European capacity and will for effective aggression overseas. A feature prominent from phase 1 onward but less prominent or absent in preceding centuries is a strong candidate for inclusion as a contributing cause.

Does the theory avoid overshooting the mark spatially? That is, does it explain not only why Europeans founded overseas empires but also why other societies with the maritime capacity to do so did not? The best way to answer this question is to compare western Europe with Arab-speaking peoples and China around the start of phase 1. A feature present in Europe but less prominent or absent in the other two leading candidates for global dominance helps account for the direction world history actually took.

So many factors vie for inclusion as important contributing causes that the search for explanation threatens to become unmanageably complex.[1] If some factors can be discounted for failure to pass the "both phases" temporal comprehensiveness test, then the task becomes more tractable. Expansion occurred in the preindustrial era, during the first Industrial Revolution of iron, textiles, and steam power, and during the second industrial revolution of steel, chemicals, and electricity. Expansion took place when capitalist institutions were in nascent form and when they reached the advanced "finance capital" stage described by Lenin; when Europe produced little for export and when it faced periodic overproduction crises. Colonies were founded during periods of intense intra-European warfare and decades of unusually peaceful interaction; during periods of rising and falling prosperity; before nationalist ideas gained currency and after they became popular; when settlers were integral to the process and when they were absent. It follows that a theory of European imperialism cannot plausibly identify industrialization, advanced capitalism, overproduction, war, a particular phase of the business cycle, populist nationalism, or settler activity as essential causal agents. There are simply too many instances when expansion occurred in the absence of these factors for any of them to be conducive to a process lasting five centuries.

By the same logic, variations among metropoles can be used to rule out otherwise plausible causal factors for failing to pass the spatial comprehensiveness test. Empires were constructed by states that were large and small (by European standards), rich and relatively poor, industrialized and agrarian, monarchical and republican, democratic and authoritarian, feudal and postfeudal in social structure. The size, wealth, level of industrial development, type of political system, degree of democratization, or social structure of metropoles cannot be considered necessary, sufficient, or even conducive conditions for European global dominance. There is simply too much variation in each category among states sharing the capacity and will to establish overseas possessions. To say this is not to deny that each metropole differed in important ways from the others. Chapter 9 discusses these distinctive features, showing how they help account for variations in the extent, duration, and character of various empires.

The search for dissimilarities between phases and among metropoles performs the useful function of decreasing the number of plausible causal factors. The search for widely shared features of west European geography, society, and history takes enquiry in a more positive direction. What merits inclusion as a conducive cause? The criterion is how well a given factor fares against the comprehensiveness tests just described. It would be unreasonable to expect any factor to pass all four tests. For example, a feature of European geography shared by all metropoles but not present in other world regions is too comprehensive temporally: it cannot distinguish between Europe pre- and postphase 1 because it remains constant across time. A more reasonable standard is that a causal factor pass at least one and preferably two or three tests, and that each of the four tests be passed by at least one factor. What sets modern western Europe apart, both from its medieval predecessor and from other societies that might have attained world dominance, are the conjuncture and interaction of factors noted in chapters 8–10.[2]

TECHNOLOGY AND GEOGRAPHY

The one obviously necessary condition for overseas empire is maritime capacity: ships sturdy enough to survive long journeys across rough seas, sailors with sufficient nautical knowledge and skill to reach distant destinations and return home. Western Europe was aided in meeting this condition by being a peninsula surrounded on three sides by ocean waters. For centuries peoples living along its coastlines made a living, directly or indirectly, from the sea. By the fifteenth century information and technologies imported from the Middle East and Asia greatly increased European seafarers' confidence that they could take to the high seas and return safely.

But west Europeans were by no means the only candidates for overseas initiatives early in phase 1. Long-standing traditions of maritime trade evolved in East and Southeast Asia, along the vast arc of the Indian Ocean basin, and in the eastern Mediterranean.[3] Large polities with some state-controlled naval capacity included China and the Ottoman Empire.[4] Numerous smaller polities looked out to sea: city-states along the Arabian peninsula's southern and eastern edges, in Gujarat, on southern India's Malabar and Coromandel coasts, and bordering the Strait of Malacca. The Chinese (Ming) imperial court dramatically demonstrated that it could show the flag far from home by sponsoring seven major expeditions to the Indian Ocean between 1405 and 1433. Egypt's Mamluk rulers dispatched ships to the Indian Ocean in the early sixteenth century. Arab seafarers traveled widely, founding city-states along the East African coast. By the eighteenth century Oman, on the Arabian peninsula, claimed quasi-formal authority over several East African ports.

If other polities and peoples had substantial maritime capacity, why did they not compete more effectively with west Europeans for control of the seas? One answer, advanced by Carlo Cipolla, is that in the fourteenth and fifteenth centuries European societies fronting the Atlantic greatly improved the quality and versatility of their ships. The key innovation was to carry guns and, later, cannon fixed to the deck. Thus equipped, ships could sink enemy vessels at a distance and intimidate rulers of port cities by launching artillery without disembarking.[5] This method of warfare contrasted with one favored in the Mediterranean by the Ottomans as well as by Venice and Genoa: oar-propelled galleys that rammed and boarded enemy vessels. When ships with sails and guns confronted galleys, their speed, mobility, and ability to inflict damage from afar gave them a decisive edge. For long-distance voyages ships designed for the Atlantic's rough waters held enormous advantages over vessels better suited for the calmer Mediterranean. Polities facing the Atlantic consequently enjoyed a geostrategic lead over Mediterranean counterparts. This helps to explain the northwestward power shift within Europe during phase 1.

Sailing ships with guns could outdo sailing ships without them, as shown in the Portuguese victory over a much larger Egyptian and Gujarati fleet near Diu in 1509. This was a turning point in world history, enabling Portugal's ships to sail essentially uncontested thereafter throughout the Indian Ocean. Cipolla contends that Europeans enjoyed a comparative advantage in sea warfare long before they developed this advantage on land. Hence they were able to expand overseas while Ottoman armies advanced into southeastern and central Europe from the fifteenth century until well into the seventeenth.[6]

Cipolla's argument leads to a more general point. From early phase 1 onward west Europeans invested time, ingenuity, and resources to improve the means of transport and warfare. Whether by design or accident, these improvements made it much easier to attain overseas political goals. Progress in transportation was obviously important given the immense distances between a metropole's capital city and its colonial frontiers. The carrying capacity, speed, and safety of European ships improved dramatically after the fifteenth century, as caravels were succeeded by carracks, galleons, and steamships. Steam-driven railroads permitted access to continental interiors in phase 3, paralleling Europe's access to continental coastlines in phase 1. Progress on the military front was likewise crucial, with continuous improvements in deployment of soldiers, in battle tactics, and in the distance, accuracy, destructive power, and firing speed of artillery.[7] No comparable technological breakthroughs occurred among non-European peoples to counter the latest round of innovations launched against them.

Further distinguishing Europeans from other societies was the practice of combining improvements in mobility and firepower. The *Diana*, which wreaked so much damage in the first Anglo-Burmese war, was the latest version of the gunned ship that produced victory off Diu three centuries earlier. With the coming of the railroad, troops and repeating rifles could be moved quickly from place to place to quell uprisings. Unusually mobile firepower encouraged Europeans to take the offensive in land warfare despite their unfamiliarity with the local terrain. Mobility gave them the advantage of tactical surprise, as the sudden arrival of troop or matériel reinforcements upset enemy battle plans. In the Battle of Plassey in 1757, for example, English East India Company troops taken by ship from Madras to Bengal were invisible to enemy forces before they disembarked yet extremely effective once deployed in battle. The ability to move quickly while killing efficiently was a pivotal factor in Europe's global dominance.

Virtually uncontested control of the high seas offered advantages on land as well. Europeans could select among invasion sites, avoiding hostile places and favoring ones in which resistance was known to be weak or nonexistent.

The vehicle of choice for moving Europeans inland in phase 1, the horse, was ideally suited for conquest in the Americas. Because the animal was not native to that hemisphere, European horsemen enjoyed an immediate and usually decisive advantage over local warriors. The sixteen horses accompanying Cortés's men to Tenochtitlán in 1519 figured prominently in the victory over the Aztecs. Pizarro's reliance on horses for overland transport and warfare was vital to his men's success over vastly larger Inca forces at the Battle of Cajamarca (1533). These creatures were truly "the tanks of the Conquest." Incan soldiers "thought little of a Spaniard on foot, cumbersome in armor and breathless from the altitude; but the horses filled them with dread."[8] Europeans did not enjoy a comparable advantage in the Old World, where many other peoples were as skilled as they in horsemanship, in some cases more so. In other Old World areas diseases threatened the animal's survival. Europeans consequently remained confined to coastal enclaves in many parts of Africa and Asia until the nineteenth century, when the railroad made interior penetration possible. The sequence of reliance on the horse and then on the iron horse helps explain the New World thrust of phase 1 and the Old World emphasis of phase 3.

The New World's indigenous peoples were not technically equipped to take to the high seas and discover the Old World. But several Old World societies were equipped to make voyages to the New World and back. Whichever society first made sustained contact with the New World was in a position to gain enormously. Conquest and settlement would be facilitated by the vulnerability of New World peoples to imported diseases. The "horse differential" has been noted. Concentration of mineral wealth in the hands of Aztec and Inca political elites gave outsiders incentives and opportunities to acquire these resources for themselves through military victory. Maize and potatoes, the New World's fecund and nutritious staple crops, could be literally transplanted to the Old World with positive effects on agricultural yields and population growth. There was of course no guarantee that invaders from the other hemisphere would reap all these potential benefits. But considering the sheer magnitude of possible gains one could conclude that the pioneer would be strengthened politically and economically. Enhanced strength could then influence relations with other societies in its own hemisphere

West Europeans gained the New World prize, benefiting greatly in phase 1 from the "Columbian exchange" of people, raw materials, diseases, plants, and animals. Exploitation of indigenous and African slave labor gave Europe access to silver, sugar, tobacco, animal hides, and other commodities at high volume and low cost.[9] Bullion from New World mines stimulated monetization of the European economy and growth of its market system.[10] New World bullion stimulated European consumption as well as production by enabling its holders to pay for Asian luxury and consumer goods. Silver from the rich mines of Potosí, Zacatecas, and Guanajuato helped phase 1 Europe make up a perennial trade deficit with Asia. Such economic gains in turn increased Europe's capacity to confront Old World societies that had hitherto been able to hold their own. There is thus a logic to the temporal/spatial sequence outlined in part 2. European states' formal control of much of the Old World might not have occurred had their power not been enhanced by prior formal control of the New.

The logic of this sequence is illustrated and symbolized by the story of quinine (see chapter 5). Europeans could not safely enter the malarial zones of Africa and Asia until they became aware of the beneficial effects of a substance—quinine—derived from bark of a tree whose original habitat is the South American forest. Access to a New World tropical plant became a necessary condition for the penetration, conquest, and administration of Old World tropical interiors.

But why did west Europeans reach the Americas while other Old World maritime powers did not? Here geography figures as a conducive condition. With the possible exception of the Chinese, other societies with seafaring experience plied waters in which additional profits could be gained by expanding and diversifying trade among Old World regions. The Mediterranean was basically a closed sea connecting European, African, and western Asian port cities, which relied in turn on trade with their respective hinterlands. The Red Sea linked the coasts and interiors of Africa and Arabia. The Indian Ocean, in premodern times far more deserving of the "middle of the earth" moniker than the Mediterranean, offered enormous opportunities for gainful trade in ordinary consumer goods as well as luxury items. East Africa, Arabia, the Indian subcontinent, and mainland and insular Southeast Asia could be reached by short voyages from one port to another. Or connections could be made by longer open-sea voyages relying on well-known, predictable monsoon winds that shifted back and forth depending on the season.[11] Even assuming that Ottoman, Arab, Indian, or Indonesian sailors had the capacity to reach the Americas, they would have had no incentive to do so given the still untapped potential for profit in waters close to home.

Arabs might have sponsored a New World expedition. After all, for centuries they controlled large portions of the Iberian peninsula, the same area from which Europeans set off on epochal exploratory voyages. Arabs in the late medieval period, moreover, were world leaders in the practical arts of seafaring and its more abstract dimensions, notably astronomy and cartography.[12] European rulers and mariners were aware of this. Prince Henry did not hesitate to borrow liberally from the Arabs' maritime inventory for expeditions he sponsored.

The Arabs, however, relied far more upon land than sea power as they sped across North Africa and into Iberia in the seventh and eighth centuries. The conquerors were peoples of the desert. Their mobility was based on the horse and camel, not the ship. When it came to sea power Iberia and northwest Africa remained peripheral. The Arab and indigenous Berber inhabitants of Morocco, who were able to keep Europeans from conquering the hinterland until the end of phase 3, offered no resistance to European ships sailing past their Atlantic coastline. Had Gil Eannes been intercepted he might never have made it to Cape Bojador, much less back from the cape to Portugal. Prince Henry's ambitious plans would have been thwarted at the outset, when prospects for success were most tenuous. And Europe's global expansion might not have occurred. The Arab maritime presence was most impressive far to the east: in the Red Sea, Persian Gulf, and Indian Ocean.[13] These were waters so distant from the New World that efforts to reach, much less cross, the Atlantic were out of the question. Moreover, at the outset of phase 1 Arab sailors and merchants were active in the Indian Ocean, the very region Europeans were trying so desperately to reach. Why should Arabs want to circumvent Africa in the opposite direction, abandoning a profitable trade zone for no known or even imagined destination?

Peoples at Eurasia's edges—Europeans facing the Atlantic, Chinese facing the Pacific—enjoyed a geographic advantage in access to the New World. But in the fifteenth century it was the Indian Ocean and adjacent Spice Islands, not an unknown hemisphere, that attracted sailors from the two edge societies. Cheng Ho's and Vasco da Gama's voyages mark the convergence of East and West on the same area. A major difference, however, was that Europeans had to circumvent a huge land mass to reach the Indian Ocean, whereas it was relatively easy for Chinese ships to reach the Spice Islands, Strait of Malacca, and points further east. For Europeans to bypass Africa they had to mount a sustained, risky, and expensive exploratory campaign. This entailed ventures financially supported by a government. Wealth seekers needed power holders. Power holders figured they could share in the profits if wealth seekers reached the source of Asia's fabled riches. An early basis was laid for collaboration across sectoral lines. This gave European overseas operations the empowering combination of institutional backing, strong and complementary motivations for aggression, and tactical flexibility (see chapter 10).

The serious obstacles fifteenth-century Europeans confronted in sailing so far south to travel east gave rise to the idea that their ultimate destination could be reached by sailing west. Once Columbus persuaded public officials in Spain to finance a venture based on this idea, the epic voyage accidentally linking Europe with the New World could take place.

By contrast, the relatively short distance between China and lucrative trade sites to the south and southwest meant that China's government and private merchants could gain access to these areas without having to cooperate. Indeed, noncollaboration between the two sectors was the norm. The Ming court was sole sponsor of Cheng Ho's voyages. When in the 1430s imperial officials chose to discontinue these remarkable initiatives, there were no interests outside the court actively pressing it to reconsider what in retrospect was a momentous decision to abandon maritime outreach. Merchants from southern China were active throughout Southeast Asia for centuries. But they operated on their own as participants in what Philip Curtin terms a "trade diaspora." They neither requested nor received support from an imperial court that, in any case, was located hundreds of miles from their hometowns.[14] If anything, the Ming court tried periodically to restrict Chinese merchants' international activities. The same geographical factors that encouraged cross-sector alliances in western Europe discouraged them in China.

A similar point applies to Chinese settlers, whose migration from (primarily) southern China to many parts of mainland and insular southeast Asia took place over several centuries. These emigrants' departure was not approved by court officials in Beijing. Neither did the court take special notice of the economic activities of Chinese communities overseas or try to protect their interests. Rulers in territories in which overseas Chinese communities formed did not perceive them as advance agents of Chinese imperial ambitions. In sharp contrast, migration from Europe was accompanied from the outset by metropolitan claims to possess territory the newcomers occupied. Whether deliberately or unintentionally, European settlers were advance agents of distant polities. Chinese settlers were not.

Migratory movements across Eurasia account in part for the contrasting attitudes of Chinese and European rulers toward overseas initiatives. Nomads originating in Central and Eastern Asia were directly or indirectly responsible for some of the world's greatest land empires: Mongol, Mughal, and Ottoman. Being close to the nomads' steppes, China has historically confronted military threats from its hinterland, as witness the enormous efforts across two millennia to construct and maintain the Great Wall. The danger of invasion was not hypothetical: Mongol rule lasted almost a century and was not terminated until 1367.[15] It would be quite understandable if Ming officials opposed Cheng Ho's expeditions for diverting resources and attention from defense against highly mobile peoples living to the north and west. By contrast, western Europe was not threatened by nomadic groups after the Arab invasion from Morocco in the eighth century and Magyar advances to the middle Danube in the ninth and tenth. Mongol armies advanced no closer than Hungary, the Ottomans no closer than Vienna's outskirts. Europeans did not construct a Great Wall to repel invaders from the east because they never considered "steppe imperialism"[16] a clear and present danger. Being distant from the Eurasian heartland, west European polities were more readily disposed than the Chinese to face away from it. Rulers could sustain maritime initiatives once threats from quite another direction—Viking raids on coastal zones—had subsided.

Europe and China differed in another respect. The Mongol Empire greatly facilitated overland contact between China, the Middle East, and Europe. The opportunity this offered for long-distance trade was seized by the Venetian merchant family, the Polos, among others. Europeans knew of "Cathay" through Marco Polo's well-known account of his Asian travels in the late thirteenth century. He conveyed the image of an imperial court with far greater wealth and artistic treasure than any European monarch, or even the pope, possessed. Europeans thus had strong economic incentives to reach Cathay.[17] Ming dynasty rulers had no comparably detailed knowledge of Europe prior to phase 1. Even if they had they would not have learned of a single source of wealth so impressive they would have wanted to dispatch expeditions to acquire it. In Europe wealth was more dispersed, geographically and among sectors and classes, than in China.[18] Europe had the will as well as the capacity to reach China. China had the capacity but not the will to reach Europe.

It was much more likely that a European sailing west to reach Cathay would have chanced upon the New World than that a Chinese ship sailing east would have done so. Columbus's route across the Atlantic was less than half the distance of a voyage from East Asia to Central or South America, using the most favorable wind patterns across the Pacific.

In summary, for both technical and geographical reasons sailors from Eurasia's western extremity were more likely than those based elsewhere in the Old World to set up the first two-way ties with the New World. As these ties deepened and broadened they enhanced Europe's wealth and power, strengthening its capacity to take over Old World societies at a later point. Sailors from the Eurasian far west also had more economic incentive to reach the Indian Ocean and China than mariners from those regions had to reach Europe. The unequal distribution of perceived opportunities for wealth helps explain why westerners sought the East and not the reverse.

GEOSTRATEGIC CONSIDERATIONS

West European states were surrounded by states with relatively well equipped armies. This made territorial expansion at the expense of neighbors problematic and costly in men and matériel. Advocates of expansion were therefore inclined to look outside the region. Arab and Chinese armies found it easier to extend their political boundaries or conquer and administer neighboring areas because large portions of their borderlands were lightly populated and culturally and politically fragmented. The expansionist impulses of Arab and Chinese rulers could be satisfied close to home without recourse to the sea.

The centuries-long struggle of Iberian Christians to wrest control of the peninsula from Muslims concluded successfully in 1492 with victory over the kingdom of Granada. After that point all of western Europe was ruled by Christians, and it experienced no invasion threat from outside forces. The cultural as well as military foundations of their civilization having been secured at home, the region's rulers were more favorably disposed to sponsor activities far afield. The clearest illustration of this point is the decision by Queen Isabella and King Ferdinand to support Columbus's westward voyage to the Indies almost immediately following their armies' victory over Granada. The intimate connection between these two world-historical events is noted in the opening paragraph of Columbus's log:

> Most Christian, exalted, excellent, and powerful princes, King and Queen of the Spains and of the islands of the sea, our Sovereigns: It was in the year of 1492 that Your Highnesses concluded the war with the Moors who reigned in Europe. On the second day of January, in the great city of Granada, I saw the royal banners of your Highnesses placed by force of arms on the towers of the Alhambra, which is the fortress of the city. And I saw the Moorish king come to the city gates and kiss the royal hands of your Highnesses, and those of the Prince, my Lord. Afterward, in the same month, based on information that I had given your Highnesses about the land of India and about a Prince who is called the Great Khan, which in our language means "King of Kings," Your Highnesses decided to send me, Christopher Columbus, to the regions of India, to see the Princes there and the peoples and the lands, and to learn of their disposition, and of everything, and the measures which could be taken for their conversion to our Holy Faith.[19]

In contrast, from the thirteenth through sixteenth centuries the Arabs and Chinese periodically experienced the threat—and at times the reality—of invasion. Mongol armies captured Baghdad, seat of the Abbasid caliphate, and took over

China. Ottoman Turks subdued Egypt and occupied the Fertile Crescent. The potential of borderlands to pose strategic dangers as well as opportunities partly accounts for Arab and Chinese rulers' disinclination to use their ships for expeditions of conquest. The risk of diverting scarce resources to distant places when the home base was not secure outweighed gains anticipated from overseas ventures.

AN ASSERTIVE WORLDVIEW

Was expansion aided by the way empire builders perceived the world and the place of human beings in it? Were psychological and cultural factors widely shared by Europeans conducive to global dominance? People's worldviews doubtless influence their will to act in specific situations. The will to act is a component of power. And empires are products and expressions of power. But how can one ever know the worldviews or motives of persons separated from us by time, societal setting, and subtle differences in assumptions about reality? From what is known about prominent empire builders one can infer that their motives and their understandings of what they were doing varied greatly. Are generalizations about their states of mind more liable to mislead than enlighten?

If one can identify broad perspectives that underlie and encompass the wide range of motives operating at the personal level, the risks of making unsupportable, overgeneralized claims are reduced. If there is evidence from phases 1 and 3 of worldviews compatible with expansion; if these worldviews were more prevalent in European society during the past five centuries than in premodern times; and if they were more prevalent in Europe than in other societies that might have formed overseas empires but did not, then a causally meaningful cultural factor is at work.

Widely shared among empire builders was the view that life was most meaningful when actively engaged, for the dual purpose of understanding the world and changing it. I term this assertive stance the explore-control-utilize syndrome (see chapter 2). Its first component was exploration: the practice of leaving familiar settings to learn about unfamiliar and often unknown places. In taking this initiative, explorers implicitly affirmed the importance of other places and people. For if there were no reason to fill gaps of knowledge about them there would be no grounds for leaving home. Exploration affirmed the importance of curiosity and the value of satisfying it. Turning the unknown into the better known was for many a desirable goal in its own right. But if curiosity, once satisfied, could be the means to other ends, so much the better.

The second component was control. Empire builders wanted to possess distant places and people. Possession might result from subduing others through force, but it was perceived as more than sheer coercive superiority. It had a legal and normative dimension as well, linked to deeply engrained notions of property. The European state, which ensured private property rights in its domestic domain, felt itself entitled to exercise collective property rights abroad.

The third component was utilization, the realization of imagined potential. Europeans expressed activism not only by going out to create empires but also by what they did with what they claimed to possess. A recurring pattern was the deliberate, systematic attempt to transform the social structure, economy, culture, and physical environment of other places. These invaders were perpetually restless, dissatisfied with what they found, and anxious to put it to more effective or efficient use. The principal though not exclusive beneficiary of the transformation project was themselves. Cortés's remark to the first messengers sent by Moctezuma sums up the insatiable appetites impelling so many Europeans in his day and afterward. After being presented fabulous gifts of gold he asked in apparent indignation, "And is this all?"[20]

The forms these multiple transformations took differed in phase 1 and phase 3, if only because industrialization enormously increased Europe's capacity to alter physical landscapes and social and psychological patterns. But the dream of radical change was there from the early years. Within hours of Columbus's first landfall in what turned out to be the New World, he mused in his journal about what could be done with the land and people he had just claimed on behalf of King Ferdinand and Queen Isabella:

> I went this morning, that I might be able to give an account of all to Your Highnesses and also say where a fort could be build. I saw a piece of land, which is formed like an island although it is not one, on which there were six houses; it could be converted into an island in two days, although I do not see that it is necessary to do so, for these people are very unskilled in arms, as Your Highnesses will see from the seven whom I caused to be taken in order to carry them off that they might learn our language and return. However, when Your Highnesses so command, they can all be carried off to Castile or held captive in the island itself, since with fifty men they would be all kept in subjection and forced to do whatever we wished.[21]

Columbus and the millions of Europeans crossing the oceans after him had a profoundly teleological conception of the world. Their task was to bridge the gap between the realities they experienced and their idealized versions of reality by reshaping what they found to become what it could and should be. This perspective is well illustrated in Sir Walter Raleigh's widely read account of his quest in the jungles of Guiana for the mythical golden city of Manoa (1596). Raleigh spelled out the tempting possibilities if only England possessed the land: "To conclude, Guiana is a countrey that hath yet her Maydenhead, never sacked, turned, nor wrought, the face of the earth hath not beene torne, nor the vertue and salt of the soyle spent by manurance [cultivation], the graves have not beene opened for golde, the mines not broken with sledges, nor their Images puld down out of their temples."[22]

Writing of merchants, whalers, settlers, missionaries, soldiers, and administrators who came to the Marquesas Islands from the eighteenth century onward, Greg Dening concludes, "There were very few outsiders who came to [this island chain] who did not want to remake it."[23] The same could be said of many other parts of the world.

Europeans were hardly unique in wanting to control physical and human environments. What made them distinctive, from phase 1 onward, was their reliance on exploration to gain political control and then to put available resources to use in new ways. The cumulative and interactive effects of the syndrome's three components were extraordinarily empowering. The link between exploration and control was well expressed by the chronicler of Prince Henry's expeditions, Gomes Eanes de Zurara, who wrote of captains of caravels sailing for Cape Verde saying, "Great is the desire of our Senhor the Infante to learn something of the Land of the Negroes, especially of the Nile; let us then go forth to conquer until we have found the Earthly Paradise."[24] A similar link was referred to in phase 3 by the French geographer La Roncière de Noury: "Providence has dictated to us the obligation to know the world and to conquer it."[25] Cecil Rhodes took this self-designated obligation to its logical conclusion. "Expansion is everything," said the great imperialist. But then, writes Hannah Arendt, he "fell into despair, for every night he saw overhead 'these stars . . . these vast worlds which we can never reach. I would annex the planets if I could.' "[26]

The link between control and utilization was expressed in British colonial secretary Joseph Chamberlain's oft-cited reference to the world's tropical areas as "undeveloped estates." Implicit in this phrase is the view that humans enjoy the privilege but also bear the moral responsibility of turning the potential of their physical surroundings into something useful to themselves or others. Non-Europeans, in this view, have abdicated that responsibility. For eons they moved lightly across the land or squatted upon it, letting its abundant resources lie unused. In striking contrast—so the argument goes—Europeans have shown the capacity and will to realize nature's untapped potential. They therefore have the right to take possession of land others failed to utilize, transforming it into a productive estate. In Lockean terms, Europeans have progressed far beyond a State of Nature. They are entitled to take whatever they want from those who remain in that primitive condition or not far removed from it. In effect, Europeans have use rights to vast portions of the globe.

From phase 1 onward this argument was advanced by settlers to justify seizing land from indigenous occupants, expelling "useless" non-European peoples, and forcibly mobilizing their labor. "That which lies common, and hath never beene replenished or subdued is free to any that possesse and improve it."[27] These words by the Puritan leader John Winthrop summarized the doctrine of *vacuum domicilium,* according to which undeveloped land occupied by people could be deemed unin- habited, hence rightfully seized. A phase 3 example comes from Sir Charles Eliot, high commissioner for the East African Protectorate (Kenya) from 1901 to 1904. Eliot wrote in 1905, "We must assist Europeans to develop the fine land the Protectorate contains, and must not allow nomadic tribes to monopolize huge areas of which they can make no real use."[28]

Does the explore-control-utilize syndrome distinguish phase 1 from prephase 1 Europe? To be sure, there is no precise break in modes of consciousness from one century to another, and thinking of 1415 or any other date as a decisive turning point in all aspects of European life, especially subjective ones, is unwarranted. Yet there is a shift in mentality between the closest prephase 1 equivalent to imperialism—the Crusades—and empires described in this book. The military expeditions west Euro- peans launched between 1096 and 1291 had a control objective: wresting possession of Jerusalem and the tomb of Christ from Muslim rulers. But control was in the hands of soldiers on the spot or of military/religious orders—notably Knights of Malta and Templars—not sovereign states administering conquered areas from afar. And the Crusaders' travels did not qualify as exploration. Warriors left Europe not for places whose location and potential were unknown, but for well-known lands perceived to be the religious center of the world. The Crusaders' interest in conquest was unmedi- ated by curiosity about other people, and control was not as prominently linked to utilization as in later empires. The principal artifacts crusading armies left in the Levant were fortified castles, designed to hold conquered territory against implacable foes. Crusaders had neither the means nor the desire to transform the Levant's economic, social, and cultural landscape. Control was decoupled from exploration and utilization. Motivations driving the Crusades were less complex and synergistic than in the empire-building projects—which may explain why the earlier outward- facing ventures failed while those from phase 1 onward fared much better.

Were Europeans more likely to exhibit the explore-control-utilize syndrome than other peoples? A majority of the world's great explorers of seas, continents, and polar regions was born in western Europe.[29] Travel to distant places was socially understood and accepted in Europe, often conferring fame. This social role had institutional backing, most expeditions being financed by government officials or scientific societies or both. Government sponsorship greatly increased the likelihood that knowledge generated from exploration would be followed by political claims in newly discovered areas.

In most other societies, by contrast, the explorer role did not emerge, and scientific societies designed to learn about unknown places were not formed. The

Islamic world had a tradition of travel accounts by Abu al-Idrisi, Ibn Hawqal, Abu al-Hasan al-Masudi, and the incomparable Ibn Battuta (1304–77), at more than seventy thousand miles the greatest explorer of all time. But these men generally confined themselves to areas inhabited by fellow Muslims. A recent account of Ibn Battuta's travels notes that "almost everywhere [he] went he lived in the company of other Muslims, men and women who shared not merely his doctrinal beliefs and religious rituals, but his moral values, his social ideals, his everyday manners."[30] The compulsion to visit places and people manifestly foreign—a prominent motivation among many European travelers—apparently was much less strong among their Muslim counterparts. Moreover, Ibn Battuta and his predecessors traveled on their own, covering expenses through their own initiatives. Lack of institutional support meant that the knowledge they generated did not lead to expansionist claims by rulers of Muslim states.

The closest Chinese parallel is Cheng Ho, whose expeditions were officially sponsored and reached lands of which the Ming court had been at most dimly aware. But the Chinese admiral was a historical anomaly, not a contributor to an ongoing, socially acknowledged tradition of exploration. Whatever he learned had no policy impact once his sponsors lost interest in convincing foreign potentates of China's greatness. Even when the court was interested, its goal was not to assert power through military and administrative means but to enhance status and encourage trade through symbolic government-to-government tribute relations. Thus, in the exceptional Chinese instance when exploration was valued, formal control was not, at least in the way Europeans understood and practiced it.

Exploration from the Islamic world and China was on the decline when west Europeans began to reach outward. Ibn Battuta and Cheng Ho were the last of their kind rather than pioneers inspiring successors to build on their findings. The contrast with the cumulative acquisition and wide dispersal of knowledge from European exploration is clear.

Links between control and utilization were also less evident in the great non-European overland empires. The tendency was for rulers to extract resources from the populace without trying to change what their subjects produced or how they produced it. The idea of remaking the natural environment and rearranging the way people lived so as to realize a vision of a more perfect order of things did not figure prominently in the thinking of non-European elites.

One reason the explore-control-utilize syndrome could emerge is that exploration and utilization become more highly valued in a particular era, hence more readily linked to control objectives, which can be assumed to be fairly constant over time. That phase 1 Europeans placed a higher priority than their predecessors on exploring the world and putting new knowledge to practical use is demonstrated in the domains of science and technology. Advances in theoretical and experimental science and the impact of scientific thinking on everyday life accelerated during the Renaissance, about the time the early explorations took place. Like imperialism, the ascendant scientific worldview set modern Europe apart from its premodern predecessor. Over time it increasingly set European societies apart from non-European ones. According to this way of thinking human beings are not simply immersed in Nature; they are in some sense distanced or alienated from Nature. The key to scientific knowledge is systematic observation, which assumes some distance between observer and observed yet posits that this distance can be traversed through careful observation. Another mental distancing operation involves distinguishing between Nature as what is apprehended by the senses and Nature as what lies behind signals the senses convey. The essence of Nature in this latter manifestation is conveyed by comprehensive, unchanging, abstract laws, typically expressed in mathematical form.[31]

Having postulated various kinds of distance between the observing mind and Nature, the modern scientific enterprise tries to reduce that distance as much as possible through systematic exploration. This may involve traveling to places the scientist wants to reach or devising sophisticated instruments to observe distant or very small objects. Scientific exploration probes beyond the empirically observable level to reveal or "dis-cover" natural laws. These laws subsume a confusing array of sensory data under patterns that are at once comprehensive and comprehensible.

Knowledge obtained from scientific exploration has long been considered instrinsically desirable by its practitioners. Yet there has been a strong tendency in modern European society to view basic knowledge in instrumental, utilitarian terms. Technological innovation has flourished, bringing closer to fulfillment Nature's imagined potential to enhance human well-being. Since the Renaissance a series of research and development cycles may be observed in which basic knowledge stimulated technological advances, which in turn permitted further exploration at the more fundamental theoretical level.

That Europe began to project political power outward at about the time its innovations in scientific thinking and technological application were accelerating is not a coincidence. New levels of activism in these two domains, from early in phase 1 and continuing through succeeding centuries, reflect a close, mutually supportive linkage among exploration, control, and utilization. Imperial expansion and scientific/technological innovation share an underlying logic because both are derived from the same syndrome of attitudes.

Interaction between these separate yet similar domains was synergistic and mutually reinforcing. Explorers of seas and continents accumulated a vast amount of information that enriched basic and applied scientific work at home. Their early findings may have fostered qualities of mind essential for scientific advance. Germain Arciniegas argues that because ancient classical and medieval Christian scholars were unaware of the New World, its discovery increased skepticism about the claims of received wisdom from whatever source and led Europeans to ask more insistently whether statements about the world were supported by evidence. Maritime exploration having paid rich and unexpected dividends, scholars were emboldened to apply its unabashedly empiricist approach to other endeavors as well.[32]

Some revenues extracted from the colonies were invested in scientific research and development at home. The quest for natural laws in turn unearthed knowledge leading to breakthroughs in transport and communication, which made it easier for Europeans to conquer other people. Sometimes geographical exploration combined imperial and scientific motives. Back of Captain Cook's first voyage to the South Pacific in 1768, for instance, lay the geostrategic goal of finding a southern continent to which Britain might lay claim. Accompanying Cook was the young naturalist Joseph Banks, who won a well-deserved reputation for his careful observation and impressive collection of flora and fauna. Banks became first director of the famed botanical garden at Kew, outside London, and was president of the Royal Society for forty years.[33] The network of botanical gardens connecting metropoles and colonies further illustrates the fusion of imperial and scientific enterprises. Botanists at Kew, the Jardin d'Essai Colonial in Paris, and government-sponsored gardens in Buitenzorg (Dutch East Indies), Calcutta, Peradiniya (Ceylon), Singapore, Libreville (Gabon), Saigon, and elsewhere collected and classified specimens. Much of the botanists' work was then put to commercial use. Cinchona, rubber, and sugarcane were transplanted from continent to continent and stimulated economic development far from their places of origin.[34]

In retrospect, advances in knowledge leading to the gunned ship of early phase 1 were not accidental or isolated. They were the opening rounds in a series of advances that progressively enlarged the technology gap between Europeans and others. By phase 3, when the gap had become a chasm, Europeans saw their scientific and technological accomplishments as evidence of their across-the-board superiority over others. Empire was explained as a manifestation of that superiority and justified as a way to civilize materially less advanced cultures. A growing capacity to understand and manipulate the physical world thus reinforced the will to dominate the human world (see table 8.1).[35]

A society with the will to explore, control, and utilize its environment is well positioned to conquer societies less inclined to think in this way. If in addition the more assertive society can call upon a steady stream of advances in science and technology while others cannot, its prospects for political dominance are even better. From the fifteenth century western Europe linked control vertically to exploration

TABLE 8.1.

Syndrome	Imperialism		Stance Toward Nature
Explore	expeditions by sea, land ↓	↔	basic and experimental science ↕
Control	colonial rule ↓	↔	applied science; technology ↓
Utilize	economic, social transformation of colonies; transfer of resources, profits to metropole	↔	higher standard of living via reliance on technology and its products

and utilization *and* laterally to advances in the exploration, control, and utilization of Nature. The combination was hard to resist.

SECTORAL INSTITUTIONS

Are there features of west European society that permit one to think of the region as a single, coherent unit? If so, do they help explain why the region had such an impact elsewhere? We do speak, after all, of European civilization, culture, and empires; when traveling abroad, Europeans persistently referred to their continent of origin as a source of identity and loyalty. In a sense, an entire region, not simply the political units embedded within it, projected power and influence overseas.

Here I stretch the concept of sector to refer to functionally specific activities within western Europe as a whole. When one examines recurring patterns of government, economic activity, and religious belief and ritual, one sees underlying themes conducive to global dominance: each sector displays a high level of institutionalization, autonomy, and will to extend itself overseas.

Public Sector: The Bureaucratic State

Europeans were long accustomed to living within territorially bounded polities and under rulers with substantial power and moral authority. The sequence was from one unit to a multitude to a few: from an immense empire centered in Rome to hundreds of small feudal principalities to a much smaller number of states. At all times, however, could be found specialists in rule visibly presiding over a public realm.

Given this experience, Europeans defined living in a polity as a defining feature of civilized life. It is not accidental that the Latin root for civilization is *cives*, "citizen." Europeans looked down upon societies that lacked recognizable, specialized political structures as uncivilized—Rudyard Kipling's "lesser breeds without the law."

The Spanish, for example, called stateless New World peoples savages (*indios salvajes*), as distinct from *indios policías* who lived under identifiable governance structures. By conceptualizing differences in the way societies performed political functions as inequalities between superior and inferior ways of life, Europeans handed themselves a powerful moral justification for imperialism. Placing stateless peoples under the jurisdiction of political institutions was deemed an essential part of the noble task of improving the lives of savages. In many parts of the world the European state was a symbol of the purpose of empire as well as the tool for constructing it.

The line separating a feudal principality from a modern state is blurred, conceptually as well as in actual historical circumstances. Generally speaking, however, early in phase 1 western Europe began to accelerate the transition across that line. Modern state formation involved a shift in power and status from physically dispersed, rural-based aristocrats to court officials in a capital city; codification and territory-wide application of legal norms and procedures; the growth of standing armies to defend rulers against domestic and external challengers; and a functionally specialized bureaucracy largely recruited, trained, compensated, and directed through the central government.[36] Modern state building involved the elimination of many small units by incorporation into larger ones. By Charles Tilly's estimate, western Europe had some five hundred political units at the start of the sixteenth century and about twenty-five early in the twentieth.[37]

Modern states were far better positioned than their feudal predecessors to construct overseas empires. Their greater size and population, their rulers' capacity to amass taxes and borrowed capital in central treasuries, and their control of standing armies gave them more human and financial resources to deploy, abroad as well as at home. Had Europe remained as politically fractured after the fifteenth and sixteenth centuries as it was in the feudal era the region could not have had the global impact it did. The external projection of power was facilitated by the internal consolidation of power by centralizing dynasties: the House of Aviz in Portugal, the Aragón-Castile merger followed in 1516 by Habsburg rule in Spain, the Bourbons in France, the Tudors in England, and subsequently the Prussian Hohenzollerns in Germany.

The prospect that colonies might enrich a metropolitan government's coffers was, of course, a strong incentive to look abroad. State building in Europe was an extremely expensive proposition. Funds had to be raised to induce or coerce otherwise unwilling subjects to obey the government as well as to wage war against neighboring enemies. Resources from abroad could help resolve the state's perennial fiscal crisis.[38]

European colonies may be considered protostates. Territorial boundaries, capital cities, defense forces, functionally specialized bureaucracies—these features were transferred deliberately from metropolitan core to imperial periphery. Construction of protostates abroad could not occur until the modern state was in place as a model for export.[39]

The sequence of European political evolution from one unit to hundreds to a few affected relations among sectors. Private profit and religious institutions that emerged prior to modern state building had opportunities to take root in society, gain legitimacy on their own terms, and enjoy autonomy from political control. From the feudal era came a tradition of largely unfettered entrepreneurial activity in urban areas. Among the Roman Empire's legacies was the Catholic Church. The autonomy of urban capitalist institutions was clearly a factor in Europe's sustained economic development. The autonomy of its religious institutions—Roman Catholic and eventually Protestant—limited the arbitrary and authoritarian exercise of power by state officials. Sectoral autonomy also influenced the way Europeans acted overseas. Capitalist and Christian institutions had the leeway to set their own foreign policy agendas and the financial and personnel resources to carry them out. This meant that the number of actors and the range of motivations and incentives operating overseas at any given time was far greater than a survey of government actions alone would suggest. It also meant that Europeans could exert influence even when the states from which they came were unable or unwilling to govern specific overseas territories (see chapter 10).

The Roman Empire was far enough removed in time to pose no challenge to Europeans constructing states out of the huge territory Rome once controlled, yet sufficiently recent to be on state builders' minds. Its legal and architectural legacies affected the way European polities operated at home. Rome also served as a role model for external relations. Modern empire builders, familiar with classical history through their formal education, often described their actions as replicating Rome's accomplishments. Patricia Seed observes that every imperial power in the New World between 1492 and 1640 invoked Rome. Doing so "served to foster the sense that Europe was indeed engaged upon a single legitimate project—domination of the peoples/lands/commerce of the New World in the name of recreating the imagined ideal of the Middle Ages—the medieval dream of a single unified Rome."[40] The ancient empire cast a shadow even in phase 3, though the medieval ideal had by then been discarded.

Luis Vaz de Camoëns's sixteenth-century poem *The Lusiads,* written in praise of early Portuguese explorers, is filled with references to classic mythology and history. The poet writes that Venus "was attracted to the Portuguese, seeing in them many of the qualities of the ancient Rome she had loved so much." Jupiter promises Venus, "You shall see Greeks and Romans cast into oblivion by the great deeds this people will perform in the East."[41]

The British in phases 3 and 4 were especially fond of comparing their accomplishments to those of Rome, as seen in the phrase *pax britannica*. Classical studies (*litterae humaniores*) were popular among students at Oxford and Cambridge, and colonial officials from these elite institutions frequently referred to Greek and Roman themes. Cecil Rhodes liked to be told that his bust resembled that of a Roman emperor. Richard Symonds writes that Rhodes, "brooding often on the lessons of Rome for Britain, . . . had the books Gibbon used as sources for the *Decline and Fall of the Roman Empire* translated into English for his personal use."[42] In *The Ancient Roman Empire and the British Empire in India* (1914), Lord Bryce compared Rome's impressive road network with the British feat of crisscrossing India by railway.

In both expansionist phases the Roman Empire was an exemplar for several states whose territories had been incorporated within it centuries earlier. Rome's lesson was not so much that Europe could again be unified as that its people could again perform great deeds on other continents.

Private Profit Sector: Urban Capitalist Institutions

Western Europe developed a regionwide private profit sector through the institutions and values of capitalism. As the word "bourgeoisie" indicates, the key to this outcome was the rise of urban areas specializing in production of marketable goods and services. Cities have been to the region's economy what states have been to its politics. As Tilly puts it, "Europe's system of cities represented the changing relations among concentrations of capital, its system of states the changing relations among concentrations of coercion."[43] Before the Industrial Revolution rural areas accounted for a sizable proportion of handmade goods. But even then, "wherever physical production might take place, the intangible processes of information flow, decision making, and exchange concentrated firmly in cities."[44] The onset of factory-based industry in phases 2 and 3 led to a dramatic urbanization of nonagricultural production.

In the late Middle Ages European towns and cities enjoyed considerable political autonomy from neighboring barons—a legacy that insulated them to some extent from the centralizing activities of state builders in phase 1.[45] Another feature of late medieval life was the dense network of trade and credit linking cities throughout the region. These two features were interdependent. Autonomy within a polity was enhanced by flows of valuable resources across political boundaries. Partial insulation from external political control enabled cities to concentrate on economically productive activities and to maintain direct trade ties with other regional urban centers.

Although much of this trade took place overland, western Europe's extensive coastline encouraged reliance on ships to transport bulk as well as luxury goods. Douglass North and Robert Thomas observe that during the sixteenth century a thriving trade along the Atlantic coast "tended to join together the greater commercial loops of the Mediterranean and the Baltic regions until these three loops became one chain of commerce."[46] Merchants and traders were ideally positioned by early phase 1 to extend to other continents patterns of maritime activity already serving their own region.

Europe's urban population was driven primarily by the imperative of economic survival, considering that the time-honored means of subsistence—land—was inaccessible to the great majority. For a growing number of city dwellers, however, accumulation of wealth over and above subsistence became an attainable goal. Such a goal was hardly unique to European society. What was distinctive was the high priority placed on acquiring wealth and the innovative techniques used to do so.

European capitalism was marked, first, by societal acceptance of private ownership of property (including land) and by effective enforcement of claims to property rights. As the legal system developed, public sector officials came to acknowledge private claims even when these were directed against the government itself. Second, the search for profit was linked to an interest in technological innovation that might lower production costs or generate new products. Third, wealth was valued not only for the goods and services it could purchase but also as a means to generate even more wealth in the future. The idea that capital derived from putting resources to use should itself be put to use was consistent with the explore-control-utilize syndrome. Rapid, efficient recycling of capital into subsequent rounds of production was an enormously potent stimulant of economic life and technological change over the long run.

Fourth, urban political autonomy enabled entrepreneurs to avoid being crushed by taxes and regulations imposed by central governments. The will of urban capitalists to generate profits was complemented by their capacity to retain substantial portions of what they accumulated.

Fifth, although a driving force in Europe as elsewhere was the self-interest of individuals and families, a large and growing role was played by institutions whose organizing principle transcended individualism and kin loyalties. Examples were artisans' guilds, joint-stock trading companies, and banking houses. Once established they could grow, taking advantage of economies of scale in ways not open to individual or family enterprises. They could also extend their territorial scope, competing effectively with enterprises elsewhere whose outreach and personnel recruitment policies were limited by dependence upon kinship.

Sixth, people engaged in making a profit—from artisans and tinkers to traders, industrialists, and bankers—were not relegated to inferior status. Skilled manual labor and the drive for material possessions were respectable. The stratification system was sufficiently flexible that ambitious persons from lower-class backgrounds could move upward, spending wealth to acquire higher status.[47]

Western Europe's merchants favored overseas exploration as opening up additional sources of profit. Lands distant from Europe were especially attractive if they produced commodities unavailable at home. The will to reach beyond Europe was coupled with capacity to do so, especially through joint-stock companies whose capital assets were pooled from many private investors. The autonomy capitalist institutions enjoyed gave them latitude to act overseas on their own and with their own interests uppermost in mind rather than as agents of a metropolitan government.[48] The trade frontiers along which they operated might coincide with the political boundaries of empire. But they need not. During phase 1 they extended well beyond de facto political frontiers in such diverse places as Canada, Brazil, India, the West African coast, and the Dutch East Indies.

Religious Sector: Euro-Christian Missionary Agencies

Christianity was an enormously important cultural unifier in western Europe,[49] even after the Protestant Reformation ended the Roman Catholic Church's virtual monopoly of religious life. For one thing, Catholicism retained widespread support. Three of the five phase 1 imperial powers were officially Catholic, and a substantial Catholic population lived in England and Holland long after rulers there broke with the papacy. For another, Protestant reformers, whether they retained much of the Catholic liturgy (as in the Church of England) or rejected the old tenets and rituals (as in the more radical dissenting sects), could never fully disentangle themselves from Rome. The Protestant/Catholic divide added an element of competition to overseas initiatives—but it should not obscure beliefs and practices that made western Europe, on balance, remarkably homogenous in religious terms.

Christianity is an institutionalized religion whose governance structures are separate from those of secular political authority. Even when European governments formally adhered to a branch of the faith and had a say in promotion to top ecclesiastical posts within their borders, religious structures maintained autonomy from the state. The Roman church's autonomy was aided by several factors: its universalistic (catholic) claims; a historical pedigree far more ancient than any European government; a centralized, transnational bureaucracy; recognition by late medieval and early modern national legislatures of the clergy as a separate corporate estate; and location of the Papal See in Rome, far from the emerging centers of European power and an autonomous polity in its own right. Most Protestant sects enjoyed independence from government control for a quite different reason: a high degree of self-government at the local congregational level. Whether autonomy was derived from suprastate centralization or substate decentralization, the freedom Europe's Christian institutions enjoyed gave them leeway to set their foreign agenda and act on it.

The agenda always had an outward-oriented dimension, for Jesus directed his followers to "go out to all the world" and convey the Good News. His command took institutional form in denominational agencies specializing in conversion: for example, Jesuits, Franciscans, Augustinians, and White Fathers for Catholics, the Church Missionary Society for Anglicans, the English Baptist Mission, and so forth. Mission agencies were headquartered in Europe and found recruits there to send forth with instructions to report on what they accomplished. European soldiers, administrators, merchants, and settlers did convert the occasional individual to Christianity. But the vast bulk of the work was done by missionaries because their reason for being where they were was to persuade others to replace false beliefs with true ones. This motive being separate from political control—though not necessarily incompatible with it—mission agencies had strong reasons to set up distant outposts regardless of whether a colonial regime was in place there. What Alistair Hennessy calls "the mission frontier" extended well beyond de facto political frontiers in Canada, Brazil, and Paraguay in phase 1 and in many parts of Africa in phase 3.[50] The parallel with the overseas ventures of European capitalists is obvious.

It is one thing for European Christians to want to convert people to their faith. It is quite another to think of the faith as distinctly European, a factor setting the region apart from and above other parts of the world. Yet several developments converged to produce just this way of thinking, with the result that missionaries consciously spread the gospel of European civilization as well as of personal salvation. In this respect they served, deliberately or unconsciously, as advance agents of regional aggression.

In its early years Christianity could not possibly have been identified as a west European cultural artifact. It originated, after all, in Western Asia, spread north to Armenia, south to Abyssinia, and southeast to Mesopotamia and India as well as to the Mediterranean basin. Conversion of Europe's northern areas to Roman Catholicism was not completed until the fourteenth century. But ways of thinking began to change with the rise of Islam, which severed or severely frayed links between Catholics and non-European Christians. The initial wave of Arab conquests led many Western Asian and North African Christians to convert to the new faith. It isolated Christian communities in Asia and Africa (Nestorians and Monophysites, for example) from those living north of the Mediterranean. Subsequent advances of Seljuk and then Ottoman Turks into Asia Minor challenged the Eastern Roman (Greek Orthodox) Church, official faith of the Byzantine Empire. This branch of Christianity was dealt a tremendous blow in 1453 with the capture of the imperial capital, Constantinople.

Largely because of Islam's rise, inhabitants of western Eurasia began to think of themselves as having a shared European identity. The first use of the term "European" has been traced to the Battle of Tours in A.D. 732, when Romano-Gallic and so-called barbarian armies came together to defeat Muslim forces invading France.[51] Because the challenge was religious as well as political and military, Europeans came to regard their regional identity as intimately connected to their faith. The origins of this subjective change long preceded phase 1, being traceable to the Arab conquest of the Holy Land and invasion of Iberia. What was new about the early years of phase 1 was the Islamic challenge's next round under Turkish leadership. Ottoman advances through the Balkans and into central Europe led people living close to the Atlantic to perceive western Europe as the cultural heartland of the entire continent. With the fall of Constantinople Roman Catholics saw themselves as the only Christians left to combat the infidel. Pope Pius II, who took office five years after Constantinople's fall, was a leading proponent of the idea that Europe was a single entity unified by its Roman Catholic faith.[52] Increasingly the broad, pre-Ottoman category of Christian Europe was displaced by a narrower Roman Catholic western Europe.

The Ottoman Turks' role in spreading Islam made that faith more cosmopolitan because no longer could it be seen as the ethnic property, so to speak, of Arabs who originated and initially spread it. Paradoxically, the Ottomans made Christianity *less* cosmopolitan by further reducing the already limited contact among Christians on different sides of Muslim-controlled lands. Roman Catholics in early phase 1 had a vague sense that Christian communities existed south and east of the line, an awareness expressed in the myth of Prester John. But the myth's appeal lay precisely in the absence of hard evidence to support it. Even if Prester John existed, Catholics could not assume the priest-king would reach out to find them. It was they who had to take the initiative to locate him and form a grand anti-Islamic alliance. An idea one may term Euro-Christianity gradually took shape: if the faith was to flourish, Europeans had to shoulder the responsibility for going out to all the world.

The reality of Ottoman military power, coupled with knowledge of a wider world conveyed by explorers, persuaded fifteenth-century Europeans that it was time to change strategy and tactics from crusading days. The earlier goal had been to conquer the Holy Land. Conversion was an incidental aim because Crusaders were realistic: even if defeated on the battlefield, Muslims were not going to become Christians. The new goal was to bypass the Holy Land and place top priority on converting pagans in areas far from it. The task was assigned not to warriors but to missionaries. If Christians could not control sites central to their faith, they could compensate (and retaliate) by mounting conversion campaigns elsewhere.[53] The prospect of finding non-Muslims in other regions was appealing, as they would be less inclined than Muslims to reject the Good News out of hand. This proselytizing impulse, seen in the despatch of friars to the Mongol court in the thirteenth century, became pronounced in the fifteenth and sixteenth centuries. Changing attitudes took institutional form with creation of the Jesuit order (in 1540) and redirection of the Franciscan and Dominican orders toward overseas work.

Adding impetus to this new approach was the conquest of Granada. Religious zeal generated in the final round of the long crusade to retake Iberia was there to be tapped and redirected at the very moment Spain's rulers decided to sponsor a major overseas venture. One can see this clearly in the selection from Columbus's log cited earlier.

To summarize, several features of western Europe made it a distinct, relatively homogeneous, integrated regional system. Its political life was organized around territorially bounded states, its economic life around urban-based private actors seeking and recycling profit, its religious life around versions of Christianity grounded in Roman Catholicism. Regionwide sectoral activity was institutionalized in the Middle Ages but became even more so from phase 1 onward with the centralization and bureaucratization of state structures, increased use of joint-stock corporations to amass and invest capital, and formation of specialized mission agencies. All three sectors had the organizational capacity to project themselves overseas while retaining control of operations from region-based headquarters.

Europe's private profit and religious sectors were relatively autonomous from its state structures. Autonomy was aided by separate institutions and by a widely held view that each sector could perform its specialized functions best when given a large measure of freedom. The sequence of European political development was crucial in making sectoral autonomy possible. The politically fragmented feudal era that followed Rome's collapse was conducive to the rise of capitalism; the earlier concentration of power under Rome and Emperor Constantine's conversion were conducive and perhaps necessary conditions for Christianity's spread. Because capitalism and Christianity took root before modern states were formed, they could protect themselves from autocratic state builders and limit the scope and arbitrariness of public sector power. Geographic factors were also important. Capitalism was based in urban centers considerably smaller than the states into which cities were eventually incorporated. The Roman Catholic Church had a hierarchy and base of believers far more extensive than any one state. Many denominations formed from the Protestant Reformation stressed local congregational self-government. Whether the key sectoral unit was smaller or larger than the state, the fact that it did not coincide with state boundaries helped insulate it from political control.

Sectoral autonomy meant that states were not the only actors able to assert themselves abroad and that nongovernment agencies could act without waiting for home governments to approve what they proposed. The fact that many kinds of institutions operated overseas, with varying but complementary goals in mind, gave

Europeans a wide range of options for penetrating and influencing other societies (see chapter 10).

A high capacity for overseas initiatives was complemented by will. Political control, commercial gain, conversion—all could be achieved by looking abroad. At the outset of phase 1 the image of the Great Khan attracted rulers and merchants, while the image of Prester John attracted rulers and supporters of Christianity's global mission. These myths did not correspond to reality. But their allure helped shape the way the modern world emerged.

The features discussed here have sufficiently broad geographic range to apply to all eight metropoles. Are they sufficiently narrow temporally to distinguish between western Europe before phase 1 and afterward? If one focuses on capitalism the answer is a qualified no. Its orientation and urban base were in place well before the fifteenth century, but its reliance on corporate structures to accumulate and recycle profit accelerated after that time. With Christianity the answer is a qualified yes. Its institutional and ideological roots were obviously premodern. But the way its adherents associated region with religion—what I term Euro-Christianity—was a response to Ottoman advances early in phase 1. And the emergence of specialized missionary agencies is a feature of the imperial era. Emergence of the modern state coincides most clearly with the early years of phase 1. Empire building depended on state building, in that small feudal principalities had insufficient resources to administer colonies. The point is not that all three sectors changed radically in the fifteenth century but that when the public sector was finally ready to act the other two sectors were ready as well. The triple assault could then be launched.

The political dominance of several European states becomes more understandable in the context of multisectoral activity based in an entire region.

A revealing indicator of regional identity is the willingness of individuals born in one part of Europe to work for "foreign" sponsors. One sees this in the Ceuta expedition. Ferdinand Magellan was born in Portugal and claimed the Philippines for Spain. Italian-born explorers found sponsors where they could, Columbus visiting royal courts in France and England before winning support from Ferdinand and Isabella. Amerigo Vespucci and Giovanni da Verrazzano worked for Spanish monarchs, John Cabot (Giovanni Caboto) for England. So many Venetians did early exploratory work for Spain off the South American coast that Venezuela (Little Venice) was named for them. The Englishman Henry Hudson came upon the river named after him while reporting to the Dutch East India Company. The Bavarian count Prince Rupert was an architect of the Hudson Bay Company. In phase 3 Italian-born Savorgnan de Brazza worked for France, Welsh-born Henry Morton Stanley for Belgium's Leopold II. The German explorers Heinrich Barth and Carl Weiss helped Britain and Portugal, respectively. Recruitment of Catholic missionaries shows another form of cosmopolitanism. Father Eusebio Kino, for example, a pioneer in northern New Spain, was born in the Tyrolean Alps.

Nothing confirmed identification with one's continent so much as leaving it. People describing themselves as French, English, or German at home became Europeans abroad. In Camoëns's *Lusiads,* commonly seen as an ardent patriot's tribute to Portugal, Vasco da Gama is asked by the ruler of Malindi where he comes from. "We hail from the proud continent of Europe," the explorer replies. He goes on to give his African host a detailed description of European geography.[54]

Over a long time lines of causation become very complex and may indeed be circular. Such was the case with imperialism. The convergence of state building, urban capitalism, and Euro-Christianity was conducive to expansion. But the reverse was also true. Resources extracted from colonies were available for state building at home; profits accumulated overseas were available for recycling in later rounds of domestic private investment; ready access to raw materials from colonial plantations and mines facilitated the Industrial Revolution; opportunities for mass conversion overseas helped revitalize Christianity in Europe, substituting forward-looking, positive goals for the earlier defensive aim of halting Islam. Once circular causality came into play, powerful forces sustained patterns of dominance that were fast becoming the status quo.

A CROSS-CULTURAL COMPARISON

If these features of modern Europe are found in other societies that might have established overseas empires but did not, the argument that they were conducive to empire is spatially overstretched and hence weakened. If the features were absent or less strongly felt elsewhere, the argument is strengthened. A brief look at the two peoples most likely to have competed successfully for global dominance—the Arabs and the Chinese—supports the argument.[55]

Arabs and Europeans alike followed missionary religions and had active private profit sectors with merchants traveling far afield. But the polities Arabs founded during their initial drive into the Fertile Crescent and across North Africa seem to have been weaker and less internally stable than states emerging in modern western Europe. On the one hand, suprastate constraints on sovereignty were set by incorporation into overarching political-religious structures: the Umayyad and Abbasid caliphates, later the Ottoman sultanate. On the other hand, rulers of many Islamic polities found it difficult if not impossible to control nomadic peoples in their domains' vast, dry hinterlands.[56] Effective governance was more elusive than in Europe, where the population consisted mainly of sedentary agriculturalists. The daunting challenge of subjecting urbanites and pastoralists to common bureaucratic structures left few resources and limited energy for administering territories elsewhere.

Arab long-distance trade was less hierarchically structured and metropole centered than trade patterns Europeans devised. Many Arab merchants set out on their own or joined sea voyages or caravans. They were not employed by firms headquartered in the Arabian peninsula, Egypt, or Fertile Crescent. The Islamic world did not have its Dutch or English East India Company. Less able than Europeans to accumulate gains from physically dispersed activities in one place, the Arab private profit sector was less able to place profits at the disposal of governments.

The religious sector offers an additional contrast. Islam's initial advance was simultaneously the expansion of Arab-speaking conquerors. But expansion was of a people on the move, not of a defined home state dispatching soldiers, bureaucrats, and settlers to implement an ambitious foreign agenda. The closest Arab equivalent to European metropoles was the administratively decentralized Umayyad and Abbasid caliphates. But even this (somewhat forced) parallel disappeared with the decline of the Baghdad-based Abbasids in the tenth century and their decisive defeat by Mongol/Turkic forces in 1258. The rise of the Ottoman Empire, in many areas at the expense of Arab elites, hastened the decoupling of Islam from its Arab progenitors. Moreover, in the eastern edges of the Muslim world the original Muslim dynasties were not Arab. Facing Mecca in prayer had everything to do with a transcendent faith and nothing to do with acknowledging Arab ethnic superiority, much less Arab political hegemony.

The cosmopolitan trend in Islam reversed the tendency toward parochial association of region with religion that I have called Euro-Christianity. Both religions spread, each in keeping with its proselytizing mission. But over time Christianity became linked to the political project of one region, whereas Islam became increasingly disconnected from any particular region or people.

The conversion imperative took different institutional forms in the two religions. Heavy Christian reliance on missionary bodies permitted monitoring and control of operations from mission headquarters in Europe. With Islam, conversion was more the responsibility of specialists in nonreligious activities ranging from warriors to merchants. Islam did not generate orders like the Jesuits, White Fathers, or Church Missionary Society whose primary task was converting unbelievers. Its spread during and after phase 1 was a more diffuse, decentralized operation, with pressures for reform and mass conversion often coming from areas distant from the Arabian core zone. In the absence of missionary agencies based in a distant state, Muslims had no reason to take the promotion of that state's interests as their moral responsibility. What Cardinal Lavigerie said of the White Fathers—"We also work for France"—had no parallel in the Islamic world.

The Chinese empire had impressive, centralized, respected public sector institutions during the Ming (1368–1644) and Ch'ing (1644–1911) dynastic eras spanning the centuries of European advance. Yet the very strength and historical continuity of these institutions may have hampered emergence of a private profit sector with the autonomy, social status, and incentives to stimulate growth at home and sponsor extensive activities beyond China's borders. The imperial bureaucracy was recruited largely from local landowning elements, and its revenues were derived primarily from agriculture. With its vast territory and agrarian fiscal base, China's central government had less incentive than rulers of smaller, ocean-oriented polities like Portugal and England to seek additional revenues from abroad. Cities lacked the degree of insulation from imperial control they enjoyed in feudal Europe. For these reasons, groups that led the drive for development in western Europe—urban-based artisans, traders, financiers, and manufacturers—played a more peripheral role politically and economically in China.

China's religious sector was integrated with the public sector through the practice of staffing the bureaucracy with scholars trained in the Confucian classics. None of the religions practiced in China had a hierarchical structure or degree of autonomy from state control equivalent to that of the Roman Catholic Church. Neither was there a strong will to go abroad. Confucian doctrines did not call for conversion of unbelievers elsewhere. If anything, Confucianism was a civil religion, supporting a domestic social and political order that was considered unique—and clearly superior to other societies. Uniqueness was a reason to stay home, not to reach out.

Joseph Levenson draws the contrast in these words:

> From the point of normative Confucianism, wedded to culture and history and antimessianic to the core, the barbarians are always with us. From the point of view of normative Christianity, transcending culture and history . . . the pagans are not always with us; let missionaries go overseas, seek them out, convert them. The "Kingdom of God" was nowhere in the world. But the "Middle Kingdom," the point of balanced perfection in the world, under Heaven, was at home. Whatever it was that sent Chinese into Southeast Asia before the Portuguese ever got there, it had nothing to do with any pretensions to bearing out a Word.[57]

Subordination of the private profit and religious sectors to an inwardly directed public sector meant that people who in Europe had opportunities and incentives to go overseas, on their own or in cooperation with government, in China stayed home.

The contrast may be traced to patterns of overland migration and conquest preceding phase 1. The Roman Empire was the closest European parallel to the Chinese in territorial scope and the belief that it was a center of civilization. But the Roman *imperium* was broken into fragments by invaders, giving urban capitalists and the Roman Catholic Church the political space to develop largely on their own in the millennium after the fall. China also experienced invasion. But the Mongols, instead of fragmenting China as the Huns, Vandals, Goths, and others did to the Roman domains, ruled it as a component of their vast Eurasian empire. China emerged from invasion and conquest an intact polity, with a government strong enough to limit the autonomous development of urban mercantile and religious institutions.

Ironically, the invasions which destroyed western Eurasia's greatest empire laid the foundations for new rounds of empire building centuries later. The Mongol invasion, by failing to dismantle eastern Eurasia's greatest empire, reinforced Chinese tendencies to avoid overseas involvement.

In brief, Arabs and Europeans possessed an outward-looking private profit sector and a missionary religion. But compared to western Europe, Arab states were weak and Arab economic and religious activities less institutionalized and more cosmopolitan. China and western Europe were similar in that their people lived under relatively centralized bureaucratic structures. But compared to western Europe, China's private profit and religious sectors were less autonomous and less institutionalized. To the extent that China had an official religion, its message was that adherents should stay home. Taken together, these factors point to substantial differences between Europeans and the other two societies in the capacity and will of sectoral institutions to exert influence overseas. Evidence from crucial non-European cases thus supports the argument being advanced.

The separation of public, private profit, and religious sector institutions in western Europe was instrumental in placing limits on the arbitrary exercise of power by state rulers. One consequence of a distinctive regional pattern of sectoral relations was enhanced prospects for constitutional regimes respecting individual and group liberties. This same sectoral pattern had quite different, indeed opposite, consequences abroad. There, the triple sectoral assault facilitated formation of empires whose agents had substantial latitude arbitrarily to restrict the liberties of non-European peoples. Institutions conducive to a politically liberal order in one part of the world were the instruments of authoritarian control elsewhere.

9
Western Europe as a System of Competing States

Imperial expansion was driven not only by features widely shared throughout western Europe but also by the region's deep divisions. Europe was fragmented into states, each of which felt insecure because it was embedded in a larger system of units much like itself.[1] Each state claimed sovereignty, the legal and moral authority to steer its own course. Yet the system guaranteed continual threats and limits to sovereignty. Not even the most powerful state was sufficiently dominant to be confident that it would not be invaded or blockaded by some combination of its neighbors. Alliances forged with other states in the past could not be counted upon in future crises, when the alignment of international forces and interests might be changed. The interstate system was fluid and anarchic. It lacked overarching institutions to ensure that the regional status quo would be maintained or that disputes among member states would be peacefully adjudicated.

Insecurity caused by the dispersal of political power within a single economic and cultural system generated enormous amounts of nervous energy. Much of this energy was recycled within the region. Preparing for defensive or offensive war against a nearby foe, waging war, recovering from it, and financing its unexpectedly heavy costs—these have historically been the principal challenges facing European rulers. Indeed, state building was more likely driven by the need to counter external threats than by rulers' desires to repress or coopt domestic challengers. By one estimate, during the past seven centuries between 70 and 90 percent of European states' financial resources were deployed to prevent or fight wars among themselves.[2]

At first glance these expensive, destructive efforts to cope with the region's problems seem at odds with initiatives elsewhere. In several respects, however, Europe's political disunity was conducive to imperialism. First, the security problems all states faced gave them strong incentives to adopt new military technologies. From the medieval period to the present a steady stream of innovations profoundly altered the way defensive and offensive warfare was waged.[3] Fully as important as the invention of new weapons and ways of organizing armed forces was the rapid diffusion of these innovations throughout Europe.[4] Innovation gave the first user a military advantage. Diffusion had the opposite effect, tending to equalize armies' capacity to withstand each other's attacks. As Europeans traveled overseas they brought weapons employed in intra-European wars, including ones developed by other states. Empire builders from several countries thus enjoyed a marked military advantage, one they did not hesitate to put to use. The very process that tended to equalize armies within the region increased the military gap between soldiers from that region and soldiers outside it.

As Europeans became more aware of distant lands, overseas aggression became attractive as a way of easing, though never ultimately resolving, a metropole's security dilemma. The cost of surviving as a state within the European system increased dramatically over time as rulers felt obliged to replace small ad hoc forces with large standing armies equipped with the most advanced weapons. If revenue a colony generated for a metropole's government exceeded the cost of setting up and maintaining a colonial administration, the net gain could help finance wars fought on European soil. Moreover, revenue from overseas sources reduced pressures to extract funds internally. Rulers knew that increases in domestic taxes might trigger unrest or outright revolt among their subjects. Repressing these challenges was politically risky, both in its own right and because it diverted resources from defense. The revenue-raising imperative, driven by military insecurity, encouraged European rulers to seek lucrative possessions abroad.

The same factors led them to articulate mercantilist doctrines justifying empire. The model in this respect was phase 1 Spain, whose Habsburg rulers used New World bullion to finance numerous wars throughout western Europe. The search for a comparable source of readily accessible wealth lay behind exploration and settlement by Spain's rivals. The Jamestown settlement (1607), for example, was sponsored by the Virginia Company of London, whose shareholders "had invested their capital in the hope that the English could duplicate the remarkable success of the Spanish and Portuguese in Mexico, Peru, and Brazil."[5] Profits accruing to Portugal from the Indian Ocean and Spice Islands encouraged the Dutch to become involved. The influential tract by Hugo Grotius entitled *The Freedom of the Seas* (1608), though phrased in the universalistic language of natural law, was in fact an argument for Holland's interests against Portugal's monopolistic claims. The essay's subtitle spells out the jurist's purposes: "The Right Which Belongs to the Dutch to Take Part in the East Indian Trade."

Interstate competition also stimulated imperialism by increasing the stakes of engaging in conquest. When one state advanced an overseas claim it typically did not know whether the gains it expected or desired would be realized. But whatever they might turn out to be, they were in effect doubled by the fact that the state's rivals were deprived of access to them. Conversely, if a state did not act when rivals were making overseas claims it risked a double loss: deprivation of potentially valuable resources and the expense of fending off a rival strengthened by access to them. Empire building was a competitive process driven as much by anxiety over loss as by hope of gain. Referring to inter-European rivalries in Asia in phase 1, David Fieldhouse notes that "fear of exclusion generated aggression which ambition might not have done."[6] A similar dynamic was at work in phase 3 when Cecil Rhodes lobbied to place the Tswana under British South Africa Company protection to forestall direct territorial links between Germany's colony in South West Africa and the independent Boer republics.[7]

Interstate competition accelerated the pace of overseas activity, leading at times to scrambles for territory whose dynamics resemble a spiraling arms race. If state A has no rival it may take its time deciding whether to expand. But if A fears that a rival, B, also covets overseas territory, A is likely to give the issue higher priority and treat it with greater urgency. The presence of additional rivals C, D, and E only increases pressure to act quickly to preempt similarly preemptive action by others. The existence of many states in Europe explains why expansion proceeded in spurts, several empires growing simultaneously as each metropole responded to the real or imagined overseas initiatives of rival neighbors.

In such a situation it is not enough for A's citizens to exercise informal influence overseas, for example, through trade or missionary work in an area unclaimed by an outside power. Influence A's citizens exert there must be translated into formal power by A's government lest takeover of the area by B lead to replacement of A's traders and missionaries by those from B. Referring to the late nineteenth-century scramble, William Langer notes that Britain's needs for new markets and investment opportunities "had been met in the past without any corresponding expansion of territory. It was the embarkation of France, Germany, and other countries in the course of empire that brought the British to the conviction that only political control could adequately safeguard markets."[8]

A scramble may prompt prominent actors in A's private profit and religious sectors who have been operating overseas on their own to change their tune, calling upon the home government to guarantee their future operations by advancing imperial claims.[9] When externally generated competition for territory activates domestically based sectoral actors to become pressure groups for expansion, A's government is pushed in an aggressive direction from within its borders as well as outside them.

Once a scramble gets under way it can take on a life of its own, driven by the growing sense of insecurity each party feels should it fail to assert itself as vigorously and quickly as possible. Decision makers adopt a zero-sum mentality, reasoning that if their country does not win today it will be counted tomorrow among the losers. This view was well expressed by Premier Jules Ferry, the architect of French imperialism in the late phase 3 scramble. In a speech to the Chambre des Députés in 1885 Ferry declaimed,

> In the contemporary reality of Europe, in this competition among so many rivals that we see ever-intensifying around us . . . a policy of introversion or abstention is nothing more nor less than the road to decadence! Nations in our time only become great by the activity which they generate.
>
> To radiate influence without acting, without involving oneself in the world's affairs, staying aloof from all the various European [diplomatic] combinations, seeing as a trap or misguided adventure all expansion into Africa or the Orient—to live in this manner for a great nation, I tell you, is to give up, and in less time than you would think possible it is to fall from being a first-rate power to the third or fourth rank.[10]

The premier warned, "If the French flag should be withdrawn . . . from Tonkin, Germany or Spain would replace us within the hour."[11]

Rulers may enter the fray out of resentment at rivals' efforts to keep them out of a rapidly globalizing competitive arena. Francis I of France is said to have reacted to the Spanish-Portuguese Treaty of Tordesillas by remarking wryly, "I should very much like to see the clause in Adam's will that excludes me from a share of the world." As the pace of overseas acquisitions accelerates, so does the tendency of competing parties to extend the scope of their activities. Suddenly it seems sensible to include areas previously considered unimportant. A frontier once deemed safe now needs to be protected by another frontier, which in turn has to be protected by a third.[12] The admonition to "Grab now; check later to see if what you took was worth grabbing" rings ever louder in the ears of harried decision makers.

States in a territorial scramble engage in "defensively aggressive" behavior. Actions that from the victims' perspective look unmistakably like aggression are driven from the aggressors' perspective by the opposite motivation: desire for protection against threats to key interests. Objectively powerful actors exert themselves to counteract a subjectively feared *loss* of power and prestige.

This point suggests a more general one. Competition among states in the same system leads each unit continually to compare itself to its rivals. Its sense of self-worth depends greatly on where it believes it is ranked relative to the other units. Imperial expansion can be driven by desire to *reflect* the high standing a state thinks it possesses: Spain, for example, in the sixteenth century, Britain in the nineteenth. But expansion can also be driven by desire to *compensate* for a real or perceived decline in status. A phase 1 example of compensatory imperialism was the arrival in the East Indian islands of well-armed Dutch ships as a result of Spain's decision in the 1590s to exclude Dutch merchants from the Lisbon spice market.[13] Perhaps the clearest phase 3 example was France's burst of activism in Africa and Southeast Asia following defeat in its war with Prussia. Gains in the Sahara or Tonkin might make up for—and momentarily deflect public attention from—the humiliating loss of Alsace and Lorraine. Paul Leroy-Beaulieu, one of France's most ardent imperialists, wrote an article in 1881 urging annexation of Tunisia. Referring to the lost territories, he admitted that "all hopes of forceful revenge are vain dreams in the face of a Germany of 55,000,000 inhabitants." In contrast, "Africa is open."[14] Britain's success at excluding France from Egypt in 1879–82 only fueled the desire of French policy makers to stake ambitious claims elsewhere.

But Britain itself offers a pertinent illustration. Its economic preeminence at the outset of phase 3 permitted it to break with mercantilist doctrine and concentrate on exerting informal influence. Why, then, did it revert later in the nineteenth century to the traditional pattern of claiming territory? A clue is provided by comparing its manufacturing output to the combined total of that of France and Germany (or Germany's predecessor states). The ratio rises dramatically from .28 in 1750 to 1.09 in 1830 to 1.55 in 1860. But after that point it declines—to 1.4 in 1880 and .93 in 1900.[15] The Berlin Conference took place when Britain equaled France + Germany and was starting to fall behind them. Britain's participation in the scramble suggests that its rulers considered formal empire necessary to protect an economic hegemony that its major continental rivals were swiftly undermining.

Another effect of interstate competition is imperial inertia. Once a colony has been established the metropole comes to value it for more than the economic benefits it confers. If in fact the only consideration driving imperialism were narrow cost-benefit calculations, one would expect a metropole to shed possessions whose costs, contrary to expectation or hope at the moment of acquisition, turned out to exceed benefits. Virtually all Germany's colonies fit this description. But governments do not voluntarily abdicate power at home or abroad even if it makes eminent economic sense to do so. At some point colonies become important as symbols of international status. To abandon even one unviable colony might signal to competitors a declining capacity or will to behave assertively and thereby weaken the metropole's international position.

Inertia played a role in late phase 3 expansion into North Africa. British forces invaded Egypt in 1882 at the invitation of its ruler, Khedive Tawfiq, who at the time faced serious domestic threats to his authority. Tawfiq expected the British to depart after they had imposed order, and the London government itself initially assumed it was carrying out a brief rescue and retire mission. But once in place as de facto rulers the British refused to leave even though they repeatedly assured others they would.

France was particularly upset at Britain's refusal to leave a country—and a canal—in which substantial French funds had been invested. The Marchand expedition that reached Fashoda in 1898 deliberately challenged British control of the Upper Nile. London's determination to stand firm, coupled with some embarrassment over its unwillingness to honor its promises to leave, led to the Anglo-French Entente of 1904. In exchange for French recognition of British primacy in Egypt, Britain supported France's plans to intervene in Moroccan affairs. Imperial inertia in one territory thus contributed to imperial advance in another.

Interstate competition assumed its most dramatic form when two or more states scrambled for new lands, as in the following examples from phases 1 and 3:

- in the late fifteenth century, when Spain countered Portugal's steady advance around Africa toward India by supporting Columbus's proposal to reach Asia by an alternative route. Rival claims of Portugal and Spain following Columbus's first voyage were only temporarily resolved by the Tordesillas Treaty of 1494 dividing the non-European world between them;
- in the late sixteenth and seventeenth centuries, when England and Holland challenged the Iberian powers and each other, producing new settlements in North and South America, South Africa, and Java;
- in the eighteenth century, when England and France penetrated the interiors of North America and India in a duel for global hegemony;
- in the late nineteenth century, when newly formed states joined the original phase 1 metropoles in occupying territory in Africa, Southeast Asia, and Oceania.

Sometimes a scramble was triggered by a state's entry into the imperial game: Spain in the first example, England and Holland in the second, Germany in the fourth. The assertive newcomer's presence elicited defensively aggressive responses by others. Sometimes competition was played out far from the area where it began. The Tordesillas line, though initially drawn with the New World and Africa in mind, girdled the earth, leading Spain and Portugal to vie in the early sixteenth century for spice-rich islands off Asia's southeast coast close to where the line supposedly passed.

In the first and fourth examples the scramble proceeded with little or no violence among metropoles. Indeed, the papal bulls preceding Tordesillas and the Berlin Conference some four centuries later can be seen as efforts to create an overarching framework for interstate conflict resolution. By contrast, in the second and third examples warfare was the order of the day both in Europe and overseas. But the underlying competitive dynamic was similar in all four examples, whether or not it took the form of war.

After the Protestant Reformation created a permanent schism in Euro-Christianity, rivalry between two states on grounds unrelated to religion assumed greater intensity if one was officially Protestant and the other officially Catholic. This factor was operative when England and Holland encountered Spain in the New World in phase 1.[16] Dutch-Spanish rivalry was especially fierce because of the eighty years' war the Dutch fought to rid themselves of Habsburg rule. Dutch leaders were products of the Reformation; Habsburg rulers took the lead in the Counter Reformation. Religious rivalry played a more muted but not insignificant role in British-French struggles during the eighteenth century and in their phase 3 contest for preeminence in Madagascar and Uganda. In these instances forces fragmenting Europe along religious as well as political lines were at work. When domestic mobilization of support for expansion involved two sectors, it enhanced institutional capacity in both sectors and ensured more intense popular support for a metropole's foreign policy.

Europe's interstate system was unlike that in the Islamic world and in East Asia. The close proximity of many units within a small, self-contained area is the geographical basis both for the system's unifying features and for its disunity. By contrast, Islamic states established by Arabs and other peoples stretched for thousands of miles along an east-west axis from Morocco through the East Indies. Physical dispersion did not permit a dense network of continuous interaction, either cooperative or hostile, among polities sharing the same faith.

For most of the past two millennia the Chinese have not experienced the tension between cultural unity and political fragmentation that was such a distinctive feature of Europe. Rather, culture and politics reinforced each other to create a unit, the Middle Kingdom, considered the epicenter of civilized life. Polities around it, including Japan, were deemed inferior. Devising regular diplomatic interactions among neighbors on the basis of the sovereignty each possessed was not an option because the very idea assumed an equality of status rejected by the reigning ideology. The Chinese emperor was not just another ruler but the Son of Heaven, the link between humans and the cosmos.[17]

Had China been fragmented into two or more states during the past five centuries, as was the case earlier, it is conceivable that these units would have come to accept competition among themselves and other neighbor states as the norm. They might have vented shared insecurities by launching rival overseas expeditions. But this was not to be. Following Cheng Ho's voyages the Ming and then Ch'ing imperial dynasties adopted a far less activist course in foreign policy. The court valued occasions when envoys of other polities arrived, bearing tribute and acknowledging inferior status by kowtowing. The ideal relationship was one in which the world outside the Middle Kingdom made its respectful way to the imperial capital. To reverse the procedure by dispatching emissaries abroad on a mission to change the rest of the world would be unseemly and undignified.

That the west European pattern of intense competition among polities comprising a single economic and cultural system was not replicated in either the Arab/ Islamic or Chinese cases supports the proposition that interstate rivalry played a key role in the formation of European empires.

SPECIFIC METROPOLES

Refocusing the zoom lens on units smaller than an entire region, namely, countries that became metropoles, one sees that each had a distinctive profile. This was a composite of its location, size, population, ethnic and religious mix, natural resources, level and rate of economic development, social structure, political institutions, key historical events, and so forth. Each metropole's empire was also unique, unlike others in the timing and circumstances of its formation, its duration, size, number and location of colonies, roles played by settlers, and so on. A metropole's special characteristics shaped the kind of empire it governed. But because I am interested not in any one empire but in the process of parallel empire building by several states, the question is how features marking one metropole off from others shed light on the larger phenomenon of European dominance. One answer is that innovative or unusual activities on the part of one metropole were noted and then emulated by rivals. Europe was in effect a learning laboratory in which a variety of experiments in techniques of overseas domination was performed, with results diffused throughout the region.

Portugal

Portugal's most distinctive feature was its role as precedent setter. Indeed, in the three-quarters of a century between the conquest of Ceuta and the Spanish monarchs' sponsorship of Columbus's voyage, Portugal was the only European country whose rulers were serious about long-distance maritime initiatives. Its location— close to Africa and the Mediterranean basin, yet with a coastline facing westward— gave it a head start. Its explorers showed how Europeans could reach the fabled lands of Asia and profit from direct access to its spices, precious stones, and textiles. Portugal pioneered in demonstrating the military potential of highly mobile sailing ships armed with guns. Projection of Portuguese power into the Indian Ocean basin was marked by strong anti-Muslim sentiments, doubtless influenced by centuries of struggle to expel Muslim rulers from the home country. Portugal's early successes showed what can happen when political and commercial motives are reinforced by religious ones. The first empire builder taught others the synergistic effects of the triple assault.

Within a century of the conquest of Ceuta, Portugal had enclaves in the New World as well as in Africa and Asia. A European country became, with surprising ease and speed, literally a world power. That a small, relatively weak polity was able to accomplish so much virtually invited more powerful European states to emulate it, in the reasonable expectation that deploying more resources would produce even more spectacular results. Had a major state set the imperial precedent, smaller states might not have joined in. Because a small state took the lead, the system in which it was embedded ensured that larger states would follow suit.

Portugal offers the first instance of compensatory imperialism. Overseas expansion bolstered its otherwise marginal position within Europe, enhanced national identity and pride, and imbued a tiny country with a spirit of global mission. But the impressively wide range of Portugal's holdings could not hide the reality of military and economic weakness, dramatized by its inability to avoid being incorporated into Spain from 1580 to 1640. That period aside, Portuguese rulers tried to protect a vulnerable independence by forming an alliance with England. As the phase 3 scramble for Africa accelerated, the British were willing to support Portuguese claims to the interior of Angola and Mozambique provided their own Cape-to-Cairo ambitions were not thwarted. Portugal remained an imperial actor longer than might have been expected by playing the game of European balance-of-power politics. Indeed, in some respects it became a client of the regional system's most powerful member. Portugal showed how, through diplomacy, a state could operate within the region to effect gains outside it.

Spain

Spain's first great contribution to the European imperial project was, of course, sponsorship of the epic voyage that made the Old World aware of the New. Spain enjoyed the advantage over Portugal of direct access to both the Atlantic and the Mediterranean. Having extensive political responsibilities in Italy, Spain's rulers were ideally placed to facilitate transfers of Mediterranean knowledge and technology to the wider world of the Atlantic. Columbus's life dramatically illustrates this lateral transfer. The Spanish capitalized on the Genoese explorer's findings by concentrating on the Americas. Their pioneering work led other metropoles to focus attention on the New World during phase 1.

A second accomplishment was to demonstrate that a small number of highly disciplined European soldiers mounted on horses and armed with guns could defeat vastly larger Amerindian forces. Conquest of the Aztec and Inca empires by troops led by Cortés and Pizarro ranks among the decisive events in world history. Yet these triumphs were also among history's more improbable events. Had the first Spanish invaders been defeated it is by no means clear that Europeans of any nationality could have dominated New World hinterlands as rapidly and decisively as they did. To understand the conquistadors' success one must turn to Spain's history. Owing in part to the prolonged struggle against the Moors that culminated in the defeat of

Granada in 1492, many men were trained in the arts of combat. They expected material gain and enhanced social status from daring military accomplishments. The Americas were a vast arena in which to distinguish themselves for those ends.

Spain showed that colonies could enrich a metropole in the versatile, fungible form of gold and silver. Abundant early evidence from the mines of New Spain and Peru that colonies can pay stimulated other countries to seek new possessions. A motivator in some instances—for example, Sir Walter Raleigh's expedition up the Orinoco River in 1595 and the Jamestown settlement in Virginia—was hope that unexplored lands would likewise yield precious metals.[18] That this expectation usually proved illusory did nothing to undermine its centrality as an incentive driving early expansion. Spanish settlers further demonstrated the economic value of colonies by setting up sugar plantations and cattle ranches, mass producing for export plants and animals initially imported from the Old World. That overseas possessions might profitably produce commodities not native to them was a lesson widely learned.

Spain was the first European power to dispatch large numbers of people to live in its colonies. The settlers' ability to adjust to new environments and in some cases to prosper probably encouraged other phase 1 metropoles to deploy settlers as an integral part of their own New World strategies. The settlers' insistent demand for land and inexpensive non-European labor proved enormously disruptive to indigenous societies. Through the settlers' example, the Spanish empire was the first to demonstrate the will and capacity to transform the economic, social, and demographic environment of other continents.

Spreading the Roman Catholic faith was an integral part of Spain's imperial project and a primary justification for it. Spain's monarchs worked to link state structures with the hierarchy of the Catholic Church at home and abroad. The resulting cross-sector coalition was one reason for their success at undermining indigenous resistance in many areas. Not until the rise of evangelical Protestantism in Britain during phases 2 and 3 did commitment to religious activism figure so prominently in a metropole's overseas agenda.[19]

France

France, by virtue of its location in the heart of western Europe, centralized public sector, and sizable standing army, was the most powerful state on the mainland from the seventeenth through the mid–nineteenth centuries. Given the nature of the interstate system, France's very prominence presented it with an acute security dilemma. But its location and military resources also offered excellent opportunities for overland expansion in several directions. This ambiguous situation led the country's rulers at times to adopt a defensive military posture and at others to attack their neighbors. An understandable preoccupation with diplomatic and military developments in the European region made it unlikely that France's rulers would take the lead in sponsoring overseas ventures. But once the Iberian countries set precedents in this respect and showed that empire could generate material and status benefits, France was fully prepared to follow suit.

In phase 1 the French concentrated on thinly populated North American areas largely neglected by other metropoles. To some extent this resulted from the private actions of fishermen and trappers rather than deliberate state policy. Still, focusing on what became eastern Canada might be termed an instance of emulation by avoidance. Likewise, France acquired enormous chunks of Saharan and Sahelian West Africa during the phase 3 scramble, knowing that much of this desolate land was not desired by its major rivals, Britain and Germany. The tendency to claim large, underpopulated areas not highly valued by other metropoles reflected a certain ambivalence about overseas empire. On the one hand, France wanted possessions whose cumulative size signaled its great-power status. There was also a certain appeal in expanding holdings abroad to compensate for military defeat at home. This factor influenced policy making after Alsace and Lorraine were lost to Germany in 1871. On the other hand, the security problems France faced on its borders prevented it from committing substantial resources to acquire distant holdings.[20] The effect of this ambivalence was that many parts of the world that from a European perspective appeared economically or strategically marginal were acquired by a decidedly non-marginal state. France thus contributed substantially to the globalization of Europe's impact.

Following the French Revolution the country's leaders pioneered the appeal to and manipulation of public opinion for expansionist purposes. An early instance was Napoleon Bonaparte's effort to advance his political ambitions by leading the ill-fated invasion of Egypt in 1798. In 1830 the restored Bourbon monarch, Charles X, facing growing popular opposition, ordered the occupation of Algiers that commenced French rule in North Africa. This initiative, notes Raphael Danziger, "was largely the product of domestic political considerations, primarily the calculation that a spectacular expedition would give the declining Bourbon monarchy enough prestige to defeat the opposition and win the coming election."[21] In the 1880s Premier Ferry tried to rally popular as well as parliamentary support for expansion in Indochina.

Efforts to link popular nationalism with specific imperial goals were not all that successful. At most they produced a temporary surge of interest and pride in the nation's overseas accomplishments. But France demonstrated that democratization was quite compatible with imperialism, a lesson not lost on politicians in other countries like Benjamin Disraeli, Otto von Bismarck, and Joseph Chamberlain. The populist dimension in phase 3 imperialism made leaders of Europe's metropoles more unwilling than ever to risk the public humiliation of backing down once they were committed to an aggressive foreign policy.

Holland

Holland's population was traditionally oriented to waterborne trade. Several rivers flow into the North Sea in Holland, and it is close to the British Isles and the passage to the Baltic Sea. During the first half of the seventeenth century the Netherlands, having large numbers of technically advanced, skillfully manned ships at its disposal, played a critically important role as integrator of the world economy. "The Dutch maritime zone," writes Jonathan Israel, "moved to the top of the global hierarchy of exchanges, emerging as the hub of what was now definitely a 'mono-nuclear' system, the first and, for most of early modern times, the only true world entrepôt."[22] This achievement was all the more impressive considering the territory's small size and population and the fact that for much of the period its people were fighting for independence from Habsburg Spain. The unusually efficient institutions the Dutch developed in the private profit sector enabled them to mobilize and gainfully invest resources from other parts of Europe as well as from their own society. The Dutch state, controlled by urban interests specializing in production and international exchange of a wide array of consumer goods, was far less inhibited by the agrarian feudal structures of medieval Europe than Portugal, Spain, and France. The Reformed Protestant faith of Holland's elites sanctioned unabashedly acquisitive behavior. Dutch actions and motivations in phase 1 prefigured those of leading participants in phase 3, when capitalist-led economic growth became a dominant motif in European life.[23]

The Dutch copioneered with the English the classic institutional link between public and private profit sectors: the officially chartered company. The United East India Company (Vereenigde Oost-Indische Compagnie, or voc), established by the Estates General in 1602, was intended to function as a trading enterprise and, if necessary or convenient, as a government. In dealings with Japan the voc was strictly confined by the Tokugawa rulers to trade. But in the East Indies economic transactions went hand in hand with political control backed by force. Jan Pieterszoon Coen, considered the founder of the East Indies empire, wrote in 1614 to the board of directors that trade "must be conducted and maintained under protection and favor of your own weapons and . . . the weapons must be supplied from the profits enjoyed by the trade, so that trade cannot be maintained without war or war without trade."[24] Appointed governor-general three years later, Coen put his philosophy into practice. Inhabitants of the nutmeg-producing Banda Islands were almost wiped out and the islands resettled by others willing to sell their crops solely to voc agents. A company monopoly in cloves was obtained by launching violent attacks on producers in the Moluccas and against all ships serving rival clove traders.[25] The Dutch consolidated political power slowly on Java. But by the end of phase 1 they were recognized as direct or indirect rulers of much of the island.

As these examples illustrate, an important advantage of the chartered company was its tactical flexibility. When faced with effective resistance to its political ambitions, the VOC defined itself as a trading firm and was content to exert informal influence. Externally imposed constraints did not humiliate the Dutch state, for the state was only indirectly involved, its presence buffered by the corporate front it had set up. If indigenous resistance was ineffective, however, the company could proceed to assert control. Areas it governed were transferred to the Dutch state after the VOC was abolished in the war years of phase 2. In large part because of the flexibility it offered, the chartered company model was adopted by other European states. Chartered companies were especially active during the middle years of phase 1 and the latter half of phase 3.[26]

The VOC was widely regarded in its heyday as a cost-conscious, efficient, carefully managed company. But even this paragon of a profit-driven institution was unwilling to rely solely upon market forces. Its founding charter officially designated the VOC a monopoly, the goal being to eliminate competition among Dutch traders in Asia. The idea of negotiating prices with willing sellers was anathema. The belief that market share could be increased and assured by forcibly asserting political control over the market made eminent sense to VOC entrepreneurs. It made sense to the Dutch in phase 3 as well. By ensuring order at the cost of crushing local uprisings, the colonial state helped an efficient plantation system run by Dutch private interests to prosper. The Schumpeterian notion that capitalists are inherently peaceable did not apply to the Dutch in distant lands, where the perils and uncertainties of operating in what seemed like a Hobbesian "war of each against all" were self-evident. If western Europe's most efficient private profit sector relied so heavily upon soldiers and administrators to ensure overseas profits, it is all the more understandable why private entrepreneurs in other European metropoles pressed their governments to take up the imperial cause. The Dutch experience illustrates more clearly than any other the symbiotic relationship between private profit and public sectors in European expansion. Capitalist institutions were driven not by free market ideology but by a persistent tendency to act politically and to call upon state institutions for assistance.

Britain

Britain was inescapably oriented to the sea and hence exceptionally well positioned to enlarge its colonial holdings once the Tudor monarchs had consolidated political control at home. Whereas the military strategies of mainland countries required heavy spending on armies, Britain's best means of defense was to expand and modernize its navy. Once in place a strong navy was far better suited than a large European-based army to claim and defend overseas colonies and to expand trade ties with them.[27] Given the importance of ships for commercial as well as military ends, the British had strong incentives to increase the speed, maneuverability, carrying capacity, safety, and firing range of their vessels. A striking consequence of their numerous technological breakthroughs in the hundred years following the Industrial Revolution's takeoff was a capacity, unrivaled until the 1890s, to rule the waves. A head start in producing ships powered by steam and constructed of iron and steel helped Britain become the preeminent metropole in phase 3. Its mainland neighbors readily adopted Britain's advances in maritime (and overland) transport, giving western Europe as a whole the dramatic technological edge over other regions noted in chapter 5.

A corollary of Britain's position as the world's leading sea power was the tendency of its rulers to feel threatened by—and to want to challenge—the leading land-based power of the day. France held the title during the eighteenth century and Napoleon's reign. Its successor was Russia, which rapidly extended its hold over central and eastern Asia in phase 3. The assertion of British power in the Indian subcontinent can be interpreted in geostrategic terms as a sustained effort to counter advances by these adversaries: the French in phase 1, the Russians in phase 3. Britain's comparative advantage on the high seas was insufficient in and of itself. Land claims in many parts of the world were needed both to ensure naval supremacy and to compensate for its limits.

Millions more people left the British Isles to take permanent residence in a more dispersed set of territories, over a longer period of time, than residents of any other metropole. English-speaking settlers brought with them the institutions and values of representative government that they enjoyed at home. Strongly disposed to political and religious self-rule, they constituted fragments of the metropole with a high potential to break away from it.[28] Over the long run, settlers' insistence on transferring key features of Britain's political system to the colonies undermined metropolitan control. In the short run, however, the restless, almost insatiable demand by settlers for new land was a powerful expansionist force in its own right. Settlers extended imperial frontiers in BNA during phase 1 and in Australia, New Zealand, and Southern Rhodesia during phase 3.

Britain relied on the chartered company mechanism more widely and over a longer time than did Holland. The Virginia Company of London was short-lived (1606–24). But this joint venture of merchant capital and royal authority succeeded in founding, at Jamestown, the New World's first permanent English-speaking settlement. The English East India Company operated as a quasi government over ever-larger areas of India from the 1750s until 1858, when the British government assumed direct control in the aftermath of the Great Mutiny. The Hudson's Bay Company, chartered in 1670, controlled vast tracts of land in Canada until 1867. Late phase 3 expansion in the Niger Valley, along the East African coast, and in what became Southern and Northern Rhodesia was directed by royally chartered companies. Britain is the prime example of sustained collaboration between public and private profit sectors, with the benefits of tactical flexibility and synergistic energy this arrangement yielded. Generous representation of propertied interests in the two houses of Parliament lent itself to the creation and sustenance of a cross-sector coalition.

Britain pioneered mass production of inexpensive, machine-made consumer goods. Its leadership in the first Industrial Revolution had mixed effects, varying over time, on the will of influential economic actors to enlarge the empire. From the early nineteenth century onward British prosperity depended not only on assured access to imported primary products but also on exported manufactures. Hence factory owners joined mercantile and shipping interests in paying close attention to overseas markets. During the early decades of phase 3 British manufactures enjoyed such a competitive edge everywhere that it did not seem necessary for government to provide backup support through territorial claims. Indeed, many in the private profit sector opposed using public funds to acquire new colonies because this would entail higher taxes. But by the 1870s diffusion of industrial technologies to the European mainland and the United States undercut Britain's competitive edge. And the cumulative capacity of all the industrial powers to generate consumer and capital goods began to exceed world demand. Under these more threatening conditions Britain's private profit sector looked more favorably on imperialism. Colonies were valued as ensuring the dual access to raw materials and markets required by an industrial economy.[29]

The British case suggests that while industrialization per se need not generate imperial expansion, rivalry among several simultaneously industrializing countries can easily take the form of a colonial scramble. The world's first overproduction crisis, in the last quarter of the nineteenth century, gave powerful economic impetus to interstate rivalries for new possessions.

Britishers have had unusually diverse religious affiliations. An official Church of England was established in the 1530s in a dramatic break with Rome, yet substantial numbers remained Catholic. A variety of dissenting Protestant sects flourished. The small Jewish population was not persecuted. Religious pluralism significantly influenced British imperial expansion, albeit in varying ways depending on the time period. In phase 1 the government permitted non-Anglicans to found colonies overseas and practice their faith there, provided they acknowledge the authority of

Crown and Parliament. This policy encouraged religious minorities to seek a better life for themselves abroad, in the course of which they extended the frontiers of British power. The role of Puritans, Baptists, Quakers, and Catholics in the formation of Britain's North American colonies is well known.

The faiths most early settlers brought to the New World fostered a sense of separation from—and superiority over—indigenous peoples. Only tangentially were Anglicans, Congregationalists, Baptists, Methodists, and Presbyterians interested in converting Amerindians to Christianity. If anything there were persuasive reasons not to do so because converts might have to be treated with the respect due fellow believers. The early settlers wanted a frontier of exclusion, not of inclusion. Unconverted Indians fit the stereotype of the savage and, as such, were candidates for extermination and expulsion from land the settlers coveted. John Winthrop expressed a widely held view when he rejoiced that "God hath consumed the natives with a miraculous plague, whereby the greater part of the country is left voide of inhabitants."[30]

In this respect early English Protestantism differed from the strong conversionist ethic of the Roman Catholic Church, whose missionary orders were active from the outset in Portuguese, Spanish, and French colonies.[31]

By phase 3, however, British Protestants had become at least as interested in missionary work as western Europe's Catholics. The new orientation was a product of the evangelical movement that began in the late eighteenth century and crested in the late nineteenth. The movement's ambitious initial aims included abolishing the transatlantic slave trade, then slavery throughout the British empire.[32] After Parliament approved these measures, reformers set an even more far-reaching goal: to transform non-European societies. Of particular interest were sub-Saharan Africa, south Asia, and Oceania, deemed malleable because many of their inhabitants adhered to animist religions, were nonliterate, and employed simple technologies. Their societies were to be transfigured by a civilizing package: conversion to Christianity, formal instruction in European learning, abolition of domestic slavery, encouragement of cash-crop production, and adoption of a Victorian-era lifestyle.[33] British Catholics likewise offered the world's benighted souls not just a religion but a religion encased in a way of life. The task was daunting, not least because many of the societies to which missionaries were attracted lay outside the pale of colonial authority.

The work of conversion can proceed on its own. The work of civilizing others, at least as phase 3 British missionaries defined the task, is another matter. Close links between Christianity and commerce—or, in a widely used phrase, between "the Bible and the Plough"[34]—meant that European trading companies were needed to exchange peasant-grown cash crops for imported manufactured goods. Abolishing domestic slavery required the use of force against recalcitrant slaveholders and introduction of a new legal code. This typically meant replacing indigenous rulers with European ones. The sheer scope of the missionaries' transformative agenda led them, in short, to press other sectors to help launch a triple assault.

British Protestants in phase 3 were extraordinarily effective lobbyists for empire. Their most famous missionary, David Livingstone, played a key role in this respect.[35] Livingstone's well-publicized travels greatly increased popular interest in previously unknown parts of the African interior, and his views took antislavery sentiment in a new direction. Whereas abolitionists had earlier attacked Britain and other European powers for complicity in an iniquitous trade, now they began to support Britain's advance into the heart of Africa to end non-European complicity in the same trade. Livingstone did more than advocate an active diplomatic presence in central Africa. He acted on these beliefs, accepting appointment as British consul in Quelimane, Mozambique, in 1858. Protestant missionaries in Nyasaland, Nigeria, Uganda, and Bechuanaland—and the home-based mission societies sponsoring them—pressed vigorously for government intervention to facilitate the civilizing mission.[36]

Britain in the latter half of phase 3 provides the clearest instance of a coordinated triple assault on non-European peoples. That all three sectors were so actively involved may help explain why Britain emerged from the late nineteenth-century scramble as the premier imperial power. With officials facing insistent appeals from mercantile, financial, and missionary groups to act aggressively overseas, the empire continued to grow even when the home government lacked expansionist plans of its own. The Cambridge University historian J. R. Seeley overstated matters when claiming in 1883 that the British Empire grew "in a fit of absence of mind." If politicians and bureaucrats were looking elsewhere, their absentmindedness was more than compensated for by the close attention nongovernmental actors paid to their country's imperial role.

Belgium

Belgium represents the classic case of a determined ruler's impact on foreign policy. King Leopold II (r.1865–1909) became obsessed with acquiring overseas territory. Lewis Gann and Peter Duignan write that the king "had a personal drive so compelling that it repelled Cecil Rhodes, who was not an overly squeamish man."[37] Through sponsorship of an international conference on the Congo in 1876 and skillful diplomacy at the Conference of Berlin, Leopold obtained in the bizarrely misnamed Congo Free State a land almost eighty times larger than Belgium. The Congo was considered the king's personal property until atrocities committed in his name forced transfer of sovereignty in 1908 to Parliament.

Leopold II parlayed his country's small size and population into sources of strength by playing upon rivalries within the interstate system. France, Germany, and Britain were more willing to cede jurisdiction over an immense, strategically located territory to the Belgian ruler than to grant one another this privilege. By reducing great-power rivalry in the Congo basin Leopold assisted the rapid European takeover of Africa. Like Portugal and Holland before it, Belgium illustrates the role of compensatory imperialism—and the disproportionately large role small states played in projecting European power abroad.

Germany

Germany offers additional evidence that a leader's ability to utilize competitive features of the interstate system could have major impacts outside the system. Chancellor Bismarck's foreign policy focused principally on power relationships within Europe and only peripherally on the wider world. Bismarck aspired to serve as regional balancer while preventing formation of a coalition of other states to challenge the Second Reich's growing prominence. His interest in defusing and diverting French *revanchiste* sentiment following Germany's acquisition of Alsace and Lorraine led him to back French expansion abroad. His one brief foray into the imperial arena in 1884–85 was apparently influenced more by domestic and regional political considerations than by any analysis of global trends.

Whatever the motives may have been, the effect of German territorial claims in several parts of Africa in 1884 was to intensify and accelerate rivalry for control of Africa's coastal areas. Having raised the stakes of competition, Bismarck then took steps to regulate its form by convening the Berlin Conference. States attending this conclave not only not only devised a common set of rules for occupying large portions of Africa and Oceania, but also pledged to resolve disputes among themselves through diplomacy. The conference's routinization of the scramble for territory may be considered Germany's most important and distinctive imperial contribution.

Italy

The peninsula that eventually became the Italian state played diverse roles over time. As noted in the previous chapter, the Roman Empire created and diffused institutions, norms, and ideas that gave cultural coherence and unity to western Europe. It was an inspiration and role model for advocates of multicontinental empire in modern times.

That Italy did not become politically unified until the nineteenth century affected early European expansion in indirect but nonetheless important ways. Experienced mariners like Columbus, Vespucci, Cabot, and Verrazzano abandoned the tiny city-states of their birth and worked instead for rulers of far larger, more powerful states fronting the Atlantic. The Roman Catholic Church was able to gain sway throughout western Europe, as both an actor within countries and a comparatively autonomous supranational institution. Had Italy been unified in phase 1, people elsewhere in Europe might have eyed the Roman Church with suspicion as an agent of the Italian state. Instead, the Church's association with catholic (that is, universal) goals and its sponsorship of missionary orders operating throughout the world enabled the proselytizing element in Christianity to be harnessed to the political ambitions of several states, not just one.

When political unification did occur in the 1860s, the new state was able to play a direct role of its own. Last entrant in the competition for colonies, Italy was also the last European power to dispatch armies in search of colonial glory when Benito Mussolini launched the invasion of Abyssinia (Ethiopia) in 1935. The hostile reaction this invasion elicited from many quarters, including other metropoles, showed that actions widely supported by Europeans in phase 3 no longer had moral and emotional appeal by phase 4. Attempting to recreate the ethos of a bygone era, Abyssinia's fascist conquerors played out the final act in the drama of European expansion.

Distinctive features of each metropole influenced the behavior of others through competition or emulation. To note the uniqueness of each imperial power does not undermine the argument that all the metropoles should be seen as constituents of a larger system. One reason for the system's dynamism was a high level of interaction among units differing among themselves in important respects. These very differences enabled metropoles to learn from the successes and failures of their rivals' experiments with long-distance rule.

10
The Institutional Basis for the Triple Assault

A striking feature of European overseas initiatives is their multisectoral character. Governments, profit-oriented companies, and missionary bodies had their distinct reasons for reaching out. Each had the capacity to do so on its own. But a country's sectoral institutions often found it convenient to work in tandem. When agents of the state collaborated with private entrepreneurs and missionaries, the result was a formidable and unusually flexible type of power.

Initiatives by sectoral actors sometimes had a cumulative impact even when the actors did not deliberately collaborate. For example, merchants or missionaries working in an indigenous society could disrupt it in ways that facilitated takeover by soldiers and administrators at a later point.

Variations among metropoles in cross-sector relations account for differences in the character and durability of specific empires. But still they are variations on a common theme. The multifaceted character of *all* metropoles' activities is highlighted when one draws comparisons with the behavior of Chinese and Arabs in overseas settings.

SECTORAL INSTITUTIONS: SPECIALIZATION AND SPATIAL STRETCH

Social action in European countries was highly institutionalized. In all three sectors could be found formal organizations, each with its internal hierarchy, procedures, norms, sources of revenue, personnel recruitment policies, and mechanisms to reward and punish people impacted by its work. Institutions create power by pooling, coordinating, and directing the efforts of many human beings. The density and variety of institutions in European countries generated an enormous potential to exercise power. To the extent that institutions elsewhere were less numerous, formalized, complex, and adaptable, Europeans found it relatively easy to enter other societies, to gain influence quickly, and eventually to undermine or outflank indigenous structures.

European institutions had a high capacity to absorb and channel for their long-term benefit what the "imperial entrepreneurs" noted in this chapter accomplished. They were thus the crucial links between individuals and the larger units—country, system, region—on which attention has so far been focused. Sectoral institutions were the workhorses of empire. That so many of them flourished after transplantation overseas is the key to any effort to explain the origins and duration of European dominance.

These institutions tended toward specialization of tasks. This point should not be overstated, for functional overlap was a recurring feature of this story. Government employees routinely used public power to amass private wealth. Merchants deployed wealth to influence government decision making. An official church was in some respects part of the public sector. Churches acted as private entrepreneurs when managing land and other property bequeathed to them.[1] A certain amount of overlap may have increased the overall effectiveness of European institutions at home and abroad. Still, a broad division of labor among governmental bureaucracies, merchant houses, banks, and religious bodies was widely recognized and accepted. The division of labor enabled sectoral institutions to dispatch agents in pursuit of specific goals, whether power, profit, or proselytization. The result was a greater impact on non-European societies than if each sector had waited for others from the same country to devise a joint plan before itself taking action.

Specialization facilitated recruitment. There were careers abroad for those who wanted to dominate and to serve; for the gold hunter and the ascetic; the lustful and the chaste; the idealist, the dispenser of justice, the cynic, and the sadist; the loner and the deal maker. Europe exported its best and its worst.[2] That such a wide range of motivations could be tapped strengthened the drive for expansion by enlarging the pool of recruits for it.

The existence of many specialized sectoral institutions allowed Europeans to tap an array of sources to finance early overseas initiatives. Supplementing government tax revenues were the investable capital of private entrepreneurs and donations of Christians eager to support missionary work. The extractive capacity of European institutions, taken together, was sufficiently high to cover imperialism's initial operating expenses before gains from exploitation of colonial resources were realized.

European rulers had extra resources to spend on overseas initiatives because of what nonstate sectors did at home. Productive activities of profit-seeking individuals and institutions generated substantial tax revenue, while religious institutions carried out social service tasks—education, health, care for the poor and aged—that might otherwise have been performed and financed by government. As a bonus, nonstate sectors could be expected to perform similar services overseas once a colonial administration was in place. European or settler-run enterprises could generate taxable revenue. Official outlays for education and health could be kept low because

FIGURE 10.1.

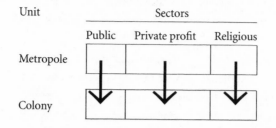

mission agencies were willing, for their own reasons, to deploy funds as well as personnel for schools and clinics. Fiscal incentives were thus tipped toward government engagement overseas.

Sectoral institutions headquartered in Europe were able to extend their reach outward, maintaining communication links and lines of authority across thousands of miles. The metropole's institutions penetrated its colonies. Once there they began to shape colonial sectoral life. But even as they were domesticated in new settings their accountability upward and outward remained. The spatial stretch of sectoral institutions is presented visually in figure 10.1.

The first step in asserting a presence abroad was to recruit individuals from the metropole as a sponsoring institution's agents. Before departure recruits were instructed what to do to realize their sponsor's objectives. But the sponsor, whatever its sectoral specialty, faced a problem. To use principal–agent terminology, people whom the principal designated as agents enjoyed unusually high levels of autonomy after reaching their overseas destination. The physical distance between principal and agent, the difficulty if not impossibility of communicating quickly between continents, the agent's need to respond at short notice to rapidly changing local conditions, serendipities built into cross-cultural encounters—all these factors gave people on the scene far greater leeway to set goals and decide how to reach them than principals wanted to acknowledge. The danger from the latter's perspective was that the agent might neglect the principal's goals and (mis)use autonomy to advance the agent's own interests. Even more serious than this risk of "moral hazard" was the possibility that the agent might openly rebel, claiming power and legitimacy the principal believed it alone possessed.[3] Recruitment for overseas careers might in fact attract precisely the kind of person inclined to reject the principal's authority once rejection became a viable option.

There is ample evidence that the self-interest of agents posed serious, recurring problems for sponsoring institutions. This was true above all early in phase 1 and whenever wealth was readily available. Royal appointees in Portuguese India, for example, routinely abused their posts for personal gain.[4] Field employees of phase 1 chartered companies frequently diverted company funds into unreported personal consumption, with a predictably negative impact on corporate profits. This pattern affected even the tightly run VOC and was a major reason the company eventually (in the late eighteenth century) declared bankruptcy.

In striking contrast, the more serious danger of agent rebellion never materialized. The Spanish conquistadors were perhaps the extreme examples of individuals able to do whatever they wanted after indigenous armies and rulers were decisively defeated. Yet Hernán Cortés did not assert authority over conquered Aztec domains in his own name. Neither did he proclaim himself founder of a breakaway royal dynasty. Instead Cortés penned lengthy letters to Emperor Charles V assuring that all had been properly done in the emperor's name and urging New Spain's incorporation into Habsburg domains. A letter written in 1524 begins, "At the time when the city of Tenochtitlán and surrounding country were recovered for your Majesty two other provinces became subject to the imperial crown."[5] Later, charged with misusing power, Cortés traveled to Spain to clear his name. On returning to the scene of his conquests he did not resist serving another man the emperor appointed viceroy.

Francisco Pizarro, whose Andean exploits took him even farther afield, could have declared himself lord of the Inca realms without fearing counterattacks from forces loyal to the Spanish Crown. But Pizarro, who had taken care to secure royal appointment as governor of kingdoms he planned to conquer, set aside the "royal fifth" of the loot from Cajamarca and sent it to Seville. He felt honored when Charles, in return, appointed him a marquis. In the mid-1540s one of Pizarro's brothers, Gonzalo, led a rebellion against Charles's viceroy. The viceroy was killed, and Gonzalo became for a time the most powerful man in Peru. J. H. Parry reflects that

> Had [Gonzalo] repudiated his allegiance altogether, as his grim camp-master Carbajal advised, he might have established an independent kingdom. Habits of loyalty to the Crown, however, though loose, were strong. Gonzalo attempted to negotiate for royal recognition of his authority, and the consequent delay enabled [the previous viceroy's] successor . . . to land in Peru . . . and eventually to raise an army which defeated him. Gonzalo and his principal lieutenants were beheaded in 1548.[6]

In these situations the sponsoring institution's hold on its agents went beyond the limited penalties and rewards at its disposal. More important was the subjective factor: agents' interpretations of the meaning and purpose of their own actions. Cortés and the Pizarro brothers fully acknowledged that legitimate authority over conquered New World lands lay in the hands of Charles V—and ultimately the pope, whose edicts sanctioned royal initiatives. The Spanish state and the Roman Catholic Church extended their authority across vast distances because a group of unruly, impetuous soldiers insisted upon acting on behalf of emperor and pope. In the final analysis the remarkable spatial stretch of European sectoral institutions was due to their agents' worldview and values.

Another aspect of spatial stretch is the emigration of settlers. In many instances a government agency or chartered company was responsible for their recruitment and transportation.[7] Once arrived in a new land, which settlers knew would have to provide their livelihood, they almost immediately began to act in their own interest rather than as agents of whomever had sponsored the voyage. Their presence reflected not so much the extension of European sectoral institutions as the relocation of fragments of metropolitan society. Settlers typically approached life in their new home with the explore-control-utilize syndrome that underlay the European expansionist project. In setting up a colony's private profit sector they employed technologies and practices from the country they or their forebears left. Whether settlers acknowledged allegiance to European religious authorities depended on the form of Christianity they practiced. At one end of the spectrum, Roman Catholics were part of a complex hierarchy culminating in the Vatican. At the other end, Calvinists and Baptists stressed local congregational autonomy.

The presence of settlers posed a potential danger to governors of colonies in which they lived. Because settlers were not agents of metropolitan institutions and did not perceive themselves as such, they enjoyed a great deal of autonomy when deciding how to make a living and manage their local affairs. With autonomy went capacity to organize and lead successful movements for independence. This was of course what eventually occurred in phase 2, then more subtly in phase 4 with Britain's white dominions.

Adding to the problem colonial governors faced, settlers threatened the indigenous population. Given their intense interest in appropriating land and using it in new ways to make a profitable living, settlers were generally far more destructive of indigenous ways of life than even the most exploitive of governors. Indeed, officials in pure and mixed settlement colonies often felt that in order to maintain peace and assure some measure of justice they had to limit settlers' proclivities to undermine if not exterminate indigenous societies. In such situations tensions developed between colonial bureaucrats, whose power reflected the spatial stretch of a European government, and a community whose presence marked the spatial diffusion of Europe's activist way of life.[8]

That these risks and tensions were inherent in state-sponsored settlement schemes makes all the more striking the willingness of early settler communities to place themselves under metropolitan authority. Had they not done so, Europe's global impact might have been quite different. A stream of emigrants might have founded polities that were independent from the outset or that broke away a few years after the first settlers arrived. Large portions of the world would still have been dominated by people of European descent—but not by European countries. That settlers acknowledged their subordination to distant rulers, despite grievances over specific policies rulers promulgated, demonstrates the spatial stretch of metropolitan public sectors. A settler presence, in turn, enhanced the credibility of metropolitan claims that an overseas territory was effectively, not just nominally, under its jurisdiction.

When sectoral institutions stretched overseas they tended to arrange themselves along national lines. This is self-evident for soldiers and administrators sent out by a monarch or central government. But the point is not obvious for the other two sectors. For, as argued in chapter 8, one reason European merchants, manufacturers, and religious leaders enjoyed substantial autonomy from their governments was that the territorial unit with which their activities were identified was not coextensive with the state but rather smaller or larger than it. In fact, in early phase 1 merchants and financiers from cities in one part of Europe assisted the imperial designs of monarchs located elsewhere. One sees this in private sector actors in Italian city-states and in the rulers of Castile and Aragon. Portugal's royal court negotiated with Antwerp merchants to sell the spices Portuguese sailors brought from Africa and Asia. A Roman Catholic missionary order like the Jesuits, operating from a pan-European institutional base, managed to avoid takeover by the governments in whose colonies its priests worked.

Increasingly, however, nongovernment actors organized overseas activities around national identities and loyalties. In part this was in response to developments within European countries, notably the growth of central government power from phase 1 onward and the spread of nationalist sentiment in phases 2 and 3. In part it was due to the tendency of merchants or missionaries to identify with their homeland when overseas work brought them into competition with people from other countries.

The nationalization of overseas economic activity can be seen in the mercantilist policies of phase 1 metropoles, restricting private trade and production in their empires to ventures run by their own citizens. In return, officials tried to limit what citizens could do outside imperial boundaries. Mercantilism strengthened mutually dependent ties between a country's public and private profit sectors. The national character of these ties is evident in the structure and names of chartered companies: *English* and *Dutch* East India Company, for example.[9] The British government in phase 3, though formally opposed to mercantilism and committed to free trade, was far more partial to British business than to merchants from other countries. Royal charters were granted only to enterprises directed by British citizens, for example, Cecil Rhodes, George Taubman Goldie, and William Mackinnon.

To varying degrees the overseas work of missionaries was nationalized as well, most obviously in state-supported Protestant denominations: the Church of England and Dutch Reformed Church. But Roman Catholicism was hardly unaffected by the growing power of European governments and the growing appeal of nationalism. That the Catholic Church was a thoroughly transnational institution did not gainsay the fact that Catholicism was the official religion of specific states. The Spanish Crown was especially effective at controlling recruitment of clergy and missionaries sent to Spain's colonies.[10] This meant that the majority of religious personnel in the empire was of Spanish birth, and that regardless of birthplace one's tenure in a post depended on the disposition of the royal court. In the phase 3 scramble for Africa the White Fathers, a missionary order founded by Cardinal Lavigerie, functioned in some places as an arm of French imperial interests, in much the same way that the (Anglican) Church Missionary Society (CMS) did for Britain's. Field agents of the White Fathers and CMS might more accurately be called Gallo- and Anglo- than Euro-Christians.

CROSS-SECTORAL LINKS

Functional specialization, autonomy, distinctive motivations for reaching out beyond Europe—these factors gave a metropole's sectoral institutions the option of acting overseas on their own. But the nationalizing trends just discussed, as well as the complementarity of function among specialists in coercive rule, commerce, and conversion, pushed sectoral institutions in the opposite direction: toward coordination and interdependence. The result of these conflicting pressures was considerable variation in the nature and extent of cross-sectoral links. Much depended, for example, on the time period in which expansion took place, the metropole involved, and the non-European society being impacted. There were variations in the degree of self-conscious, formalized collaboration; in numbers and types of sectors linked; in the degree to which the public sector dominated institutions from other sectors; in whether collaboration took place primarily in metropole or colony; and in whether sectoral institutions entered a foreign territory more or less simultaneously or at different times. At one level, these variations make generalization difficult if not impossible. At a deeper level they reveal precisely the generalization that matters. The capacity of multiple sectoral institutions to operate autonomously *and* cooperatively gave Europeans enormous tactical flexibility in penetrating other societies.

Of several patterns available one involved a coalition between government and the officially approved church. The most notable example was Spain in phase 1. At least one Catholic priest accompanied Columbus on his second voyage to the New World. There followed a steady stream of clerics to minister to settlers and convert Amerindians. The Spanish state endeavored to protect Church property in the colonies and prevent Jews and Protestants from entering overseas possessions. In turn, the Church provided the justification for conquest rulers in Spain and conquistadors in the field believed they needed. The Bulls of Donation issued by Pope Alexander VI in 1493 assigned land west of a line in the Atlantic to Spain's rulers on condition that they actively support the Church's evangelical mission. "The prime right," as one interpreter puts it, "is not conquest but conversion."[11] Subsequent interpretation of the papal proclamation by Spanish jurists led to the *requirimiento,* a statement to be read aloud to Amerindians at the moment of contact. This document

> called on the Indians to acknowledge the pope as ruler of the world and, in his stead, the king of Castile by virtue of donation. It then informed them that if they accepted the summons they would be received as loyal vassals, but if they did not they would be deprived of their liberty and property and further stated, "We protest that the deaths and losses which shall accrue from this are your fault, and not that of their Highnesses, or ours, nor of these cavaliers who came with us."[12]

Because the statement was written and read in Spanish, indigenous people could not possibly have understood what their options were, much less the reasoning behind the *requirimiento*'s grandiose claims to worldly authority. Still, the fact that it was routinely proclaimed in the early years of the Conquest shows the significance to Spanish imperialists of having a religious rationale for aggression.

The Church further served Spanish administrators by instructing young Amerindians in Spanish and Latin and compiling dictionaries of indigenous languages. It thus satisfied a necessary condition for effective colonial administration: a means of communication between rulers and ruled.

Church and state cooperated closely to assert Spain's claims to Alta (upper) California when, in the mid-1700s, the Russians and English showed signs of interest in the area. A chain of missions and forts was established, beginning at San Diego in 1769 and rapidly extending northward. Military emissaries of New Spain's government, including Gaspar de Pórtola and Juan Bautista de Anza, worked closely with Fray Junípero Serra, the Franciscan founder of California's earliest missions. The eighteen mission stations established by Serra and his successor, Fray Fermín Lasuén, were designed not only to convert local Amerindians but also to signal other great powers that Spain held vast stretches of North America's west coast.

The state was dominant partner in its alliance with the Church by virtue of patronage rights conceded Spanish monarchs by Rome. Yet the Church was no pliant agent of the state. Catholic prelates played important roles as royal advisers. Columbus might not have been granted the audience with Queen Isabella in 1491, to present his case one last time, had it not been for the influence at court of Father Juan Perez. Consolidation of royal power by Isabella and Ferdinand was itself due in large measure to Cardinal Gonzalo Ximenes de Cisneros, the queen's confessor and subsequently de facto regent of Castile.[13] In the colonies, missionaries carried out their work with minimal government supervision or intervention. Their reports on settler exploitation of Amerindians were sent directly to officials in the colonies and in Spain. The tireless lobbying of Father Bartolomé de Las Casas on behalf of indigenous peoples pressed the royal court to limit the worst abuses. Franciscans and Jesuits set up stations far beyond the effective bounds of Spanish administrative authority. Especially noteworthy were the initiatives of Father Eusebio Kino in northern New Spain and the virtually independent polity run by the Jesuits in Paraguay.

The standardized layout of a Spanish colonial city symbolically expressed the ability of state and church to cooperate and complement one another while retaining separate institutional identities. On one side of the large square in the city center—and typically the tallest structure—was the principal church. On two other sides were the governor's house and municipal council building.[14]

A second pattern was a coalition between a metropolitan government and elements of its private profit sector. For the Portuguese during the first two centuries of phase 1, individual investors and merchants were keys to expansion of intercontinental commerce. Entrepreneurs needed the state because it controlled fortified trading enclaves in Africa and Asia, and the king claimed monopoly rights to proceeds from trade. The king needed entrepreneurs because they had the strongest incentive to go out and engage in trade. The two interests were satisfied when the royal court delegated monopoly rights to traders in exchange for a share of gains from their ventures. Once access to the Indian Ocean was assured the court devised a special office, the Casa da India, to delegate these rights. Licensed merchants were given permission to sail on the king's ships and to place goods in royal storehouses.[15]

The situation changed as the volume and variety of trade goods increased and as economies of scale from corporate transactions undercut operations by individual traders. In Dutch and English hands the chartered company became the classic mechanism for forging mutually beneficial ties between public and private profit sectors.

The coalition took another form in phase 3. The emergence of large European financial institutions with considerable investable capital coincided with the rise of a new type of North African ruler, committed to modernize his country through public expenditures on railroads, ports, military training and upgrading, and public buildings. Banks made large portfolio loans to rulers in Egypt, Tunisia, and Morocco to assist their defensive modernization programs. When export revenues proved insufficient to repay these loans, financiers pressured their home governments to manage the revenue collection efforts of increasingly insolvent regimes. From fiscal intervention to comprehensive administrative and military takeover of these three territories was but a short step.[16]

Another pattern involved less formalized interaction among all three metropolitan sectors, each at times operating independently, at times taking others' activities into account when planning its own strategies. France (in phases 1 and 3), Britain (in phase 3), and Germany (in phase 3) illustrate this pattern. During phase 1, French monarchs dispatched explorers, soldiers, and administrators to North America and India. Merchants from Nantes, Rochelle, Bordeaux, Saint-Malo, and other ports traded in the Atlantic basin for furs, sugar, tobacco, and slaves. French missionaries worked among the Huron, in the Mississippi Valley, and on the other side of the world in Cochinchina.[17]

All three sectors were likewise active in constructing the virtually new French empire of phase 3. In the public sector were politicians like Léon Gambetta, Jules Ferry, and Eugène Etienne, and soldiers whose actions in the field often went well beyond marching orders. Among these were Thomas Bugeaud (Algeria), Louis Faidherbe (West Africa), Louis Archinard (West Africa), Henri Rivière (Tonkin), Joseph Gallieni (Tonkin and Madagascar), and Hubert Lyautey (Morocco).[18] Business interests in the 1880s and 1890s were anxious to carve out overseas zones in which French merchants, industrialists, engineers, shippers, and investors could be assured a protected, preferred status. They pushed for expansion through the organizations noted in chapter 5. In the religious sector Cardinal Lavigerie's aptly named Pères Blancs (White Fathers) were active in Algeria, Tunisia, and the East African interior. The Société des Missions Africaines de Lyon proselytized along the West African coast, the Société des Missions Étrangères de Paris concentrated on Indochina, and the Congrégation des Sacrés Coeurs worked in the Marquesas.[19]

Links between French missionaries and government officials were close in the Marquesas. Missionaries arrived in 1838, four years before these Pacific islands were formally annexed. Greg Dening writes, "The French government saw the missionaries as civilizing influences and precursors of the flag. They had free passage in French naval ships and from the beginning had negotiated to be fully paid and supported from public funds."[20]

The overseas role of all three British sectors in the nineteenth century was described in chapters 5 and 8. As the scramble intensified after the 1870s, coalition building across sectoral lines increased and became more formalized. In the West African interior, for example, soldiers and merchants employed by the Royal Niger Company cooperated with English and African preachers sent to the Niger Valley by the Church Missionary Society.

As if to compensate for Germany's belated entry into the imperial sweepstakes, German businessmen and missionaries entered many territories at virtually the same time as soldiers and administrators. This was the triple assault in its most literal form. An example from Kamerun (Cameroon) shows how sectoral activity assumed a national character. Shortly after setting up an administration there the German government asked the Basler Evangelische Missionsgesellschaft to take over the work and property of the English Baptists, whose presence was unwelcome. This move was supported by a syndicate of Hamburg traders, who foresaw the benefits of having Africans gain technical and German-language skills in mission schools. For its part the Basle mission, headquartered in Switzerland, established a branch in Stuttgart to portray itself as a more German institution.[21]

The autonomy European sectors enjoyed permitted several variations in the sequencing of overseas activities. One pattern—seen in France's advance from Senegal into the West African interior—was for soldiers to assert political control over a territory. Merchants and missionaries came in once pacification efforts were well advanced.[22] A more common pattern was for soldiers and administrators to enter a territory at about the same time as agents of other sectors. Normally this was done with a clear understanding of which actors would undertake which tasks. Examples were the state–Church alliance in Spain's colonies, the state–merchant coalition of Dutch, English, and French chartered companies, and the triple sector activities of the French in seventeenth-century Canada and the Germans in nineteenth-century Africa.

Another option, the reverse of the first, was for merchants or missionaries or both to ensconce themselves in an area before the arrival of soldiers and administrators. In many cases—notably in the New World in phase 1—agents of all three sectors set up headquarters in a coastal enclave. Merchants and missionaries then moved into the interior, far beyond zones protected by colonial authorities.[23] Only at a later point did soldiers and administrators catch up with them. On the West African coast, in Madagascar, Indochina, and Oceania merchants and missionaries operated, often for decades, without access to colonial enclaves.

The capacity of Europeans to assemble combinations of sectoral actors and to devise a variety of sequencing patterns for sectoral overseas activities goes far toward explaining their global dominance. Europeans had at their disposal a wider repertoire of options for organizationally outflanking other societies than anyone else. Their repertoire enabled them to be highly flexible, adapting penetrative strategies to the specific circumstances they encountered. When military conquest at the time of initial contact was possible and deemed desirable, empire could be established by the classic method of aggressive soldiering. Here the metropole's coercive and administrative resources facilitated the work of traders and missionaries. When conquest at the time of contact was not possible or advisable Europeans did not abandon overseas initiatives as not worth the effort. Instead they employed a backup strategy substituting influence for power. If a metropole's soldiers could not prevail, at least its consumer goods could be purchased and its preachers' salvationist message heard.

Informal influence by nongovernmental sectors functioned in practice as a Trojan horse. Indeed, it was instrumental in preparing many non-European societies for eventual subordination. Some takeovers were the result of mercantile and missionary activity consciously designed for that end. But to an even greater extent takeovers were the unintended and unforeseen product of activities that, while ostensibly nonpolitical, nonetheless subverted the political status quo. Examples from both expansionist phases show how different sequencing arrangements worked.

The "conquest first" option was most likely when an indigenous population's capacity to resist takeover was limited by low population density, vulnerability to imported diseases, the absence of powerful state structures, and the presence of numerous small-scale societies riven by intergroup conflicts or internal cleavages. Many of these conditions obtained along the coasts and rivers of the New World in phase 1. Another circumstance tempting would-be conquerors was the concentration of vast quantities of transportable wealth in the hands of indigenous elites. This situation—quickly redefined as the opportunity of a lifetime—faced Cortés and Pizarro.

Had European countries sent forth only soldiers it is unlikely they would have come to dominate the world. Administrators were needed to translate battlefield victories into ongoing control. But not even the ablest bureaucrats backed by the best-equipped soldiers would have sufficed. The key to dominance was the spatial stretch of all three—not just one—of several metropoles' sectors and the ability of sectoral agents to devise complementary mechanisms of control. The colonial government did what governments everywhere do, obtaining compliance by heavy reliance on the use and threat of force. Agents of the private profit sector emphasized material inducements, rewarding with imported consumer goods those who produced and sold commodities Europeans wanted. Missionaries specialized in what Émile Durkheim terms "normative pacification." They offered a sense of moral superiority now and eternal salvation later to hearers who abandoned inherited worldviews, values, and behaviors for new, civilized ones. What Amitai Etzioni terms the three forms of power—coercive, remunerative, normative—were all in play and were all backed up by home-based institutions.[24]

A colonial regime installed by conquest needed revenues to cover pacification, personnel, and infrastructure expenses. It needed non-Europeans to collaborate in such tasks as collecting taxes, implementing new laws and regulations, recruiting police forces and forced labor gangs, and keeping an eye on potential rebels. If revenues and collaborators were not found quickly, initial military victories would not translate into durable rule. Here is where agents from a metropole's private profit and religious sectors were so valuable. Traders, plantation and mine owners, and settlers set rapidly to work producing whatever might net them a profit. Because capitalists specialized in economic transformation and had personal incentives to bring it about, they were often highly efficient at generating output which could then be taxed. Many of their activities were export-oriented, which cut revenue collection costs by concentrating tax collection in a few sites—notably port cities—where commodities were shipped.

Fully as important was the missionaries' contribution: training and socializing collaborators. To be effective agents of religious conversion missionaries had to become linguistic intermediaries, learning indigenous languages, translating the Bible into them, and teaching the metropole's official tongue. Missionaries in turn trained students in catechism classes and schools as linguistic intermediaries. School graduates were in great demand by governments whose top officials all too often could not speak directly and intelligibly to the subject population. Mission schools taught literacy and numeracy, skills required for many bureaucratic positions.

Missionaries dispensed a cultural as well as religious doctrine. To the extent that they converted indigenous people to the colonizer's lifestyle and values, making European civilization the normative reference point, they increased the likelihood that some of their converts would actively wish to collaborate. Products of missionary schools often possessed the school-based knowledge and compliant demeanor administrators considered ideal for effective grassroots work.

Sir Harry Johnston, whose late nineteenth-century exploits in southern Africa certify him as an archetypal soldier-administrator, was not alone in recognizing the contributions agents of Euro-Christianity made to empire. Writing in 1890, he waxed almost rhapsodic: "The missionary is really gaining your experience for you without any cost to yourself. . . . They strengthen our hold over the country, they spread the use of the English language, they induct the natives into the best kind of civilisation, and, in fact, each Mission Station is an essay in colonisation."[25]

But sometimes administrators found the missionary presence inconvenient, if not downright subversive. An obvious example was a colony in which another highly institutionalized, cosmopolitan religion, with its own sacred texts, was widely practiced. Active proselytizing for Christianity might trigger a revolt by adherents of the other religion that would be difficult to repress. The autonomy of sectors within European society permitted adaptability in this situation. Lack of fusion between state and church in the metropole made it possible for colonial administrators to restrict missionary activity if there were persuasive political reasons to do so.

Thus British officials in India adopted a distinctly more critical stance toward Christian missionaries after the Great Mutiny than they had in the quarter century before it. Behind the uprising was growing suspicion among Hindu and Muslim sepoys that the British were trying to convert them to Christianity by forcing them to violate religious practices. To help counter this impression among Muslims the raj went so far as to subsidize an elite secondary school in Aligarh to teach Islamic principles alongside the standard English curriculum.[26] In Nigeria and the Sudan the British devised a dual policy, permitting missionary activity in the predominantly animist southern regions while virtually prohibiting it in the overwhelmingly Islamic northern areas. For the same pragmatic reason the French were tolerant of missionaries in Dahomey and Gabon yet wary of them in the Soudan and Niger.[27] Where missionaries were not wanted, administrators met the need for educated indigenous personnel by founding government schools.

More frequent than conquest first was a pattern in which soldiers bearing the flag followed traders bearing manufactures and missionaries bearing redemption messages. This was the typical sequence during phase 1 in the Old World as well as in the New World interior. During phase 3 the same sequence played out in the African interior and Oceania. This pattern took advantage of the autonomy of nongovernmental sectors, which could send out their agents even if the home government was unable or unwilling to do likewise.

When merchants or missionaries were the first Europeans to reach other societies, they helped in several ways to facilitate subsequent imposition of European rule. Posing a less immediate and obvious threat to indigenous authorities than foreign soldiers or administrators, they could gain entrée in ways not possible for a metropolitan government's agents. Once installed within a foreign society merchants and missionaries reported their observations and activities to sponsoring agencies. Many reports were read by others as well. C. R. Boxer notes that the Jesuits "enormously enlarged the scope and depth of Europe's knowledge of Asia by the letters and reports which they sent from their mission-fields, and which were widely circulated through the medium of the principal European presses."[28] Information that such reports conveyed about local political conditions, natural resources, social customs, and languages proved invaluable to empire builders at a later point.

In some cases missionaries provided intelligence directly to government officials. In 1815 directors of the London Missionary Society wrote Lord Somerset, governor of South Africa's Cape Colony, requesting assistance in sending a mission to the Tswana people, who lived north of the colony's boundaries. The directors observed, "We hope that the information which [this mission] may obtain respecting remote nations will be gratifying to your Excellency."[29] David Livingstone's well-publicized writings and speeches on the depredations of Arab and Swahili slave raiders increased popular pressure on the British government to intervene in central Africa.

As a joint public–private profit venture, a chartered company was able to penetrate other societies more readily than public sector agents acting on their own. Non-European rulers might regard the company as a trading operation whose occasional resort to force was only a means to the end of profit. If rulers believed they themselves could profit by trading with the company they might tolerate its troops on their territory as a minor strategic risk outweighed by economic gain. The troops could even be a strategic asset if borrowed to help the ruler against local rivals. But if at some point the company reversed means and ends and used its wealth to obtain power, its troops would be ideally positioned to conquer a polity from within. According to Jawaharlal Nehru this is how the English East India Company entrenched itself in India. The company "had originally established itself for trading purposes, and its military establishment was meant to protect this trade. Gradually, and almost unnoticed by others, it had extended the territory under its control, chiefly by taking sides in local disputes. . . . People looked upon [the company's] troops as mercenaries to be hired. When it was realized that the British were playing nobody's game but their own, and were out for the political domination of India, they had already established themselves firmly in the country."[30]

Agents of nongovernment institutions who had won the confidence of indigenous elites were able to use their influence to facilitate the transfer of power. Their role as cultural intermediaries was ready-made for cross-cultural deception. Leaders of New Zealand's Maoris were persuaded to sign the Treaty of Waitangi (1840) with British officials by Archdeacon Henry Williams, who understood the Maoris' language after years of working among them. The archdeacon's Maori-language version of the treaty, however, conveniently glossed over the clear delegation of sovereignty to Queen Victoria's government contained in the English-language version. Lobengula, ruler of the Ndebele, was induced in 1888 by the Revs. C. D. Helm and John Moffat, whom he considered trustworthy friends, to sign agreements granting the British South Africa Company concessions far more sweeping than the missionaries led Lobengula to understand.[31] When the extent of the deception became known it was too late. Heavily armed soldiers and settlers had moved into Maori and Ndebele territory. The invaders were well positioned to suppress indigenous uprisings that took place within a few years of the signing of deliberately misleading treaties.

Consumer goods introduced by missionaries as well as merchants almost invariably proved popular. Woollen cloth, needles, mirrors, iron pots, and kerosene lanterns may at first have been considered novelties and luxuries—but they quickly became conveniences, then were seen as satisfying basic needs. A seventeenth-century traveler in North America, Nicolas Denys, observed that nearly all Amerindians aware of European ways were affected "by the need for the things which come from us, the use of which has become to them an indispensable necessity. They have abandoned all their own utensils, whether because of the trouble they had as well to make as to use them, or because of the facility of obtaining from us, in exchange for skins which cost them almost nothing, the things which seem to them invaluable, not so much for their novelty as for the convenience they derived there-from."[32] In order to obtain imported goods people expanded traditional production patterns and grew new crops in response to external demand. They began, in other words, to look outside their society, turning to the nearest representatives of the outside world to satisfy new notions of the good life. A parallel process of external dependence occurred in the religious sphere when people converted to Christianity, since foreigners now became the arbiters of acceptable religious belief and practice.

Non-Europeans looking to Europeans to satisfy their material and spiritual needs were prime candidates for directing political loyalties outwardly as well. They were inclined to disparage indigenous rulers unable to furnish desired material benefits and to disrespect or even disavow rulers whose legitimacy rested on non-Christian foundations. Sensing the inadequacies of non-European rule, they were more likely to consider the colonial alternative with an open mind or even with eagerness. Whether by design or accident European nongovernmental sectors produced collaborators-in-waiting.

At some point rising European influence within a society became a source of discord in its own right, pitting those prepared to cooperate with Europeans against others counseling caution, noncollaboration, or resistance. Cleavage lines could take highly visible form, as when Christian converts abandoned their communities to enter mission stations restricted to those who had been "saved." Examples of cultur-ally and economically insulated Christian communities were the Jesuit *congrega-ciones* in Paraguay, *aldeias* in Brazil, and Livingstonia Mission in Nyasaland. In many instances externally generated cleavages reduced a society's capacity and will to unite against the sources of those very cleavages.

Newly introduced consumer goods could undermine the old order. Distilled alcohol contributed to loss of personal self-control and family cohesion, and guns to societal disintegration. European travelers and missionaries routinely recounted the devastating human toll of gin, rum, brandy, wine, and whiskey.[33] As for guns, Keith Sinclair reports in his *History of New Zealand* that by the 1820s:

> the Maoris had entered not a money but a musket economy. When they had got enough guns, they set off to even old scores. Because of the ramifications of kin-ship, each new death . . . spread out like waves from a stone dropped in the pool of tribal society. . . . In the twenties and early thirties these savage civil wars led to heavy casualties and cannibal feasts unprecedented in pre-European battles fought with stone-age weapons. It is estimated that about forty thousand people were slaughtered. . . . The traders gave the Maoris the means of self-destruction.[34]

When guns were more readily available to one indigenous group than to others, the newly strengthened group sometimes launched more frequent and destructive attacks on neighbors. Examples were slave raids by West African coastal peoples on residents of the interior and Iroquois attacks on the Huron. The desire of these groups to ally against a shared threat from distant shores was thereby undercut.

Missionary preaching had a subtler but potentially more corrosive impact on indigenous life. A case in point was Tahiti. Alan Moorehead writes of missionaries who arrived there early in the nineteenth century that "they meant the Tahitians nothing but good, and when all their righteous follies have been ignored, one is still left with a sense of astonishment at their success. Nothing dismayed them. Nothing turned them away from their purpose. Resolutely and persistently they kept hammering away at the Tahitian way of life until it crumbled before them, and within two decades they had achieved precisely what they set out to do."[35]

By physical self-destruction or normative pacification, the way was cleared for empire builders to march in and impose their own version of law, order, and civilization.

On several occasions indigenous elites, accurately assessing the political dangers posed by Europe's nongovernmental sectors, launched counteroffensives. In the most successful instance, Japan's Tokugawa regime in the early seventeenth century persecuted Catholic missionaries and their local followers and severely restricted the travel of European merchants. In phase 3, as European trading houses extended operations from West Africa's coast into the interior they encountered growing resistance from Africans who had earlier, when trade was confined to the coast, been partners in mutually beneficial transactions. Missionaries to the Yoruba, Baganda, and Vietnamese experienced hostile backlashes by local rulers.

An underlying dynamic was at work in these cases. To attain their goals agents of European private profit and religious sectors had to disrupt the societies they entered. If anything, agents tended to underestimate the extent of the transformations set in motion by their presence and activities. Societal disruption in turn placed at risk the work agents were sent out to perform. As merchants and missionaries faced a growing array of obstacles, ranging from persecution to the anarchy loosed by breakdown of local authority structures, they turned to their metropole's public sector for help. A colonial regime that earlier had appeared unnecessary or even undesirable now was attractive if not essential. European rule could restore a vanishing political stability and permit traders and missionaries to move freely about the territory on their business.

How a metropolitan government responded to pleas for intervention from its other sectors depended largely on conditions in a given territory—a point elaborated in chapter 11. Suffice it to say that Japan's rulers were capable of repelling European invaders in the early seventeenth century while this was not so for Yoruba, Baganda, and Vietnamese elites confronting far stronger European states more than two centuries later. Another factor was a government's relations with the other two sectors. Sometimes the decision to advance imperial claims was influenced by private lobbying, as when British missionaries urged London in the 1890s to intervene in Buganda. Sometimes complaints that merchants or missionaries were being unfairly treated gave officials a pretext for action impelled by quite different motives. A case in point was the French invasion of Cochinchina's Mekong delta in 1858–60. Ostensibly troops went in to help beleaguered French missionaries. More likely were geostrategic calculations having nothing to do with the agendas or problems of Roman Catholics. Even here, however, the religious sector mattered. Lacking persecuted missionaries, French politicians would have lacked the excuse they needed to justify naked aggression.

Examples from many places and times show how the multisectoral character of European overseas activities was conducive to empire. With a repertoire of mixtures and sequences of sectoral activity at their disposal, outsiders were able to adapt flexibly to the enormous range of overseas situations they faced.

From the perspective of non-European peoples, even if agents of three sectoral institutions had acted independently the cumulative effect of their activities was often as disruptive of precolonial ways of life *as if* their penetrative strategies *had* been carefully coordinated. Whether invasion was a single three-pronged assault or three distinct single-pronged assaults, it was eventually experienced as having a triply threatening impact. Nothing in the old way of life was safe from challenge.

A CROSS-CULTURAL COMPARISON OF SECTORAL LINKS: MALACCA

The multifaceted nature of Europe's assault is highlighted when contrasted with the overseas activities of the Chinese and the Arabs. The ideal site for comparison would be a place distant from Europe, China, and Arabia, hence unlikely to be controlled by any of them, where people arriving by sea from all three areas were present at about the same time. That such stringent conditions could be met seems highly unlikely. But in fact they do apply to one case: Malacca during roughly the first century of phase 1.[36] This city, located on the Malayan side of the narrow strait named after it, was founded in the late fourteenth century and rapidly became the principal center for maritime trade among Indian Ocean emporia, the Spice Islands, and China. Malacca benefited from the weather as well as from its location. Because of monsoonal winds, vessels sailing from the Indian Ocean to China (and vice versa) had to lay over for a few months before continuing the journey. An alternative was for ships to unload their wares in Malacca, returning to their respective home ports with goods from the others' ships as well as gold, spices, and precious woods from the offshore islands.

The city and strait of Malacca were extraordinarily cosmopolitan places several centuries ago. A well-placed Portuguese observer wrote in the 1570s, "One may well and truly say that Malacca, in point of fact, and merchant trade, is the most extensive place in the world."[37] The city was visited by Cheng Ho on at least two of his voyages and thereafter by many Chinese sailors and traders. The great Arab traveler Ibn Battuta passed through the strait in 1345–46, and several thousand Muslims, including some from Arabia, resided in the city in the early 1500s. Ibn Battuta's Italian counterpart, Marco Polo, passed through the Malacca Strait in 1292 on his return to Europe from China. As noted in chapter 3, the Portuguese captured Malacca in 1511, holding it until the Dutch replaced them in 1641. Thus people from all three regions converged around the start of phase 1 on the same small area.

By studying Malacca in 1511 one comes as close as possible to a historical laboratory experiment. Are sectoral features of European countries present as well in China and in Arab (and, more generally, Muslim) societies? If so, for reasons given in chapter 2 my argument about the importance of sectors is weakened. If not, the argument is strengthened.

The Chinese government's impact on Malacca was far more limited in scope and duration than might be expected given the country's size and wealth. Cheng Ho's armada of huge junks, with thousands of well-armed soldiers aboard, was designed to ensure attention and respectful deference to China's rulers from elites elsewhere. Presumably Admiral Ho was instructed to urge monarchs he met to establish symbolic tributary relations with the Celestial Court. But the admiral was unwilling to use the military might at his disposal to conquer Malacca, there being no plan to claim and administer distant lands as integral parts of the emperor's domains.[38] Moreover, as noted earlier, the impressive voyages undertaken by Cheng Ho ended abruptly in 1433. The emperor politely received the king of Malacca when the king later journeyed to Beijing, bearing tribute. But assertion of China's superior political status was made by the inferior party visiting the Celestial Court, not by the latter reaching out aggressively beyond its borders. The contrast with the European pattern is obvious.

China's private profit sector had a more substantial and long-lasting impact on Malacca. One indicator was the existence, as of the early 1500s, of a separate section of the city reserved for Chinese merchants. These traders were on their own when residing overseas. This was manifestly the case after 1433 when they could not count on even an intermittent visit of ships to demonstrate the home government's power. If anything, Malacca's Chinese merchants carried on their business despite the imperial court, which launched periodic efforts to restrict economic ties with the outside world. The court controlled government-to-government trade, expressed through the tributary system. Nonofficial trade, which it was unable to regulate, was perceived as an unwelcome challenge to its power and authority.[39] That many Chinese merchants in Malacca were long-term residents did not signify that they were over-seas agents of Chinese power. On the contrary, it reflected recognition of obstacles bureaucrats would have placed in their way had they based their international opera-tions on the Chinese mainland.[40] A common pattern for the Chinese in sixteenth-century Malacca and elsewhere in southeast Asia was to conduct clandestine com-merce with the home country. Alternatively, they concentrated on trade among ports scattered about the Nanyang (Southern Seas). In both cases they tried to avoid contact with Chinese officials rather than work with them.

The imperial court disapproved of Chinese settling elsewhere because this meant abandoning the graves of their ancestors. The court took this view to its logical conclusion in 1712 with an edict forbidding its subjects to live or trade in Southeast Asia. Though poorly and inconsistently enforced, the edict nonetheless expressed an attitude toward overseas settlers diametrically opposite to that of west-ern Europe's rulers.[41]

China's public and private profit sectors thus had minimal contact with each other in dealing with Malacca. When cross-sectoral contact did occur it tended to be competitive and conflictual rather than cooperative. The profit-sharing and char-tered company options were ruled out. This stands in sharp contrast with the Euro-pean pattern of linking the two sectors in mutually beneficial ways.

The Chinese did not carry a missionary religion to Malacca because they had none. As noted in chapter 8, the imperial court's Confucian creed was a civil religion, not available for export or readily separable institutionally from the public sector. Cheng Ho was dispatched as a diplomatic emissary of the court. But he could not have served as a Confucian missionary, had this unlikely possibility ever been consid-ered, because he was Muslim. Chinese merchants in Malacca practiced their own re-ligious faiths but kept to themselves when doing so. No basis existed for an outward-looking coalition between leading practitioners of China's religions and its rulers or merchants.

Arabs visited Malacca as long-distance merchants, staying in a quarter of the town set aside for Muslims. Unlike the Chinese they did bring a missionary religion. They used their wealth and external connections to persuade Southeast Asia's politi-cal elites to let them build mosques and invite *mullahs* to lead the Islamic commu-nity's religious life. In many instances Muslim merchants pressured local rulers to convert. Malacca's rulers had been Muslim for about a century before the Portuguese arrived. One may thus speak of an alliance between Arab mercantile and religious interests resembling the European pattern.

But Arabs in the Indian Ocean basin were not like Europeans. First, they were not agents of a polity eager to assert itself overseas. Home bases for Arab seafarers were port cities—Jiddah, Aden, Muscat—along the periphery of a vast, thinly populated desert peninsula not effectively governed by anyone. These cities faced outward to the sea. But they were not linked to a densely populated, economically productive, politically controlled hinterland in the way that western Europe's port cities were. They were urban areas on their own, not urban areas embedded in states.[42] Their prospects for profitable trade were most favorable if none of them advanced political claims beyond its immediate domain. Traders and sailors moved on monsoonal winds from one trading center to another, intermediaries among several autonomous units rather than agents of any particular one.[43]

Second, Arabs were not the only—or even the principal—propagators of Islam in southeast Asia. The central role they played in the religion's formation and explosive early spread into the Fertile Crescent and across North Africa was diluted in later centuries. Islam's steady advance eastward by land and sea was due mainly to initiatives by non-Arabs. Its increasingly cosmopolitan character can be seen in Malacca. The Portuguese chronicler Tomé Pires reports that shortly after the city was founded "some rich Moorish merchants moved from Pase [in Sumatra] to Malacca, Parsees, as well as Bengalese and Arabian Moors, for at that time there were a large number of merchants belonging to these three nations."[44]

The successes of traders as proselytizers meant that diffusion of Islam in Southeast Asia did not depend on soldiers and administrators brought in from outside. If public sector support was deemed necessary it was provided on site: once Malacca's ruler converted, Islam became in effect the kingdom's official faith. Further, the spread of Islam did not depend on full-time specialists in conversion recruited, dispatched, and reporting to an institution headquartered in Arabia or any other Muslim country. Islam indigenized itself as it expanded rather than serving the ambitious designs of a distant state or missionary agency.

To summarize, the Chinese public sector had only a fleeting interest in reaching out to Malacca, no interest in conquering the city, and competitive rather than cooperative relations between itself and private profit sectors; the religious sector had no will or autonomous institutional capacity to assert itself overseas. China's impact on Malacca as of the early sixteenth century was confined to the activities of a single sector functioning on its own. Arabs had two sectors interested in influencing the outside world, hence the potential for a sectoral coalition. But Islam's spread to Malacca and elsewhere in Southeast Asia was not essentially an Arab activity. Neither was it directed by religious agents accountable to their own sectoral institutions, as in the European pattern. Most important, the Arabs' mercantile and religious interests were not backed by a state able or anxious to expand overseas. What initially appears as a two-sector alliance turns out to be a phantom alliance because it lacked institutions stretching outward from a territorial base.

The limited, functionally diffuse character of Chinese and Arab/Muslim relations with Malacca posed an insoluble dilemma for the city's sultan when he encountered Europeans. The first ship sent out in 1509 from Goa, administrative capital of Portugal's Estada da India, consisted of traders. But Muslim merchants resident in Malacca who came from Gujarat and other Indian ports knew from experience that the Portuguese flag accompanied trade and that the Portuguese were Christians implacably hostile to Islam. Warned in effect that the Portuguese constituted a triple threat to his regime, the sultan imprisoned and mistreated several members of the trade mission. His actions precipitated the very attack by Portuguese soldiers two years later that he hoped to forestall. But the Muslim merchants could offer only warnings. None of the cities from which they came was in any position to supply military aid, even to coreligionists threatened by Christian infidels.

The only powerful polity to which the sultan could turn was China. But if he was able to contact the Chinese emperor his efforts were in vain. The tributary system binding Malacca to the Celestial Kingdom symbolized superior/inferior relations. But it did not contain a mutual defense clause. Help was not forthcoming. At a critical moment in world history, when Europeans first intervened in Southeast Asian affairs, the Chinese court was unwilling to assert its stake in a nearby region. The sultan faced toward Mecca when praying and toward Beijing when offering tribute. But for quite different reasons he could count on neither to help counter the new foe.

Beijing, in other words, was the capital city of a powerful state lacking both an expansionist foreign policy and an expansionist religion. Mecca was the central city of an expansionist religion but not of a state. Lisbon was the capital city of a state with an expansionist foreign policy *and* a strong commitment to spread an expansionist religion.

As the Muslim merchants predicted, the Portuguese launched a triple assault on Malacca. The city was captured in 1511 by an armada of ships carrying fifteen hundred soldiers whose commander, Viceroy Afonso d'Albuquerque, saw himself as an extension agent of the Portuguese state.[45] That the invaders intended to assert permanent political control soon became clear. Albuquerque allegedly cried out to his men in the heat of battle, that "We [should] build a fortress in this city . . . and sustain it, and . . . this land [should] be brought under the dominion of the Portuguese, and the King D. Manuel be styled true king thereof."[46] Construction of a stone fortress was begun as soon as the battle was won, and it was kept well supplied with soldiers and cannon. The city was a Portuguese possession until the Dutch took it in the seventeenth century. Once secured, Malacca became a vital outpost used to establish other Portuguese enclaves in the Moluccas and on the China coast.

The conquest of Malacca, in turn, was an integral part of a grand scheme to capture gains from Indian Ocean trade. Political control of enclaves throughout the ocean basin was considered a necessary as well as desirable means to an economic end. Albuquerque appealed to the profit motive as explicitly as one could: "If we take this trade of Malacca away out of [the Moors'] hands, Cairo and Mecca are entirely ruined, and to Venice will no spiceries go except that which her merchants go and buy in Portugal."[47]

Portuguese actions also reveal the religious dimension of their drive for dominance. Albuquerque waited to launch his attack until the day of Saint James, patron saint of Iberian crusaders. That the crusading mentality was alive and well can be seen in his reference to "the great service which we shall perform to our Lord in casting the Moors out of the country, and quenching the fire of this sect of Mofamede so that it may never burst out again hereafter."[48] Non-Muslims were spared following the battle. But "of the Moors, [including] women and children, there died by the sword an infinite number, for no quarter was given to any of them."[49] A church was constructed, and in 1557 it became the Cathedral of the Bishop of Malacca. Priests working among non-Muslims in the local fishing community made many converts. The famous Jesuit missionary Francis Xavier visited the city in 1545 on his way from India to Japan.

By one estimate between half a million and a million people, from Mozambique to Japan, converted to Roman Catholicism by the end of the sixteenth century.[50] Malacca's history and its role as missionary way station to other parts of Asia illustrate the strong expansionist impulses of Euro-Christianity.

By examining actions, motivations, and institutions at a critical juncture of world history when representatives of the three leading candidates for global dominance were present at the same place and time, the case study of Malacca in 1511 tests—and supports—the book's central proposition. The Portuguese were unlike the Chinese and Arabs in the number and variety of sectoral institutions at their disposal, in the stretch of these institutions far from home base, and in the way agents of different sectors worked together for mutually beneficial ends. The Malaccan case highlights not only the contrast between Europeans and others who might have formed equivalent empires, but also the empowering effects when cross-sectoral coalitions were assembled.

The Malaccan case highlights the significance of sectors in another respect. European states were not active rivals to control the Indian Ocean when Viceroy Albuquerque launched his attack in 1511. Granting that desire to preempt Spain from controlling the nearby Spice Islands was a strategic consideration lurking in the background, interstate competition probably played a smaller role here than in any subsequent European overseas initiative. The international system's relative insignificance in this story increases one's confidence that the pattern of sectoral institutions within European states is a causal variable analytically separate from the system in which those states were embedded.

The case study helps answer a secondary question raised earlier: why Europeans concentrated phase 1 settlement and conquest activities on the New World. The point can be made by comparing the capture of Malacca with another world-historical event occurring less than a decade later: conquest of the Aztec capital, Tenochtitlán, by forces led by Cortés. Portugal's grand strategy in the Indian Ocean was to capture gains from a lucrative seaborne trade that had functioned for a long time. Malacca was valued as an enclave facing the water, where profits literally floated past in the form of ships carrying spices, precious stones, textiles, chinaware, carvings, and so on through a narrow strait. There was no economic or strategic reason for Albuquerque to invade the Malayan interior. Nor would he have been able to do so, since the key to Portugal's strategy was to disperse the small number of soldiers at its disposal to several posts separated by vast distances. A successful invasion of Malaya would have come at the unacceptable cost of abandoning Goa, Cochin, Hormuz, or Mombasa.

In contrast, Spaniards in the New World encountered no preexisting maritime trade. The wealth they sought would have to be captured at its source, deep in central and south American hinterlands. Vera Cruz, where Cortés landed in 1519, was seen not as an enclave facing the sea but as the staging area for an arduous march inland. The key to Cortés's success was not the geographic dispersal of his soldiers but sufficient concentration in one place to defeat the enemy's equally concentrated forces.

Portugal and Spain both took to the oceans in search of economic gain. But whereas Portugal could attain this goal in the Old World by controlling the high seas, Spain could attain wealth in the New World only by conquering and settling the land. Portugal's aim was not to revolutionize the Indian Ocean basin's economy but rather to extract a hefty share of gains from an existing pattern of trade. But Spain had to revolutionize the New World economies it encountered in order to gain from conquest. Portugal, having an essentially conservative economic agenda, felt no need to send settlers to Malacca or to set up plantations or prospect for minerals outside the city. Spain, facing both the necessity and the opportunity in the Americas to design radically new patterns of extraction, production, and trade, exported its people across the Atlantic and fostered large-scale, labor-intensive agricultural and mining operations.

The Portuguese in Malacca found they could prosper without altering indigenous political structures in the city's immediate environs. Not so Cortés and his successors, who could not prosper unless state structures run by Europeans were in place to coerce indigenous peoples to labor long and hard for minimal reward. It was possible for a metropole to profit from an Old World enclave while keeping political claims outside enclave boundaries to a minimum. It was not possible to profit from a New World plantation or mining economy without superimposing political control over large areas. A minimalist colonial strategy that worked well in phase 1 Malaya was insufficient for New Spain.

Not until the nineteenth century did Europeans consider the Malayan interior worthy of their attention. Under British direction, exports from rich tin mines were increased and rubber plantations laid out. The plantations marked a transfer to the Old World of a plant Europeans had found in the New (*Hevea brasiliensis*) and of a mode of production perfected earlier in the Americas. More recent Malaccan history thus illustrates, in microcosm, how Europe's concentration on transforming the New World in phase 1 facilitated conquest and transformation of much of the Old World in phase 3.

THE ROLE OF INDIVIDUALS

A final twist of the zoom lens allows one to focus on prominent individuals born in Europe who played leading roles in asserting influence and power overseas (table 10.1). Many agents of a metropole's public sector took advantage of autonomy in the field to take aggressive action not called for—or even expressly forbidden—in their instructions. Individuals who acted on their own to extend empire included Cortés (Valley of Mexico, 1519–22), Marquess Arthur Wellesley (Mysore; Marathas, 1798–1805), Sir Thomas Stamford Raffles (Singapore, 1819), Comdr. George Lambert (Burma, 1851), Adm. Pierre de la Grandière (western Cochinchina, 1867), and Gen. Charles-Emile Moinier (Meknes, 1911).

When risky initiatives by men on the spot proved successful, imperial inertia quickly set in. Home governments resisted giving up territory acquired in their name, even if without their prior knowledge and consent. Raymond Betts's assessment of French expansion in phase 3 applies to other situations as well: "Most of French imperialism was belated governmental response to activities undertaken far away from Paris by individuals who frequently altered, defied, or simply ignored official policy. That irregular band of self-seekers and noble spirits, who were soldiers, merchants, explorers and missionaries, marched on to encounter problems that the home government then felt politically compelled to resolve. . . . The reality of imperialism was in the singular person of the Frenchman who happened to be there."[51]

Some of these individuals sought public acclaim and some tried to avoid it; there were extroverts and intensely private persons; wealth seekers and ascetics; sadists, altruists, and would-be martyrs; men with strong heterosexual drives, misogynists, and latent or active homosexuals. For some an overseas career permitted

TABLE 10.1.

INDIVIDUALS ASSERTING EUROPEAN INFLUENCE AND POWER IN AREAS THAT BECAME COLONIES

NOTES: Individuals are listed in roughly chronological order for phases 1 and 2 and in alphabetical order for phase 3. Where their overseas activities were sponsored by a European-based institution, they are listed by the sector with which that institution is associated. A sponsoring organization with scientific purposes—e.g., geographical exploration—is classified as part of the public sector when its activities were approved by rulers and/or supported by public funds.

The selection criterion for leaders and agents in the public sector is whether they took initiatives to add to the overall extent of European empires. Not listed are people who engineered transfers of existing holdings from one metropole to another. To avoid confusion, the country a monarch ruled is listed after the monarch's name.

Phases 1 and 2

Public sector

Rulers/leaders/bureaucrats in the metropole:

Prince Henry; John II (Portugal); Isabella (Castile); Charles V (Hapsburg domains/ Spain); Elizabeth I (England); Philip II (Spain); Johan von Oldenbarnevelt; Louis XIV (France); Jean-Baptiste Colbert; Napoleon Bonaparte.

Overseas agents (includes officially sponsored explorers, soldiers, early colonial administrators):

Gil Eannes; Bartolomeu Dias; Christopher Columbus; Vasco da Gama; Amerigo Vespucci; Nicolas de Ovando; Afonso d'Albuquerque; Vasco Nuñes de Balboa; Hernán Cortés; Ferdinand Magellan; Juan Sebastián de Elcano; Hernando de Soto; Francisco Pizarro; Francisco de Toledo; Jacques Cartier; Samuel de Champlain; Francis Drake; Marquis de Dupleix; James Cook; George Vancouver; Arthur Phillip; Charles Cornwallis; Arthur Wellesley; Mountstuart Elphinstone.

Agents of scientific organizations:

Joseph Banks; Mungo Park.

Private profit sector

Entrepreneurs (including privateers):

Nuno Tristao; Pierre Radisson; Henry Morgan; John Hawkins; Piet Heyns.

Sponsors or agents of officially chartered companies (includes leaders of company-sponsored settlement communities):

Jan Pieterzoon Coen; Walter Raleigh; Henry Hudson; Prince Rupert; George Carteret; John Smith; John Winthrop; Jan van Riebeeck; Robert Clive; Warren Hastings; Thomas Stamford Raffles.

TABLE 10.1.

CONTINUED

Religious sector

High ecclesiastical office; founders or agents of missionary bodies:

Gonzalo Ximenez de Cisneros; Pope Alexander VI; Ignacio Loyola; Francis Xavier; Jean-Jacques Olier; François Xavier de Laval-Montmorency; Eusebio Kino; Junípero Serra; Alexandre de Rhodes; Christian Friedrich Schwartz; William Carey.

Phase 3

Public sector

Rulers/leaders/bureaucrats in the metropole:

Otto von Bismarck; Joseph Chamberlain; Charles X (France); Benjamin Disraeli; Antonio Enes; Eugène Etienne; Jules Ferry; Léon Gambetta; Leopold II (Belgium); Lord Salisbury.

Overseas agents (includes officially sponsored explorers, treaty collectors, soldiers, early colonial administrators):

Louis Archinard; Evelyn Baring (Earl Cromer); Heinrich Barth; Pierre Savorgan de-Brazza; Thomas Bugeaud; Louis Faidherbe; Joseph Gallieni; François Garnier; Pierre de la Grandière; Charles Gordon; Harry Johnston; H. H. Kitchener; Henry Lawrence; Frederick Lugard; Louis Hubert Lyautey; Jean-Baptiste Marchand; Gustav Nachtigal; Carl Peters; Frederick Sleigh Roberts; Albert Sarraut; Henry Morton Stanley; Lothar von Trotha; Garnet Wolseley.

Agents of scientific organizations:

Richard Burton; John Hanning Speke; Joseph Thomson.

Private profit sector

Entrepreneurs:

Macgregor Laird; Adolf Luderitz; Adolf Woermann.

Sponsors or agents of officially chartered companies:

George Taubman Goldie; Ferdinand deLesseps; William Mackinnon; Cecil Rhodes.

Founder of settler communities:

Edward Gibbon Wakefield.

Religious sector

High ecclesiastical office; founders or agents of missionary bodies:

François Coillard; Friedrich Fabri; C. D. Helm; Charles Lavigerie; Robert Laws; David Livingstone; Samuel Marsden; Robert Moffat; Ludwig Nommenson; John Philip; Joseph Shanahan; Mary Slessor; Alfred Tucker; Henry Venn; Henry Williams.

---

escape from the conventions and constraints of their own society or opportunity to start over following a failed early career. For others what mattered was the allure of places far away, where one could satisfy curiosity about the unknown, experience high adventure, and test the limits of endurance.[52] The impetus for action could change during a lifetime, as with Livingstone's shift from missionary work to anti-slavery lobbying to geographical exploration. Important as individuals were in asserting European dominance overseas, the enormous variations in their stories lead us away from a psychologically based theory of imperialism.

Some nonpsychological generalizations about individuals can be advanced. First, constructing empires was a gendered operation, reserved for men. The only exceptions were women monarchs in phase 1—Isabella of Castile and Elizabeth I of England played, in fact, decisive roles—and women sent out by Protestant mission agencies in phase 3—Mary Slessor, for example. The virtual male monopoly in this field is not, however, a feature distinctive of Europe. The same could be said of aggressive behavior throughout human history, whether across political boundaries or within them.

Second, aspects of west European culture and social structure were supportive of individual achievement. The Renaissance and Reformation, albeit in different ways, stressed the value and autonomy of individuals and encouraged each person to realize unmet potential by acting in the here and now. The Judeo-Christian image of a God intervening actively and redemptively in human affairs expressed a model of behavior that disparaged fatalism and passivity. In general, social stratification was sufficiently marked that persons born on the lower end of the scale were acutely aware of the rewards of living at a higher level. Yet relations among classes did not ossify into a caste system, and all three sectors offered opportunities for upward mobility. Unusual personal accomplishments were acknowledged and praised, for example, by statues in public places, commissioned works of art, folktales, biographies, and autobiographies. As the legal system developed, courts affirmed private property rights against claims by the state. This permitted entrepreneurs to accumulate and dispose of wealth without excessive fear of arbitrary property expropriation. Leaving a home town or country to venture abroad was not regarded as a violation of family obligations or religious norms. Returning home after succeeding abroad held open the prospect of societal recognition. Outward mobility could thus translate into upward mobility. To the extent that these factors were not as prominent in non-European societies, incentives were not as strong for individuals to take risks and initiatives outside their communities.

Third, overseas achievements of individuals, far from undermining metropolitan sectoral institutions, strengthened them and extended their territorial reach. To be sure, some Europeans went abroad as loners, unconnected to or only nominally supported by a sponsoring agency. Examples include *coureurs de bois* in the French Canadian interior; privateers like Henry Morgan and Piet Heyns in the Caribbean; explorer/adventurers like René Caillié, Richard Burton, Gerhard Rohlfs, and Mary Kingsley; beachcombers on South Sea islands, and James Brooke, founder of a family dynasty in Sarawak. In his final years Livingstone cut himself off from all previous sponsors, ecclesiastical, scientific, and governmental. Archetypal loners immortalized in fiction are Kurtz in Joseph Conrad's *Heart of Darkness* and Dravot in Kipling's *The Man Who Would Be King.* Still, it is striking how frequently able, ambitious individuals advanced the interests of an institutional sponsor in the course of advancing their personal careers. As noted earlier, Cortés and Pizarro could have seized power in their own names following conquests attributable in large part to their decisive, tactically brilliant leadership. Yet they insisted on portraying themselves as agents of Emperor Charles V. What at one level was a personal triumph was transmuted into a conquest for the ruler of Spain and the ruler's domains. The same holds for many other soldiers listed in the table. Founders and agents of chartered companies, while doing what they could to obtain material gain for themselves, worked to advance corporate interests. Missionaries converted people to the denomination that recruited and sent them forth.

Focusing on individuals thus takes one back to sectors. Europe's sectoral institutions offered sufficient recognition and reward to individual accomplishments that high achievers were attracted to their ranks. At the same time, ambitious individuals found ways to define personal career goals in ways compatible with advancement of larger institutional objectives. It was on the frontiers of empire that the organization man and the rugged individualist turned out to be the same person. Perhaps it was the daunting challenge of creating new organizations in unfamiliar settings that permitted the fusion of these apparently opposite personality types. In any event, the willingness of dynamic individuals to work for organized causes transcending self-interest meant that their labors outlasted their lives. If bold personal initiatives often proved decisive in the formation of overseas empires, the persistent channeling of personal initiatives into European-based institutions goes far to explain the durability of these improbable arrangements.

11
Non-European Initiatives and Perceptions

When Europeans visited other lands they simultaneously encountered other peoples.[1] Claims to possess distant places were inseparable from claims to rule their inhabitants. The scope and effectiveness of European claims were greatly affected by what indigenous peoples did. As pointed out in chapter 2, power is relational. Imperialism involves one set of actors wresting power from another. A theory of imperialism must take into account the losers as well as winners of this struggle. What was it about people who became colonial subjects that limited their capacity or their will to resist subordination?

Unfortunately, most theories of European imperialism focus primarily if not exclusively on the colonizers. Hence they provide little assistance in answering this question. And writers who do show how non-Europeans shaped their own history tend to emphasize certain activities while neglecting others. A substantial literature in what might be termed resistance studies has emerged in recent years.[2] Works in this genre show that European expansion was contested in a wide range of societies by people who were not about to concede accustomed liberties and ways of life to arrogant, disruptive invaders.

But chronicles of resistance, far from accounting for European imperialism, only deepen the mystery as to why invaders could have been so successful when confronted by determined local opposition. Resistance studies imply that imperialists were more powerful than their apologists imagined or more cleverly diabolic than their most fervent detractors asserted or both. But a theory of imperialism that treats Europeans as giants or moral monsters fails for lack of credibility. Europeans can be restored to a status at once merely and fully human by acknowledging that people in other continents responded to their initiatives in many ways, some of which had the effect of facilitating empire. Resistance was clearly an important part of this story, being at times decisive in delaying or halting conquest. But the willingness of indigenous people to collaborate was also frequently decisive in providing the territorial footholds and social leverage Europeans needed to start carrying out expansionist designs.[3] Non-Europeans contributed in important measure to their eventual colonization, even if they did not foresee or intend it.

In the hindsight of a postcolonial world with strongly held anticolonial norms, collaboration is difficult to understand and easy to condemn as the work of sellouts and traitors. But in the context of its time and place it may have made sense on moral as well as tactical grounds. Europeans' propensity to intervene in others' affairs was often supplemented by requests for intervention from local people, who hoped this would help them achieve their own goals. In many cases imperialism was the result not only of European push but also of indigenous pull.

RESISTANCE AND ITS EFFECTS

At some point west Europeans ruled most of the world, but they never ruled all of it. Japan, China, Tibet, Thailand, Persia, Afghanistan, and most of the Arabian Peninsula were not incorporated into overseas empires. To explain why one must turn first to these territories and only secondarily to Europe.

In some instances geography played an important role. The deserts and mountains of Arabia, Afghanistan, and Tibet inhibited outside penetration. On occasion these features were skillfully put to defensive use, as when Afghans humiliated the British army in 1839–42 and 1878–80. As noted earlier, diseases in the Old World tropics decimated European ranks until prophylactics were devised and mass produced.

The military, political, and administrative capabilities of non-European states were a factor. The Japanese never confronted a European invading force, primarily because their reputation for ferocity against enemies, both fellow Japanese and foreigners, was a powerful deterrent. A Spanish royal decree of 1609 directed commanders in the Pacific "not to risk the reputation of our arms and state" against Japanese soldiers.[4] Wrote the missionary pioneer Francis Xavier, "Never in my life have I met people who rely so much on their arms. . . . They are very warlike and always involved in wars."[5] When in the early seventeenth century Tokugawa rulers restricted trade with the West and persecuted European priests and local Christian converts, no European power dared launch a retaliatory strike, much less an invasion bent on conquest. Instead, the English quietly left in 1623, while the Spanish were deported in 1624 and the Portuguese fifteen years later. Only the Dutch remained, confined to a tiny artificial island in Nagasaki harbor. In 1640 the Portuguese-ruled enclave of Macao sent emissaries to press for a resumption of trade. The party was arrested on arrival, sixty-one members of the embassy and crew beheaded, and the remaining thirteen sent back to Macao to recount what had happened. Lest the message be misunderstood, a large pole at the site of the buried corpses carried the following inscription: "A similar penalty will be suffered by all those who henceforth come to these shores from Portugal.... Even more, if the King of Portugal ... or even the GOD of the Christians were to come, they would all pay the very same penalty."[6] A policy of preemptive intimidation was at work.

Japan's resistance to phase 1 European penetration was a function of its rulers' capacity and will to take decisive, timely action. Political consolidation in the early seventeenth century under the Tokugawa dynasty ended more than a century of warfare among the islands' regional lords. A centralizing regime was able to carry out a coherent foreign policy at the very point when Europeans were making their presence felt in East Asian waters. Had Japan's state-building era occurred a century later and had the civil wars continued, Europeans might have had a greater impact on Japan's domestic affairs than they did.

Moreover, the early Tokugawa rulers had the foresight to envisage that foreign merchants and missionaries would be followed by soldiers. The official rescript on the Macao mission alleged that "the worm-like Barbarians of Macao, who had long believed in the doctrine of the Lord of Heaven, wished to propagate their evil religion in our country; and for many years they sent people called 'Bateren' [Padre] on board their own ships, or in hired Chinese ships. They did this with the intention of seducing our ignorant people, thus paving the way for the eventual occupation of our country."[7] By expelling agents of the two sectors that had infiltrated Japanese society, the shoguns ensured that the triple assault they feared would not take place.

More than two centuries later the leading European countries, reinforced by the United States, announced their governments' intentions to intervene. Once again Japan's rulers carried out an effective resistance strategy. Architects of the Meiji Restoration embarked on a sustained course of technological modernization, paying special attention to upgrading the navy and army. Their policies not only held off the Western powers but also enabled Japan to form its own overseas empire. A key to the Meiji reformers' success was their borrowing of Western technology without becoming heavily indebted to Western banks. Japan avoided the debt / foreign intervention trap that ensnared modernizing rulers in Egypt, Tunisia, and Morocco.

China escaped takeover not because of its rulers, who in sharp contrast to the Japanese approached outsiders with indifference heavily laden with disdain, even after Opium War defeats and the sack of the imperial summer palace in Beijing in 1860 by a British-French expeditionary force.[8] The main factor was a durable bureaucracy linking the imperial court with the rest of the vast country. An institution using meritocratic recruitment principles supported by domestic sources of revenue and socialized to respect the emperor and his edicts was a formidable obstacle to foreign conquerors. The only comparably populous society, India, proved easier for Europeans to penetrate because Mughal rulers never imposed a unified, centrally controlled administrative apparatus on the subcontinent. The English East India

Company had room to maneuver within a public sector far more decentralized and loosely structured than that in China.

The vital role of rulers resurfaces when one examines Thailand and Abyssinia. The Thai rulers Mongkut and Chulalongkorn and the Abyssinian emperor Mene-lik II skillfully engaged in international diplomacy, taking advantage of rivalries among European powers pressing against their borders. Though neither Thailand nor Abyssinia industrialized as did Japan, both adopted aspects of defensive modern-ization. Thai rulers redesigned administrative and educational systems along Euro-pean lines. Menelik purchased from European sources the weapons his forces used to defeat the Italian army at Adowa (1896). Victory ensured Abyssinian independence for four decades.

The ability of non-European warriors to intimidate or defeat European in-vaders helps explain why some areas that were eventually colonized retained inde-pendence as long as they did. Moroccan defeat of a large Portuguese army in 1578 at El Ksar-el-Kabir abruptly ended Iberian dreams of conquering the African territory closest at hand. In the New World fierce resistance by the Carib inhabitants of Trinidad, Martinique, Antigua, St. Vincent, and St. Kitts delayed permanent Euro-pean settlement for well over a century. Araucanians in the southern extremities of South America and so-called Chichimecs in northern New Spain fended off Spanish claims for decades by launching guerrilla raids on settlers and colonial troops. Other examples come from Angola (Queen Nzinga Mbande), the Philippines (Muslim Moros of Mindanao), the West African interior (Samory and Rabeh), Sumatra (the Acheh emirate), and India's Northwest Frontier District.

In some cases indigenous forces killed or expelled Europeans who had estab-lished themselves in an area. Amerindians likely annihilated the party Columbus left at La Navidad, Hispaniola, in 1492–93 and turned Sir Walter Raleigh's Roanoke settlement (1587–91) into a lost colony. Omani Arabs dislodged the Portuguese from Muscat in 1650 and from Mombasa in 1698. Instead of a European replacement for the declining Iberian state, "in general it was Arab sea-power that dominated East African waters north of Cape Delgado throughout the eighteenth century."[9] In 1661 a large fleet and twenty-five thousand soldiers led by Cheng Ch'eng-kung (Coxinga) invaded Taiwan and expelled the Dutch from a lucrative trade enclave. Europeans never retook the island, which was later annexed to China by a Ch'ing expeditionary force. In northern New Spain Pueblos under Popé drove Spanish settlers and mis-sionaries out of their territory in 1680 and kept repacification forces at bay for more than a decade. In the Sudan the Mahdi's forces ended vestiges of British rule from the early 1880s to 1898.

Numerous revolts set back European plans to settle and administer newly claimed territories. Examples come from New Spain (Mixton War, 1540–42; Yucatan

Mayas, 1546), Brazil (Potiguar attacks on Itamaracá Island settlers, 1540s–90s); Virginia (tribes confederated by Powhatan, 1622), the New England colonies (Pequot War, 1636–37; Wampanoags under Metacom, 1675–76), Algeria (guerrillas led by Abd-al-Qadir, 1839–47), north-central India (the Great Mutiny of 1857–58), New Zealand (Maori Wars, 1865–72), German East Africa (Mkwawa, 1891–94; Maji-Maji Rebellion, 1905–06), Southern Rhodesia (Matabele [1893] and Mashona [1896] revolts), Madagascar (Red Shawl uprising, 1895), Sierra Leone (Bai Bureh's Hut Tax Rebellion, 1898), Somalia (dervishes led by Sayyid Muhammad Abdille Hassan, 1900–20), German Southwest Africa (Nama and Herero resistance, 1904–07), and Libya (Sanusi sheikhs, 1912–18).

Indigenous responses to Christian missionaries influenced the geography and timing of colonial expansion. Muslim rulers generally opposed the presence and activities of missionaries, seeing them as religious rivals and precursors of infidel rule. This limited the number of Christian converts Europeans could call upon as political collaborators. As noted, emphasis in phase 1 on exploration and settlement of the New World was initially driven by a desire to bypass powerful Islamic polities ensconced in the Mediterranean basin. Religious considerations affected European plans well into phase 3. Otherwise it is hard to explain why Arabian holy sites, the Ottoman heartland in Anatolia, and Persia were not formally taken over, and why for three decades, until strategic necessities intervened in 1914, Britain maintained the fiction that Egypt was part of the Ottoman Empire.

In colonies in which Muslims composed a high proportion of the population, administrators were alert to the possibility that insurrections would become *jihads* (holy wars) and escalate out of control. This concern may account for the fact that in many such places care was taken to keep Islamic institutions in place. Europeans exercised authority indirectly through Muslim rulers in Morocco, Tunisia, Saharan Algeria, northern Nigeria, emirates along the edges of the Arabian peninsula, Muslim (and Hindu) princely states in India after the Great Mutiny, and Malaya. The long-standing Dutch preference for indirect rule in the East Indies may have been influenced by Islam's dominant position in the Indonesian archipelago.

These examples show that there was nothing easy, automatic, or inevitable about the overseas extension of European power. Resistance delayed and in some instances prevented outsiders' claims from being realized. The battle of El Ksar-el-Kabir was not a fluke: European-led forces would in all likelihood have been routed had they tried to conquer Old World continental interiors in phase 1. There was little choice but to adopt the more subtle strategy of sending in merchants and missionaries. Formal control being out of the question, a backup strategy of informal influence would have to suffice.

Violent resistance shaped the way Europeans governed their colonies. In general, after uprisings were crushed in territories with a settler presence, settler leaders pressed for harsh restrictions on indigenous peoples' physical mobility and access to land as a deterrent to future outbreaks. Such was the case in BNA, Southern Rhodesia, Algeria, and New Zealand. On the other hand, uprisings in colonies of occupation often led European rulers to accommodate indigenous leaders and social forces. Examples are the search for collaborators in India following the mutiny of 1857–58 and in northern Nigeria following the Satiru revolt in 1906. Accommodation sensibly acknowledged the weakness of the strong. With few fellow Europeans on site to enforce compliance, rulers were acutely aware of the need for local help if the fledgling colonial enterprise was to succeed. Offering carrots seemed a more promising deterrent to future rebellion than brandishing sticks. But whatever the mix of coercion and accommodation, initiatives by the newly colonized were the driving force. Colonial policy was a response.

LIMITATIONS ON EFFECTIVE RESISTANCE

Several factors made it difficult for non-Europeans to mount sustained, united, effective opposition to the empire builders. These factors help explain why resistance seldom prevented eventual takeover. In many instances, moreover, non-Europeans unintentionally facilitated their own subjugation. These aspects of the imperial story should be stressed. They complement and challenge the Eurocentric interpretation of chapters 8–10 as well as the emphasis many writers place on resistance. Because "non-Europe" is a vast and varied residual category, attempts to generalize about it are virtually guaranteed to fail. The point is not that factors mentioned here were present in all times and places but that when and where they were they undercut resistance.

Geographical Factors

The starting point for overseas empire was the arrival of armed ships along coasts or island chains of other continents. Ship commanders held the psychological and military advantage of surprise over indigenous people.[10] The initial report to the Aztec court of the Spaniards' arrival on the gulf coast registered astonishment as well as surprise when it told of "towers or small mountains floating on the waves of the sea."[11] Inhabitants of the lower St. Lawrence River valley were amazed when they first saw a French ship, thinking it was "a moving island."[12] Europeans capitalized on the surprise/shock factor by constructing stockades or forts as soon as they could upon landing.[13] Almost before local people knew what had happened a strong, easily defended enclave had been erected on the shoreline. This became the base for subsequent movement inland.

Many non-European societies lacked ships that might have given advance notice of an invading flotilla. Those who did usually had too few to halt the invaders before they landed. The power imbalance at sea gave Europeans a decisive advantage at the moment of first encounter on land.

In the centuries following that first encounter other ships arrived with fresh surprises. On board might be immigrants eager to farm the land, preachers from a newly formed missionary body, soldiers and administrators with new policies to carry out. In the hold might be crates of the most advanced repeating rifles, equipment to lay the colony's first railroad track, the first consignments of iron bars, quinine pills, kerosene lamps, bicycles, and the like. Indigenous peoples lacked intelligence networks that could report what was about to hit them next. When they did find out it was usually too late.

In many cases, notably in the Indian Ocean basin, the early explorers landed in established port cities. Indigenous rulers might have better withstood onerous demands or seaborne assaults had they been aligned to a large inland state whose army could come to their rescue. But the most powerful non-European armies usually belonged to states figuratively as well as literally grounded in continental interiors, with little or no access to the coast. Examples of hinterland polities are the Aztec and Inca empires; Mali, Songhai, Bornu, and the Sokoto caliphate in western Africa; the Shona and interlacustrine Bantu kingdoms, Mahdist state, and Abyssinia in eastern Africa; and the Delhi Sultanate and Mughal Empire, centered in the northern Indian heartland.[14] Rulers of inland states were minimally concerned about developments in maritime trade or naval warfare. They were in no position to appreciate the changed relationship between land and sea power effected by Europe's takeover of the oceans because, from their vantage point, the maritime takeover was invisible.

Thus the armies most capable of defeating Europeans in their coastal enclaves were too far away, and their commanders too ill-informed or unconcerned, to be effective. Almost by accident, Europeans in phase 1 possessed the optimal level of coercive power. They were strong enough to gain footholds along coasts and rivers but too weak to pose serious, immediate threats to hinterland states.[15] Rulers of coastal ports consequently had to fight on their own.

Most of western Europe's Atlantic ports, by contrast, were embedded in larger states. In some instances ports were created or developed by monarchs as part of the state-building project.[16] The seaward orientation of major ports was complemented by the landward orientation of the polity as a whole. The west European state was Janus-faced, its rulers looking to sea *and* soil for sources of revenue and power. European ports derived cash, raw materials, and recruits for overseas voyages from the hinterland. In return, ports sold what they imported to a large inland market. The port–state nexus thus stimulated overseas trade and empire building. Imperialism may have been further aided by the absence of similarly close links elsewhere.

Where people were vulnerable to European diseases because their homelands were distant from the Eurasian-African land mass, their capacity to resist was drastically undercut by epidemic outbreaks. Warrior ranks were decimated. Anomie and social disarray came to the fore just when a well-organized collective response was needed. By felling leaders at key moments an imported disease may have been decisive in the fall of the two most powerful New World empires. Cuitlahuac, an Aztec warrior who warned against allowing Cortés to enter Tenochtitlán and directed a charge against the Spaniards, was chosen ruler after his brother Moctezuma died under "protective custody" of the Spaniards. Cuitlahuac had the personal qualities to mobilize the city's defenses and mount a major counterattack. But he died of smallpox less than three months after assuming the throne. It is likely that the last great ruling Inca, Huayna Capac, was also a victim of smallpox, which spread inland before Pizarro and his men arrived. Huayna Capac's death triggered a succession struggle between his sons Huascar and Atahualpa, a political crisis the astute Pizarro was quick to manipulate.[17] Epidemics also lowered the will of indigenous peoples to fight back. Everyone in an affected group had to concentrate on the daunting challenge of surviving. Morale was doubtless lowered by a disaster inexplicably engulfing an entire society. Traditional medicines, religious rituals, and the wisdom of respected elders were to no avail. It must have been especially demoralizing to realize that Europeans were far less likely to die from these diseases. Missionaries and traders sometimes seized on this fact as evidence of their group's religious and biological superiority. In a setting of unprecedented crisis with familiar ways of life disappearing all around them, many people may have been persuaded not only to concede power to Europeans but also to regard the new rulers as cultural role models.

Attitudes, Values, Worldviews

Many non-Europeans were proud of their custom of offering hospitality to passing strangers. To cite three among numerous examples, generous provisions of food and drink may have saved the lives of Magellan's crew in the Philippines and permitted the Jamestown settlers and Massachusetts Bay Pilgrims to survive their first months ashore. All too often Europeans took this hospitality for granted and did little to requite it.[18] What indigenous peoples did not realize is that these strangers were not just passing through but in many instances intended to stay. Had the newcomers' goal of occupying and permanently settling land been known at the outset, the first indigenous response would likely have been hostility. And more would-be settlements would have joined Raleigh's ill-fated ventures at Roanoke on the lost colony roster. When indigenous people realized their mistake it was often too late. Newcomers were settled in for the duration.

In a show of generosity with enormous historical ramifications, the Aztec ruler Moctezuma sent an extravagant array of gifts to Cortés shortly after the Spanish expedition reached Vera Cruz and was still encamped along the shore. Intricately wrought gold objects, emeralds, and tropical feathers were presented by royal messengers to propitiate Cortés should he turn out to be the returning god Quetzalcoatl, as was widely rumored. This was surely the most inappropriate, self-defeating hospitality Moctezuma could have bestowed. For it only enflamed the avaricious spirits of the Spaniards, further strengthening their resolve to conquer and loot the Aztec capital. Moctezuma repeated his mistake as the Spaniards and their Amerindian allies advanced toward Tenochtitlán. An indigenous account relates that chiefs dispatched by Moctezuma

> went out to meet the Spaniards . . . there in the Eagle Pass. They gave the "gods" ensigns of gold, and ensigns of quetzal feathers, and golden necklaces. And when they were given these presents, the Spaniards burst into smiles; their eyes shone with pleasure; they were delighted by them. They picked up the gold and fingered it like monkeys; they seemed to be transported by joy, as if their hearts were illumined and made new.
>
> The truth is that they longed and lusted for gold. Their bodies swelled with greed, and their hunger was ravenous; they hungered like pigs for the gold. They snatched at the golden ensigns, waved them from side to side and examined every inch of them.[19]

The more obvious it became that Cortés was not satisfied by the finest offerings and would not go away, the more disheartened Moctezuma grew. The king's will to resist collapsed just when he might have put a highly militarized regime on full alert. The account continues, "When he learned that the 'gods' wished to see him face to face, [Moctezuma's] heart shrank within him and he was filled with anguish. . . . He had lost his strength and his spirit, and could do nothing. . . . Now he was weak and listless and too uncertain to make a decision. Therefore he did nothing but wait. He did nothing but resign himself and wait for them to come. He mastered his heart at last, and waited for whatever was to happen."[20]

Indigenous conceptions of the proper relationship between human beings and land had the unintended effect of empowering European settlers. It was widely believed that land was available for collective use and that its allocation to families or lineages should be set on a need-specific, revocable basis by group leaders. Land was not perceived as a commodity that could be permanently owned by individuals or traded in a market. Nor was permission to use it seen as entitling occupants to do whatever they wanted on it. In many instances European settlers simply took land without going through the motions of bargaining with local people. But even when bargaining did occur, indigenous leaders agreeing to part with land did not assume that something of value had been irrevocably lost. Land alienation was not part of their worldview, much less their vocabulary. Settlers for their part considered land a commodity which became its owner's personal property once purchased and legally registered. What one side considered a loan hedged with qualifications the other interpreted as an unqualified, permanent transfer. What for one was a use permit was for the other a right of full possession.

Given their conception of property rights, settlers thought it proper to delineate the precise boundaries of land to which they had title, to place fences or other markers along boundary lines, and then to prevent other people from entering without permission. The Lord's Prayer notwithstanding, trespassing was a sin these Christians were not inclined to forgive. With monotonous regularity in all continents and expansion phases, land was taken before indigenous people realized what had happened. Guns protected the boundaries of settler property against local people who had no idea the land was not also theirs to occupy. The armed defense of land that had just been declared off-limits gave Europeans an advantage of surprise equivalent to the advantage of arriving suddenly by sea. Little wonder that colonial land transfers were so consistently one-sided. An African saying puts it well: "Before the white man came we had the land and they had the Bible. Now the white man has the land and we have the Bible." The clear implication is that the exchange was not based on free-market principles—and that whites gained far more than blacks.[21]

The explore-control-utilize syndrome that marked modern European thought and action was less prevalent in other societies. There was no such thing as a single, commonly held non-European worldview. Still, values embedded in many indigenous cultures questioned or directly countered the syndrome's empirical and normative assumptions. Emphasis was frequently placed on adapting to a group's physical surroundings rather than struggling against them; being an integral part of the natural world rather than observing nature from an analytically distant vantage point; enjoying what the environment provided rather than trying continually to develop its presumed potential to produce something more; experiencing the present in the context of the past rather than reaching out toward an imagined future. For many people the way to influence an uncertain, potentially hostile environment was to propitiate powerful unseen spiritual forces that were believed to affect what happened in the observable world. This belief was at odds with the increasingly prevalent European view of nature as a despiritualized realm governed by impersonal universal laws. From one perspective, ritual appeals to spiritual forces could harness the capricious character of the universe for desired ends. From the other, it was precisely the *un*capricious, lawlike character of the universe that permitted people to manipulate nature for their own ends. There was no need to resort to superstitions that at best were useless, at worst dangerous.

Other things being equal, when a society that is comfortable with its natural environment encounters a society that is uncomfortable unless actively attempting to control and improve its environment, the former is likely to lose out to the latter. One reason is that scientific and technological advance is more likely in the second situation, with technologies to put Nature to use being readily adaptable to dominate other people. To the extent that non-European cultures fit the first situation while modern European cultures fit the second, one has a plausible cultural explanation for Europe's rise to power.

RELATIONS AMONG INDIGENOUS SOCIETIES[22]

Chapter 9 showed how rivalries among west European states stimulated and accelerated formation of parallel empires. Ironically, expansion was given an added boost by rivalries among non-European societies. Learning what these rivalries were, what was at stake, and who was on what side often constituted the most important information Europeans learned when reaching a distant destination. Gaining power depended in large measure on the newcomers' ability to take advantage of local cleavages. Once a conflict had been identified, the critical question was whether European interests would be served by allying with one of the parties to it. If an alliance was negotiated it was considered purely tactical, to be adjusted or abandoned once the newcomers achieved their goals.

European intervention abroad is often described as divide and rule. The phrase implies that Europeans created divisions among others which were then used to take power. Although accurately describing what happened in some cases, divide and rule is implausible as a description of the typical state of affairs. It implies that indigenous peoples were extraordinarily naive and malleable, with so weak a sense of who they were that they were easily persuaded to accept identities invented on the spot with outsiders' interests primarily in mind. A more accurate description is manipulate and rule. In general, people Europeans encountered had well-formed and only marginally adjustable identities and interests. It was the newcomers' skill at using what they found that mattered, not their ability to sell unsuspecting customers a bill of identity goods never heard of before.

Even more significant, imperial expansion was frequently the result not just of European push but also of indigenous pull. We can see how the latter factor operated by imagining a simple scenario: rivalry between non-European polities *A* and *B*. Their relationship takes a new turn when Europeans enter the scene. If *A* and *B* are commercial competitors each could gain by fostering stable trade relations with the outsiders, whose ships bring an attractive array of consumer goods and offer potentially lucrative outlets for local commodities. If *A* and *B* are at war each could gain at the expense of the other if it got access to European guns. It is easy to understand why emissaries from *A* (or *B* or both) would make their way to the European encampment, offering to form an alliance on terms the outsiders would find attractive.

Suppose that *A* offers the most favorable terms and succeeds in negotiating an alliance. One may assume that *A* regards the alliance as purely tactical, to be adjusted or abandoned once its objectives have been attained. Both parties to the negotiations thus have something in common: each wants to use the other for its own short-term advantage. *Mutual* manipulation is the name of this diplomatic game. That Europeans will usually get the best of the arrangement can be known only at a later point. At the time negotiations take place *A*'s decision makers convince themselves it is they who stand to gain, certainly relative to *B* and probably relative to the Europeans as well. *A*'s top priority, after all, is to outdo known rival *B*. The capabilities and intentions of Europeans are not yet well known. If anything, the newcomers' willingness to form an alliance is taken as a portent of future friendship, not enmity. How can *A* know at the outset that the outsiders will eventually take *A* as well as *B* under their custody?

The point is borne out by examples from both expansionist phases. G. V. Scammell writes that on India's western coast "the governor of Diu . . . abandoned (1508) the 'league of all Muslims' which was to have overthrown the Portuguese and hastened to secure the best commercial terms he could from them, while the King of Cochin was happy to welcome strangers rejected by his fellow Hindu, but age-old rival, the Samorin of Calicut. Thereafter Portuguese penetration of Asia owed much, and in some cases everything, to indigenous disunity and consequent indigenous approval or support."[23] In the 1660s the Dutch inserted themselves into western India by reversing the pattern and allying with Calicut against Cochin.

Bitter enmity between the people of Tlaxcala and their Aztec rulers in Tenochtitlán was a critical factor in Hernán Cortés's subjugation of the Aztec capital. After an initially hostile response to the Spanish soldiers Tlaxcalan leaders negotiated an alliance with Cortés that remained intact throughout the conquest's tumultuous events. About 6,000 Tlaxcalan warriors joined a Spanish force of fewer than 350 on the march to Tenochtitlán. It was to Tlaxcala that the Spaniards retreated after the *noche triste* (sad night) when half their army was annihilated. Without Tlaxcalan cooperation it is virtually inconceivable that Cortés could have completed the audacious mission that changed world history.

On the island of Java the kingdom of Mataram appealed in 1675 for Dutch assistance against its enemy, Banten. In return, Mataram "was obliged to give the Dutch a monopoly over the cloth and opium trades. Dutch help was purchased again and again by tributes and concessions of land until, in 1755, with the partition of

Mataram into two kingdoms, Surakarta and Jogyakarta, the Dutch became suzerains of both."[24] Clive Day concludes that the Dutch in Java "were never carrying on a war of conquest against the natives; they were always fighting *for* the natives, and their territorial gains came to them from the interested party as compensation for services rendered. It was the ceaseless quarreling among the native states that enabled the Dutch always to find a party or a person to champion . . . their candidate was generally successful, and he was not allowed to forget to whom his success was due."[25]

Rivalries among local people permitted early European settlers of North America to entrench themselves on the coast and push inland. The Wampanoags signed a treaty with the Pilgrims in 1621 offering protection against the Narragansetts. The settlers later paired with the Narragansetts against the Pequots, then with the Mohegans against the Narragansetts. Settlers in Pennsylvania found the Iroquois eager to ally with them against the Delawares. In the Mississippi valley the French collaborated with Choctaws to subdue the Natchez.[26]

In phase 3 the Fanti of the Gold Coast sought British help to ward off a growing threat from their northern neighbors the Ashanti. One of the first British representatives in the area wrote in 1853, "The necessity of a protector against the power and ambition of the Ashantees . . . the mutual fear and jealousy of rival chiefs [and other factors] all conspired to influence the minds of every class, to elevate us into power, and to make common cause in maintaining our authority."[27] Sikh soldiers assisted British troops in suppressing Muslim and Hindu forces in India's Great Mutiny.[28] Afrikaner and British migration into the South African interior during the 1830s and 1840s was facilitated by the unwillingness of non-Zulu groups to join Zulu *impis* (warriors) in opposing white settlement. The Zulus' neighbors could not forget the aggressiveness of Shaka's armies and the social dislocation accompanying his state-building tactics. The first white settlers in what became Southern Rhodesia benefited from rivalry between the Ndebele and the Ngwato branch of the Tswana. Chief Kgama of the Ngwato provided soldiers for the Pioneer Column of 1890 and helped settlers crush a major Ndebele uprising three years later.[29] In Mozambique almost half the soldiers employed in Portugal's campaign to conquer the Zambezi Valley in 1888 were recruited from two African states, whose leaders favored cooperation with the Portuguese as an opportunity to gain advantage over neighboring enemies.[30]

The more strongly people identify with their group and the more physically insulated and culturally distinct that group is, the greater the challenge of forging bonds of identity and loyalty with neighbors. This was a formidable challenge in many non-European areas, making it difficult for large numbers of people to unite, or even coordinate activities, around the common cause of resisting colonial takeover. To take an extreme form of a recurring scenario, imagine that societies *C* and *D* are located a hundred miles apart. Each is unaware of the other's existence because of the terrain, the absence of connecting trade routes, and rudimentary methods of transport and communication. Each is economically self-reliant and has its own customs regarding marriage and inheritance. C's and D's people practice different religions and speak mutually unintelligible languages. The two societies have never been incorporated into a larger indigenous polity. In this scenario, had C and D interacted they would have found they had little in common. Whereas A and B in the earlier hypothetical case are rivals, C and D are strangers, distanced from one another in many more ways than physical space.

C regards Europeans entering its territory as strangers. But it would think the same of D's people if it knew of their existence. To C, Europeans and D are Others, just as for Europeans C and D are Others.[31] European offers to recruit C's young men on a campaign to conquer D would not be met with indignant refusal on grounds that C and D have too many things in common to betray each other. The comprehensive racial, continental, and national identities that evolved in the colonial era and gave birth to anticolonial solidarity movements did not exist before the onset of European rule. Whether D is subjugated is a matter of indifference to C, whose young men may feel no qualms at joining a force marching on D. Any qualms might be overridden by anticipated gains from victory, which can be foreseen since the advancing army deploys powerful weapons unavailable to D's defenders.

This hypothetical example helps one understand why Europeans consistently found indigenous people to fight for them. Successful recruitment drives enabled European soldiers to overcome the initial handicaps of small numbers and unfamiliarity with the local terrain, languages, and customs. Though the armies that built overseas empires were commanded by European officers, they were typically manned on the front lines by local foot soldiers. As long as C's recruits were not asked to subdue their own people they were ready to march a hundred miles and wage war on D. Parochial identities and loyalties induced many non-Europeans to take a leading part in their subjugation.

To take a few examples, Indian soldiers (sepoys) recruited by the English East India Company enabled the company to move inland from the coastal "presidencies" of Bombay, Madras, and Calcutta. Young men who joined the famed Tirailleurs Senegalais helped the French pacify areas of West Africa hundreds of miles from their homelands. Senegalese and Algerians fought for France in Morocco. The Zimbabwean historian Stanlake Samkange asserts that "European armies had to depend on Africans for foot soldiers and carriers, for intelligence and food supplies. Without other Africans supplying these services, Europeans would never have been able to mount the campaigns by which they conquered the continent."[32]

DIVISION AND WEAKNESS WITHIN INDIGENOUS SOCIETIES

Cleavages within indigenous social/political units offered additional opportunities for Europeans to establish and extend a power base. To revert to hypothetical mode, imagine that polity E has recently conquered its neighbor, F. E has begun to treat F as part of its regular domain, forcibly extracting resources and labor from F. When Europeans arrive F's leaders understandably consider Europeans potential allies in a movement to regain lost freedom. It was exactly this kind of alliance that European commanders welcomed.

Such an opportunity arose when Pizarro and his band of adventurers took on the mighty Inca Empire. The Huanca Indians had been recently defeated by an army from Quito and incorporated into the empire. John Hemming writes that when the Quitan army engaged Pizarro's men in 1534 at the Battle of Jauja, the Huancas "made no move against the Spaniards. . . . They even provided two thousand auxiliaries for [the Spanish commander's] army. Their action was partly revenge for the Quitan occupation during the past year, but it was also a more fundamental revolt . . . against the rule of the Incas from Cuzco. The hostile attitude of powerful tribes such as the Huanca was a decisive factor in the overthrow of Inca rule in Peru."[33]

A large indigenous polity lacking strong bonds of common loyalty was in a vulnerable position, for parts of it could be taken without necessarily precipitating a hostile response from other parts. The decentralized structure of the Mughal Empire in the eighteenth century made it problematic to devise a common strategy against advances by the British East India Company into outlying Mughal provinces. In West Africa, the Sokoto Caliphate was unable to coordinate resistance to British forces led by Frederick Lugard (1900–03). Each major city within the caliphate fought its own defense with minimal assistance from others. What appeared initially as one large obstacle to the conquest of northern Nigeria turned out to be several small, separate challenges, each manageable given the military resources at Lugard's disposal.[34]

Another kind of internal cleavage open to outside manipulation was a struggle for political leadership. A contestant might seek or be offered European assistance to come out on top. The British acquired Singapore by such means. Though the island belonged to the sultan of Johore, succession to the sultan's throne was disputed when Stamford Raffles, an agent of the English East India Company, arrived on the scene in 1819. Raffles sided with one of the two claimants, installing his man as sultan in an elaborate ceremony and offering him a handsome yearly stipend. The condition was that the new ruler formally request British protection. In western Senegal after the 1860s "succession conflicts were increasingly taken to the French. . . . Every time there was a succession conflict in Siin, [French headquarters in] Goree received letters, often promising things like new posts that the French had not even requested."[35] These vignettes suggest that societies lacking widely accepted rules for handling political succession were vulnerable to outside intervention whenever contenders for office looked around for powerful supporters.

A different sort of leadership struggle gave the British the pretext they wanted to occupy Egypt in 1881. Popular opposition to the corrupt, bankrupt government of Khedive Tawfiq coalesced around Col. Ahmad Urabi. When riots broke out to protest the government's supine acquiescence to stiff British and French financial demands, the khedive feared he would be overthrown by nationalists led by Urabi. Tawfiq secretly suggested that the Anglo-French fleet, anchored offshore from Alexandria, bombard the city and land marines to save his throne. The French declined, but the British acted on the request. In the short run Tawfiq triumphed over his challenger: Colonel Urabi surrendered to British officers and was dispatched to exile in the Seychelles. But in the long run Tawfiq and his successors lost out. A. L. Al-Sayyid Marsot notes that the khedive made a major miscalculation in expecting the British rescue operation "to be carried out expeditiously, after which the British forces would then evacuate the country. The British occupation of Egypt was to last until 1954."[36]

When ethnically distinct groups with origins outside a territory specialized in trade and finance, they sometimes found it convenient to collaborate with agents of European firms and governments. This was the case with long-established Chinese communities scattered throughout the Southeast Asian mainland and East Indian and Philippine archipelagos. As the Malaccan episode indicated, overseas Chinese lacked ties to their home government. The government in turn was indifferent to what happened to them.[37] Hence they were vulnerable to extortion and persecution in areas where they lived. Many Chinese merchants were amenable to a European takeover provided they could be assured a profitable, protected niche in the local economy. Instead of serving as advance agents of China's power, as European settlers did for their metropoles, overseas Chinese communities helped Europeans consolidate power by serving as intermediaries between rulers and local people in the colonial division of labor.

Christian missionaries often directed conversion campaigns toward low-status groups in the understandable hope that these people would welcome a gospel of liberation from oppression, slavery, and neglect. Target groups included untouchable and low-caste Hindus in India and slaves and repatriated former slaves in Africa.[38] Converts were able to raise their position in society—or even declare independence from the old stratification system in which they had been trapped—by attending mission schools and moving up the mission agencies' alternative hierarchy. These people's linguistic and cross-cultural skills made them especially desirable employees in European firms and government offices. They knew they owed their position in life to the new order brought by outsiders. It is not surprising that the collaborators so essential for consolidating European rule were drawn disproportionately from their ranks.[39]

SECTORS

The type of political system a non-European society possessed was a poor predictor of ability to resist European aggression. Some centralized polities, notably China and Japan, retained independence. Others such as the Aztecs and Incas quickly succumbed. Some stateless societies—Araucanians, Chichimecs, Indians of the Brazilian hinterland, Tuareg and Somali pastoralists, Naga Hill tribes, among others—were remarkably successful at using guerrilla tactics to postpone the day of defeat. Other stateless societies like the Caribbean Arawaks, Australian aborigines, and Nigeria's Bauchi Plateau peoples were easily subdued. The quality of leadership and a society's geographical location probably counted for more than whether its public sector was institutionalized, centralized, or well armed.

Especially in phase 3, the capacity of indigenous rulers to control their subjects was weakened by the disintegrative societal impact of European trading and missionary activity. Efforts to reassert authority by persecuting outsiders or local collaborators often had the opposite effect of further dividing the populace and strengthening opposition to the old order. These efforts dramatized for all how weak the rulers really were. Awareness of the power vacuum tempted ambitious Europeans to move in. In these situations the indigenous pull factor was not the deliberate policy of political elites, but a condition affecting society at large that elites were unable effectively to address.[40]

How a precolonial public sector was organized affected colonial policies. A centralized state that was defeated often retained social control mechanisms that the new rulers could put to use. Mark Burkholder and Lyman Johnson note that "compulsory labor service had been common in both the Aztec and Inca empires, and Spaniards had used it from the beginning of the colonial period for the construction of roads, aqueducts, fortifications, and public buildings and for some agricultural purposes."[41] The compulsory labor draft for Peru's silver and mercury mines imposed by Viceroy Francisco de Toledo in the 1570s was modeled and even named after the *mita* system devised by the Incas. A colonial regime might choose to rule subjects of a defeated polity indirectly, through pliable officials of the old regime. Indirect rule was an option where indigenous states existed. It was not feasible for stateless societies—unless, that is, colonial officials were prepared to invent traditional rulers lacking any shred of precolonial legitimacy.[42]

Many non-European societies operated close to the margin of subsistence, recognized communal use rights rather than individual property rights, were primarily rural dwellers, and depended minimally on goods traded with other societies. To assert that a private profit sector existed in these cases stretches the meaning of the term past the breaking point. In other cases, however, people were able and eager to accumulate income over and above subsistence. The rise of an indigenous private profit sector was associated, as in western Europe, with the growth of urban areas and with networks of middle- and long-distance trade.[43]

Whether or not a private profit sector existed in a particular society prior to contact with Europeans, there is overwhelming evidence that indigenous people welcomed European consumer goods when these were introduced to local markets. The rare instances when officials tried to limit or proscribe trade with Europeans only reinforce this point, since restrictions would not have been needed had there not been high demand for what foreigners had to offer. From the outset Europeans held a monopoly over the sale of a wide range of products, if only because local artisans lacked the raw materials and technical means to make them. Europeans did not have to wait until the Industrial Revolution to shape other people's consumption patterns. Early New World encounters showed that iron bars and glass beads were highly valued. Europeans were referred to as "iron people" and "cloth makers."[44] Bottled alcoholic drinks were in demand on the West African slave-trading coast as well as among Amerindians.

The more limited the capacity of indigenous artisans to compete with European traders in making goods for the local market, the more easily could agents of foreign trading companies carve out influential market niches. Force was often used at the start to gain access to local buyers. But no force was needed to sustain a niche once imported items were valued as elements of the good life. Many items were attractive because of their uniqueness, utility, quality, and low cost. If local artisans had been able to meet growing demands for goods in their own societies or if structures and incentives had been in place to generate a steady stream of new technologies, non-European societies would have been less vulnerable to the seductive appeal of European goods. This speculation suggests that the relative underdevelopment of indigenous private profit sectors may have facilitated European imperialism by not limiting penetration of local economies by outside commercial agents.

Imported goods conferred special status on their producers, an advantage Europeans were happy to put to noneconomic use. James Axtell's discussion of phase 1 North America identifies a subtle process at work in other times and places as well: "The Europeans quickly realized that technological advantage could be turned to spiritual and political profit. As Captain George Waymouth cruised St. George's River in 1605, he performed various feats of technological and scientific wizardry for the visiting Indians, such as picking up a knife with a magnetized sword, in order, he said, 'to cause them to imagine some great power in us; and for that to love and feare us.' The heavy salesmanship of the fur trade, the religious proselytizing of the missions, and the political push of the farming frontier all depended for their initial success on that foundation of love and fear."[45] From monopoly of a market niche to domination of a political system could be a short step.

Some societies were more open to the Euro-Christian message than others. In general, religions most likely to succumb to Christianity were polytheistic, stressed kinship obligations, had no sacred texts, and lacked specialized cadres of priests to administer rituals. Religions were also vulnerable if their spiritual forces were parochial—if, that is, influential spirits were believed to reside in nearby mountains, rivers, trees, or caves or represented a group's ancestors. The more parochial a religion the less credible it was once the autonomy and inherited lifestyles of local communities gave way under multiple assaults from outside. As old faiths lost their hold people were drawn to religions whose transcendent God and universalistic appeal would not change despite the mercurial twists and turns of history. Christianity benefited from the rapid decline of what was variously called animism and paganism. But so did Islam. Societies in which many people converted to Christianity and in which European missionaries were able to operate freely were especially vulnerable to European rule and to thoroughgoing cultural penetration. Societies in which pagans converted to Islam were not immune to European rule. But they had a greater capacity to resist cultural penetration because their religious sector offered a coherent, viable alternative to the European model. Attending a Koranic school, learning Arabic, and facing daily toward Mecca were all acts restricting the extent of a person's political subordination.

In some cases indigenous religious beliefs had the effect, though not the intent, of facilitating European takeover. Already noted were the momentous consequences of the view held by Aztec elites that Cortés should be treated with generosity and deference because he might be the returning god Quetzalcoatl. In a quite different place and time (South Africa, 1856–57) many Xhosa-speakers were persuaded by a young woman's prophecies that their ancestors would return and that hard times—including the recent imposition of British rule—would be ended if they sacrificed their cattle. An estimated four hundred thousand cattle were slaughtered, all to no avail. The ensuing desperate situation accelerated alienation of Xhosa land and pushed millions of Africans into the white-controlled South African labor market.[46]

THE ROLE OF INDIVIDUALS

On many occasions exceptional non-Europeans determined the outcome of early cross-cultural encounters. Employing an admittedly imprecise classification scheme whose categories are not mutually exclusive,[47] one may identify four types:

1. *Preservers:* Rulers who used diplomatic and governing skills to try to preserve a polity's independence. In some cases the effort was successful. In the many cases in which it was not, the individual's actions affected how and when the takeover occurred. In phases 1 and 2 the preservers included Hideyoshi and Ieyasu (Japan), Powhatan (Virginia), Gia Long (Vietnam), and Kamehameha I and II (Hawaii). In phase

3, Ranjit Singh (Punjab, India), Moshoeshoe (Sotho; Basutoland), Lewanika (Lozi; Northern Rhodesia), Mongkut, Chulalongkorn and Prince Devawongse (Thailand), Ismail (Egypt), Menelik II (Abyssinia), Mutesa (Buganda; Uganda), Radama I, Ranavalona I, and Premier Rainilaiarivony (Imerina; Madagascar), Kgama (Ngwato branch of Batswana; Bechuanaland).

2. *Resisters:* Rulers whose armies fought Europeans and leaders in early violent resistance movements against settlers or colonial administrators. In phases 1 and 2, Cuitlahuac (Mexica Aztec; New Spain), Manco Inca (Inca; Peru), Metacom (Wampanoag; Massachusetts Bay Colony), Popé (Pueblo Indians; New Spain), Nzinga Mbande (Angola), Coxinga (Taiwan), and Tipu Sultan (Mysore). In phase 3, Bagyidaw (Burma), Abd al-Qadir (Algeria), Dingane (Zulu; South Africa), Lakshmi Bai and Rani of Jhansi (India), Te Ua Haumene and Te Kooti (Maori; New Zealand), Samory (sudanic West Africa), Rabeh (sudanic West-Central Africa), Muhammad Ahmad and Ibn Abdallah, proclaimed the Mahdi (Sudan), Ahmad Urabi (Egypt), Mkwawa (Hehe; German East Africa), Béhanzin (Dahomey), Bai Bureh (Temne; Sierra Leone), Sayyid Muhammad Abdille Hassan (British Somaliland), and Samuel Maherero (Herero; German Southwest Africa).

3. *Facilitators:* Individuals who assisted European explorers, soldiers, traders, mission agencies, or settlers (for example, as guides, translators, or missionaries). In phases 1 and 2 Ahmad ibn Madjid (Vasco da Gama; Indian Ocean), Malinche (Doña Marina) (Hernán Cortés), and Squanto (Wampanoag; Pilgrims). In phase 3, Samuel Adjai Crowther (missionary pioneer, Nigeria), James Chuma (guide for David Livingstone), and Munisi (Matabeleland guide; Southern Rhodesia).

4. *Collaborators:* Politically prominent individuals who formed alliances with Europeans to increase their power or to ward off challenges from others. In phases 1 and 2, Sultan of Malindi (Vasco da Gama; East Africa), Mir Jafar (Robert Clive; Bengal), and Sultan of Kedah (Penang). In phase 3, Tawfiq (Egypt) and Akitoye (Lagos, Nigeria).

CONCLUSION

This chapter illustrates the multiple ways in which non-Europeans shaped their own history. Clearly, a theory of European imperialism that ignores the rest of the world is inadequate. Likewise, an account that concentrates only on resistance fails to capture the indigenous "pull" factor, which in turn affected the timing, location, and overall results of the European "push." Indigenous actors are not in danger of being ignored when the topic is the end of empire. But the danger *is* present when one is trying to explain the outset of empire. Hence the need for this chapter as a supplement to the three Eurocentric chapters preceding it.

Part IV

CONSOLIDATING POWER

(*Overleaf*) Missionary in German Kamerun prepares to baptize a woman by immersion. From National Archives and Records Administration, Washington, D.C., courtesy of Instructional Resources Corporation.

12
Sectoral Institutions and Techniques of Control

An overseas empire gained is not necessarily an empire retained. If anything, geographic and demographic realities would lead one to expect a brief life for such an improbable, manifestly contrived arrangement. In the vast majority of cases metropoles were separated from colonies by thousands of miles of ocean. In colonies of occupation Europeans were a tiny fraction of the population. Even where settler communities were present their numbers were usually modest compared to indigenous peoples or imported slaves, who lacked racial and cultural ties to the metropole and could hardly be expected to welcome subordination to an acquisitive, racially distinct oligarchy.

Yet that oligarchy prevailed for a long time. The duration of metropolitan rule in the 125 member states of the United Nations (as of 2000) that at one time were governed by European countries is shown in the appendix. I estimate, on the basis of criteria spelled out there, that overseas rule lasted

- more than 500 years in two countries (Cape Verde; São Tomé and Príncipe);
- more than 300 years in 18 countries;
- more than 200 years in 37;
- more than 100 years in 60; and
- more than 60 years in 105.

Only two states—Egypt and Ethiopia—were colonies for fewer than 10 years.

How did a handful of states manage to defy the odds and govern so many distant territories for so long? Part IV addresses this question. Chapter 12 continues the sectoral theme developed earlier, showing how institutions that figured in imperial expansion were critical in colonial consolidation as well. European-led institutions transformed initially inflated political claims into effective control. They made control durable by recruiting and training new cadres to replace older ones. They used positive and negative incentives to get individual employees to work toward sectoral goals and comply with terms of employment. Even if institutions from one or two sectors took an early lead in an area, it was not long before the remaining sector(s) also became active. Sooner or later colonized peoples experienced the triple assault of specialists in power, profit, and proselytization. Sectoral institutions stretched not only from metropoles to colonies but also, increasingly, from capital cities and major ports to hinterlands. The cumulative, synergistic effects of their extended geographical reach, functional specialization, and ability to work in mutually reinforcing ways proved tremendously empowering.

Chapter 13 complements the top-down approach of this chapter by examining what colonial subjects did and thought. Attention is focused on non-Europeans though settlers are also discussed. Colonial subjects were not utterly powerless and passive. They continually took initiatives to which rulers had to respond. But sometimes initiatives driven by opposition to some aspect of foreign dominance had the unintended effect of reinforcing dominance. Colonial residents also disagreed among themselves over identities, goals, and appropriate tactics for organizing themselves and confronting rulers. Recurring debates over these matters undercut serious challenges to the status quo from below.

In many respects governing a colony is like governing other collections of human beings. I focus here on features specific to the colonial situation, notably the physical distance between metropole and colony and the racial/cultural distance between rulers and non-European subjects. What did metropolitan governments do to ensure that administrators dispatched to far-off lands complied with their directives? What did top administrators in a colony do to ensure that non-Europeans complied with their directives? How did institutions imported from a metropole become domesticated and begin to shape colonial society? How was the public sector reinforced by European-led private profit and religious sectors?

The character of sectoral institutions varied from one metropole to another, from one region to another, and from one expansionist phase to another. The variations were noted in previous chapters and will be discussed in passing here. They have been studied in a number of insightful works.[1] It would be a mistake, however, to emphasize obvious differences while ignoring features that cut across the dividing lines of geography, culture, and time. In what follows I employ an abstract, ideal-type analysis to identify frequently recurring institutional patterns. The claim is not that every pattern appears in every colony but that the frequency with which they appear in diverse settings helps explain the surprising durability of the colonial project.

RETAINING METROPOLITAN CONTROL

Ultimate authority to set imperial policy usually lay with a metropole's ruler, whether a monarch or an elected politician. Ultimate responsibility to execute policy lay with political leaders and bureaucrats in a metropole's capital city who were assigned this task. Over time agencies specializing in imperial defense, trade and tariffs, shipping, legal matters, labor policy, and issues involving settlers evolved. Specialists often had a hand in designing the policies they were expected to implement. In some cases an empirewide civil service was established, permitting recruitment of young men from the metropole who could envisage career assignments in several colonies.

Metropolitan officials faced a dilemma in deciding how to control distant possessions. They wanted the administrators they sent out to perform the basic tasks of governments everywhere: defining and defending borders, maintaining order, interpreting and enforcing laws, collecting taxes, regulating individual and group activities, providing basic services. The easiest way to create an effective public sector overseas was to transfer institutions and practices metropolitan officials were most familiar with: those in their own country. This meant turning a colony into something like its metropole, with a boundary, a capital city, an official language and currency, and functionally specialized, bureaucratically structured agencies transplanted from the imperial center. Because transplants might not take unless adapted to new and unfamiliar local environments, top administrators in the colonies required authority to make adjustments on the spot.

But replicating the metropole overseas and delegating authority to colonial governors posed obvious problems. The more closely a colony resembled the metropolitan state the greater the risk that its inhabitants—perhaps even its administrators—would demand the one attribute of statehood the metropole insisted on reserving for itself: sovereignty. A metropole's success at replicating itself could set in motion centrifugal forces pulling the empire apart. Granting colonial governors leeway to adapt to local conditions risked giving them permission to become too autonomous. The point of having an empire, after all, was not to delegate power but to wield it.

The only way to resolve this dilemma was to make colonies protostates. They should look like states—but without the crowning attribute of sovereignty. Their governors should govern, but only in accord with policy guidelines set by faraway superiors. A colonial edifice was to be constructed. But the carpenters would be ordered to lay down their tools if they came too close to completing the task.

How assure that a colonial governor follows instructions when one instruction is to live thousands of miles away? The classic principal–agent problem was magnified in the imperial setting by the distance separating principals from agents. Several policies and mechanisms were devised to retain control. Imperial officials insisted on the right to appoint, transfer, and dismiss governors. Seldom did a governor remain in the same post for more than four or five years. With few exceptions governors were recruited from the metropole, it being understood that they would return home when their tours of duty were over.[2] The same applied to officials in charge of internal security, finance, the judicial system, and communications. Teams were dispatched to monitor the performance of top administrators and report on their findings. Spain's Council of the Indies, for example, arranged occasional general inspections by *visitadores,* who had authority to examine the files of any official, including a viceroy. The council arranged *residencias,* judicial reviews at the end of officials' terms of office. These could result in punishment for serious misuse of power. British authorities from phase 3 onward sent out commissions of enquiry after uprisings, massacres, and riots. Governors knew they would be held account-able, and their careers adversely affected, for actions running counter to London's policies that may have triggered these events. All colonies developed legal institu-tions, charged among other things to apply metropolitan laws and procedures to certain kinds of disputes. If decisions by colonial judges were contested the final court of appeal was located in the metropole.

In order to assert authority as well as clarify policy, metropolitan rulers issued edicts and legislatures passed laws governing a wide range of activity throughout an empire. The history of mercantilist policy cannot be written without reference to these edicts. Even when trade restrictions were disregarded or openly disobeyed in the colonies, everyone was aware of them because there was always a chance that officials would identify an infraction and press charges based on the regulations. Metropoles took care to enforce prohibitions on exporting advanced technology to the colonies, fearing this could undermine the desired imperial division of labor.

Considering the interest colonial residents had in retaining economic surplus for themselves, some metropoles did an impressive job of transferring wealth back to Europe. Spain's rulers extracted massive amounts of bullion from the Americas in phase 1 despite losses on sea and land. Dutch officials took a great deal from the East Indies, indirectly through the East India Company in phase 1 and directly in phase 3. Under the so-called culture system in place from 1830 to the 1870s, peasants were forced to grow export crops and sell them to government buyers for a fraction of market value. By 1877, writes Robert McMahon, this system "had paid off all of the East India Company's debts and was bringing a sizable amount of additional revenue into The Hague's home treasury. The East Indies, between 1831 and 1877, earned on the average 18 million guilders a year in profit; in view of a national budget that did not exceed 60 million guilders a year during the same period, the considerable contribution of the colony to the health of the home economy is unmistakable." One minister for the colonies declared that "Java pours riches upon the homeland as if by a magician's wand."[3]

As these examples show, one way a metropole acquired wealth from its colo-nies was to orient them toward exports. A wide range of commodities was then available to the home market as consumer goods or industrial inputs. High levels of intra-imperial trade offered a fiscal advantage as well. Taxes on a colony's exports and imports could be more easily and cheaply collected than head or hut taxes directly levied on colonial residents. Concentration of tax revenues in a few port cities made it relatively easy for a metropole's agents to collect their share and send it home.

PENETRATING AND GOVERNING COLONIAL SOCIETY

For a governor and leading officials around him in a colonial capital city, the challenge of consolidating power was defined rather differently. Here the problem was to gain compliance not across seas but across land: specifically, how to govern people living hundreds of miles away and unconnected by road or other means with the outside world. An administration that eventually covered the entire territory had to be assembled. Agents had to be recruited and assigned to distant outposts to show the flag, keep the peace, settle local disputes, interpret new legal codes, recruit labor, supervise road construction, stimulate production for the international market, and the like. The cost of this operation could be high, and it was usually borne by the colony itself. Hence the imperative to mobilize its natural and human resources for taxable development. A political risk of extending public sector institutions throughout a colony was that development was socially destabilizing and some forms of resource mobilization (notably forced labor) deeply unpopular. If the desired goal was stable, legitimate government, the means employed to get there could push the goal out of reach.

A related challenge in constructing the protostate was how to bridge racial and cultural distance. The demographic composition of colonies was enormously varied. But differences and inequalities among groups were more visible, numerous, and generally more pronounced than in the metropole. A striking feature of many colonial societies was not only the number of distinct groups but also the range of reasons given for drawing distinctions among them. If one imagines a territory whose population reflects the colonial world's diversity, group identity was based on

- race: inhabitants came from Europe, from the continent where the colony was located, and from one or more other continents from which third parties migrated;
- race and power: the dominant race (European) vs. subordinate races (all others)— this was the fundamental cleavage between colonizer and colonized;
- racial descent: people wholly descended from a continental "stock" vs. those of mixed race;
- place of birth and territorial affinity: metropole-born Europeans temporarily residing in the colony vs. people born in the colony who regarded it as home;
- legal status: free or slave;
- political status: those with voting rights and/or metropolitan citizenship vs. those without them;

- economic function: for example, third parties serving as intermediaries between Europeans and indigenous groups;
- class: those with property and high income vs. poor people lacking property;
- attributes distinguishing indigenous groups from each other: language, religion, homeland, livelihood, social customs, and precolonial political history.

Figure 12.1 maps this composite society. It locates groups along a horizontal axis of difference—race, religion, language, geographical location, and so forth—and a vertical axis of inequality—power, income, wealth, and status. As may be seen in the figure, group differences and inequalities were systematically linked, Europeans typically clustering in the highest property and income categories, third-party groups in the middle, indigenous people and imported slaves at the bottom. In the colonial situation a group was *defined* by socially acknowledged characteristics setting it apart from others and simultaneously *slotted* in a hierarchy in which the rank ordering of groups was more or less fixed.

Of course, not all colonies possessed all groups noted in figure 12.1. But in most there was sufficient heterogeneity to pose problems for anyone charged with governing the entire population. The challenge was to penetrate diverse groups and control their behavior in spite of knowing little about their social structure, values, and opinions of Europeans. Heterogeneity presented opportunities as well as obstacles for rulers. If differences and inequalities could be manipulated by pitting groups against each other, rulers could keep the populace subdued and deflect resentment that might otherwise be directed at themselves.

Efforts to control more people and more aspects of people's lives produced violent backlashes. The rebellions noted in chapter 13 often occurred at early stages of power consolidation, when it became clear that the European presence was not temporary and that subjugation had serious costs, including taxation and forced labor. But the government had ready responses to rebellion. The key to victory was swift, decisive applications of force. Rulers took out the most advanced weapons available, stored in armories for just such emergencies, and turned them on warriors whose arsenal was far inferior. The government mobilized groups not involved in the revolt, gave them arms, and turned them loose on rebel forces. A central player in consolidating British rule over India, Gen. Frederick [Lord] Roberts, wrote of the Great Mutiny of 1857–58 that "Delhi could not have been taken without Sikhs and Gurkhas; Lucknow could not have been defended without the Hindustani soldiers who so nobly responded to Sir Henry Lawrence's call, and nothing that Sir John Lawrence might have done could have prevented our losing, for a time, the whole of the country north of Calcutta, had not the men of the Punjab and the Dejerat remained true to our cause."[4]

FIGURE 12.1.

CLEAVAGES IN COLONIAL SOCIETY

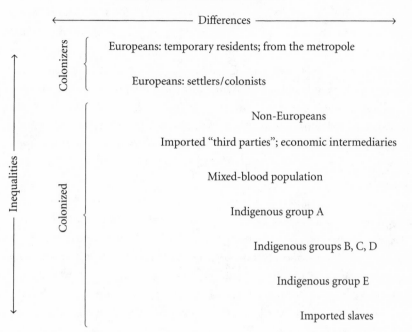

Once rebellion was crushed its leaders were punished in settings that signaled in unmistakable terms to the populace what would happen to anyone contemplating treason in the future. The two most significant resistance movements in colonial history were the Tupac Amaru Rebellion in Peru and Upper Peru (1780–83) and the Great Mutiny in India. Reasons for their failure are discussed in chapter 13. Here I note that Tupac Amaru II was drawn and quartered in the Cuzco public square and that Indian sepoys condemned by court martial were tied over the barrel of a gun and, to the roll of drums, blown to pieces. The point is not that Europeans were more cruel than the rebels but that their retaliatory cruelty was given a public face to forestall future outbreaks. In some cases punishment was visible and collective, as when BNA settlers massacred and expelled rebellious Pequot Indians (1636) or when German troops led by Gen. Lothar von Trotha pushed thousands of Hereros into the Kalahari Desert to perish of starvation and thirst (1905).[5]

In areas wracked by war or anarchy prior to European rule, imposition of order was often greeted with relief by colonial subjects. As personal security increased and freedom of movement throughout a colony became possible, many people acknowledged that in these respects the new rulers made a positive difference.

Here, coercion became a basis for legitimacy rather than serving, as it usually did, as a method of retaining illegitimate rule.

The search for collaborators in time of peace was just as marked as the decisive application of force against rebels. The two tasks were intimately linked when non-Europeans were recruited to police and border-defense forces. A common practice was to favor poor, low-status groups with reputations for martial prowess. Their loyalty could be counted on because recruitment raised their income, social status, and power. Examples include Ambonese in the Dutch East Indies; Sikhs, Pathans, Gurkhas, and Baluchis in post-1857 India; Karens in Burma; Hausa, Tiv, and Kanuri in Nigeria; Temne in Sierra Leone; Kamba and Kalenjin in Kenya; Acholi and Langi in Uganda; Azande and Batetela in the Belgian Congo's early years; and Berbers in Morocco.[6]

On the public sector's civilian side non-European collaborators were essential as linguistic intermediaries, interpreters of the customs and beliefs of local people, spies who identified and kept tabs on troublemakers, low- and middle-level government functionaries working at low cost, and proxies carrying out the dirty work of colonialism by collecting tribute and hut taxes and rounding up forced-labor brigades. By taking on unpopular assignments they became targets of anger that might otherwise have been directed at European overseers. Collaborators in turn could count on certain benefits, including high income by local standards, exemption from forced labor, high status associated with bureaucratic office, permission to grow crops normally reserved for Europeans, and opportunities to use official positions for illicit personal enrichment. Colonial governments offered compensation packages whose benefits to collaborators were designed to outweigh the costs.

When indigenous polities survived into the colonial era and their rulers were willing to work with Europeans, a policy of ruling through traditional authorities had much to recommend it. Indirect rule was adopted in the Americas by the Spanish, who worked through *caciques* and *kurakas;* by the Dutch in the East Indies; by the French in Vietnam, Morocco, Saharan Algeria, Tunisia, Guinea, and Tchad; and by the British in India (which had more than 560 princely states), Malaya, Borneo, Nigeria, the Gold Coast, Uganda, and many other places. By retaining elements of preexisting polities, colonial rulers focused local energies on local issues and away from matters affecting the colony as a whole. Indirect rule was particularly useful in the early stages of power consolidation, when few Europeans were available for local-level assignments. The legitimacy indigenous rulers carried over from an earlier era could be symbolically transferred to the colonial regime through participation in the regime's structures and rituals. Europeans could not forget that traditional rulers were prime candidates to lead anticolonial movements. This risk was reduced by giving them positive incentives to cooperate. A steady, generous income and support against other claimants to the throne helped turn potential enemies into cooperative subordinates.

How could rulers use a colony's racial and cultural pluralism to undercut challenges from below? Three techniques were widely employed: insulation, competition, and stratification. Keeping groups separated from each other made it less likely that they would unite in opposition. As people from many areas migrated to cities, governments passed regulations creating quarters segregated by race and on occasion by religion and ethnic identity as well. A common pattern was to recruit certain groups for specialized tasks on the basis of stereotypes colonizers believed to be valid. Thus, "martial race" X came to predominate in the military, "clever group" Y was favored for clerical posts, and "strong, hard-working, docile group" Z was heavily represented on road gangs. Even though members of X, Y, and Z worked for the same employer, their interaction was limited by structural and functional differentiation within the public sector. Geographic insulation was another approach, as when Britain administered northern and southern portions of the Anglo-Egyptian Sudan and Nigeria for decades as virtually separate entities. A policy that initially reflected preexisting distinctions between north and south in these huge territories had the effect of accentuating regional cleavages as time went on.

But diverse groups could not be indefinitely insulated from each other, if only because economic and social changes induced by European rule produced unprecedented interactions, especially in growing urban centers. When this occurred a strategy was to make group relations competitive rather than cooperative. Government was aided here by its role as a major employer. Groups which in precolonial times had neither opportunity nor inclination to interact now came together as competitors for scarce, prestigious, high-paying posts within the same sector. When one group held an advantage in job recruitment because of its greater access to primary or secondary schools, other groups often reacted by founding schools for their young people. The result was a larger cadre of Western-educated people than colonial rulers considered politically safe. Still there was something reassuring about colonized peoples competing to enter a sector the rulers themselves controlled. Winners in this competition were not likely to join with the losers to oust foreigners paying their salaries.[7]

Given the substantial economic inequalities in colonial society and their close correlation with the divide separating colonizer from colonized, rulers faced the possibility of class-based revolt. This risk was reduced if non-European society was itself highly stratified. In many instances colonial policy recognized existing inequalities and then reinforced them. Thus in Ruanda-Urundi Germans and Belgians favored aristocrats among the minority Tutsi over Hutu peasants for access to schooling and government posts. In Senegal a school was founded for the sons of chiefs.

When special benefits were conferred on a group by assisting its next generation, that group had strong incentives not to challenge the status quo.

European rule, being a quintessentially male activity, enabled colonized men to become more dominant over women than in the precolonial period. When a district officer needed collaborators or wanted to find out about local customs, he almost invariably turned to fellow males, who he assumed held dominant positions among their people. Armed with the formidable power to interpret one's society to an ignorant foreigner, an indigenous man found it in his interest to describe traditional gender roles in ways most favorable to males. Likewise European anthropologists, the vast majority of them men, obtained information primarily from male informants. Colonial regulations concerning the right to use and own land, grow and sell cash crops, and so forth, were often strongly biased against indigenous women.[8] In a sense, men forged an unspoken coalition under colonialism, their common gender transcending the racial differences and power inequalities separating them. To the extent that this coalition gave colonized men special benefits, it may have reduced the will to rebel within the gender category most likely to do so.

In other instances colonial policy helped construct a new stratification system. People of mixed blood in Portugal's American, African, and Asian colonies; freed slaves in phase 1 plantation colonies; Indians in Fiji, Kenya, Uganda, Trinidad, and Guyana; Lebanese in French West Africa; Chinese in Malaya and the Dutch East Indies—these groups were not only allowed but actively encouraged to occupy niches in the colonial economy below Europeans and above the indigenous or slave majority. If they specialized in retail trade and banking, the nature of their work and their apparent monopoly of certain jobs made them intensely unpopular among groups at the low end of the hierarchy. The result was triply advantageous to colonial rulers: important economic functions were performed by specialists; the colonized were at odds with one another; and intermediate groups looked upward to government for protection from those below them.

In short, colonial policies reinforcing existing group insulation limited the capacity of colonized people to form a united opposition front. Policies encouraging competition for scarce resources lowered the will of colonized people to form a united front. Policies reinforcing existing inequalities and creating new ones limited both the capacity and will of subject peoples to organize. The cumulative result was a remarkably stable system of rule.

CONSOLIDATING CONTROL OVER SETTLERS: POLICY DILEMMAS

How to govern Europeans who considered a colony their permanent home presented quite another challenge to officials sent out from the metropole, whom I term metropolitans. Settlers, lying on the colonizer's side of the racial divide, viewed themselves as civilized and were acknowledged as such by metropolitans. Hence a major justification for colonial rule—civilizing the uncivilized—did not apply to them. Being culturally as well as racially similar to metropolitans, settlers in rural areas above all, likely the only Europeans for miles around, saw themselves as the extension agents of colonialism. They were primary actors in the private profit sector, colonial treasuries depending heavily on income generated by their plantations, farms, artisanal activities, and commercial houses. Officials held limited political leverage over settlers because settlers held substantial economic leverage over them.

Gaining compliance was even more problematic if settlers had their own institutions of self-government, transplanted from the metropole to a new land. Metropolitans could not question the legitimacy of institutions that replicated those seen as legitimate at home. But self-government by one segment of the population conflicted in theory and practice with metropolitan control over the whole population. If the political tradition settlers brought with them stressed self-rule at the local but not territory-wide level, a workable division of responsibilities could be designed, metropolitans running the central bureaucracy while settlers ran local government affairs. This was generally speaking the pattern in Spain's phase 1 colonies. The dominant position accorded creole interests in elected town councils (*cabildos*) helps to account for the longevity of Spanish rule despite grievances creoles held against metropolitans (*peninsulares*) in top public sector posts.

But if the metropole's political tradition was to elect representatives to a national parliament, the only way settlers could continue the tradition was to set up colonywide legislatures and choose their members. This was the pattern in phase 1 BNA and in Britain's white dominions in phases 3 and 4. The fact that BNA settlers controlled both local government and colonywide elected bodies gave them an advantage compared to creoles in Spain's colonies. It gave them leverage over colonial governors, whose salaries were not paid unless the legislature approved. The location of representative institutions at the center rather than periphery of the public sector enabled the thirteen BNA colonies to break with their metropole in phase 2 before Spain's possessions did with theirs.

Governing settlers would be less of a challenge if metropolitans and settlers had identical or compatible interests. That there was compatibility will be seen later in this chapter. Indeed, it was the key to mutually reinforcing relationships between public and private profit sectors in colonies with substantial settler presence. But interests were not identical, and in some respects they conflicted. As in any political system a contentious issue was how to allocate gains from economic activity. How much should be taxed by government and how much retained in the private profit sector? A special feature here was that not one government but two—in the metropole and in the colony—made compelling fiscal claims. Hence the distribution struggle was between public sectors as well as between government and private interests.

Another recurring point of tension, one distinctive of multiracial colonial situations, was over land and labor policy. Settlers' livelihoods depended on access to plentiful supplies of commercially viable land. Their interests directly conflicted with those of indigenous peoples occupying good land. Where settlers depended on plentiful supplies of cheap non-European labor, the coercive techniques they used— and called on government to employ on their behalf—were deeply resented by indigenous or slave populations. If settlers insisted on working the land themselves indigenous peoples faced the even more disastrous option of expulsion from their homes or extermination.

A colonial regime had economic incentives of its own to support these harsh measures. But beyond a certain point metropolitans felt they should intervene on behalf of the colonized. The more non-Europeans suffered at the hands of Europeans the more unsustainable became the civilizing rationale for colonialism. And the less plausibly could administrators project to themselves and others the image of benevolent paternalism. Practical concerns intervened as well. Brutal treatment of non-Europeans might produce violent rebellion. This rebellion might be an uprising of peasants legally bound to work hacienda fields, a revolt among plantation slaves, or murderous raids by people forced to retreat behind an inexorably advancing settler frontier. Whatever the form, a colonial government had to take punitive action. But repression might only inflame a condition driven by widespread desperation. It would consume revenue administrators might prefer to spend on civil service salaries or development. A badly handled war could net a governor unfavorable publicity at home and damage his career prospects. For these reasons top administrators almost invariably favored less harsh land and labor policies than those demanded by settler leaders.

When the interests of metropolitans and settlers diverged, officials had a limited repertoire of options. Harsh repression of settlers was out of the question, given racial and cultural similarities and shared economic stakes. Even moderate measures to limit settler privileges could produce an unpleasantly loud response. Settlers typically had well-placed friends and relatives in the metropole's capital city. Complaints lodged in high places could get a governor recalled.

If repression was ruled out, governors could still deploy symbols, offer rewards, and make arguments. Ceremonies stressing the metropole—its power, its cultural appeal, important events in its past, the virtues of its current monarch—told settlers that the country they came from should continue to hold center stage in their identities and loyalties. Appeals to monarchical legitimacy were salient in the Spanish colonies, given the doctrine that colonies were possessions of Spain's ruler. But appeals could be effective even when no such doctrine was in force—as witness the enormous affection and esteem in which Queen Victoria was held throughout Britain's white dominions. The idea of rebelling against the queen was never discussed because it was unthinkable. Unusually cooperative settlers were awarded titles and offered the highest administrative posts to which nonmetropolitans could aspire. A governor could manipulate cleavages within settler society, favoring the side most inclined toward his own.

Settlers were reminded that without the metropole's military assistance they were unable to repress rebellions from below or repel invasions from outside. Indeed, when rebellions did occur they often pushed a sobered and scared settler community closer to the metropole. Tupac Amaru's rebellion had this effect in Peru and Upper Peru. One reason so many phase 1 plantation colonies in the Caribbean remained under European control until phase 5 may have been settlers' desires for protection in case the African-descended majority revolted as it had in Haiti.

By adopting the Durham Report's recommendations for Canada, Britain's Parliament signaled willingness to accede to settler demands for more self-government. Anticipating and in effect planning for the eventual loss of power as the Westminster model took root in white dominions, Britain's leaders redefined imperial goals to include transplantation of parliamentary institutions. Responsible government was an artful compromise by which settlers set domestic policy while war powers, defense, currency, and other foreign affairs remained in London's hands. If this arrangement gave up a great deal it was also the most London could expect under the circumstances.

NONGOVERNMENT SECTORAL INSTITUTIONS

Virtually all colonies could point to evidence—from trading firms to mining companies and plantations to banks—of some sort of private profit sectoral stretch. Europe-based enterprises often extended operations inland as transport networks grew. As Europe industrialized, the range of their agricultural and mining operations increased to keep up with an ever-greater range of needed commodities.[9]

When an enterprise headquartered outside a colony played an important role within it for an extended time, many people came to regard it as an integral part of the colony's economy. In this respect foreign enterprises were gradually domesticated, the process paralleling that of public sector institutions. Indeed, to the extent that public and private profit sector institutions imported from Europe were the only ones whose reach extended throughout a colony, to that extent their presence shaped and even defined the contours of a territory's *domestic* life. Europeans enjoyed a power edge over colonized peoples when their sectoral institutions had a spatial range that no institution controlled by the colonized could match.

The European-directed portion of a colony's private profit sector had several effects on economic and social life. Given a commitment to rearrange natural and human resources in the search for profit, entrepreneurs had few compunctions about disrupting past ways of doing things if disruption was expected to produce future gain. Just as capitalism continuously remade modern European economies, so it had ongoing impacts on colonies. Over the five-century span of this book, dramatic change took place in ocean and land transport, communications, mining technology, transfers of plants and animals to new areas, and applications of scientific research to agricultural production. These kinds of changes accelerated from phase 3 onward, but events and trends in phase 1 mattered also. Galleons had far greater carrying capacity than caravels. Printing breakthroughs led to mass production of newspapers and books. The patio process for separating silver from ore with mercury (1556) made American silver mining viable. Importation of horses, cows, pigs, sugar, and citrus fruits to the New World forever changed a hemisphere's economy. Colonies were laboratories for production experiments taking advantage of economies of scale. Sugar and coffee plantations, silver and copper mines were enormous operations compared to anything done before.

Land and labor requirements of colonial capitalists substantially impacted non-European ways of life. Many people were driven from their lands and had to devise new ways to survive, including working for European employers on the latter's terms. Many were kidnapped and shipped over the high seas as slaves. Many were enticed from homelands by the prospect of cash and consumer goods if they worked in large-scale enterprises. Where migrant labor arose to meet the heavy demand of mines and plantations for unskilled labor, economic life in areas the migrants left was profoundly altered by their absence. The shock waves of capitalist development thus spread far beyond the sites where Europeans supervised extraction and production for the market.

Employers used varying mixes of coercion and inducement to get the amount of non-European labor they needed. For activities dependent on slavery and forced labor, government's police units and courts were invaluable supplements to methods employers were prepared to use. But the persuasive power of material reward was great. Europeans monopolized the supply of many products desired by their subjects. In numerous instances the only way to earn cash to buy these products was to be employed in European-owned operations. As a metropole's output of consumer goods increased so did the extent to which colonial employers could rely on inducement to attract, train, and even discipline their work force. Colonial development was not simply pushed along by the restless striving of employers after profit: it was also pulled along by employees' strong preferences for imported goods and a diffusion throughout society of consumerist values.

Christian missionary bodies greatly extended their reach during the colonial era. The typical pattern was for an organization based in the metropole (or at the Vatican) to set up branches overseas. These were led by Europeans the organization recruited, trained, funded, and instructed to follow policy guidelines. The Roman Catholic Church and its missionary orders are the clearest illustrations of the religious sector's institutional stretch. The situation was more ambiguous among Protestant denominations, particularly those with strong traditions of congregational autonomy. But when Anglican, Dutch Reformed, Lutheran, Methodist, Presbyterian, and Baptist missionaries in the field received funds from sponsoring home agencies, used agency-provided Bibles and tracts, returned home for leave and retirement, and were reassigned from one place or task to another, they demonstrated the considerable hold European institutions had on agents operating far afield.

A missionary's ultimate mission was not, however, to set up branch headquarters but to reach people not converted to the true faith. An already stretched institution was called upon to stretch further, this time into the periphery of colonial society. If conversion was successful the emphasis shifted to sustaining and deepening the faith of believing communities clustered around mission stations. As the geographic scope and range of activities increased, non-European converts were recruited to preach, teach, and assist in translating the Bible into local languages. Some began to look to mission agencies as sources of employment and upward mobility, just as others sought employment opportunities in the public and private profit sectors.

Missionaries concentrated on people most likely to convert. In practice, this meant those not already committed to Islam, Hinduism, Buddhism, or other faiths based on sacred texts. Missionaries relied heavily on persuasion, advancing arguments favoring their own salvationist creed and attacking what they called heathen beliefs. But they were not above using or appealing to force, as when "pagan idols" were collected and destroyed.[10] And material inducements in the form of trade goods were frequently offered the unconvinced. By providing services that met peoples' needs missionaries were able to make converts and retain them in the fold. Schools taught literacy and numeracy, tools crucial for upward mobility in all three sectors. By diffusing the colonizer's culture schools helped people understand why the ruling racial caste was so powerful, with implications for how the colonized might increase their own power. In many areas mission clinics were the only sources of Western-style medicine. Many missionaries felt called to make services available to everyone regardless of religious convictions. Their work touched a wider population than the numbers of Christians would indicate.

A parallel pattern thus emerges for each of the three sectors. Specialized institutions stretched from metropole to colony, then outward from nodes of concentrated activity toward a colony's peripheral areas. Each sector had distinctive reasons for wanting to reach ever-larger numbers of colonial residents. But all reasons had something to do with changing how residents acted and thought. The cumulative impact of institutional dynamism expressed simultaneously on several fronts enabled colonizers to consolidate an already dominant position.

SECTORAL AUTONOMY

The tendency of metropolitan sectoral institutions to retain autonomy yet cooperate with each other carried over from the empire-building era into the years of colonial consolidation. The same tendency marked the way institutions transferred from the metropole functioned within colonial boundaries.

To address autonomy first, the colonial government and various missionary bodies retained separate structures, each with its own jurisdictional units, personnel system, financial accounts, holdings and rights in land, and revenue-raising techniques.[11] Church–state links were doubtless closest in Iberian phase 1 colonies. Yet even there missionary bodies (especially the Jesuits) retained substantial autonomy. It was precisely the Jesuits' freedom from royal control that led to their expulsion from Iberian colonies in the 1750s and 1760s, when centralizers in Lisbon and Madrid set out to tighten control over overseas possessions.

The distinction between a colony's public and private profit sectors was less sharply drawn in the phase 1 mercantilist era than subsequently. In Spain's colonies, the distinction was blurred because the state was itself a major profit maximizer, owning mines, handling the transport of bullion to Spain, exercising monopoly rights over the sale of certain commodities, and the like. Sectoral lines were crossed in a different way with the officially chartered companies of the British, Dutch, and French.

Even in phase 1, however, private entrepreneurs played their own hand. Much of what appears as statism in the Spanish colonies is economic activity directed by private groups, the government formally asserting control but then subcontracting with capitalists to do the real work. Thus in 1543 the Crown's *Casa de Contratación* (House of trade) granted the *consulado* (wholesale merchants' guild) of Seville a monopoly of trade with the Americas. As merchant guilds arose in the colonies they pressed successfully for a share of business: in 1592 and 1613 *consulados* in Mexico

City and Lima were granted monopolies over trade in their respective viceroyalties.[12] Grants of this sort showed a clear recognition by public sector officials that colonial economies could not thrive unless individuals and organizations had ample leeway to seek their own gain.[13]

By phase 3 the public–private profit distinction was more clearly drawn. The old chartered companies had been disbanded or were in the process of dissolution, replaced by institutions more obviously on one side or the other of the sectoral divide.

Sectoral autonomy in the colonies facilitated power consolidation in several ways. Each institution specialized in what it did best, leading to efficient deployment of the resources available to it. Autonomy ensured the persistence of vigorous assaults on a broad range of non-European institutions, behavior patterns, and beliefs. The intensity and scope of the triple assault, its synergistic character, its power to subvert the ways other peoples used to arrange their lives, increased with the passage of time. Colonized peoples found themselves continually responding to the latest round of plans to change them. Being forced on the defensive on many fronts at the same time hindered any sustained counteroffensive.

Multiple institutions of dominance created many targets of anger and frustration. European merchants, settlers, and missionaries could not avoid experiencing some of the disruptive consequences of their activities. As long as popular resentments were focused on these groups and did not take the form of open rebellion, colonial administrators had some measure of respite from unpopularity.

The presence of sectoral actors may have prolonged colonialism by enabling some of its worst excesses to be reformed. Many missionaries felt called by their faith to protect the rights of victims of exploitation. In some cases missionaries lobbied on behalf of the colonized. The Dominican friar Bartolomé de Las Casas was largely responsible for the New Laws of 1542, which tried to limit abuses of power by settlers and royally appointed officials in the Americas. In Brazil the Jesuit priest Antonio Vieira opposed enslavement of Amerindians. Later named court preacher and counselor to King John IV, Vieira persuaded the king to modify an edict of 1653 that permitted de facto Indian slavery.[14] Missionaries in many colonies spoke out against land alienation, extortionate taxing of indigenous communities, forced labor, unfair trading practices, and encouragement of alcoholism through sales of cheap liquor. Because they had their own sponsoring agencies they could communicate complaints directly to the metropole. They thus brought to the attention of officials in Europe issues that would likely have been ignored or repressed had there been only one communication channel from a colony to the imperial center. When a metropole took corrective action in response to informed criticism it forestalled worse scandals that might have imperiled its hold on power.

COOPERATION ACROSS SECTORAL LINES

As in the empire-building era, so too during the years of colonial consolidation institutions specializing in power, profit, and proselytization worked in mutually supportive ways. That their autonomy spurred experiments in cooperation across sectoral lines rather than constituting a barrier to it goes far to explain the longevity of colonialism. Cross-sector networks produced a structurally integrated arrangement more powerful and flexible than the sum of its parts. Networks focused Europeans' attention on shared interests in maintaining colonial rule despite their differing motivations for doing so. Cooperative ties allowed Europeans to project the appearance of a united front even when there was none. The image of unity impeded colonized peoples' efforts to undermine the system by playing factions within the dominant elite against each other.

Government support for the private profit sector took several forms. When officials could ensure order and the safe movement of people and goods throughout a colony, they created conditions conducive to long-term investment in productive assets. Soldiers and police protected traders, land-hungry settlers, and missionaries from physical attack. Gendarmes helped provide low-cost labor for private enterprises, if need be by evicting locals from their land and turning them into a dependent labor force on the same land, now placed under European ownership. Official edicts and court decisions affirmed the private property claims of Europeans while frequently denying that indigenous peoples had comparable rights, especially against settlers' land claims. When roads and railroads were preconditions for profitable activity back of coastal areas, governments bore the heavy initial cost of constructing them. A high portion of the burden was then passed on to the subject population through forced labor and direct taxes. Government-administered botanical gardens and agricultural research stations tested whether species imported from one area would flourish elsewhere and improved yields on plantation crops like cinchona, coffee, rubber, and palm oil.

Through the chartered company mechanism and grants to groups of merchants, metropolitan rulers assigned private actors monopoly powers over a colony's imports and exports. Officials favored European firms when awarding contracts to carry the mails and construct public buildings, port facilities, roads, railroads, and utilities.[15] Metropolitan banks profited from loans colonies took out to finance infrastructural improvements. Government regulations prevented non-Europeans from growing lucrative cash crops,[16] taking designated high-paying jobs, and otherwise competing for a more equitable share of gains from capitalist activity. At racially restricted social clubs government officials and businessmen discussed the terms of their alliance, usually over drinks at day's end.

Colonial governments assisted missionary bodies by enforcing social order and making it safer to set up mission stations and easier to launch mass conversion campaigns. Many regimes allotted tax revenues for the educational and health work of religious agencies. In 1618 the Spanish Crown, ever anxious to spread the Roman Catholic faith abroad, exempted laypersons with designated church responsibilities from paying tribute and meeting personal service obligations. This aided recruitment of indigenous church officers like *fiscales*, whose task was to see that the congregation attended Sunday mass.[17]

European control of government may have been an indirect stimulus to conversion. With few exceptions top officials were nominally Christian; many were genuinely and deeply committed to the faith. Christianity was thus closely associated in the minds of colonized peoples with worldly power. A convert might have a better chance to partake of power than a nonconvert, especially when rulers openly preferred Christians to fill government jobs. Did not political realities prove that the Christians' God was more powerful than indigenous pantheons of spirits and deities? If so—and missionaries were only too eager to assert that it was—here was one more reason to convert.

The private profit sector's principal contribution to colonial government was the taxes that financed public sector functions. By combining natural resources, capital, advanced technology, and labor in efficient, productive ways, European capitalists helped generate an unprecedented volume of wealth compared to other empires. Because so many commodities were involved in international trade, colonial and metropolitan governments could collect taxes on these items easily and at relatively low cost. It stretches the point to describe tax payments as a form of cooperation with government. Private actors had an obvious interest in keeping rates low, passing on more of the costs of government to non-Europeans, and, if possible, evading their assessed share. Still, in the vast majority of situations European private interests acknowledged, however grudgingly, the appropriateness of transferring some portion of accumulated gains. The reason was straightforward: their taxes enabled government to help them carry on with business.

Willingness of the private profit sector to support missionaries was by no means universal. The two sectors had grounds for mutual suspicion, given the conflicting priorities they placed on material acquisition and devotion to spiritual matters. Suspicion often verged on open antagonism in settler colonies, for settlers feared that non-Europeans would rebel if given too much Western learning and the "wrong" interpretation of the Bible. Settlers nonetheless recognized that missions turned out literate, numerate young people whom they could then employ. Wealthy individuals made donations and bequests to religious bodies. Of course, when Christian denominations functioned as support groups for settlers—as did Protestant sects in BNA and Dutch South Africa—the community reciprocated by enthusiastically supporting the church's work.

Missionaries, though critical at times of other sectors for exploiting and neglecting colonized peoples, assisted them in several ways. First, mission schools trained indigenous youth for low-level posts in a wide range of institutions. The products of these schools were linguistic and cultural intermediaries between rulers and ruled, extended the penetrative reach of all sectoral institutions, and worked for considerably lower pay than Europeans in the same posts would have tolerated. Second, missionaries provided services in education, health, and social welfare that the colonial government might have otherwise had to cover from its own resources. Religious bodies recouped a high proportion of operating expenses through their own revenue collection system, including donations from churches in Europe and Sunday offerings and school fees from local congregants. Missionaries limited personnel costs by living, in general, more simply than Europeans in other sectors. Catholic priests kept expenses unusually low by their commitment to celibacy and austerity. In these ways mission agencies reduced pressures on government to take the unpopular step of raising taxes to pay for basic services.

Third, missionaries often felt that a frontal assault on other people's beliefs was required for mass conversion to take place. To the extent that this assault succeeded, it called into question the legitimacy and effectiveness of other aspects of life closely linked to indigenous beliefs. The disintegrative multiplier effect of mission preaching probably made it harder for indigenous political and religious leaders to organize sustained popular resistance movements.[18] Familiar ways of life were further disrupted when converts were urged to abandon their homes and form new settlements of believers. This was a particularly important objective and accomplishment of phase 1 Catholic missionaries in the New World. Convert communities were called *aldeias* in Brazil and *reducciones* in Spanish colonies. Phase 3 Protestant missionaries likewise founded communities around their churches and schools; a well-known example was Livingstonia in Nyasaland.[19] Relocating people from widely dispersed, often highly mobile rural settings into villages and towns made it easier for government to tax them, force them to supply labor for various projects, and regulate their behavior. A policy inspired by proselytizing motives thus aided political consolidation.

Fourth, many missionaries delivered a message justifying colonialism on theological and moral grounds. The rationale might be based on a specific biblical passage. The statement in St. Paul's Letter to the Romans (13:1–4) that existing authorities "have been instituted by God" was cited. Or the rationale might be linked to more general features of the Christian faith. Through its most important symbol, a cross, Christianity posits the centrality, unavoidability, and redemptive potential of suffering. The suffering colonized peoples experienced at European hands could be interpreted as an opportunity to gain individual and collective salvation by bearing patiently with tribulation.

Missionaries preached a more secular gospel as well: that of the culture from which they came. They associated civilization with polities ruled by Christians and with a private sector whose driving motive was generating wealth by making the most of the world God gave human beings. As many missionaries saw it, colonial rule granted precisely these benefits. Consider the dismal alternative: in its absence non-Europeans would be consigned to the anarchy of statelessness or the despotism and idolatry of pagan rulers. In either case the option of sustained economic development was foreclosed.

These justifications of colonialism doubtless failed to convince many people who heard them in churches and mission schools. There was a suspiciously high coincidence between the way biblical passages were interpreted and the self-interest of the interpreters. Jesus warned against an obsessive, never-satisfied desire for material possessions—the very thing the colonizers' behavior epitomized. And the liberatory and egalitarian aspects of the biblical message pointed in a strongly anticolonial direction (see chapter 15).

Nonetheless, missionaries performed a vital role in the normative pacification of colonized peoples. In so doing they complemented the coercive forms of pacification used by government police and settler vigilantes. Whatever the reasons for conversion, when non-Europeans took this step they became in varying degrees converts to the larger European civilizational agenda colonialism was pledged to advance. Converts found it more difficult to reject all aspects of colonialism once they accepted the religion that accompanied it.

Religious justifications for colonialism may have had a more pervasive impact on the colonizers than on the colonized. Imposing political, economic, and cultural changes from above systematically violated the moral injunction to treat fellow human beings fairly and respectfully. Members of the dominant racial group needed a constant infusion of messages validating their behavior. They felt better about pursuing self-interested goals when preachers praised the imperial project for improving the lives of subject peoples. How reassuring to hear from the pulpit, "Whatever you are doing, it is the Lord's work! Keep on with it!"

Figure 10.1 visualized sectoral penetration of colonial society as a series of vertical lines. Figure 12.2 superimposes upon these a series of horizontal lines across sectoral boundaries with arrows pointing in both directions to signify mutual support.

FIGURE 12.2.

Sectors

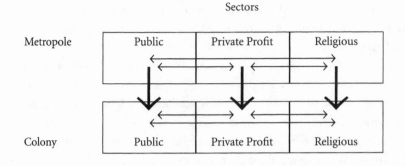

The resulting institutional grid combines functional pluralism, structural strength, and tactical flexibility. Once imposed upon a society, it can remain in place for years.

EUROPEANS AS A RACIAL CASTE

Regardless of their sectoral affiliation, Europeans living in colonies constituted a single community. Their physical features set them off from those they dominated. They had a common cultural frame of reference, based on shared ties to a distant continent. Because their version of civilization had political, economic, and religious components and because colonialism's underlying rationale was civilizational, they saw themselves as part of a comprehensive project involving each sector yet transcending them all. Most Europeans took as an article of faith that they were superior to other people in intelligence, morality, self-control, and governing skills. Where they lived as a small group scattered among a non-European majority, they shared fears of what might happen should a violent uprising break out.

Whether from a sense of superiority or a sense of fear or both, Europeans distanced themselves from their subjects. A recurring practice was to take small differences between individuals on different sides of the racial dividing line and magnify them into significant differences between races. The goal was to transmute observed or imagined differences from normatively neutral descriptors into normatively and emotionally loaded badges of unequal value. To be colonized was to be subaltern—that is, beneath one's superiors *and* other than them.[20] Social distance was symbolized and reinforced by physical distance. A British missionary in early twentieth-century New Guinea, Rev. W. J. Saville, had pertinent advice on this subject: "Never touch a native, unless to shake hands or thrash him."[21]

The political advantage of a superiority complex was that it could be used to teach colonized peoples their inferiority. If the colonized accepted this message much of their anger at being subordinated and exploited could be deflected inward. The dominant race took care to promulgate an inferiority complex. Europeans often referred to themselves as adults and to non-Europeans of all ages as children. Children were expected to use deferential terms when speaking to adults, while adults could address children by first name. Terms of abuse described colonized peoples as not fully human, and in extreme cases as animals. Through official regulations and informal pressures Europeans went to extreme lengths to ensure that no non-European gave orders to anyone with a white skin.

Europeans learned to address their subjects in peremptory fashion and imperative mode. An English–Swahili phrase book published in 1944 listed instructions a white person could be expected to use when landing from a canoe: "Here we are. I will get out first. Push the boats further up. Carry me on your shoulders. Go steadily. Don't let me fall. There are six boxes, two bags, and a chair. Take them all out. Don't make a noise. Come here, you and you and you. Carry these things for me."[22]

Schoolchildren were taught about European accomplishments in literature, art, architecture, science, technology, and government. Little or nothing was said about the values or precolonial achievements of non-European cultures. The silences blared a loud message: there was nothing outside the colonizer's culture worth learning. Sometimes the indigenous past was addressed, but with the intent of demeaning it while elevating those in power. Writing in the late 1950s, the Dahomean writer and political activist Albert Tevoedjre recalled a song he and his classmates were taught in the 1930s:

> France, ta main puissante a brisé nos liens
> Des tyrans nous vendaient comme bêtes de somme.
> Ils tuaient nos enfants et ravagaient nos biens,
> Mais tu nous délivras et fis de nous des hommes.[23]
> [France, your powerful hand destroyed our bonds to tyrants who sold us like
> beasts of burden. They killed our children and destroyed our belongings. But
> you delivered us and made us into men.]

In the colonial setting race became a proxy for class, and the two became markers of caste. Caste lines permanently marked off groups defined as unequally valuable. These features gave the system a coherence and durability quite apart from the institutional features emphasized in this book. But the elements were complementary. Europeans' sense of their racial solidarity and superiority reinforced at the subjective level the cross-sectoral institutional alliances that constituted objective bases for dominance.

13
Sources of Colonial Weakness

Europeans did not deploy everywhere the full battery of institutions and techniques noted in chapter 12. Their goals varied according to the funds and technologies at their disposal and their estimates of how much economic and social change was needed to consolidate political power. But colonizers' goals were also shaped by local circumstances beyond their control, such as a territory's resource base, the religious orientation and cultural diversity of its population, and the presence or absence of indigenous institutions on which rulers could build.

Even when goals were adjusted downward to take realities on the ground into account, a large gap often separated what colonizers attempted to do from what they achieved. This was due in part to the serendipitous nature of cross-cultural inter-actions under colonialism. Unexpected results were, in fact, to be expected when unequally powerful actors tried to communicate across dividing lines of worldview, language, religion, and social custom. British soldiers employed by the East India Company, for example, had no idea that the new Enfield rifle they introduced to Indian infantrymen (sepoys) in 1857 might be culturally problematic. The rifle's cartridges were coated with grease and had to be bitten open for powder to be released. How could company officers have anticipated reactions to a rumor that animal tallow in the grease came partly from pigs, abominable to Muslims, and partly from cows, sacred to Hindus? Suspicion that the British were trying by this subtle tactic to force sepoys to violate religious norms, and hence become vulnerable to Christian missionaries' appeals, triggered the Great Mutiny.

Sometimes a policy had counterproductive results. An example is the public torture and death of Tupac Amaru II, noted in chapter 12. The goal was to terrify the rebel leader's followers into submission. "The effect of these cruelties was cata-strophic," writes John Crow,

> and was the exact opposite of what the Spaniards had anticipated. The Indians of
> the mountain country rose in spontaneous masses and continued the war. They

captured one Spanish town and beheaded every one of the inhabitants, and an army of several thousand besieged La Paz for one hundred and nine days before it was finally relieved by troops from Argentina. It was not until 1783, two years after the death of Tupac Amaru, that order was finally restored. The civil war had cost approximately eighty thousand lives, and the country was devastated.[1]

No matter how powerless a colony's residents might appear to be, they never fully lost opportunities to assert their interests and affirm their values. What they did affected their rulers and helped shape the colonial experience for rulers and ruled alike. Part 5 shows how residents' initiatives undermined the imperial status quo and led to the formation of independent states. This chapter takes the opposite tack, pointing out ways in which residents reinforced the system controlling them. Such an outcome seems obvious in the case of collaborators but counterintuitive for armed resistance, at the other end of the spectrum of available options. Here too the serendipitous character of colonialism is highlighted. Just as rulers' efforts to consolidate power underscored contradictions in the system which their subjects were able to exploit (see chapter 14), so efforts of subject peoples to advance their individual and collective interests sometimes proved self-defeating. The law of unintended consequences could—and did—work in both directions. The very range of behavioral options noted in this chapter could itself be disempowering, by preventing people from reaching consensus on the principal problems they faced and the most appropriate tactics for resolving problems.

A colony's residents could be settlers as well as non-Europeans. I focus here on the latter, with comments on settler communities in a concluding section.

COLLABORATION AND ACCOMMODATION

Indigenous collaborators often played essential roles in maintaining the colonial system. Especially valuable to Europeans were traditional rulers willing to hold office under indirect rule arrangements even though prevented from exercising the full range of powers held by their predecessors. Their presence transferred legitimacy to the new order of things and symbolized continuity with the past rather than a sharp break from it. Recruits to armies and police forces were the shock troops that suppressed rebellions and the enforcers of government edicts in time of peace. Non-Europeans collaborated for a variety of reasons, not all of them reflecting selfishness and disloyalty to others. Indeed, a prominent motive may have been to soften and deflect the impact of unpopular policies on people for whom collaborators were responsible. A local chief ordered to collect tribute or recruit a road gang was better placed than anyone else to moderate government's harmful impact on his charges. In this respect collaborators may have made colonialism more tolerable. But a more tolerable system was probably also a more durable one.

The number of active collaborators in any given situation was typically small. The number of accommodators was considerably larger. Accommodation did not imply approval of colonial rule in general or of specific features such as the legal code, employment in mines and plantations, or mission schooling. Neither did it imply disapproval. Rather it was an intensely pragmatic response to circumstances considered unlikely to change whatever one did and thought. Accommodation was an attractive coping mechanism for those who were not politically inclined. It also appealed to the vast numbers who had no time or energy for political activity because the struggle to survive from one day to the next took everything they had. These people adapted with enterprise and resilience—and a minimum of moralizing—to realities confronting them, figuring that the alternative was even more untenable.

The accommodationist attitude was eloquently expressed in *Ambiguous Adventure*, by the Senegalese writer Cheikh Hamidou Kane. In this novel the Royal Lady of the Diallobé urges her brother the chief to send his young cousin, Samba Diallo, to a school just established by the French:

> A hundred years ago our grandfather, along with all the inhabitants of this countryside, was awakened one morning by an uproar arising from the river. He took his gun and, followed by all the elite of the region, he flung himself upon the newcomer. His heart was intrepid, and to him the value of liberty was greater than the value of life. Our grandfather, and the elite of the country with him, was defeated. Why? How? Only the newcomers know. We must ask them: *we must go learn from them the art of conquering without being in the right.* Furthermore, the conflict has not ceased. The foreign school is the new form of the war which those who have come here are waging, and we must send our elite there, expecting that all the country will follow them.[2]

Accommodation entailed active engagement with the new rulers in hopes that it would empower the disempowered. Samba Diallo was sent to school to learn how his conquerors managed to win despite being in the wrong. Knowing France's secret, he might some day be able to end French domination. Harboring expectations of increased power, wealth, and status, many people went to work for European employers in all sectors, took up cash-crop farming, purchased imported consumer goods, converted to Christianity, and enrolled their children in school.

Did accommodation strengthen or undermine European rule? The most general answer is that it did both. In the short to medium run it helped the three sectors function effectively. Had there been no accommodators, colonialism's startup costs could not have been paid. In the medium to longer run, however, active engagement with sectoral institutions had the empowering, enriching, and enlightening consequences people hoped for when they decided to participate in the new order. The

Royal Lady of the Diallobé was prescient about the distant future even if early battles of the war she referred to were lost.

As sectoral institutions penetrated colonial society, non-Europeans identified and seized opportunities to use them for their own ends. The legal system was one arena in which each side tried to manipulate the other. Paradoxically, the more effective the colonized were in using externally imposed laws, the less likely they were to challenge colonialism's basic institutions and values. Noting that during the first century of Spanish rule Peru's Indians tried with increasing frequency to advance their interests through legal appeals, Steve Stern makes a broader point: "A strategy of defense which depended upon colonial institutions to resist exploitation tied the natives more firmly than ever to Hispanic power. . . . To the extent that reliance on a juridical system becomes a dominant strategy of protection for an oppressed class or social group, it may undermine the possibility of organizing a more ambitious assault aimed at toppling the exploitative structure itself. When this happens, a functioning system of justice contributes to the hegemony of a ruling class."[3]

EXIT, AVOIDANCE, SABOTAGE

Because collaboration and accommodation accepted some aspects of the colonial situation, it is not surprising that these strategies helped consolidate European control. Less plausible is the notion that strategies premised on negative responses also had system-maintaining effects. But there are grounds for making this argument.

Some colonized people exercised the exit option literally: they physically escaped. Indigenous groups in frontier zones relocated deep in forests, swamps, mountains, and deserts, where the environment was so harsh that invaders dared not follow. Amerindians in northern South America have retreated into the rain forest from their earliest contacts with Europeans to the present day.[4] Along the forested eastern flank of the Andes Inca elites fleeing the conquistadors established a kingdom whose centers in Machu Picchu and Espíritu Pampa were so well insulated they were not identified by outsiders until the twentieth century.[5]

Exit is a recurring theme in the history of African slaves in the New World. Escapees formed self-governing communities in the mountainous hinterlands of Caribbean islands and in South America's interior. They were called maroons, and their communities were known as *quilombos, palenques, mocambos,* and *mambises.* The best-known maroon polity was Palmares, in Brazil's Pernambuco region. Formed in the early 1600s and composed of several thousand people, it retained independence for almost a century despite repeated assaults by Portuguese expeditionary forces. In Jamaica, maroons led by Cudjoe launched guerrilla attacks on plantation owners and colonial troops between 1729 and 1739. The English government had to sign a peace treaty in 1739 acknowledging the autonomy of several maroon settlements.[6]

Physical escape was less frequent in the Old World than in the New. But it was not unknown. The crude methods associated with power consolidation in Belgian and German Africa led Africans to flee across untended borders to places where they would be less vulnerable to forced labor, mutilation, and rape. In Algeria, several thousand Muslims opposing conscription into the French army emigrated to (Ottoman) Syria between 1910 and 1912 despite efforts by French authorities to prevent their departure. Emigrés heeded the call by one of their leaders to emulate Muhammad's *hejira* (flight) from Mecca to Medina.[7]

The ultimate—and ultimately tragic—escape was suicide. An unknown number of Amerindians in Hispaniola, confronted with the dual disaster of slaughter by Spanish settlers and decimation of entire communities by disease, killed themselves by jumping off cliffs or eating poisonous plants. Some Africans committed suicide shortly after arriving in the New World rather than submit to enslavement in a strange land.

Other people resorted to psychological rather than physical forms of exit. Some believed that if they acted in a certain way Europeans would disappear, and they could return to an idealized precontact existence. Expectations of this sort led many South African Xhosa-speakers in 1856–57 to kill their own cattle. Similar hopes of restoring a bygone era were evoked in the Ghost Dance movement, which arose in the late nineteenth century among North American Plains Indians. Some prophets spoke of a millennium in which Europeans would all be killed or driven away. This was the appeal of Kitawala, a version of the Jehovah's Witnesses Watch Tower message that spread rapidly throughout southern Africa in the early twentieth century.[8] Alcohol and drugs offered individuals other kinds of escape from the demoralizing circumstances of their lives.

Those who took the exit option challenged European control in several ways. The existence of an Inca government-in-exile and of independent maroon communities showed that it was possible to construct alternatives to subjugation. Survival of these polities under extraordinarily harsh conditions belied the notion that non-Europeans were unable to govern themselves. Stories celebrating the accomplishments of escapees were circulated among the colonized population, boosting morale and in some cases inspiring later resistance movements.[9] Whatever the form physical escape took, it deprived Europeans of manual labor they needed to prosper. In the Jamaican case noted above as well as in many others, maroons raided European settlements in valleys below their hideaways. Here, exiting the system was a prelude to reentry in order violently to resist it. Such attacks placed European slaveholders, already terrified of revolts, even further on the psychological defensive. Resources spent to improve internal security were unavailable for other purposes elites might have preferred.

In other respects, however, the exit option may have had the unintended effect of maintaining European control. Its appeal as an alternative to the presumably hopeless route of mass rebellion affirmed the coercive edge rulers held over their subjects. However appropriate exit may have appeared as the only thing left under the circumstances, still it was a tactic of evading rather than confronting the enemy. The enemy may in fact have been strengthened when some of its ablest and bravest foes left. The most maroons could expect in relations with a slaveholding regime was coexistence: acknowledgment of their autonomy on condition that they cease raiding areas Europeans controlled and return newly escaped slaves. These were the terms of the treaty between Cudjoe and the English in Jamaica.

Exit held high potential for self-inflicted harm, most obviously with suicide. Alcoholism hurt not only the individual addict but also the family and community that had to cope with the addict's behavior. When Xhosas killed their cattle they only increased dependence on whites, the very people their sacrifice was intended to expel. Kitawala's dramatic predictions may have encouraged fatalism and passivity, for nothing anyone might do could alter the imminent arrival of a cosmic event that, as it turned out, never took place.

For those wanting to resist exploitation yet unable or unwilling to exit the system, avoidance and sabotage were attractive options. They were what James Scott aptly terms "weapons of the weak."[10] Individuals, even entire communities, might mysteriously disappear when the tax collector or labor recruiter showed up. On occasion religious leaders urged followers not to contaminate themselves by using European consumer goods.[11] A person might agree to carry out a command, then do so as slowly as possible or deliberately disobey. A classic avoidance technique was pretending to be too stupid or insufficiently fluent in the colonizer's language to understand orders. People learned the enormously useful skill of lying with a straight face when asked if they knew about a crime or an alleged plot. As for sabotage, miners withheld some of the precious metals and stones they were expected to turn over to supervisors. Plantation slaves burned cane fields, tossed objects into intricate machinery, and laced owners' food with poison and ground glass. Domestic servants took home small amounts of flour and cooking oil when the day's work in their employers' kitchens was done. Accountants altered financial records. The possibilities for disruptive initiatives were legion.

Avoidance and sabotage undermined the colonial enterprise by denying colonizers resources they might have obtained had their exploitation methods been more efficient. Such actions also helped the colonized. They reduced burdens and redistributed resources from rich to poor. They gave otherwise powerless people the quiet satisfaction of having once in a while turned the tables on their oppressors.

At the same time, avoidance and sabotage may have had unintended system-stabilizing effects. Though marginally hurting the colonial economy, they did virtually nothing to challenge the political status quo. By making intolerable situations more tolerable they probably undercut the appeal of more genuinely threatening forms of resistance. When colonized people conveyed the false impression of being stupid and ignorant, they reinforced the rulers' view that native non-Europeans were children unable to govern themselves and in need of paternalistic oversight.

Avoidance and sabotage were typically the work of individuals acting quietly and furtively in one small place. They were typically ad hoc responses to specific opportunities for subversion rather than components of a long-term strategy for societal change. As such they were the antithesis of the sustained, coordinated, overt, collective action needed to liberate an entire territory. These options did not produce institutions. Hence they were unable effectively to challenge institutions commanding colonialism's sectoral heights. For these reasons rulers generally perceived avoidance and sabotage as tolerable inconveniences, not calamities calling for drastic countermeasures.

DISPLACEMENT, SELF-ABASEMENT

When a dominant society adds insult to injury by humiliating those it rules, the ensuing frustration and anger cannot be vented directly at the oppressor because that invites repression and might make the weak even worse off. The temptation is to displace anger on other targets less able to retaliate. Obvious candidates in the colonies were immigrant groups positioned between indigenous peoples and Europeans in the economic and status hierarchy. Indigenes angry over rising prices of consumer goods found it easy and relatively safe to take out hostility on Chinese retail merchants in Southeast Asia and Indian and Levantine merchants in sub-Saharan Africa. Another candidate was an indigenous group whose members were adept at seizing new opportunities for upward mobility—Kasai Baluba in theBelgian Congo, for example. Although the role of displacement in intergroup hostility cannot be convincingly shown, it probably escalated the level and intensity of many conflicts. When colonized groups were pitted against each other in riots, arson, and looting, Europeans may have had a difficult time restoring order—but a relatively easy time retaining a dominant position above the fray.

A subordinated group can focus anger on another target: itself. Colonized peoples were told repeatedly and in all sorts of ways that they were inferior. Some people hated their rulers for saying this. Others came to believe that the charge contained elements of truth, and as a result they felt shame, humiliation, embarrassment, and self-doubt.[12] The more they valued imported consumer goods and technologies the more susceptible they were to the taunt that their culture was a failure because it had not been as inventive as that of Europeans. A damaging further implication was that racial disparities in material and scientific achievement mirrored unequal accomplishment in all spheres of life, including intellectual development, morality, spiritual insight, language, and political organization.

Once implanted in the mind, collective self-doubt is hard to eradicate. One does not have to believe that all accusations of inferiority are true, but only to suspect that some of them might be. People are haunted by a nagging question: Could it be that our inferior political status is the result rather than the cause of our low standing in the human race? The damaged self, moreover, could be an individual as well as a collectivity. If I believe that a racial or ethnic group to which I belong is inferior, it is but a short step to believing that I personally am unworthy.

The Tunisian writer Albert Memmi analyzes the psychology of self-abasement in these terms:

> Constantly confronted with this [negative] image of himself, set forth and imposed on all institutions and in every human contact, how could the colonized help reacting to his portrait? It cannot leave him indifferent and remain a veneer which, like an insult, blows with the wind. He ends up recognizing it as one would a detested nickname which has become a familiar description. The accusation disturbs and worries him even more because he admires and fears his powerful accuser. "Is he not partially right?" he mutters. "Are we not all a little guilty after all? Lazy, because we have so many idlers? Timid, because we let ourselves be oppressed?" Willfully created and spread by the colonizer, this mythical and degrading portrait ends up by being accepted and lived with to a certain extent by the colonized. It thus acquires a certain amount of reality and contributes to the true portrait of the colonized.[13]

Self-abasement can have serious political implications. When people believe they are unable to govern themselves and would make a mess of things if they replaced those in authority, their desire for autonomy is undermined. E. F. E. Douwes Dekker, a Eurasian who founded the Indische Party in the Dutch East Indies in 1912, put the problem this way: "There is nothing we need so much as self-assurance and self-confidence. We must get rid of our timidity. It is a hindrance to us, it damages us. On the contrary, we must feel in us a strong sense of our own worth, a realization that we are not inferior to anybody."[14]

REBELLION

To rebel against the colonial regime was to confront it directly and violently through structured collective action (table 13.1). Rebellions thus had a potential for institutional development lacking in the options just discussed. Rebel movements varied greatly in their objectives. In fact, goals could shift during a single uprising as

TABLE 13.1.

COLONIAL REBELLIONS BY INDIGENOUS OR SLAVE POPULATIONS

Date	Colony	Leadership (if known); other data
	Phases 1 and 2	
1637	Connecticut	Pequots
1680–92	New Spain (northern)	Popé; Pueblos
1712	New Spain (Chiapas)	Tzeltal and Tzotzil Mayas
1742–50s	Peru (eastern)	Juan Santos Atahualpa; Campa
1750	Peru (Huarochiri)	
1763–65	British North America (Great Lakes region)	Pontiac; Shawnees, Chippewas, Hurons, Miamis, etc.
1777	Upper Peru	Tomás Katari; Aymaras
1780–83	Peru, Upper Peru	José Gabriel Condorcanqui (Tupac Amaru II)
1791+	Saint Domingue	Toussaint L'Ouverture; slaves
1795	New Granada (Coro)	Blacks and mulattoes, slave and free
1811	New Spain	Miguel Hidalgo; Indians, mestizos
1811–15	New Spain	José María Morelos; Indians and mestizos
	Phases 3 and 4	
1825–30	Dutch East Indies (Java)	Prince Dipanagara
1857–59	India (north-central)	sepoys; Muslim and Hindu rulers
1860–65	New Zealand	Maoris
1895	Madagascar	Red Shawl movement
1896–97	Southern Rhodesia	Lobengula; Ndebele. Mashona
1899–1900	India (Chota Nagpur)	Birsa Rising
1900–20	Somaliland (British)	Sayyid Muhammad Abdille Hassan
1904–06	German South West Africa	Samuel Maherero; Herero. Hendrik Witbooi; Nama
1905–06	German East Africa (central)	Maji Maji
1906	South Africa	Bambatha; Zulus
1906	Nigeria (northern)	Satiru town
1912–18	Libya	Sanussi sheikhs
1915	Nyasaland	John Chilembwe
1921–26	Morocco (Spain, France)	Abd el-Krim; Berbers. Rif War.
1922–31	Libya	Sanussi sheikhs
1930–31	Vietnam	VNQDD uprising; Nghe-An and Ha-Tinh Soviets
1930–32	Burma	Saya San

TABLE 13.1.

CONTINUED

Date	Colony	Leadership (if known); other data
1930s–48	Palestine	Arabs vs. Jews vs. British
	Phase 5	
1945–49	Dutch East Indies	Sukarno, Mohammad Hatta
1946–54	Vietnam	Ho Chi Minh, Vo Nguyen Giap; Viet Minh
1947	Madagascar	
1948–54	Malaya	Malayan Communist Party (mostly Chinese)
1952–56	Kenya (central)	Mau Mau
1954–61	Algeria	FLN collective leadership
1961–75	Angola	Holden Roberto (GRAE); Agostino Neto (MPLA); Jonas Savimbi (UNITA)
1962–75	Mozambique	Eduardo Mondlane; Samora Machel; FRELIMO
1963–75	Guinea-Bissau	Amilcar Cabral; PAIGC
1972–79	Rhodesia	Robert Mugabe; ZANU. ZAPU

Note: This list includes major rebellions threatening European control of a colony, as well as several minor ones confined to a portion of a colony. Except for the Hidalgo revolt, leadership in all cases was provided by non-Europeans (mestizos included).

Sources: Michael Adas, *Prophets of Rebellion;* Kevin Gosner, *Soldiers of the Virgin: The Moral Economy of a Colonial Mayan Rebellion;* C. L. R. James, *The Black Jacobins;* Brian Lapping, *End of Empire;* Gary B. Nash, *Red, Black, and White: The Peoples of Early America;* Robert I. Rotberg, ed., *Rebellion in Black Africa;* James C. Scott, *The Moral Economy of the Peasant;* Karen Spalding, *Huarochiri: An Andean Society under Inca and Spanish Rule;* Steve J. Stern, ed., *Resistance, Rebellion, and Consciousness in the Andean Peasant World.*

circumstances and leaders changed. Still, a recurring theme was the need to challenge not just specific actions or policies deemed objectionable, but the regime's basic character. Because of their violent means and far-reaching goals, rebellions had an unmatched capacity to grip the attention of Europeans.

Major rebellions fought in the colonies by non-European peoples[15] put rulers tactically and psychologically on the defensive, at least for a time.[16] They undermined colonizers' assiduous efforts to depict themselves as invincible. Rebel leaders' accomplishments became sources of inspiration for subsequent generations of nationalists. In the two most dramatic cases—the Andean uprising led by Tupac Amaru II and the Great Mutiny in India—revolt was so widespread that it was unclear at times whether the metropole could hold on.

Yet prior to phase 5 not a single rebel movement calling for independence attained it. The two that came closest to proclaiming independence—movements led by Hidalgo and Morelos in New Spain—were crushed and their leaders executed. The others were not seen by their leaders or followers as leading to sovereign statehood in the sense that we now think of it. Tupac Amaru II, who claimed direct descent from Inca royalty, implied to his Amerindian followers that the old empire might be restored in some form. But he also persistently proclaimed loyalty to the Spanish king, leaving unclear what his ultimate aims were. A similar ambiguity over goals can be seen in the Indian Mutiny, if only because the groups arrayed against East India Company rule were so diverse. Each was trying to restore a past differing in crucial respects from the restoration plans of others. Stanley Wolpert writes of leaders in the revolt,

> It was not simply the decayed and dying Great Mughal Empire that they wanted to restore in all its glory, but a past symbolized by Shivaji Maharaj, who hated all Mughals as well, the Maratha Confederacy, and King Rama himself, a golden age of Hindu myth when Gods walked on earth miraculously to save their devout supplicants from demon darkness. It was all of these incompatible eras and dreams divided by centuries or millennia, each with its clamoring band of dedicated loyalists clutching tattered banners of faded fortune. . . . They were all divided by unbridgeable gulfs of belief, by doctrines that taught them to hate or mistrust one another.[17]

This was not exactly a propitious setting for appeals to Indian unity or to a future that would mark a great improvement over the past.

The Haitian revolt aimed to change the social status of persons—by ending slavery—but not the political status of the colony. Toussaint L'Ouverture wanted to retain Saint Domingue's dependence on France to protect the revolt's achievements. An appeal to French revolutionary ideals, in Toussaint's view, was the best insurance against reinstatement of a practice violating the rights of man. Other New World slave revolts were likewise focused on social revolutionary goals rather than changes in territorial governance. Indeed, demands that authorities scrap old laws and enforce new ones assumed that the government would remain in place. The most socially radical of colonial revolts were in this respect politically conservative.

Many rebellions brought about a tightening of European control so as to prevent a repeat performance. Peru's creole population, for example, became decidedly more royalist after the early 1780s because it feared another uprising like Tupac

Amaru's. Spain's hold over one of its most important viceroyalties thus became stronger. In New Spain, *peninsulares* and creoles came together in horrified reaction to the mobilization of Indian and mestizo masses by Fathers Hidalgo and Morelos. At least for a while, elites saw retention of the tie to Spain as a way to protect themselves against a threat from below. After India's Great Mutiny was crushed the British Parliament abolished the East India Company, ending the loose administrative methods associated with company rule. A more bureaucratic, centralized structure was established with direct accountability to officials in London.

In putting down rebellions, colonial authorities harshly repressed the most active groups. Rebel leaders were executed or permanently exiled. Rulers thus managed to undermine if not destroy whatever institutional capacity these movements had developed.

Many rebellions were weakened by failure to articulate what they wanted as clearly as what they opposed. Lack of clarity about alternatives to the colonial order could reflect genuine ambivalence on a leader's part, as was probably the case with Tupac Amaru II. It could reflect military realities. When placed on the defensive, as inevitably occurred, rebels were preoccupied with holding their own and had little time to speculate on what might happen if they won. But a more serious problem was also at work. Given the complex, pluralistic character of many colonial societies, it is not surprising that several groups within a territory might be ready to claim self-determination rights. How could people decide which claims were valid and which were not? Even under optimal circumstances of political freedom (which did not obtain), the choice of electoral or negotiating techniques for resolving the problem would be hotly contested. Under these circumstances it made sense for rebels to *avoid* clarifying what size of unit or type of polity should replace the system they opposed. But what makes tactical sense in the short term can be a fatal flaw in the longer run. Jawaharlal Nehru wrote of the revolt of 1857–58, "There was hardly any national and unifying sentiment among the leaders, and a mere anti-foreign feeling, coupled with a desire to maintain their feudal privileges, was a poor substitute for this."[18]

What distinguishes pre–phase 5 rebellions from modern nationalist movements is the willingness of rebel leaders to experiment with alternatives to the colonial/national self. Early rebellions failed because their alternative identities were even more problematic as mass mobilizers than national ones. Most revolts were highly localized, a consequence of the small scale of many indigenous societies (see chapter 10). Appeals directed to one group embedded in a larger colony often failed to attract a wider following. The Tzeltal Revolt of 1712, for example, involved a small segment of New Spain's Mayan population. The rebellion led by Juan Santos Atahualpa in Peru appealed to people on the Andes' forested eastern slopes but failed to attract a mass following in the more densely populated sierra regions. Bambatha's rebellion did not spread beyond the Zulus; indeed, it was confined to certain regions of Zululand. The more restricted an uprising's base of support, the broader the base from which government could recruit forces to suppress it.

An obvious way to overcome limitations of small scale was to resurrect a large indigenous polity. Appealing to a real or imagined precolonial past had the advantage of evoking a society uncontaminated by the Europeans' presence and evil ways. But how appealing would an earlier empire be to those whose ancestors had been conquered and unwillingly incorporated into it? When Tupac Amaru II tried to rally Amerindians by emphasizing his descent from rulers of the Inca Empire two centuries earlier, he alienated Aymaras in Upper Peru (Bolivia) who had kept alive memories of heroic resistance to Inca conquerors.[19] The prospect of a revived Mughal Empire inspired many Indian rebels in 1857. But this very prospect alarmed Sikhs and people identifying with the Mughal Empire's historic nemesis, the Maratha Confederacy. Sikhs helped the British crush the rebellion; Maratha-speakers helped fragment the movement from within.

Failure of the two most significant pre–phase 5 uprisings in colonial history suggests that symbols of resistance appealing to selected aspects of indigenous history are not guaranteed broad popular support. They are at least as likely to divide as to unite, because the very feature that attracts some people can repel others with dissimilar backgrounds and interpretations of the past. Nationalists searching for nondivisive symbols may have to delve so far back in time that their choices are irrelevant to their major constituencies. A politically inspired choice for the center of independent India's flag was the wheel associated with the great Buddhist emperor Ashoka. The wheel not only evoked pride that India gave birth to a major world religion. It also avoided reliance on a symbol based on Hinduism or Islam that might offend whichever of the two religious communities was left out. A similarly inspired choice was the name Ghana to replace Gold Coast. Reference to the West African kingdom, which existed from the fourth through eleventh centuries A.D., evoked the image of sustained, successful African self-government. No Gold Coast groups were likely to object because the ancient kingdom was located hundreds of miles from its modern successor.

Effective mobilization for independence evidently requires extensive reference to colonialism as the generator of identities the masses share. Fundamental to the nationalist message is a claim that the negative experience of subjugation by foreigners can play a positive role in creating the nation. One reason nationalist rebellions of phase 5 succeeded whereas nonnationalist rebellions of earlier phases failed may be that the former directly acknowledged the realities and impacts of colonialism in ways that the latter did not.

NATIONALISM: OBSTACLES ALONG THE ROAD TO SUCCESS

Nationalist ideas and movements were driving forces behind the independence wave of phase 5.[20] Yet the limitations of anticolonial nationalism and the obstacles non-European nationalists confronted when trying to displace their rulers were serious. The more numerous and daunting the obstacles, the easier it was for rulers to maintain the status quo.

Non-European nationalism, as defined here, identifies the colony as the national unit that is entitled to form an autonomous state.[21] Typically the nation comprises all residents of a colony regardless of race. The nation may also be equated, however, with all its non-European or indigenous residents. Given that the vast majority in phase 5 new states fits one or both of the latter categories, non-European nationalism is democratic in aspiration, its inclination toward inclusiveness contrasting sharply with the exclusivist, antidemocratic premises of colonialism. Its inclusiveness also sets it apart from settler nationalism, which from phase 2 through 4 (in the white dominions) and 5 (in Rhodesia) tended to define the nation as residents of European descent. Where settlers constituted the vast majority of the population their nationalism was consistent with democratic, albeit racially discriminatory, forms of government. Where settlers were in the minority their nationalism shared colonialism's antidemocratic character.

Non-European nationalism was unlike collaboration and accommodation in opposing foreign control of a colony's leading institutions, particularly in the public sector, and in proposing that the nation's citizens control these institutions. It differed from exit, avoidance, sabotage, and displacement in directly and openly challenging the holders of power. Nationalists inveighed against individual and collective self-abasement, preaching confidently that the nation could do a better job of governing itself than foreigners. Nationalism sometimes took the form of violent rebellion. But the nonviolent path was far more typical in phase 5. Whatever the tactics employed, the goal was to advance toward a modernizing future, not to turn the clock back to a premodern past.

In most territories gaining independence in phase 5, a substantial time gap separated imposition of European rule from the spread of nationalist ideas and movements. In Portugal's African colonies the interval extended from early phase 1 to the 1950s and 1960s, in many Caribbean islands from mid–phase 1 to phase 4. If one dates British intrusion in Indian affairs to the 1750s, more than a century elapsed before the INC was formed in 1885 and more than a century and a half before it became a mass movement and declared independence as the goal in 1929. In sub-Saharan Africa nationalist mobilization in the late 1940s and 1950s came four to six decades after European rule was imposed. Once articulated, nationalist ideas did not automatically generate mass support and in many instances were contested by movements appealing to other identities. The puzzle is why nationalism took so long to emerge, and why when it did the journey to the political kingdom was often long and hazardous.

One answer is that nationalist ideas could not gain widespread acceptance until colonial rule was firmly consolidated. Because a territory's non-European residents differed from each other in many ways, such as language and social custom, if they were to press at an early point for self-determination they would appeal to multiple selves and hence split colonial society into hostile fragments. Not until later, when foreign rule impacted the lives of ordinary people, could they take seriously the argument that their shared political subjugation was more important than the factors keeping them apart. Asking residents of a territory whose boundaries were externally and often arbitrarily imposed to think of themselves as one nation was asking a lot. Why should an identity traceable to European aggression be more highly valued than identities rooted in people's culture and precolonial history?

Once nationalist ideas took hold the most obvious obstacle to their spread was opposition from government, to say nothing of settlers. Top administrators saw nationalists as critics with dubious credentials, who applied inappropriate political standards and persistently invented or exaggerated facts. Even worse, nationalists aspired to the jobs power holders occupied. Officials with careers at stake and a civilizational project at risk were not about to let themselves be displaced without a struggle. Their aim was to weaken and divide and divert nationalist movements, if not repress them. Metropoles with no plans to devolve power to colonial residents favored outright repression. Examples from phase 4 and the early years of phase 5 were the Dutch in the Dutch East Indies, Belgians in the Congo, the Portuguese in all their colonies, and the French in Indochina, Algeria, and Madagascar. When a movement was declared illegal, its leaders jailed and followers harassed, its headquarters infiltrated by spies, all protest marches and demonstrations banned, the press censored, and public speech unprotected, the obstacle course to national liberation was formidable indeed.

The British, by contrast, having devised in phase 3 a policy of shifting power to settler communities that culminated in the Statute of Westminster (1931), were open to pressures from colonies of occupation to apply similar policies to non-Europeans. In the typical British colony it was easier than in territories ruled by other metropoles for nationalists in phases 4 and 5 to form legally recognized organizations and address public gatherings. Political parties could contend for votes in elections to colonial legislatures assigned meaningful policy-making responsibilities.[22]

But London's willingness to transfer power to nationalist politicians should not be overstated. Prior to phase 5 indirect rule was the dominant policy in many colonies, and administrators made it clear they regarded traditional rulers of small units embedded within a colony as the legitimate representatives of indigenous views. Because many traditional rulers benefited from the status quo and felt threatened by the populist appeals and organizing tactics of nationalist movements, nationalists had to contend with the localized opposition of indigenous elites as well as with the colonywide opposition of British administrators. Even when indirect rule was jettisoned and the Labour Party took power after World War II, nationalists could not count on the cooperation of those they aimed to replace. Policy makers in London valued colonies as sources of raw material exports earning dollars and aiding Labour's plans for postwar reconstruction. Fears were expressed that independence would expose ex-colonies to the influence of one or both superpowers, thereby accelerating Britain's decline in world affairs. The case for holding on was particularly strong in colonies with a settler presence, strategically significant naval facilities, and substantial metropolitan investment in productive assets.

In general, Britain's strategy in phase 5 was to delay the transfer of power as long as was prudent. One part of the strategy, paradoxically, was to insist that its successors prove they represented a plurality if not a majority of the population. Nationalists could not come to power on a vehement claim to represent the voiceless masses. They had to go out and win contested elections organized and supervised by colonial administrators. Both sides converged in appealing to the popular will as arbiter of a colony's future.

Regardless of the metropole in charge and the extent of opposition from above, nationalists confronted additional obstacles. They had to convince substantial numbers of people that their analysis of history and the contemporary political situation was valid and that their proposed plan of action made sense. Among problems nationalists encountered were (1) difficulties in communicating their message to the masses; (2) the attractiveness of alternative coping mechanisms; and (3) claims to identity and loyalty by other collective units.

Many of the early nationalists were physically, culturally, and psychologically distanced from the people they sought to reach. Nationalists clustered in cities, while the vast majority in most colonies was dispersed throughout the countryside. Where transport was rudimentary it proved difficult if not impossible to reach outlying areas. Where people spoke many languages a speaker might address an audience in a tongue it did not understand—and hope for an accurate translation. The magnitude of the challenge was concisely expressed by Julius Nyerere, founder of Tanganyika's nationalist party TANU: "Other nations try to reach the moon. TANU tries to reach the villages." For Nyerere the two tasks were equivalent in magnitude, scope, and complexity.

Nationalists tended to assume that the desperate poverty of the masses made for a high level of discontent that could be easily tapped and mobilized for political ends. But it was not that simple. As Eric Hoffer has observed, "Misery does not automatically generate discontent; nor is the intensity of discontent directly proportional to the degree of misery. Discontent is likely to be highest when misery is bearable; when conditions have so improved that an ideal state seems within reach."[23] Hoffer's words suggest why nationalist leaders were often angrier at colonial rule than were the ordinary folk they set out to reach. The initial challenge was to describe reality in a way that made the audience as angry as the speaker was. Only then could popular discontent be channeled in the desired direction.

A second obstacle is implicit in the earlier discussion of coping mechanisms. The sheer number and variety of options made it likely that colonized people would move not in one direction but many. To some people in some circumstances each option made sense, both in its own right and in comparison with nationalist appeals. Collaborators presumably found nationalists too negative. Accommodators probably worried that benefits enjoyed under a stable regime might be lost in the transition to a future that looked bright but might never arrive. Those leaning toward exit, avoidance, sabotage, and displacement were doubtless put off by the high cost of directly challenging powerful rulers. People harboring an inferiority complex might find the appeal to self-confidence unrealistic. Nationalists had to fend off the substantive objections of people who examined their arguments and then declined to go along.

A third obstacle is implicit in the observations of this and earlier chapters. Phases 4 and 5 witnessed a proliferation of collective identities. Some had precolonial roots. Others resulted from the penetrative activities of public, private profit, and religious sector institutions. Many identities combined old and new, as when small ethnic groups and subcastes banded together to gain better access to public sector jobs and social services. What outsiders called traditional groupings were often recent creations responding to new forms of competitive interaction among the colonized.[24] Organizations arose to speak on behalf of racial and ethnic groups, residents of districts and regions, religious communities, castes and subcastes, occupational categories like plantation workers, miners, traders, farmers, teachers, junior civil servants, and the like.

These organizations were not necessarily rivals of nationalist movements. After all, people can hold several identities simultaneously. Ardent nationalists saw no incompatibility between their appeals to national unity and the undeniable fact that as individuals they too belonged to certain linguistic or religious groups and not others. In numerous cases organizations representing specific groups functioned as local level building blocks for nationalist parties. The trade union movement, for example, was the base for the Parti Démocratique de Guinée, a farmer's association for the Parti Démocratique de la Côte d'Ivoire.[25] In any event few nonnationalist organizations went so far as to press for their own independent state. The Muslim League's call in 1940 to carve an independent Pakistan out of British India was the rare exception, not the general rule.

These points granted, nationalists often found themselves competing with groups they deemed either subnational or antinational. Nationalists were trying to reach the same people the other organizations were eager to proselytize. The target audience was unlikely to accept and act positively on all messages sent its way. Could the call for national self-determination even be heard amid the cacophony of voices appealing to multiple selves?

Especially worrisome to nationalists were movements that mobilized large groups concentrated in distinctly defined regions within a territory. The fear was that such groups might come to regard themselves as nations, entitled to their own independent states and capable of forming them. A recurring nationalist nightmare was civil war prompted by the attempted secession of would-be nations within the larger one. A version of this scenario did in fact play out when India was partitioned at independence. After independence, secessionist revolts shook Nigeria, the Congo (Zaire), and Pakistan.

Some nationalist movements were weakened by being perceived as agents of one group's political agenda. In India from the late 1930s onward, M. A. Jinnah was able to rally many Muslims to forsake the INC for the Muslim League. Jinnah's argument was that the INC, for all its inclusive rhetoric, was a communal party representing the Hindu majority. Jinnah was disturbed by Gandhi's reliance on the Hindi language and Hindu religious symbolism to mobilize the peasant masses. The Muslim League leader derisively termed Gandhi "that Hindu revivalist."[26] Jinnah feared that if the INC controlled an independent government Muslims would be permanently marginalized. From the INC's perspective, Jinnah's call for a separate Muslim state delayed and ultimately derailed the drive for a united, independent, secular India.

In Nigeria, the National Council of Nigeria and the Cameroons (NCNC) failed to gain broad support in all parts of the country consistent with its self-image. Nnamdi Azikiwe, who became NCNC president shortly after its formation in 1944, was a dedicated nationalist who eventually became Nigeria's first president. But he was also an Igbo, and Igbos were the party's most active supporters. Azikiwe seriously hurt his cause by becoming president of the Ibo State Union in 1948 and declaring, "It would appear that the God of Africa has created the Ibo nation to lead the children of Africa from the bondage of the ages."[27] This convinced prominent figures in other regions that the NCNC was really an ethnic chauvinist organization

317

masquerading under nationalist colors. Subsequent formation of the Action Group and Northern People's Congress to represent other ethnic and regional interests slowed the drive for independence in Africa's most populous territory.

Nationalists did not need to capture the institutional heights of all three sectors in order to gain independence. Taking over top executive positions in the public sector was a necessary and often sufficient condition. In the struggle to control this sector European power holders enjoyed a clear institutional advantage. The bureaucracies they directed reached throughout the colony and covered a wide range of activities, including ones people wanted like social services and utilities. Taxes were a steady revenue base, enough to pay high salaries to civil servants.

In sharp contrast, the typical nationalist movement found it difficult to set up and staff branches throughout the territory. It lacked the expertise of specialists in public policy issues, and it had no regular source of income. Some non-Europeans might occupy midlevel civil service positions, but their numbers were usually small and their policy-making experience minimal. A political party might hold seats in an elected legislature. But even in the most favorable situation—where the Westminster model was being transferred—a legislature's powers were far more limited than those of its European role model. In the worst cases a movement had to operate underground, its leaders behind bars or continually on the run. In all cases nationalists lacked experience in governance. All they could do was promise they would do a better job if they came to power. But the promise of performance is not the same as demonstrated performance. Nationalists scored high on the will for political autonomy, but their institutional capacity to achieve it was limited, especially when compared to that of rulers they opposed.

THE SETTLER POPULATION

Settler communities were in a stronger position than non-Europeans to become autonomous if they chose to do so. Settlers usually outnumbered metropolitans and hence constituted a majority of a territory's colonizers. Even if they felt metropolitans looked down on them (as did Spanish American creoles), settlers never had to bear the heavy burden of inferior status which they themselves did so much to place on people not of pure European descent. The absence of a deep-seated inferiority complex meant that many of the self-destructive behavior patterns noted among non-European peoples did not inhibit settlers from working toward goals consistent with their interests.

When settlers began to think in nationalist terms they regarded themselves as the nation deserving of self-determination. Except for colonies in which there were two distinct European communities, as in Canada and South Africa, the settler nation was strikingly homogeneous in terms of race, language, and cultural patterns.

In Iberian colonies the settler nation was homogeneous in religion as well. Mobilizing settlers to act was thus not nearly as great a challenge as mobilizing a far more diverse colonized population.

Settlers were far better positioned than non-Europeans to gain access to and influence over critical sectoral institutions. There were important cross-national differences in this respect, Spanish American settlers in phases 1 and 2 possessing less leverage than English-speaking settlers in phases 1 through 4. Nonetheless, if one focuses on the two groups' common denominators, in the public sector they controlled local government structures and were members of local militia, with the important right, denied ordinary non-Europeans, to carry weapons. Limits to upward mobility within the bureaucracy were set much higher than for non-Europeans. In some colonies settlers became influential insiders in the policy process. Perhaps the extreme case was their virtual monopoly of bureaucratic and legislative posts in Southern Rhodesia from 1923, when it became a so-called self-governing colony, until the late 1970s. Because of their race settlers enjoyed informal social relations with top metropolitan administrators that were simply out of the question for non-Europeans.

Settlers were if anything even more active players in the other sectors than in government. They owned productive assets: land for commercial agriculture and ranching as well as slaves when this practice was permitted. They had access to credit from European banks, when comparable lines of credit were unavailable to non-European entrepreneurs. They were sometimes involved in international commerce. Many small and medium enterprises were directly under their control. In colonies where Protestants were dominant, settlers controlled local denominational structures and church-managed educational systems.

The institutional leverage settlers held meant that they did not need to struggle as hard as non-Europeans to infiltrate key colonial structures—to say nothing of having to develop elaborate underground institutions to sabotage these structures. This factor helps explain why settlers led the initial round of independence movements while non-European nationalists did not enjoy comparable success until much later.

The puzzle is why settlers remained formally dependent on metropoles for as long as they did. That dependence lasted for roughly 250–300 years in the New World colonies of Spain and Portugal, for more than 150 years for English-speakers in Canada (if we take the Statute of Westminster as the marker of independence for white dominions), for more than 140 years in Massachusetts and Virginia, and for longer than a century in Australia. Why did settlers accept the authority of a distant power for so long when it appears they could have captured the levers of state power and gained independence with relatively little difficulty whenever they wanted?

The principal obstacle to autonomy was not capacity but will. Strong identity ties to the metropole led settlers to regard themselves as part of a great civilizing and modernizing project managed from the imperial center. The metropole was not simply a political entity, a government ruling an empire. It was also a principal source of settler culture, lifestyle, identities, values, and memories. As new waves of immigrants came out over the years their presence reinforced the metropole's position as a civilizational reference point. The stronger the emotional bonds to the mother country, the less ready communities of European descent were to sever ties with it.

Such reluctance can be seen with special vividness in Britain's white dominions during phases 3 and 4. As long as settlers[28] in Canada, Australia, New Zealand, and South Africa had authority to manage domestic affairs through imported parliamentary institutions, their leaders were unwilling to push for the formal separation from Great Britain that the term "independence" denoted. The Statute of Westminster granted the reality of sovereignty desired by dominion leaders. But these leaders were anxious to play down the significance of the statute. They studiously avoided references to independence, emphasizing common interests with Great Britain rather than the freedom to go their own way. During the 1920s and 1930s they worked closely with officials in London to design a Commonwealth giving new institutional form to long-standing ties. The unwillingness of Britain's diaspora communities to announce a formal break with the mother country in 1931 contrasts strikingly with the way independence was celebrated in phase 5.

In both Spanish and British empires the monarchy played a large role in retaining settler loyalties (see chapter 12). Spanish American creoles remained loyal even when the ruling dynasty shifted in the early eighteenth century from one non-Spanish line (Habsburg) to another (Bourbon). On occasion creoles rebelled against policies they did not like, as in Paraguay in 1732–33, New Granada (Venezuela) in 1749, and New Granada (Colombia) in 1781. But anger was directed at agents the monarch appointed to govern them, not at the distant ruler himself. The most popular slogan of the *comunero* rebellion of 1781 was "Long live the king, and death to bad government."[29]

British monarchs lacked constitutional authority overseas equivalent to that of Spain's rulers. And George III's unstable personality did not help him as disputes with the thirteen North American colonies escalated in the 1760s and 1770s. The contrast with phase 3 is striking. During the years when English-speakers in Canada and Australasia might have pressed for autonomy, Queen Victoria became a revered figure at home and abroad. During the final quarter century of her long reign (1837–1901) the queen saw herself as the living symbol of a vast, unified empire.[30] She was perceived that way by millions of her far-flung subjects, of all racial backgrounds.

In phase 4 Parliament's leaders skillfully transformed the monarchy into the embodiment of British Commonwealth unity. The very institution that in phase 3 represented the metropole's dominance was redefined to soften the blow of the decline from dominance. At Imperial Conferences held in London during the 1920s dominions were assured that affirmations of loyalty to the Crown would not prevent them from exercising the full panoply of sovereign rights. In a feat of verbal legerdemain, the Balfour Report to the conference in 1926 described the United Kingdom and overseas dominions as "autonomous communities within the British Empire, equal in status, in no way subordinate one to another in any aspect of their domestic or foreign affairs, though united by a common allegiance to the Crown, and freely associated as members of the British Commonwealth of Nations."[31] The Crown thus came to symbolize a new relationship among political equals.

Settler dependence on the metropole had practical as well as symbolic advantages. Its troops could be called on to suppress internal rebellion and ward off invasion by land or sea. The nature of the threat varied depending on the colony. In Iberian phase 1 New World possessions and Caribbean slave-based plantation colonies, where hierarchically arranged racial groups lived in close proximity, rebellion was the principal threat. In BNA cross-frontier raids by Indians and the French were the main danger. Strategic concerns were less important for the white dominions. Still, Canadians fearful that an expanding United States would look north as well as west had reason to retain close ties with the world's greatest naval power.

CONCLUSIONS

Chapter 12 offered Eurocentric explanations for the unusually lengthy span of European rule in many parts of the world. Chapter 13 offers complementary explanations based on the actions and perceptions of colonial residents, showing that non-European peoples and European settlers alike faced serious obstacles to the successful assertion of autonomy. Maintenance of the status quo was due not only to the rulers' high capacity and will to consolidate power, but also to limits on the capacity and will of colonial subjects to seize power. In general, non-Europeans' desire to terminate foreign control was higher than their institutional capacity to carry it out. Settlers had a higher capacity for autonomous action, but their will to break with the metropole was relatively low.

A major obstacle to autonomy was the complexity, group insulation, and intergroup competition built into most colonial societies. Residents found it difficult to reach agreement over strategies and tactics even when they concurred on what they did not like. Neither could they readily agree on the kind of polity that should replace what was there. Another set of obstacles was psychological. Among non-European peoples there were recurring patterns of self-destructive behavior, and among settlers a pronounced unwillingness to break with the country that served as their civilizational frame of reference.

Obstacles to autonomy had an institutional dimension. Although the challenge of collective self-determination was far more daunting for non-Europeans than for settlers, both groups had to design strategies to gain control of key sectors. This might mean infiltrating from below the very institutions whose stretch from Europe empowered the metropole to shape colonial life. Or it might mean creating new institutions wholly controlled from the start by colonial residents. In either case it was problematic for residents to attain independence until they had effective institutional leverage of some kind as a counter to the sectoral power held by metropolitans. Many of the problems described in this chapter derive precisely from the effectiveness of the stretched sectoral institutions discussed in chapter 12.

The differential impact of these factors may help explain broad patterns in the history of overseas empires. Because non-Europeans faced more serious problems than settlers in asserting autonomy, one can understand the outcome of the initial round of independence movements. In phase 2 settler elites directed the movements in all cases except one, then subjugated or marginalized non-Europeans in the decades following independence. For the same reason one can understand why Britain's white dominions attained de facto sovereignty before Britain's colonies of occupation. And one can see why colonies in which non-Europeans constituted the vast majority could not easily translate numbers into political power. The demographic edge held by the colonized could in fact be a disadvantage for would-be leaders, who had to design common goals around which to mobilize diverse and competitive constituents.

Part V

ACCOUNTING FOR
IMPERIAL CONTRACTION

(*Overleaf*) Contemporary engraving of the Battle of Bunker Hill, June 1775. "Drawn by Mr. Miller." Courtesy Massachusetts Historical Society.

14
Colonialism as a Self-Defeating Enterprise

Part 5 proposes to account for the decline and fall of European empires. Given the obstacles to colonial autonomy noted in earlier chapters, it is not obvious why independence movements succeeded. Why were any new states formed, let alone more than a hundred?[1] A theory of decolonization should also explain why new-state formation was so heavily concentrated in two relatively brief time periods. What factors stimulated the large number of successful breakaway movements in phases 2 and 5? Other questions refer to differences between decolonization phases. Why was the initial round of independence movements led almost exclusively by settlers while comparable movements by non-Europeans did not arise until much later? Why did metropoles in phase 2 so frequently fight to hold on, while the typical phase 5 pattern was a peacefully negotiated transfer of power?

A theory of European imperialism must use evidence culled from several centuries. It is bound to be more general, complex, and inclusive of a variety of causal factors than a theory of decolonization, which must account for the compression of independence movements into phases 2 and 5 and the years immediately preceding these phases. A theory of imperialism focuses attention on characteristics of Europe and the world that persisted over time. It is the continuity of these features that permits recurring expansionist activities. In contrast, a theory of decolonization draws attention to conditions in which the world changed quickly—that is, to discontinuities. The implication is that overseas empires rose because of deep-seated structural and cultural attributes, whereas their fall was dependent on catalytic, unpredictable, contingent events.

Is it reasonable, however, to posit a theory of decline comprehensive enough to apply to trends in phases 2 *and* 5? To explain changes in the size of empires one should concentrate on those areas in which key initiatives for change were concentrated. With respect to imperialism this means focusing on one compact region, Europe. This book emphasizes developments in European political history, economics, and culture even as it argues that Eurocentrism alone is insufficient and misleading. To explain contraction one must focus on the principal sources of pressure to change the status quo, namely, territories that gained independence. The number of independent countries in each phase greatly exceeded the number of metropoles. New states were dispersed throughout the world. Differences among them—in size, population, demographic complexity, natural resources—were far greater than differences among metropoles. Moreover, chapters 4 and 7 identified important differences between the decolonization phases. Among these were the geographically more confined range of phase 2, contrasts between settler and non-European political elites, and a far more complex international system in phase 5 that included international organizations. Chapter 13 further emphasized objective and subjective differences between settler communities and non-European populations. Taking all these kinds of variation into account, one could understandably decide to write off the search for a general theory of decolonization.

Part 5 argues, to the contrary, that such a theory can be devised, as long as one bears in mind that what is being explained is broad historical patterns and not specific events. Back of differences between phases are underlying similarities in the nature of European colonialism which, over time, contributed to its demise. It is not so much the overextension of empire as the contradictions of empire that eventually destabilized this system of global dominance. The more these contradictions were noticed by colonial residents, and the more troubled residents became because of what they noticed, the more vulnerable to collapse the system became.

Back of differences between non-Europeans and settlers were factors that led them to become more similar over time. The previous chapter argued that non-Europeans and settlers differed not only racially and culturally but also in the key factor blocking successful demands for autonomy. This chapter shows that as non-Europeans raised their capacity to control colonial public sector institutions, and as settlers demonstrated a greater will to press for independence, the two groups converged in having the level of capacity and will needed effectively to challenge their rulers.

A crucial question is how decolonization phases begin, given the forces at work to maintain imperial control. An examination of developments in BNA in late phase 1 and India in phase 4 reveals that the precedent-setters of phases 2 and 5 were similar in important ways. Settlers in the BNA colonies and Indians in India had unusually high levels of institutional leverage in the public sector. Moreover, mutually beneficial relations developed between political leaders and prominent business figures that became in effect cross-sector alliances. Just as these alliances were empowering to Europeans in the drive for expansion, so they were to colonial residents in the drive for autonomy. Precisely because BNA and India differ in so many ways—

hemisphere, decolonization phase, the racial composition of their elites, and so forth—one would not expect to find these sectoral similarities. That they are there lends support to the argument that cross-sector alliances are conducive to the initiation of decolonization waves.

Chapter 15 shifts attention to the international scene, pointing out additional similarities between phases 2 and 5. Hegemonic wars shifted power relations within empires and produced high levels of uncertainty and expectation on all sides concerning the character of imperial relations after wars ended. However, it was not wars themselves but political crises immediately *following* them that triggered independence movements. These crises had a remarkably similar form, causing leaders in otherwise very different colonies to share the belief that they and their people had been betrayed by the metropole. With the sense of betrayal came a rapid escalation in the popular demand for separation from the betrayer. Once the independence precedent was set, international demonstration effects took over, accounting for the rapidity with which a large number of new states was formed. Over time the factors driving decolonization shifted from the domestic politics of specific colonies to international events beyond the control of any one colony or metropole.

CONTRADICTIONS OF COLONIALISM

Consolidation of colonial rule had the unintended effect of magnifying and highlighting problems inherent in systems of overseas governance. These problems made it more difficult for administrators to know what to do and became sources of conflict with colonial residents. Consolidation eventually undercut itself.

As the colonial government extended its sway throughout a territory, extracting resources, regulating behavior, adjudicating disputes, and providing services through bureaucratic agencies, the public sector came to look increasingly like the metropole's. But the more closely the public sectors resembled each other in function and structure, the more obvious to all was the essential dissimilarity between them: the metropole's monopoly of sovereignty. The colony was supposed to be a protostate, not a complete state. In order to create a protostate the metropole's agents set themselves an ambitious agenda for change (see chapter 13). Once the apparatus of control was in place rulers favored not change but the status quo. They thus shifted from a radical to a conservative stance toward the role of government in colonial society.

But as government tried to slow down political change, growing numbers of colonial residents asked why their protostate should not move more rapidly toward state sovereignty. Critics complained, in effect, "The metropole has taken us 80 percent of the way. Why not finish the task? If our rulers won't do it we will." As a political movement, nationalism represented a challenge to colonial rulers. As an ideology, however, it was a pledge not to abandon the metropole's agenda but to complete it. The European state was the normative reference point, the standard to which nationalists appealed when critiquing the way their territory was governed.

If colonial rulers acquiesced to nationalist demands they sped up the transfer of power and their own eventual departure. If rulers held firm they were charged with refusal to accept the logical conclusion of what they had been doing all along. Anger over failure to transfer power intensified nationalist desires to challenge the system. Either way rulers found themselves under seige by their subjects.

In one instance a metropole's struggle for freedom was cited to support the claim that its colony should likewise be free. In 1913 officials and settlers in the Dutch East Indies proposed to celebrate the centenary of the Netherlands' independence from French rule. I. R. M. Soewardi Soerjeaningrat, secretary of the newly formed Indische Party, wrote an essay--tongue firmly in cheek—warning against this plan: "If I were a Netherlander I would not celebrate the commemoration of independence in a country where we refuse to give the people their freedom. . . . Especially in these times when the people of the Indies are engaged in finding their feet, although they are only half awakened, it would be a tactical mistake to show this people how it should eventually celebrate its independence."[2]

Disagreement over the locus of ultimate political authority was reinforced by conflict over the basis of political legitimacy, conflict not only between metropolitan authorities and nationalists but also between norms and practices applied by metropoles at home and those applied abroad. In theory and practice colonialism was authoritarian. The matter was straightforward: the strong took possession of a distant land, and decisions affecting it were made at the imperial center, from the top down. Yet the theory and practice of domestic politics in many metropoles were antiauthoritarian. From the seventeenth century onward a powerful theme in European political thought was the idea that legitimacy inhered not in monarchs by divine right but in the people, expressed through legislatures representing the popular will. Such ideas were institutionalized in England's Glorious Revolution of 1688 when Parliament successfully limited royal prerogatives, and in France in 1789 with the onset of a social revolution that abolished the monarchy, appealed to Liberty, Equality, and Fraternity, and vested ultimate power in a people's assembly. When a metropole's colonial policy was top down while its domestic institutions reflected representative ideals, it could be accused of hypocrisy and worse for refusing to implement its fundamental political norms overseas. The more democratic the metropole, the greater the contradiction between domestic and colonial practice.

Through education, travel, and word of mouth politically conscious individuals in colonies became aware of these trends in Europe. They demanded that the colonial nation be represented in an elected legislature, either its own or the metropole's. The principle of consent from below applied whether the nation was defined restrictively (as by settlers in phase 2) or inclusively (as by non-Europeans in phase 5). Again Europe was the normative reference point. Colonial elites wanted their territories to replicate not only the sovereignty but also the populism of European states.

Political developments in England pushed BNA opinion leaders toward forming the first new state. In a stream of pamphlets that became a torrent following the Seven Years' War, writers asserted the principle, reaffirmed by Parliament in 1688–89, that only a body representing the people had the right to impose taxes. Parliament's failure to apply this principle when imposing new taxes on North American colonies after the war set off the first serious organized opposition to metropolitan policies. The American Declaration of Independence eloquently affirmed the principle of consent of the governed and notions of social contract articulated around the time of the Glorious Revolution. Samuel Eliot Morison observed that "the principles and language of John Locke's *Second Treatise of Government* (1690) were so much a part of [Thomas Jefferson's] mind that unconsciously [Jefferson] thought and wrote like Locke."[3] Independence was seen by its architects as a way to fulfill values the metropole rhetorically affirmed but refused, in practice, to respect.

In what became the second new state, Haiti, the timing of the slave revolt in 1791 was strongly influenced by the opening rounds of revolution in France. White plantation owners and free mulattoes used the revolution's rhetoric of equality and human rights to improve their positions within the colonial hierarchy. Revolt was triggered by the slaves' realization that whites and mulattoes had no intention of applying these universal ideals to the slaves' situation. Leaders of the revolt obtained critical support from a general the Jacobins dispatched to Saint Domingue, Sonthonax, who in 1793 announced the abolition of slavery. C. L. R. James asserts, "The history of liberation in France and slave emancipation in Saint Domingue is one and indivisible."[4] Haitian independence was premised on affirmation of French liberatory ideals, in the context of an invading French army committed to violating them by reimposing slavery.

French revolutionary ideals appealed to Spanish Americans who went on to lead independence movements. The Argentine nationalist Manuel Belgrano wrote, "As I was in Spain in 1789, and the French Revolution was then causing a change in ideas, and especially in the men of letters with whom I associated, the ideals of liberty, equality, security, and property took a firm hold on me, and I only saw tyrants in those who opposed man's enjoying, wherever he might be, those rights with which God and Nature endowed him."[5]

Phases 3 and 4 saw increased participation in European national legislatures through progressive extensions of the right to vote. This trend did not go unnoticed in the colonies. Most directly affected were Britain's white dominions, many of whose residents had recently left the mother country and were unwilling to accept more restrictive franchise rules for themselves than for British elections. When the first substantial influx of settlers took place in Australia and New Zealand in the mid–nineteenth century, democratization of British political institutions was well under way. These dominions consequently experienced more rapid transitions to responsible government than did Canada, whose founding occurred in a predemocratic era.

In Britain's colonies of occupation politicians pressed in phases 4 and 5 for a broadened franchise paralleling developments in the metropole and in Canada, Australia, and New Zealand. The argument was that granting all adult residents of a territory the right to vote regardless of race or culture was the ultimate fulfillment of a movement for participation that had already broken down restrictive barriers of education, class, and gender.

Concepts of nation and nationalism became more appealing in colonies as they became more popular in Europe. It is well known that the French Revolution ushered in an era of heightened nationalist sentiment throughout Europe. The initial impact of its appeal to fraternity was on the French people, mobilized to carry out radical change domestically and wage war against neighboring monarchical regimes. A second impact was on peoples whose lands were invaded, whether by revolutionary forces or Napoleon's armies. The warlike form French patriotism took stimulated patriotic anti-French fervor in countries as far afield as Russia and Spain. It is not a coincidence that independence movements flourished in the Americas between the start of the French Revolution and the end of Napoleon's rule. Year after year, leaders of New World movements were exposed to the emotional rhetoric of European nation-states at war. Hence they found it increasingly "natural" to think in nationalist terms about their own circumstances.

The experiences of colonial subjects living in Europe during this tumultuous period had a radicalizing effect. Francisco de Miranda, a legendary figure in Spanish American revolutionary history, was a general in France's army in the early 1790s. José de San Martín served as a lieutenant colonel in the Spanish army that fought desperately to repel France's invasion of Iberia. Simón Bolívar resided in Europe in 1799–1802 and 1803–07. It was during his travels there that he swore (in Rome) to devote his life to the independence cause. José Bonifacio de Andrade, the main figure urging Brazil's Dom Pedro to declare independence, was studying in Portugal when the French Revolution broke out. Though appalled at the revolution's excesses, he saw, in the words of John Crow, "how a social order rebels, how it fights and conquers when it has a strong purpose and audacious leadership. From that time forward, José Bonifacio undoubtedly had in the back of his mind the liberation of Brazil."[6]

The legacy of French revolutionary nationalism was felt well into the twentieth century. Writing in Paris in 1922, Ho Chi Minh referred to "the people of France . . . who have won their freedom through revolution, shattering the despotic yoke of emperors and kings so that they might become rulers of their own destiny."[7] Already an ardent patriot before leaving Vietnam for France, the young man was further inspired by the history of the country that had conquered his own.

But metropoles whose people regarded themselves as nations were generally unwilling to grant that colonies had this same attribute or might some day acquire it. The unwillingness was understandable because nationhood was equated with shared racial and cultural features, and colonies were generally far more heterogeneous than their metropoles. But Europeans also saw nationhood as the product of shared historical experience. Metropolitan officials typically reacted with skepticism if not outright rejection to the argument that their own rule was a sufficiently important shared experience to create a colonial nation. From the colonial perspective it was abundantly clear that Europeans wanted nationhood for themselves but not for others.

Sovereignty, popular representation in government, national identity were ideas integral to European political development from the eighteenth century onward. Colonial elites were so favorably impressed by them that they wanted to apply them to their own territories. Here the contradictions of overseas empire came into play. Metropoles refused to grant these ideas an export permit, claiming their inapplicability abroad. A break from Europe became the best way to affirm ideas Europeans were eloquently articulating.

That these ideas were also ideals enabled colonial nationalists to seize the offensive in the normative arena. Empires had been constructed on the premise that Europeans were morally superior to other peoples. Colonial nationalists turned the tables by accusing Europeans of being morally deficient, hypocrites who denied their own principles when these conflicted with narrow self-interest. Nationalists in phases 2 and 5 had a strong sense that their cause was just, both because it embraced universalistic values and because independence would move humanity closer to acknowledging those values. As the high ground was seized by colonial activists, supporters of empire found themselves on the moral defensive.

NEW-STATE ELITES: MAKING UP THE DEFICIT

Colonial rule was most effectively challenged when a group of colonial residents had (1) the capacity to administer one or more of the colony's public sector institutions,

(2) a strong will to control the public sector, and (3) the will to terminate dependent status and form an independent state. Absence of these three conditions was a sufficient condition for maintaining the status quo. Presence of the three was a necessary though not sufficient condition for substantial change.

This conclusion applies equally to settlers who led independence movements in phase 2 and to non-Europeans who led them in phase 5.[8] But each group had to call upon a distinctive experience to reach the necessary-condition threshold. To state this in another way, each had to satisfy different conditions to converge with the other in satisfying all three. Settlers were least likely to meet the third condition, non-Europeans the first. To the extent that colonized peoples identified with subnational groups more than with the colonial nation as a whole, their interest in organizing these groups detracted from an interest in controlling public sector institutions and hurt prospects for meeting the second condition. The critical factor permitting settlers to satisfy their missing will for independence condition was the passage of time, which gradually shifted identities and loyalties away from the metropole and toward the territory where settlers resided. The critical factor permitting non-Europeans to satisfy their missing capacity to control the public sector condition was diffusion of secondary- and university-level Western education to a few individuals. The experience of attending schools, combined with the content of curriculum taught there, gave the best-educated elements the capacity and will to focus on public sector institutions with the intent of capturing them.

The passage of time was, of course, something over which neither phase 1 settlers nor European states had any control. During their first decades overseas settlers had strong reasons to identify with the mother country and more broadly with Europe as the "mother continent." By doing so they could emphasize their distinctness from and superiority over indigenous peoples. One alleged difference was that Europeans had a meaningful past while indigenous peoples did not. Newly settled areas "were perceived by the settlers as having had no history prior to their arrival; the history of the mother country remained the salient history to them."[9] But as decades passed a growing number came to identify the colony as a homeland with its own past, defined as the heroic efforts of settlers to develop the land and tame or exterminate uncivilized peoples. The metropole continued to play a familiar role as civilizational reference point. But this did not mean that its political and economic interests should take precedence over the colonial homeland's when interests diverged. Over time, settlers became increasingly sensitive to policies that appeared to benefit the metropole at their expense. Assertions of imperial authority accepted grudgingly in an earlier period risked a far more hostile reception later on.

By the mid–eighteenth century New World settler colonies were long established; in the Iberian empires they had been in place for more than two centuries. But several generations of residence should be seen as the precondition not of independence but of settler interest in it, and the latter depended on metropolitan policies as well as the passage of time. The impetus shifting opinion toward separation was a metropolitan initiative to assert new forms of control or challenge settlers' economic or security interests. In chapter 15 I show how such initiatives, in the context of the Seven Years' and Napoleonic wars, raised settler discontent and pushed it in a separatist direction.

In Old World colonies of occupation,[10] resentment at being subjugated was hardly a scarce commodity. And desire for freedom from European rule was intense at the outset. In this sense the third condition was readily met.

The will to control public sector institutions depended on a degree of identification with an externally defined territory and diverse population that initially made no sense. In chapter 13 I showed that before the twentieth century most indigenous leaders working for freedom did not think of the colony as the unit that should be free. Early struggles for self-determination were typically waged for and by a subset of the population. Whether the response to subjugation was exit (as with maroon communities) or rebellion (as with Tupac Amaru II or the north Indian mutineers of 1857–58), the operation was designed to *bypass* colonial-level structures, not confront them.

The failure of rebellions and the steadily growing impact of sectoral institutions on the lives of ordinary people led many non-Europeans to view the colony as the unit over which struggles for power and autonomy should be waged. This meant that it was crucial to interact with the public sector as Europeans defined it. Relevant institutions might be the civilian bureaucracy, police, or courts. They might be the fledgling legislatures established in British colonies or tightly disciplined underground movements aiming forcibly to overthrow the government. Forms of engagement ranged from infiltration of the civil service to speeches by party leaders in legislative budget sessions to setting bombs in public buildings to organizing underground nationalist networks. What these forms shared was the goal of eventually controlling the public sector. When opinion leaders began to think in these terms—and a growing number did by phase 4—the second condition for independence was met.

The passage of time, which helped settlers meet the third condition, helped non-Europeans meet the second. Settlers took the colony for granted as an appropriate political unit but needed time to decide that it should be free (under their leadership, of course). Many non-Europeans took it for granted that they should be free but needed time to decide that freedom should come about by capturing the colonial government. Paradoxically, the more actively European-run sectors impacted society, enabling subjects to see that the "colonial nation" was a meaningful category, the less time was needed for this change to occur.

EFFECTS OF WESTERN EDUCATION

In occupation colonies the most difficult condition to satisfy was the first. Capacity to administer public sector institutions depended on holding responsible positions within them, thereby accumulating experience in shaping and implementing policies. But rulers excluded non-Europeans from the upper rungs of bureaucratic, military, and judicial hierarchies, the usual rationale being that colonized people lacked the civilizational prerequisites. How could someone not fluent in the official language, unable to read and write and do sums, and unfamiliar with the metropole's culture and values be expected to handle major administrative responsibilities? The obvious retort was that young people who attended Western schools learned precisely these skills. Western education—hereafter described simply as education—was an unrivaled device for spreading what colonizers valued. Well-educated non-Europeans felt their training entitled them to high-level posts. If they were excluded the reason could not be their alleged civilizational deficit but rather their membership in the wrong nationality and race. Such a reason was not only patently immoral. It also violated the norm of individual achievement measured by universalistic standards, a norm Europeans repeatedly claimed set their civilization above others. Here was another example of self-serving hypocrisy.

Primary and secondary school enrollments grew dramatically throughout the colonial world in late phase 3 and phase 4. They did so in response to demand from below, the link between formal educational qualifications and access to responsible jobs in all three sectors being obvious. Changes on the supply side also contributed. Mission agencies, noting the popularity of schooling, expanded enrollments in order to convert more young people. Governments became active in their own right, establishing secondary schools and technical training institutes in agriculture, civil engineering, and public health. Over time education became the responsibility of two sectors, not one.

The enrollment explosion dramatically increased the capacity of colonized peoples to capture the public sector. Particularly empowered were those attending secondary schools and postsecondary institutions. The vast majority of independence leaders in phase 5 received secondary school diplomas. Many had university and postgraduate degrees, having attained them when such accomplishments were virtually unheard-of among their peers. A survey of 107 chief executives of sub-Saharan and Southeast Asian countries between 1958 and 1973 listed the following distribution for highest level of education: postgraduate, 22 percent; university, 24 percent; secondary school, 49 percent; primary school, 4 percent; no formal schooling, 1 percent.[11] Thirty-four chief executives attended universities in the metropole. These included H. Kamuzu Banda (Malawi), Amilcar Cabral (Guinea-Bissau), Mohammed Hatta (Indonesia), Jomo Kenyatta (Kenya), Seretse Khama

(Botswana), Milton Margai (Sierra Leone), Agostino Neto (Angola), Julius Nyerere (Tanzania), Tunku Abdul Rahman (Malaya), Leopold Senghor (Senegal), and Lee Kuan Yew (Singapore). Others studied in another foreign country, among them Nnamdi Azikiwe (Nigeria) and Kwame Nkrumah (Ghana) in the United States. First-generation executives outside sub-Saharan Africa and Southeast Asia who were educated in metropolitan universities include Grantley Adams (Barbados), S. W. R. D. Bandaranaike (Ceylon/Sri Lanka), Habib Bourguiba (Tunisia), M. A. Jinnah (Pakistan), Norman Manley (Jamaica), Jawaharlal Nehru (India), and Eric Williams (Trinidad and Tobago).[12]

The principal figure undermining French rule in Vietnam, Ho Chi Minh, lived in Paris from 1917 through 1923. Known then as Nguyen Ai Quoc, he never formally enrolled as a student. But he educated himself, becoming a voracious consumer of classics in Western literature and political thought. A fellow Vietnamese who knew him at the time described him as "a wraithlike figure always armed with a book—who read Zola, France, Shakespeare, Dickens, Hugo and Romain Rolland."[13] When Emperor Khai Dinh visited France in 1922 the young radical wrote him a hostile letter. "Has your august attention ever once been drawn," he asked, "to the existence and achievements of Pasteur, Voltaire, Victor Hugo, and Anatole France?"[14] During his Paris years Ho Chi Minh became acquainted with the syndicalist ideas of Sorel and the revolutionary writings of Marx and Lenin. He had no compunction about marshaling Western ideas against Western dominance.

Postprimary education increased the capacity of non-Europeans to capture state power by giving them the formal qualifications to hold responsible positions in dominant institutions. It trained and certified lawyers, engineers, journalists, doctors, and other professionals who could take up employment outside of government and hence be better positioned than civil servants to speak out against the regime, become active in political parties, and run for office.

Schooling imparted fluency in the ruler's language, enabling people to communicate with officials in informal as well as formal settings. Command of the colonizer's language was virtually a precondition for legislative office, as parliamentary business was normally carried on only in that tongue.

Schooling increased the capacity of individuals to organize colonywide political movements. A territory's leading secondary school recruited young people from many parts of the colony and from diverse ethnic, religious, and class backgrounds. Examples from Africa were Achimota College (Gold Coast), Alliance High School (Kenya), Gordon Memorial College (Sudan), King's College, Lagos (Nigeria), and École Normale William-Ponty (Senegal). Shared memories of hazing, eccentric teachers, athletic endeavors, school pranks, and the like created lifelong emotional bonds cutting across colonial society's cleavage lines. Social networks formed in school—and reinforced at class reunions nostalgically recalling the good old days—could be activated when the time came to found nationalist movements and parties. Those who shared the old school tie also shared a European language, which permitted easy communication among people from diverse linguistic backgrounds. People with mutually unintelligible mother tongues had to converse in the foreign ruler's language before they could develop a sense of national identity.

École William-Ponty recruited throughout French West Africa. Personal ties among its graduates help explain why the Rassemblement Démocratique Africain (RDA) functioned for years after its founding in 1946 as the dominant party in several territories. School ties made for more amicable communication among political rivals, as Ruth Schachter Morgenthau notes: "That at Ponty an RDA leader saved the life of an IOM man; that as students RDA Ivory Coast leaders learned to have confidence in the integrity of a Progressiste leader, facilitated the quick transfer of partisan loyalties which occurred periodically among French West African party leaders after the war."[15]

A similar integrative process, at a transnational as well as national level, occurred when students from several colonies came to the metropole to study. The West African Students' Union in London, for example, ran a hostel for young people from several English-speaking colonies. Ladipo Solanke, the union's most outstanding figure from 1925 to 1945, encouraged hostel residents to think along pan-African lines.[16] Young intellectuals from France's colonies met in Paris. There they evolved the negritude movement in the 1930s and founded the influential journal *Présence Africaine*. After World War II students from Portugal's three African colonies met in Lisbon, where they discussed shared problems and began to devise common strategies for the armed struggles to come. Networks initiated in the metropole permitted rapid spread of information and morale-boosting support from one colony to another. When nationalists from several territories acted in concert they increased leverage on the metropole. When a territory became independent the prior existence of interterritorial networks gave added impetus to the international demonstration effect.

Students' overseas experiences could directly increase their capacity for effective action later on. Nkrumah writes that during his years at Lincoln University in Pennsylvania

> I made time to acquaint myself with as many political organizations in the United States as I could. These included the Republicans, the Democrats, the Communists and the Trotskyites. It was in connection with the last movement when I met one of its leading members, Mr. C. L. R. James, and through him I learned how an underground movement worked. . . . My aim was to learn the

technique of organization. I knew that when I eventually returned to the Gold Coast I was going to be faced with this problem. I knew that whatever the programme for the solution of the colonial question might be, success would depend first of all on the organization adopted. I concentrated on finding a formula by which the whole whole colonial question and the problem of imperialism could be solved. I read Hegel, Karl Marx, Engels, Lenin and Mazzini. The writings of these men did much to influence me in my revolutionary ideas and activities.[17]

In many ways education increased the will of colonized peoples to assert autonomy. Young people in schools staffed by European instructors and administrators had rare opportunities to see colonizers up close. Upon inspection, Europeans failed to live up to their carefully projected self-image of mental and moral superiority, becoming instead mere human beings with the full range of failings and foibles humans exhibit. The less intimidated school graduates were by their rulers, the more willing they were to consider challenging the status quo.

Advanced study abroad entailed extensive interaction with Europeans or, in the United States, with people of European descent. The results were decidedly mixed. Many white people treated colonial students decently and respectfully, while others practiced discrimination and sought to humiliate them. It was not possible to forget the bitter experiences even if one wanted to. A single incident could have a formative impact on a young person's political outlook. Tunku Abdul Rahman, first prime minister of the Federation of Malaya, recalled at independence in 1957 that as a young man he journeyed to England to study at St. Catherine's College, Cambridge. When he tried to find rooms at the college he was repeatedly turned down. One person told him he was not eligible because "this college is built for Englishmen." "I was offended at the time," said Rahman, "but that soon passed. I was a good mixer and popular, so it did not matter. Nevertheless, the incident made me decide for the first time that I must help make my country my own."[18]

Blatant racial discrimination against students from Africa and the Caribbean convinced many to struggle not just for their territory's independence but also for liberation of black people everywhere from colonialism and racism. The pan-African component of nationalism in these two regions markedly accelerated decolonization in both once Ghana, under Nkrumah's leadership, became the first independent sub-Saharan state. Another ardent pan-Africanist, the Trinidadian George Padmore, was among Nkrumah's closest confidantes and political advisers.

Living in the metropole gave students occasion to reflect on its political, economic, and cultural relations with their homelands. The metropole was politically free and economically affluent. Why should not the colony be the same? Could the colony's poverty have been caused by the drain of its resources to the metropole and the undercompensation of its labor force for their economic contributions? If Europeans were not the superior beings they pretended to be, how could they justify subjugating people elsewhere?

The effort to answer such questions was, for many, profoundly radicalizing. Young people from the Dutch East Indies studying in Holland were the first to use the term "Indonesia" and the first to call publicly (in 1924) for independence.[19] Four Indian Muslims living in England coined the term "Pakistan" and in 1933 issued the first call for a separate Pakistani state.[20] For some, residence in the metropole redefined how colonialism was understood. To live in the imperial center was to be intensely aware that one's homeland was part of a transcontinental empire. To participate in European intellectual life was to be exposed to theories by figures on the ideological left, such as John Hobson, Rosa Luxemburg, and Lenin, linking colonialism to capitalist exploitation. These theories appealed because they combined a searing moral critique of colonialism with a historically grounded explanation for European global dominance, while confidently asserting that the future lay with the oppressed. The fusion of particularist nationalism with broader anti-imperial and anticapitalist themes is well illustrated in *Le Procès de la Colonisation Française*, a book Ho Chi Minh wrote while living in Paris. Writes Jean Lacouture,

> The title on the cover was written in three languages—Arabic, Chinese and French. Vietnam was given the most space because the author had more experience with the abuses of colonialism there, but he tried scrupulously to cite other examples of colonial abuses from Dahomey, Madagascar and the West Indies.
>
> The book was not a nationalist protest which cited the case of a single oppressed country, but an indictment of an international system which the author felt should be opposed on an equally international scale. He ends the penultimate chapter with a manifesto for the Intercolonial Union, concluding with Karl Marx's famous "Workers of the world, unite."[21]

Many young people returned home from years abroad with more deeply engrained anticolonial convictions than when they set out for Europe. That return was often a deeply unsettling experience, for it highlighted the Western-educated elite's double alienation: politically from the metropole and culturally from its own society. Individuals who had studied in Oxford, Paris, Louvain, or the Hague were themselves more fluent in a European language than in their mother tongue,[22] more accustomed to the lifestyle of affluent Europe than to the austere ways of impoverished homelands. Earnest idealists who felt called to lead their people to freedom found the sense of cultural and psychological distance from the people very painful. In Nehru's words,

I have become a queer mixture of the East and West, out of place everywhere, at home nowhere. Perhaps my thoughts and approach to life are more akin to what is called Western than Eastern, but India clings to me as she does to all her children, in innumerable ways; and behind me lie, somewhere in the subconscious, racial memories of a hundred ... generations of Brahmins. I cannot get rid of either that past inheritance or my recent acquisitions. They are both part of me, and, though they help me in both the East and the West, they also create in me a feeling of spiritual loneliness not only in public activities but in life itself. I am a stranger and alien in the West. I cannot be of it. But in my own country, sometimes, I have an exile's feeling."[23]

It did not help when officials scornfully charged that "overeducated natives" could not possibly represent the masses because they had become so westernized.

The emotional intensity with which many highly educated persons strove for independence may have been driven by a need to compensate for the alienation schooling produced. Intellectuals may have wanted to demonstrate to themselves as well as to sneering critics that the long years of distancing from their cultural roots had not obscured their vision so much as afforded them a platform from which to articulate the emerging nation's deepest yearnings.

Schoolchildren whose lessons dispensed steady doses of Eurocentrism were more directly exposed than the unschooled to ideas instilling an inferiority complex. Yet the most effective antidote to this complex was more education. Precisely because schooling propagated European culture, each additional year brought students closer to cultural equality with their mentors. Equality came at a high price: acceptance of the colonizer's standards and a more or less explicit rejection of one's own culture. Nonetheless, when non-Europeans won diplomas that rulers had to acknowledge as valid measures of intellectual achievement, the notion of European racial superiority was weakened. Those who did well academically could go about their lives less burdened by doubts about their intrinsic worth.

Research conducted in the Gold Coast in the early 1950s by Gustav Jahoda confirms the connection between educational level and psychological outlook. Illiterates in Jahoda's sample, having essentially nothing in common culturally with their rulers, felt dependent on Europeans but not inferior to them. Those with primary education were most likely to exhibit an inferiority complex. Those who had attended secondary or postsecondary institutions had a greater sense of autonomy and felt confident that they could replace Europeans in positions of responsibility as the colony evolved toward self-government.[24]

Additional schooling increased one's ability to analyze the situation with an independent, critical mind. When Albert Tevoedjre cited the poem he learned as a schoolchild, his goal was to attack colonial education for deliberately undermining the self-confidence of young Dahomeans. One of the most accomplished products of the education system had the intellectual tools and psychological outlook to argue persuasively that the system was bankrupt.

Mission schools contributed to independence movements by teaching people about the Bible. Granted, the Book of books contains narratives and sayings that can be put to almost any purpose. As noted earlier, apologists for colonial rule often cited the Pauline injunction to obey constituted authority. But ultimately the Bible contains messages of liberation and hope for all human beings. All are created in God's own image, affirms Genesis. All are freed from the bonds of sin by the life and death of God's son, Jesus, preaches Paul. The Bible says too much about the divine yearning for human self-fulfillment to be a comfort to repressive rulers, be they Nebuchadnezzar or Herod or those of a later era.

For many colonized peoples the Bible offered an extended, theologically grounded argument for individual and collective liberation from foreign rule. When a catechist learned that the people of Israel were subjected to forced labor under pharaoh, removed from their promised land to Babylon, and incorporated into a European empire centered in distant Rome, it was easy to draw parallels with the modern colonial situation. And God clearly sided with the disempowered nation of Israel. When in 1921 the Congolese prophet Simon Kimbangu acted out the story of David and Goliath in front of a Belgian district officer, both men knew the drama's political implications. The understandably worried administrator had Kimbangu arrested for subversive activities soon afterward. Even so, the imprisoned prophet and his followers remained confident that the God of David was on their side. Throughout southern Africa from the early twentieth century onward and in Kenya in phase 4, independent religious movements affirmed the Bible but rejected European dominance of church structures. Indigenous versions of liberation theology promulgated by these movements shaped subsequent nationalist discourse.[25]

The Zimbabwean nationalist Ndabaningi Sithole cogently summarizes the destabilizing effects of mission education on colonial rule:

> The Christian Church has introduced a new spirit of learning without which no nation can have a truly balanced progress. It is this creative spirit which helped to sustain African nationalism and without which the whole idea would end in dismal failure. . . .
>
> The Bible redeemed the African individual from the power of superstition, individuality-crushing tradition, witchcraft, and other reactionary forces. The same Bible helped the African individual to reassert himself above colonial powers! If the Bible teaches that the individual is unique, of infinite worth before God, colonialism in many respects said just the opposite, and it became only a matter of time before one ousted the other. The Bible-liberated African reasserted himself not only over tribal but also over colonial authority.[26]

Sithole quotes a South African: "When Europeans took our country we fought against them with our spears, but they defeated us because they had better weapons and so colonial power was set up against our wishes. But lo the missionary came in time and laid explosives under colonialism. The Bible is now doing what we could not do with our spears."[27] Not just Africans but the colonized in all lands were set on the path to freedom by the Bible.

That Christianity was an integral component of the triple assault demonstrates the self-defeating nature of European colonialism. When products of mission schools cited biblical chapter and verse to argue that colonialism ran counter to God's plan, rulers were placed on the defensive. Would-be civilizers found it uncomfortable enough to be called uncivilized. The critique was even more biting when the moral standards used to reach this harsh judgment were their own. The religion that inspired Europeans to go out to all the world eventually inspired people in other lands to indict the messengers for behavior contradicting the message.

In summary, continuity of overseas empires was threatened when colonial residents began to overcome the most serious obstacles to organizing for independence. For settlers in phases 1 and 2 the prime obstacle was unwillingness to break with the metropole. The passage of time made that break less unthinkable. For non-Europeans in phases 4 and 5 the prime obstacle was low capacity to capture public sector institutions. Diffusion of Western education greatly enhanced this capacity. Knowledge of European history and the Bible is incompatible with a permanently submissive stance.

Nationalist leaders in phases 2 and 5 did not feel ready for independence until they had become intensely ambivalent about the metropole. Settler elites moved toward autonomy when they experienced psychological *distance* from lands to which they had long felt close emotional affinity. Non-European elites were ready for independence when their educational experiences brought them *close*—psychologically, culturally, in many cases physically—to a metropole that had hitherto been distant in these respects. It was precisely the positive identification with many aspects of the colonizer's lifestyle and values that made racial discrimination all the more painful and unjustifiable when it occurred. Positive identification with the ideals of European civilization sensitized non-European elites to contradictions between these ideals and colonial domination. The only way to uphold ideals colonizers claimed to value was to reject colonizers' claims to rule.

THE PRECEDENT-SETTERS: BRITISH NORTH AMERICA AND INDIA

Back of the obvious differences between the two decolonization phases are similarities that drove parallel processes of change. But this conclusion remains vague. How much time did settler communities need to change their attitudes, other than a few decades? How much education did non-European populations need to take on the government, other than some postprimary education for a few people? There is too much variation in the historical record to permit one to advance beyond these imprecise statements. Duration of rule and extent of education, however, are not triggers of independence movements but conditions highly conducive to their formation. So it is unreasonable to expect a close correlation between duration or education and the timing of independence. The triggers were events, discussed in the next chapter, which impacted colonies at very different points in their political evolution.

Approaching decolonization phases from an alternative angle enables one to be more specific. If the question is not why these phases occurred but how and why they began, one can focus attention on territories whose independence helped set off a series of political transitions. The thirteen BNA colonies and India were precedent-setters in their respective phases.[28] A search for similarities between them might seem pointless because there are so many obvious and important ways in which they differ. But rough parallels do exist, which help explain the parallel roles of political activists separated by half a globe and more than a century.

BNA settlers in late phase 1 were in a stronger position to capture the colonial public sector than settlers elsewhere in the New World at that time. They elected representatives to legislatures functioning at a colonywide level, in contrast to Spanish American creoles, whose power base was limited to local government assemblies. BNA legislatures had the authority to tax and the power to approve the salaries of Crown-appointed governors. Settlers controlled community policing and frontier security operations. Leaders in several colonies took the initiative in 1765 to convene the Stamp Act Congress to devise a common stance against Parliament's tax measures. As tensions with the metropole escalated Committees of Correspondence were formed to exchange information and coordinate activities across colonial lines. In these ways settlers created the institutional basis for a new public sector representing many colonies rather than just one. This new sector they controlled from the start, since there were no comparable coordinating structures among officials representing the Crown in the thirteen colonies. Only a few administrators were directly accountable to colonial governors. Of these a high proportion came from the settler community and favored its interests.

Indian political leaders in phase 4 were in a stronger position to capture the colonial public sector than non-Europeans elsewhere in the colonial world at that time. An electorate of many millions sent representatives to legislatures operating at provincial and all-India levels. By 1937 elected politicians took full control of provincial assemblies. This contrasted sharply with the situation in non-British colonies, which lacked equivalent representative bodies, and in other British colonies in which appointed European administrators still dominated fledgling legislative councils. In

the early 1920s Gandhi, Nehru, and others transformed the INC into a mass movement, organizing throughout the subcontinent and challenging the raj on many
fronts. No social movement or political party in phase 4 came close to the INC in size,
tactical creativity, and clearly articulated nationalist goals. The INC was controlled
from top to bottom by Indians, as were other populist movements like the Muslim
League and Hindu Mahasabha. In contrast to BNA there was a powerful bureaucracy,
the Indian Civil Service, accountable to top British officials. But here too, as noted
in chapter 6, the indigenous presence was felt, rising in the interwar years from about
a fifth to a half. The extent to which the bureaucracy was infiltrated from below
was unique in colonies of occupation, reflecting the large number of Indians qualified for top posts through their education in Indian and British universities. Thus by
phase 4 some Indians had substantial experience in party organizing, electoral campaigning, legislative debates and policy making, and national-level administration.
Like BNA leaders a century and a half earlier, they were ready to govern should the
opportunity arise.

BNA settlers played a more conspicuous role in the private profit and religious
sectors than settlers in other New World territories. They dominated small-scale and
plantation agriculture, fishing, forestry, handicrafts, and commerce among the thirteen colonies. Entrepreneurs were active in international shipping and small-scale
industrial production, fields normally reserved for a metropole's private profit sector. In fact, by the mid–eighteenth century the settler-owned economy was as diversified, industrialized, and wealthy as any in the world, including England. Settlers
were competent in so many facets of the economy that Benjamin Franklin said, "I do
not know a single imported article into the northern colonies, but what they can
either do without or make themselves."[29] In the Spanish colonies settlers predominated in agriculture, but there was less small-scale industry. Bureaucrats controlled
the sale of many commodities and tried to enforce regulations restricting creole
commercial autonomy.

The great majority of BNA settlers was Protestant, with many from dissenting
sects constituting self-governing congregations. Religious autonomy was far higher
than in officially Catholic Spanish America, where a hierarchy headquartered in
Rome and sensitive to the Spanish Crown's interests controlled sectoral life. The BNA
religious sector was a model for political independence rather than a barrier to it.

Segments of the public and private profit sectors that BNA settlers controlled
overlapped in the sense that those who organized politically and engaged in debates
over public issues earned income from self-employment or ownership of large plantations. Political leaders could tap their own resources to cover expenses as they
devoted time to the unpaid career of challenging colonial authority. Those who
needed help could obtain it from affluent businessmen. Once fighting broke out in

1775, settlers' resources were deployed in various ways to cover the costs of recruiting and training soldiers. The emergence of new public sector institutions—Continental Congress, Continental Army—was greatly aided by settlers' dominance of the private profit sector.

Indians in phase 4 played a more prominent role in the private profit sector— and in the Christian segment of the religious sector—than did non-Europeans in any other Old World colony. Substantial wealth was held by a landowning and money-lending elite. In chapter 6 I noted that Indian entrepreneurs owned and managed iron and steel plants, cotton yarn and cloth factories, and shipping companies. Such large-scale industrial activities were either nonexistent in other colonies or owned by Europeans. Also noteworthy was the role Indian clergy played in Christian churches.

The private wealth some Indians possessed gave nationalism a headstart by generating university-trained people decades earlier than in other occupation colonies. The three outstanding figures at independence and partition—Gandhi, Nehru, Jinnah—received university training in England prior to World War I, at their families' expense. Nehru went the others one better by attending Harrow, the exclusive secondary school. A highly educated cadre was ready by the 1920s to join nationalist ranks and enter the Indian Civil Service.

The high profile of Indians in the private profit sector meant that resources were available to political activists when the INC took a populist turn in phase 4. Landed elites were a vital support base in the rural areas. Big industrialists were divided in their views of the INC and its civil disobedience tactics. But some were supportive, and millowners in Ahmedabad helped finance civil disobedience campaigns.[30] Gandhi maintained close ties with Indian business leaders even when they did not agree with him. The INC's emergence as a new kind of public sector institution was facilitated by Indian prominence in the private profit sector. There is no parallel in other colonies.

The unusually influential position BNA settlers and Indian entrepreneurs held in their colonies' private profit sectors is shown by the successful campaigns their politicians launched to boycott imported consumer goods. The BNA and Indian economies were sufficiently diversified and self-reliant to sustain these campaigns. And at least some local entrepreneurs stood to benefit from a boycott of East India Company tea, in the first instance, and Lancashire cloth, in the second. Cross-sector coalitions empowered the two precedent-setting nationalist movements, just as cross-sector coalitions strengthened Europe's drive for expansion.

This chapter provides background evidence making imperial decline understandable. But it does not account for the specific timing or compressed nature of developments in phases 2 and 5. To address those issues an analysis of broad trends should be complemented by a search for politically transformative events.

15
The International Dimension: War as the Catalyst for Independence

What turned precariously poised relationships into unsustainable ones were crises impacting several empires at the same time, crises whose course and outcome no one metropole could control. Since the mid–eighteenth century four wars were fought to determine which states would dominate world affairs: the Seven Years' War (1756–63), the Napoleonic Wars (intermittently between 1799 and 1815), and World Wars I (1914–18) and II (1939–45). Each of these struggles became a catalyst for imperial decline, suddenly and dramatically reinforcing from outside the boundaries of empire trends that had quietly evolved within those boundaries. Wars altered power relations in one or more of the following ways: (1) they lowered metropolitan capacity to retain overseas possessions, (2) they diminished metropolitan will to retain them, (3) they increased colonial capacity for autonomy, and (4) they intensified colonial will for autonomy. The most important was the fourth.

Each struggle for global hegemony had distinctive, unique features. Are there any broadly similar patterns in the conduct and aftermath of these four wars? If so, the parallels may account for shared postwar outcomes of imperial decline.

Phases 2 and 5 were each preceded by a war that stimulated formation of a colonial protest movement, though protest was not initially manifested as a drive for independence. These preparatory wars set the stage for follow-up struggles which engaged many movements aiming explicitly at sovereignty. The Seven Years' War had a catalytic—albeit indirect and delayed—effect on the independence movement in BNA. Its impact was similar in many ways to World War I's effect on the INC in India. The Napoleonic Wars and World War II can be seen as follow-up conflicts. Each built on changes introduced by the war preceding it. Each had a more direct, immediate, and wide-ranging impact on decolonization than its predecessor. The implication is that it took not one hegemonic war but two to undermine overseas empires. The cumulative repercussions of the Seven Years' and Napoleonic wars ended European dominance in most New World mainland settler colonies. The cumulative effect of

World Wars I and II ended European dominance in the vast regions ruled at the start of phase 4.

In another recurring pattern, major contestants in hegemonic wars selectively supported movements for independence from other metropoles. In some cases support was tendered during wartime, as when British diplomats early in World War I offered to assist Arabs in throwing off Ottoman rule. Declarations of American support for the principle of national self-determination—somewhat qualified in President Wilson's Fourteen Points, unequivocal in the Atlantic Charter—were widely welcomed by nationalists. In other cases assistance was extended after a war was over. Examples are French military intervention on behalf of American revolutionaries— in effect repaying England for France's defeat in 1763—the thousands of British volunteers in Spanish American liberation struggles, and British Foreign Secretary George Canning's threat of naval intervention to prevent Spain from trying to reconquer its former colonies. In these situations interstate competition helped dissolve empires, whereas in other situations examined in chapter 9 it was a force driving imperial construction.

Victory in war often precipitated imperial decline. This outcome is less paradoxical than might appear. Metropoles proud of having triumphed on the world scene felt entitled to assert authority in their own domains. They also wanted to extract resources to pay for the war, whose costs were reflected in heavy postwar debt burdens. In asserting control over affairs they in effect turned the clock back to prewar days. Their reactionary policies in turn generated immediate, intense opposition from colonial elites. The primary triggers of independence movements were not wartime crises at moments when metropoles were unusually weak, but postwar crises at moments when metropoles wanted to be seen as unusually strong. Pressures for independence intensified when metropolitans balked at reform and insisted on remaining dominant. Increased metropolitan will should thus be added to the ways in which war weakened empire.

This is not to deny that defeat contributed to imperial decline. An empire losing a major war cannot avoid confronting internal shocks and external pressures sufficient to break it up. This occurred after World War I with two land-based empires, Austro-Hungarian and Ottoman. When European states lost to one another their possessions frequently changed hands, as in the wars of phases 1 and 2 and in modified form in phase 4 when Germany's possessions passed to the victors via League of Nations mandates. Temporary loss of Southeast Asian colonies to Japan clearly accelerated the demise of European rule there. Still, what is striking is that victory in struggles for global hegemony not only failed to guarantee dominance within the victor's overseas domains but actually undermined it.

Another recurring problem is that independence movements in phases 2 and 5 went through similar sequences of change. The most immediate effect of war was on the capacity of metropoles to control colonies and of colonies to assert autonomy. In many instances wars lowered the former and raised the latter. In contrast, postwar crises were primarily conflicts of will. As these crises unfolded, each side displayed increased resolve to resist the claims of the other. Willingness to compromise dissolved at a time when the capacity gap between imperial center and periphery was smaller than ever before.

The following sequence can be observed in diverse times and places: During wartime a metropole experienced loss of control over a colony. Needing to defeat its enemy, it called on the colony for assistance. Colonial elites were prepared to help if they could be assured that the colony would be at least as well off politically after the war as before, and hopefully in a better position to chart its future. Colonial elites did their part, thinking that such a bargain had been struck. But once the war was won the metropole no longer needed help to survive. It tried to compensate for earlier losses of control by reasserting authority, in effect abandoning its part of the bargain. Colonial elites did not expect this. They felt they and their people had been unfairly used during the war and let down, if not betrayed, afterward. Angered that the political situation was regressing rather than progressing, elites created new institutions or activated existing ones, using them to mobilize mass protest. At some point these institutions shifted from protest to the goal of capturing the public sector.

In broad terms, this sequence proceeded from reduced metropolitan capacity to increased metropolitan will to increased colonial will to increased colonial capacity. The components of power changed for both sides. But they did so in a pattern that gave a colony greater leverage in the postwar setting than before the war because both components of its power were on the rise. Metropolitan will rose to compensate for loss of capacity. Colonial capacity to organize for independence rose in response to rising will, the two components synergistically reinforcing each other.

CHANGES IN CAPACITY

Hegemonic wars were titanic conflicts weakening all European parties, including the eventual victors. Workers and material resources were diverted from productive to destructive uses. Lives and property were destroyed, sometimes in massive campaigns that decided nothing. Some areas were especially hard hit: Spain in the struggle for liberation from Napoleon's armies, northern France and what in 1830 became Belgium in three of the four wars. Britain came off best overall, being on the winning side in all four conflicts. Yet victory came at enormous cost. Its national debt rose by an unprecedented 78 percent during the Seven Years' War,[1] and it had to call in massive foreign investments to finance World War I. Its maritime dominance was effectively challenged in World Wars I and II. Loss of the Singapore naval base in 1942 was described by Prime Minister Churchill as "the greatest disaster and worst capitulation in the history of the British Empire."[2] Major urban centers were decimated by Nazi missile and air attacks.

The capacity of metropoles to govern colonies was severely impaired in wartime. In several cases metropoles were invaded and became temporarily unable to govern themselves, much less others: Portugal, Spain, and Holland in the wars of phase 2, Belgium in World War I, and France, Belgium, and Holland in World War II. England's blockade of continental ports during the revolutionary and Napoleonic Wars prevented France and, at times, Holland and Spain from linking up with their overseas possessions. Naval warfare frayed and sometimes severed shipping ties connecting far-flung empires. The usual trade flows were disrupted, and administrators did not circulate between metropoles and colonies as they did in peacetime. Japan's invasion of Southeast Asia removed metropolitan officials from top decision-making posts.

In contrast, many colonies were economically stimulated and politically empowered by war. Transport and communications lines were improved to facilitate movement of war-related matériel and troops. Areas not invaded or directly involved in fighting had opportunities to develop, particularly if their exports helped the war effort and were in great demand. Some colonies adopted economic policies consistent with their own interests. With commercial ties to Spain cut off during the Napoleonic Wars, Spanish American colonies could violate mercantilist policies with impunity, and trade with Britain and the United States flourished. Industrialization in India accelerated in World War I, increasing economic self-reliance while assisting the war effort. Young men who had never held a rifle were recruited to fight. Their training and experiences prepared them for postwar nationalist activities, whether as soldiers or political activists. Of vital importance in the Indonesian struggle against Holland after World War II were young soldiers trained by the Japanese.

The power vacuum created by loss of metropolitan control was filled in some cases by colonial residents. After King Ferdinand VII was dethroned by Napoleon, creole-led *cabildos* in Buenos Aires, Mexico City, and Lima exercised executive functions previously reserved for royal appointees. Japan's invasion of the Dutch East Indies gave nationalists interned by the Dutch opportunities to move about and spread their message. The invasion also increased the capacity of local people to manage the public sector. Robert McMahon writes,

> Expediency led the new Japanese administration to effect a tremendous rise in
> socioeconomic status for the educated class of Indonesians. Within six months

of the invasion, the Japanese interned practically the entire Dutch population of the Indies, opening up thousands of mid- and upper-level administrative and technical jobs. Since the Japanese had only a limited number of military personnel, Indonesians, out of necessity, filled many of the vacated jobs. This new mobility became a significant factor after the war: now there was a large class in the East Indies whose rapid elevation in status would be threatened by a return to Dutch rule and repressive prewar conditions.[3]

WARTIME EXPECTATIONS

In the Seven Years' War England relied on BNA assistance to drive France from North America. Because BNA settlers stood to gain if France was expelled they made substantial military and financial contributions to the war effort when asked to do so. London officials did not promise future benefits in return, feeling that a successful North American campaign would benefit the colonies at least as much as the metropole. Still, settlers had good reason to expect that they would be thanked when victory was won. They would then return to the all-but-complete autonomy they had enjoyed before the French and Indian troubles broke out.

In Saint Domingue expectations were high that slavery would be permanently outlawed following its formal abolition by the Jacobins in the 1790s. Toussaint believed in France and was unwilling to break with it even when Napoleon, who was more conservative than the Jacobins, came to power.

Spanish America faced a legitimacy crisis after King Ferdinand VII's forced abdication. While many creole leaders used the occasion to organize for independence, others remained loyal to Ferdinand. They looked forward to his return to the throne, expecting that he would listen to their pleas. The hope was that in reward for their loyalty the king would affirm the autonomy that creoles exercised during his years of confinement. Colonial political advance would thus be legitimized.

Twentieth-century wars involved explicit offers of a better postwar future by metropoles desperate for assistance from strategically essential possessions. The most important promissory note was the Montague Declaration of 1917 favoring an accelerated pace toward Indian self-government. World War I also saw assurances to Vietnamese, Algerians, and Dutch East Indians of an improved postwar political situation. A variation on this theme was British backing of Arab self-determination if Arabs took up arms against Ottoman overlords. In all these situations the bargain entailed non-European help now in exchange for metropolitan concessions later.

Transcending specific World War I commitments were the broad principles embodied in the Fourteen Points. Percival Spear notes that Wilson's speech in 1917

> contained the declaration on self-determination and this, Indian opinion noted, had been accepted by the British willy-nilly. The Americans talked about rights,

it was further observed, while the British talked about concessions and safe-guards. The whole Indian mental outlook became more radical and a sense of expectancy, of a new dawn breaking, filled the air. What before 1914 would have been regarded as a gracious concession was now looked upon as little short of an insult. The [Gopal] Gokhale gasp of "so much" gave place to the [Bal] Tilak snort of "so little!"[4]

In World War II the Atlantic Charter was seen by many colonial subjects as a promissory note applicable everywhere. "Join the struggle against the Axis powers," the charter proclaimed in effect, "and you can decide your own future after we have jointly achieved victory."

World War II was a great leveler. Soldiers of all races died under horrendous circumstances; bodies of all colors lay exposed to the elements. Belkacem Krim, who became a leader in the Algerian revolution, fought with the Free French. "My brother returned from Europe with medals and frost-bitten feet!" he once noted. "There everyone was equal. Why not here?"[5]

The dramatic, zigzag course of World War II's campaigns in North Africa and the Pacific gave rise to a view that the near future would bring further surprises. Sylvia Leith-Ross noted that before the war educated Nigerians "wanted independence, they looked forward to it in some foreseeable but still indeterminate future. Then all of a sudden, from one day to another, it almost seemed from one hour to another, they wanted it at once, the next day, that very evening."[6]

POSTWAR CRISES: THE COLONIAL MOBILIZATION OF ANGER

Postwar realities were quite another matter, as metropoles took a harder line than expected once the emergency was over. Within two years of England's victory in the Seven Years' War a series of unprecedented restrictions on BNA colonies was announced. King George III proclaimed areas west of the Appalachians off-limits to settlers. Parliament imposed new taxes on internationally traded goods (Sugar Act) and domestically produced items (Stamp Act). English troops were to be quartered in the colonies at settlers' expense, even though France had just been eliminated as a threat to colonial security. The implication was that settlers were themselves security risks.

In 1801–02 Napoleon marked a truce in the fighting in Europe by dispatching a large force to invade Saint Domingue and reimpose slavery. Ferdinand VII, restored to the throne in 1814, promptly sent an army to crush rebellions in his American possessions. Spanish soldiers became known for the atrocities they committed against suspected as well as real enemies in the creole population.

India a year after World War I ended was politically in an altogether different space than in 1918, to say nothing of prewar years. Constitutional reforms proposed by British officials were more modest and slow-paced than many Indians expected. The Rowlatt Acts, retaining martial law after the wartime need for it ended, were harshly enforced. Above all the Amritsar Massacre shocked the Indian public by the extent of its brutality and the arrogance toward Indians displayed by General Dyer and his vocal supporters.

In Algeria, Vietnam, and the Dutch East Indies, wartime assurances that colonial subjects would be more actively involved in policy making were abandoned by the early 1920s. The Versailles Conference of 1919 made it clear that Wilsonian principles of national self-determination applied to residents of the former Austro-Hungarian empire but not to non-Europeans.

The Middle East following World War I witnessed abrupt policy reversals. Britain and France soon revealed that they had their own territorial ambitions, which took precedence over notions of Arab self-determination they had invoked earlier. Added to the forced imposition of mandates on large chunks of former Ottoman territory was British equivocation about the rights of Palestinian Arabs, since Zionists had been promised a national home for Jews in Palestine.

Political developments in France at the end of World War II and shortly afterward raised and then lowered expectations in the overseas possessions.[7] Algerian Muslims who used Victory in Europe Day as the symbolically powerful occasion to march for freedom in their own country were massacred at Sétif. Independence was not an option in Algeria or elsewhere; what politicians termed Greater France and the Fourth Republic's constitution termed the French Union was considered indivisible. At issue, rather, was whether colonial subjects would be accorded French citizenship, whether that status entailed equal rights with French citizens, and what functions were to be exercised by officials in Paris and the overseas territories. The assembly that convened in 1945 to write a constitution for the Fourth Republic issued a draft containing several relatively liberal provisions on these matters. The draft said the French Union was "freely consented to," implying that its constituent parts would at some point be asked to express their views on it.

The draft was rejected, however, by an electorate heavily weighted toward voters in France. The second version, written by another constituent assembly and approved by the same electorate in October 1946, was much more conservative in tone and content than the first. It "made the cornerstone of the French Union not free consent but domination by France."[8] In response to concerted pressure from French settlers and business interests, it reduced the size of the African electorate, allocated fewer colonial seats to the French National Assembly, concentrated decision-making power in Paris, limited prospects for changed political status, and

set up an electoral system giving hugely disproportionate weight to Europeans resident overseas. The French historian Yves Person describes the October version as
"simply verbiage intended to impede political progress."[9]

Colonial reactions to postwar metropolitan initiatives came swiftly and were
overwhelmingly negative. Shock, anger, disillusionment, and a sense of betrayal are
recurring themes in speeches and writings of prominent individuals. In BNA the
principal target was the Stamp Act, though anger was probably intensified by other
policy moves announced at about the same time. This was hardly the thanks settlers
expected for work well done. "Perhaps more than any other single factor," writes Jack
Greene, "the sense of betrayal, the deep bitterness arising out of the profound
disjunction between how, on the basis of their performance during the Seven Years'
War, they thought they deserved to be dealt with by the metropolis and the treatment
actually accorded them, supplied the energy behind their intense reactions to the
Grenville program in 1765–66."[10]

The Stamp Act crisis raised larger constitutional issues and led to new ways of
organizing across colonial boundaries. The Stamp Act Congress, convened in late
1765 by representatives of eleven colonies, was markedly more effective at directing
colonial energies toward shared objectives than the most serious previous attempt at
Albany, New York, in 1754. Committees of Correspondence were formed to communicate information and proposals for action among town, county, and colonial
assemblies. Parliamentary repeal of the Stamp Act in 1766 was due in large measure
to the settlers' capacity to mobilize public opinion and direct it toward policy makers
in London. Richard Merritt concluded from a content analysis of leading BNA newspapers that the Stamp Act crisis had a strong and lasting impact in shifting settlers
toward American identities and loyalties.[11]

The significance of organizational and attitudinal changes in the mid-1760s
should not be overstated. Opposition to specific actions of Parliament did not imply
assertion of a right to autonomy. The Stamp Act Congress affirmed its loyalty to King
George III. Parliament's Regulating Act of 1773 and the Boston Tea Party, which
pushed the settlers from protest to violent confrontation, lay several years ahead.
Colonial leaders hesitated even after fighting broke out; more than a year elapsed
between the battle at Bunker Hill and the Declaration of Independence.

Granting these points, disputes that erupted shortly after the Seven Years' War
ended marked decisive first steps on the road to independence. The British historian
P. D. G. Thomas describes the events of 1763–67 as "the first phase of the American
Revolution."[12] The American scholars Robert Tucker and David Hendrickson assert
that "all the essential elements that led to the fall of the First British Empire—
the conflicts of interest, the rival ambitions, the profoundly disparate estimates of
power—were present in the crisis over the Stamp Act."[13]

Evidence of reaction to the French army's invasion of Haiti is clear-cut. Former slaves, their status as free persons at stake, fought intensely, launching guerrilla attacks from mobile mountain bases on a force initially numbering more than twenty thousand. Attacks continued after Toussaint was seized and deported to Europe. Unable to prevail militarily and decimated by yellow fever, French forces withdrew, leaving Haitian patriots to declare independence.

Spain's American colonies began moving toward independence when Ferdinand VII's removal from power gave creoles political space and a constitutional pretext for action. But the king's unwillingness to consider creole proposals when he returned to the throne in 1814, coupled with his dispatch of ten thousand soldiers to impose royal authority over rebellious New Granada and Venezuela, were last straws. The army commander's tendency to treat all creoles as enemies turned many with royalist sympathies into patriots. Spanish forces initially won the day, forcing Bolívar to take refuge in Jamaica. But their tactics proved self-defeating. Patriotic forces in New Granada and Venezuela fought back with renewed determination. Creole leaders in Argentina, Chile, and elsewhere could see that negotiating with the king for a power-sharing compromise was doomed to fail, hence that independence was their only option. In exile, Bolívar wrote in 1815, "Now we have seen the light; yet they want to plunge us back into darkness. Our chains have been broken and we have been freed; yet now our enemies seek to enslave us anew. For this reason America fights desperately, and seldom has desperation failed to win victory."[14] Eventually it did.

More than a century later, in India, a metropole's regressive postwar policies once again generated widespread popular protest. Many Indians assumed from the Montagu Declaration that Indians would soon be controlling legislative business at the central government level, where ultimate power lay. But the Government of India Act (1919) proposed power sharing in the provinces, not at the center. At this rate of progress, people asked, would not dominion status be decades rather than years away? Even conservatively inclined Indians were shocked that the raj's first order of business in 1919 was to replace wartime internal security arrangements with the Rowlatt Acts. Indian powerlessness was put on display as these bills were passed by the British official majority in the central legislature despite unanimous opposition by the body's Indian members.

The repressive content of this legislation and the process by which it was passed transformed Gandhi's political attitudes. Gandhi had been in many respects a loyal subject of the British Empire. While in South Africa he was awarded medals for supporting the British in the Boer War and the Zulu uprising of 1906. As late as the summer of 1918 he courted unpopularity among Indian radicals by campaigning for unconditional support of the British war effort, including more volunteers for the army. Gandhi had faith that the British would grant Indian home rule if they saw how bravely the recruits fought. But his faith was dashed by the raj's actions after the war. "Compared with the man who had merely been called in to advise on passive resistance in 1917, the Gandhi who got up from a sick bed to fight the Rowlatt bills at the beginning of 1919 was an all-India figure of considerable stature," writes his political biographer Judith Brown.[15] Calling for a week of peaceful nationwide protests in April, he traveled widely to mobilize popular support for the cause. "For a brief time he engineered an agitation whose reverberations were felt throughout the subcontinent, from the North-West Frontier to Madras, from Sind to Bengal."[16] Something deeper than politics was at stake here. Writing to Edwin Montagu in June 1919, Gandhi stated, "The retention of the Rowlatt legislation in the teeth of universal opposition is an *affront* to the nation. Its repeal is necessary to appease national honour."[17]

General Dyer's order to fire on a crowd assembled in Amritsar to protest British policy reflected a resolute will to assert control. But mass killings that in other contexts might have cowed the colonized population had exactly the opposite effect in a politicized postwar atmosphere. Changes in Indian public opinion were channeled into organized action. The ambitious *satyagraha* campaigns Gandhi launched in 1920–22 broadened the territorial and class base of the INC, transforming it into a mass-based national movement. A new constitution adopted in 1920 expanded the party's ability to make day-to-day policy decisions at the top and enroll new members at the district level. The noncooperation campaign was called off in 1922 when it turned violent, and the INC lost much of its momentum until the next anticolonial surge in the late 1920s. Nonetheless, the opening round in the struggle for a democratic, self-governing India had been fought. Indian politics would never again be the same.

Parallels with the Stamp Act crisis come to mind. As in BNA a century and a half earlier, so in British India the reaction of colonial subjects to metropolitan assertions of authority showed a new will and capacity to set the political agenda. It quickly became the colonizer who reacted to colonial initiatives rather than the reverse. People increasingly thought of themselves as part of a larger national community, called American and Indian. Important advances in institutional capacity were made with the convening of the Stamp Act Congress and the organizational reforms and outreach campaigns of the INC. Colonial capacity was enhanced in both instances by networks of mutual support between politicians and elements of the private profit sector. Mobilization against the Stamp Act and the *satyagraha* campaigns of 1920–22 were basically protest movements; in neither was independence called for. In both cases political mobilization peaked and declined, with a lull of several years before picking up again. Nonetheless, movements launched in the immediate aftermath of war marked a decisive break with the past. They revealed popular forces at work that would, after a series of subsequent crises, be crucial to the independence drive.

Egypt is another example of the radicalizing effect of wartime expectations dashed. Afaf Marsot summarizes the situation in 1918–19:

> The various declarations made by the Allies during the war aroused hopes that independence might be in the offing, especially when President Wilson made public his Fourteen Points. Self-determination became the keyword in everybody's mouth, and a group of politicians met to plan the future of Egypt as an imminently independent country, or at least one that would have a modicum of home-rule. That group of men constituted themselves into a delegation, in Arabic a *wafd,* and in November 1918 met with Sir Reginald Wingate, the British High Commissioner, to request that they be allowed to proceed to the Paris Peace Conference and present Egypt's case. The British government in London refused the request of the *wafd* in no uncertain terms and agitation broke out in the country, encouraged by the nationalists and the government of the day and the sultan. . . . Throughout 1919 Egypt was rife with agitation. [*Wafd* leader Saad] Zaghlul was arrested and deported to Malta, which signalled an explosion of violence in all regions in support of the national leader.[18]

Before the war Zaghlul had been a somewhat conservative lawyer and a personal friend of Lord Cromer, de facto proconsul of Egypt. His political metamorphosis paralleled Gandhi's in timing, rapidity, and direction. The upsurge of anticolonial activity Zaghlul orchestrated and the outbreaks following his deportation had an unprecedentedly broad popular base. Supporters emerged in cities and rural areas and included large landowners, peasants, Bedouin nomads, students, the urban poor, and the intelligentsia. The breadth and depth of discontent indicated a capacity for asserting Egyptian interests that surprised the British and placed them on the defensive. The high commissioner relented, released political prisoners, and allowed *Wafd* leaders to proceed to Paris. Nothing came of their appeals. In 1922, following further unrest which could not be controlled, Britain announced Egypt's independence. A postwar crisis that increased colonial will and capacity to reject the status quo ended the shortest instance of formal European rule on record.

In World War II as in its predecessor expectations were raised and then dashed, giving rise to anger and political mobilization. One can see this pattern during the war itself in the hostile reaction of Indians, Nigerians, and others to Prime Minister Churchill's emphatic denial that the Atlantic Charter's promise of self-determination applied to the British Empire. As French public opinion shifted rightward between 1945 and 1946, the reaction in France's African colonies was one of dismay. A majority of indigenous voters in these territories approved the liberal first draft and opposed the second. Voters in France followed the opposite course—and prevailed because of the unequal voting system in place. Africans expressed their frustrations in various ways. In late 1946 an interterritorial party, the Rassemblement Démocratique Africain (RDA), was formed. This party, which dominated French West African politics for a decade, worked to maximize African influence on French colonial policy through its elected representatives to the Assemblée Nationale in Paris. In Madagascar a major revolt broke out in 1947, repressed at the cost of an estimated eighty thousand lives. Whether the response was to work peacefully within Fourth Republic institutions or to revolt, France's African subjects in 1946–47 organized for political action in ways without prewar precedent.

Trained, disciplined soldiers were decisive organizational weapons in Vietnam's and Indonesia's independence struggles. Ho Chi Minh and Sukarno seized the opportune moment to declare independence: the brief period when Japanese forces were demoralized and confused following Emperor Hirohito's surrender, yet before Allied forces arrived in sufficient numbers to take over. Had trained soldiers not been available to secure a territorial base for these fledgling governments, the new regimes would probably have succumbed—in Vietnam to French and Kuomintang Chinese armies, in Indonesia to Dutch troops. Guerrilla bands trained and brilliantly led by Vo Nguyen Giap used weapons captured from other armies and smuggled in from China. The communist-led Viet Minh controlled a base of operations in Tonkin (northern Vietnam) which it never ceded. To the discipline and opportunistic tactics of the guerrillas should be added their skill at using nationalist appeals to win peasant support. This combination kept them from being decimated at the outset of France's reconquest drive in late 1946 and enabled them by 1954 to deal the French a humiliating defeat. In Indonesia, Japanese-trained forces constituted the nucleus of the new republic's army as it fought two concerted Dutch reconquest campaigns. Indonesian troops held their ground long enough to permit United Nations diplomacy to pressure the Dutch to leave.

The decisive contribution of politically conscious soldiers to independence in Vietnam and Indonesia becomes clearer when one realizes that all phase 4 efforts to organize civilian-led nationalist movements in these territories were crushed. With the path toward evolutionary advance blocked and efforts at violent revolution aborted, it is difficult to see how decolonization could have occurred unless an external factor intervened. Hegemonic war was that factor. By providing opportunities to expand indigenous military capacity in Vietnam and Indonesia, war was a surrogate for the subversive role Western education played in colonies in which more peaceful political evolution was possible.

Each of the four hegemonic wars thus illustrates a pattern of crises in which postwar metropolitan efforts to reassert control generated strong opposition. The belief that colonial populations had been manipulated and betrayed intensified this opposition. People do not like being used by others. Especially intolerable are situations in which they feel they have been deceived into making sacrifices for the sake of a future reward that is then denied them. Opposition had an unusually broad popular base because leaders reached out to followers in innovative ways through existing or newly created institutions. What is striking about the cases cited above is the speed with which political mobilization took place. If colonies did not expect the metropole's reactionary turn at war's end, neither did metropoles expect the speed, intensity, magnitude, and institutionalized character of nationalist responses.

One reason BNA and India were precedent-setters in their respective decolonization phases was their headstart in postwar crises. The Stamp Act crisis emerged from the Seven Years' War; the Rowlatt Acts protest and Amritsar Massacre followed World War I. More tightly controlled colonies apparently needed the combined effects of two wars—first and second or third and fourth—to set up effective nationalist movements.

This analysis indicates why BNA and India were followed by other territories, including non-British possessions. Postwar crises affected colonies of France and Spain in phase 2 and those of France and Holland in phase 5. Hegemonic wars preceding these crises served as external destabilizers of empires in which opportunities to capture the public sector were far more limited than under the British. By mobilizing people to fight, wars created opportunities for rapid institutional development in the coercive arena. Where a Western-educated elite was not permitted to form or was severely circumscribed, military units filled the organizational gap.

THE INTERNATIONAL DEMONSTRATION EFFECT

The timing of hegemonic wars makes the timing of decolonization phases more understandable. But wars by themselves cannot account for the magnitude and temporal compression of these phases. New-state formation had a transformative effect in its own right on the interstate system. Chapters 4 and 7 gave numerous instances of the impact independence in one territory had on the drive for independence elsewhere. If anything, changes at the international level played an even more important part in decolonization than suggested thus far. Once war-related independence movements succeeded, demonstration effects sustained and even accelerated the momentum for change in territories not so directly affected by war.

Independence of the United States and India had far-reaching observation effects, emboldening people elsewhere to act once they could point to real examples of political change. Leaders of other phase 2 movements were impressed, among other things, that Americans were willing to fight for freedom. Many phase 5 nationalists were impressed by the peaceful mass mobilization techniques pioneered by Gandhi and adopted them in their own work. That phase 5 was more peaceful than phase 2 may owe something to the types of struggles the precedent-setters modeled.

Observation effects crossed imperial lines. What BNA colonists achieved was noted in Haiti and Spanish America; what India did was noted in Indonesia and Indochina. Francophone Africans noted Ghana's independence; residents of Leopoldville in the Belgian Congo heard of General de Gaulle's independence offer, made across the river in Brazzaville. If postwar crises were intra-imperial, pitting colonies against their metropoles, observation effects had wide-ranging impacts on two or more empires.

The direct influence effect also crossed imperial lines. Haitians assisted Bolívar when he was in dire straits. U.S. citizens supported Spanish American liberation struggles, and the Monroe Doctrine formally committed the U.S. government to oppose Spanish reconquest efforts. Guerrilla fighters in Portugal's African colonies received help from Algeria and other former French colonies, the former Belgian Congo, and Tanzania. These interventions helped nationalist movements struggling under highly repressive regimes.

There were no international organizations in phase 2 to bring diplomatic pressures from many sources to bear, either to limit or prevent vertical violence. The presence of international organizations in phase 5 added the indirect influence option. The United Nations was very important both in accelerating new-state formation and in limiting the violence associated with power transfers. The U.N. Charter embodied principles of national self-determination articulated earlier by President Wilson and the Atlantic Charter, ensuring efforts to apply them universally. In this setting defenders of overseas empires were placed ideologically and morally on the defensive. As each new state entered the United Nations, the organization became even more a forum for anticolonial lobbying. It hastened the Dutch departure from Indonesia (see chapter 7). The trusteeship system subtly but surely forced Belgium and France to abandon adamant opposition to independence in their sub-Saharan possessions. Another international structure, the Commonwealth, pressured Britain to move its colonies more rapidly toward self-government and to intervene to end the Rhodesian civil war.

The American War of Independence had two observation effects, initially on Canada and then on Britain. The result, as unexpected as it was unintended, was a set of procedures permitting the peaceful breakup of Europe's greatest empire. English-speakers in Canada reacted against the American Revolution, especially after the influx of Loyalists bitter over mistreatment by the revolution's supporters. This negative response kept Canada within the empire, giving Britain opportunities to experiment with new ways of treating settler communities. British officials could see what went wrong in BNA and resolved to avoid the same mistakes elsewhere. The Durham Report can be seen as the application of a metropolitan learning process to a territory kept within the imperial fold by rejection of America's revolutionary past and worry over its expansionist designs. Canada became the precedent-setter for political evolution within the British Empire. In this respect it may have influenced the course of European empire as much as its southern neighbor. Successful transfer of the Westminster model to Canada was followed by transfer to other white dominions, then to Britain's occupation colonies. With the passage of time English-speaking settlers pushed to extend control over public policy from domestic to foreign affairs. With the expansion of education non-European nationalists pushed to emulate the white dominion example. Peaceful negotiation of de facto independence for the dominions in 1931 became the model in India, Ghana, Tanganyika, Jamaica, and many other territories. One reason the British Empire unraveled peacefully in phases 4 and 5 is that its initial loss in phase 2 was violent.

Cross-phase variations in international demonstration effects are not accidental. They illustrate international learning, the formation of new institutions to avoid the repetition of problems encountered in the past. Britain learned from its BNA losses to treat settlers in the white dominions with greater caution. Non-Europeans in Britain's colonies, observing the white dominions' evolution toward autonomy, shaped goals and tactics to follow up the precedents set by settler communities. The Commonwealth was the result of continual, incremental redefinitions of empire to adjust gracefully to the leading metropole's loss of dominance. The League of Nations and United Nations were born in the aftermath of hegemonic wars, their purpose being to avoid more of the same. The United Nations' availability as a forum for peacefully arranging transfers of power contributed to a less violent decolonization process after 1945 than in the earlier phase, when no comparable mechanism for indirect influence was in place.

CONCLUDING REFLECTIONS

Focusing on the connection between hegemonic war and decolonization enables one to see the importance of political and military factors in phases 2 and 5. The role played by economic trends, actors, and interests is somewhat less clear. David Strang reaches a similar conclusion in a statistical study of twentieth-century decolonization, arguing that it "arises from characteristics of the larger political context, while more purely economic factors have a modest impact. Metropolitan political institutions and military power clearly matter, as do the pronouncements of the United Nations. The economic transformation of the dependency and global economic conditions seem less relevant."[19]

In contrast, imperial expansion was strongly influenced by economic considerations, as evidenced by the explore-control-utilize syndrome and the key role private profit sector institutions played in phases 1 and 3. An implication is that expansion was more driven by economic factors than was contraction. "It may thus be fruitful," Strang writes, "to separate the conditions that produce colonization from those that produce decolonization. The processes that lead to the breakdown of empires may be intrinsically different from those that construct them."[20]

My discussion of the rise of European empires began by referring to the international system. My discussion of imperial decline concludes by referring to the international system. But the two systems are not the same, precisely because of the expansionist dynamic in modern European life. Whereas the system referred to in chapter 8 consisted of west European countries, the political setting for events discussed here was transcontinental. Creation of overseas empires *was* the process by which a regionalized system became a global one. Wars over the global distribution of power were the only events of sufficient magnitude to impact the imperial edifice from outside. When metropoles trying to counter slowly evolving forces for internal dissolution were forced to confront rapidly moving external threats as well, it is not surprising that cracks appeared in the edifice of domination.

Part VI

CONSEQUENCES OF
EUROPEAN OVERSEAS RULE

(*Overleaf*) Prime Minister Jawaharlal Nehru of India addresses the United Nations General Assembly, 1960. United Nations Photo Library, courtesy Instructional Resources Corporation.

16
Legacies

Identifying the legacies of European rule is fraught with conceptual and methodological perils. I construe colonialism narrowly as control of a territory's public sector by a metropole. Instances in which informal influence was exercised apart from formal governance are not considered. I focus on what Europeans did in trying to carve out and consolidate dominant positions for themselves. If one broadened the definition of colonialism and equated it with westernization or modernization, its impact would be considerably greater than claimed here. But so many things would have been tossed into the causal side of the equation that sorting out which aspect of westernization had which effects would become an unmanageable operation.[1] Likewise, if one considered everything that occurred during the colonial era, including responses and initiatives of colonized peoples, the independent variable would be too comprehensive and complex to generate meaningful cause-effect statements. It is more appropriate, for instance, to treat anticolonial nationalism as a significant legacy of colonialism than to regard the two as part and parcel of the same thing.

To assert that colonialism had consequence X or Y is not to claim that it is the only cause of X or Y. Indeed, a safer assumption is that outcomes noted here were shaped by many factors. Clearly, the greater the time gap between the end of colonial rule and events or patterns one wants to explain, the less plausible the claim that colonialism was the sole or even principal cause. The colonial impact on today's world is more obvious and direct for phase 5 states than for those gaining independence in phase 2. Effects on the latter have been filtered through personalities, events, and trends in postindependence decades that had little or nothing to do with the time when Europeans were formally in charge.

No one can confidently assert what kind of world would have emerged had Europeans *not* projected power to other continents. To identify legacies of empire is implicitly to contrast what occurred in modern world history with speculation about what would have happened in the absence of empire. Different scenarios of the likely course of counterfactual history account for many of the differences in people's assessments of European rule. Counterfactual thinking is inherently contestable. But can efforts to account for the past do without it? "We can avoid counterfactuals only if we eschew all causal inference . . . ," assert Philip Tetlock and Aaron Belkin. "Everyone [carrying out historical analysis] does it and the alternative to an open counterfactual model is a concealed one."[2] Where appropriate, assumptions about alternative pasts are made explicit rather than concealed.

European rule affected more than colonies. It helped shape Europe's own development and eventually influenced worldwide patterns of thought and action. Propositions about each of these categories are arranged in the same sequence: impacts on society, politics, economics, religion, culture, and psychology. References to politics, economics, and religion parallel the analysis of the triple assault.

IMPACTS ON COLONIZED PEOPLES AND TERRITORIES

—*European rule led to large-scale redistributions of the world's peoples. The population of many colonies—and of their new-state successors—was far more racially and culturally diverse than in precolonial times.*

Prior to the fifteenth century all or almost all inhabitants of a given continent could trace their ancestry to people from that continent. Formation of European empires made possible, and greatly facilitated, massive flows of people from continents of origin to other regions. Over a five-century period tens of millions of Europeans emigrated, substantial settler communities being established only in areas claimed by metropoles. Over a four-century period tens of millions of Africans were transported as slaves to plantation-based colonies in the Americas. In phase 3 Indians and Chinese migrated as indentured servants to colonies in Africa, Southeast Asia, the Indian Ocean, and the Caribbean.

These movements altered the demographic composition of many regions. Especially affected were areas in which diseases carried by newly arriving groups decimated indigenous peoples. The New World and Oceania were radically changed in this respect, Africa and Asia far less so.

To the extent that race denotes continental origin, European empires made race relations a persistently significant issue for the modern world. The multiracial character of many colonies profoundly affected the way social relations and political life were organized after independence. It was difficult for people visibly unlike each other as well as culturally diverse to feel part of the same country, with citizenship rights in common. In phase 2 states it was impossible for indigenous peoples and those of African descent to belong to the country in which they lived because people of European descent denied them basic political and legal rights. This exclusivist attitude to citizenship postponed until the twentieth century a serious commitment by most phase 2 states to incorporate non-European groups into national life.

In European countries religious, class, and regional cleavages have historically been sources of conflict. Not so with race. In sharp contrast, colonies were arenas of interracial contact and conflict from the moment the first Europeans arrived. Race relations was a contentious issue that could not be ignored and did not go away, particularly in territories with large settler populations.

By phase 5, however, metropoles were no longer insulated from the racial pluralization their presence and policies produced elsewhere. Whereas the state spread from Europe to the colonies, the plural society spread from the colonies to Europe. Since the end of World War II hundreds of thousands of people have migrated from newly independent countries to former metropoles. Extensive communities from the West Indies, India, and Pakistan now reside in Great Britain; likewise Algerians, Moroccans, Senegalese, and Malians in France, Zaireans in Belgium, and Indonesians in Holland. As "the empire strikes back" through these migrations, Britain and France above all have wrestled with problems arising from growing heterogeneity. Contemporary Europe has a great deal to learn from former colonies about how to manage the subtle tensions and overt conflicts experienced by multiracial societies.

—*The racially based stratification system of the colonial era is a primary determinant of social relations today.*

In European history struggles for equality occurred among people with the same racial background. These struggles were bitter at times. But they lacked the emotional intensity of comparable struggles in colonies and their independent successors, where race not only marked observable biological differences but also signified economic and status inequalities. Close links between difference and inequality produce an unusually durable stratification system. Once a racial category becomes a socioeconomic caste it is extremely difficult for those at the scale's lower end to move up, and potentially explosive of social relations if they do. In territories where settlers were preoccupied with maintaining racial purity, sexual anxieties and rivalries added fuel to an already combustible mix. Where settlers inherited the public sector at independence—as in phase 2 states and South Africa—non-Europeans found it even more difficult to raise their collective position because the power of government was used to reinforce colonial-era inequalities.

—*Colonial rule begat anticolonial nationalism and hence eventually undermined itself. But since virtually all nationalists wished to retain key aspects of the public sector Europeans put in place, many features of colonial government carried over to successor regimes. The territorially bounded, bureaucratic, sovereign state is the joint product of colonialism and nationalism, a dialectical synthesis of two apparently opposed forces.*

Metropoles turned colonies into protostates by transferring many of their public sector institutions. Metropoles also spread the idea that a state was the most advanced political form devised by humanity. The one thing colonies lacked—sovereignty—was the one thing nationalists demanded. In effect, nationalists criticized not the fact of public sector transfer but its incompleteness, insisting on nothing less than full replication of the metropole's status. At one level the demand for independence was a rejection of foreign rule. At another level it was a ringing affirmation of the structural and ideological form foreign rule took. The goal was to capture the protostate, not to dismantle or fundamentally rearrange it. Hence a paradox: The result of the nationalists' success at terminating European global dominance was global diffusion of Europe's governance model.

The spread of this model has produced a far more homogeneous pattern of political organization than would have existed in the absence of overseas empires. Five centuries ago many of the world's peoples lived in stateless societies, small-scale chiefdoms, and self-governing cities. These forms became increasingly rare as they were encompassed by colonial boundaries and their autonomy undercut by externally imposed bureaucracies. Today's world is a collection of states; its peoples define themselves, among other things, as citizens of states.[3] That this observation is now little more than a truism underlines the distance humanity has traveled in a few centuries, from many governance modes to one overwhelmingly predominant one.

—The colonial origin of public sector institutions often reduces their effectiveness and legitimacy.

An imperial legacy in many parts of the world is a lack of fit between social structure and political institutions. Society has become more heterogeneous owing to demographic changes noted earlier. But public sector institutions have become more homogeneous, in the double sense that the same institutions govern citizens with diverse racial and cultural backgrounds within a country and that governing institutions in very different countries resemble each other. Where government has been shaped more by external forces than by its own society, rulers may not consider themselves accountable to those they rule, and citizens may regard government procedures and policies as illegitimate.

In countries where colonial administrators, judges, and police were harsh and unpopular, retention of the institutions that employed them can undermine legitimacy even when the offending foreigners have been replaced by local personnel. The perception that government is an alien force can last a long time. It can encourage pillage of public funds for private purposes, pillagers regarding the treasury as the possession not of the nation but of foreign exploiters who deserve to be robbed.[4] This practice further lowers support for government by diverting resources officials might have devoted to the collective good.

—Whether a new state becomes democratic depends in large measure on whether colonywide representative institutions were in place and functioning effectively before independence. While the presence of colonial legislatures cannot ensure democracy in later years, its absence appears to be a sufficient condition for maintenance of authoritarian rule.

By their nature colonial regimes were authoritarian: bureaucracies carried out decisions made by foreigners who were unaccountable to local people. The top-down character of government was bequeathed to new states. The Nigerian historian Stephen Akintoye's description of the African scene applies to other regions as well: "The isolation of the government from the governed, the refusal to tolerate opposition or criticisms, the fear of delegating authority, the branding of all virile opposition as treasonable action—all these were learned from Africa's colonial masters by the Africans who took over African governments at independence."[5]

The most effective counterweight to authoritarian rule after independence was an elected legislature capable of restraining the executive branch. If a legislature was in place at independence and had shown that it could influence decisions of colonial authorities, then it had a reasonable chance of survival. In this respect Britain's possessions differed significantly from the rest. That the Westminster model should have been transferred to settlers is not surprising; that it was eventually transferred to occupation colonies at the insistence of nationalists is more so. But importing this particular foreign institution made sense because, unlike a bureaucracy, a legislature comes ready-made for rapid capture.

How long the Westminster model lasted after Britain left depended on many factors, including the personalities and values of political leaders. Jawaharlal Nehru was committed to a multiparty electoral system and open parliamentary debate. Kwame Nkrumah was not, and by the mid-1960s he had become a dictator eagerly fanning the flames of his own personality cult. The opposing strategies of the two men account in part for the diverging political trajectories of India and Ghana. An effectively functioning colonial legislature does not guarantee competitive electoral systems, as the large number of undemocratic ex-British colonies in 1980 shows (table 16.1).

But *absence* of such a legislature is virtually a sufficient condition for *failure* of competitive elections to take root. To confine discussion to the quarter century after independence, these two negative features are found in all phase 2 countries except the United States and in such phase 5 countries as Vietnam, Indonesia, Zaire, Algeria, and Angola. (Spain permitted settlers representative government at the local level but not in larger administrative units.)

Further support for the double negative hypothesis comes from an analysis of patterns in phase 5 new states. Freedom House's annual survey *Freedom in the World*

TABLE 16.1.

POLITICAL RIGHTS IN PHASE 5 NEW STATES AS OF 1980

| Former metropole | Number of ex-colonies ranked | Rankings | | | | | |
| | | 1 or 2 | | 3 or 4 | | 5, 6, or 7 | |
		#	%	#	%	#	%
Britain	53	22	42	7	13	24	45
France	25	0	0	5	20	20	80
Portugal	5	0	0	0	0	5	100
Belgium	3	0	0	0	0	3	100
Holland	2	0	0	0	0	2	100
Italy	2	0	0	0	0	2	100
Spain	1	0	0	0	0	1	100

Source: Raymond Gastil, Freedom in the World (1980), tables 1, 3, pp. 14–18.

ranks countries on a 1–7 scale according to political rights their citizens exercise. Countries rated 1 and 2 conduct regular competitive elections. Those rated 5 through 7 lack formal mechanisms for meaningful electoral choice and are typically governed by single parties or despots. Countries ranked 3 and 4 lie between these extremes. In 1980 all former colonies of metropoles ruling in a clearly authoritarian manner— Portugal, Belgium, Holland, Italy, and Spain—scored in the 5–7 range. The same applies to all these countries as of 1990. Britain's former colonies are about evenly divided between the 1,2 and 5,6,7 categories. The ratio improves to 22:18 if one excludes the six Arabian peninsular quasi colonies whose domestic affairs Britain never firmly controlled. France occupies an intermediate position, consistent with an intermediate pattern of representation in the Fourth Republic: colonies could send delegates to the Assemblée Nationale in Paris, though not until the late 1950s were territorial legislatures with any real authority established.

To know what leads new states toward or away from democracy, a starting point is to examine what kinds of representative institutions, if any, were established by former metropoles.

—Colonial administrative boundaries have proven unusually durable. With few exceptions they constituted territorial borders at independence, and they define the size and shape of the great majority of states today.

Among phase 2 countries the United States is a partial exception to this generalization. It is a postcolonial invention, both because the shift from confederation to a federal system did not occur until the late 1780s and because boundaries steadily expanded westward for decades after independence. But even here the old boundaries mattered, for it was the thirteen ex-colonies that debated and authorized the union's formation and became its original constituents. As for other phase 2 states, Haiti and the Dominican Republic retain the border between French- and Spanish-ruled portions of Hispaniola. Brazil closely resembles the late phase 1 Portuguese viceroyalty. Boundaries of ex-Spanish states were drawn along familiar lines, in some instances replicating viceroyalties, in others captaincy-generals and *audiencias*.

The generalization fits phase 5 states. Major exceptions are in South Asia: the last-minute partition of India that produced Pakistan, followed in 1971 by secession of East Pakistan to become Bangladesh. Separate colonial units were consolidated when Cameroon, Somalia, and Malaysia were formed. But consolidation efforts such as the Guinea-Ghana Union, Mali Federation, and East African Federation lasted only a short time before the territorial units of colonial days reasserted themselves as separate states.

One reason for continuity is that a colony's public sector was structured to administer the territory demarcated by its boundaries. Once the geographic and functional scope of their activities was fixed, bureaucrats found it convenient and in their interest to maintain the status quo. They also did what bureaucrats everywhere are famous for doing: fighting with skill, determination, and the resources at their disposal to protect their turf. With independence the personnel of central government agencies changed. But discontinuity in a bureaucracy's staffing patterns was fully compatible with continuity in its geographic scope. If anything, people newly installed in government posts were determined to preserve inherited job descriptions. Central government employees generally favored keeping the independent state as it was, neither dividing it into smaller units nor merging with other states. Ambitious or idealistic politicians might on occasion call for such changes, but the collective weight of national bureaucracies was arrayed on the side of conservatism.

The most striking evidence of boundary continuity comes from sub-Saharan Africa. Here one would expect the greatest change in the number, size, and shape of postindependence states, because borders were externally imposed and in most cases bore no relationship to social and political realities on the ground. Independent African states might have fragmented into units based on ethno-linguistic identities. Or they might have joined to form larger entities, consistent with pan-African ideology and with the argument that existing states were far too small to be economically viable. Instead old patterns were maintained virtually intact into the 1990s. Secessionist movements in the Congo, Nigeria, and the Sudan failed. Rebels fought not in the name of ethnic autonomy but on behalf of multiethnic administrative units—Katanga, Nigeria's Eastern Region (Biafra), Southern Sudan—whose boundaries had been arbitrarily set by Europeans. Had secession succeeded, the new boundaries would have been just as artificial and externally imposed as the old ones. Almost all efforts at supranational political integration also failed.

A plausible explanation is that civil and military bureaucracies, entrenched at independence, constituted a country's most powerful domestic interest group. Rapid personnel growth immediately following independence gave these institutions additional clout.[6] There was little political leaders could do when confronted by the preference of strategically placed groups for existing boundaries.

The experience of the first independence movement supports this argument in a reverse way. Of all the colonies Europeans formed, the thirteen in BNA had perhaps the most rudimentary bureaucracies. The colonies thus lacked interest groups that might have pressed successfully for thirteen separate territories following England's defeat at Yorktown. In these circumstances politicians had an unusually high level of freedom to experiment with new forms of government, including changes in boundaries. The least bureaucratized of Europe's colonies generated the most far-reaching challenge to inherited institutions and boundaries.

—*A substantial majority of new states retained the language of the former metropole when they conducted official business.*

One would expect linguistic continuity in countries governed by people of European descent. Since independence English has been the sole language of central government in the United States and Australia, Spanish in Mexico and Argentina, Portuguese in Brazil. Countries with a dual-settler heritage retained both languages: Canada (English and French) and white-ruled South Africa (Afrikaans and English). Of greater interest is that many states ruled by non-European elites opted to retain the colonial language. These include Asian and African countries in which a substantial majority do not speak a European tongue. In about half of the more than eighty phase 5 states for which information is available, the only language accorded official status is that of the former metropole. In an additional sixteen countries it shares that status with an indigenous language.[7]

One reason for retaining the colonial language in a multilingual country is that it may be the only one known to everyone in the political and bureaucratic elite. And some ex-colonies are exceedingly multilingual: in fifteen more than a hundred languages are spoken.[8] Another reason is that selecting a non-European alternative can prove contentious, alienating speakers of languages not chosen. That Arabic is the sole official language of the Sudan has long angered those in the three southern provinces, only about 1 percent of whom speak it. This grievance figures prominently in the civil war afflicting the country for most of the last four decades. The Indian government's commitment to Hindi as a co-official language with English met tremendous resistance in southern regions, where Hindi was not commonly spoken. Mauritania's adoption of Arabic in 1966 as a co-official language with French triggered riots by non-Arab speakers. Togo removed two indigenous languages shortly after independence and has kept only one—French—ever since.[9]

A consequence of retaining the colonial language in countries where most people do not speak it is that only a minority of the population is eligible for election or appointment to central government posts.[10] This limits the pool of talent available to serve the public at home and abroad. And it raises the question posed of educated nationalists in an earlier period: whether leaders are so acculturated to Western ideas, values, and consumption patterns that they poorly represent the interests of people on whose behalf they speak.

—*Colonial rule spread the idea that continuous economic development is possible and desirable.*

The explore-control-utilize worldview impelled much European activity overseas and contributed hugely to colonial economic development. Europeans vastly increased the volume and range of marketable output. They did so by assembling a transformational package of available natural resources, a local and imported labor force, imported plants and animals, capital, new technologies, profit-driven organizations, and intercontinental trade networks.

Phase 2 settler nationalists shared this commitment to realize the economic potential of their environment—they were, after all, themselves bearers of European attitudes to distant frontiers. But non-European nationalists in phases 4 and 5 adopted the same stance. Their education, their awareness of economic and technological advances in other parts of the world, and their knowledge of wealth-generating activities in their own territories led them to place high priority on development. Colonizers were criticized not for trying to stimulate growth but for imposing so many of its costs on the colonized population and allotting most of its benefits to themselves. If anything, twentieth-century nationalism had a more ambitious transformative agenda than its phase 2 predecessor. The greater the economic gap separating imperial centers from peripheries, the more pressing the need to catch up.

Industrialization was attractive to non-European nationalists because they felt the value added from factory production had been appropriated by metropoles and deliberately denied the colonies. The radical demand to bring heavy industry and hydroelectric power to new states was also conservative, in the sense that its goal was to emulate the most advanced countries' experience. Just as nationalists embraced the European state as a political model while rejecting European control of the state, so they embraced European industrialization as an economic model while rejecting European appropriation of gains from mass-production technologies.

Japan's and Russia's launching of industrialization drives in phase 3 reinforced nationalists' arguments that independence was a precondition for industrial development. Meiji and tsarist reformers took advantage of their countries' sovereignty to promote rapid defensive modernization. Such policies could not be adopted in colonies because control over economic affairs lay in the hands of metropoles threatened by defensive modernization.

The explore-control-utilize syndrome was conducive to imperial expansion. Its diffusion to colonized peoples contributed to imperial decline. Diffusion also affected postcolonial relationships. Because colonized peoples became more like Europeans in adopting a developmental stance to Nature, the basis was laid for extensive international economic ties after political ties were severed. Phase 5 new states, like their phase 2 predecessors, wanted European capital and technology. The desired transfers were primarily through the private profit sector for phase 2 states (portfolio investment) and largely through the public sector (foreign aid) for phase 5 states. But behind different modes of transfer lay the fundamental similarity that transfer was taking place, and on terms both sides could live with. Ex-metropoles learned they could deal profitably with ex-colonies because ex-colonies wanted what was needed to catch up to them. The shared commitment to make nature useful moderated old antagonisms and made postcolonial relations more congenial and interdependent than might have been expected.

Cutting political ties with a metropole made it possible to arrange economic exchanges with numerous European countries. The independence of South American countries enabled British private interests to invest profitably in the continent's mines, railroads, and utilities. Phase 5 states negotiated aid agreements with many European countries as well as with the two superpowers. As transnational European institutions developed, diplomats from new states negotiated with people representing the region and not simply its individual countries. Several rounds of negotiations between the European Economic Community and African, Caribbean, and Pacific states produced conventions governing trade, investment, and aid.[11] In both decolonization phases the end of empire meant that Europe mattered more to ex-colonies even as ex-metropoles mattered less.

—*Colonial-era patterns of extraction, production, transport, and trade carried on into independence. In general, this economic legacy was even more durable than the political one.*

Earlier chapters noted the emergence of open colonial economies with high ratios of trade to gross domestic product and exports consisting mainly of unprocessed or semiprocessed primary products. When new-state elites had little interest in changing this arrangement, as in nineteenth-century Latin America, the fact that it continued should not be surprising. But even phase 5 nationalists committed to reversing inherited patterns found it difficult if not impossible to do so once they came to power. Earlier investments in mines, plantations, roads, railways, and port facilities constituted sunk costs that could be recovered and generate profits only if they continued to operate much as they had. New governments anxious to industrialize had to decide how to finance the heavy up-front costs of new factories and related infrastructure. Borrowing abroad was risky, especially if loans could not be repaid. High debt levels could lead not only to economic crisis as scarce resources were diverted to repayment but also to loss of sovereignty as lenders imposed macroeconomic policy conditions on "structural adjustment" bailout packages. Foreign exchange generated through the existing export base had the advantage of preserving a semblance of policy autonomy. Thus, in order to change the composition of imports and domestic output many new states found they had little choice but to retain the composition of exports. A planned break with the past entailed unexpected continuity with the past. Only in rare instances was a phase 5 country able substantially to increase the manufactured component of exports within the first quarter century of independence.

New states generally avoided lowering the levels of external exposure they inherited. In rare cases such as Haiti and Burma small countries turned inward. India had a sufficiently large domestic market and industrial base to shift toward self-reliance after 1947. But these are exceptions. Most new states remained highly vulnerable to external economic trends. They benefited if terms of trade rose but lost out if terms declined, as happened over the long term for many countries. The elaborate multiyear plans announced with fanfare by phase 5 states were in effect efforts to hide, through largely symbolic rituals, inability to chart the economic future.

Once large-scale colonial operations like mines, plantations, and ranches were in place, there were strong economy-of-scale arguments to retain them after independence. It made little difference in this respect if ownership passed from private to public hands. Nationalization might be politically radical. But it was economically conservative, in the sense that new public sector owners only confirmed colonial-era patterns of commodity production. Returning to small-scale, localized, kin-based units of precolonial days was out of the question, at least for goods traded on the world market.

—*Imperial rule helped Christianity become a world religion.*

What I have termed Euro-Christianity spread with the dispersal of settler communities, and some version of it was adopted as the official faith of most phase 2 regimes. But it spread as well among non-Europeans in response to the work of missionaries. The sectoral autonomy of religious bodies and their calling to go out to all the world meant that they did not confine their work to areas incorporated into overseas empires. But it is in these areas that their campaigns were most successful over the long term, in large part because public sector resources and protection sustained missionary endeavors. Who governed the state affected how people worshiped. Euro-Christianity's spread was hindered in noncolonized areas like Japan and China, where ruling elites saw its doctrine and its followers as political threats.

—*For many intellectuals and other opinion leaders in new states, the struggle for psychological independence was more protracted and emotionally exhausting than the struggle for political independence. Images people held of themselves and their abilities continued to be affected by negative stereotypes derived from the colonial era.*

The superiority complex was a legacy centuries of global dominance bequeathed to Europeans. The inferiority complex was a legacy with which many residents of colonies and ex-colonies have had to grapple. One response of people to being told repeatedly that they were inadequate was angrily to deny the charge. Resentment at being humiliated by colonial authority figures was salient in the discourse of nationalist movements. One sees it in the reaction of Spanish American creoles to the slights of *peninsulares,* and even more so in the rage non-Europeans expressed over racially based taunts and acts of discrimination.

In general, leaders of independence movements did not try to replace one superiority complex with another. They argued not that the colonial nation was morally, intellectually, or culturally better than the metropole but rather that it deserved to be treated as the equal of nations elsewhere. Phase 5 movements phrased the crusade for equality in universalistic terms. All human beings possessed certain rights, above all the right not to be treated as subhuman. Independence was the political manifestation of the fundamental claim to dignity, as well as a way of ensuring that the claim would not be violated again. In Nkrumah's words, "It is only when people are politically free that other races can give them the respect that is due to them. It is impossible to talk of equality of races in any other terms. No people without a government of its own can expect to be treated on the same level as peoples of independent sovereign states."[12]

Another response, found among non-Europeans who attended Western-style schools, was to concede that the colonizer's civilization was superior but to insist that they be offered opportunities to become part of it through cultural assimilation. This approach internalized the inferiority complex at the collective level of indigenous culture while rejecting it at the individual level. In territories in which colonial rulers adopted assimilationist policies, postcolonial elites consisted primarily of individuals who had struggled to cross the cultural line—and succeeded. These people might use populist rhetoric on appropriate public occasions. But how plausible was their national leadership when they had devoted so much effort to rejecting the culture of their fellow citizens? Neither were they inclined to ask how indigenous ways of thinking and acting might resolve their country's problems. Intent on modernization, they tended to regard traditional rulers, folk religions, herbalists and their remedies, old patterns of dress, traditional handicrafts and the like as relics of a primitive past that did not deserve to survive.

Another response among non-Europeans was to believe the claim that they were individually and collectively inferior. This was of course a deeply disturbing thought. Subconscious internalization of the inferiority complex was the most pernicious outcome of all.

The inferiority complex could coexist with other responses, including anger at the way one's people were being humiliated and exploited. Frantz Fanon writes bitterly in *The Wretched of the Earth* of the evils of colonialism, urging the colonized to take up arms against their white oppressors. The same author, in *Black Skin, White Masks*, writes in tortured prose about the self-hatred he cannot escape because his whole social environment relentlessly conveys the message of black inferiority.

However they coped with accusations of inadequacy, non-Europeans had to devise coping mechanisms of some sort, which took time and emotional energy. The existential challenge of battling what the Indian cultural theorist Ashis Nandy calls "the intimate enemy: the loss of self" threatened to distract individuals from the challenge of making the most of their country's newly won independence.[13] Excitement about shaping a better future was less intense when demons from the past had to be exorcised.

Stephen Jay Gould eloquently describes the effects of doubting one's competence and feeling ashamed of a group with whom one is identified. Gould's words apply to more than colonial and postcolonial situations. But European overseas rule did more than anything else to shape the racial and cultural forms self-hatred takes in the modern world. "We only get to go through this world once, as far as we know," Gould writes, "and if our lives are thwarted, if our hopes are derailed, if our dreams are made impossible by limitations imposed from without, but falsely identified as residing within us, then in a way that's the greatest tragedy one can imagine. And millions—hundreds of millions—of human lives have been so blighted."[14]

IMPACTS ON WESTERN EUROPE
—State formation was accelerated.

Empire building abroad had to await formation of centralized states at home. But the two processes became mutually reinforcing once some measure of control was gained in overseas lands. When colonies yielded net gains to a metropole's treasury, extra resources were available to strengthen its bureaucracy and armed forces. In effect, an increase in a state's international extractive capacity raised its ability to regulate domestic affairs.[15] Castile's Queen Isabella and England's Queen Elizabeth I were skilled at using foreign initiatives to enhance their power. Spain's

Philip II liberally dispensed Mexican silver pesos to influential Portuguese to bolster his successful claim (1581) to the Portuguese throne.[16] Access to overseas resources gave monarchs an edge over local nobles, whose resource base was confined to their own domains. Colonies gave rulers valuable patronage opportunities.[17] A land grant charter or governorship could reward supporters. Overseas posts could buy off rivals or dispatch them to virtual exile. Such forms of patronage typically came at no cost to the metropole, as colonies were expected to cover their own administrative expenses.

Charles Tilly's assertion that in western Europe "war made the state, and the state made war"[18] should be complemented by the observation that the European state made the overseas empire, and the empire helped make the European state.

—*Domestic political stability was enhanced.*

Overseas possessions and issues relating to empire enabled rulers to deflect, divert, and undercut domestic opposition. This reduced the likelihood of unrest and revolt from below and made it easier for those in power to retain it.

Absorption of settlers by selected colonies probably increased metropolitan stability by lowering population pressures in overcrowded areas and removing troublesome minorities, notably Puritans, Baptists, and Quakers to BNA and French Huguenots to Dutch South Africa. Moreover, all imperial powers used colonies as dumping grounds for persons convicted of criminal offenses. "With rare exceptions after the initial conquest of Ceuta in 1415," writes Gerald Bender, "every [Portuguese] ship involved in the discoveries and conquests held a contingent of *degradados* (convicts). . . . Laws governing the use of *degradados* in the conquests date back to 1434." The overwhelming majority of Angola's Portuguese residents from the initial explorations to the early twentieth century were exiled convicts.[19] Britain found it convenient to establish Georgia and Australia as penal colonies at a time when private enclosure of communally shared lands and the rapid growth of newly industrializing urban centers produced enormous social dislocation and economic inequality.

Following the massive workers' uprising in Paris in 1848, "the Second Republic felt itself called upon to solve the underlying social problem," writes Charles-Robert Ageron, "and the Assembly voted 50 million francs to clear the capital of subversive elements. Unemployed artisans and labourers made over 100,000 applications for free grants of land in Algeria; in the end there were 20,000 such emigrants, 15,000 of them from Paris, who settled in Algeria in forty-two new villages."[20] Ex-revolutionaries quickly became reactionaries, ardently supporting French rule in Algeria. In one stroke the government turned enemies at home into agents of expansion abroad.

A long-term effect of Britain's industrial development was a surge in population. Having to absorb all entrants to the labor force would have been difficult, particularly when the business cycle turned downward in the 1870s. More than twelve million people left Great Britain in the nineteenth century. Most emigrated to the United States, where the predominance of English-speakers was an enduring colonial legacy; others went to Canada, Australia, New Zealand, and South Africa. In the absence of these vents for surplus population, Britain might have experienced urban unrest and a more radical working-class movement. The United States and the white dominions in turn sent vast quantities of wheat, beef, lamb, and dairy products to Britain, making staple foods available at low cost to a country no longer able to feed itself.

When politics took a populist turn in phase 3 the quest for overseas territory was used to generate mass support or to mute or deflect criticism of a government's performance at home. Among the earliest examples of an overseas "circus" designed primarily for domestic consumption was the French invasion of Algiers in 1830.[21] Politicians seizing on imperial issues for electoral purposes included Benjamin Disraeli, Jules Ferry, Otto von Bismarck, and Joseph Chamberlain.[22] It is unclear whether their actions had the desired effect. Ferry's Vietnam policy, in fact, backfired on him. But major expansionist initiatives were taken in phase 3 in the expectation that they would increase popular support for the government of the day.

If expansion helped stabilize metropolitan regimes, the impending loss of empire could destabilize them, as occurred twice in phase 5, with the fall of France's Fourth Republic in 1958 over Algeria and the coup in 1974 against the Caetano government over the Portuguese armed forces' inability to defeat African nationalist movements. Both instances involved a change of regime as well as of national leadership and hence represented a major break with politics as usual.

—*How metropoles fared overseas influenced membership and status in the European interstate system and affected procedures for handling relations among states in war and peace.*

Having overseas possessions may have influenced whether a polity survived or disappeared. Profits generated by the Dutch East India Company doubtless helped Holland win the long struggle for independence from Habsburg rule. Holland's status as a player in Southeast Asian trade and politics must have counted for something when independence was internationally acknowledged in 1648. Not by accident are all five phase 1 metropoles still functioning as states, as are the three new-state metropoles of phase 3. On the other side of the ledger, of hundreds of phase 1 polities that failed to survive only two made halfhearted efforts to establish trading enclaves outside the Mediterranean basin.[23] None administered territories back of a coastal port. In one case noted earlier, failure to capture overseas territory led directly to loss of sovereignty: Portugal's incorporation into Spain following its defeat at the Battle of El Ksar-el-Kabir.

Metropoles with access to colonies during wartime enjoyed a strategic edge. In this respect the distribution of imperial power influenced the outcome of hegemonic wars. England's victories over France in the Seven Years' and Napoleonic Wars owe a great deal to its ability to trade with far-flung colonies while using seapower to curtail France's ability to do likewise. Writing after World War I, the French colonial administrator Albert Sarraut stressed how important France's possessions had been:

> When after the attack of 1914 the first batallions of black troops arrived, immediately followed by those disembarking from Asia, Antilles, and Madagascar, when our industries became full of hardworking and silent Indochinese workers, when our harbors and storehouses were stocked with abundant products from our overseas possessions, when successive war borrowing recorded hundreds of millions of subscriptions by French and indigenous peoples from our colonies, everyone noticed suddenly that the efforts of our soldiers and administrators and colonizers, ignored until then, were not worthless.[24]

Germany and its allies could not extract comparable resources from outside the war theater.

Did competition for colonies raise the propensity of European states to go to war? This was quite likely the case in phases 1 and 2 but not in phase 3, so the evidence is mixed. The answer appears to depend on whether mechanisms were in place for resolving a wide range of interstate conflicts. The limited number of such mechanisms in phase 1 may have caused competition overseas to intensify and lengthen wars fought on European soil. The greater number of diplomatic mechanisms in phase 3 may have had the opposite effect, permitting territorial scrambles to deflect rivalries to areas of the world not threatening any metropole's vital interests.

A colony could stabilize international relations by being used as a pawn in diplomatic negotiations. Exchanges of non-European territory in the last decade of phase 3 reduced the level of tension among great powers and postponed the day of reckoning. After the French declared a protectorate over Morocco very little additional real estate was available, either to reward the winner of a peaceful great-power confrontation or to compensate the loser. The competition for colonies did not cause World War I, as Lenin argued; more likely the termination of the scramble for colonies depleted available buffers against the resort to violence and made war more likely.

Europeans gained valuable diplomatic experience as they negotiated overseas claims. They attended conferences and signed treaties—as at Tordesillas (1494), Brussels (1876), Berlin (1885), and Algeciras (1906)—that addressed disputes over foreign lands. Formal settlements of major European wars in 1714, 1763, 1815, and 1914 contained protocols redistributing governance rights over colonies. Imperial issues enabled diplomats to hone their skills, develop widely accepted procedures for conflict management in their own region, and learn about the capacity and will of other governments to implement agreements.

Possession of territories outside the European system had symbolic value, enhancing the status of countries so obviously able to make their presence known in the larger world. Not all metropoles were great powers. But all European countries aspiring to become great powers acquired colonies. The tendency to associate greatness with empire can be traced to the major metropoles of phase 1: Spain, France, and England. But once the association was made it affected foreign policies of states in subsequent phases. This is best shown by Germany under Bismarck. The chancellor was far more interested in consolidating and preserving Germany's leadership within Europe than in extending its power overseas. But the fact that he became a reluctant imperialist only demonstrates the point: he came to believe that Germany would not be acknowledged a great regional power until it acquired possessions outside the region.

—*The private profit sector was strengthened.*

Capitalism and imperialism were mutually reinforcing enterprises. Private profit sector institutions played leading roles in founding and consolidating empire. Empire in turn strengthened the sector and set west European countries even more firmly along the path of capitalist development. Not all, but a great many metropolitan-owned colonial ventures turned a profit. These included firms handling shipping, insurance, wholesale and retail trade, corporations owning mines and plantations, banks lending large sums to governments for infrastructure projects, and exporters of capital goods like railroad equipment and structural steel. A portion of gains from overseas activities was presumably invested in profitable ventures in Europe, thereby fortifying the sector in its home base.

Colonial governments helped capitalist institutions by providing physical security, protecting property claims, financing construction of port facilities and transport networks, and ensuring access to desired amounts of low-cost labor (see chapter 12). In these ways governments lowered the risks and costs of private ventures and raised profit margins. In many cases overseas private investment would not have occurred had the government not been run by Europeans. When the bulk of a colony's public revenue was generated by non-Europeans, a subject population living close to subsistence involuntarily subsidized wealthy foreign enterprises.

A legacy of colonial rule was ex-colonies whose elites eagerly sought European private investment. Phase 3 offers an instructive contrast between former colonies in the New World and colonies-to-be in the Old. European investors in the Americas gained handsome profits from assets like mines and utilities and returns on portfolio loans to new governments. They saw no need to recolonize New World states because, with elites of European descent running government, the political conditions were in place for outsiders to make secure, profitable transactions. At the same time many European investors pressured their governments to claim territory in Africa and Asia. There the desired political conditions were absent because rulers of indigenous polities were ambivalent toward foreign investment or hostile to it. The different attitude of European private sectors toward ex-colonies and what might be called prospective colonies partly explains why phase 3 metropoles did not try to reconquer independent countries in the Americas while simultaneously sponsoring conquest in Africa and Asia. An apparently inconsistent foreign policy was in fact quite consistent. It followed the maxim that profit seekers could do far better in areas that were colonies or had been so than in places never brought under metropolitan rule.

Some of the gains capitalists made from the colonies were spent for political ends at home. Money financed electoral campaigns and, whether placed on top of the table or under it, swayed politicians in their decision making. Lobbying efforts helped ensure that restrictive regulations and high tax rates were not imposed or, if on the books, not assiduously enforced.[25] In these ways business interests maintained the high level of influence over—and autonomy from—the public sector that has long marked west European societies.

—*European economic development was stimulated.*

It is beyond the scope of this book to estimate how much the colonies contributed to European economic growth. Some scholars conclude that the impact was significant, others that on balance it was negligible.[26] The more modest goal here is to trace how resources extracted from colonies stimulated metropolitan growth and structural change. At issue is the nature if not the magnitude of the contribution.

Two caveats are in order. Colonies varied enormously in the capacity to assist development outside their borders. Clearly, much depended on factor endowments, population, location, and the role (if any) of settlers. Moreover, the most a colony could contribute were *potentially* productive resources. There was no guarantee that potential would be realized. For evidence of missed opportunities one has only to observe the Habsburgs, who squandered vast supplies of New World bullion on wars and anti-Reformation propaganda campaigns. Whether a metropole made good use of its empire's resources depended on how its society, polity, and economy were structured.

An obvious rationale for colonies was that they supplied valued commodities unobtainable at home. Cinnamon, pepper, tobacco, tea, coffee, cocoa, and cane sugar were consumed by growing numbers of Europeans. Other commodities were inputs in manufacturing operations. Cotton and tropical dyes were essential components in Britain's early textile-based industrialization. Tin, rubber, chrome, copper, bauxite, and petroleum were likewise crucial at later stages of European industrial development. Gum arabic was used in the manufacture of textiles, paper, medicines, confections, and cosmetics. Palm oil literally lubricated the wheels of industry and, as an ingredient in soap, kept the industrial work force clean. Colonies were important sources of all these commodities, in some instances the only areas where they could be obtained. Political control over the source increased assurance of future access and made it easier for metropolitan manufacturers to invest large sums in factories dependent on imported inputs.

Slave labor in phase 1 plantation colonies kept production costs of sugar, indigo, tobacco, and cotton artificially low, enabling the emerging European middle class to consume more of these commodities. In *Capitalism and Slavery* Eric Williams shows how profits amassed by slave traders and owners of West Indian sugar plantations were invested in new technologies. Capital from the West Indian trade financed Boulton and Watt, the first firm to manufacture the steam engine.[27]

Government policies regulating trade between Britain and India gave early industrialization a boost. Lightweight, brightly colored cotton cloths imported from India, known as calicoes, became popular in the early eighteenth century and threatened English wool interests. Responding to pressure, Parliament in 1721 passed the Calico Act prohibiting display or consumption of printed cotton goods. This constructed a barrier behind which the infant industry of cotton textile manufacturing, using imported raw cotton, got its start.[28] Given the critical importance of cotton textiles to the first Industrial Revolution, what might have happened had free-trade principles been applied and Indian competition not been restricted? A century later the East India Company took the opposite approach and removed duties on British textiles entering India. This assured Lancashire's mills a valuable overseas market and further undercut competition from Indian handloom weavers. Had Indians set tariffs on goods entering their country they would presumably have acted to protect endangered domestic interests in the way that Parliament did. But the British were in charge at home *and* in India. Tariff policies in both settings had the effect of industrializing one country and pushing the other toward rural stagnation.

In both the colonial and independence eras, settler communities were closely tied to the European economy as exporters of primary products and avid importers of the latest consumer goods. To the extent that settlers and their descendants became wealthier overseas than if they had not emigrated, they stimulated Europe's development by spending additional income on its exports.

—*Empire helped create and reinforce a superiority complex.*

In many situations Europeans quickly and easily subdued indigenous peoples.

Those early encounters took place not simply across lines of racial and cultural difference but also across the gap of power inequality. Europeans found it difficult to separate observations about difference from those about inequality—and many observers had an active interest in blurring that very distinction. It was but a short mental leap for people superior in power to infer that they were superior in intellect, morality, and civilization as well. The superiority complex served as a rationalization for colonial rule and, by reducing qualms over the rightness of dominating other people, was empowering in its own right.

The inequality built into cross-cultural encounters affected what European observers saw, did not see, and imagined or fantasized that they saw. More important, it affected the meaning of the observers' experience, which was then conveyed through words and pictures to a broad reading public at home. Edward Said's influential study *Orientalism* emphasized how perceptions shaped by power and self-interest distorted Europeans' views of themselves and the colonized Other. This idea is a leitmotif in the rapidly growing field of cultural and postcolonial studies.[29]

Power asymmetry reinforced a recurring human tendency to describe real or imagined cultural dissimilarities in normatively loaded language. European travelers sometimes used complimentary terms to describe people they met. Political theorists relying on travelers' reports sometimes emphasized positive features, as when they referred to the nobility and generosity of New World peoples. But more often what was strange to the traveler and armchair philosopher was described as repulsive, barbaric, irrational, and uncivilized. Or unfamiliar customs were deemed bizarre, implying that their practitioners were not fully human.

Colonial rule made negative stereotyping easy and relatively costless. The deepening and broadening of dominance described in part 4 increased the range of settings in which Europeans could express a superiority complex without fear of retaliation. Their control of the means of coercion made it dangerous for colonial subjects to question, much less confront, the complex's assumptions and claims. When Europeans could largely shape the form cross-cultural interaction took, they came to believe that negative stereotypes were not instances of self-serving prejudice but documentable matters of fact. The ruling caste's prejudices, in other words, were reinforced by judgments made after observing group relations in the colonial situation.

How the superiority complex was phrased and justified varied over time and from one metropole to another. But a theme constantly emphasized from phase 1 well into the twentieth century was that Europeans were especially skilled at governance. They took pride in a long tradition of founding polities, ranging in scale from Greek and Italian city-states to postfeudal national states to the vast Roman empire. A colonial administration, once installed, gave Europeans additional cause to believe they were good rulers. For not only did they know how to govern themselves; they also knew how to rule alien people in places far from the civilizational center. What is more, went the claim, Europeans knew how to govern others better than others could ever govern themselves. Colonial rule did its subjects a favor for which they should be grateful.

Sentiments and values nurtured on imperial frontiers were conveyed to people who never left home. Colonial rule shaped Europe's self-image by juxtaposing its civilized self to the uncivilized existence of subordinate peoples abroad.

This legacy carried over to the postcolonial era. Just as formerly colonized peoples struggled to throw off an internalized inferiority complex, so those who once ran the world found it difficult to abandon the belief that they were truly superior to everyone else.

—*Empire contributed to a guilt complex.*

Some Europeans appealed to core values of Western civilization in bitterly criticizing what their compatriots were doing overseas. There is a long tradition of carefully documented attacks by insiders on European greed, cruelty, exploitation, sexual misconduct, and hypocrisy. It dates to the first years of settlement in the Americas with the sermons of Father Antonio Montesino and the impassioned lobbying of Bishop Bartolomé de Las Casas. It can be traced through the writings of William Wilberforce and other Abolitionist crusaders to the nineteenth-century Dutch administrator and novelist Eduard Douwes Dekker to twentieth-century critics like E. D. Morel, André Gide, Norman Leys, Fenner Brockway, and Jean-Paul Sartre. Critics did not necessarily conclude that the colonial enterprise should be abandoned: Las Casas and Morel called for reform despite impressive evidence they themselves amassed that human rights abuses were intrinsic to foreign rule. In some cases, however, Europeans supported movements for independence against their own countries. Annie Besant and Rev. Charles Andrews were active in Indian nationalist circles in phase 4. Sartre and Brockway were articulate, impassioned critics of French and British colonial policies, respectively.

With the final collapse of empire in phase 5, a desire to atone for past sins has probably played a role, however sublimated, in the foreign policy of former metropoles. It may have been a factor in the establishment of foreign aid programs. It may also account for reluctance by many European officials and intellectuals to criticize the human rights violations of new-state leaders.[30] One sees this, for example, in the cordial relations between France's presidents—from de Gaulle through Mitterand—and leaders of repressive military and one-party regimes in francophone Africa.

A sense of guilt does not entail the absence of a sense of superiority. The two may coexist, as when Europeans (or westerners generally) use demanding moral standards to criticize their own countries' domestic and foreign policies and lower standards to evaluate non-European regimes. That the superiority complex continues into the present is most unmistakable in the rhetoric of some on the political right. The complex is more subtly manifested but nonetheless present in the double moral standards sometimes employed by the left.

GLOBAL IMPACTS

—An interstate system once confined to Europe has been enlarged to cover the world.

The combination of European imperialism and anticolonial nationalism globalized the idea and institutions of the territorial, bureaucratic, sovereign state. The original interstate system, whose existence was so conducive to imperialism, was transformed by the addition of polities whose very formation signaled imperial decline. Yet characteristics of the old system persist in the new, expanded version: the exchange of diplomats, for example, the principle of diplomatic immunity, and treaty-drafting conventions. International negotiations are for the most part conducted in metropolitan languages. The idea that sovereign states are equal in key respects despite glaring inequalities in others is universally accepted. Thus, state A is accorded the legal and moral right not to be invaded by state B even if A is small, poor, and weak while B is a great power. This egalitarian feature of the old system is particularly welcomed by new states, the great majority of which are far poorer and weaker than their former rulers. Application of the one state–one vote principle in international meetings gives each unit a sense that it matters, whatever its resources or the capacity of its rulers to govern.[31] Today's global system, like the old European one, is ultimately anarchic and potentially unstable. Yet widespread acceptance of multiple sovereignties tends to reduce insecurity and routinizes relations among the system's component parts.

Colonialism had contradictory effects on the numbers of units in the interstate system. As just noted, it led eventually to a far larger and more geographically dispersed membership than obtained in a system initially confined to one region. But European rule decimated hundreds of polities by incorporating them, often summarily and brutally, within colonial boundaries. Among the most obvious instances were New Spain, British India, the Dutch East Indies, Nigeria, and German East Africa. Had the system evolved to include all indigenous polities functioning when Europeans first encountered them, there might be one or two thousand states today. It is difficult to imagine how—or whether—that many units could regulate their relations in any meaningful way. Paradoxically, forcible incorporation of myriad small polities into larger ones during earlier centuries may have made possible relatively stable interactions among sovereign states in modern times.

—Empires stimulated an enormous rise in long-distance trade, resulting in a global economy.

The volume and variety of commodities transported from one continent to another rose dramatically during the centuries of European dominance. One should not attribute this phenomenon wholly to colonial rule. Europe's private profit sectors were more directly involved in overseas commerce than public sectors, and maritime trade did not always require the flag. But metropolitan governments did a great deal to influence the extent, direction, and composition of trade. This was most obvious with mercantilist policies in phase 1, but no less important in phases 3 and 4 when decisions based on a Eurocentric interpretation of comparative advantage created and then reinforced the concentration of industrial production in metropoles.

The persistent tendency of Europeans to assert formal control over other parts of the world is itself the clearest indication that, despite the technological and economic advantages they so often enjoyed over others, in the final analysis they lacked confidence in the workings of the free—that is, uncoerced and politically unregulated—market. Public sector institutions were set up to ensure a higher prominence for trade and to guarantee Europeans a higher portion of gains from it than would have occurred had outcomes been driven by the market alone.

Much is made today of globalization as if it were a recent phenomenon. To say this is to ignore the history of most of the world. For most ex-colonial countries a high degree of openness and vulnerability to economic trends elsewhere—including flows of capital and advanced technology—has been a reality for centuries. Political independence may be a necessary condition for changing an inheritance of economic dependence, but it is by no means a sufficient condition. Trade patterns between an industrialized north and a primary product-producing south are difficult to change in the postcolonial era, in large part because they have deep roots in the formative colonial stage of the globalization process.

—Overseas empires spread a transformative stance toward nature. As rapid economic development becomes a universal goal, an urgent question is whether the physical environment can withstand the sustained assaults mounted on it in all countries.

The development ethos pervading today's world can be traced to the explore-control-utilize syndrome impelling five centuries of European expansion. Settler nationalists in phase 2 and non-European nationalists later (with the virtually unique exception of Gandhi) did not critique this syndrome. Instead they enthusiastically adopted it, viewing independence as a way to continue and if possible accelerate the transformation of nature. This point was eloquently made by the Indonesian nationalist Soetan Sjahrir in his intellectual biography *Out of Exile:*

For me, the West signifies forceful, dynamic, and active life. It is a sort of Faust that I admire, and I am convinced that only by a utilization of this dynamism of the West can the East be released from its slavery and subjugation. The West is now teaching the East to regard life as a struggle and a striving, as an active movement to which the concept of tranquillity must be subordinated. . . . [Struggle and striving] signify a struggle against nature, and that is the essence of the struggle: man's attempt to subdue nature and to rule it by his will.[32]

The larger the number of people holding this view, the more must one question the confident assumption of earlier eras that nature can be manipulated with impunity. The harmful environmental consequences of colonial development were manageable for the most part. The same cannot be said of the postcolonial world, in which ex-metropoles and ex-colonies alike redesign the landscape so their citizens can live longer, more comfortable lives. Might nature, under continuous and accelerating assault, launch a lethal counterattack? The triumph of the syndrome that drove imperialism may at some point become a Pyrrhic victory.

17
The Moral Evaluation of Colonialism

Was European colonial rule good or bad? The subject matter invites normative judgments, for at issue are the lives and livelihoods, the well-being and worldviews of hundreds of millions of human beings. People do not need to know much about colonialism to hold strong opinions about its moral status.

It is one thing to say that an ethical evaluation of colonialism is appropriate. It is quite another to decide how to carry out that evaluation in a thoughtful, sensitive, consistent, and thorough way. The good or bad question is deceptively simple. Even if one retains the narrow definition of colonialism used in chapter 16, the subject's scope is so vast and the forms colonial rule took so varied that rendering an overall verdict seems fruitless. Edmund Burke told Parliament that "I do not know the method of drawing up an indictment against a whole people." Is there a method of indicting—or vindicating—the peoples and governments of western Europe for an immense range of activities spanning several centuries? The answer, from the standpoint of social science methodology, is that there is not. But from a broader standpoint this response is unsatisfactory, especially if it excuses one from moral reflection on the past. People make ethical judgments not only on personal and interpersonal matters but also on large-scale phenomena like imperialism and colonialism. The issue is not whether they should engage in macro-level moralizing but how carefully and persuasively they do so. What is their frame of reference? What standards do they use? What evidence do they cite to support their position? How well do they deal with opposing viewpoints?

One way to proceed is to convene, as it were, leading critics and defenders of empire and construct a debate between them. Placing their arguments next to one another permits a close examination and critique of each side's evidence, logic, normative standards, and visions of what might have happened had overseas empires not existed. One can see whether critics and defenders directly engage or talk past each other, are deeply and irreconcilably at odds or agree on many points. The imagined debate that follows shows that protagonists argue past each other much of the time, each side ignoring the claims of the other when it is convenient to do so. This implies that if both sides addressed the same features of colonialism, took evidence from the same historical cases, and were prepared to accept each other's counterfactual assumptions, they would find they were not as far apart as they think they are.

WHERE DO CRITICS AND DEFENDERS DISAGREE?

In constructing this imagined debate I rely heavily on twentieth-century authors located at one end or the other of the spectrum of informed opinion. Although their examples are taken mainly from Asian and African territories acquired in phase 3, the basic arguments apply to other times and places as well. Prominent critics include Aimé Césaire, Walter Rodney, Frantz Fanon, Kwame Nkrumah, and Andre Gunder Frank. Among prominent defenders are P. T. Bauer, L. H. Gann and Peter Duignan, Alan Burns, Margery Perham—and, earlier in the century, Albert Sarraut and Frederick Lugard.[1] I then turn to authors occupying a middle ground. Some conduct cost-benefit analyses and identify features on both sides of the ledger. Others stress the moral ambiguities and contradictions inherent in colonial rule.[2]

Critics and defenders of empire accentuate their differences. But agreement exists and should be identified because it shows that the debate is not all-encompassing. The two sides concur that colonial rule should be judged by whether it helped or harmed the non-European subject population. Neither side disputes that governments and private interests in metropoles acquired valuable resources that would not have been as readily or cheaply available had empires not been in place. Neither side denies that European settlers generally fared quite well, at least after the initial hardships of relocating in strange lands. There is debate over how much metropolitans and settlers gained in income, wealth, and status, with gains set far higher by critics than by defenders. But from the standpoint of moral judgment this disagreement is immaterial. Defenders do not argue that colonialism was justified solely or primarily because Europeans benefited from it. Rather, they try to show that, in situations in which one assumes or can demonstrate that rulers did gain, non-European subjects also benefited. For critics the key issue is what happens to non-European peoples—and does not happen to them, to the extent that resources non-Europeans rightfully possessed were wrongly taken away. Since both sides concentrate on how the colonized fared under European rule, so shall I.

To a surprising degree critics and defenders concur over factual matters. When disputes over facts do arise they are treated as peripheral to the main argument. In one such dispute, the French government estimated the number of Algerian Muslims killed following the Sétif massacre of 1945 at 1,020 to 1,300, while nationalists in

Algeria and other Arab countries placed the toll between 45,000 and 50,000.[3] But numbers were not really, or ultimately, the issue. Algerian nationalists would have been outraged had a thousand compatriots been killed. And even if the French government had conceded the 50,000 figure, officials would have defended their actions as the regrettably necessary response to a savage, unprovoked uprising in one of France's *départements*. In order to highlight more important issues I assume that neither side disputes—or wants to spend time disputing—the other's factual claims.

Disagreements arise over the following issues:

—Definition and measurement of terms

A major reason colonial rule was unjust, according to critics, was that it facilitated and profited from extensive economic exploitation of non-Europeans. Defenders do not disagree that exploitation, when it occurs, is morally repugnant. Rather, they argue that exploitation did not occur or was far less extensive than critics assert and that in many instances colonized peoples benefited from foreign rule. How can the two sides diverge on this basic point if, as I posit, they do not part company over the facts? The answer is that they have different understandings of "exploitation," based on differing conceptions of how value is added in economic activity. Critics emphasize the role non-European labor played in generating wealth and the colonial origin of natural resources that became marketable commodities. Critics charge that labor was systematically denied proper compensation, not only in systems employing slavery and forced labor but also in ostensibly free-market settings. Likewise, colonies were denied a just return on their natural resources when profits from resource extraction were reinvested or consumed elsewhere. Defenders, in contrast, stress factors of production supplied by the colonizers—capital, technology, organization, transnational market links—arguing that the distribution of gains from development accurately reflected the enormous contribution of these factors. No wrong was done if a metropole's public and private profit sectors enjoyed high rates of return on their investments in colonial development.

Critics and defenders also part company over how to measure exploitation. To take a simple hypothetical example, say both sides agree that table 17.1 accurately describes the per capita income of non-European residents of an island and of Europeans about to land there, just before initial contact. Fifty years after the island has become a colony the incomes of non-European and European residents are assessed. Assume agreement by both sides that changes over the five decades were due solely to activities of colonized and colonizers on the island and that these activities were not undertaken prior to foreign rule.

Critics see in these figures unassailable evidence of exploitation. Europeans gained three times more than indigenous people, and the income gap between the two groups rose from $300X$ to $700X$. Looking at the same figures, defenders would

TABLE 17.1.

	Per capita income	
	Before contact	Fifty years later
Indigenous people	100 (in currency X or its equivalent)	300 X
Europeans	400 X	1,000 X

see evidence not only that exploitation had not occurred but that the opposite was at work. Indigenous per capita income rose, so the colonized were better off than before contact. Indigenous people gained by a higher percentage over the precontact base than did Europeans (200 percent to 150 percent), and the ratio of indigenous to European income rose from 1:4 to 3:10. Different operational indicators of a term thus permit the two sides to keep arguing despite their agreement that exploitation is immoral.

Did colonial government contribute to economic exploitation? Critics point out that government's coercive powers were used to support private profit ventures, including land alienation by settlers. Where official policies had their intended effect of keeping indigenous labor costs below free-market levels, forcing people to carry out unwanted tasks, restricting the best-paying jobs and contracts and the most productive land to Europeans, undercutting local artisans through discriminatory tariff policies, and so forth, the public sector made possible otherwise unattainable levels of exploitation. Defenders see government using its coercive and legal powers to create orderly, predictable, relatively peaceful settings conducive to productive activity. Without protection for private property rights, they argue, far less European capital and technology would have been invested overseas, with results benefiting all parties.

Should exploitation be measured in subjective as well as objective terms? Suppose the hypothetical island's indigenous inhabitants did not consider themselves poor before contact but did do so afterward, because of their close proximity to far wealthier Europeans. A growing sense of impoverishment thus coincided with rising prosperity. For critics, the way people think and feel about their circumstances should count, in this case on the negative side of the ledger. Defenders tend to discount subjective factors as irrelevant or misleading, especially when objectively measurable indicators point in the opposite direction.

Disagreement over how much exploitation occurred leads critics and defenders to use different terms to describe conditions in ex-colonized countries. Critics refer to *underdevelopment,* seen as economic stagnation or regression linked to highly unequal distributional outcomes as a result of advanced capitalist countries' actions. In Rodney's words,

All of the countries named as "underdeveloped" in the world are exploited by others; and the underdevelopment with which the world is now preoccupied is a product of capitalist, imperialist and colonialist exploitation. African and Asian societies were developing independently until they were taken over directly or indirectly by the capitalist powers. When that happened, exploitation increased and the export of surplus ensued, depriving the societies of the benefit of their natural resources and labour.[4]

From this perspective, even if incomes of colonized people on the island rose from $100X$ to $300X$, the gap that matters is between $300X$ and the far higher income the colonized should have received had the surplus over subsistence not been so unfairly distributed and so much of it siphoned off to the metropole.

Defenders reject the concept of underdevelopment because it ignores the contributions of European factors of production, relies on questionable zero-sum assumptions, and depends too heavily on counterfactual speculation. Defenders prefer "development," referring to actual as opposed to hypothetical increases in per capita production and consumption.

An advantage of using these two terms is that semantic and measurement disagreements between critics and defenders are made explicit. The extent of disagreement is less clear when both sides use the same word—like "exploitation"—to point to different phenomena.

—*Selection of comparative frames of reference*

Evaluation is ultimately an act of comparison. In effect, one places phenomenon X next to a real or imagined scenario suggested by standard Y and concludes that X is better or worse than the situation derived from standard Y. Obviously, the standard selected can profoundly influence the judgment reached. The opposite can also be true. That is, people may start with their conclusions, then work backward to select the standard leading them toward those conclusions. Critics and defenders of colonialism are highly selective in choosing comparison standards, employing those that reinforce conclusions each side has already reached. For example, critics describe non-European societies in positive ways, leading the colonial experience to look bad by comparison. Defenders describe non-European societies in negative ways, enabling European takeovers to appear as an improvement over pre-colonial realities.

Here is the contrast as drawn by Césaire:

Every day that passes, every denial of justice, every beating by the police, every demand of the workers that is drowned in blood, every scandal that is hushed up, every punitive expedition, every police van . . . brings home to us the value of our old societies. They were communal societies, never societies of the many for the few. . . . They were democratic societies, always. They were cooperative societies, fraternal societies. I make a systematic defense of the societies destroyed by imperialism.[5]

While Rodney does not portray the past in such glowing terms, he stresses the organizational and technological achievements of African peoples, using Europeans' descriptions to support his argument:

> Indeed, the first Europeans to reach West and East Africa by sea were the ones who indicated that in most respects African development was comparable to that which they knew. To take but one example, when the Dutch visited the city of Benin they described it thus:
>
> "The town seems to be very great. When you enter into it, you go into a great broad street, not paved, which seems to be seven or eight times broader than the Warmoes street in Amsterdam. . . . These people are in no way inferior to the Dutch as regards cleanliness; they wash and scrub their houses so well that they are polished and shining like a looking glass."[6]

In contrast, defenders of colonialism use a standard relying heavily on worst-case scenarios. Their precolonial world is better described in Hobbesian than Rousseauian terms. Among features described are social practices repressed on humanitarian grounds when Europeans took over, including human sacrifice, slavery, killing of twins, persecution on allegations of witchcraft, widow burning, and live burial of criminals. Civil war, brigandage, anarchy, and despotism figure prominently in the story. Here is how Lord Lugard frames the comparison:

> When I recall the state of Uganda at the time I made the treaty in 1890 which brought it under British control, or the state of Nigeria ten years later, and contrast them with the conditions of today, I feel that British effort—apart from benefits to British trade—has not been in vain. In Uganda a triangular civil war was raging—Protestants, Roman Catholics, and Muslims, representing the rival political factions of British, French, and Arabs, were murdering each other. Only a short time previously triumphant paganism had burnt Christians at the stake and reveled in holocausts of victims. Today there is an ordered Government with its own native parliaments. Liberty and justice have replaced chaos, bloodshed, and war. The wealth of the country steadily increases.[7]

When compared with this panoply of evils European rule appears quite attractive.

Justifying British rule in India, Theodore Roosevelt wrote, "There is now little or no room for the successful freebooters, chieftains, and despots who lived in gorgeous splendor, while under their cruel rule the immense mass of their countrymen festered in sodden misery. But the mass of the people have been, and are, far better off than ever before, far better off than they would be if English control was overthrown or withdrawn."[8]

Critics regard the denial of self-government as one of colonialism's most pernicious features. In their view, forcibly preventing people from shaping their collective affairs is intrinsically wrong, regardless of whether popular engagement in civic life has results an outside observer may or may not like. Denial of self-government was especially obvious in colonial situations, where the power gap between rulers and ruled was marked by observable racial and cultural differences. Insult was added to injury when Europeans claimed colonized peoples were incapable of governing themselves. How could non-Europeans refute these insulting charges—or at least test their validity—when the very people leveling the accusation refused to permit experiments in self-rule?

While not denying that power passed at some point from a few non-Europeans to a few Europeans, defenders doubt that political participation was widespread in precolonial times, above all in large states where democratic norms were unknown and communications technologies too poorly developed to gauge popular opinion even if rulers wanted to do so. Defenders question whether, from a democratic perspective, replacement of autocratic indigenous monarchs by autocratic Europeans was a retrograde step.[9] Defenders add that when non-European rulers were culturally or physically distinct from their subjects—as in the Ottoman, Mughal, and Inca empires—their replacement by another group of foreigners, this time from Europe, did not constitute a loss of political autonomy. Autonomy had already been lost. Karl Marx, in some respects a defender of British rule in India as well as a penetrating critic, wrote of the subcontinent that "what we call its history, is but the history of the successive intruders who founded their empires on the passive basis of that unresisting and unchanging society. The question, therefore, is not whether the English had a right to conquer India, but whether we are to prefer India conquered by the Turk, by the Persian, by the Russian, to India conquered by the Briton."[10]

When discussing economic changes introduced under colonial rule, critics point to instances in which land and other productive assets used by indigenous peoples were confiscated. People deprived of their traditional means of livelihood suffered declines in living standards as well as a profound threat to their way of life. Critics contrast precolonial patterns in which people worked for their own benefit with colonial economies in which slave and corvée labor further enriched the most privileged elements.

Defenders tend to ignore such instances or minimize their economic and moral meaning, dwelling instead on the introduction of technologies, commodities, animals, and crops that improved living standards for many non-Europeans.

Adam Smith's chapter entitled "On Colonies" in *The Wealth of Nations* draws this comparison:

> Before the conquest of the Spaniards there were no cattle fit for draught either in Mexico or in Peru. The lama was their only beast of burden, and its strength seems to have been a good deal inferior to that of a common ass. The plough was unknown among them. They were ignorant of the use of iron. They had no coined money, nor any established instrument of commerce of any kind. Their commerce was carried on by barter. A sort of wooden spade was their principal instrument of agriculture. . . . In this state of things, it seems impossible, that either of those empires could have been so much improved or so well cultivated as at present, when they are plentifully furnished with all sorts of European cattle, and when the use of iron, of the plough, and of many of the arts of Europe, has been introduced among them. . . . In spite of the cruel destruction of the natives which followed the conquest, these two great empires are, probably, more populous now than they ever were before.[11]

Another way to evaluate European rule is to compare colonies with territories not formally taken over. This raises the question whether colonial rule was a necessary condition for sustained economic development in non-European regions. Twentieth-century critics and defenders alike concur that economic development is desirable.[12] They agree that economic and cultural interchange between Europeans and other peoples can have positive outcomes for all concerned. The debate is whether development would have taken place to the extent and at the pace it did had the informal influence of European merchants and missionaries not been reinforced by formal rule. Césaire writes of the nineteenth century that "the technical outfitting of Africa and Asia, their administrative reorganization, in a word, their 'Europeanization,' was (as is proved by the example of Japan) in no way tied to the European *occupation*. . . . the Europeanization of the non-European continents could have been accomplished otherwise than under the heel of Europe."[13] Japan's successful defensive modernization thus becomes a standard for comparison with territories deprived of similar opportunities for self-initiated development. For Césaire, Japan demonstrates that a bad means (colonialism) is not necessary for a good end (economic development).

In contrast, Gann and Duignan cite Ethiopia, where defensive modernization did not occur despite external security threats, as the standard for comparison with European accomplishments in Southern Rhodesia.[14] By implication the Ethiopian case shows that in many places modernization would not have taken place had Europeans not initiated it. Defenders throw out a challenge to critics: "If you accept modernization as a desirable goal, you may have to accept a means to attain it in materially and technically backward societies that you find abhorrent. If you reject the colonial means you should admit that you are also rejecting backward societies' most likely prospect of realizing a goal you favor."

Another way to draw comparisons is to contrast a society's experience of colonial rule with what one imagines its history would have been had it remained independent. There is no way, of course, to prove or disprove the validity of counterfactual thought experiments. But it is the very freedom to unfold a favored scenario without fear of contradiction that makes hypothetical speculation so attractive when contentious issues are debated. Nothing can prevent colonialism's critics from imagining a rosy alternative past, or its defenders from imagining a grim alternative one. In general, critics posit a non-European setting in which the costs of Europe's political dominance are absent but the benefits of its informal influence are present. This scenario leaves open the option of defensive modernization by indigenous leaders if only Europeans had not prematurely grabbed power. The Malaysian scholar Hussein Alatas writes,

> It was colonial bondage which blocked the flow of assimilation from the Western world. Had there been a free intercourse between independent Acheh and the Western world from the 16th century onward, Acheh and similarly other Indonesian states would have reached an advanced state of development by now. Instead, the Dutch destroyed Acheh by a prolonged war. Until now, Acheh has not recovered its former status. . . . Like Japan, Russia, Turkey, and Thailand, by the 19th century [Indonesian] states would have recognized the benefits of modern science and technology from the West, as they did recognize similar benefits from other societies in the past.[15]

In contrast, defenders assume that had Europeans not ruled, their presence in other sectors of overseas societies would have been minimal. The defenders' scenario is the Hobbesian state of nature allegedly obtaining in the precontact period. Defenders lament that colonial officials are not given credit for preventing bad things that would have occurred absent foreign rule. G. B. Masefield of Britain's Colonial Agricultural Service writes, "No glory attached to the service for the famines that never occurred, the pests and diseases that did not devastate crops, and the steep hillsides that were prevented from being exposed to the disaster of soil erosion by their painstaking labours."[16]

—*Emphasis on selected aspects of the colonial situation*

The vast scope of the colonial enterprise permits critics and defenders to focus on those features that strengthen their respective cases while deemphasizing or ignoring features stressed by the other side. Thus critics underscore psychological and cultural dimensions, above all else the legacy of humiliation and individual and collective self-hatred among the colonized. Loss of pride in one's culture and the declining integrity and autonomy of non-European cultural life under the triple assault are deemed among the most morally indefensible consequences of colonialism. Defenders spend virtually no time discussing such matters, focusing rather on European economic and technological accomplishments. During the first 50 years of rule in colony X, goes the usual defense, 3,100 miles of railroad track were laid, 16,480 children attended secondary schools, 6 new crops were introduced, and exports rose fourfold. These changes benefited everyone, including non-Europeans.[17]

This is a classic instance of protagonists arguing past each other. Critics emphasize subjective aspects of colonialism that are difficult to measure, while defenders cite readily measurable objective indicators. Critics praise cultural practices and values abandoned as societies set out toward European-style modernization. Defenders praise adoption of cultural practices and values consistent with modernization. Critics mourn the precipitate decline of cultural diversity. Defenders celebrate the global spread of a few cultures they consider superior and the cross-cultural communication made possible by widespread adoption of European languages. Critics talk about what happened *to* the colonized, defenders about what colonizers did *for* the colonized. Critics view the world from the ground-up perspective of subject peoples coping with deeply disruptive changes arbitrarily imposed by foreigners. Defenders view the world from the top-down perspective of rulers working diligently, under trying circumstances, to bring about progress in societies incapable of transforming themselves.

Césaire contrasts the way evaluation is framed by opposing sides:

> They talk to me about progress, about "achievements," diseases cured, improved standards of living. *I* am talking about societies drained of their essence, cultures trampled underfoot, institutions undermined, lands confiscated, religions smashed, magnificent artistic creations destroyed, extraordinary possibilities wiped out. They throw facts at my head, statistics, mileages of roads, canals, and railroad tracks. . . . I am talking about millions of men torn from their gods, their land, their habits, their life—from life, from the dance, from wisdom. . . . I am talking about millions of men in whom fear has been cunningly instilled, who have been taught to have an inferiority complex, to tremble, kneel, despair, and behave like flunkeys.[18]

Even when the two sides converge on the same topic and appeal to shared values, they manage to evade each other's arguments. Césaire and Rodney mourn the deaths of thousands in forced-labor railroad construction gangs. The French, writes Rodney, "got Africans to start building the Brazzaville to Pointe Noire railway, and it was not completed until 1933. Every year of its construction, some 10,000 people were driven to the site—sometimes from more than 1,000 kilometres away. At least 25% of the labour force died annually from starvation and disease."[19] On the other side, Gann and Duignan write that "an ordinary freight train used nowadays in Africa will do the work of 15,000 to 20,000 carriers for one-fifth to one-tenth the cost. The steam engine thus relieved the sweating African porter from his age-old labors. . . . Africa's scarce manpower could at last be used in pursuits more profitable to the economy than head porterage."[20]

These writers agree that reducing the burden of exhausting physical labor is a good thing. Critics correctly point out the increase in this kind of labor, leading to tragic loss of life, during the railroad's construction. Defenders correctly point out the reduction in heavy labor, leading to widely shared economic gains, after construction was completed. One side examines railroads before they were operative but not afterward; the other does the reverse. Neither directly engages valid observations made by the other.

Nor does either side seriously engage the problem of morally assessing technologies with multiple, contradictory uses. A rail line carries trade goods that undermine some occupations and foster others. It can end the economic and intellectual isolation of a hinterland and simultaneously integrate a colony with the international economy on unequal, dependent terms. Trains carry troops dispatched to crush a colonial rebellion and nationalists bent on mobilizing mass disaffection. Can condemnation or praise summarize the complex, often unintended impacts of new transport and communication technologies?

Railways, telegraphs, wireless, and the like, writes Jawaharlal Nehru in his autobiography, *Toward Freedom,*

> were welcome and necessary, and because the British happened to be the agents who brought them first, we should be grateful to them. But even these heralds of industrialism came to us primarily for the strengthening of British rule. They were the veins and arteries through which the nation's blood should have coursed, increasing its trade, carrying its produce, and bringing new life and wealth to its millions. It is true that in the long run some such result was likely, but they were designed to work for another purpose—to strengthen the imperial hold and to capture markets for British goods—which they succeeded in doing. I am all in favor of industrialization and the latest methods of transport, but sometimes, as I rushed across the Indian plains, the railway, that life-giver, has almost seemed to me like iron bands confining and imprisoning India.[21]

—Interpretation of Europeans' stated intentions

In assessing the morality of an action one can focus on the intentions of the actor or on the consequences of the act, whether intended or not. Critics and defenders of colonialism disagree on both counts, but their perspectives on intentionality are instructive. Critics highlight situations in which European motives are crudely self-serving or opposed to the rights and interests of colonized peoples. The implication is that colonialism cannot be good because the motives driving it are bad. Defenders highlight rulers' claims that they are trying to benefit their subjects, for example, by spreading a superior civilization, saving souls, stimulating economic growth, and bringing law and justice and order to societies lacking them. Colonialism cannot be all that bad, defenders imply, if many of the motives driving it are good—or are believed to be so by those whose behavior one is judging.

The debate is joined over statements justifying colonial rule on grounds of altruistic intentions. A typical formulation is by Sir John Malcolm, governor of Bombay in the early nineteenth century. Britain's aim in India, said Malcolm, is "to pour the enlightened knowledge of civilisation, the arts and sciences of Europe, over the land, and thereby improve the condition of the people."[22] Was this a typical example of hypocritical rhetoric, designed more to mislead than enlighten? Or did the governor genuinely believe what he was saying? If Malcolm was sincere, was this goal uppermost in his mind or far down on his list of reasons for Britain's presence? Supposing Malcolm was sincere and that the goal was primary, was it proper or improper to propose "pour[ing]" his country's civilization over the civilization(s) of another land? Critics and defenders disagree on all these counts, especially the last. Critics see Malcolm's project as ethnocentric, brazenly arrogant, and ignorant, hence morally indefensible. Defenders see the project as praiseworthy to the extent that Malcolm was motivated by the desire to do good, whether or not one shares his conception of the good. Defenders consider it inappropriate, if not unfair, retroactively to apply the enlightened standards of present-day times and places to the actions of a man in phase 2 Bengal. Defenders might add that policies consistent with Malcolm's goal were moral if they actually did "improve the condition of the people."

HOW FAR APART ARE CRITICS AND DEFENDERS?

The recurring tendency of critics and defenders to talk past each other rather than directly to challenge the other's assumptions and arguments suggests that their positions may not be as diametrically opposed as they imagine. Each side's emphasizing of certain aspects of the colonial situation while ignoring others implies an acknowledgment that its case is strongest on the issues stressed and weakest on those ignored. Likewise, when each side selects a comparative frame of reference that strengthens its position, it implicitly grants that alternative frames of reference might lead to other, unwelcome conclusions. For obvious tactical reasons the two sides prefer *not* to employ the same assumptions and comparative frameworks. But if they had to do so their views might converge.

Suppose both sides refrained from generalizing about colonialism as a single, unvarying phenomenon and focused on circumstances under which European rule was least (or most) justifiable. Critics and defenders might agree that each of the following conditions, if it obtained in a territory, would strengthen the case against colonial rule there. By extension, the case against foreign rule would be strongest if all these conditions obtained:

- Prior to takeover there were no customs violating basic human rights.
- Prior to takeover people governed themselves at the local level. If a larger political entity existed its elites were of the same race or culture as their subjects.
- Had Europeans not intervened politically, the territory would have had a good chance of modernizing under indigenous leaders.
- Policies of colonial rulers led to substantial loss of life among the indigenous population (massacres, planned starvation, deliberate introduction of fatal diseases, and so on).
- Colonial policies deprived indigenous peoples of land and other resources necessary to sustain familiar ways of life.
- Colonial rule was marked by high levels of forced labor, non-Europeans being compensated at rates well below those they would have received in a free labor market.
- Forced labor was legally reinforced by slavery.
- Virtually all gains from economic activity accrued to Europeans.
- Non-European per capita income and other quality-of-life indicators fell over time.
- The value of assets transferred from the metropole and invested in the colony was dwarfed by the value of assets transferred to the metropole.
- Europeans did little to develop indigenous human resources over and above whatever maximized their economic gain.
- Non-Europeans were systematically discriminated against in recruitment to high-paying positions in all sectors.
- Rulers were contemptuous of the race, cultural practices, and historical accomplishments of peoples they ruled, leading many among the colonized to internalize an inferiority complex.
- Rulers failed to introduce institutions permitting subjects to air grievances on a regular basis and in a peaceful manner. Opponents of official policies were harshly repressed.

Critics and defenders would probably agree that the case for colonialism would be strongest if these conditions were absent or the circumstances reversed. Thus people diverging in their overall evaluation of colonialism nonetheless share a substantial set of values.

EVALUATION BETWEEN THE EXTREMES

Not all writers cluster around the far ends of the opinion spectrum. Many occupy positions between the extremes in portraying colonialism as having both costs and benefits. Exemplifying this balance-sheet approach is Kenneth Kaunda, Zambia's first president, who writes of

> a strange mixture of advantages and disadvantages, curses and blessings. Colo-nialism brought greater freedom yet more servitude. The peoples of Africa were freed from certain enemies—disease, ignorance, superstition and slavery—the horizons of their lives were lifted, offering new areas of choice and fresh possibil-ities of material and spiritual enrichment. Yet the colonialism which threw open certain doors slammed others shut. It engendered in the African peoples a deepening awareness of servitude. New forms of power cast a web about them, hemming them in and subjecting them to strange constraints. . . . all too often [the dominant position Europeans held in positions of leadership and control] was transformed into a philosophy of racial dominance. It appeared that the colonialists had freed them in order to make them servants.[23]

The Congo's first premier, Patrice Lumumba, shifted from one end of the spectrum to the other as political conditions changed. Writing in the mid-1950s, when he believed that Belgium would develop the country in the interests of all and that *évolués* like himself would serve as intermediaries between top officials and the populace, Lumumba was almost obsequious in praise of Belgian rule:

> To whom do we owe our liberation from that odious trade practiced by the bloodthirsty Arabs and their allies, those inhuman brigands who ravaged the country?
>
> At a time when our people were suffering from these atrocities, when they were being decimated by sleeping sickness and . . . when thousands of the inhabitants of the country were being carried away in chains to be sold like cattle in gruesome markets . . . Belgium, moved by a very sincere and humanitarian idealism, came to our help and, with the assistance of doughty native fighters, was able to rout the enemy, to eradicate disease, to teach us and to eliminate certain barbarous practices from our customs, thus restoring our human dignity and turning us into free, happy, vigorous, civilized men. . . .
>
> As regards the mistakes that were made, I have already said that they are inherent in any human activity, be it in Africa, Europe, or any other country of the world. . . . Let us stop railing against these few mistakes.[24]

Subsequent events in the Congo and elsewhere in Africa profoundly radi-calized Lumumba's views. Responding at Independence Day celebrations to a pa-tronizing address by King Baudouin, the premier departed from the program to launch an impassioned attack on the departing rulers:

> [Our struggle was] noble and just, a struggle indispensable for ending the humil-iating slavery that was imposed upon us by force.

Considering what we went through during 80 years of colonial rule, our wounds are still too fresh and too painful to be erased from memory. We have known exhausting labor, extracted in exchange for wages too low to enable us to satisfy our hunger, or decently clothe and house ourselves, or raise our children as loved ones.

We have experienced sarcastic remarks, insults, beatings morning, noon, and night, because we were niggers [nègres]. Who can forget that a black person was addressed as "tu"—most certainly not as one would speak to a friend—but because the honorific "vous" was reserved only for whites? . . .

We have known that in the towns there were magnificent homes for the whites and ramshackle huts for the blacks, that blacks couldn't be admitted to the cinemas, the restaurants, and the stores designated for Europeans. . . .

Finally, who can forget the gunshots that killed so many of our brothers, the prison cells into which were brutally thrown those who refused to submit any more to a system of oppression and exploitation?[25]

A regime that at one point was perceived as a liberator from slavery became at a later point, under other circumstances, an agent of enslavement.

Karl Marx's writings on the British in India illustrate a different kind of cost-benefit analysis. For Marx it is not that some of colonialism's features are positive and others negative, but that the same features assume variable meanings depending on the time frame employed to interpret them. The costs imposed by capitalism and British rule were severe in the short term. But they were also a necessary condition for India's eventual escape from economic and social stagnation. Marx subjects the greedy and often cruel behavior of the British to withering condemnation. But he does the same for traditional social structures the new rulers and industrial magnates are undermining. He writes in 1853 of India's villages,

These small family-communities were based on domestic industry, in that peculiar combination of hand-weaving, hand-spinning and hand-tilling agriculture which gave them self-supporting power. English interference having placed the spinner in Lancashire and the weaver in Bengal, or sweeping away both Hindoo spinner and weaver, dissolved these small semi-barbarian, semi-civilized communities, by blowing up their economic basis, and thus produced the greatest, and, to speak the truth, the only *social* revolution ever heard of in Asia.

Now, sickening as it must be to human feeling to witness these myriads of industrious patriarchal and inoffensive social organizations disorganized and dissolved into their units, thrown into a sea of woes, and their individual members losing at the same time their ancient form of civilization and their hereditary means of subsistence, we must not forget that these idyllic village communities, inoffensive though they may appear, had always been the solid foundation of Oriental despotism, that they restrained the human mind within the smallest possible compass, enslaving it beneath traditional rules, depriving it of all grandeur and historical energies. . . . We must not forget that these little communities were contaminated by distinctions of caste and by slavery, that they subjugated man to external circumstances instead of elevating man to be the sovereign of circumstances, that they transformed a self-developing social state into never-changing natural destiny, and thus brought about a brutalizing worship of nature, exhibiting its degradation in the fact that man, the sovereign of nature, fell down on his knees in adoration of Hanuman, the monkey, and Sabbala, the cow.

When uninvited outsiders use morally flawed methods to destroy a morally flawed social structure, what judgment should be passed? Marx continues:

England, it is true, in causing a social revolution in Hindostan, was actuated only by the vilest interests, and was stupid in her manner of enforcing them. But that is not the question. The question is, can mankind fulfill its destiny without a fundamental revolution in the social state of Asia? If not, whatever may have been the crimes of England she was the unconscious tool of history in bringing about the revolution.[26]

Marx advanced what might be termed the doctrine of regrettable yet progressive necessity. We hear echoes of this doctrine when Nehru writes decades later, "I feel sure that it was a good thing for India to come in contact with the scientific and industrial West. Science was the great gift of the West; India lacked this, and without it she was doomed to decay. The manner of our contacts was unfortunate and yet, perhaps, only a succession of violent shocks could shake us out of our torpor."[27]

In Marx's view, "England has to fulfill a double mission in India: one destructive, the other regenerating—the annihilation of old Asiatic society, and the laying of the material foundations of Western society in Asia." This latter mission did not preclude industrial development. On the contrary,

when you have once introduced machinery into the locomotion of a country, which possesses iron and coals, you are unable to withhold it from its fabrication. You cannot maintain a net of railways over an immense country without introducing all those industrial processes necessary to meet the immediate and current wants of railway locomotion, and out of which there must grow the application of machinery to those branches of industry not immediately connected with railways. The railway system will therefore become, in India, truly the forerunner of modern industry.[28]

These views placed Marx sharply at odds with his putative disciple Lenin. The German revolutionary theorist insisted that capitalist colonialism plays a historically progressive role, at least in its initial impact on agrarian societies. The Russian revolutionary activist insisted that the impact of advanced capitalism was harmful in all circumstances, and only harmful. Marx envisaged the diffusion of industrial development to some backward areas under colonialism; Lenin denied such a possibility. As the Marxist writer Bill Warren points out, Lenin's views prevailed in subsequent socialist and communist interpretations of capitalism even though Marx's analysis and predictions were far closer to the mark.[29]

A PERSONAL PERSPECTIVE

It would be convenient to side with balance-sheet moderates against proponents of either extreme position as a way to resolve—or evade—unending controversy. But this move is too convenient. I find myself returning to arguments between colonialism's critics and defenders, in large part because persuasive arguments are advanced by both sides. How can this be? One possibility is that I hold mutually incompatible values and am unwilling to make painful choices among them. Another is that, as argued earlier, the two sides are much closer than they imagine and that the zone of agreement between them is terrain I too wish to occupy. Whether explicitly or implicitly, critics and defenders agree that it is morally preferable for people to live rather than to die or be killed; to gain experience in collective self-government; to enjoy a rising material standard of living; and to choose how to allocate their labor rather than have it coercively extracted at below-market rates. Both sides value enhanced opportunities for personal advancement, free of arbitrary discrimination rejecting individuals on grounds irrelevant to a job's responsibilities. Both sides value the exchange of ideas, goods, and services across cultural and racial lines in an open, mutually beneficial manner. Critics affirm the right of individuals and groups not to be humiliated. Though defenders generally do not bring up this matter, their silence when it is raised implies tacit agreement that human dignity has intrinsic moral value.

These widely shared norms are appropriate ones to reframe as evaluation criteria. One way to proceed is to say that in times and places where colonial rule had, on balance, a positive effect on training for self-government, material well-being, labor allocation choices, individual upward mobility, cross-cultural communication, and human dignity, compared to the situation that would likely have obtained absent European rule, then the case for colonialism is strong. Conversely, in times and places where the effects of foreign rule in these respects were, on balance, negative compared to a territory's likely alternative past, then colonialism is morally indefensible.

This way of framing the issue takes into account the enormous variability of colonial situations and permits ethical judgments distinguishing one metropole from another, one time period from another, and one colonized society from another. Using the self-government criterion, for example, one can conclude that in colonies of occupation Britain did a distinctly better job than other metropoles because representative institutions were available through some variant of the Westminster parliamentary model. By the labor allocation criterion, regimes permitting the slave trade and enforcing domestic slavery were worse than regimes, from phase 3 onward, that outlawed such practices. By the same criterion, colonies that routinely relied on forced labor were more oppressively governed than colonies that did not.

By the material well-being standard, a colony in which indigenous claims to land were respected and non-European incomes rose was better governed than one in which land was alienated and non-European living standards fell. A colony with minimal prospects for modernization under indigenous leadership, whose indigenous incomes were raised by investment of European capital and technology, was better administered than a colony in which the opposite conditions applied.

By the human dignity standard, a regime practicing overt discrimination on the basis of race—which may be considered invariant for a given individual and is presumably irrelevant to job performance—was more immoral than one practicing discrimination on cultural grounds, at least in cases in which cultural assimilation was possible. Both regimes were worse than one practicing less discrimination on either racial or cultural grounds. A colony whose rulers suppressed human sacrifice and widow burning was better governed than one in which such practices were tolerated.

There is, to be sure, plenty of room for dispute over the application of these criteria to particular situations. Even if critics and defenders agreed on what colonial rulers did in a certain time and place, they could still offer very dissimilar assessments of precolonial society. And they could invoke very different scenarios of what would have occurred had a society retained its autonomy. The grounds for contention are legion. Nonetheless, progress will have been made if people with widely divergent worldviews are willing to share criteria for making moral judgments.

Another approach is to assess how well colonial regimes, considered collectively, performed in each major issue area. The obvious problem here is overgeneralization: whatever is said might apply to an imagined "typical" situation but definitely not to all situations. This approach has the advantage, however, of permitting us to identify arenas in which European rulers frequently performed well and others in which their behavior was consistently indefensible. What follows is my attempt to draw up a moral balance sheet, proceeding from most positive to most reprehensible aspects of the overall record.

Colonial rulers performed best in the economic arena. The explore-control-utilize syndrome led them actively to manipulate the natural environment so as to enhance people's material well-being. By introducing capital, advanced technology, new flora and fauna, and profit-seeking individuals and institutions to overseas territories, Europeans took the lead in generating unprecedented wealth there. To the extent that these factors of production would not have been exported had Europeans not controlled the public sector, colonial rule can be considered close to a necessary condition for sustained economic growth. To the extent that wealth generation depended upon utilizing hitherto untapped resources, Europeans increased the productive capacity of colonies without depriving non-Europeans of resources they would have enjoyed absent foreign rule. In numerous instances—especially territories gaining independence in phase 5—such indicators of non-European well-being as per capita income, access to a wide range of consumer goods, literacy, availability of health facilities, and life expectancy were substantially higher when colonial rule ended than when it began.

The record was clearly worse when it came to distributing gains from growth. Because Europeans controlled the public as well as private profit sector and because the two sectors regularly collaborated for mutual benefit, Europeans could and did allocate themselves most of the benefits of development. In effect they unilaterally decided that factors of production they contributed should be generously compensated while the labor contributions of local people should be assigned low priority. A related distributional issue is geographical: a high proportion of the profits from colonial natural and human resources was sent to Europe and not consumed or productively reinvested in lands generating these profits.

The record was mixed with respect to labor allocation choices and personal upward mobility. Slavery and forced labor severely constrained peoples' freedom to work for their own benefit and deprived them of income they should have earned from their labors. Discriminatory policies limited upward mobility on grounds that were arbitrary and unrelated to personal qualifications or performance. On the other hand, economic development opened up new occupational options. Even when discrimination limited access to top positions in sectoral institutions, the existence of these institutions created new opportunities for advancement in low- and middle-level ranks.

The colonial record was mixed but, on balance, poor with respect to cross-cultural communication. Diffusion of European languages permitted people from diverse backgrounds who otherwise would not have understood each other to share a lingua franca. Diffusion of literacy and numeracy to societies lacking them permitted a wider expression of ideas across barriers of time and space. All too frequently, however, communication was a one-way street: Europeans commanded, but they did not listen. They insisted that colonial subjects assimilate to their culture while looking askance at assimilation in the opposite direction. When visible differences of race and culture were closely linked to substantial inequalities of power, wealth, and status, the colonized ran a terribly high risk if they dared speak candidly to their rulers. The situation for people on both sides of the dividing line is aptly summarized by an African proverb: "I cannot hear what you are saying, because who you are is thundering in my ears."

The overall record is uneven but generally poor when it comes to training for self-government. This is not surprising, for administrators had an active interest not only in making key policy decisions but also in retaining the power to make them. Metropoles varied greatly in the training function. Britain did considerably better than Portugal and Belgium, which refused to acknowledge self-government as a legitimate goal and did virtually nothing to prepare subject populations for it. But even the British record is mixed. Where settlers were present indigenous prospects for autonomy were severely set back, permanently and fatally so in North America and Australasia. Britain's indirect rule policies often had the effect, intended or not, of making self-government at the colonywide level more problematic.

On the positive side, colonial public sector institutions operated over a wider area and affected far more people than did most precolonial stateless societies. Local communities with poorly institutionalized governance mechanisms cannot hope to survive in a world of states. Colonialism extended the "self" in self-government far beyond the level of face-to-face interaction. It was the colonial state, moreover, that nationalist movements targeted for capture. Nationalists were able to use available civil and military bureaucracies to govern large areas once they replaced Europeans in top policy posts. In a sense, colonial sectoral institutions played a positive historic role by being vulnerable to capture and redirection by independence movements.

Among the most reprehensible aspects of colonialism, in my judgment, were its deliberate, systematic, and sustained assaults on human dignity. The assertions of cultural and racial superiority accompanying European rule had devastating effects on the self-respect of many peoples. In myriad, unsubtle ways rulers violated the right of their subjects not to be individually and collectively demeaned. The point was well put in a memorandum from one English official to another in early nineteenth-century India: "Foreign conquerors have treated the natives with violence, and often with great cruelty, but none has treated them with so much scorn as we; none has stigmatised the whole people as unworthy of trust, as incapable of honesty, and as fit to be employed only where we cannot do without them."[30] The harmful effects of such attitudes were further magnified when colonized peoples learned the lesson too well and came to accept the charge that they were indeed inferior. This psychological complex hampered their will and limited their capacity to live full, satisfying lives.

The imperial project consumed the lives of millions of human beings and blighted the lives of millions more. Its worst aspects—the transatlantic slave trade, plantation slavery, forced labor, sexual exploitation—should not be forgotten or excused. The forests of the Amazon and Congo basins were killing fields, as were the Banda islands and Tasmania and lands inhabited by Araucanians, Pequots, and Hereros. A recurring corollary of land acquisition by settlers was that indigenous peoples deprived of access to land lost inherited ways of life and patterns of thought and belief as well. Alienated lands should be thought of as dying fields. Things fell apart for non-Europeans—many things—under the triple assault. But colonialism was not just the sum total of its worst-case scenarios. New crops, medicines, and occupations extended the life spans and enhanced the welfare of millions of subject peoples. New ideas and beliefs were not only comforting and enlightening but also empowering.

These personal assessments may or may not resonate with other people. By its very nature European colonialism ensures continuing controversy not only over its causes, characteristics, and consequences but also over its morality. The challenge in today's postcolonial era is to frame the debate so that arguments are more informed and directly engaged, assumptions and normative standards more explicit, than they were in the past when west European powers confidently strode the world.

APPENDIX
SPATIAL AND TEMPORAL DIMENSIONS
OF THE OVERSEAS EMPIRES

Listed here are the 188 states belonging to the United Nations on January 1, 2000. Of these, 125 are countries outside of Europe that were once colonies of one or more European metropoles. Bold and light lines mark the duration of imperial rule in these countries. Also listed is Tuvalu, an island chain that gained independence from Great Britain in 1978 but did not join the United Nations until 2000.

Each vertical bar represents two decades, beginning with 1460–79. A country has a line for a twenty-year period if a portion of its currently defined territory—beyond small coastal enclaves—was governed by a metropole during part or all of that period. The test of governance is whether officials appointed by metropolitan authorities (a government or a government-approved charter company) collected taxes or imposed some degree of order through recognizable bureaucratic structures and were formally authorized to control a territory's foreign relations as well as to regulate aspects of its domestic affairs. For more on the definitions of colony and metropole, see chapter 2.

Deciding when colonial rule begins is problematic, especially in the Old World during phase 1. Contestable judgment calls are unavoidable whatever one's criteria. One reason I use twenty-year segments rather than assigning specific starting dates is to avoid conveying an inappropriately concise impression of the takeover process. Even this arrangement risks making a process that was often gradual and subtle appear more precipitate—and more obvious to the parties involved—than it actually was.

For small islands I take the year of European arrival if this is marked by territorial claims and/or the start of continuous settler presence. Where the initial European presence on a larger island or continental mainland involved control of a coastal port, I focus on the period when Europeans exercised governmental powers *outside* the original enclave rather than on the date a port city was founded or taken over. Thus I date colonial rule in India from the 1750s, when the English East India Company began collecting taxes in Bengal, not from the early 1500s, when Portugal carved out trading enclaves on the Malabar coast. The colonial era in the East Indies is dated from the 1680s (Dutch control over the Javanese sultanates of Mataram and Bantam), not from the founding in 1619 of the company's administrative center, Batavia, or from early sixteenth-century Portuguese spice-trading activities.

These criteria generally understate the duration of European informal influence overseas, since even a tiny enclave could have substantial influence on its hinterland. Examples were the slave-trading "factories" along West Africa's coast from the sixteenth through nineteenth centuries. On the other hand, the criteria overestimate the duration of formal colonial rule in many territories because inhabitants of hinterland areas may have evaded European control for many decades after people in more accessible regions had become colonial subjects.

A country's final bold segment marks the transition from colonial status to independence. Independence could be dated from the year a territory's leaders declared it, the metropole acknowledged it, or the first sovereign state officially recognized it. In the vast majority of phase 5 cases these three criteria produce identical results. Where results diverge I pick the self-selected date, if only because this is what a country's citizens celebrate. The independence date for the United States is listed as 1776, and that for Haiti as 1804, even though Britain and France did not formally acknowledge the change in status until 1783 and 1825, respectively.

A United Nations member state that was part of a larger unit when that unit became independent is assigned the latter's independence date. Thus, Central American countries which in the colonial era were components of New Spain are deemed independent when Mexico broke from Spain, not several years later when they broke from Mexico. Bangladesh is assigned the date for Pakistan, Singapore the date for Malaysia.

Tanzania consists of two territories—Tanganyika and Zanzibar—that united after gaining independence separately.

A country has a light line for the period when it was a quasi colony. This category covers a wide range of relationships with one metropole, Great Britain. I classify Canada, Australia, New Zealand, and South Africa as shifting from colonial to quasi-colonial status when domestic control of internal affairs in these settler-led territories was formally recognized by Dominion status: 1867 for Canada, 1901 for Australia, 1907 for New Zealand, 1910 for South Africa. These states' de facto independence is set at 1931, when the Statute of Westminster relinquished London's control over foreign affairs. Cyprus and Egypt are considered quasi colonies during the decades when they were technically under Ottoman suzereignty while their foreign relations were determined by agents of the British Crown. Their ambiguous status ended with formal annexation by Britain at the start of World War I.

Three states—Kuwait, Qatar, and the United Arab Emirates—were not formally incorporated into overseas empires and are not counted among the United Nations' 125 ex-colonies. But they are classified as quasi colonies because their rulers negotiated treaties retaining control over domestic affairs while ceding jurisdiction over foreign affairs to Great Britain. This status lasted while these treaties were in force. Afghanistan, Bhutan, and Oman might be listed as quasi colonies, on these same grounds, for short periods in late phase 3 and phase 4. But I do not do so because Britain's control over their foreign relations appears to have been more tenuous than with the Arab sheikhdoms.

Countries attaining independence from a non-European state following a period of European rule have a bold line only for the years when governed by a European metropole. These countries are Cuba (Spain to 1898; United States), Philippines to 1898 (United States), Eritrea (Italy to World War II, British trusteeship to 1952; Ethiopia), and German possessions turned over to League of Nations mandatory powers following World War I: Papua New Guinea (including former German New Guinea; Australia), Namibia (South Africa), and several Pacific island chains: Marshall Islands (Japan; U.S. after World War II), Micronesia (Japan; U.S. after World War II), Nauru (Australia, with United Kingdom and New Zealand), Palau (Japan; U.S. after World War II), and Samoa (New Zealand). Ethiopia excepted, all non-European powers that were terminal colonial rulers were themselves once European colonies.

	1460–79	1500–19	1600–19	1700–19	1800–19	1900–19	1980–99
Afghanistan							
Albania							
Algeria						▬	
Andorra							
Angola						▬	
Antigua and Barbuda			▬				
Argentina		▬					
Armenia							
Australia					▬		
Austria							
Azerbaijan							
Bahamas							
Bahrain		▬			▬		
Bangladesh				▬			
Barbados			▬				
Belarus							
Belgium							
Belize			▬				
Benin						▬	
Bhutan							
Bolivia		▬					
Bosnia and Herzegovina							
Botswana						▬	
Brazil		▬					
Brunei						▬	

	1460–79	1500–19	1600–19	1700–19	1800–19	1900–19	1980–99
Bulgaria							
Burkina Faso						——	
Burundi						——	
Cambodia					——		
Cameroon						——	
Canada			——————————————			–	
Cape Verde	———————————————————————————————————						
Central African Republic						——	
Chad						——	
Chile			—————————————————————————				
China							
Colombia			—————————————————————————				
Comoros						————	
Congo						——	
Congo (ex-Zaire)						——	
Costa Rica			————————————————————————				
Cote d'Ivoire						——	
Croatia							
Cuba		——————————————————————————————————					
Cyprus						——	
Czech Republic							
Denmark							
Djibouti							
Dominica			———————————————————————————				
Dominican Republic		———————					
Ecuador		———————————————————————————————					
Egypt						——	
El Salvador		———————————————————————————————					
Equatorial Guinea						————	
Eritrea						——	
Estonia							
Ethiopia						——	
Fiji						————	
Finland							
France							
Gabon						————	
Gambia						——	

412

	1460–79	1500–19	1600–19	1700–19	1800–19	1900–19	1980–99
Georgia							
Germany							
Ghana					███	███	
Greece							
Grenada			███	███	███	███	
Guatemala		███	███	███			
Guinea						███	
Guinea-Bissau						███	
Guyana				███	███	███	
Haiti	███	███	███	███			
Honduras		███	███	███	███		
Hungary							
Iceland							
India				███	███	███	
Indonesia			███	███	███	███	
Iran							
Iraq						█	
Ireland							
Israel						█	
Italy							
Jamaica		███	███	███	███	███	
Japan							
Jordan						█	
Kazakhstan							
Kenya						███	
Kiribati						███	
Korea, Democratic People's Republic							
Korea, Republic							
Kuwait						█	
Kyrgyzstan							
Laos						███	
Latvia							
Lebanon						█	
Lesotho					███	███	
Liberia							
Libya						█	

	1460–79	1500–19	1600–19	1700–19	1800–19	1900–19	1980–99
Liechtenstein							
Lithuania							
Luxembourg							
Macedonia							
Madagascar						▬▬	
Malawi						▬▬	
Malaysia					▬▬▬		
Maldives				▬▬▬▬▬▬▬			
Mali						▬▬	
Malta				▬▬▬▬▬▬▬▬▬			
Marshall Islands						▬	
Mauritania						▬▬▬▬	
Mauritius					▬▬▬▬▬▬		
Mexico		▬▬▬▬▬▬▬▬▬▬▬▬▬▬					
Micronesia						▬	
Moldova							
Monaco							
Mongolia							
Morocco						▬▬	
Mozambique						▬▬	
Myanmar							
Namibia						▬	
Nauru							
Nepal							
New Zealand					▬▬▬		
Nicaragua		▬▬▬▬▬▬▬▬▬▬▬▬					
Niger						▬▬▬▬	
Nigeria						▬▬▬▬	
Norway							
Oman		▬▬▬▬					
Pakistan					▬▬▬		
Palau						▬	
Panama		▬▬▬▬▬▬▬▬▬▬▬▬					
Papua New Guinea						▬	
Paraguay		▬▬▬▬▬▬▬▬▬▬					
Peru		▬▬▬▬▬▬▬▬▬▬▬▬					
Philippines			▬▬▬▬▬▬▬▬▬				

	1460–79	1500–19	1600–19	1700–19	1800–19	1900–19	1980–99
Poland							
Portugal							
Qatar						■	
Romania							
Russian Federation							
Rwanda						■	
St. Kitts and Nevis			■■■■■■■■■■■■■■■■				
St. Lucia			■■■■■■■■■■■■■				
St. Vincent and the Grenadines			■■■■■■■■■■■				
Samoa						■	
San Marino							
Sao Tomé and Principe		■■■■■■■■■■■■■■■■■■■■					
Saudi Arabia							
Senegal					■		
Seychelles				■■■■■■■■■			
Sierra Leone						■	
Singapore				■■■■■■■			
Slovakia							
Slovenia							
Solomon Islands						■	
Somalia						■■	
South Africa				■■■■■■		■	
Spain							
Sri Lanka		■■■■■■■■■■■■■■■■■■					
Sudan						■	
Suriname			■■■■■■■■■■■				
Swaziland						■	
Sweden							
Syria						■	
Tajikistan							
Tanzania						■	
Thailand						■■	
Togo						■	
Tonga							
Trinidad and Tobago		■■■■■■■■■■■■■■■■■■					
Tunisia						■	

	1460–79	1500–19	1600–19	1700–19	1800–19	1900–19	1980–99
Turkey							
Tuvalu						■	
Turkmenistan							
Uganda						■	
Ukraine							
United Arab Emirates							
United Kingdom of Great Britain and Northern Ireland							
United States of America			■				
Uruguay				■			
Uzbekistan							
Vanuatu						■	
Venezuela		■					
Vietnam						■	
Yemen					■		
Yugoslavia							
Zambia						■	
Zimbabwe						■	

NOTES

Chapter 1. Ceuta, Bojador, and Beyond

1. The official version of Ceuta's capture is recounted in Zurara, *Conquests and Discoveries*, 31–115. Boxer, *Portuguese Seaborne Empire*, 15–19, discusses the significance of the expedition.

2. According to Zurara, King John considered waging war against Portugal's nearer rival, Castile. But his youngest son pressed the case for attacking the Moors. Castile's king, argued Prince Henry, is an enemy "only so by accident (being a Christian like ourselves), whereas the Infidels are our enemies by nature." *Conquests and Discoveries*, 41. For the larger setting, see Kedar, *Crusade and Mission*.

3. Overviews of early European maritime initiatives are Scammell, *The World Encompassed*, Scammell, *The First Imperial Age*, and Phillips, *Medieval Expansion of Europe*. Detailed studies include Roesdahl, *The Vikings*, and Lane, *Venice*.

4. "Portugal was the first European country in which oversea exploration, whether with trade or conquest in mind, was actively supported over a long period by government." Parry, *Discovery of the Sea*, 89.

5. Mauny, *Navigations Médiévales*, discusses maritime exploration in this area before ships rounded Cape Bojador and returned to Europe.

6. See Zurara, *Conquests and Discoveries*, 119–253, and Parry, *Discovery of the Sea*, 89–107, on explorations sponsored by Prince Henry. For Cape Bojador's reputation as the Cape of Fear and the significance of Gil Eannes's voyage for later maritime exploration, see Chaunu, *European Expansion in the Later Middle Ages*, 111–16.

7. Braudel, *The Mediterranean and the Mediterranean World*.

8. There is, of course, no distinct boundary between Europe and Asia. Neither does any clear geographic or political marker separate Europe's western portion from the rest of the continent. By "western Europe" I mean the eight countries noted here, or more generally the segment of Europe west of 14 degrees of latitude east of Greenwich. I call people from western Europe Europeans. This reflects the way they often thought of themselves when interacting with people from other continents, and by using it I avoid undue reliance on the awkward term "west European."

9. Parry, *Discovery of the Sea*; Wilford, *The Mapmakers*, 7–86. The evolving European worldview

as explorers conveyed their findings to cartographers is beautifully illustrated in Campbell, *Early Maps*.

10. Alhough Russia and Japan held overseas possessions, their empires differed from west European ones in important respects. Russia's expansion was overwhelmingly overland. Its North American possessions, held for less than a century, were economically and strategically peripheral and not central to Russia's image of itself as a vast multicultural empire. In contrast, overseas possessions *constituted* the west European empires. Japan's overseas empire comes closest to systems of rule discussed in this book. Japan could not have expanded except by sea, and its foreign policy initiatives from the 1870s onward were deliberately patterned on the west European model. But the scope of Japan's power was regional rather than global, as seen by its proximity to its principal possessions: Korea, Shantung, and Taiwan. In the late sixteenth century the great military leader Hideyoshi devised a plan of conquest that included India, Southeast Asia, and the Philippines and would have made Japan an imperial power on a par with any European state had it been carried out. But Hideyoshi failed to develop the navy his plan required. And his army failed to subdue the Koreans, first on the list of peoples marked for subjugation. Hideyoshi's plan was abandoned at the very time several European powers were asserting themselves overseas. Kuno, *Japanese Expansion on the Asiatic Continent*, 143–77.

11. A strength of the world-system approach pioneered by Immanuel Wallerstein is its tendency to regard western Europe as a unit, with patterns of production and trade that enabled it to become the globe's "core" economic zone. But this tendency also weakens world-system theorizing. The political fragmentation of western Europe and rivalries among its leading states, though noted, are relegated to the background when the question arises why the core came to dominate the modern world economy. See the critique by Zolberg, "Origins of the Modern World System."

12. The career of Central Asian conqueror Timur (ca. 1336–1405) provides horrific examples. Timur was famous for erecting towers from the skulls of enemy soldiers killed in battle and of civilians slain en masse following his army's victories.

13. Steve Stern's description of the Inca empire fits many non-European cases: "As a 'redistributive' state, the Inca Empire absorbed surplus labor from a self-sufficient peasantry and dispensed the fruits of this labor to the royal population and its retainers, the army, peasants on corvee duty, strategic beneficiaries, and so forth, but without in general transforming local modes of production." Stern, *Peru's Indian Peoples*, 22.

14. Crosby, *Ecological Imperialism*, 75.

15. For fascinating discussions of these transfers, see two works by Alfred Crosby—*The Columbian Exchange* and *Ecological Imperialism*—and Hobhouse, *Seeds of Change*. On the role of botanical gardens in improving and transferring tropical export crops in the nineteenth and twentieth centuries, see Headrick, *Tentacles of Progress*, chap. 7, and Brockway, *Science and Colonial Expansion*.

16. For the transformative character of European rule in a wide variety of settings, see Bakewell, *Miners of the Red Mountain*; Curtin, *Rise and Fall of the Plantation Complex*; Davis, *Modern Industry and the African*; Drabble, *Rubber in Malaya*; Gide, *Travels in the Congo*; Hecht, *Continents in Collision*; Hulme, *Colonial Encounters: Europe and the Native Caribbean*; Keith,

Conquest and Agrarian Change . . . on the Peruvian Coast; Moorehead, *Fatal Impact: . . . the Invasion of the South Pacific;* Murray, *Development of Capitalism in Colonial Indochina;* Schwartz, *Sugar Plantations in the Formation of Brazilian Society;* Sherman, *Forced Native Labor in Sixteenth-Century Central America;* and van der Kraan, *Lombok.*

17. Among numerous accounts of the disruptive effects of European settlement on indigenous societies are Chevalier, *Land and Society in Colonial Mexico;* Hecht, *Continents in Collision;* Hemming, *Red Gold: The Conquest of the Brazilian Indians;* Kanogo, *Squatters and the Roots of Mau Mau;* Plaatje, *Native Life in South Africa;* and Price, *Western Invasions of the Pacific and Its Continents.*

18. Erickson, *Emigration from Europe, 1815–1914.* For comparative studies of European overseas settlement, see Hartz et al., *The Founding of New Societies;* Denoon, *Settler Capitalism: . . . Dependent Development in the Southern Hemisphere;* and Platt and di Tella, eds., *Argentina, Australia, and Canada.*

19. "To consolidate their gains . . . the pastoral conquerors usually adopted the administrative models of the peoples that they had overcome. In practice this meant that the nomads of the western steppe followed Islamic prototypes, while those of the eastern steppe and desert borrowed the models of the Han Chinese." Wolf, *Europe and the People without History,* 33. On Aztec adaptation to the cultural patterns of settled urban populations in the Valley of Mexico, see Fagan, *The Aztecs,* 27–63.

20. Exceptions, from the early period of expansion I term phase 1, include the syncretistic culture of British East India Company officials in India, Dutch East India Company officials in Java, and Portuguese *prazeros* in Mozambique. Other examples are adoption of Amerindian lifestyles by some English and French colonists on the North American frontier. See, for example, Isaacman, *Mozambique: Africanization of a European Institution,* and Axtell, *The Invasion Within,* "The White Indians," 302–27. In the nineteenth and twentieth centuries Europeans were much less inclined to adjust to other cultures or engage in sex across racial lines than in phase 1. Changing attitudes as they affected India are described in Ballhatchet, *Race, Sex, and Class under the Raj.*

21. Effects of the colonizers' attitudes on colonized peoples' self-images are sensitively discussed in Fanon, *Black Skin, White Masks;* Memmi, *The Colonizer and the Colonized;* Mazrui, *The African Condition;* Manganyi, *Looking through the Keyhole;* and Nandy, *The Intimate Enemy.*

22. See the appendix for these countries and criteria employed to assign starting and ending points of European rule. Different criteria would, of course, produce different results. I classify under the imperial heading territories with a wide range of legal statuses, including protectorates (e.g., French Morocco and the informal British protectorates over small emirates on the Arabian peninsula), mandate territories of the League of Nations (e.g., French Syria, British Transjordan, and Belgian Ruanda-Urundi), and U.N. trusteeship territories.

23. "International relations" and "international system" are more familiar terms than "interstate relations" and "interstate system," hence will generally be used in this text. The latter terms, however, are more accurate and will be used as well. The world's key political units are the territorially bounded, bureaucratically administered entities called states, not groups of people regarding themselves as historically coherent, culturally integrated nations. Indeed, the vast

majority of the world's states have not been nations for most of their history and are not so now. Most political movements designating themselves nationalist are formed to create a nation, not to celebrate its prior existence. See Seton-Watson, *Nations and States,* and Anderson, *Imagined Communities.* I maintain the distinction between "state" and "nation" when discussing internal affairs of polities. But with regret I abandon it when discussing so-called international relations.

24. Huntington, *The Clash of Civilizations.* Huntington acknowledges western Europe's historical dominance. But in my view he understates the extent to which ideas and institutions accompanying Western expansion influenced the subsequent development of non-Western civilizations.

25. An official language is one approved by central government for use in its administrative offices and for printing official documents. Of the eighty-eight former colonies, sixty list a west European language as the only one with official status. Sixteen share a west European language with a non-European, noncreole language. Three (Haiti, Seychelles, white-ruled South Africa) share it with a creole language having European roots. Three (Cameroon, Canada, Vanuatu) employ two European languages. Four (Somalia, Singapore, Zaire, democratic South Africa) have more than two official languages, at least one of which is that of the ex-metropole. The United States has no official language but employs English de facto in that role. Figures calculated from Gunnemark, *Countries, Peoples, and Their Languages,* 172–81 and ff.; as revised in a few cases by information in Morrison et al., *Black Africa: A Comparative Handbook.*

26. Gunnemark, *Countries, Peoples, and Their Languages,* 172–81.

27. The distinction between Asia and Oceania is necessarily vague and arbitrary. "Oceania" refers to islands of the central and south Pacific located a considerable distance from mainland Asia and influenced slightly, or not at all, by the major religions of mainland Asia. The term covers Australia, New Zealand, and the islands of Micronesia, Melanesia, and Polynesia. By "Asia" I mean the mainland plus the islands currently comprising Indonesia and the Philippines.

28. Betts, *Uncertain Dimensions: Western Overseas Empires in the Twentieth Century,* 213.

Chapter 2. Why Did the Overseas Empires Rise, Persist, and Fall?

1. Lenin, *Imperialism, the Highest Stage of Capitalism.*

2. On the dangers of stretching a concept beyond its original meaning, see Sartori, "Concept Misformation in Comparative Politics," *American Political Science Review.*

3. A devastating critique of Lenin's methods and conclusions, from within the Marxist tradition, is Warren, *Imperialism: Pioneer of Capitalism.* According to Warren, Marx's nuanced analysis of the causes and effects of European overseas political conquests was more accurate than Lenin's attack on anything and everything conceivably attributable to advanced capitalism. Yet it was Lenin whose views prevailed in the Communist and non-Communist Third World for decades, while Marx's views were ignored by many who called themselves Marxist.

4. My conception parallels Doyle's; see *Empires,* 12.

5. Gallagher and Robinson, "The Imperialism of Free Trade," *Economic History Review.* The authors argue persuasively that informal economic influence should be considered along with the British government's formal political claims if one is to understand "the history of an

expanding society" in the nineteenth century and "the radiations of the social energies of the British peoples" (5). The problem is not with their substantive argument but with their semantics: appropriating a single term, "imperialism," to cover both phenomena.

6. Baumgart, *Imperialism: The Idea and Reality of British and French Colonial Expansion, 1880–1914*, 6.

7. The most famous Phoenician colony, in this sense, was Carthage. Greek settlers founded Constantinople, Naples, Palermo, and Marseilles.

8. Almond, "Approaches to Developmental Causation," in Almond et al., *Crisis, Choice, and Change*, 22, 24. Tilly, *Big Structures*, 2.

9. Works of this genre published since 1980 include Abu-Lughod, *Before European Hegemony;* Barkey and von Hagen, eds., *After Empire: Multiethnic Societies and Nation-Building;* the English translation of Braudel, *Civilization and Capitalism;* Bull and Watson, eds., *The Expansion of International Society;* Cooper et al., *Confronting Historical Paradigms;* Crosby, *Ecological Imperialism;* Curtin, *Cross-Cultural Trade in World History;* Curtin, *Rise and Fall of the Plantation Complex;* Denoon, *Settler Capitalism;* Diamond, *Guns, Germs, and Steel;* Downing, *The Military Revolution and Political Change;* Doyle, *Empires;* Ferro, *Colonization: A Global History;* Gilpin, *War and Change in World Politics;* Goldstein, *Long Cycles: Prosperity and War in the Modern Age;* Hall, *Powers and Liberties: Causes and Consequences of the Rise of the West;* Hodgson, *Rethinking World History: Essays on Europe, Islam, and World History;* Holland, *European Decolonization, 1918–81;* Huff, *Rise of Early Modern Science: Islam, China, and the West;* Jones, *The European Miracle;* Kennedy, *Rise and Fall of the Great Powers . . . 1500 to 2000;* Kindleberger, *World Economic Primacy, 1500 to 1990;* Landes, *The Wealth and Poverty of Nations;* Levy, *War in the Modern Great Power System, 1495–1975;* McNeill, *The Pursuit of Power;* Mann, *Sources of Social Power*, 2 vols.; Marx, *Making Race and Nation;* Ralston, *Importing the European Army . . . into the Extra-European World, 1600–1914;* Rosenberg and Birdsell, *How the West Grew Rich;* Scammell, *The First Imperial Age;* Scammell, *The World Encompassed;* Smith, *Creating a World Economy . . . 1400–1825;* Stavrianos, *Global Rift;* Tilly, *Coercion, Capital, and European States, A.D. 990–1992;* Tracy, ed., *Political Economy of Merchant Empires . . . 1350–1750;* Tracy, ed., *Rise of Merchant Empires: Long-Distance Trade . . . 1350–1750;* von Laue, *World Revolution of Westernization;* Wolf, *Europe and the People without History;* and Young, *The African Colonial State in Comparative Perspective.* Works from the 1960s and 1970s include Almond et al., *Crisis, Choice, and Change;* Black, *Dynamics of Modernization;* Chinweizu, *The West and the Rest of Us;* Crosby, *The Columbian Exchange;* Davis, *Rise of the Atlantic Economies;* Eisenstadt, *The Political Systems of Empires;* Fieldhouse, *The Colonial Empires: a Comparative Survey from the Eighteenth Century;* Frank, *World Accumulation, 1492–1789;* Lang, *Conquest and Commerce: Spain and England in the Americas;* Hartz, ed., et al., *Founding of New Societies;* Hennessy, *Frontier in Latin American History;* North and Thomas, *Rise of the Western World—a New Economic History;* Wallerstein, *The Modern World-System, The Modern World-System II,* and *The Capitalist World-Economy.* For conceptual and methodological problems involved in comparative historical analysis of large units, see Tilly, *Big Structures, Large Processes, Huge Comparisons.*

10. For a clear, cogent statement of what a theory is and what strengthens or weakens its explanatory power, see Przeworski and Teune, *Logic of Comparative Social Inquiry,* chap. 1.

11. This is an instance of the "principal-agent" problem, to employ legal terminology used in the current literature on organizations. See Wilson, *Bureaucracy,* 154–58, and Pratt and Zeckhauser, *Principals and Agents,* 1–35.

12. Bendix, *Nation-Building and Citizenship,* 13.

13. These observations permit critical reflection on the fit between question, argument, and evidence in Jared Diamond's acclaimed *Guns, Germs, and Steel.* The book's central puzzle is posed by Yali, a New Guinea politician: why were his people colonized by Europeans and not the reverse? Diamond's answer takes readers on a fascinating excursion through thirteen thousand years of history, with special emphasis on Eurasia's advantages in the development and diffusion of innovations in agriculture, livestock management, and the like. But is not a thirteen-thousand-year answer far too comprehensive, considering that Europe's expansion was compressed into a fraction of that time? Is not Eurasia too spatially comprehensive an explanatory category, considering that it was not people from any part of that vast land space, but only those from its distant western periphery, who came to dominate New Guinea's indigenous peoples? Yali's intriguing question could be more directly addressed by focusing on the last five centuries and on developments in Eurasia's far western edge.

14. This line of reasoning employs John Stuart Mill's method of agreement. If two effects are similar in an important respect, one searches for factors associated with both effects that plausibly helped cause both effects. In the complex, multiple-causation situations found in human societies, one should avoid claiming with certainty that all such factors are important causal agents. But it makes sense to privilege these factors over others associated with one effect but not the other, to say nothing of factors associated with neither. Mill, *A System of Logic,* book 2, chap. 8, 279–91.

15. A more rigorous test of temporal comprehensiveness would examine phases 2 and 4 as well, since expansion also occurred in these periods. To keep an already formidable operation from becoming unmanageable, I focus on phases covering over 80 percent of the fifty-two decades separating Portugal's conquest of Ceuta from Italy's conquest of Abyssinia. Expansion in phases 1 and 3 is most amenable to analysis, moreover, because unmediated by trends in the other direction that mark phases 2 and 4.

16. Major theories are summarized in Wright, ed., *The "New Imperialism."* See the critical discussion in Fieldhouse, *Economics and Empire, 1830–1914,* 3–87; and Mommsen, *Theories of Imperialism.*

17. This line of reasoning follows what J. S. Mill terms the indirect method of difference. When two effects differ in the respect one wants to study, one searches for factors associated with one effect but not both. These factors are highlighted because their presence in one situation and absence in the other may help account for the different outcome. This is the method underlying experimental designs. J. S. Mill, *A System of Logic.*

18. As Doyle (*Empires,* 12) argues, in order to understand interactions between a dominant metropole and a subordinate periphery, "it is quite as necessary to explain the weakness of the periphery as it is to explain the strength and motives of the metropole."

19. Hobson, *Imperialism: A Study;* Schumpeter, *Imperialism and Social Classes.* Works by Lenin and Wallerstein are cited in notes 1 and 9, respectively.

20. Frank, *Capitalism and Under-Development in Latin America*. The ideas of late nineteenth- and early twentieth-century British imperialists are discussed in Semmel, *Imperialism and Social Reform*, and Symonds, *Oxford and Empire*.

21. I define an institution as a complex organization with an identifiable hierarchy, a primary purpose relating to the world outside the organization's boundaries, and procedures and norms giving individuals associated with the organization incentives to support its primary purpose through their own actions. This definition is more structural and less comprehensive than the one North offers in *Institutions, Institutional Change, and Economic Performance*, 3: "humanly devised constraints that shape human interaction." But it benefits from North's emphasis on individual incentives and the role organizational procedures and norms play in shaping them.

22. I do not assume that all societies share the same set of functional requisites for maintaining themselves over time. The notion of sectoral activities employed here is derived from an examination of historical events and sequences in several European countries. It is not deduced from macrofunctionalist premises about how every society operates.

23. In all the cases just noted, except France and Haiti, the metropole emerged on the winning side. Though France eventually lost the Napoleonic Wars, it lost Haiti at a time when it had fought well enough in Europe to manage a stalemate with its enemies.

Chapter 3. Phase 1: Expansion, 1415–1773

1. Columbus, *The Journal of Christopher Columbus*, 23, 29.
2. McAlister, *Spain and Portugal in the New World, 1492–1700*, 111.
3. Hennessy, *Frontier in Latin American History*, esp. chap. 3, "Types of Frontier," 54–109.
4. Because England's rulers steadily extended their jurisdiction within the British Isles during phase 1, it is unclear at what point the polity ceases to become England and is more accurately designated Britain. For phase 1 I use "England" unless the reference is to Parliament following the Union of England and Scotland in 1707. I use "Britain" and "Great Britain" for subsequent phases.
5. Data from Kohn, *Dictionary of Wars*. For an overview, see Kaiser, *Politics and War: European Conflict from Philip II to Hitler*, parts 1 and 2. During the half century preceding its internationally recognized independence from Spain, Holland conducted foreign affairs as a de facto independent state.
6. Data from Kohn, *Dictionary of Wars*. For detailed accounts of selected conflicts, see Andrews, *Trade, Plunder, and Settlement . . . 1480–1630;* Boxer, *The Dutch Seaborne Empire, 1600–1800;* Furber, *Rival Empires of Trade in the Orient, 1600–1800;* and Earle, *The Sack of Panama*.
7. Davis, *Rise of the Atlantic Economies*, 54–55. Volume 1 of Cook and Borah, *Essays in Population History: Mexico and the Caribbean*, provides estimates cited here of population declines in Hispaniola (401) and New Spain (viii).
8. McAlister, *Spain and Portugal*, 121.
9. Headrick, *Tools of Empire*, 59–73; Curtin, *Image of Africa: British Ideas and Actions, 1780–1850*, 483–87; Curtin, *Death by Migration*, chap. 1.
10. By "race" I mean a socially defined category assigning special importance—typically, unequal social status—to physical differences among people with different continental origins. Race

has a subjective component, permitting definitions of its boundaries to change over time and from one place to another. But it also has an objective component, pointing to observable features that vary systematically among groups tracing ancestry to different continents. Racial categories are constructed. But they are not invented. That is, they are not based solely on the "inventing" group's interests, projected desires, or misconceptions.

11. McAlister, *Spain and Portugal,* 344, gives estimates for the Iberian empires. Estimates for Peru are from Anna, *Fall of the Royal Government in Peru,* 16–17.

12. Perkins, *Economy of Colonial America,* 1–2. See also Nash, *Red, White, and Black: the Peoples of Early America.*

13. Estimates for Spanish and Portuguese territories are taken from McAlister, *Spain and Portugal,* 344. Estimates for the British West Indies and southern BNA colonies are from Engerman, "Notes on the Patterns of Economic Growth in the British North American Colonies in the Seventeenth, Eighteenth, and Nineteenth Centuries," in Bairoch and Levy-Leboyer, eds., *Disparities in Economic Development Since the Industrial Revolution,* 47. See also Nash, *Red, White, and Black,* chap. 7.

14. Estimates for 1650 for the Iberian colonies are from McAlister, *Spain and Portugal,* 344; for Peru from Anna, *Fall of the Royal Government,* 17. Estimates of mestizos in New Spain vary widely. MacLaclan and Rodriguez, *The Forging of the Cosmic Race,* 197, cite Gonzalo Aguirre Beltrán's estimates (1972) of 6 percent in 1646, 10 percent in 1742, and 11 percent in 1793. The much higher figure in the text is from Cook and Borah, *Essays in Population History: Mexico and the Caribbean* 2:266. See James, *The Black Jacobins: Toussaint Louverture and the San Domingo Revolution* for the social and economic role of mulattoes in Saint Domingue.

15. Fieldhouse, *The Colonial Empires,* 11–13.

16. Hennessy, *Frontier in Latin American History,* 19 and *passim.*

17. Ibid.

18. Two stimulating comparisons of South African and U.S. history are Fredrickson, *White Supremacy,* and Lamar and Thompson, eds., *The Frontier in History.* On early cross-cultural encounters, see Elphick, *Khoikhoi and the Founding of White South Africa.*

19. Crosby, *The Columbian Exchange.* Not all items exchanged were deliberately transferred— disease viruses, for example. Neither were they all commercially viable. See the chapter entitled "Weeds" in Crosby, *Ecological Imperialism.*

20. Schurz, *The Manila Galleon.* New World bullion stimulated not only a direct lateral trade with East Asia but also a substantial increase in vertical trade between Europe and East Asia. About half the four hundred million silver dollars imported from South America and Mexico into Europe between 1571 and 1821 was used to purchase Chinese products. Gernet, *A History of Chinese Civilization,* 485.

21. Tracy, *Rise of Merchant Empires,* 291.

22. An exception is sugar grown on New World plantations. Sugar shifted from a luxury to a middle-class consumption good because of the technical efficiency of plantation operations, the artificially low cost of slave labor, and the enormous volumes exported. See Mintz, *Sweetness and Power,* and Curtin, *Rise and Fall of the Plantation Complex.*

23. The Industrial Revolution's start is conventionally dated at about 1750. Its impact on England's economy and society was minimal, however, until early phase 2. Steam engines incorporating James Watt's invention in 1765 of a separate condensing vessel were not produced commercially until 1775. The first yarn-spinning mill employing Richard Arkwright's spinning frame and carding machine began operations in 1772. Mass production of cotton in the Americas, complementing the new spinning and weaving technologies, awaited widespread adoption of Eli Whitney's cotton gin, invented in 1793.

24. James, *The Black Jacobins*, 66.

25. Parry, *The Discovery of the Sea*, 177.

26. Elkiss, *Quest for an African Eldorado*, 20.

27. Panikkar, *Asia and Western Dominance*, 50.

28. Quoted in Teng and Fairbank, *China's Response to the West*, 19.

29. Axtell, *The Invasion Within*, 11.

30. Bakewell, *Miners of the Red Mountain: Indian Labor in Potosí, 1545–1650*; Cole, *The Potosí Mita*; Stern, *Peru's Indian Peoples and the Challenge of Spanish Conquest*. See Wallerstein, *The Modern World-System*, 65–74, and *passim* for the contrast in modes of mobilizing and organizing labor in the west European "core" and the American colonial "periphery."

31. Craton, *Testing the Chains: Resistance to Slavery in the British West Indies*.

32. Sources on phase 1 chartered companies include Blusse and Gaastra, eds., *Companies and Trade*; Chaudhuri, *The English East India Company . . . 1600–1640*; Furber, *Rival Empires of Trade in the Orient, 1600–1800*; Haudrère, *La Compagnie Française des Indes aux XVIIIème Siècle, 1719–1795)*; Israel, *Dutch Primacy in World Trade, 1585–1740*; Newman, *Company of Adventurers: The Story of the Hudson's Bay Company*; Steensgaard, *The Asian Trade Revolution of the Seventeenth Century*; Tracy, ed., *Rise of Merchant Empires*; and Tracy, ed., *Political Economy of Merchant Empires*.

33. Lippy et al., *Christianity Comes to the Americas, 1492–1776*, 58, 137.

34. For far-flung Jesuit activities, see Alden, *The Making of an Enterprise: The Society of Jesus*.

Chapter 4. Phase Two: Contraction, 1775–1824

1. Indirect beneficiaries of phase 2 independence movements are territories that broke from previously independent countries to become sovereign states on their own. Costa Rica, El Salvador, Guatemala, Honduras, and Nicaragua defected peacefully from Mexico in 1823 as the United Provinces of Central America and became separate states in 1838. Panama was part of Colombia until, under intense U.S. pressure, it became a republic in 1903. Colombia, Venezuela, and Ecuador were joined as Gran Colombia during the struggle for independence. But Simón Bolívar's experiment in pan-American solidarity collapsed when Venezuela and Ecuador seceded in 1830.

2. The battle was actually fought on Charlestown's Breed's Hill, less elevated than Bunker Hill but closer to the harbor, which British troops controlled.

3. The phrase is Lipset's; see *The First New Nation: The United States in Historical and Comparative Perspective*.

4. Quoted in Crow, *The Epic of Latin America*, 526. See Bethell, "The Independence of Brazil," in Bethell, ed., *The Independence of Latin America*, 155–94.

5. Kennedy, *The Rise and Fall of British Naval Mastery*, chaps. 4–6.

6. The so-called Straits Settlements included Penang (acquired 1786), Singapore (1819), and Malacca, ceded by Holland to Britain in 1824.

7. War was waged for twenty-six of the forty-nine years: 1778–83, 1793–1802, 1803–14, and 1815.

8. For overviews, see Kennedy, *British Naval Mastery*, 123–47, and his *Rise and Fall of the Great Powers*, 115–39. Kaiser, *Politics and War*, 212–63, focuses on Europe; Sherwig, *Guineas and Gunpowder: British Foreign Aid in the Wars with France, 1793–1815*, on areas outside Europe.

9. The now-sovereign states where these conflicts occurred are Bolivia, Chile, Colombia, Ecuador, Haiti, Panama (as part of Colombia), Peru, the United States, and Venezuela. Because forces loyal to the metropole included soldiers recruited from a colony as well as those dispatched by a metropole, many independence struggles were simultaneously civil wars. The socially radical revolts led by Hidalgo and Morelos in New Spain may be considered incipient independence movements even though the leaders did not explicitly advocate a break with Spain.

10. Interestingly, the short-lived capture of Buenos Aires by a British naval force in 1806 triggered the first major movement in that city for freedom from *all* European powers. Individual Europeans acting on their own assisted independence movements against other metropoles. Perhaps most significant was Britain's Lord Cochrane, a brilliant and daring sea commander who kept the Spanish navy at bay off the coasts of Chile and Peru at a critical juncture. Cochrane subsequently helped the Brazilians expel Portuguese land and sea forces that were unwilling to accept Brazil's independence.

11. Palmer, *The Age of the Democratic Revolution*, 188–89, and Higgonet, *Sister Republics: The Origins of French and American Republicanism*, 193; cited in Lipset, *Continental Divide: The Values and Institutions of the United States and Canada*, 11.

12. Act of September 15, 1821, cited as the original independence document for Costa Rica, Guatemala, Honduras, and Nicaragua in Blaustein et al., *Independence Documents of the World* 1: 138.

13. Davis, *Slavery and Human Progress*, 294. See the insightful comparison of slavery and abolition in Brazil, the United States, and South Africa in Marx, *Making Race and Nation*.

14. Stein and Stein, *The Colonial Heritage of Latin America*, 158–62. Burns, *Poverty of Progress: Latin America in the Nineteenth Century*. On the link between postindependence liberalism and land tenure policy in Mexico, see Hale, *Mexican Liberalism in the Age of Mora, 1821–1853*, 224–34. The disastrous impact on El Salvador's Indians of late nineteenth-century alienation of their communal lands is noted in Durham, *Scarcity and Survival in Central America*, 39–43 and *passim*.

15. See Prucha, *The Great Father: The United States Government and the American Indians* 1: esp. 21–88, 183–213. As Prucha documents, pronouncements in the Republic's early years showed willingness to include Indians as citizens if they abandoned their old ways and assimilated to the dominant culture as individuals. But assimilationist policies could not be implemented. Federal and state politicians persistently supported "their own kind," settlers whose hunger for land on the Indian side of an ever-moving frontier was insatiable. For the triumph of

Indian-removal policies even where Indians were prepared to assimilate to settler culture, see McLoughlin, *Cherokee Renascence in the New Republic, 1794–1833.*

16. Lynch, *The Spanish American Revolutions, 1806–26,* 29. On the impact of the American Revolution on events elsewhere in the hemisphere, see Whitaker, *The United States and the Independence of Latin America, 1800–1830;* Knight, "The American Revolution and the Caribbean," in Berlin and Hoffman, eds., *Slavery and Freedom in the Age of the American Revolution,* 237–61; and Rodriguez, "The Impact of the American Revolution on the Spanish- and Portuguese-Speaking World," in Library of Congress, *The Impact of the American Revolution Abroad,* 101–25.

17. Quoted in Rodriguez, "The Impact of the American Revolution," 116.

18. Ibid., 117.

19. In Blaustein, *Independence Documents,* 194.

20. Davis, *The Problem of Slavery in the Age of Revolution,* 152.

21. Lynch, *Spanish American Revolutions,* 29.

22. Clark, *The Developing Canadian Community,* 190–91, quoted in Lipset, *Continental Divide,* 10. Moore, *The Loyalists: Revolution, Exile, Settlement,* describes the experience of those who left for Canada. Loyalists also settled in the British West Indies, bringing with them similar antirepublican sentiments.

23. By increasing the proportion of English-speakers in Canada, the Loyalist influx probably increased Britain's capacity to control Quebec's French-speakers. Moreover, concentrations of Loyalists in New Brunswick and Upper Canada meant that the francophone community was flanked on both east and west by people opposing uprisings or secessionist attempts on its part.

24. Craton, *Testing the Chains.*

Chapter 5. Phase 3: Expansion, 1824–1912

1. Estimates compiled from Clark, *Balance Sheets of Imperialism,* 6, 31. See table 1, 23–28, for more details. Square kilometers are recalculated as square miles.

2. The British already held the Straits Settlements, including Singapore, acquired in 1819. Until late phase 3 these possessions were valued as ports ensuring Britain's dominance of the seas, not as entry points to the interior. Britain broke with the traditional enclave pattern in acquiring Arakan and Tenassirim, which stretched for hundreds of miles down the Bay of Bengal's eastern edge and along the Malay Peninsula. The war in 1824–26 was the first of three. Subsequent conflicts in the 1850s and 1880s incorporated the entire Kingdom of Burma and numerous neighboring, mountain-dwelling ethnic groups into British India.

3. Headrick, *Tools of Empire,* 21. On the background to the first Anglo-Burmese War, see Cady, *A History of Modern Burma,* 68–75.

4. Landau, *Moroccan Drama, 1900–1955,* 53–82, describes the backdrop to formation of the protectorate. Porch, *The Conquest of Morocco,* stresses the military dimension.

5. Morris, *Heaven's Command: An Imperial Progress,* 204. Morris adds that the railway image was "readily adopted by the Church of England too as a figure of salvationary progress:

> The line to heaven by Christ was made
> With heavenly truth the Rails are laid.
> From Earth to Heaven the line extends
> To Life Eternal where it ends."

On the railway boom and its overseas impact, see Headrick, *Tools of Empire*, chaps. 13, 14; and Headrick, *Tentacles of Progress*, chap. 3.

6. Figure estimated from Clark, *Balance Sheets*, table 1, 23. I classify the Anglo-Egyptian Sudan as a British colony though Clark lists it as an "international area." White-ruled dominions—Canada and associated provinces, Australia, New Zealand, and South Africa—accounted for 60 percent of the empire's territory. South Africa became a dominion in 1910 when its four provinces formed a union. Whites controlled political life in South Africa as in the other dominions. But in contrast to the other cases whites were a minority group, with slightly over 20 percent of the population when the union was created.

7. Technically, the Congo Free State was under the personal rule of the Belgian king, Leopold II, until 1908. In that year formal control passed to the Belgian Parliament.

8. Barraclough, *Introduction to Contemporary History*, 36–38. What the author called the First Industrial Revolution, led by Britain, was based on iron, steam power, and mass-produced textiles. For a slightly different distinction between the two revolutions see Hobsbawm, *Industry and Empire* 2, chaps. 3, 6.

9. On the most important acquisition, see Miller, *"Benevolent Assimilation": The American Conquest of the Philippines.*

10. Black, *Dynamics of Modernization*, 71 and *passim*.

11. Myers and Peattie, eds., *The Japanese Colonial Empire, 1895–1945*. The chapter by Lewis Gann compares Japanese and European empires. Duus, *The Abacus and the Sword: The Japanese Penetration of Korea, 1895–1910.*

12. From Clark, *Balance Sheets*, table 1, 23–24. I adjusted Clark's data to exclude the metropole's land area. The figure for Great Britain includes the Anglo-Egyptian Sudan. The U.S. figure does not include Alaska.

13. An international regime is defined by Stephen Krasner as "sets of implicit or explicit principles, norms, rules, and decision-making procedures around which actors' expectations converge in a given area of international relations." Krasner, ed., *International Regimes*, 2. For colonialism from 1870 to 1914 as an instance of an international regime, see the essay by Donald J. Puchala and Raymond Hopkins in ibid.

14. Quoted in Langer, *European Alliances and Alignments, 1871–1890*, 122.

15. For the complex diplomacy involved, see Taylor, *The Struggle for Mastery in Europe, 1848–1918*, chaps. 4, 11.

16. On the strategic rivalry between Britain and Russia that was called at the time "the Great Game in Asia," see Gillard, *The Struggle for Asia, 1828–1914*, and Meyer and Brysac, *Tournament of Shadows.*

17. Quoted in Crosby, *Ecological Imperialism*, 208. On U.S. Indian policy in the nineteenth century, see Prucha, *The Great Father: The United States Government and the American Indians* 1, chaps. 8, 9; and Hecht, *Continents in Collision*, chaps. 7–12.

18. Quoted in Moorehead, *The Fatal Impact: An Account of the Invasion of the South Pacific, 1767–1840*, 212. Morris, *Heaven's Command*, 447–67, graphically describes the genocidal assault on Tasmania's aboriginal population.

19. Headrick, *Tools of Empire*, 58–79. Curtin, *Death by Migration*.

20. Data derived from Clark, *Balance Sheets*, table 21, 52. These are gross emigration figures. Net outflow was substantially lower, as many would-be emigrants returned home. A comparative study of settler-controlled societies in South America, South Africa, and Australia in late phase 3 is Denoon, *Settler Capitalism*.

21. Mansergh, *The Commonwealth Experience*, chaps. 2, 4.

22. Tinker, *A New System of Slavery: The Export of Indian Labour Overseas, 1830–1920*; Miège, *Indentured Labour in the Indian Ocean*; Sandhu, *Indians in Malaya*; Emmer, *Colonialism and Migration*, part 2. With British encouragement Indians also migrated to the Caribbean basin, replacing former slaves on plantations in Trinidad and Guiana. The novelist V. S. Naipaul is descended from an Indian who migrated to Trinidad on a labor contract. See Naipaul, *A House for Mr. Biswas*.

23. On biological and cultural racist thinking in phase 3 and its justification on allegedly scientific grounds, see Curtin, ed., *Imperialism*, and Adas, *Machines as the Measure of Men: Science, Technology, and Ideologies of Western Dominance*, part 2. See also Bolt, *Victorian Attitudes to Race*. Ballhatchet discusses changing sexual attitudes in India in *Race, Sex, and Class under the Raj*.

24. Mixed-blood groups were more numerous in parts of colonies of occupation that had been trading enclaves in phase 1. Examples include Goans descended from Indians and Portuguese, descendants of Sinhalese and Dutch in the vicinity of Colombo (Ceylon/Sri Lanka), Eurasians in Java, the Coloured population in and around South Africa's Cape Town, and mestizos in the Angolan capital, Luanda. Mixed-blood populations emerged in these places not only because of the long period during which various groups interacted but also because Europeans in phase 1 were less obsessed than their nineteenth-century successors with maintaining racial purity.

25. Wolf, *Europe and the People Without History*, chaps. 9, 11, gives an excellent summary of changes in international commodity movements effected by the Industrial Revolution.

26. Data compiled from tables in Bairoch, "The Main Trends in National Economic Disparities since the Industrial Revolution," in Bairoch and Levy-Leboyer, eds., *Disparities in Economic Development since the Industrial Revolution*, 7, 8, 12, 14.

27. The extent of deindustrialization in India, and the extent to which this was due to deliberate British policy as distinct from market forces, are matters of debate. See Bagchi, "Deindustrialization in India in the Nineteenth Century: Some Theoretical Implications," *Journal of Development Studies*. Bagchi estimates (139–40) that 18.5 percent of Gangetic Bihar's population was engaged in handicraft industries in 1809–13, a figure that fell to 8.5 percent by 1901.

28. Cited in Nzemeke, *British Imperialism and African Response: the Niger Valley, 1851–1905*, Appendix B, 361.

29. Landes, *The Unbound Prometheus*, 42.

30. Paul Bairoch, "International Industrialization Levels from 1750 to 1980," *Journal of European Economic History*, 277, 279.

31. Bairoch, "International Industrialization Levels," 275.

32. In one important respect rising European demand for raw materials increased lateral links among non-European continents. With far more conscious intent and scientific rigor than in phase 1, nineteenth-century Europeans transferred plants from one place to another where it was hoped plants would thrive in plantation settings. Transferred crops included cinchona (for quinine), sugar cane, rubber, sisal, and tea. See the chapter entitled "Economic Botany and Tropical Plantations" in Headrick, *Tentacles of Progress*, 209–58.

33. Headrick, *Tools of Empire*, 100. Chap. 5 discusses the nineteenth-century "breechloader revolution."

34. Churchill, *The River War: An Account of the Reconquest of the Sudan*, quoted in ibid., 118–19.

35. For an example of the intimidation effect, see the conclusion to *Things Fall Apart*, the historical novel by one of Africa's leading writers, Chinua Achebe.

36. Hartz et al., *The Founding of New Societies*.

37. Brunschwig, *French Colonialism, 1871–1914*, 111–34; Persell, *The French Colonial Lobby, 1889–1938*, chaps. 2, 3. Especially influential were business interests from Marseilles and Lyon. See also Coquery-Vidrovitch, *Le Congo au Temps des Grandes Compagnies Concessionaires, 1898–1930*.

38. Hynes, *The Economics of Empire: Britain, Africa and the New Imperialism, 1870–95*, 50–54. "There can be no doubt," Hynes concludes (54), "that the government's decision to annex Upper Burma in 1886 was influenced by pressure from commercial circles in Britain."

39. Figures calculated from Oliver, *The Missionary Factor in East Africa*, 299–302. The opening chapter is appropriately entitled "The Missionary Occupation of East Africa."

40. O'Donnell, *Lavigerie in Tunisia: Interplay of Imperialist and Missionary*. Fabri's influence is noted in Stoecker, ed., *German Imperialism in Africa*, 21. David and Charles Livingstone, *Narrative of an Expedition to the Zambesi and its Tributaries*, 634, and *passim*.

Chapter 6. Phase 4: Unstable Equilibrium, 1914–39

1. For wartime diplomacy regarding Arab-speaking parts of the Ottoman Empire, see Monroe, *Britain's Moment in the Middle East, 1914–1956*, 23–49, and Hurewitz, ed. and comp., *The Middle East and North Africa in World Politics* 2, documents 8, 10, 13, and 15.

2. From Article 22 of the Covenant, reprinted in Hurewitz, *The Middle East and North Africa in World Politics* 2:61–62 (document 24). The classic study is Wright, *Mandates under the League of Nations*. See also Chowduri, *International Mandates and Trusteeship Systems*.

3. Baer, *The Coming of the Italo-Ethiopian War*, and *Test Case: Italy, Ethiopia, and the League of Nations*. For the traditional European conception of the international political community and twentieth-century challenges to it, see Bull and Watson, eds., *The Expansion of International Society*, esp. chaps. 6–8.

4. The evolution from British Empire to British Commonwealth is traced in Mansergh, *The Commonwealth Experience*, chaps. 1–8, and Judd and Slinn, *The Evolution of the Modern Commonwealth, 1902–80*, parts 1–3. The interwar period is covered in Holland, *Britain and the*

Commonwealth Alliance, 1918–1939. By the Anglo-Irish Treaty of 1921 Ireland also became a dominion. But its nationalist movement, Sinn Fein, regarded this status as a trick to sidetrack popular pressures for a complete break from London. Southern Ireland's Constitution of 1937 made it a republic in all but name. Its declaration of neutrality in 1939 effectively took it out of the Commonwealth, an action formally acknowledged by all parties ten years later.

5. Cited in Yapp, *Making of the Modern Middle East, 1792–1923*, 293.

6. Monroe, *Britain's Moment in the Middle East*; Darwin, *Britain, Egypt, and the Middle East . . . 1918–1922.* As Monroe notes (65) of Great Britain's policies toward its Palestinian mandate, "The speculation and confusion of mind into which the indeterminate and multiple promising of Palestine had thrown everyone cannot be overstressed."

7. Monroe, *Britain's Moment in the Middle East*, 72. For the background to Britain's unilateral grant of independence, see Darwin, *Britain, Egypt, and the Middle East.*

8. The context for the Montagu statement is laid out in Robb, "The British Cabinet and Indian Reform, 1917–1919," *Journal of Imperial and Commonwealth History*, and Robb, *The Government of India and Reform . . . 1916–1921.* See also Ellinwood and Pradhan, eds., *India and World War I.*

9. Draper, *The Amritsar Massacre.*

10. For interwar relations between Congress and British authorities in New Delhi and London, see Low, ed., *Congress and the Raj . . . 1917–47*; Moore, *The Crisis of Indian Unity, 1917–1940*; and Tomlinson, *The Political Economy of the Raj, 1914–1947.* For Gandhi as thinker and political activist, see Brown, *Gandhi's Rise to Power: Indian Politics 1915–1922*, and Brown, *Gandhi and Civil Disobedience: The Mahatma in Indian Politics, 1928–34.* Hutchins, *India's Revolution: Gandhi and the Quit India Movement*, discusses the events of 1942 and their broader significance.

11. Fishel, *The End of Extraterritoriality in China*; Susa, *The Capitulatory Regime of Turkey.* An observation effect was at work in these cases. Susa notes (x) that a Chinese envoy visited Ankara, the new Turkish capital, in the 1920s to study abolition of the capitulatory regime. His aim was clearly to apply lessons from Turkish experience to China.

12. British Empire figures from Barnett, *The Collapse of British Power*, 73. Wartime contributions of France's colonies are summarized in Sarraut, *La Mise en Valeur des Colonies Françaises*, 40–51.

13. Tomlinson, *Political Economy*, 109; Spear, *A History of India* 2:183.

14. Sarraut, *La Mise en Valeur*, 86 (translation supplied). Lugard, *The Dual Mandate in Tropical Africa.* Sarraut was governor-general of Indochina before the war and from 1920 to 1924 was France's minister for the colonies. Lugard was the first governor-general of Nigeria and a key figure in formulating and articulating British colonial policy in the interwar years. Cooper, *Decolonization and African Society: The Labor Question in French and British Africa*, chaps. 2, 3, discusses a theme linked to the new emphasis on colonial development: reconceptualization of colonial subjects as units of labor not substantially different from the metropole's working classes. On the "development of development" as a rationale for British rule in the interwar period, see Constantine, *The Making of British Colonial Development Policy, 1914–1940*, and vol. 1 of Morgan's five-volume *Official History of Colonial Development.*

15. An overview of private and public investment in European, American, and Japanese overseas empires in the mid-1930s is Royal Institute of International Affairs, *The Colonial Problem*, 275–85. See also Frankel, *Capital Investment in Africa*, and Fieldhouse, *Unilever Overseas: The Anatomy of a Multinational, 1895–1965*.

16. Headrick, *Tentacles of Progress*, chap. 9. Pim, *Colonial Agricultural Production*.

17. World trade data are not classified in terms of colonized vs. noncolonized areas. However, the three most colonized regions in phase 4—Oceania, Africa, and Asia—together accounted for 24 percent of global exports of primary products in 1913, 29 percent in 1928, and 34 percent in 1938. Figures from Yates, *Forty Years of Foreign Trade*, table 19, 47. See also Royal Institute, *The Colonial Problem*, 288–93.

18. Figures calculated from appendix 11, 196–200, in Latham, *The Depression and the Developing World, 1914–1939*.

19. Plantation data from von Albertini, *European Colonial Rule, 1880–1940*, 175. For Burma, see Adas, *The Burma Delta . . . 1852–1941*. For Southeast Asia generally, see Scott, *The Moral Economy of the Peasant*.

20. Betts, *Uncertain Dimensions: Western Overseas Empires in the Twentieth Century*, 8.

21. Pacification campaigns were by no means easy or quick. Not until 1934 was all of Morocco brought under French control (Wesseling, *Divide and Rule*, 355). For other examples of pacification campaigns, attempts to apply regulations throughout a territory, and difficulties Europeans encountered in implementing these projects, see Collins, *Shadows in the Grass: Britain in the Southern Sudan, 1918–1956*, and Fuglestad, *A History of Niger, 1850–1960*.

22. See, for example, Crowder, "The White Chiefs of Tropical Africa," in Gann and Duignan, eds., *Colonialism in Africa, 1870–1960* 2:320–50.

23. Collins, *Shadows in the Grass*, 174–75, discusses the role of E. E. Evans-Pritchard, the eminent British anthropologist, in the administration of the Sudan. An example of officially sponsored anthropological research prompted by an unexpected popular revolt—the Aba Women's War of 1929 in southeastern Nigeria—is Green, *Ibo Village Affairs*.

24. Stocking, ed., *Colonial Situations*.

25. Latourette, *Advance through Storm: A.D. 1914 and After* (a volume in his *History of the Expansion of Christianity*), 282, 240, 277, 326. Figures for French Indochina are for Catholics only; Protestant activity there was minimal. For English, Scottish, Dutch, and other Protestant mission agencies, see Parker, *Directory of World Missions*. Among those founded in phase 4 were the Congo Evangelistic Mission, Friends Service Council, Methodist Missionary Society, and United Society for Christian Literature.

26. An insightful description of the impact of mission schooling in rural Africa is Murray, *The School in the Bush*.

27. Fédération des Anciens Coloniaux, *Le Livre d'Or de l'Exposition Coloniale de Paris 1931*.

28. Royal Institute of International Affairs, *The Problem of International Investment*, 130–31.

29. Clough and Rapp, *European Economic History*, 419. Kennedy, *Rise and Fall of the Great Powers*, documents the post-1914 ascent of Japan (298–303) and the United States (327–32).

30. Quoted in von Albertini, *Decolonization*, 11–12.

31. Furnivall, *Colonial Policy and Practice: A Comparative Study of Burma and Netherlands India*,

NOTES TO PAGES 119–128

291, 296. Though published in 1948, this book was based on observation of prewar trends, and its conclusions echoed those of other European analysts in the interwar years. Britain's Royal Institute of International Affairs noted in its 1937 survey, *The Colonial Problem* (2), that "anthropological studies on the effects of the impact of Western civilization on more primitive ways of living have aroused serious anxiety among those interested in colonial administration."

32. Concern about the alleged detribalization of African mine workers is expressed in Davis, *Modern Industry and the African*. Scathing attacks by European officials on Western-educated politicians are cited in Coleman, *Nigeria: Background to Nationalism*, 145–59, and Draper, *Amritsar Massacre*.

33. Hobsbawm and Ranger, eds., *The Invention of Tradition*.

34. Ibid., 249–50.

35. Royal Institute, *The Colonial Problem*, 2, 264. See also Furnivall's comments in *Colonial Policy and Practice*, 290–303, on trends in southeast Asian colonies. "The desire for gain tends to subordinate all social relations to individual economic interest, and, unless kept under control, leads . . . to general impoverishment. . . . It seems . . . to be generally true in tropical dependencies that western law encourages litigation, crime, and corruption." Ibid., 291, 296.

36. Deutsch, "Social Mobilization and Political Development," *American Political Science Review*. Lerner, *The Passing of Traditional Society: Modernizing the Middle East*, makes similar observations. The multiple transformations subsumed under social mobilization occur, of course, in all kinds of societies. Their effects are shaped by the political situation in which people find themselves. In a colonial situation social mobilization has typically generated a mass base of support for independence movements.

37. Figures from Misra, *The Bureaucracy in India*, 232, 235, 291. Included are holders of listed as well as regular ICS posts. The Indian proportion of provincial administrations and centrally administered agencies like the Agricultural Service, Educational Service, and Society of Engineers was considerably higher than in the ICS.

38. Latourette, *Advance through Storm*, 304. Data from chaps. 9, 11, 12.

39. Ibid. 411.

40. See Cooper, *Decolonization and African Society*, chaps. 2, 3, for the rise of labor unions in British and French Africa and efforts of colonial officials to understand and confront challenges the unions posed.

41. An overview of Indian as well as British industrial investments is Bagchi, *Private Investment in India, 1900–1939*. See also Markovitz, *Indian Business and Nationalist Politics, 1931–1939*, and Leadbeater, *The Politics of Textiles*. Appendix D in Harris, *Jamsetji Nusserwanji Tata*, 319–27, details the twentieth-century diversification of the House of Tata into locomotive and truck production, chemicals, cement, tinplate, air travel, insurance, and the like.

42. Woolman, *Rebels in the Rif: Abd el Krim and the Rif Rebellion*, 82–102.

43. Marr, *Vietnamese Traditions on Trial, 1920–1945*, 5–6.

44. The Pan-African Congress was a transcontinental gathering, with twenty-one delegates from the West Indies, sixteen from the United States, and twelve from nine African countries. For Du Bois's assessment of the Congress and its attempt to influence postwar colonial policy, see "The Pan-African Movement," in Kedourie, ed., *Nationalism in Asia and Africa*, 372–77.

45. M. Rollin, cited in Royal Institute, *The Colonial Problem*, 311.

46. Lamming, *In the Castle of My Skin*, 91.

47. The phrase is from Anderson's brilliant book, *Imagined Communities: Reflections on the Origin and Spread of Nationalism*.

Chapter 7. Phase 5: Contraction, 1940–80

1. Zanzibar gained independence from Britain in 1963 and merged the next year with Tanganyika to form the United Republic of Tanzania. I classify independence for Malaya and Malaysia as two separate events because Malaysia included the previously dependent territories of Singapore, Sabah, and Sarawak. Britain's figure would be higher if one included British Somaliland, merged with Italian Somaliland in 1960 as Somalia. Libya is considered an Italian colony, as Italy ruled it at the start of World War II and played a minor role along with Britain and France in its postwar administration under U.N. auspices.

2. The principal examples were Portuguese Goa and French Pondicherry (to India); Dutch West New Guinea and Portuguese East Timor (to Indonesia); Eritrea, an Italian colony governed after World War II by Britain (to Ethiopia); and Spanish Western Sahara (to Morocco). In 1993 Eritrea gained independence after a thirty-year war against the Ethiopian government. Whether the Western Sahara should be independent or absorbed into Morocco remains a matter of dispute. The people of East Timor won independence from Indonesia in 1999.

3. When French troops entered Hanoi in late 1945 they found the statue of the colonial administrator Paul Bert lying in pieces on the ground. The statue's fate symbolized what the war had done to France's power in Vietnam. Betts, *Uncertain Dimensions*, 189.

4. Ranger, *Peasant Consciousness and the Guerrilla War in Zimbabwe*; Martin and Johnson, *The Struggle for Zimbabwe: The Chimurenga War*; Stedman, *Peacemaking in Civil War: International Mediation in Zimbabwe, 1974–1980*.

5. The shift from formal rule to informal influence is discussed by Scott, *The Revolution in Statecraft*, and in Bull and Watson, eds., *The Expansion of International Society*. For contrasts between European colonialism and the more informal mechanisms of post-1945 superpowers, see Abernethy, "Dominant-Subordinate Relationships," in Triska, ed., *Dominant Powers and Subordinate States*, esp. 108–23.

6. Lebra, *Japanese-trained Armies in Southeast Asia*. Austin, *Politics in Ghana 1946–1960*, 11.

7. For tensions between British and American perspectives on empire as the two allies began thinking about the postwar world, see Louis, *Imperialism at Bay*.

8. Quoted in Coleman, *Nigeria: Background to Nationalism*, 239. Nigeria's leading nationalist, Nnamdi Azikiwe, referred to the charter in his influential pamphlet, *Political Blueprint of Nigeria* (1943).

9. Coupland, *The Cripps Mission*, 22. Ba Maw, *Breakthrough in Burma*, 37, 39.

10. Quoted in Hutchins, *India's Revolution*, 197.

11. Césaire, *Discourse on Colonialism*, 14.

12. See, for example, Devillers and Lacouture, *End of a War: Indochina 1954*, and Bender, "American Policy Toward Angola: A History of Linkage," in Bender, Coleman, and Sklar, eds., *African Crisis Areas and U.S. Foreign Policy*, 110–28. In 1947 and 1948 the United States was uncertain

whether to support the Dutch or the Indonesian republican government headed by the nationalist Mohammad Hatta. Hatta's suppression of the communist-led Madiun rebellion in 1948 was decisive in tilting the United States toward the nationalists. McMahon, *Colonialism and Cold War: The United States and the Struggle for Indonesian Independence*, 243–44.

13. Kent, *The Internationalization of Colonialism: Britain, France, and Black Africa, 1939–1956*.

14. Newitt, *Portugal in Africa: The Last Hundred Years*. esp. 219–47; Davidson, *The People's Cause: A History of Guerrillas in Africa*; Birmingham, *Frontline Nationalism in Angola and Mozambique*. A detailed study of Angola prior to independence is Marcum, *The Angolan Revolution*.

15. There is a vast literature on decolonization in British India. Sources include Hodson, *The Great Divide: Britain-India-Pakistan*; Hutchins, *India's Revolution*; Inder Singh, *The Origins of the Partition of India, 1936–1947*; Menon, *The Transfer of Power in India*; Gopal, *Jawaharlal Nehru: A Biography* 1:1889–1947; Moore, *Escape from Empire: The Attlee Government and the Indian Problem*; and the twelve-volume compilation of primary sources in Mansergh and Lumby (later Moon), eds., *Constitutional Relations between Britain and India: The Transfer of Power*.

16. Mansergh, *The Commonwealth Experience*, 145–60. India's decision in 1949 to adopt a republican form of government might have led to withdrawal, since the Commonwealth's formal head was an unelected monarch. But Prime Minister Nehru made clear India's desire to remain within the Commonwealth if constitutionally possible. Adroit diplomacy produced a mutually acceptable description of the British monarch as "the symbol of the free association of its independent member nations, and as such the Head of the Commonwealth." This wording enabled India and other republics to affirm their complete sovereignty while participating in Commonwealth affairs.

17. Louis, *The British Empire in the Middle East, 1945–51*; Louis and Stookey, eds., *The End of the Palestine Mandate*; Hurewitz, *The Struggle for Palestine*; Wasserstein, *The British in Palestine... 1917–1929*.

18. Quoted in von Albertini, *Decolonization*, 493.

19. Kahin, *Nationalism and Revolution in Indonesia*; McMahon, *Colonialism and Cold War*; Ricklefs, *A History of Modern Indonesia*, 187–221.

20. Kahler, *Decolonization in Britain and France*; Smith, *The French Stake in Algeria*.

21. For the siege of Dien Bien Phu, see Fall, *Hell in a Very Small Place*. For the national and international context, see Devillers and Lacouture, *End of a War: Indochina, 1954*.

22. Naroun, *Ferhat Abbas ou les Chemins de la Souveraineté*, 93–94. Murphy, *Diplomat Among Warriors*.

23. Khenouf and Brett, "Algerian Nationalism and the Allied Military Strategy and Propaganda during the Second World War: The Background to Setif," in Killingray and Rathbone, eds., *Africa and the Second World War*, 267.

24. Horne, *A Savage War of Peace*, 23–28.

25. Reforms included ending the citizen-subject distinction in France's colonies, abolition of forced labor, extension of the franchise, and equal pay for equal work regardless of race. Morgenthau, *Political Parties in French-Speaking West Africa*, chap. 3.

26. Ibid., chap. 6; Berg, "The Economic Basis of Political Choice in French West Africa," *American Political Science Review*.

27. Of these, Cameroun and Togo were administered as United Nations trust territories.

28. White, *Black Africa and de Gaulle.* For policy continuities between colonial and postcolonial eras, see Corbett, *The French Presence in Black Africa,* and Chipman, *French Power in Africa.*

29. Young, *Politics in the Congo: Decolonization and Independence;* Centre de Recherche et d'Information Socio-Politiques, *Congo 1959;* Gerard-Libois and Verhaegen, *Congo 1960;* Gerard-Libois, *Katanga Secession.*

30. The principal non-British case was Rwanda, where Belgian indirect rule policies favoring the Tutsi minority were challenged by politicians from the 85 percent majority Hutu population. Several hundred people were killed and some 220,000 internally displaced in the ethnically charged run-up to Rwanda's first local elections in 1960. Vassall-Adams, *Rwanda: An Agenda for International Action,* 9. Prunier, *The Rwanda Crisis: History of a Genocide,* 48–49. Belgium transferred power to Hutu leaders when it departed in 1962.

31. For descriptions of the communal violence and refugee crisis by persons involved in negotiations among the British, INC, and the Muslim League, see Menon, *Transfer of Power,* 417–36 and Hodson, *Great Divide,* chaps. 16, 18, 22. A powerful journalistic account is Collins and Lapierre, *Freedom at Midnight.*

32. Among the best-known nationalists who came to power were, by year of independence, Jawaharlal Nehru (India), M. A. Jinnah and Liaqat Ali Khan (Pakistan), Sukarno (Indonesia), David Ben-Gurion (Israel), Ho Chi Minh (Vietnam), Sultan Sidi Mohammed ben Youssef (Morocco), Habib Bourguiba (Tunisia), Kwame Nkrumah (Ghana), Tunku Abdul Rahman (Malaya), Sékou Touré (Guinea), Patrice Lumumba and Joseph Kasavubu (Congo-Leopoldville), Archbishop Makarios (Cyprus), Félix Houphouët-Boigny (Ivory Coast), Modibo Keita (Mali), Nnamdi Azikiwe and Abubakar Tafawa Balewa (Nigeria), Léopold Senghor and Mamadou Dia (Senegal), Sylvanus Olympio (Togo), Julius Nyerere (Tanganyika/Tanzania), Ahmed Ben Bella (Algeria), Norman Manley (Jamaica), Eric Williams (Trinidad & Tobago), Milton Obote (Uganda), Jomo Kenyatta (Kenya), Kenneth Kaunda (Zambia), Hastings Banda (Malawi), Seretse Khama (Botswana), Forbes Burnham (Guyana), Francisco Macias Nguema (Equatorial Guinea), Amilcar Cabral (Guinea Bissau), Samora Machel (Mozambique), and Robert Mugabe (Zimbabwe). Three prominent nationalists killed shortly before their countries attained independence were Aung San (Burma), David Dacko (Central African Republic), and Eduardo Mondlane (Mozambique).

33. A classic expression of this view is Lord Lugard's pronouncement in 1920: "It is a cardinal principle of British Colonial policy that the interests of a large native population shall not be subject to the will . . . of a small minority of educated and Europeanized natives who have nothing in common with them, and whose interests are often opposed to theirs." Quoted in Coleman, *Nigeria: Background to Nationalism,* 156.

34. When this did occur, in revolts led by Fathers Hidalgo and Morelos, it pushed creoles fearful of social revolution to seize independence so as to prevent a repeat performance. An exception to this generalization is the recruitment of mixed-blood *llaneros* into Bolívar's army.

35. Marshall, "Citizenship and Social Class," in Marshall, *Class, Citizenship, and Social Development,* 71–134.

36. Figures from Bairoch, "The Main Trends in National Economic Disparities since the Industrial Revolution," in Bairoch and Levy-Leboyer, eds., *Disparities in Economic Development since the Industrial Revolution,* 7, 8, 12, 14. Asia includes China and other areas not incorporated into European empires.

37. Nehru, *Nehru, the First Sixty Years,* 210.

38. Nigeria, Western Region, *Proposals for an Education Policy,* 6.

39. Smith, *We Must Run While They Walk: A Portrait of Africa's Julius Nyerere.*

40. Achebe, *A Man of the People,* 34.

41. Nkrumah, *Ghana: The Autobiography of Kwame Nkrumah,* 111–12. On Kaunda, see Rotberg, *The Rise of Nationalism in Central Africa,* 164.

42. See, for example, *L'Afrique Révoltée,* by the Dahomean intellectual Albert Tevoedjre.

43. Press release of July 28, 1947, quoted in Nehru, *India's Foreign Policy: Selected Speeches, September 1946 to April 1961,* 159.

44. Mortimer, *The Third World Coalition in International Politics.* Kahin, *The Asian-African Conference, Bandung, Indonesia, April 1955.*

45. For the impact of the Accra conference on Roberto's thinking and subsequent activities, see Marcum, *Angolan Revolution* 1:64–70. Among leaders Roberto met were Nkrumah (Ghana), George Padmore (Trinidad; Nkrumah's adviser on pan-African affairs), Sékou Touré (Guinea), Kenneth Kaunda (Northern Rhodesia), Tom Mboya (Kenya), and Frantz Fanon (Martinique and Algeria).

46. McMahon, *Colonialism and Cold War,* 179–85; Taylor, *Indonesian Independence and the United Nations.* George, *Krishna Menon: A Biography,* 177–79.

47. Hovet, *Africa in the United Nations*; El-Ayouty, *The United Nations and Decolonization.*

48. From Article 76b of the United Nations Charter.

49. Listowel, *The Making of Tanganyika,* 239–51.

50. Morgenthau, *Political Parties,* 64, notes the impact of political advances in Togo in the mid-1950s on the thinking of French West African leaders.

Chapter 8. Western Europe as a Region

1. This is a classic problem for causal theorizing in the social sciences. In Arend Lijphart's words, "The principal problems facing the comparative method can be succinctly stated as: many variables, small number of cases." Lijphart, "Comparative Politics and the Comparative Method," *American Political Science Review,* 685. One response is to increase the number of cases. This is the methodological advantage of treating European imperialism as two distinct expansionist phases rather than a single half-millennial episode. Even then, so many plausible independent (causal) variables remain that imperialism remains overdetermined, i.e. explained several times over. Here the challenge is as much to eliminate contenders from serious consideration as it is to identify those remaining after passing a series of plausibility tests.

2. On multiple conjunctural causation, see Ragin, *The Comparative Method,* chaps. 1–3.

3. Polynesians were the world's premier long-distance sailors in the premodern era, their ships covering enormous distances throughout the Pacific. I do not list them here because it is

not clear their vessels would have been able consistently to return to home port had this been the goal.

4. "In the four and a half centuries from the consolidation of the Sung empire to the great period of expansion of the Ming empire China was the greatest maritime power in the world." Gernet, *A History of Chinese Civilization*, 326. See also Needham, *The Grand Titration: Science and Society in East and West*, 109.

5. Cipolla, *Guns, Sails, and Empires*, 137 and *passim*.

6. Ibid., 138–40.

7. Parker, *The Military Revolution*.

8. Hemming, *Conquest of the Incas*, 112.

9. Crosby, *The Columbian Exchange*. Williams, *Capitalism and Slavery*, discusses gains to Great Britain from the transatlantic slave trade and the slave-based plantation economies of the Americas.

10. McAlister, *Spain and Portugal in the New World*, 468; Landes, *The Unbound Prometheus*, 36.

11. Chaudhuri, *Trade and Civilisation in the Indian Ocean*, esp. chaps. 5, 6. Abu-Lughod, *Before European Hegemony*, 251–59. Meilink-Roelofsz, *Asian Trade and European Influence in the Indonesian Archipelago*.

12. Al-Hassan and Hill, *Islamic Technology: An Illustrated History*, chap. 5.

13. Hourani, *Arab Seafaring*. Boorstin, *The Discoverers*, chap. 24 discusses Arab seafaring priorities.

14. Curtin, *Cross-Cultural Trade in World History*, 1–3 and *passim*.

15. Barfield, *The Perilous Frontier: Nomadic Empires and China*.

16. Jones, *The European Miracle*, xix.

17. Columbus took a heavily annotated copy of Marco Polo's *Voyages* on his first transatlantic voyage. Following landfall he kept looking for the Great Khan as he sailed from one unpromising island to the next. The great mariner was off target by about twelve thousand miles, half the earth's circumference.

18. Jones, *European Miracle*. Jones argues that the concentration of wealth in many Asian courts resulted from the conquest of agrarian societies by traditionally pastoral groups. Alien dynasties had opportunities and incentives to extract economic surplus from the agarian base. In the process they enriched the court while keeping the base in essentially unchanged conditions of poverty. Jones contends that Europe's failure to experience nomadic invasions permitted evolution of a more equitable distribution of resources than in the great Asian polities. Europe's image of Asian affluence in early phase 1 was in reality the image of wealth concentrated in the hands of Asian rulers.

19. Columbus, *The Log of Christopher Columbus*, 51.

20. Quoted in León-Portilla, ed., *The Broken Spears: The Aztec Account of the Conquest of Mexico*, 26.

21. Columbus, *The Journal of Christopher Columbus*, 28 (entry for October 14, 1492).

22. Raleigh, *The Discoverie of the Large and Bewtiful Empire of Guiana*, 73. The sexual reference here is clear: imperialism is analogized to rape.

23. Dening, *Islands and Beaches . . . Marquesas, 1774–1880*, 206.

24. Zurara, *Conquests and Discoveries of Henry the Navigator*, 14.

25. As quoted in (and translated from) Girardet, *L'Idée Coloniale en France de 1871 à 1962*, 63.

26. Quoted from Millin, *Rhodes*, 138; cited in Arendt, *The Origins of Totalitarianism*, 124.

27. Quoted in Axtell, *The Invasion Within*, 137. See also Pearce, *The Savages of America*, 3–24.

28. Eliot, *The East Africa Protectorate*, 104.

29. See capsule biographies in Waldman and Wexler, *Who Was Who in World Exploration*.

30. Dunn, *The Adventures of Ibn Battuta*, 7.

31. See Collingwood, *The Idea of Nature*. The author asserts (11) that this view of Nature became prominent during the Renaissance—i.e., early in phase 1.

32. Arciniegas, *America in Europe: A History of the New World in Reverse*, chap. 4.

33. MacLeod and Rehbock, eds., *Nature in its Greatest Extent: Western Science in the Pacific*; Mackay, *In the Wake of Cook: Exploration, Science, and Empire, 1780–1801*.

34. Brockway, *Science and Colonial Expansion: The Role of the British Royal Botanic Gardens*; Headrick, *The Tentacles of Progress*, chap. 7.

35. Adas, *Machines as the Measure of Men*.

36. On European state formation from phase 1 onward, see Poggi, *Development of the Modern State*; Tilly, ed., *Formation of National States in Western Europe*; Hall, *Powers and Liberties: Causes and Consequences of the Rise of the West*; Bendix, *Nation-Building and Citizenship*; Anderson, *Lineages of the Absolutist State*; and Barker, *Development of Public Services in Western Europe, 1660–1930*. My debt to Max Weber is obvious.

37. Tilly, ed., *Formation of National States*, 15.

38. On the fiscal crisis, see Gabriel Ardant's essay in ibid. North and Thomas, *The Rise of the Western World*, part 3, discuss how early modern European governments tried to resolve the crisis. A rational-choice perspective on the recurring extractive and distributive dilemmas confronting rulers is Levi, *Of Rule and Revenue*.

39. The impressive exploratory activities of Norse/Viking sailors in the North Atlantic did not produce colonies, in the sense in which I employ the word, because there was no significant metropole to administer the scattered settlements settlers founded.

40. Seed, *Ceremonies of Possession in Europe's Conquest of the New World*, 184.

41. Camoëns, *The Lusiads*, 64.

42. Symonds, *Oxford and Empire*, 33–34, 161, 162. See also Betts, "The Allusion to Rome in British Imperialist Thought of the Late Nineteenth and Early Twentieth Centuries," *Victorian Studies*.

43. Tilly, *Coercion, Capital, and European States, A.D. 900–1992*, 47. For the economic role of European cities in the late Middle Ages, see Braudel, *The Perspective of the World*, chaps. 2, 3; Abu-Lughod, *Before European Hegemony*, chaps. 2–4; North and Thomas, *Rise of the Western World*, chaps. 6, 7; and Tilly, *Coercion, Capital, and European States*.

44. Hohenberg and Lees, *The Making of Urban Europe, 1000–1994*, 131.

45. Poggi, *Development of the Modern State*, 36–42.

46. North and Thomas, *Rise of the Western World*, 113.

47. By focusing on urban-based institutions and values favoring productive recycling of profit, I associate capitalism with European history from the late Middle Ages onward. This approach differs from Marx in stressing the bourgeoisie's insulation from state control in the crucial initial phases of capitalist development, rather than bourgeois control of the state. It differs

from Weber in not identifying capitalism so closely with Protestant northern Europe. The problem with Weber's analysis is that key procedures for recording, generating, and recycling commercial gain were developed in Catholic, pre-Renaissance Italian cities, long before Calvin elaborated the predestinarian ideas Weber considers so important. My approach differs from Immanuel Wallerstein in not defining capitalism in terms of relations of trade. Wallerstein is clearly on the mark, however, in emphasizing the profitable role played by intraregional and global trade. See stimulating discussions of the emergence of European capitalism in Rosenberg and Birdzell, *How the West Grew Rich,* chaps. 1–4; North and Thomas, *Rise of the Western World,* parts 2, 3; and Baechler et al., *Europe and the Rise of Capitalism.*

48. For examples, see Andrews, *Trade, Plunder, and Settlement,* and Israel, *Dutch Primacy in World Trade, 1585–1740.*

49. See the insightful discussion in Mann, *Sources of Social Power* 1, chap. 10. Jews inhabiting various urban centers of western Europe comprised a visible and often prominent community. But their small numbers and strong pressures from Christians to isolate and discriminate against them limited the pluralizing effect of their presence on European religious life.

50. Hennessy, *The Frontier in Latin American History,* 54–60; Clarke, *West Africa and Christianity,* chaps. 1–3; Ajayi, *Christian Missions in Nigeria, 1841–1891.*

51. Hay, *Europe: The Emergence of an Idea,* 25.

52. Ibid., 83–87.

53. For a survey of Christian–Muslim relations from the seventh through the sixteenth centuries, see vols. 2 and 3 of Kenneth Latourette's monumental *History of the Expansion of Christianity: The Thousand Years of Uncertainty: A.D. 500–A.D.1500,* esp. chaps. 6, 7; and *Three Centuries of Advance: A.D. 1500–A.D. 1800,* esp. chap. 1. Also Malouf, *Crusades Through Arab Eyes.*

54. Camoëns, *The Lusiads,* 70, 78–80.

55. This discussion benefits from the stimulating comparisons of European, Arab/Islamic, and Chinese civilizations in Hall, *Powers and Liberties,* chaps. 2, 4, 5; and Levenson, ed., *European Expansion and the Counter-Example of Asia.*

56. Abun-Nasr makes this point with respect to North Africa west of Egypt in *A History of the Maghrib in the Islamic Period,* 12. In the *Muqadimma,* the great historian Ibn Khaldun (1332–1406) advanced a theory of the rise and fall of Islamic dynasties based on the sharp contrast in lifestyles between urban dwellers and pastoralists.

57. Levenson, *European Expansion,* 45.

Chapter 9. Western Europe as a System of Competing States

1. In this discussion "state" refers to a central government, in particular to civilian and military agencies charged with formulating and implementing policies toward governments of other countries. More generally, "state" denotes a territorially bounded unit recognized by others as having sovereignty, and the people living within that unit.

2. Mann, *The Sources of Social Power* 1:511. "Preparation for war," writes Charles Tilly, "has been the great state-building activity. The process has been going on more or less continuously for at least five hundred years." Tilly, ed., *The Formation of National States in Western Europe,* 74.

3. McNeill, *The Pursuit of Power: Technology, Armed Force, and Society since* A.D. 1000; Parker, *The Military Revolution.*

4. This process is copiously illustrated in Cipolla, *Guns, Sails, and Empires*. See also Parker, *The Military Revolution*, esp. chap. 1. For diffusion of military technology among major European powers during phase 3, see Headrick, *The Tools of Empire*, chaps. 4, 5.

5. Nash, *Red, White, and Black*, 45.

6. Fieldhouse, *The Colonial Empires*, 159.

7. Maylam, *Rhodes, the Tswana, and the British . . . 1885–1899.*

8. Langer, *The Diplomacy of Imperialism, 1890–1902*, 95.

9. An example is the Liverpool merchant John Holt, who traded along the West African coast for years prior to the 1880s. In a letter to British foreign secretary Lord Granville in 1882, Holt warned of growing French and Portuguese political interest in Africa and urged that Britain "not allow the trade at present possessed by her to be confiscated for the benefit of protectionist competitors; but that the influence due to her by virtue of her great colonial and trading interests in Western Africa . . . will be maintained, and, if necessary, her territory extended, in order to prevent the encroachments of those foreign powers whose interests are antagonistic to those of Great Britain." Cited in Chamberlain, *The Scramble for Africa*, 121.

10. Quoted in Girardet, *L'Idée Coloniale en France de 1871 à 1962*, 85–86 (translation supplied).

11. Quoted in Ibid., 85.

12. Robinson and Gallagher, with Denny, *Africa and the Victorians*, illustrate this kind of thinking among British officials at the time of the scramble. Defense of India, so the reasoning went, entails control of South Africa and Egypt. Defense of Egypt entails control of the source of the Nile--that is, Uganda. Access to Uganda entails control of Kenya, and so forth. In the authors' felicitous phrase, the British government advanced along "new frontiers of insecurity."

13. Israel, *Dutch Primacy in World Trade*, 68.

14. Quoted in Betts, *Tricouleur: The French Overseas Empire*, 43.

15. Ratios derived from estimates in Bairoch, "International Industrialization Levels from 1750 to 1980," *Journal of European Economic History*, table 10, 296.

16. Andrews, *Trade, Plunder, and Settlement*; Earle, *The Sack of Panama*; Lang, *Conquest and Commerce: Spain and England in the Americas*. Writing in 1629, a year before setting out to found "a plantation in New England," John Winthrop asserted that "it will be a service to the church of great consequence, to carry the gospell to those parts of the world, and to raise a bulwarke against the kingdom of Antichrist which the Jesuits labour to rear up in all places of the world." Massachusetts Historical Society, *Winthrop Papers* 2:117.

17. Fairbank, ed., *The Chinese World Order: Traditional China's Foreign Relations*, 1–14 and *passim*.

18. Hemming, *The Search for El Dorado*, chap. 10, describes Raleigh's futile attempts to find what he called "that great and golden city which the Spaniards call El Dorado and the naturals Manoa."

19. McAlister, *Spain and Portugal in the New World*, 166–74; Latourette, *Three Centuries of Advance: A.D. 1500–A.D. 1800*, chaps. 3, 12. See also de la Costa, *The Jesuits in the Philippines, 1581–1768*, and Duviols, *La Lutte Contre les Religions Autochtones dans le Perou Coloniale.*

20. This helps explain the limited number of settlers from France as compared to those from Spain (in phase 1) and England/Britain (in phases 1 and 3). The largest concentration was in Algeria, a territory sufficiently close at hand that settlers could readily be mobilized to fight on French soil should this become necessary—as it was in World War I.

21. Danziger, *Abd al-Qadir and the Algerians: Resistance to the French and Internal Consolidation*, 38. See also Girardet, *L'Idée Coloniale en France*, 25.

22. Israel, *Dutch Primacy*, 6. See also Wallerstein, *The Modern World-System II*, chap. 2, "Dutch Hegemony in the World-Economy."

23. Holland's pioneering role in west European economic modernization is stressed in North and Thomas, *Rise of the Western World*, chap. 11.

24. Quoted in Day, *Policy and Administration of the Dutch in Java*, 45.

25. Meilink-Roelofsz, *Asian Trade and European Influence in the Indonesian Archipelago*, chap. 9.

26. See the comparative studies of phase 1 chartered companies in Blusse and Gaastra, eds., *Companies and Trade*; and two works edited by Tracy, *The Rise of Merchant Empires* and *The Political Economy of Merchant Empires*.

27. Kennedy, *The Rise and Fall of British Naval Mastery*, chaps. 1–7. Whereas Spain's phase 1 heroes were conquistadors whose exploits took place on land, most of Britain's early heroes were seafarers. Sir Francis Drake, Sir Walter Raleigh, Henry Morgan, Sir John Hawkins, Capt. James Cook, and (in phase 2) Admirals George Rodney and Horatio Nelson come to mind.

28. Hartz et al., *The Founding of New Societies*, 3–16 and ff. The case studies here show that British settlers were more inclined to insist on self-government than settler fragments from Spain, Portugal, and France.

29. Hynes, *The Economics of Empire: Britain, Africa, and the New Imperialism 1870–95*; Thornton, *The Imperial Idea and its Enemies*, chap. 1.

30. *Winthrop Papers* 2:120. See Nash, *Red, Black, and White*, chaps. 3, 4; and Vaughan, *New England Frontier: Puritans and Indians, 1620–1675*.

31. Axtell, *The Invasion Within*, contrasts the missionary work of English-speaking Protestants in seventeenth- and eighteenth-century BNA with the far more extensive—and considerably more successful—efforts of Jesuit contemporaries in French Canada. For a New World overview see Latourette, *Three Centuries of Advance*, 186.

32. Anstey, *The Atlantic Slave Trade and British Abolition, 1760–1810*, chaps. 5, 7–9.

33. The ambitious agendas and self-assured moralism of British Protestant missionaries are conveyed in such works as Johnston, *Missionary Landscapes in the Dark Continent*; Lovett, *History of the London Missionary Society, 1795–1895*, 2 vols.; Pitman, *Central Africa, Japan, and Fiji: A Story of Missionary Enterprise, Trials and Triumphs*; and Stock, *History of the Church Missionary Society*. See Morris, *Heaven's Command*, chaps. 2, 16, for the religious dimensions of Victorian Britain's "improving instinct." Studies of phase 3 missionary activity dealing primarily or exclusively with British-based Protestant agencies include Ajayi, *Christian Missions in Nigeria, 1841–1891*; Comaroff and Comaroff, *Of Reason and Revelation . . . in South Africa*, vol. 1; Goodall, *A History of the London Missionary Society, 1895–1945*; Gow, *Madagascar and the Protestant Impact*; Kalu, ed., *History of Christianity in West Africa*; Kent, *Company of Heaven: Early Missionaries in the South Seas*; Langmore, *Missionary Lives: Papua, 1874–1914*;

Oliver, *The Missionary Factor in East Africa;* Ross, *John Philip (1775–1851);* Rotberg, *Christian Missionaries and the Creation of Northern Rhodesia, 1880–1924;* Sanderson and Sanderson, *Education, Religion, and Politics in Southern Sudan, 1899–1964;* and Temu, *British Protestant Missions.*

34. This phrase summed up the arguments of Thomas Fowell Buxton's widely read tract, *The African Slave Trade and its Remedy* (1840). Buxton's ideas were elaborated and put into practice by Henry Venn, the influential secretary of the (Anglican) Church Missionary Society from 1841 to 1872. See Webster, "The Bible and the Plough," *Journal of the Historical Society of Nigeria.*

35. A biographer calls him "one of [nineteenth-century] imperialism's earliest proponents and advocates." Jeal, *Livingstone,* 188.

36. See works by Ajayi, Oliver, and Ross cited in n. 33.

37. Gann and Duignan, *The Rulers of Belgian Africa, 1884–1914,* 29. See also Hochschild, *King Leopold's Ghost;* Ascherson, *The King Incorporated: Leopold II in the Age of Trusts.*

Chapter 10. The Institutional Basis for the Triple Assault

1. On this last point, see Schwaller, *Origins of Church Wealth in Mexico . . . 1523–1600.* Alden, *The Making of an Enterprise: The Society of Jesus . . . 1540–1750,* part 4, discusses the Jesuits' wide-ranging economic activities.

2. Porch described Tangier's European population as falling "broadly into two categories: the celestial and the criminal." Porch, *The Conquest of Morocco,* 14.

3. For a discussion of principal-agent relations, see Milgrom and Roberts, *Economics, Organization, and Management,* esp. chap. 6, "Moral Hazard and Performance Incentives," 166–98. Moral hazard is "the consequence of postcontractual opportunism that arises because actions that have efficiency consequences are not freely observable and so the person taking them may choose to pursue his or her private interests at others' expense." Ibid., 167. Moral hazard is most likely to occur under conditions of long-distance institutional stretching analyzed here.

4. Referring to the early seventeenth century, Winius observes, "While official India drifted in military and financial crisis, the bureaucracy went shamelessly about its private business. Shielded by the distance from Portugal, the deliberate weakness of the viceregal office, and the restricted personnel policy, its members connived to pursue their private fortunes in as many ways as individual, traditional, or collective ingenuity could devise." Winius, *The Fatal History of Portuguese Ceylon,* 99.

5. Cortés, *Five Letters of Cortés to the Emperor,* 243. Cortés was not, strictly speaking, an agent of royal power, as his expedition left Cuba for the mainland in defiance of orders from the island's governor. He is better described as a self-designated agent. This makes even more striking his insistence on conquering on behalf of a distant ruler who could not possibly have known what was happening in the field.

6. Parry, *The Spanish Seaborne Empire,* 92–93.

7. European governments frequently sponsored overseas settlement of people they least wanted to have living at home. Convicted criminals, sentenced in British courts to "transportation," formed the core of settler society in Georgia and Australia. Other territories serving as penal

colonies were Angola, New Caledonia, and French Guyana. Opponents of Napoleon III's rule were consigned to political exile in Algeria. For the Australian case, see Hughes, *The Fatal Shore*, chaps. 2, 4–6, 13. For *degredados* (exiled criminals) in Angola, see Bender, *Angola under the Portuguese*, chap. 3.

8. An early instance of metropolitan intervention against settler interests was the Spanish Crown's edict of 1542, elaborated in 1549, restricting *encomenderos'* power to exploit Amerindian labor. This triggered settler revolts in Peru and Nicaragua. But opposition was quickly quelled and metropolitan authority reasserted.

9. The VOC's structure acknowledged the urban base of mercantile activity by permitting several cities to select representatives to the company's ruling Council of 17. But the very fact that these municipalities were willing to subordinate commercial rivalries and form a single company demonstrates the growing appeal of the Dutch nation relative to the smaller units—Amsterdam, Middelburg, Delft, Hoorn, etc.—in which merchants conducted business.

10. "From the beginning [the popes] realized that an apostolic mission in America could be organized only by the Spanish Crown." Parry, *Spanish Seaborne Empire*, 153. See also Shiels, *King and Church: The Rise and Fall of the Patronato Real*. Beginning in 1508, a series of papal bulls conceded the Crown's right to select missionaries, name all bishops, heads of religious houses, and parish priests, and create new dioceses. The Jesuits were perhaps most successful among Catholic orders at retaining control over what they did and who did it.

11. Shiels, *King and Church*, 78. See pages 72–81 for the text and interpretation of the papal proclamation, *Inter caetera divinae*.

12. McAlister, *Spain and Portugal in the New World*, 90. See also Seed, *Ceremonies of Possession in Europe's Conquest of the New World*, chap. 3.

13. Merton, *Cardinal Ximenes and the Making of Spain*. An interesting commentary on the Church's role in European imperialism is the fact that Ximenes organized, with financial aid from church funds, and personally accompanied a military expedition to Oran (Algeria) in 1509. The city was captured and remained in Spanish hands until destroyed by an earthquake in 1790. Ibid., chap. 9.

14. Lockhart and Schwartz, *Early Latin America: A History of Colonial Spanish America and Brazil*, 66–67. Shops and the homes of prominent citizens occupied the square's remaining side. In effect, two sides of the square were allotted to the public sector, one side each to the private profit and religious sectors.

15. Meilink-Roelofsz, *Asian Trade and European Influence in the Indonesian Archipelago*, 167ff.

16. Abun-Nasr, *A History of the Maghrib in the Islamic Period*, 272–314; Ganiage, *Les Origines du Protectorat Français en Tunisie, 1861–1881*, chaps. 4–7; Miège, *Le Maroc et l'Europe (1830–1894)*, vol. 3. On international financiers in Egypt before the British occupation, see Landes, *Bankers and Pashas*.

17. Axtell, *The Invasion Within*, and Moore in his carefully researched novel *Black Robe* describe interactions among seventeenth-century French colonial officials, fur traders, missionaries, and Amerindians in what is now eastern Canada.

18. Brunschwig, *French Colonialism, 1871–1914*, 102–11; Persell, *The French Colonial Lobby, 1889–1938*; Betts, *Tricouleur*, chaps. 1, 3.

19. Miège, *Expansion Européenne et Décolonisation de 1870 à nos Jours*, 174. See also Cohen, *The French Encounter with Africans . . . 1530–1880*, 275–79.

20. Dening, *Islands and Beaches . . . Marquesas, 1774–1880*, 192.

21. Rudin, *Germans in the Cameroons, 1884–1914*, 363–64.

22. Klein, *Islam and Imperialism in Senegal;* Kanya-Forstner, *The Conquest of the Western Sudan;* Roberts, *Warriors, Merchants, and Slaves: The State and the Economy in the Middle Niger Valley, 1700–1914.*

23. A similar situation obtained in south-central Africa from the 1820s onward—though the portion of South Africa under British rule was by then far larger than a coastal enclave. The Cape Colony was a secure base from which Robert Moffat, David Livingstone, and others launched missionary initiatives into the interior further north. The European penetration of China in phase 3 also fits this pattern. China's coastal and riverine treaty ports, where citizens of Britain, France, and other states enjoyed extraterritorial legal rights, were staging areas from which their merchants and missionaries left for the interior. In this case, however, informal influence foreigners exercised outside the treaty ports was never translated into formal rule.

24. Etzioni, *A Comparative Analysis of Complex Organizations*, 5 and *passim*.

25. Quoted in Oliver, *The Missionary Factor in East Africa*, 128.

26. Metcalf, *Aftermath of Revolt: India, 1857–1870*, 47–48, 92–110, 129–30. Lelyveld, *Aligarh's First Generation: Muslim Solidarity in British India.*

27. For Nigeria, see Buell, *The Native Problem in Africa* 1:728–37; and Ayandele, *The Missionary Impact on Modern Nigeria, 1842–1914*, chaps. 3, 4. For the Sudan, see Daly, *Empire on the Nile: The Anglo-Egyptian Sudan, 1898–1934*, 240–59. Growing anticlerical sentiment in France toward the end of the nineteenth century reinforced official suspicion of missionary work. French West African authorities were more willing to countenance Islamic religious education, provided it contained pro-French instruction, than to support Catholic schools. Harrison, *France and Islam in West Africa, 1860–1960*, 18, 63–65.

28. Boxer, *Portuguese Seaborne Empire, 1415–1825*, 83.

29. Quoted in Comaroff and Comaroff, *Of Revelation and Revolution* 1:253.

30. Nehru, *The Discovery of India*, 274.

31. On the Treaty of Waitangi, see Sahlins, *Islands of History*, 67–71. Deception over consumer goods was another feature of this treaty. As one Maori participant in the negotiations put it, "We had less tobacco and fewer trinkets and other European goods than formerly and we saw that the first Governor had not spoken the truth, for he told us that we should have a great deal more" (quoted in ibid., 70). On negotiations between Lobengula and the British, see Samkange's *Origins of Rhodesia* and his novel *On Trial for My Country.* Samkange describes Reverend Helm, who knew the Ndebele language and served as translator in the negotiations, as "a Rhodes man in missionary clothing" (*Origins*, 67).

32. Quoted in Martin, *Keepers of the Game*, 61.

33. For examples, see Axtell, *Invasion Within*, 64–68; Ayandele, *Missionary Impact*, chap. 10; and Moorehead, *The Fatal Impact*, 118, 124. Alcoholism, it should be noted, was more often the consequence than the cause of demoralization. As Gary Nash noted of North American native peoples, "When tribes lost their land, their autonomy, and their confidence in their traditional

belief system, drinking could change from a form of social relaxation to a solvent for internalized aggressive impulses against whites." Nash, *Red, White, and Black,* 244.

34. Sinclair, *A History of New Zealand,* 41–42.

35. Moorehead, *Fatal Impact,* 108–09.

36. The following discussion relies heavily on the account of Malaccan history in the Sixth Book of Tomé Pires's monumental *Suma Oriental of Tomé Pires.* Pires was sent from Goa to Malacca shortly after the Portuguese captured the city in 1511. He was accountant for the trade factory the new rulers established, later serving as the first Portuguese ambassador to the Chinese imperial court. A description of the city's capture, written in the 1570s by the son of the soldier/administrator directing the assault, is found in Albuquerque, *Commentaries of the Great Afonso Dalboquerque, Second Viceroy of India* 3:66–146. Other sources consulted include Abu-Lughod, *Before European Hegemony;* Boxer, *Portuguese Seaborne Empire;* Chaudhuri, *Trade and Civilisation in the Indian Ocean;* Gernet, *A History of Chinese Civilization;* Lapidus, *A History of Islamic Societies;* Meilink-Roelofsz, *Asian Trade and European Influence;* Panikkar, *Asia and Western Dominance;* and Reid, ed., *Southeast Asia in the Early Modern Era,* chap. 3.

37. Quoted from Viceroy Afonso d'Albuquerque's son in *Commentaries* 3:88.

38. The apparent exception to this generalization is Vietnam, which experienced centuries of Chinese rule. Ming armies occupied Vietnam in 1406, coincident with Admiral Ho's early voyages, holding it until 1427. But governing a neighbor was essentially an overland operation. Vietnam is not an instance of overseas empire.

39. On the separate, essentially competitive character of official and private trade, see Fairbank, *Trade and Diplomacy on the China Coast . . . 1842–1854,* 37. Meilink-Roelofsz notes another source of tension between the two sectors in the fifteenth century: "the government's tendency to prevent precious metals from leaving China, as these were being exported by the merchants on a large scale." *Asian Trade and European Influence,* 74.

40. Boxer notes that as of the early sixteenth century Chinese merchants and mariners from the coastal provinces of Fukien and Kwantung were trading in the Philippines, the Indonesian islands, and Malacca. But "their activities were either ignored or disowned by the Imperial government." Boxer, *Portuguese Seaborne Empire,* 44.

41. Wickberg, *The Chinese in Philippine Life,* cited in Levenson, *European Expansion and the Counter-Example of Asia,* 68.

42. If there was a dominant polity in the Near East early in phase 1 it was the Ottoman Empire, whose rulers were not Arab. After conquering Lower Egypt and the Arabian holy places in 1516–17, the Ottomans controlled shipping in the Red Sea. But even with Egyptian ships at their disposal Ottoman rulers were unable to block Portugal's entry to the Indian Ocean.

43. Chaudhuri, *Trade and Civilisation,* and Abu-Lughod, *Before European Hegemony.*

44. Tomé Pires, *Suma Oriental* 2:240. The author's use of the term "Moorish" to refer to Muslims reflects, of course, his Iberian background. It also reinforces the point about the cosmopolitan character of Islam. Adherents of the faith included Moroccans (the vast majority of whom were not descended from Arabs) and Sumatrans living more than seven thousand miles east of Morocco.

45. "The importance of Malacca had been recognized in King Manuel's instructions to the commanders of the fleets which left Lisbon in 1509 and 1510, though it fell to Albuquerque to achieve the actual conquest." Boxer, *Portuguese Seaborne Empire,* 47.

46. Albuquerque, *Commentaries* 3:119. This, at least, is a paraphrase of the viceroy's words by his admiring son, writing years later.

47. Ibid. 3:118.

48. Ibid. 3:116.

49. Ibid. 3:127.

50. Boxer, *Portuguese Seaborne Empire,* 80.

51. Betts, *Tricouleur,* 20–21.

52. Escape from Europe's alienating confines was evidently a motivator for Hubert Lyautey, who according to Douglas Porch was an open homosexual. This status "condemned him to be a perpetual outcast, a man on the margins of many worlds but belonging to none. . . . Moving from the minutiae and the parochial concerns of garrison life in France to the giant tasks of empire-building was like stepping from a small room into the open air." Porch, *Conquest of Morocco,* 86, 87. Christopher Columbus seemed driven less by desire to escape home than by the allure of the unknown. The journal entry for December 26, 1492, expresses his perpetual restlessness: "For it was always with the intention of discovering that he voyaged and not delaying more than a day in any place, save for lack of wind." Columbus, *The Journal of Christopher Columbus,* 128.

Chapter 11. Non-European Initiatives and Perceptions

1. Rare exceptions were isolated chains of tiny islands—the Azores, Malvinas/Falklands, Seychelles—and Antarctica.

2. Examples include Adas, *Prophets of Rebellion: Millenarian Protest Movements against the European Colonial Order;* Aptheker, *American Negro Slave Revolts;* Campbell, *Rasta and Resistance from Marcus Garvey to Walter Rodney;* Craton, *Testing the Chains: Resistance to Slavery in the British West Indies;* Crowder, ed., *West African Resistance: The Military Response to Colonial Occupation;* Drechsler, *"Let Us Die Fighting": The Struggle of the Herero and Nama against German Imperialism (1884–1915);* Isaacman, *The Tradition of Resistance in Mozambique;* Jones, *Maya Resistance to Spanish Rule;* Josephy, *The Patriot Chiefs: A Chronicle of Indian Resistance;* Nonini, *British Colonial Rule and the Resistance of the Malay Peasantry, 1900–1957;* Ohadike, *The Ekumeku Movement: Western Igbo Resistance to the British Conquest of Nigeria, 1883–1914;* Ranger, "Connexions between 'Primary Resistance' Movements and Modern Mass Nationalism in East and Central Africa; Part I," *Journal of African History,* and *Revolt in Southern Rhodesia, 1896–7;* Rotberg and Mazrui, eds., *Protest and Power in Black Africa;* Sariola, *Power and Resistance: The Colonial Heritage in Latin America;* Scott, *The Moral Economy of the Peasant: Rebellion and Subsistence in Southeast Asia,* and *Weapons of the Weak: Everyday Forms of Peasant Resistance;* Stern, ed., *Resistance, Rebellion, and Consciousness in the Andean Peasant World, 18th to 20th Centuries;* Welch, *Anatomy of Rebellion;* and Wolf, *Peasant Wars of the Twentieth Century.*

3. Ronald Robinson makes this point persuasively in "Non-European Foundations for European Imperialism: Sketch for a Theory of Collaboration," in Owen and Sutcliffe, eds., *Studies in the Theory of Imperialism*, 117–42.

4. Perrin, *Giving up the Gun: Japan's Reversion to the Sword, 1543–1879*, 35.

5. Quoted in Cooper, ed., *They Came to Japan: An Anthology of European Reports on Japan, 1543–1640*, 41.

6. Ibid., 402. See also Boxer, *The Great Ship from Amacon: Annals of Macao and the Old Japan Trade*, 163–65, 331–33.

7. From the rescript of 1640 as reprinted in Boxer, *The Great Ship from Amacon*, 331–32. This policy may be attributed less to foresight than to careful observation of what was happening on other islands further south. Japan's rulers were acutely aware of the triple assault Spain had successfully launched on the Philippines.

8. For this contrast, see Schirokauer, *Modern China and Japan: A Brief History*, chaps. 3–7.

9. Oliver and Atmore, *The African Middle Ages, 1400–1800*, 181.

10. Describing Napoleon's invasion of Egypt in 1798, a local historian of that era noted that residents of the great port of Alexandria were surprised by the arrival of French ships. Jabarti, *Napoleon in Egypt*, 20–22. This observation is itself surprising, considering that Alexandrians had ships of their own and centuries of experience with European vessels and crews.

11. León-Portilla, ed., *The Broken Spears: The Aztec Account of the Conquest of Mexico*, 13.

12. Axtell, *The Invasion Within*, 9.

13. Writes Bernal Díaz of the founding of Vera Cruz, from which he set off with Cortés to Tenochtitlán: "We planned a church, a market-place, arsenals, and all the other features of a town, and built a fort. From the moment of laying the foundations till the walls were high enough to receive the woodwork, loopholes, watchtowers, and barbicans we worked very fast." Bernal Díaz, *The Conquest of New Spain*, 114.

14. The Ottoman Empire and Japan do not qualify as hinterland polities, especially after their capitals were moved to the ports of Istanbul and Edo, respectively. However, in important respects both were oriented to the land rather than the sea. The Ottomans' sixteenth-century preoccupation with expansion into southeastern Europe, the Arab Middle East, and Persia weakened their maritime capacities just when European ships were entering the Indian Ocean. Had Ottoman navies successfully retaliated for the Egyptian-Gujarati loss to the Portuguese in the Battle of Diu (1509) or won the Battle of Lepanto (1571) in the Mediterranean, western Europe's rise to Old World dominance might have been thwarted. Tokugawa centralizers concentrated on strengthening Japan's army while neglecting naval forces. This made it impossible for Hideyoshi even to begin to achieve his grandiose goal of conquering India, China, Mongolia, Korea, southeast Asia, and the Philippines. The Japanese historian Yoshi Kuno states that "in his continental [Asian mainland] campaign Hideyoshi had not entirely disregarded the need of a naval force, yet it is undeniable that he did not consider the navy an essential factor in his military organization. In so thinking he was only following what had long been a military tradition in Japan. Throughout the seven hundred years of the feudal military period, all national difficulties were settled by land battles." Kuno, *Japanese Expansion on the Asiatic Continent*, 152. This is a classic case of the will to create empire not being

matched by capacity. For Hideyoshi's plan and its outcome—his armies wreaked havoc on Korea but never got beyond Korea's borders—see ibid., 143–77.

15. The Aztec case is an exception. Moctezuma was deeply concerned about the news that strange beings (men? gods?) had landed on the coast, some two hundred miles away. The striking fact remains that the Aztec ruler did not mobilize his troops to fight the Spaniards at Vera Cruz or at any point along the lengthy route between the coast and Tenochtitlán.

16. Konvitz, *Cities and the Sea: Port City Planning in Early Modern Europe*.

17. León-Portilla, ed., *The Broken Spears*, 61, 91–92. Hemming, *Conquest of the Incas*, 28–29.

18. For examples, see Kupperman, *Settling with the Indians: The Meeting of English and Indian Cultures in America, 1580–1640*.

19. Quoted in León-Portilla, *The Broken Spears*, 51–52.

20. Ibid., 35, 36.

21. Many economic historians argue that a precondition for economic development is legally secure private property rights. See, for example, North and Thomas, *Rise of the Western World*, and Rosenberg and Birdzell, *How the West Grew Rich*. This point is valid for European empires if one adopts the perspective of colonizers, who routinely assigned themselves land rights, enforced them through the colonial legal system, and proceeded to develop what they owned. The same economic historians seem less willing to grant the corollary proposition that in the course of securing European property rights an indigenous system of property rights was systematically destroyed. Colonial development occurred at the expense of an established set of rules and understandings about land. It is not secure property rights per se that matter for economic development. Rather it is the assignment of such rights to people committed to raising the commercial value of property by realizing its potential to produce items for sale in the market.

22. I use "societies" to encompass the enormous variety of organized units Europeans encountered. These ranged from stateless societies to states with stable, specialized public sector institutions; from nomadic societies to polities with sedentary populations and stable boundaries; and from small-scale units with hundreds of members to empires whose bureaucracies exerted influence over tens or even hundreds of millions of people. One of the most profound adjustments overseas Europeans had to make was to realize that the state, whose structure and legitimating rationale were so familiar to them, was but one of many devices people have invented to satisfy collective needs. Organizational models that seemed natural and civilized to Europeans struck many people elsewhere as deviant, and vice versa.

23. Scammell, *The First Imperial Age . . . c.1400–1715*, 79.

24. Lapidus, *A History of Islamic Societies*, 473.

25. Day, *Policy and Administration of the Dutch in Java*, 48.

26. For these and other examples, see Nash, *Red, White, and Black*, chaps. 3–6. Sometimes more complex alliance patterns emerged. Thus competition for trade in the second quarter of the seventeenth century pitted the Dutch and Iroquois (based in the Hudson River region) against the French and Hurons (based in the St. Lawrence River region). Ibid., 90–91. Indigenous groups could retain autonomy longer if their leaders played off European powers contending for dominance.

27. Cruickshank, *Eighteen Years on the Gold Coast of Africa* 2:10–11, cited in Doyle, *Empires*, 355.

28. "Without martial Sikh assistance the British might not have recaptured their proudest jewel to set in Victoria's Imperial Crown." Wolpert, *India*, 109.

29. Chirenje, *Chief Kgama and His Times, c.1835–1923*, 28.

30. Isaacman, *Tradition of Resistance*, 38.

31. A recurring theme in the literature on subaltern and postcolonial studies is the pernicious tendency of Europeans to regard indigenous people as Others, not entitled to receive the rudiments of respect because of their differences from the civilized European Self. See, for example, Said, *Orientalism*, and Guha and Spivak, eds., *Selected Subaltern Studies*. The point is well made. But it is also incomplete and therefore misleading. The larger truth is that groups on both sides of a racial/cultural divide regard those on the opposite side as Others. Indigenous peoples perceived Europeans as different from them in significant ways and often considered European behavior barbaric. Alterity should be seen as a shared feature of cross-cultural interaction, not as a characteristic confined to the interaction's dominant party.

32. Samkange, *Origin of African Nationalism in Zimbabwe*, 46–47.

33. Hemming, *Conquest of the Incas*, 140.

34. On the Sokoto Caliphate, see Ikime, *The Fall of Nigeria: The British Conquest*, chap. 5 and episodes 10–12. The Nigerian historian concludes (189), "Common loyalty to Sokoto did not exclude hostility between those who gave this loyalty. We have to realize that relations between the various Hausa states of the period before the jihad [in the early nineteenth century] were carried over to the period after the jihad. So there were enmities which a common loyalty to Sokoto did not necessarily remove."

35. Klein, "Colonial Rule and Structural Change: The Case of Sine-Saloum," in Cruise O'Brien, ed., *The Political Economy of Underdevelopment: Dependence in Senegal*, 70.

36. Marsot, *A Short History of Modern Egypt*, 74.

37. More than twenty thousand Chinese residents of Manila were killed by the beleaguered Spanish community following an uprising in 1603. Yet the Chinese court took no measures to protect them and did not even protest what happened. The court again took no notice when thousands were slaughtered in 1629. Beijing officials could not have been unaware of events in a thriving center of Chinese–European trade less than eight hundred miles off the mainland (Schurz, *The Manila Galleon*, 89, 93). It is inconceivable that a European government would have been so indifferent to a massacre of its people overseas. On the vulnerability of Chinese overseas communities, see Wang Gunwu, "Merchants without Empire: The Hokkien Sojourning Communities," in Tracy, ed., *The Rise of Merchant Empires*, 400–21.

38. On Francis Xavier's successful work among India's low-caste fishing communities, see Latourette, *Three Centuries of Advance*, 253–54. In the nineteenth century Wesleyan Methodists in Hyderabad concentrated upon Malas (outcaste agricultural laborers) and Madigas (outcaste scavengers and leather workers). Latourette, *The Great Century*, 153–54. The Holy Ghost Society began its work in Africa by buying slaves; see P. B. Clarke, "The Methods and Ideology of the Holy Ghost Fathers in Eastern Nigeria, 1885–1905," in Kalu, ed., *The History of Christianity in West Africa*, 36–37.

39. Harris, *Repatriates and Refugees in a Colonial Society: The Case of Kenya*, gives examples from late phase 3.

40. Disintegration of old socioeconomic structures is stressed as a pull factor in Fieldhouse, *The Colonial Empires*.

41. Burkholder and Johnson, *Colonial Latin America*, 112.

42. In Nigeria Sir Frederick Lugard attempted to apply indirect rule principles developed among Muslim emirates of the far north to the stateless peoples of the southeast. For the failure of this effort, see Afigbo, *The Warrant Chiefs: Indirect Rule in Southeastern Nigeria, 1891–1929*.

43. See Curtin, *Cross-Cultural Trade in World History*, and Abu-Lughod, *Before European Hegemony*, for long-distance trade networks.

44. Axtell, *The Invasion Within*, 11.

45. Ibid., 11–12.

46. Peires, *The Dead Will Arise: Nongqawuse and the Great Xhosa Cattle-Killing Movement of 1856–7*.

47. An individual's role can, of course, change as time passes and circumstances shift. An example is Chief Maherero, who initially collaborated with the British and Germans in what became Southwest Africa (Namibia) but later led a revolt against them. I classify individuals according to what I consider to be their most significant historical contribution.

Chapter 12. Sectoral Institutions and Techniques of Control

1. A classic early study is Furnivall, *Colonial Policy and Practice: A Comparative Study of Burma and Netherlands India*. Later works include Fieldhouse, *The Colonial Empires*; Gann and Duignan, *The Rulers of Belgian Africa, 1884–1914*; Lang, *Conquest and Commerce: Spain and England in the Americas*; Lang, *Portuguese Brazil*; Crowder, *West Africa under Colonial Rule*; Pagden, *Lords of all the World: Ideologies of Empire in Spain, Britain, and France c1500–1800*; and Young, *The African Colonial State in Comparative Perspective*.

2. Exceptions should be noted. Governors in BNA colonies were frequently American born. To a degree unique in Europe's overseas experience, BNA governors and judges were beholden to elected colonial assemblies, which voted on their salaries. Ambrosio O'Higgins (ca. 1720–1801) left his native Ireland for South America at an early age. O'Higgins rose to become governor of Chile and viceroy of Peru. Felix Eboue, a black man from French Guiana, was appointed governor of Guadeloupe (1936) and Tchad (1939), then was governor-general of French Equatorial Africa from 1940 until his death in 1944. For Eboue's career, see Brian Weinstein, *Eboue*.

3. McMahon, *Colonialism and Cold War*, 24.

4. Lord Roberts of Kandahar, *Forty-One Years in India: From Subaltern to Commander-in-Chief*, viii. The Dejerat lay beyond the Indus River, more than a thousand miles from "the country north of Calcutta" where its men fought.

5. For the genocidal attack on the Hereros, see Drechsler, *Let Us Die Fighting*.

6. See Horowitz, *Ethnic Groups in Conflict*, 445–49, for recruitment of so-called martial races or martial classes into colonial police forces and armies. For India, see Mason, *A Matter of Honour: An Account of the Indian Army, Its Officers and Men*, esp. 341–61; and Farwell, *Armies of the Raj: From the Mutiny to Independence, 1858–1947*, 179–90.

7. McCully, *English Education and the Origins of Indian Nationalism,* and Lelyveld, *Aligarh's First Generation: Muslim Solidarity in British India,* discuss competition among India's Hindus and Muslims in the educational arena. Abernethy, *The Political Dilemma of Popular Education,* does the same for Yorubas and Igbos in Nigeria.

8. A growing literature documents this observation. See Etienne and Leacock, eds., *Women and Colonization: Anthropological Perspectives;* Knibiehler, *La Femme au Temps des Colonies;* Ollenburger and Moore, *A Sociology of Women: The Intersection of Patriarchy, Capitalism, and Colonization;* and Devens, *Countering Colonization: Native American Women and Great Lakes Missions, 1630–1900.*

9. Over time some firms transformed themselves by expanding territorial coverage or increasing their scope of activities. For an enterprise that grew prodigiously as it diversified from trade into plantation management and low-level manufacturing, see Fieldhouse, *Unilever Overseas . . . 1895–1965.* Profitable activities of foreign investors in a settler-dominated territory are examined in Swainson, *Development of Corporate Capitalism in Kenya, 1918–77.* Frankel, *Capital Investment in Africa,* gives an overview of foreign capital in the region as of late phase 4.

10. See, for example, Duviols, *La Lutte Contre les Religions Autochtones dans le Perou Colonial . . . entre 1532 et 1660.*

11. An effective fund-raising mechanism for Catholic parishes in Spanish American colonies was the *cofradía,* a lay brotherhood. Settlers, Amerindians, and blacks organized their own brotherhoods to raise funds for church construction, pay the priest's fee on Sunday and holy days, support impoverished congregants, and organize street celebrations on saints' days. See Farriss, *Crown and Clergy in Colonial Mexico, 1759–1821,* for judicial mechanisms created by the Catholic Church to discipline its personnel. This system operated essentially on its own, parallel to the colonial state's laws and courts, until challenged by the Bourbon centralizer, King Charles III, in the mid–eighteenth century.

12. Burkholder and Johnson, *Colonial Latin America,* 137–38.

13. Schurz, *The Manila Galleon,* shows how leading Spanish families in the Philippines, acting purely in a private capacity, facilitated trade between China and the Americas.

14. On Bishop de las Casas (1474–1566), see Wagner, *The Life and Writings of Bartolomé de las Casas.* On Father Vieira (1608–97), see Lippy et al., *Christianity Comes to the Americas, 1492–1776,* 103–06.

15. For examples from nineteenth- and twentieth-century British India, see the introduction in Ray, ed., *Entrepreneurship and Industry in India, 1800–1947,* 1–69.

16. Responding to settler pressures, twentieth-century colonial regimes passed regulations to prevent Africans from growing coffee (Angola and Kenya), sisal (Tanganyika), and tobacco (Southern Rhodesia).

17. Gosner, *Soldiers of the Virgin: The Moral Economy of a Colonial Maya Rebellion,* 83. In Amerindian communities the posts of *fiscal, maestro de coro,* and sacristan were held by indigenous Catholics. Appointed by the parish priest, these persons were important intermediaries between the local community and Europeans atop the religious hierarchy.

18. Achebe's novel *Things Fall Apart* graphically depicts these aspects of the missionary impact on Igbos in Nigeria.

19. Jack, *Daybreak in Livingstonia: The Story of the Livingstonia Mission in British Central Africa;* Rotberg, *Christian Missionaries and the Creation of Northern Rhodesia, 1880–1924,* chap. 3.

20. This dual identity is stressed in *Subaltern Studies,* an Indian journal founded in 1982 to critique European colonialism and its postcolonial legacies. Said makes a similar point in *Orientalism* and other works.

21. Quoted in Stocking, "Maclay, Kubary, Malinowski," in Stocking, ed., *Colonial Situations,* 38.

22. *English-Swahili Phrase Book,* 9.

23. Tevoedjre, *L'Afrique Révoltée,* 72. After independence Dahomey was renamed the Republic of Benin.

Chapter 13. Sources of Colonial Weakness

1. Crow, *The Epic of Latin America,* 407–08.

2. Kane, *Ambiguous Adventure,* 37. Emphasis added.

3. Stern, *Peru's Indian Peoples and the Challenge of Spanish Conquest,* 135, 137.

4. Hemming, *Red Gold: The Conquest of the Brazilian Indians, 1500–1760,* discusses the escape option Indians took as they sought, often successfully, to avoid enslavement and slaughter. The journal *Cultural Survival* describes a similar pattern today as the settler frontier presses deeper into the Amazonian forest.

5. Hemming, *Conquest of the Incas,* chaps. 16, 25.

6. Price, ed., *Maroon Societies: Slave Communities in the Americas;* Price, *The Guiana Maroons;* Campbell, *The Maroons of Jamaica, 1655–1796.*

7. Abun-Nasr, *A History of the Maghrib in the Islamic Period,* 329–30.

8. Peires, *The Dead Will Arise.* Shepperson, "Nyasaland and the Millennium," in Thrupp, ed., *Millennial Dreams in Action,* 144–59.

9. Campbell, *Rasta and Resistance,* links slave revolts and maroon activity to subsequent movements for black emancipation. He argues (39) that in the twentieth century, as blacks returned to their Caribbean homelands from education and work abroad, "the legacy of Tacky, Cudjoe, Nanny, Paul Bogle and Sam Sharpe was linked [in people's minds] to the struggles of Harriet Tubman, Sojourner Truth, King Ja Ja, Chaka Zulu and King Menelik of Ethiopia."

10. Scott, *Weapons of the Weak: Everyday Forms of Peasant Resistance.* I apply Scott's ideas to colonized peoples while recognizing that the tactics he discussed were used in all sorts of noncolonial situations as well.

11. In the 1760s a Delaware Indian prophet named Neolin urged Indians to revitalize their culture by abandoning material objects associated with whites and forswearing rum. Nash, *Red, White, and Black,* 262. In Kenya in the late 1920s, members of the Watu wa Mngu (People of God) sect among the Kikuyu threw away all utensils of foreign origin. According to Jomo Kenyatta, sect leaders "say emphatically that foreign goods are full of defilements." Kenyatta, *Facing Mt. Kenya,* 265.

12. The colonizer's message could produce *both* reactions within the same person. In a brilliant essay, "The Fact of Blackness," in *Black Skin, White Masks,* Fanon describes the devastating effect the white person's negative image of blacks has on him, even as he resolutely rejects that image as false and immoral.

13. Memmi, *The Colonizer and the Colonized*, 87–88.

14. Quoted in Penders, ed., *Indonesia: Selected Documents on Colonialism and Nationalism, 1830–1942*, 230.

15. I classify mestizos as non-Europeans, especially since they fought alongside indigenous peoples in the two rebellions in which they were most active: those led by Hidalgo and Morelos. Morelos and Tupac Amaru II were mestizo; the latter had a Spanish wife. People of European descent played a part in some cases. A few creoles assumed local leadership roles in Tupac Amaru's rebellion. The creole priest Miguel Hidalgo was acknowledged leader of the rebellion in New Spain's Bajío region. The vast bulk of the army assembled under his banner, however, was Amerindian and mestizo.

16. The longest-lasting was the campaign led by Sayyid Muhammad 'Abdille Hassan to oust foreigners from Somalia. The man the British exasperatedly called the Mad Mullah kept British, Italian, and Ethiopian forces on the defensive from 1900 until 1920. Lewis, *A Modern History of Somalia*, chap. 4.

17. Wolpert, *India*, 53–54.

18. Nehru, *The Discovery of India*, 325.

19. Leon Campbell, "Ideology and Factionalism During the Great Rebellion, 1780–82," in Stern, ed., *Resistance, Rebellion, and Consciousness in the Andean Peasant World*, 110–39; and Stern, "Introduction to Part I," 32.

20. There is a vast literature on anticolonial nationalism within the even larger corpus on nationalism. Works I found helpful include Anderson, *Imagined Communities;* Breuilly, *Nationalism and the State;* Deutsch, *Nationalism and Social Communication;* Emerson, *From Empire to Nation;* Gellner, *Nations and Nationalism;* Hodgkin, *Nationalism in Colonial Africa;* Kohn, *The Idea of Nationalism;* Ronen, *The Quest for Self-Determination;* Seton-Watson, *Nations and States;* Smith, *Theories of Nationalism;* Snyder, *Varieties of Nationalism;* and Ward, *Five Ideas that Change the World.*

21. Some nationalists supplemented the claim to statehood by a sweeping, usually vaguer, claim about the rights of larger categories of people. The prime examples are pan-Africanism and pan-Arabism. I see these as supranationalist doctrines because they served primarily to give significance to the struggle for statehood in specific territories.

22. Studies of nationalist social movements and parties in British colonies include Sisson and Wolpert, eds., *Congress and Indian Nationalism;* Tomlinson, *The Indian National Congress and the Raj, 1929–1942;* Austin, *Politics in Ghana, 1946–1960;* Sklar, *Nigerian Political Parties;* Bienen, *Tanzania: Party Transformation and Economic Development;* and Mulford, *Zambia: The Politics of Independence, 1957–1964.*

23. Hoffer, *The True Believer*, 27.

24. See Young, *The Politics of Cultural Pluralism,* and Horowitz, *Ethnic Groups in Conflict,* for analyses and examples of changes in group identity when people compete for centrally distributed resources in modernizing Third World states. Case studies of identities that appear traditional but are not include Rudolph and Rudolph, *The Modernity of Tradition: Political Development in India;* Epstein, *Politics in an Urban African Community;* Mitchell, *The Kalela*

Dance; Ranger, *The Invention of Tribalism in Zimbabwe;* and Vail, ed., *The Creation of Tribalism in Southern Africa.*

25. Morgenthau, *Political Parties in French-Speaking West Africa,* chaps. 5, 6.

26. Bolitho, *Jinnah, Creator of Pakistan,* 84.

27. Coleman, *Nigeria: Background to Nationalism,* 347; chaps. 15–18.

28. In phase 4 it seems inappropriate to describe as settlers people whose ancestors may have migrated from the British Isles a century or more earlier. But the same problem arises when one uses the term to describe late phase 1 Spanish American creoles. Despite its obvious limitations, "settlers" captures the dual identity of persons permanently ensconced in one territory yet able (and often eager) to trace genealogical and cultural descent to the metropole.

29. Phelan, *The People and the King: The Communero Revolution in Colombia, 1781,* xvii.

30. See Morris's evocative description of her Diamond Jubilee in 1897 as "an imperial fulfillment" in *Heaven's Command,* chap. 27.

31. For text and background, see Mansergh, *The Commonwealth Experience,* 233–36.

Chapter 14. Colonialism as a Self-Defeating Enterprise

1. By "new states" I mean polities that declared independence from a European metropole and were internationally recognized as possessing sovereignty. I do not refer to states formed under other circumstances, such as the collapse and fragmentation of large land-based polities like the Austro-Hungarian Empire, Ottoman Empire, and Union of Soviet Socialist Republics. A comparative study of state formation in these situations is Barkey and von Hagen, eds. *After Empire: Multiethnic Societies and Nation-Building.*

2. From "If Only I Were a Netherlander," quoted in Penders, ed., *Indonesia: Selected Documents on Colonialism and Nationalism, 1830–1942,* 233.

3. Morison, *Oxford History of the American People,* 222. Hartz emphasizes the close correspondence between Lockean thinking and BNA settler worldviews in *The Liberal Tradition in America.* On eighteenth-century settler pamphlets, which echoed contemporary complaints in England about an arbitrary and unrepresentative Parliament, see Bailyn, *Ideological Origins of the American Revolution.*

4. James, *The Black Jacobins: Toussaint L'Ouverture and the San Domingo Revolution,* 46.

5. Quoted in Crow, *The Epic of Latin America,* 416–17.

6. Ibid., 526.

7. Quoted in Lacouture, *Ho Chi Minh: A Political Biography,* 35.

8. To simplify matters I discuss only settler-led movements in phase 2, leaving the Haitian exception aside, and only non-European-led movements in phase 5, leaving the Rhodesian exception aside.

9. Singer, *Weak States in a World of Powers,* 173. See the title of Wolf's book: *Europe and the People without History.*

10. Comments here are more applicable to Old World than New World phase 5 states. Non-European populations in the Caribbean basin were exposed to Western education, Christianity, and European lifestyles much earlier and more intensively than people in Asia, Africa,

and Oceania. Hence the rapid growth of secondary- and university-level enrollment in phases 4 and 5 probably had a less revolutionary impact—politically as well as culturally—in the Caribbean than in the Old World.

11. Baum and Gagliano, *Chief Executives in Black Africa and Southeast Asia,* appendix B, tables 5, 6. Considering the prominent role Christian missions played in colonial education, it is significant that twenty-eight of the forty-eight African leaders stating a religious affiliation listed Christianity. Comparable figures for Southeast Asia were five of twenty-seven—a lower proportion but still far higher than the percentage of Christians in the region. Ibid., table 4.

12. If one broadens the criteria to include prominent nationalists trained in Europe or the United States who did not become chief executives at independence, the list includes Obafemi Awolowo (Nigeria), Ba Maw (Burma), Subhas Chandra Bose (India), J. B. Danquah (Ghana), Mamadou Dia (Senegal), M. K. Gandhi (India), Cheddi Jagan (Guyana), V. K. Krishna Menon (India), Tom Mboya (Kenya), Eduardo Mondlane (Mozambique), and Soetan Sjahrir (Indonesia). One could add a long list of politically active intellectuals as well, such as Caribbean-born pan-Africanists Aimé Césaire, Frantz Fanon, C. L. R. James, and George Padmore.

13. Ho Van Tao, quoted in Lacouture, *Ho Chi Minh,* 21.

14. Ibid., 35.

15. Morgenthau, *Political Parties in French-Speaking West Africa,* 19.

16. Olusanya, *The West African Students' Union and the Politics of Decolonisation, 1925–1958.*

17. Nkrumah, *Ghana: The Autobiography of Kwame Nkrumah,* 44, 45.

18. This incident is recounted in the essay on Prime Minister Rahman in *Current Biography Yearbook, 1957,* 444.

19. Dahm, *Sukarno and the Struggle for Indonesian Independence,* 52–54.

20. Hodson, *The Great Divide,* 81. "Pakistan" is a linguistic amalgam of the northern Indian provinces of Punjab, Afghan or Northwest Frontier, Kashmir, Sind, and Baluchistan.

21. Lacouture, *Ho Chi Minh,* 35. Ho Chi Minh's perspective was based not only on his years in France but also on experiences from 1911 to 1913 as a laborer on French ships. Lacouture notes (18) that he went ashore "at all the principal ports of Africa and the Mediterranean; Oran, Dakar, Diégo-Suarez, Port Said, Alexandria, where he observed conditions closely akin to those in Vietnam, and these findings were to constitute the factual basis" of his book.

22. Jawaharlal Nehru studied in England from 1905 to 1912, enrolling at Harrow, the elite secondary school, then at Cambridge University, and reading law and economics in London. He gave few public speeches in the early years after returning to India, in large part because "I felt that public speeches should not be in English, and I doubted my capacity to speak at any length in Hindustani." Nehru, *Toward Freedom,* 42–43. Because of schooling given M. A. Jinnah, the Muslim League leader and founder of Pakistan, by an early point in his life "English had become his chief language, and it remained so, for he never mastered Urdu; even when he was leading the Muslims into freedom, he had to define the terms of their emancipation in an alien tongue." Bolitho, *Jinnah, Creator of Pakistan,* 14.

23. Nehru, *Toward Freedom,* 353. Nehru wrote the original edition of his autobiography in 1934 and 1935 while in prison.

24. Jahoda, *White Man.*

25. See, for example, Sundkler, *Bantu Prophets in South Africa;* Shepperson and Price, *Independent African: John Chilembwe and . . . the Nyasaland Native Rising of 1915;* and Rosberg and Nottingham, *The Myth of "Mau Mau": Nationalism in Kenya,* chap. 4.

26. Sithole, *African Nationalism,* 85, 86.

27. Ibid., 86.

28. I treat British India as the phase 5 leader even though Jordan, Syria, and Lebanon preceded its independence by a year. I do so because of the prominence of India's nationalist movement in phase 4, the enormous publicity attending its run-up to independence and partition, and the great impact Indian independence had elsewhere. Independence for the three Middle East mandate territories was little noticed by the world at large.

29. Quoted in Cochrane, *Frontiers of Change: Early Industrialism in America,* 54. Perkins estimates that by the 1770s the typical BNA family maintained a material standard of living about a fifth higher than its counterpart in England. Perkins, *Economy of Colonial America,* 145.

30. Markovitz, *Indian Business and Nationalist Politics, 1931–1939.* Leadbeater, *The Politics of Textiles.*

Chapter 15. The International Dimension: War as the Catalyst for Independence

1. Brewer, *The Sinews of Power: War, Money and the English State, 1688–1783,* table 2:1, 30. Debt rose by £58 million between 1756 and 1763. In the two principal previous wars it rose by £29 million (1739–48) and £22 million (1702–13).

2. Quoted in Lapping, *End of Empire,* 156.

3. McMahon, *Colonialism and Cold War,* 35.

4. Spear, *A History of India* 2:182. Spear writes (246) that Nehru "had a deep suspicion of the designs of European powers in Asia and Africa. His ideas in this sphere may be said to have been influenced by President Wilson's Fourteen Points."

5. Quoted in Horne, *A Savage War of Peace,* 77.

6. Leith-Ross, *Stepping-Stones: Memoirs of Colonial Nigeria,* 119. The author notes (119) that newspaper reports of Sir Stafford Cripps's mission to India in early 1942, holding out the prospect of postwar Indian political advance to leading politicians, "sent as it were an electric shock throughout Lagos. . . . India was going to have complete independence. Then why not Nigeria?"

7. "Overseas possessions" includes territories with different constitutional statuses: (a) associated territories, i.e., those initially established as protectorates: Tunisia, Morocco, Cambodia, Laos, Vietnam (minus Cochinchina); (b) overseas departments considered parts of France itself: Caribbean possessions like Martinique and Guadeloupe, and Algeria; (c) overseas territories, i.e., dependent possessions of metropolitan France in sub-Saharan Africa and Madagascar. The rightward shift in French politics affected overseas territories most directly. But leaders in other possessions followed this trend closely and with growing dismay.

8. Morgenthau, *Political Parties in French-Speaking West Africa,* 48. See 41–54 for a comparison of the two constituent assemblies' proposals regarding African colonies.

9. Yves Person, "French West Africa and Decolonization," in Gifford and Louis, eds., *The Transfer of Power in Africa . . . 1940–1960,* 146.

10. Greene, "The Seven Years' War and the American Revolution," *Journal of Imperial and Commonwealth History*, 101.

11. See postwar identity changes as reported in Merritt, *Symbols of American Community, 1735–1775*, 74, 76, 215.

12. See the title of his *British Politics and the Stamp Act Crisis: The First Phase of the American Revolution, 1763–1767*. Thomas emphasizes "the almost universal consensus of opinion in Britain on the question of Parliamentary supremacy over America" (364) during these years. Thus, despite repeal of the Stamp Act, "the lesson of the Stamp Act crisis was that there would be very few 'friends of America' in Britain in any future clash with the colonies" (371).

13. Tucker and Hendrickson, *Fall of the First British Empire: Origins of the American War of Independence*, 3.

14. Quoted in Humphreys and Lynch, eds., *Origins of the Latin American Revolutions, 1808–1826*, 262.

15. Brown, *Gandhi's Rise to Power: Indian Politics 1915–1922*, 159.

16. Ibid., 185.

17. Quoted in ibid., 164. Word underlined by Gandhi.

18. Marsot, *A Short History of Modern Egypt*, 80.

19. David Strang, "From Dependency to Sovereignty: An Event History Analysis of Decolonization, 1870–1987," *American Sociological Review*, 858.

20. Ibid.

Chapter 16. Legacies

1. Wide-ranging discussions of the West's global impact include Toynbee, *The World and the West;* Dawson, *The Movement of World Revolution;* von Laue, *The World Revolution of Westernization;* and works on modernization by the social scientists C. E. Black, Karl Deutsch, S. N. Eisenstadt, Alex Inkeles, Daniel Lerner, Lucian Pye, and Dankwart Rustow. In the humanities, scholars in the rapidly growing field of postcolonial studies, while suspicious of social scientific approaches, share with modernization theorists an extremely broad conception of the West and its impacts. See, for example, Young, *White Mythologies: Writing History and the West,* and Prakash, ed., *After Colonialism: Imperial Histories and Postcolonial Displacements*. One reason it is difficult to know what to make of claims by postcolonial theorists is that colonialism is a vast, catchall category with virtually no conceptual boundaries because it is not clearly defined. Understanding cannot advance if writers fail to specify what their key terms mean.

2. Tetlock and Belkin, eds., *Counterfactual Thought Experiments in World Politics*, 3, 4.

3. Stateless peoples like Palestinians and Kurds lack a polity they control. But their problem is not that they are not subject to state authority. On the contrary, they have been incorporated into states—Israel, Iraq, Iran, Turkey—whose governments oppress them. Marginalized peoples commonly respond to oppression by demanding statehood for themselves. If their demands were granted the world would become even more politically homogenous.

4. These issues are insightfully analyzed by the Nigerian sociologist Peter Ekeh in "Colonialism and the Two Publics: A Theoretical Statement," *Comparative Studies in Society and History*.

5. Akintoye, *Emergent African States*, 9–10. The authoritarian dimension of colonialism is emphasized in Young, *The African Colonial State in Comparative Perspective*.

6. See my "Bureaucratic Growth and Economic Stagnation in Sub-Saharan Africa," in Commins, ed., *Africa's Development Challenges and the World Bank*, 179–214. I estimate (189) that employment in regular-line agencies of central and local government grew from 1.9 to 6.5 million between 1960 and 1980. If one adds nonfinancial parastatal organizations, public sector employment rose from roughly 3.8 to 10 million during this period. By 1980 the public sector, including parastatals, probably accounted for half the people formally employed outside agriculture.

7. Data calculated from Gunnemark, *Countries, Peoples, and Their Languages*.

8. Calculated from ibid. Russia is the only noncolonized country in which more than one hundred languages are spoken.

9. Information on Sudan, Mauretania, and Togo from Morrison et al., *Black Africa: A Comparative Handbook*, 631, 560, 660–61.

10. About 5 million Indians in a population of more than 850 million are said to know English well. This tiny pool presumably supplies the bulk of the central government's bureaucrats, scientists, and diplomats. (Estimates from Gunnemark, *Countries, Peoples, and their Languages*, 88–90.) As of 1985 only a quarter of those school-age and older in Africa's officially francophone countries was literate in French. Manning, *Francophone Sub-Saharan Africa 1880–1985*, 168.

11. Zartman, *The Politics of Trade Negotiations Between Africa and the European Economic Community*; Davenport et al., *Europe's Preferred Partners? The Lomé Countries in World Trade*.

12. Nkrumah, *Ghana: The Autobiography of Kwame Nkrumah*, x.

13. Nandy, *The Intimate Enemy: Loss and Recovery of Self under Colonialism*.

14. Stephen Jay Gould, lecture at the College of Wooster in 1987, quoted in Tom Wicker, "The Greatest Tragedy," *New York Times*, Jan. 21, 1988.

15. For international extractive capability, see Almond and Powell, *Comparative Politics: A Developmental Approach*, 195–205.

16. McAlister, *Spain and Portugal in the New World, 1492–1700*, 292.

17. For the large number of posts at the gubernatorial level, see Henige, *Colonial Governors from the Fifteenth Century to the Present*. This study provides data on almost four hundred European possessions.

18. From the introduction to Tilly, ed., *Formation of National States in Western Europe*, 42.

19. Bender, *Angola Under the Portuguese*, 60.

20. Ageron, *Modern Algeria*, 30. See Porch, *The Conquest of Morocco*, 67, for recruitment of social undesirables in France's African Light Infantry, which played a key role in the invasion of Algeria in 1830 and subsequent pacification campaigns.

21. "The expedition . . . was a make-shift expedient for internal political consumption, carried out by a government in difficulty seeking the prestige of a military victory. . . . As the minister of

war had written as long before as 1827, 'it would be a useful distraction from political troubles at home' and would allow the government 'to go to the country at the next election with the keys of Algiers in its hand.'" Ageron, *Modern Algeria*, 5.

22. Of these, Bismarck was the least favorably disposed to overseas expansion. But there is evidence that he thought an assertion of German claims in Africa would help him in the Reichstag elections of 1884. Stoecker, ed., *German Imperialism in Africa*, 33.

23. The Duchy of Kurland (in present-day Latvia) and the Electorate of Brandenburg (after 1701 the Kingdom of Prussia). Henige, *Colonial Governors*, appendix, 361. Venetian sailors made trade contact with islands off the North African Atlantic coast early in phase 1. Venice and Genoa, of course, controlled extensive networks of trading enclaves in the Mediterranean and the Black Sea.

24. Sarraut, *La Mise en Valeur des Colonies Françaises*, 37–38 (translation supplied).

25. For the influence of West Indian sugar planters and merchants on Britain's Parliament in the eighteenth century, see Williams, *Capitalism and Slavery*, 92–93. Persell describes the political influence of French business interests in *The French Colonial Lobby, 1889–1938*.

26. Advocates of the high-gain position include Wallerstein, in *The Modern World-System II*; Frank, in *World Accumulation, 1492–1789*; and Williams, in *Capitalism and Slavery*. Advocates of the low- or minimal-gain position include Rosenberg and Birdzell, in *How the West Grew Rich*, esp. 16–20; North and Thomas, in *Rise of the Western World*; and Bairoch, *Economics and World History*, part 2.

27. Williams, *Capitalism and Slavery*, 102; see chap. 5, "British Industry and the Triangular Trade."

28. Cameron, *A Concise Economic History of the World*, 160; Landes, *The Unbound Prometheus*, 82–83.

29. Said, *Orientalism* and *Culture and Imperialism*. See also Mudimbe, *The Idea of Africa*; Mitchell, *Colonising Egypt*; and Pratt, *Imperial Eyes: Travel Writing and Transculturation*. Discussing Victorian England in *Imperial Leather: Race, Gender, and Sexuality in the Colonial Context*, McClintock argues that the perceived exoticism of the colonial Other enabled some Europeans to indulge in a highly racialized and sexualized fantasy life.

30. For a critique of Western intellectuals' unwillingness to apply to non-Europeans behavioral standards routinely applied to their own societies, see P. T. Bauer, "Western Guilt and Third World Poverty," in Bauer, *Equality, the Third World, and Economic Delusion*, 66–85.

31. This point applies with particular force to territories in Africa and islands in the Caribbean and Oceania that became independent in phase 5. See Jackson, *Quasi-States*, and Jackson and Rosberg, "Why Africa's Weak States Persist: The Empirical and the Juridical in Statehood," *World Politics*.

32. Sjahrir, *Out of Exile*, 144–45.

Chapter 17. The Moral Evaluation of Colonialism

1. Works by critics include Alavi and Shanin, eds., *Introduction to the Sociology of "Developing Societies"*; Césaire, *Discourse on Colonialism*; Fanon, *The Wretched of the Earth* and *Black Skin, White Masks*; Rodney, *How Europe Underdeveloped Africa*; Nkrumah, *Ghana* and *I Speak of Freedom: A Statement of African Ideology*; Frank, *Capitalism and Underdevelopment in Latin*

America and *World Accumulation, 1492–1789;* and Murdoch, *The Poverty of Nations.* For defenders, see Bauer ("The Economics of Resentment" and "Western Guilt and Third World Poverty," in *Equality, the Third World, and Economic Delusion;* Burns, *In Defence of Colonies;* Perham, *The Colonial Reckoning: The End of Imperial Rule in Africa in the Light of British Experience;* Gann and Duignan, *Burden of Empire;* Kat Angelino, *Colonial Policy;* Ryckmans, *Dominer Pour Servir;* Sarraut, *La Mise en Valeur des Colonies Français;* and Lugard, *The Dual Mandate in Tropical Africa.* Though many of these works focus on the colonial experience in nineteenth- and twentieth-century Africa, the basic arguments can be readily extended to other times and places. Not surprisingly, many of the critics are non-Europeans who grew up in the colonies, while most of the defenders are Europeans who grew up in metropoles. As the adage goes, where one stands is strongly influenced by where one sits.

2. These authors include Nehru, *Toward Freedom,* chap. 41; Kaunda, *A Humanist in Africa,* chap. 3; Marx, "The Future Results of British Rule in India," and other selections in Avineri, ed., *Karl Marx on Colonialism and Modernization;* Isichei, *The Ibo Peoples and the Europeans;* and Warren, *Imperialism: Pioneer of Capitalism.* For a carefully reasoned discussion by an eminent philosopher, see Plamenatz, *On Alien Rule and Self-Government.*

3. Horne, *A Savage War of Peace,* 27.

4. Rodney, *How Europe Underdeveloped Africa,* 22.

5. Césaire, *Discourse,* 23. See also Rodney, *How Europe Underdeveloped Africa,* chap. 2. Rodney cites (40) the Gold Coast nationalist J. E. Casely-Hayford, who wrote in 1922, "Before even the British came into relations with our people, we were a developed people, having our own institutions, having our own ideas of government."

6. Rodney, *How Europe Underdeveloped Africa,* 57–83; quotation on 81.

7. Lugard, *The Dual Mandate,* 617.

8. Cited in Lewis, ed., *The British in India: Imperialism or Trusteeship?* 8. See the French poem cited earlier, contrasting cruel Dahomean rulers who sold their subjects into slavery with the French, "who delivered us and made us into men."

9. In several situations European rulers took advantage of and further refined exploitative labor recruitment practices dating from precolonial times. Examples are the Inca Empire's *mita* system and the compulsory labor policies of Vietnamese emperors. In such situations, defenders would insist that if Europeans are to be judged harshly the same judgment should apply to their predecessors as well. Defenders would not deny that Europeans violated the moral norm of nonexploitation. But they would argue that this did not, in and of itself, make colonial rule any worse for the subject population than the practices of noncolonial regimes.

10. Marx, "The Future Results of the British Rule in India," in Avineri, ed., *Karl Marx on Colonialism,* 132. The issue is not whether Marx's historical assessment was correct but whether, if one believed that it was, one would be less inclined to criticize any specific foreign elite in India, the British included, on grounds that it *was* foreign.

11. Smith, *An Inquiry into the Nature and Causes of the Wealth of Nations,* 535. It should be noted, however, that Smith attributes these benefits to the initiatives of settlers, not to the policies of colonial regimes. Indeed, his chapter "On Colonies" is an attack on the mercantilist policies and practices of the leading metropoles. Smith thus occupies an ambivalent if not contradic-

tory position: he welcomes the economic activities of European private profit actors overseas yet criticizes public sector rule that was often a precondition for these very activities.

12. Though Gandhi and Césaire (in the latter's early poems) question the high priority westerners place on material possessions and technological progress. The argument is that materialism undermines other desirable values such as social solidarity, happiness, and spiritual enlightenment.

13. Césaire, *Discourse*, 24.

14. Gann and Duignan, *Burden of Empire*, 365–67.

15. Alatas, *The Myth of the Lazy Native*, 216, See similar statements about late nineteenth-century African rulers and Western-educated intellectuals in Boahen, *African Perspectives on Colonialism*, 1–27.

16. Masefield, *A History of the Colonial Agricultural Service*, 102.

17. See, for example, Bauer on the growth of production, trade, and school enrollment in the Gold Coast from the 1890s to the mid-1950s. Bauer, "The Economics of Resentment," *Journal of Contemporary History*, 53–54.

18. Césaire, *Discourse*, 21, 22.

19. Rodney, *How Europe Underdeveloped Africa*, 182. Césaire, *Discourse*, 21–22, speaks of "thousands of men sacrificed" in the construction of this railroad line.

20. Gann and Duignan, *Burden of Empire*, 241.

21. Nehru, *Toward Freedom*, 277.

22. Cited in Moon, *The British Conquest and Dominion of India*, 428.

23. Kaunda, *A Humanist in Africa*, 50.

24. Lumumba, *Congo, My Country*, 12, 13.

25. Presence Africaine, *La Pensée Politique de Patrice Lumumba*, 198, 199 (translation supplied). King Baudoin described the Congo's independence as "the crowning achievement of the mission conceived by the genius of King Leopold II, undertaken by him with a tenacious courage . . . not as a conqueror, but as a civilizer." Quoted in Young, *Politics in the Congo*, 50–51.

26. Marx, "The British Rule in India," (*New York Daily Tribune*, June 25, 1853), in Avineri, ed., *Karl Marx on Colonialism*, 93–94.

27. Nehru, *Toward Freedom*, 278.

28. Marx, "The Future Results of British Rule in India," in Avineri, *Karl Marx on Colonialism*, 132–33, 136.

29. Warren, *Imperialism: Pioneer of Capitalism*, esp. chaps. 1–5.

30. Thomas Munro to Warren Hastings, quoted in Moon, *British Conquest and Dominion of India*, 427.

BIBLIOGRAPHY

Abernethy, David B. *The Political Dilemma of Popular Education: An African Case.* Stanford: Stanford University Press, 1969.

Abu-Lughod, Janet L. *Before European Hegemony: The World System, A.D. 1250–1350.* New York: Oxford University Press, 1989.

Abun-Nasr, Jamil M. *A History of the Maghrib in the Islamic Period.* Cambridge: Cambridge University Press, 1987.

Achebe, Chinua. *A Man of the People.* Garden City: Doubleday, 1967.

———. *Things Fall Apart.* London: Heinemann, 1958.

Adas, Michael. *The Burma Delta: Economic Development and Social Change on an Asian Rice Frontier, 1852–1941.* Madison: University of Wisconsin Press, 1974.

———. *Machines as the Measure of Men: Science, Technology, and Ideologies of Western Dominance.* Ithaca: Cornell University Press, 1989.

———. *Prophets of Rebellion: Millenarian Protest Movements Against the European Colonial Order.* Chapel Hill: University of North Carolina Press, 1979.

———, ed. *Islamic and European Expansion: The Forging of a Global Order.* Philadelphia: Temple University Press, 1993.

Afigbo, A. E. *The Warrant Chiefs: Indirect Rule in Southeastern Nigeria, 1891–1929.* New York: Humanities Press, 1972.

Ageron, Charles-Robert. *Modern Algeria: A History from 1830 to the Present.* Translated by Michael Brett. Trenton: Africa World Press, 1991.

Ajayi, J. F. A. *Christian Missions in Nigeria, 1841–1891: The Making of a New Elite.* Evanston: Northwestern University Press, 1965.

Akintoye, S. A. *Emergent African States: Topics in Twentieth-Century African History.* London: Longman, 1976.

Alatas, Hussein. *The Myth of the Lazy Native.* London: Frank Cass, 1977.

Alavi, Hamza. "The State in Post-Colonial Societies." *New Left Review* 74 (July 1972): 58–82.

———, and Teodor Shanin, eds. *Introduction to the Sociology of "Developing Societies."* New York: Monthly Review Press, 1982.

Albertini, Rudolf von. *Decolonization: The Administration and Future of the Colonies, 1919–1960*. New York: Holmes & Meier, 1982.

——. *European Colonial Rule, 1880–1940*. Westport: Greenwood Press, 1982.

——. "The Impact of Two World Wars on the Decline of Colonialism." *Journal of Contemporary History* 4:1 (January 1969): 17–36.

Albuquerque, Affonso de. *Commentaries of the Great Afonso Dalboquerque, Second Viceroy of India*. Vol. 3. London: Hakluyt Society, 1880.

Alden, Dauril. *The Making of an Enterprise: The Society of Jesus in Portugal, Its Empire, and Beyond, 1540–1750*. Stanford: Stanford University Press, 1996.

Almond, Gabriel A., and G. Bingham Powell. *Comparative Politics: A Developmental Approach*. Boston: Little, Brown, 1966.

Almond, Gabriel A., and James S. Coleman, eds. *The Politics of the Developing Areas*. Princeton: Princeton University Press, 1960.

Almond, Gabriel A., et al. *Crisis, Choice, and Change: Historical Studies of Political Development*. Boston: Little, Brown, 1973.

Altbach, Philip, and Gail Kelly, eds. *Education and the Colonial Experience*. 2d rev. ed. New Brunswick: Transaction Books, 1984.

Amin, Samir. *Unequal Development: An Essay on the Social Formations of Peripheral Capitalism*. New York: Monthly Review Press, 1976.

Anderson, Benedict. *Imagined Communities: Reflections on the Origin and Spread of Nationalism*. London: Verso, 1983.

——. *Java in a Time of Revolution: Occupation and Resistance, 1944–1946*. Ithaca: Cornell University Press, 1972.

Anderson, Fred. *Crucible of War: The Seven Years' War and the Fate of Empire in British North America, 1754–1766*. New York: A. Knopf, 2000.

Anderson, Lisa. *The State and Social Transformation in Tunisia and Libya, 1830–1980*. Princeton: Princeton University Press, 1986.

Anderson, Perry. *Lineages of the Absolutist State*. London: Verso, 1979.

Andrews, Kenneth R. *Trade, Plunder, and Settlement: Maritime Enterprise and the Genesis of the British Empire, 1480–1630*. Cambridge: Cambridge University Press, 1984.

Anna, Timothy E. *The Fall of the Royal Government in Mexico City*. Lincoln: University of Nebraska Press, 1978.

——. *The Fall of the Royal Government in Peru*. Lincoln: University of Nebraska Press, 1980.

——. *Spain and the Loss of America*. Lincoln: University of Nebraska Press, 1983.

Ansprenger, Franz. *The Dissolution of the Colonial Empires*. London: Routledge, 1989.

Anstey, Roger. *The Atlantic Slave Trade and British Abolition, 1760–1810*. Atlantic Highlands: Humanities Press, 1975.

Apter, David. *Ghana in Transition*. Rev. ed. New York: Atheneum, 1963.

Aptheker, Herbert. *American Negro Slave Revolts*. New York: International, 1963.

Arciniegas, Germain. *America in Europe: A History of the New World in Reverse*. New York: Harcourt Brace Jovanovich, 1986.

Arendt, Hannah. *The Origins of Totalitarianism.* New ed. New York: Harcourt Brace Jovano-vich, 1973.

Arrighi, Giovanni. *The Long Twentieth Century: Money, Power, and the Origins of Our Times.* London: Verso, 1994.

Asad, Talal, ed. *Anthropology and the Colonial Encounter.* New York: Humanities Press, 1973.

Ascherson, Neal. *The King Incorporated: Leopold II in the Age of Trusts.* London: Allen & Unwin, 1963.

Atieno Odhiambo, E. S. *Siasa: Politics and Nationalism in East Africa, 1905–1939.* Nairobi: Kenya Literature Bureau, 1981.

Austen, Ralph A., ed. *Modern Imperialism, Western Overseas Expansion, and its Aftermath, 1776–1965.* Lexington: D. C. Heath, 1969.

Austin, Dennis. *Politics in Ghana, 1946–1960.* London: Oxford University Press, 1964.

Avineri, Shlomo, ed. *Karl Marx on Colonialism and Modernization.* Garden City: Doubleday, 1969.

Axtell, James. *After Columbus: Essays in the Ethnohistory of Colonial North America.* New York: Oxford University Press, 1988.

——. *The Invasion Within: The Contest of Cultures in Colonial North America.* New York: Oxford University Press, 1985.

Ayandele, E. A. *The Missionary Impact on Modern Nigeria, 1842–1914.* London: Longmans, 1966.

Azikiwe, Nnamdi. *Political Blueprint of Nigeria.* Lagos: African Book Co., 1943.

——. 1937. Reprint, *Renascent Africa.* London: Frank Cass, 1968.

Aziz, Muhammed A. *Japan's Colonialism and Indonesia.* The Hague: M. Nijhoff, 1955.

Ba Maw, U. *Breakthrough in Burma: Memoirs of a Revolution, 1939–1946.* New Haven: Yale University Press, 1968.

Baechler, Jean, John Hall, and Michael Mann, eds. *Europe and the Rise of Capitalism.* Oxford: Basil Blackwell, 1988.

Baer, George. *Test Case: Italy, Ethiopia, and the League of Nations.* Stanford: Hoover Institution Press, 1976.

——. *The Coming of the Italian-Ethiopian War.* Cambridge: Harvard University Press, 1967.

Bagchi, Amiya K. "Deindustrialization in India in the Nineteenth Century: Some Theoretical Implications." *Journal of Development Studies* 12:2 (January 1976): 135–64.

——. *Private Investment in India, 1900–1939.* Cambridge: Cambridge University Press, 1972.

Bailyn, Bernard. *The Ideological Origins of the American Revolution.* Cambridge: Belknap Press of Harvard University Press, 1992.

Bairoch, Paul. *Economics and World History: Myths and Paradoxes.* Chicago: University of Chicago Press, 1993.

——. "International Industrialization Levels from 1750 to 1980." *Journal of European Economic History* 11:2 (Fall 1982): 269–333.

——, and Maurice Levy-Leboyer, eds. *Disparities in Economic Development Since the Industrial Revolution.* New York: St. Martin's Press, 1981.

Baker, Geoffrey L. *Trade Winds on the Niger: The Saga of the Royal Niger Company, 1830–1971.* London: Radcliffe Press, 1996.

Bakewell, Peter. *Miners of the Red Mountain: Indian Labor in Potosi, 1545–1650.* Albuquerque: University of New Mexico Press, 1984.

Balandier, Georges. "La Situation Coloniale: Approche Théorique." *Cahiers Internationaux de Sociologie* 11 (1951): 44–79.

Balesi, Charles John. *From Adversaries to Comrades-in-Arms: West Africans and the French Military, 1885–1918.* Waltham: Crossroads Press, 1979.

Ballhatchet, Kenneth. *Race, Sex, and Class under the Raj: Imperial Attitudes and Policies and their Critics, 1793–1905.* London: Weidenfeld & Nicolson, 1980.

Barbier, Maurice, ed. and comp. *Voyages et Explorations au Sahara Occidentale au XIXe Siècle.* Paris: Editions L'Harmattan, 1985.

Barfield, Thomas J. *The Perilous Frontier: Nomadic Empires and China.* New York: Basil Blackwell, 1989.

Barker, Ernest. *The Development of Public Services in Western Europe.* Hamden: Archon, 1966.

Barkey, Karen, and Mark von Hagen, eds. *After Empire: Multiethnic Societies and Nation-Building. The Soviet Union and the Russian, Ottoman, and Habsburg Empires.* Boulder: Westview Press, 1997.

Barman, Roderick J. *Brazil: The Forging of a Nation, 1798–1852.* Stanford: Stanford University Press, 1988.

Barnes, Leonard. *The Future of Colonies.* London: Hogarth Press, 1936.

Barnett, Corelli. *The Collapse of British Power.* New York: William Morrow, 1972.

Barraclough, Geoffrey. *An Introduction to Contemporary History.* London: Pelican Books, 1967.

Bauer, P. T. "The Economics of Resentment: Colonialism and Underdevelopment." *Journal of Contemporary History* 4:1 (January 1969): 51–71.

——. *Equality, the Third World, and Economic Delusion.* Cambridge: Harvard University Press, 1981.

——. *The Rubber Industry: A Study in Competition and Monopoly.* Cambridge: Harvard University Press, 1948.

——. *West African Trade.* Cambridge: Cambridge University Press, 1954.

Baum, Edward, and Felix Gagliano. *Chief Executives in Black Africa and Southeast Asia: A Descriptive Analysis of Social Background Characteristics.* Athens: Ohio University Center for International Studies, 1976.

Baumgart, Winfried. *Imperialism: The Idea and Reality of British and French Colonial Expansion, 1800–1914.* Oxford: Oxford University Press, 1982.

Bayly, C. A. *Imperial Meridian: The British Empire and the World, 1780–1830.* London: Longman, 1989.

——. *Indian Society and the Making of the British Empire.* Cambridge: Cambridge University Press, 1988.

Beach, Harlan P., and Charles H. Fahs, eds. *World Missionary Atlas.* New York: Institute of Social and Religious Research, 1925.

Beaglehole, J. C. *The Exploration of the Pacific*. 3d ed. Stanford: Stanford University Press, 1966.

Beckford, George L. *Persistent Poverty: Underdevelopment in Plantation Economies of the Third World*. New York: Oxford University Press, 1972.

Beidelman, T. O. *Colonial Evangelism: A Socio-Historical Study of an East African Mission at its Grassroots*. Bloomington: Indiana University Press, 1982.

Belaunde, Victor A. *Bolívar and the Political Thought of the Spanish American Revolution*. Baltimore: Johns Hopkins University Press, 1938.

Bender, Gerald J. *Angola under the Portuguese: The Myth and the Reality*. Berkeley: University of California Press, 1978.

——, James Coleman, and Richard Sklar, eds. *African Crisis Areas and U.S. Foreign Policy*. Los Angeles: University of California Press, 1985.

Bendix, Reinhard. *Nation-Building and Citizenship: Studies in Our Changing Social Order*. New York: Wiley, 1964.

Bennoune, Mahfoud. *The Making of Contemporary Algeria, 1830–1987*. Cambridge: Cambridge University Press, 1988.

Bentley, Jerry H. *Old World Encounters: Cross-Cultural Contacts and Exchanges in Pre-Modern Times*. New York: Oxford University Press, 1993.

Berg, Elliot. "The Economic Basis of Political Choice in French West Africa." *American Political Science Review* 54:2 (June 1960): 391–405.

Bergeson, Albert, ed. *Studies of the Modern World-System*. New York: Academic Press, 1980.

Berkes, Ross N., and Mohinder Bedi. *The Diplomacy of India: Indian Foreign Policy in the United Nations*. Stanford: Stanford University Press, 1958.

Berlin, Ira, and Ronald Hoffman, eds. *Slavery and Freedom in the Age of the American Revolution*. Charlottesville: University of Virginia Press, 1983.

Berman, Bruce J. *Control and Crisis in Colonial Kenya: The Dialectics of Domination*. London: J. Currey, 1990.

Bethel, Leslie, ed. *The Independence of Latin America*. Cambridge: Cambridge University Press, 1987.

Betts, Raymond F. "The Allusion to Rome in British Imperialist Thought of the Late Nineteenth and Early Twentieth Centuries." *Victorian Studies* 15:2 (December 1971): 149–59.

——. *The False Dawn: European Imperialism in the Nineteenth Century*. Minneapolis: University of Minnesota Press, 1975.

——. *Tricouleur: The French Overseas Empire*. London: Gordon & Cremonesi, 1978.

——. *Uncertain Dimensions: Western Overseas Empires in the Twentieth Century*. Minneapolis: University of Minnesota Press, 1985.

Biarnes, Pierre. *Les Français en Afrique Noire, de Richelieu à Mitterand*. Paris: A. Colin, 1987.

Bienen, Henry. *Tanzania: Party Transformation and Economic Development*. Princeton: Princeton University Press, 1970.

Birmingham, David. *Frontline Nationalism in Angola and Mozambique*. Trenton: Africa World Press, 1992.

Birnberg, Thomas B., and Stephen Resnick. *Colonial Development: An Econometric Study*. New Haven: Yale University Press, 1975.

Black, C. E. *The Dynamics of Modernization: A Study in Comparative History*. New York: Harper & Row, 1967.

Blaustein, Albert P., et al. *Independence Documents of the World*. 2 vols. Dobbs Ferry: Oceana, 1977.

Blussé, Leonard, and Femme Gaastra, eds. *Companies and Trade: Essays on Overseas Trading Companies during the Ancient Regime*. Leiden: Leiden University Press, 1981.

Boahen, A. Adu. *African Perspectives on Colonialism*. Baltimore: Johns Hopkins University Press, 1987.

——, ed. *Africa Under Colonial Domination, 1880–1935*. (Unesco *General History of Africa*, Vol. 7.) Paris: UNESCO and London: Heinemann, 1985.

Bolitho, Hector. *Jinnah, Creator of Pakistan*. London: John Murray, 1954.

Bolt, Christine. *Victorian Attitudes to Race*. London: Routledge & Kegan Paul, 1971.

Boorstin, Daniel J. *The Discoverers*. New York: Random House, 1983.

Boswell, Terry. "Colonial Empires and the Capitalist World-Economy: A Time Series Analysis of Colonization, 1640–1960." *American Sociological Review* 54 (April 1989): 180–96.

Boxer, C. R. *The Church Militant and Iberian Expansion*. Baltimore: Johns Hopkins University Press, 1978.

——. *The Dutch Seaborne Empire, 1600–1800*. London: Hutchinson, 1965.

——. *The Great Ship from Amacon: Annals of Macao and the Old Japan Trade*. Lisbon: Centro de Estudos Históricos Ultramarinos, 1963.

——. *The Portuguese Seaborne Empire, 1415–1825*. 2d ed. London: Hutchinson, 1969.

Brading, D. A., and Harry Cross. "Colonial Silver Mining: Mexico and Peru." *Hispanic American Historical Review* 52 (November 1972): 545–79.

Braudel, Fernand. *Civilization and Capitalism, 15th-18th Century*. Translated by Sian Reynolds. 3 vols. New York: Harper & Row, 1981–84.

——. *The Mediterranean and the Mediterranean World in the Age of Philip II*. New York: Harper & Row, 1972.

Brereton, Bridget. *Race Relations in Colonial Trinidad, 1870–1900*. Cambridge: Cambridge University Press, 1979.

Brett, E. A. *Colonialism and Underdevelopment in East Africa: The Politics of Economic Change, 1919–1939*. New York: NOK Publishers, 1973.

Breuilly, John. *Nationalism and the State*. 2d ed. Chicago: University of Chicago Press, 1993.

Brewer, John. *The Sinews of Power: War, Money, and the English State, 1688–1783*. Cambridge: Harvard University Press, 1990.

Bridgman, John M. *The Revolt of the Hereros*. Berkeley: University of California Press, 1981.

Brockway, Lucile H. *Science and Colonial Expansion: The Role of the British Royal Botanic Gardens*. New York: Academic Press, 1979.

Brown, Ian, ed. *The Economies of Africa and Asia in the Inter-War Depression*. London: Routledge, 1989.

Brown, Judith M. *Gandhi and Civil Disobedience: The Mahatma in Indian Politics, 1928–34*. Cambridge: Cambridge University Press, 1977.

——. *Gandhi's Rise to Power: Indian Politics, 1915–1922*. Cambridge: Cambridge University Press, 1972.

——, and Wm. Roger Louis, eds. *The Twentieth Century* (*The Oxford History of the British Empire*, Vol. 4). Oxford: Oxford University Press, 1999.

Brunschwig, Henri. *L'Afrique Noire au Temps de l'Empire Français*. Paris: Denoel, 1988.

——. *French Colonialism, 1871–1914: Myths and Realities*. New York: Praeger, 1966.

Buell, Raymond L. *The Native Problem in Africa*. 2 vols. 1928. Reprint, London: Frank Cass, 1965.

Bull, Hedley, and Adam Watson, eds. *The Expansion of International Society*. London: Oxford University Press, 1984.

Burkholder, Mark A., and Lyman L. Johnson. *Colonial Latin America*. 2d ed. New York: Oxford University Press, 1994.

Burns, Alan. *In Defence of Colonies*. London: Allen & Unwin, 1957.

Burns, E. Bradford. *The Poverty of Progress: Latin America in the Nineteenth Century*. Berkeley: University of California Press, 1980.

Buttinger, Joseph. *Vietnam: A Dragon Embattled*. Volume 1: *From Colonialism to the Vietminh*. London: Pall Mall Press, 1967.

Buxton, Thomas Fowell. *The African Slave Trade and its Remedy*. London: John Murray, 1840.

Cady, John F. *A History of Modern Burma*. Ithaca: Cornell University Press, 1960.

——. *The Roots of French Imperialism in Eastern Asia*. Ithaca: Cornell University Press, 1954.

Cain, P. J., and A. G. Hopkins. *British Imperialism: Innovation and Expansion, 1688–1914*. London: Longman, 1993.

Cameron, Rondo. *A Concise Economic History of the World*. 2d ed. New York: Oxford University Press, 1993.

Camoëns, Luis vaz de. *The Lusiads*. Translated by William C. Atkinson. New York: Penguin, 1952.

Campbell, Horace. *Rasta and Resistance: From Marcus Garvey to Walter Rodney*. Trenton: Africa World Press, 1987.

Campbell, Mavis C. *The Maroons of Jamaica, 1655–1796*. Granby, Mass.: Bergin & Garvey, 1988.

Campbell, Tony. *Early Maps*. New York: Abbeville Press, 1981.

Canny, Nicholas, and Anthony Pagden, eds. *Colonial Identity in the Atlantic World, 1500–1800*. Princeton: Princeton University Press, 1987.

Centre de Recherche et d'Information Socio-Politiques (CRISP). *Congo 1959: Documents Belges et Africains*. Brussels: CRISP, 1960.

Centre for Contemporary Cultural Studies, University of Birmingham. *The Empire Strikes Back: Race and Racism in 70's Britain*. London: Hutchinson, 1983.

Césaire, Aimé. *Discourse on Colonialism*. Translated by Joan Pinkham. New York: Monthly Review Press, 1972.

——. *Cahier d'un Retour au Pays Natal*. Paris: Présence Africaine, 1956.

Chabal, Patrick. *Amilcar Cabral: Revolutionary Leadership and People's War*. Cambridge: Cambridge University Press, 1983.

Chamberlain, M. E. *The Scramble for Africa*. London: Longman, 1974.

Chandavarkar, Rajnarayan. *The Origins of Industrial Capitalism in India: Business Strategies and the Working Classes in Bombay, 1900–1940*. Cambridge: Cambridge University Press, 1994.

Chatterjee, Partha. *Nationalist Thought and the Colonial World: A Derivative Discourse?* London: Zed Books, 1986.

——. *The Nation and its Fragments: Colonial and Postcolonial Histories*. Princeton: Princeton University Press, 1993.

Chaudhuri, K. N. *The English East India Company: The Study of an Early Joint Stock Company, 1600–1640*. New York: A. M. Kelly, 1965.

——. *Trade and Civilization in the Indian Ocean: An Economic History from the Rise of Islam to 1750*. Cambridge: Cambridge University Press, 1985.

Chaunu, Pierre. *European Expansion in the Later Middle Ages*. Translated by Katharine Bertram. Amsterdam: North Holland, 1979.

Chevalier, François. *Land and Society in Colonial Mexico: The Great Hacienda*. Berkeley: University of California Press, 1963.

Chinweizu. *The West and the Rest of Us: White Predators, Black Slavers, and the African Elite*. New York: Random House, 1975.

Chipman, John. *French Power in Africa*. Oxford: Basil Blackwell, 1989.

Chirenje, J. Mutero. *Chief Kgama and His Times, c.1835–1923: The Story of a Southern African Ruler*. London: Rex Collings, 1978.

Chowduri, Ramendra Nath. *International Mandates and Trusteeship Systems: A Comparative Study*. The Hague: M. Nijhoff, 1955.

Churchill, Winston S. *The River War: An Account of the Reconquest of the Sudan*. London: Eyre & Spottiswoode, 1933.

Cioffi-Revilla, Claudio. *The Scientific Measurement of International Conflict: Handbook of Datasets on Crises and Wars, 1495–1988 A.D.* Boulder: Lynne Rienner, 1990.

Cipolla, Carlo M. *Before the Industrial Revolution: European Society and Economy, 1000–1700*. 3d ed. New York: W. W. Norton, 1994.

——. *Guns, Sails, and Empires: Technological Innovation and the Early Phases of European Expansion, 1400–1700*. New York: Pantheon, 1966.

Clark, Grover. *The Balance Sheets of Imperialism: Facts and Figures on Colonies*. New York: Columbia University Press for Carnegie Endowment for International Peace, 1936.

Clark, S. D. *The Developing Canadian Community*. Toronto: University of Toronto Press, 1962.

Clarke, Peter B. *West Africa and Christianity*. London: Edward Arnold, 1986.

Claypole, William, and John Robottom. *Caribbean Story*. 2 vols. London: Longman, 1980–81.

Clayton, Anthony, and David Killingray. *Khaki and Blue: Military and Police in British Colonial Africa*. Athens: Ohio University Center for International Studies, 1989.

Clough, Shepard B., and R. T. Rapp. *European Economic History*. 3d ed. New York: McGraw Hill, 1975.

Cochrane, Thomas C. *Frontiers of Change: Early Industrialism in America*. New York: Oxford University Press, 1981.

Cohen, William B. *The French Encounter with Africans: White Response to Blacks, 1530–1880.* Bloomington: Indiana University Press, 1980.

——. *Rulers of Empire: The French Colonial Service in Africa.* Stanford: Hoover Institution Press, 1971.

Cole, Jeffrey A. *The Potosí Mita, 1573–1700: Compulsory Indian Labor in the Andes.* Stanford: Stanford University Press, 1985.

Coleman, James S. *Nigeria: Background to Nationalism.* Berkeley: University of California Press, 1958.

Collier, Ruth B. *Regimes in Tropical Africa: Changing Forms of Supremacy, 1945–1975.* Berkeley: University of California Press, 1982.

Collingwood, R. R. *The Idea of Nature.* London: Oxford University Press, 1945.

Collins, Larry, and Dominique LaPierre. *Freedom at Midnight.* New York: Avon Books, 1975.

Collins, Robert O. *Shadows in the Grass: Britain in the Southern Sudan, 1918–1956.* New Haven: Yale University Press, 1983.

Collis, Maurice. *Raffles.* Singapore: Graham Brash, 1982.

Columbus, Christopher. *The Journal of Christopher Columbus.* Translated by Cecil Jane. London: Anthony Blond, 1968.

——. *The Log of Christopher Columbus.* Translated by Robert Fuson. Camden, Me.: International Marine Publishing, 1992.

Comaroff, Jean, and John Comaroff. *Of Revelation and Revolution: Christianity, Colonialism, and Consciousness in South Africa.* Vol. 1. Chicago: University of Chicago Press, 1991.

Commins, Stephen K., ed. *Africa's Development Challenges and the World Bank.* Boulder: Lynne Rienner, 1988.

Conser, Walter H., Jr., et al., eds. *Resistance, Politics, and the American Struggle for Independence, 1765–1775.* Boulder: Lynne Rienner, 1986.

Constantine, Stephen. *The Making of British Colonial Development Policy, 1914–1940.* Totowa: Frank Cass, 1982.

Cook, Sherburne F., and Woodrow Borah. *Essays in Population History: Mexico and the Caribbean.* 2 vols. Berkeley: University of California Press, 1971–74.

Cooper, Frederick. "Africa and the World Economy." *African Studies Review* 24:2/3 (June-September 1981): 1–86.

——. *Decolonization and African Society: The Labor Question in British and French Africa.* Cambridge: Cambridge University Press, 1996.

——. *From Slaves to Squatters: Plantation Labor and Agriculture in Zanzibar and Coastal Kenya, 1890–1925.* New Haven: Yale University Press, 1980.

——, and Ann Laura Stoler, eds. *Tensions of Empire: Colonial Cultures in a Bourgeois World.* Berkeley: University of California Press, 1996.

Cooper, Frederick, et al. *Confronting Historical Paradigms: Peasants, Labor, and the Capitalist World System in Africa and Latin America.* Madison: University of Wisconsin Press, 1993.

Cooper, Michael, S.J., comp. and ed. *They Came to Japan: An Anthology of European Reports on Japan, 1543–1640.* Berkeley: University of California Press, 1965.

Coquery-Vidrovitch, Catherine. *Le Congo au Temps des Grandes Compagnies Concessionnaires, 1898–1930.* Paris: Mouton, 1972.

Corbett, Edward. *The French Presence in Black Africa.* Washington, D.C.: Black Orpheus Press, 1972.

Cortés, Hernando. *Five Letters of Cortés to the Emperor.* Translated by J. Bayard Morris. 1928. Reprint, New York: W. W. Norton, 1962.

da Costa, Emilia V. *Crowns of Glory, Tears of Blood: The Demerara Slave Rebellion of 1823.* Oxford: Oxford University Press, 1994.

de la Costa, Horacio. *The Jesuits in the Philippines, 1581–1768.* Cambridge: Harvard University Press, 1961.

Coupland, Reginald. *The Cripps Mission.* London: Oxford University Press, 1942.

Craton, Michael. *Sinews of Empire: A Short History of British Slavery.* Garden City: Anchor, 1974.

——. *Testing the Chains: Resistance to Slavery in the British West Indies.* Ithaca: Cornell University Press, 1982.

Crosby, Alfred W. *The Columbian Exchange: Biological and Cultural Consequences of 1492.* Westport: Greenwood Press, 1972.

——. *Ecological Imperialism: The Biological Expansion of Europe, 900–1900.* Cambridge: Cambridge University Press, 1986.

Crow, John A. *The Epic of Latin America.* 3d ed. Berkeley: University of California Press, 1980.

Crowder, Michael. *West Africa Under Colonial Rule.* London: Hutchinson, 1968.

——, ed. *West African Resistance: The Military Response to Colonial Occupation.* New York: Africana, 1971.

Cruickshank, Brodie. 1853. Reprint, *Eighteen Years on the Gold Coast of Africa.* 2 vols. 2d ed. London: Frank Cass, 1966.

Cruise O'Brien, Rita, ed. *The Political Economy of Underdevelopment: Dependence in Senegal.* Beverly Hills: Sage, 1979.

Curtin, Philip D. *The Atlantic Slave Trade: A Census.* Madison: University of Wisconsin Press, 1969.

——. *Cross-Cultural Trade in World History.* Cambridge: Cambridge University Press, 1984.

——. *Death by Migration: Europe's Encounter with the Tropical World in the Nineteenth Century.* Cambridge: Cambridge University Press, 1989.

——. *The Image of Africa: British Ideas and Actions, 1780–1850.* Madison: University of Wisconsin Press, 1964.

——. *The Rise and Fall of the Plantation Complex: Essays in Atlantic History.* Cambridge: Cambridge University Press, 1990.

——, comp. and ed. *Imperialism.* New York: Harper & Row, 1971.

Dahm, Bernhard. *Sukarno and the Struggle for Indonesian Independence.* Ithaca: Cornell University Press, 1969.

Daly, M. W. *Empire on the Nile: The Anglo-Egyptian Sudan, 1898–1934.* Cambridge: Cambridge University Press, 1986.

Danziger, Raphael. *Abd al-Qadir and the Algerians: Resistance to the French and Internal Consolidation.* New York: Holmes & Meier, 1977.

Darwin, John. *Britain, Egypt, and the Middle East: Imperial Policy in the Aftermath of War, 1918–1922.* New York: St. Martin's Press, 1981.

———. *The End of the British Empire: The Historical Debate.* Oxford: Basil Blackwell, 1991.

Davenport, Michael, et al. *Europe's Preferred Partners? The Lomé Countries in World Trade.* London: Overseas Development Institute, 1995.

Davidson, Basil. *The People's Cause: A History of Guerrillas in Africa.* London: Longman, 1981.

Davies, James C. "Toward a Theory of Revolution." *American Sociological Review* 27:1 (February 1962): 5–18.

Davis, David Brion. *The Problem of Slavery in the Age of Revolution, 1770–1823.* Ithaca: Cornell University Press, 1975.

———. *Slavery and Human Progress.* New York: Oxford University Press, 1984.

Davis, J. Merle. *Modern Industry and the African.* London: Macmillan, 1933.

Davis, Ralph. *The Rise of the Atlantic Economies.* Ithaca: Cornell University Press, 1973.

Dawson, Christopher. *The Movement of World Revolution.* New York: Sheed & Ward, 1959.

Day, Clive. *The Policy and Administration of the Dutch in Java.* New York: Macmillan, 1904 (reprinted by Oxford University Press as *The Dutch in Java,* 1966).

Delavignette, Robert L. *Christianity and Colonialism.* Translated by J. R. Foster. New York: Hawthorn Books, 1964.

———. *Freedom and Authority in French West Africa.* Translated by J. R. Foster. London: Frank Cass, 1968.

Denevan, William M., ed. *The Native Population of the Americas in 1492.* 2d ed. Madison: University of Wisconsin Press, 1992.

DeNevi, Don, and Noel Moholy. *Junipero Serra.* San Francisco: Harper & Row, 1985.

Dening, Greg. *Islands and Beaches: Discourses on a Silent Land: Marquesas, 1774–1880.* Honolulu: University of Hawaii Press, 1980.

Denoon, Donald. *Settler Capitalism: The Dynamics of Dependent Development in the Southern Hemisphere.* Oxford: Clarendon Press, 1983.

Désribes, Abbé E. *L'Evangile au Dahomey et á la Côte des Esclaves.* Clermont-Ferrand: Imprimerie Centrale, Mensboode, 1877.

Deutsch, Karl W. *Nationalism and Social Communication.* Cambridge: MIT Press, 1953.

———. "Social Mobilization and Political Development." *American Political Science Review* 55:3 (September 1961): 493–514.

Devens, Carol. *Countering Colonization: Native American Women and Great Lakes Missions, 1630–1900.* Berkeley: University of California Press, 1992.

Devillers, Philippe, and Jean Lacouture. *End of a War: Indochina 1954.* New York: Praeger, 1969.

Dewey, Clive, and A. G. Hopkins, eds. *The Imperial Impact: Studies in the Economic History of Africa and India.* London: Athlone Press for the Institute of Commonwealth Studies, 1978.

Diamond, Jared. *Guns, Germs, and Steel: The Fates of Human Societies.* New York: W. W. Norton, 1997.

Díaz del Castillo, Bernal. *The Conquest of New Spain*. Translated by J. M. Cohen. Harmondsworth: Penguin, 1963.

Dike, K. Onwuka. *Trade and Politics in the Niger Delta, 1830–1885*. Oxford: Clarendon Press, 1956.

Dilks, David, ed. *Retreat from Power: Studies in Britain's Foreign Policy*. Vol. 2. London: Macmillan, 1981.

Dodge, Ernest S. *Islands and Empires: Western Impact on the Pacific and East Asia*. Minneapolis: University of Minnesota Press, 1976.

Dominguez, Jorge I. *Insurrection or Loyalty: The Breakdown of the Spanish American Empire*. Cambridge: Harvard University Press, 1980.

Downing, Brian M. *The Military Revolution and Political Change: Origins of Democracy and Autocracy in Early Modern Europe*. Princeton: Princeton University Press, 1992.

Doyle, Michael W. *Empires*. Ithaca: Cornell University Press, 1986.

Drabble, J. H. *Rubber in Malaya, 1876–1922: The Genesis of an Industry*. Kuala Lumpur: Oxford University Press, 1973.

Draper, Alfred. *The Amritsar Massacre: Twilight of the Raj*. London: Buchan & Enright, 1985.

Drechsler, Horst. *"Let Us Die Fighting:" The Struggle of the Herero and Nama against German Imperialism (1884–1915)*. Translated by Bernd Zollner. London: Zed Press, 1980.

Duffy, James. *Portuguese Africa*. Cambridge: Harvard University Press, 1959.

Dunn, Ross E. *The Adventures of Ibn Battuta, a Muslim Traveler of the 14th Century*. Berkeley: University of California Press, 1986.

Duong, Pham Cao. *Vietnamese Peasants Under French Domination, 1861–1945*. Lanham, Md.: University Press of America, 1985.

Dupree, Louis. *Afghanistan*. Princeton: Princeton University Press, 1978.

Durham, William H. *Scarcity and Survival in Central America: Ecological Origins of the Soccer War*. Stanford: Stanford University Press, 1979.

Duus, Peter. *The Abacus and the Sword: The Japanese Penetration of Korea, 1895–1910*. Berkeley: University of California Press, 1995.

Duviols, Pierre. *La Lutte Contre les Religions Autochtones dans le Perou Coloniale: Extirpation de l'Idolatrie entre 1532 et 1660*. Lima: Institut Français d'Etudes Andines & Paris: Editions Ophrys, 1971.

Duyvendak, J. L. L. *China's Discovery of Africa*. London: Arthur Probsthain, 1949.

Earle, Peter. *The Sack of Panama*. New York: Viking, 1981.

Echenberg, Myron J. *Colonial Conscripts: The Tirailleurs Senegalais in French West Africa, 1857–1960*. Portsmouth, N.H.: Heinemann, 1991.

Edelstein, Michael. *Overseas Investment in the Age of High Imperialism: The United Kingdom, 1850–1914*. New York: Columbia University Press, 1982.

Eisenstadt, S. N. *The Political Systems of Empires*. London: Free Press, 1969.

Ekeh, Peter. "Colonialism and the Two Publics in Africa: A Theoretical Statement." *Comparative Studies in Society and History* 17:1 (January 1975): 91–112.

El-Ayouty, Yassin. *The United Nations and Decolonization: The Role of Afro-Asia*. The Hague: M. Nijhoff, 1971.

Eliot, (Sir) Charles. *The East Africa Protectorate*. London: Edward Arnold, 1905.

Elkiss, T. H. *The Quest for an African Eldorado: Sofala, Southern Zambezia, and the Portuguese, 1500–1865*. Waltham, Mass.: Crossroads Press, 1981.

Ellinwood, DeWitt C., and S. D. Pradhan, eds. *India in World War I*. Columbia, Mo.: South Asia Books, 1978.

Elliott, John H. *Imperial Spain, 1469–1716*. New York: St. Martin's Press, 1964.

Ellis, Stephen. *The Rising of the Red Shawls: A Revolt in Madagascar, 1895–1899*. Cambridge: Cambridge University Press, 1985.

Elphick, Richard. *Khoikhoi and the Founding of White South Africa*. Johannesburg: Ravan Press, 1985.

Elsbree, Willard H. *Japan's Role in Southeast Asian Nationalist Movements, 1940 to 1945*. Cambridge: Harvard University Press, 1953.

Emerson, Rupert. *From Empire to Nation: The Rise to Self-Assertion of Asian and African Peoples*. Boston: Beacon Press, 1960.

Emmer, P. C., ed. *Colonialism and Migration: Indentured Labour Before and After Slavery*. Dordrecht: M. Nijhoff, 1986.

——, and H. L. Wesseling, eds. *Reappraisals in Overseas History*. Leiden: Leiden University Press, 1979.

Epstein, A. L. *Politics in an Urban African Community*. Manchester: Manchester University Press, 1958.

Erickson, Charlotte. *Emigration from Europe, 1815–1914*. London: A. and C. Black, 1976.

Etienne, Mona, and Eleanor Leacock, eds. *Women and Colonization: Anthropological Perspectives*. New York: Praeger, 1980.

Etzioni, Amitai. *A Comparative Analysis of Complex Organizations*. New York: Free Press, 1961.

——, ed. *A Sociological Reader on Complex Organizations*. 2d ed. New York: Free Press, 1969.

Fagan, Brian M. *The Aztecs*. New York: W. H. Freeman, 1984.

Fairbank, John K. *Trade and Diplomacy on the China Coast: The Opening of the Treaty Ports, 1842–1854*. Stanford: Stanford University Press, 1964.

——, ed. *The Chinese World Order: Traditional China's Foreign Relations*. Cambridge: Harvard University Press, 1968.

Fall, Bernard. *Hell in a Very Small Place: The Siege of Dien Bien Phu*. Philadelphia: Lippincott, 1967.

Fanon, Frantz. *Black Skin, White Masks*. Translated by Charles Markmann. New York: Grove Press, 1968.

——. *The Wretched of the Earth*. Translated by Constance Farrington. New York: Grove Press, 1968.

Farriss, Nancy M. *Crown and Clergy in Colonial Mexico, 1759–1821: The Crisis of Ecclesiastical Privilege*. London: Athlone Press, 1968.

——. *Maya Society under Colonial Rule: The Collective Enterprise of Survival*. Princeton: Princeton University Press, 1984.

Farwell, Byron. *Armies of the Raj: From the Mutiny to Independence, 1858–1947*. New York: W. W. Norton, 1989.

Fédération Française des Anciens Coloniaux. *Le Livre d'Or de l'Exposition Coloniale de Paris 1931*. Paris: Honoré Champion, 1931.

Ferro, Marc. *Colonization: A Global History*. London: Routledge, 1997.

Fieldhouse, D. K. *The Colonial Empires: A Comparative Study from the Eighteenth Century*. 2d ed. London: Macmillan, 1982.

——. *Colonialism 1870–1945: An Introduction*. London: Weidenfeld & Nicolson, 1981.

——. *Economics and Empire, 1830–1914*. Ithaca: Cornell University Press, 1973.

——. *Unilever Overseas: The Anatomy of a Multinational, 1895–1965*. London: Croom Helm and Stanford: Hoover Institution Press, 1978.

Fields, Karen E. *Revival and Rebellion in Colonial Central Africa*. Princeton: Princeton University Press, 1985.

Fishel, Wesley R. *The End of Extraterritoriality in China*. Berkeley: University of California Press, 1952.

Fishman, Joshua, et al., eds. *Language Problems of Developing Nations*. New York: Wiley, 1968.

Foltz, William J. *From French West Africa to the Mali Federation*. New Haven: Yale University Press, 1965.

Forster, Stig, Wolfgang Mommsen, and Ronald Robinson, eds. *Bismarck, Europe, and Africa: The Berlin Africa Conference, 1884–1885, and the Onset of Partition*. New York: Oxford University Press, 1988.

Frank, Andre Gunder. *Capitalism and Under-Development in Latin America*. Rev. ed. New York: Monthly Review Press, 1969.

——. *World Accumulation, 1492–1789*. New York: Monthly Review Press, 1978.

Frankel, S. H. *Capital Investment in Africa: Its Course and Effects*. London: Oxford University Press, 1938.

Fredrickson, George. *White Supremacy: A Comparative Study in American and South African History*. Oxford: Oxford University Press, 1981.

Friend, Theodore. *The Blue-Eyed Enemy: Japan Against the West in Java and Luzon, 1942–1945*. Princeton: Princeton University Press, 1988.

Fuentes, Carlos. *The Buried Mirror: Reflections on Spain and the New World*. Boston: Houghton Mifflin, 1992.

Fuglestad, Finn. *A History of Niger, 1850–1960*. Cambridge: Cambridge University Press, 1983.

Furber, Holden. *Rival Empires of Trade in the Orient, 1600–1800*. Minneapolis: University of Minnesota Press, 1976.

Furedi, Frank. *Colonial Wars and the Politics of Third World Nationalism*. New York: St. Martin's Press, 1994.

Furnivall, J. S. *Colonial Policy and Practice: A Comparative Study of Burma and Netherlands India*. Cambridge: Cambridge University Press with Institute of Pacific Relations, 1948.

Gailey, Harry A. *Lugard and the Abeokuta Uprising: The Demise of Egba Independence*. London: Frank Cass, 1982.

Gallagher, John. *The Decline, Revival, and Fall of the British Empire*. Edited by Anil Seal. Cambridge: Cambridge University Press, 1982.

——, and Ronald Robinson. "The Imperialism of Free Trade." *The Economic History Review,* 2d ser., 6:1 (1953): 1–15.

Gandhi, Leela. *Postcolonial Theory: A Critical Introduction.* New York: Columbia University Press, 1998.

Gandhi, Mohandas K. *An Autobiography, or The Story of My Experiments with Truth.* Ahmedabad: Navajivan Publishing House, 1956.

Ganiage, Jean. *L'Expansion Coloniale et les Rivalités Internationales.* Paris: Centre de Documentation Universitaire, 1975.

——. *Les Origines du Protectorat Français en Tunisie (1861–1881).* Paris: Presses Universitaires de France, 1959.

Gann, L. H., and Peter Duignan. *Burden of Empire: An Appraisal of Western Colonialism in Africa South of the Sahara.* Stanford: Hoover Institution Press, 1967.

——. *The Rulers of Belgian Africa, 1884–1914.* Princeton: Princeton University Press, 1979.

——, eds. *Colonialism in Africa, 1870–1960.* 5 vols. Cambridge: Cambridge University Press, 1969–73.

Garner, Joe. *The Commonwealth Office, 1925–68.* London: Heinemann, 1978.

Geertz, Clifford. *Agricultural Involution: The Process of Ecological Change in Indonesia.* Berkeley: University of California Press, 1963.

Gellner, Ernest. *Nations and Nationalism.* Ithaca: Cornell University Press, 1983.

Genovese, Eugene. *From Rebellion to Revolution: Afro-American Slave Revolts in the Making of the Modern World.* Baton Rouge: Louisiana State University Press, 1979.

George, T. J. S. *Krishna Menon: A Biography.* New York: Taplinger, 1965.

Gerard-Libois, Jules. *Katanga Secession.* Translated by Rebecca Young. Madison: University of Wisconsin Press, 1966.

——, and Benoit Verhaegen, eds. *Congo 1960.* 2 vols. Brussels: CRISP, 1961.

Gernet, Jacques. *A History of Chinese Civilization.* Translated by J. R. Foster. Cambridge: Cambridge University Press, 1982.

Geyer, Dietrich. *Russian Imperialism: The Interaction of Domestic and Foreign Policy, 1860–1914.* Translated by Bruce Little. New Haven: Yale University Press, 1987.

Gide, André. *Travels in the Congo.* Translated by Dorothy Bussy. 2d ed. Berkeley: University of California Press, 1962.

Gifford, Prosser, and Wm. Roger Louis, eds. *Decolonization and African Independence: The Transfers of Power, 1960–1980.* New Haven: Yale University Press, 1988.

——, eds. *France and Britain in Africa: Imperial Rivalry and Colonial Rule.* New Haven: Yale University Press, 1971.

——, eds. *The Transfer of Power in Africa: Decolonization, 1940–1960.* New Haven: Yale University Press, 1982.

Gillard, David. *The Struggle for Asia, 1828–1914: A Study in British and Russian Imperialism.* London: Methuen, 1977.

Gilpin, Robert. *War and Change in World Politics.* Cambridge: Cambridge University Press, 1981.

Girardet, Raoul. *L'Idée Coloniale en France de 1871 à 1962*. Paris: La Table Ronde, 1972.

Glamann, Kristof. *Dutch-Asiatic Trade, 1620–1740*. The Hague: M. Nijhoff, 1981.

Goldstein, Joshua S. *Long Cycles: Prosperity and War in the Modern Age*. New Haven: Yale University Press, 1988.

Goldsworthy, David. *Colonial Issues in British Politics, 1945–1961*. Oxford: Clarendon Press, 1971.

Gong, Gerrit. *The Standard of "Civilization" in International Society*. Oxford: Clarendon Press, 1984.

Goodall, Norman. *A History of the London Missionary Society*. London: Oxford University Press, 1954.

Gopal, Sarvepalli. *Jawaharlal Nehru: A Biography*. Vol. 1, 1889–1947. Cambridge: Harvard University Press, 1976.

Gordon, David C. *North Africa's French Legacy, 1954–1962*. Cambridge: Harvard Center for Middle Eastern Studies, 1962.

Gosner, Kevin. *Soldiers of the Virgin: The Moral Economy of a Colonial Maya Rebellion*. Tucson: University of Arizona Press, 1982.

Gow, Bonar. *Madagascar and the Protestant Impact*. New York: Africana, 1979.

Green, M. M. *Ibo Village Affairs*. New York: Praeger, 1964.

Greenblatt, Stephen. *Marvelous Possessions: The Wonder of the New World*. Chicago: University of Chicago Press, 1991.

——, ed. *New World Encounters*. Berkeley: University of California Press, 1993.

Greene, Jack P. "The Seven Years' War and the American Revolution: The Causal Relationship Reconsidered." *Journal of Imperial and Commonwealth History* 8:2 (January 1980): 85–105.

——, ed. *Colonies to Nation, 1763–1789*. New York: McGraw-Hill, 1967.

Griffiths, Percival. *The British Impact on India*. London: Macdonald, 1952.

Grimal, Henri. *Decolonization: The British, French, Dutch, and Belgian Empires, 1919–1963*. Translated by Stephan de Vos. London: Routledge & Kegan Paul, 1978.

Grotius, Hugo. *The Freedom of the Seas: Or the Right Which Belongs to the Dutch to Take Part in the East Indian Trade*. Edited by James B. Scott. Translated by Ralph Magoffin. New York: Oxford University Press, 1916.

Grove, Charles P. *The Planting of Christianity in Africa*. 4 vols. London: Butterworth Press, 1948–58.

Guha, Ranajit, and Gayatri Spivak, eds. *Selected Subaltern Studies*. Vol. 4. New York: Oxford University Press, 1988.

Gunnemark, Erik. *Countries, Peoples, and Their Languages: The Geolinguistic Handbook*. Gothenberg: Lanstryckeriet, 1991.

Gupta, Partha S. *Imperialism and the British Labour Movement, 1914–1964*. New York: Holmes & Meier, 1975.

Gwassa, G. C. K., and John Iliffe, eds. *Records of the Maji Maji Rising*. Nairobi: East Africa Publishing House, 1967.

Hailey, William M. H. (Baron). 1939. Revised edition, *An African Survey: A Study of Problems Arising in Africa South of the Sahara*. London: Oxford University Press, 1957.

478

Hakluyt, Richard. *Voyages and Discoveries: The Principal Navigations, Voyages, Traffiques and Discoveries of the English Nation*. Edited by Jack Beeching. Harmondsworth: Penguin, 1972.

Hale, Charles A. *Mexican Liberalism in the Age of Mora, 1821–1853*. New Haven: Yale University Press, 1968.

Hall, John A. *Powers and Liberties: The Causes and Consequences of the Rise of the West*. Harmondsworth: Penguin with Basil Blackwell, 1986.

Hamill, Hugh M., Jr. *The Hidalgo Revolt: Prelude to Mexican Independence*. Gainesville: University of Florida Press, 1966.

Hancock, W. K. *Wealth of Colonies*. Cambridge: Cambridge University Press, 1950.

Hanna, Willard A. *Indonesian Banda: Colonialism and its Aftermath in the Nutmeg Islands*. Philadelphia: ISHI, 1978.

Hansen, Karen. *Distant Companions: Servants and Employers in Zambia, 1900–1985*. Ithaca: Cornell University Press, 1989.

Hargreaves, John D. *Decolonization in Africa*. London: Longman, 1988.

Harlow, Barbara, and Mia Carter, eds. *Imperialism and Orientalism: A Documentary Sourcebook*. Oxford: Basil Blackwell, 1999.

Harris, F. R. *Jamsetji Nusserwanji Tata: A Chronicle of his Life*. 2d ed. Bombay: Blackie & Son, 1958.

Harris, Joseph E. *Repatriates and Refugees in a Colonial Society: The Case of Kenya*. Washington, D.C.: Howard University Press, 1987.

Harrison, Christopher. *France and Islam in West Africa, 1860–1960*. Cambridge: Cambridge University Press, 1988.

Hartz, Louis. *The Liberal Tradition in America*. New York: Harcourt, Brace, 1955.

——, et al. *The Founding of New Societies*. San Diego: Harcourt Brace Jovanovich, 1964.

Harvey, L. P. *Islamic Spain, 1250 to 1500*. Chicago: University of Chicago Press, 1990.

al-Hassan, Ahmad Y., and Donald Hill. *Islamic Technology: An Illustrated History*. Cambridge: Cambridge University Press, 1986.

Haudrère, Philippe. *La Compagnie Française des Indes aux XVIIIème Siècle, 1719–1795*. 4 vols. Paris: Librairie de l'Inde, 1989.

Hay, Denys. *Europe: The Emergence of an Idea*. Edinburgh: Edinburgh University Press, 1957.

Headrick, Daniel R. *The Tentacles of Progress: Technology Transfer in the Age of Imperialism, 1850–1940*. New York: Oxford University Press, 1988.

——. *The Tools of Empire: Technology and European Imperialism in the Nineteenth Century*. New York: Oxford University Press, 1981.

Hecht, Robert A. *Continents in Collision: The Impact of Europe on the North American Indian Societies*. Lanham, Md.: University Press of America, 1980.

Heggoy, Alf A. *The French Conquest of Algiers, 1830: An Algerian Oral Tradition*. Athens: Ohio University Center for International Studies, 1986.

Hemming, John. *The Conquest of the Incas*. San Diego: Harcourt Brace Jovanovich, 1970.

——. *Red Gold: The Conquest of the Brazilian Indians, 1500–1760*. Cambridge: Harvard University Press, 1978.

——. *The Search for El Dorado*. New York: E. P. Dutton, 1978.

Henige, David. *Colonial Governors from the Fifteenth Century to the Present: A Comprehensive List*. Madison: University of Wisconsin Press, 1970.

Hennessy, Alistair. *The Frontier in Latin American History*. Albuquerque: University of New Mexico Press, 1978.

Heussler, Robert. *British Rule in Malaya*. Westport: Greenwood Press, 1981.

——. *Yesterday's Rulers: The Making of the British Colonial Service*. Syracuse: Syracuse University Press, 1963.

Hibbert, Christopher. *The Great Mutiny: India 1857*. Harmondsworth: Penguin, 1978.

Higgonet, Patrice L. *Sister Republics: The Origins of French and American Republicanism*. Cambridge: Harvard University Press, 1988.

Hobhouse, Henry. *Seeds of Change: Five Plants that Transformed Mankind*. New York: Harper & Row, 1986.

Hobsbawm, Eric (E. J.) *The Age of Empire, 1875–1914*. New York: Pantheon Books, 1987.

——. *Industry and Empire*. Vol. 2, *1750 to the Present Day*. New York: Pantheon, 1968.

——, and Terence Ranger, eds. *The Invention of Tradition*. Cambridge: Cambridge University Press, 1983.

Hobson, J. A. *Imperialism: A Study*. London: George Allen & Unwin, 1902.

Hochschild, Adam. *King Leopold's Ghost: A Story of Greed, Terror, and Heroism in Colonial Africa*. Boston: Houghton Mifflin, 1998.

Hodgkin, Thomas. *Nationalism in Colonial Africa*. London: Muller, 1956.

Hodgson, Marshall G. S. *Rethinking World History: Essays on Europe, Islam, and World History*. Edited by Edmund Burke III. Cambridge: Cambridge University Press, 1993.

Hodson, H. V. *The Great Divide: Britain-India-Pakistan*. Karachi: Oxford University Press, 1985.

Hoffer, Eric. *The True Believer: Thoughts on the Nature of Mass Movements*. New York: Harper & Row, 1951.

Hoffman, Ronald A., and Peter Albert, eds. *Sovereign States in an Age of Uncertainty*. Charlottesville: University Press of Virginia, 1981.

Hohenberg, Paul, and Lynn H. Lees. *The Making of Urban Europe, 1000–1994*. Rev. ed. Cambridge: Harvard University Press, 1995.

Holland, R. F. *Britain and the Commonwealth Alliance, 1918–1939*. London: Macmillan, 1981.

——. *European Decolonization, 1918–81: An Introductory Survey*. New York: St. Martin's Press, 1985.

Holsti, Kalevi J. *Peace and War: Armed Conflicts and International Order, 1648–1989*. Cambridge: Cambridge University Press, 1991.

Hopkins, A. G. *An Economic History of West Africa*. New York: Columbia University Press, 1973.

Horne, Alistair. *A Savage War of Peace: Algeria, 1954–1962*. Harmondsworth: Penguin, 1979.

Horowitz, Donald L. *Ethnic Groups in Conflict*. Berkeley: University of California Press, 1985.

Horrabin, James F. *An Atlas of Empire*. New York: A. A. Knopf, 1937.

Horsington, William. *Lyautey and the French Conquest of Morocco*. New York: St. Martin's Press, 1995.

Hourani, Albert. *A History of the Arab Peoples*. Cambridge: Belknap Press of Harvard University Press, 1991.

Hourani, George F. *Arab Seafaring*. Rev. ed. Princeton: Princeton University Press, 1995.

Hovet, Thomas. *Africa in the United Nations*. Evanston: Northwestern University Press, 1963.

Huff, Toby. *The Rise of Early Modern Science: Islam, China, and the West*. Cambridge: Cambridge University Press, 1993.

Hughes, Robert. *The Fatal Shore: The Epic of Australia's Founding*. New York: Random House, 1986.

Hulme, Peter. *Colonial Encounters: Europe and the Native Caribbean, 1492–1797*. London: Methuen, 1986.

Humphreys, R. A., and John Lynch, eds. *The Origins of the Latin American Revolutions, 1808–1826*. New York: Knopf, 1965.

Huntington, Samuel P. *The Clash of Civilizations and the Remaking of World Order*. New York: Simon & Schuster, 1996.

Hurewitz, J. C. *The Struggle for Palestine*. New York: Schocken, 1976.

——, ed. and comp. *The Middle East and North Africa in World Politics: A Documentary Record*. Vol. 2: *British-French Supremacy, 1914–1945*. New Haven: Yale University Press, 1979.

Hutchins, Francis G. *India's Revolution: Gandhi and the Quit India Movement*. Cambridge: Harvard University Press, 1973.

Huttenback, Robert A. *Racism and Empire: White Settlers and Coloured Immigrants in the British Self-Governing Colonies, 1830–1910*. Ithaca: Cornell University Press, 1976.

Hynes, William G. *The Economics of Empire: Britain, Africa, and the New Imperialism, 1870–95*. London: Longman, 1979.

Ikime, Obaro. *The Fall of Nigeria: The British Conquest*. London: Heinemann, 1977.

Iliffe, John. *A Modern History of Tanganyika*. Cambridge: Cambridge University Press, 1979.

Inder Singh, Anita. *The Origins of the Partition of India, 1936–1947*. Delhi: Oxford University Press, 1987.

Ingleson, John. *Road to Exile: The Indonesian Nationalist Movement, 1927–1934*. Singapore: Heinemann, 1979.

Isaacman, Allen. *Mozambique: The Africanization of a European Institution*. Madison: University of Wisconsin Press, 1972.

——. *The Tradition of Resistance in Mozambique*. London: Heinemann, 1976.

Isichie, Elizabeth. *The Ibo People and the Europeans*. New York: St. Martin's Press, 1973.

Israel, Jonathan I. *Dutch Primacy in World Trade, 1585–1740*. Oxford: Clarendon Press, 1989.

——. *The Dutch Republic: Its Rise, Greatness, and Fall, 1477–1806*. Oxford: Oxford University Press, 1995.

Iyer, Raghavan, ed. *The Moral and Political Writings of Mahatma Gandhi*. 3 vols. New York: Oxford University Press, 1986–87.

Jabarti, 'Abd al-Rahman. *Napoleon in Egypt: Al-Jabarti's Chronicle of the French Occupation*. Translated by Shmuel Moreh. Princeton: Markus Wiener, 1993.

Jack, James W. *Daybreak in Livingstonia: The Story of the Livingstonia Mission in British Central Africa*. Edinburgh: Oliphant, Anderson, & Ferrier, 1901.

Jackson, Robert H. *Quasi-States: Sovereignty, International Relations, and the Third World.* Cambridge: Cambridge University Press, 1990.

——, and Carl Rosberg. "Why Africa's Weak States Persist: The Empirical and the Juridical in Statehood." *World Politics* 35:1 (October 1982): 1–24.

Jahoda, Gustav. *White Man.* Oxford: Oxford University Press, 1961.

Jalée, Pierre. *The Pillage of the Third World.* Translated by Mary Klopper. New York: Monthly Review Press, 1968.

James, C. L. R. *The Black Jacobins: Toussaint Louverture and the San Domingo Revolution.* 2d ed., rev. New York: Vintage Books, 1963.

Jeal, Tim. *Livingstone.* New York: Putnam, 1973.

Jeffries, Charles. *The Colonial Empire and its Civil Service.* Cambridge: Cambridge University Press, 1938.

Johnson, G. Wesley, ed. *Double Impact: France and Africa in the Age of Imperialism.* Westport: Greenwood, 1985.

Johnston, (Sir) Harry H. *A History of the Colonization of Africa by Alien Races.* Cambridge: Cambridge University Press, 1899.

Johnston, James F. *Missionary Landscapes in the Dark Continent.* New York: A. D. Randolph, 1892.

Jones, Dorothy V. *License for Empire: Colonialism by Treaty in Early America.* Chicago: University of Chicago Press, 1982.

Jones, E. L. *The European Miracle: Environments, Economies and Geopolitics in the History of Europe and Asia.* 2d ed. Cambridge: Cambridge University Press, 1987.

Jones, Grant. *Maya Resistance to Spanish Rule.* Albuquerque: University of New Mexico Press, 1989.

Josephy, Alvin M., Jr. *The Patriot Chiefs: A Chronicle of American Indian Resistance.* New York: Viking Press, 1961.

Judd, Denis. *Empire: The British Imperial Experience, from 1765 to the Present.* London: HarperCollins, 1996.

——, and Peter Slinn. *The Evolution of the Modern Commonwealth, 1902–80.* London: Macmillan, 1982.

Kahin, George M. *The Asian-African Conference, Bandung, Indonesia, April 1955.* Ithaca: Cornell University Press, 1956.

——. *Nationalism and Revolution in Indonesia.* Ithaca: Cornell University Press, 1952.

Kahler, Miles. *Decolonization in Britain and France: The Domestic Consequences of International Politics.* Princeton: Princeton University Press, 1984.

Kaiser, David. *Politics and War: European Conflict from Philip II to Hitler.* Cambridge: Harvard University Press, 1990.

Kalu, O. U., ed. *The History of Christianity in West Africa.* London: Longman, 1980.

Kane, Cheikh Hamidou. *Ambiguous Adventure.* Translated by Katherine Woods. Oxford: Heinemann, 1963.

Kanogo, Tabitha. *Squatters and the Roots of Mau Mau, 1905–63.* London: J. Currey, 1987.

Kanwar, Pamela. *Imperial Simla: The Political Culture of the Raj.* Delhi: Oxford University Press, 1990.

Kanya-Forstner, A. S. *The Conquest of the Western Sudan: A Study in French Military Imperialism.* London: Cambridge University Press, 1969.

Kat Angelino, A. D. A. de. *Colonial Policy.* Translated by G. J. Renier. 2 vols. The Hague: M. Nijhoff, 1931.

Kaunda, Kenneth. *A Humanist in Africa.* London: Longman, 1966.

Kay, Geoffrey B., ed. *The Political Economy of Colonialism in Ghana.* Cambridge: Cambridge University Press, 1972.

Kedar, Benjamin Z. *Crusade and Mission: European Approaches toward the Muslims.* Princeton: Princeton University Press, 1984.

Kedourie, Elie, ed. *Nationalism in Asia and Africa.* London: F. Cass, 1970.

Keen, Benjamin, and Mark Wasserman. *A Short History of Latin America.* Boston: Houghton Mifflin, 1980.

Keith, Robert G. *Conquest and Agrarian Change: The Emergence of the Hacienda System on the Peruvian Coast.* Cambridge: Harvard University Press, 1976.

——, ed. *Haciendas and Plantations in Latin American History.* New York: Holmes & Meier, 1977.

Kennedy, Dane. *Islands of White: Settler Society and Culture in Kenya and Southern Rhodesia, 1890–1939.* Durham: Duke University Press, 1987.

Kennedy, Paul M. *The Rise and Fall of British Naval Mastery.* London: Ashfield Press, 1983.

——. *The Rise and Fall of the Great Powers: Economic Change and Military Conflict from 1500 to 2000.* New York: Random House, 1987.

Kenyatta, Jomo. *Facing Mt. Kenya: The Tribal Life of the Gikuyu.* New York: Random House, 1965.

Kent, Graeme. *Company of Heaven: Early Missionaries in the South Seas.* Wellington: Reed, 1992.

Kent, John. *The Internationalization of Colonialism: Britain, France, and Black Africa, 1939–1956.* Oxford: Clarendon Press, 1992.

Keyes, George S., ed. *Mirror of Empire: Dutch Marine Art of the Seventeenth Century.* Cambridge: Cambridge University Press, 1990.

Khoury, Philip S. *Syria and the French Mandate: The Politics of Arab Nationalism, 1920–1945.* Princeton: Princeton University Press, 1987.

Kiernan, V. G. *European Empires from Conquest to Collapse, 1815–1960.* Leicester: Leicester University Press/Fontana, 1982.

Killingray, David, and Richard Rathbone, eds. *Africa and the Second World War.* London: Macmillan, 1986.

Kilson, Martin, ed. *New States in the Modern World.* Cambridge: Harvard University Press, 1975.

Kindleberger, Charles P. *World Economic Primacy, 1500 to 1990.* New York: Oxford University Press, 1996.

King, Anthony D. *Colonial Urban Development: Culture, Social Power, and Environment*. London: Routledge & Kegan Paul, 1976.

Kingsley, Mary. *Travels in West Africa*. Abridged by Elspeth Huxley. London: Dent, 1987.

Kipkorir, B. E., ed. *Biographical Essays on Imperialism and Collaboration in Colonial Kenya*. Nairobi: Kenya Literature Bureau, 1980.

Kirk-Greene, A. H. M., comp. *Lugard and the Amalgamation of Nigeria: A Documentary Record*. London: F. Cass, 1968.

——, ed. *The Transfer of Power: The Colonial Administrator in the Age of Decolonisation*. Oxford: Oxford University, Inter-Faculty Committee for African Studies, 1979.

Kissling, Hans J., et al. *The Last Great Muslim Empires*. Princeton: Markus Wiener, 1996.

Kittler, Glenn D. *The White Fathers*. New York: Harper, 1957.

Klein, Martin A. *Islam and Imperialism in Senegal*. Stanford: Hoover Institution Press, 1968.

Kling, Blair B., and M. N. Pearson, eds. *The Age of Partnership: Europeans in Asia before Dominion*. Honolulu: University Press of Hawaii, 1979.

Kniebiehler, Yvonne. *La Femme au Temps des Colonies*. Paris: Stock, 1985.

Koebner, Richard, and Helmut D. Schmidt. *Imperialism: The Story and Significance of a Political Word, 1840–1960*. Cambridge: Cambridge University Press, 1964.

Kohn, George C. *Dictionary of Wars*. New York: Facts on File, 1986.

Kohn, Hans. *The Idea of Nationalism: A Study of its Origins and Background*. New York: Macmillan, 1944.

Koning, Hans. *Columbus: His Enterprise*. New York: Monthly Review Press, 1976.

Konvitz, Josef. *Cities and the Sea: Port City Planning in Early Modern Europe*. Baltimore: Johns Hopkins University Press, 1978.

Krasner, Stephen D. *Structural Conflict: The Third World Against Global Liberalism*. Berkeley: University of California Press, 1985.

——, ed. *International Regimes*. Ithaca: Cornell University Press, 1983.

Kuklick, Henrika. *The Savage Within: The Social History of British Anthropology, 1885–1945*. Cambridge: Cambridge University Press, 1991.

Kuno, Yoshi S. *Japanese Expansion on the Asiatic Continent*. Berkeley: University of California Press, 1937.

Kupchan, Charles A. *The Vulnerability of Empire*. Ithaca: Cornell University Press, 1994.

Kupperman, Karen O. *Settling with the Indians: The Meeting of English and Indian Cultures in America, 1580–1640*. Totowa: Rowman & Littlefield, 1980.

Lach, Donald F., and Carol Flaumenhaft, eds. *Asia on the Eve of Europe's Expansion*. Englewood Cliffs: Prentice-Hall, 1965.

Lacouture, Jean. *Ho Chi Minh: A Political Biography*. Translated by Peter Wiles. New York: Random House, 1968.

Lafaye, Jacques. *Quetzalcoatl and Guadalupe: The Formation of Mexican National Consciousness, 1531–1815*. Chicago: University of Chicago Press, 1976.

Lamar, Howard, and Leonard Thompson, eds. *The Frontier in History: North America and Southern Africa Compared*. New Haven: Yale University Press, 1981.

Lamming, George. *In the Castle of My Skin*. New York: Collier, 1953.

Landau, Rom. *Moroccan Drama, 1900–1955.* San Francisco: American Academy of Asian Studies, 1956.

Landes, David S. *Bankers and Pashas.* Cambridge: Cambridge University Press, 1958.

——. *The Unbound Prometheus: Technological Change and Industrial Development in Western Europe from 1750 to the Present.* Cambridge: Cambridge University Press, 1969.

——. *The Wealth and Poverty of Nations: Why Some Are so Rich and Some so Poor.* New York: W. W. Norton, 1998.

Lane, Frederic C. *Venice: A Maritime Republic.* Johns Hopkins University Press, 1973.

Lang, James. *Conquest and Commerce: Spain and England in the Americas.* New York: Academic Press, 1975.

——. *Portuguese Brazil: The King's Plantation.* New York: Academic Press, 1979.

Langer, William L. *European Alliances and Alignments, 1871–1890.* 2d ed. New York: A. A. Knopf, 1962.

——. *The Diplomacy of Imperialism, 1890–1902.* 2d ed. New York: A. A. Knopf, 1956.

Langmore, Diane. *Missionary Lives: Papua, 1874–1914.* Honolulu: University of Hawaii Press, 1989.

Lapidus, Ira. *A History of Islamic Societies.* Cambridge: Cambridge University Press, 1988.

Lapping, Brian. *End of Empire.* New York: St. Martin's Press, 1985.

Latham, A. J. H. *The Depression and the Developing World, 1914–1939.* London: Croom Helm, 1981.

Latourette, Kenneth S. *A History of the Expansion of Christianity.* 7 vols. New York: Harper and Bros., 1937–45. Vol. 2: *The Thousand Years of Uncertainty:* A.D. 500–A.D. 1500 (1938). Vol. 3: *Three Centuries of Advance:* A.D. 1500–A.D. 1800 (1939). Vol. 5: *The Great Century in the Americas, Australasia, and Africa* (1941). Vol. 7: *Advance Through Storm:* A.D. 1914 and After (1945).

Lazreg, Marnia. *The Emergence of Classes in Algeria: A Study of Colonialism and Socio-Political Change.* Boulder: Westview, 1976.

Leadbeater, Simon R. *The Politics of Textiles: The Indian Cotton-Mill Industry and the Legacy of Swadeshi, 1900–1985.* Newbury Park: Sage Publishers, 1992.

Lebra, Joyce. *Japanese-Trained Armies in Southeast Asia: Independence and Volunteer Forces in World War II.* New York: Columbia University Press, 1977.

Lee, Edwin. *The British as Rulers: Governing Multiracial Singapore, 1867–1914.* Singapore: Singapore University Press, 1991.

Lee, J. M. *Colonial Development and Good Government: A Study of the Ideas Expressed by British Official Classes in Planning Decolonization, 1939–1964.* Oxford: Clarendon Press, 1967.

Leith-Ross, Sylvia. *Stepping-Stones: Memoirs of Colonial Nigeria, 1907–1960.* Edited by Michael Crowder. London: Peter Owen, 1983.

Lelyveld, David. *Aligarh's First Generation: Muslim Solidarity in British India.* Princeton: Princeton University Press, 1978.

Lenin, Vladimir I. 1916. Reprint, *Imperialism, the Highest Stage of Capitalism.* New York: International, 1969.

Leon-Portilla, Miguel, ed. *The Broken Spears: The Aztec Account of the Conquest of Mexico.* Boston: Beacon Press, 1962.

Lerner, Daniel. *The Passing of Traditional Society: Modernizing the Middle East.* Glencoe: Free Press, 1958.

Leur, J. C. van. *Indonesian Trade and Society: Essays in Asian Social and Economic History.* Translated by James Holmes and A. van Marle. The Hague: M. van Hoeve, 1955.

Levenson, Joseph R., ed. *European Expansion and the Counter-Example of Asia.* Englewood Cliffs: Prentice-Hall, 1967.

Levi, Margaret. *Of Rule and Revenue.* Berkeley: University of California Press, 1988.

Levy, Jack S. *War in the Modern Great Power System, 1495–1975.* Lexington: University of Kentucky Press, 1983.

Lewis, Bernard. *Islam and the West.* New York: Oxford University Press, 1993.

——. *The Muslim Discovery of Europe.* New York: W. W. Norton, 1982.

Lewis, David L. *The Race to Fashoda: European Colonialism and African Resistance in the Scramble for Africa.* New York: Weidenfeld & Nicolson, 1987.

Lewis, I. M. *A Modern History of Somalia: Nation and State in the Horn of Africa.* London: Longman, 1980.

Lewis, Martin D., ed. *The British in India: Imperialism or Trusteeship?* Boston: D. C. Heath, 1962.

Lewis, W. Arthur. *Economic Survey, 1919–1939.* New York: Harper & Row, 1969.

Leys, Colin. *European Politics in Southern Rhodesia.* Oxford: Clarendon Press, 1959.

——. *Underdevelopment in Kenya: The Political Economy of Neo-Colonialism, 1964–1971.* Berkeley: University of California Press, 1974.

Leys, Norman. *Kenya.* 3d ed. London: Hogarth Press, 1926.

Library of Congress, Symposia on the American Revolution. *The Impact of the American Revolution Abroad.* Washington, D.C.: Library of Congress, 1976.

Lijphart, Arend. "Comparative Politics and the Comparative Method." *American Political Science Review* 65 (September 1971): 682–93.

Lippy, Charles H., Robert Choquette, and Stafford Poole. *Christianity Comes to the Americas, 1492–1776.* New York: Paragon, 1992.

Lipset, Seymour M. *Continental Divide: The Values and Institutions of the United States and Canada.* New York: Routledge, 1990.

——. *The First New Nation: The United States in Historical and Comparative Perspective.* New York: W. W. Norton, 1979.

Lisette, Gabriel. *Le Combat du Rassemblement Démocratique Africain pour la Décolonisation Pacifique de l'Afrique Noire.* Dakar: Présence Africaine, 1983.

Listowel, Judith. *The Making of Tanganyika.* London: Chatto & Windus, 1965.

Livingstone, David, and Charles Livingstone. *Narrative of an Expedition to the Zambesi and Its Tributaries.* New York: Harper & Row, 1866.

Livingstone, W. P. *Laws of Livingstonia: A Narrative of Missionary Adventure and Achievement.* London: Hodder & Stoughton, 1921.

Lloyd, P. C., ed. *The New Elites of Tropical Africa.* London: Oxford University Press, 1966.

Lockhart, James M. "Encomienda and Hacienda: The Evolution of the Great Estate in the Spanish Indies." *Hispanic American Historical Review* 49 (August 1969): 411–29.

——. *Spanish Peru, 1532–1560: A Social History.* 2d ed. Madison: University of Wisconsin Press, 1994.

——, and Stuart Schwartz. *Early Latin America: A History of Colonial Spanish America and Brazil.* Cambridge: Cambridge University Press, 1983.

Lonsdale, John. "Coping with the Contradictions: The Development of the Colonial State in Kenya, 1895–1914." *Journal of African History* 20:4 (1979): 487–505.

Louis, Wm. Roger. *The British Empire in the Middle East, 1945–51.* Oxford: Clarendon Press, 1984.

——. *Imperialism at Bay: The United States and the Decolonization of the British Empire, 1941–1945.* Oxford: Clarendon Press, 1977.

——, and Robert Stookey, eds. *The End of the Palestine Mandate.* London: Taurus, 1986.

Loveman, Brian. *Chile: The Legacy of Hispanic Capitalism.* 2d ed. New York: Oxford University Press, 1988.

Lovett, Richard. *The History of the London Missionary Society, 1795–1895.* 2 vols. London: H. Frowde, 1899.

Low, D. A. *Eclipse of Empire.* Cambridge: Cambridge University Press, 1990.

——. *Lion Rampant: Essays in the Study of British Imperialism.* London: Frank Cass, 1973.

——, ed. *Congress and the Raj: Facets of the Indian Struggle, 1917–47.* Columbia, Mo.: South Asia Books, 1977.

Lugard, Frederick D. *The Dual Mandate in Tropical Africa.* Edinburgh: W. Blackwood & Sons, 1922.

Lumumba, Patrice. *Congo, My Country.* New York: Praeger, 1962.

——. *La Pensée Politique de Patrice Lumumba.* Brussels: Présence Africaine, 1963.

Lustick, Ian. "History, Historiography, and Political Science: Multiple Historical Records and the Problem of Selection Bias." *American Political Science Review* 90:3 (September 1996): 605–18.

Lutz, Jessie. *China and the Christian Colleges, 1850–1950.* Ithaca: Cornell University Press, 1950.

Lynch, John. *The Spanish American Revolutions, 1808–26.* New York: W. W. Norton, 1973.

Lynn, John, ed. *Tools of War: Instruments, Ideas, and Institutions of Warfare, 1445–1871.* Urbana: University of Illinois Press, 1990.

Maalouf, Amir. *The Crusades Through Arab Eyes.* Translated by Joe Rothschild. New York: Schocken Books, 1985.

McAlister, Lyle. *Spain and Portugal in the New World, 1492–1700.* Oxford: Oxford University Press, 1984.

McClintock, Anne. *Imperial Leather: Race, Gender, and Sexuality in the Colonial Context.* New York: Routledge, 1994.

McCoy, Alfred E., ed. *Southeast Asia under Japanese Occupation.* New Haven: Yale University Southeast Asian Studies, 1980.

McCully, Bruce. *English Education and the Origins of Indian Nationalism.* New York: Columbia University Press, 1940.

Mackay, David L. *In the Wake of Cook: Exploration, Science, and Empire, 1780–1801*. London: Croom Helm, 1985.

MacKenzie, John M., ed. *Imperialism and Popular Culture*. Manchester: Manchester University Press, 1986.

MacLachlan, Colin M. *Spain's Empire in the New World: The Role of Ideas in Institutional and Social Change*. Berkeley: University of California Press, 1988.

——, and Jaime E. Rodriguez O. *The Forging of the Cosmic Race: A Reinterpretation of Colonial Mexico*. Berkeley: University of California Press, 1980.

McLane, John R. *Indian Nationalism and the Early Congress*. Princeton: Princeton University Press, 1977.

MacLeod, Roy, and Philip Rehbock, eds. *Nature in Its Greatest Extent: Western Science in the Pacific*. Honolulu: University of Hawaii Press, 1985.

McLoughlin, William G. *Cherokee Renascence in the New Republic, 1794–1833*. Princeton: Princeton University Press, 1986.

McMahon, Robert J. *Colonialism and Cold War: The United States and the Struggle for Indonesian Independence*. Ithaca: Cornell University Press, 1981.

McNeill, William H. *Plagues and Peoples*. Garden City: Anchor Press/Doubleday, 1976.

——. *The Pursuit of Power: Technology, Armed Force, and Society since A.D. 1000*. Chicago: University of Chicago Press, 1982.

——. *The Shape of European History*. New York: Oxford University Press, 1974.

Maier, Pauline. *From Resistance to Revolution: Colonial Radicals and the Development of American Opposition to Britain, 1765–1776*. New York: Vintage Books, 1974.

Makdisi, George. *The Rise of Colleges: Institutions of Learning in Islam and the West*. Edinburgh: Edinburgh University Press, 1981.

Mamdani, Mahmood. *Citizen and Subject: Contemporary Africa and the Legacy of Late Colonialism*. Princeton: Princeton University Press, 1996.

Manganyi, N. Chabani. *Looking Through the Keyhole: Dissenting Essays on the Black Experience*. Johannesburg: Ravan Press, 1981.

Mann, Kristin, and Richard Roberts, eds. *Law in Colonial Africa*. Portsmouth: Heinemann, 1991.

Mann, Michael. *The Sources of Social Power*. Vols. 1 (to 1760) and 2 (1760–1914). Cambridge: Cambridge University Press, 1986–93.

Manning, Patrick. "Analyzing the Costs and Benefits of Colonialism." *American Economic History Review* 1:2 (Fall 1974): 15–22.

——. *Francophone Sub-Saharan Africa, 1880–1985*. Cambridge: Cambridge University Press, 1988.

——. *Slavery, Colonialism, and Economic Growth in Dahomey, 1640–1960*. Cambridge: Cambridge University Press, 1982.

Mannoni, O. *Prospero and Caliban: The Psychology of Colonization*. Translated by Pamela Powesland. 2d ed. New York: Praeger, 1964.

Mansergh, Nicholas. *The Commonwealth Experience*. London: Weidenfeld & Nicolson, 1969.

——. *The Commonwealth Experience*. Rev. ed. Vol. 2. Toronto: University of Toronto Press, 1982.

——, and E. W. R. Lumby (later, Penderel Moon), eds. *Constitutional Relations Between Britain and India: The Transfer of Power*. 12 vols. London: HMSO, 1970–83.

Marcum, John. *The Angolan Revolution*. 2 vols. Cambridge: MIT Press, 1969–78.

Marcus, Harold G. *The Life and Times of Menelik II: Ethiopia, 1844–1913*. Oxford: Clarendon Press, 1975.

Markovits, Claude. *Indian Business and Nationalist Politics, 1931–1939: The Indigenous Capitalist Class and the Rise of the Congress Party*. Cambridge: Cambridge University Press, 1985.

Marks, Steven G. *Road to Power: The Trans-Siberian Railroad and the Colonization of Asian Russia, 1850–1917*. Ithaca: Cornell University Press, 1992.

Marlowe, John. *Cromer in Egypt*. London: Elek Books, 1970.

Marr, David G. *Vietnamese Anticolonialism, 1885–1925*. Berkeley: University of California Press, 1971.

——. *Vietnamese Traditions on Trial, 1920–1945*. Berkeley: University of California Press, 1981.

Marshall, Bruce. *The French Colonial Myth and Constitution-Making in the Fourth Republic*. New Haven: Yale University Press, 1973.

Marshall, T. H. *Class, Citizenship, and Social Development*. Westport: Greenwood Press, 1973.

Marsot, Afaf L. *A Short History of Modern Egypt*. Cambridge: Cambridge University Press, 1985.

Martin, Calvin. *Keepers of the Game: Indian-Animal Relationships and the Fur Trade*. Berkeley: University of California Press, 1978.

Martin, David, and Phyllis Johnson. *The Struggle for Zimbabwe: The Chimurenga War*. Harare: Zimbabwe Publishing House, 1981.

Marx, Anthony W. *Making Race and Nation: A Comparison of the United States, South Africa, and Brazil*. Cambridge: Cambridge University Press, 1998.

Masefield, G. B. *A History of the Colonial Agricultural Service*. Oxford: Clarendon Press, 1972.

Mason, Philip. *A Matter of Honour: An Account of the Indian Army, Its Officers and Men*. London: Jonathan Cape, 1974.

—— (Philip Woodruff, pseud.). *The Men Who Ruled India*. 2 vols. New York: St. Martin's Press, 1954.

Massachusetts Historical Society. *Winthrop Papers*. 2 vols. Boston: MHA, 1929–31.

Matossian, Mary. "Ideologies of Delayed Industrialization." *Economic Development and Cultural Change* 6 (April 1958): 217–28.

Mauny, Raymond. *Les Navigations Médiévales sur les Côtes Sahariennes Antérieures à la Découverte Portugaies [sic] (1434)*. Lisbon: Centro de Estudos Historicos Ultramarinas, 1960.

Maylam, Paul. *Rhodes, the Tswana, and the British: Colonialism, Collaboration, and Conflict in the Bechuanaland Protectorate, 1885–1899*. Westport: Greenwood Press, 1980.

Mazrui, Ali A. *The African Condition*. Cambridge: Cambridge University Press, 1980.

——, and Michael Tidy. *Nationalism and New States in Africa from about 1935 to the Present*. London: Heinemann, 1984.

——. *The Political Sociology of the English Language: An African Perspective*. The Hague: Mouton, 1975.

Meilink-Roelofsz, M. A. P. *Asian Trade and European Influence in the Indonesian Archipelago between 1500 and about 1630*. The Hague: M. Nijhoff, 1962.

Memmi, Albert. *The Colonizer and the Colonized*. Boston: Beacon Press, 1967.

Menon, V. P. *The Transfer of Power in India*. Princeton: Princeton University Press, 1957.

Merritt, Richard. *Symbols of American Community, 1735–1775*. New Haven: Yale University Press, 1966.

Merton, Reginald. *Cardinal Ximenes and the Making of Spain*. London: Kegan Paul, 1934.

Metcalf, Thomas. *The Aftermath of Revolt: India, 1857–1870*. Princeton: Princeton University Press, 1964.

Meyer, Karl, and Shareen B. Brysac. *Tournament of Shadows: The Great Game and the Race for Empire in Central Asia*. Washington, D.C.: Counterpart, 1999.

Meyers, Ramon, and Mark Peattie, eds. *The Japanese Colonial Empire, 1895–1945*. Princeton: Princeton University Press, 1984.

Miège, Jean-Louis. *Expansion Européenne et Décolonisation de 1870 à Nos Jours*. Paris: Presses Universitaires de France, 1973.

——. *Indentured Labour in the Indian Ocean and the Particular Case of Mauritius*. Leiden: Center for the History of European Expansion, No. 5, 1986.

——. *Le Maroc et l'Europe (1830–1894)*. Vol. 3. Paris: Presses Universitaires de France, 1962.

Milgrom, Paul, and John Roberts. *Economics, Organization, and Management*. Englewood Cliffs: Prentice-Hall, 1992.

Mill, John Stuart. *A System of Logic, Ratiocinative and Inductive*. 8th ed. New York: Harper & Brothers, 1894.

Miller, Charles. *Battle for the Bundu: The First World War in East Africa*. New York: Macmillan, 1974.

Miller, Joseph. *Way of Death: Merchant Capitalism and the Angolan Slave Trade, 1730–1830*. Madison: University of Wisconsin Press, 1988.

Miller, Stuart C. *"Benevolent Assimilation": The American Conquest of the Philippines, 1899–1903*. New Haven: Yale University Press, 1982.

Millin, Sarah G. *Rhodes*. Rev. ed. London: Chatto & Windus, 1952.

Mintz, Sidney W. *Sweetness and Power: The Place of Sugar in Modern History*. New York: Viking Penguin, 1985.

Misra, B. B. *The Bureaucracy in India: An Historical Analysis of Development up to 1947*. Delhi: Oxford University Press, 1977.

Mitchell, B. R. *International Historical Statistics: Africa, Asia, and Oceania, 1750–1988*. New York: Stockton Press, 1995.

Mitchell, J. Clyde. *The Kalela Dance*. Manchester: Manchester University Press, 1956.

Mitchell, Timothy. *Colonising Egypt*. Cambridge: Cambridge University Press, 1988.

Moffat, Abbot L. *Mongkut, the King of Siam*. Ithaca: Cornell University Press, 1961.

Mommsen, Wolfgang J. *Theories of Imperialism*. Translated by P. S. Falla. Chicago: University of Chicago Press, 1980.

Monroe, Elizabeth. *Britain's Moment in the Middle East, 1914–1956*. London: Chatto & Windus, 1963.

Moon, Parker T. *Imperialism and World Politics*. New York: Macmillan, 1926.

Moon, Penderel. *The British Conquest and Dominion of India*. London: Duckworth, 1989.

deMoor, J. A., and H. L. Wesseling, eds. *Imperialism and War: Essays on Colonial Wars in Asia and Africa*. Leiden: Leiden University Press, 1989.

Moore, Brian. *Black Robe*. Harmondsworth: Penguin, 1987.

Moore, Christopher. *The Loyalists: Revolution, Exile, Settlement*. Toronto: Macmillan, 1984.

Moore, R. J. *The Crisis of Indian Unity, 1917–1940*. Oxford: Clarendon Press, 1974.

——. *Escape from Empire: The Attlee Government and the Indian Problem*. Oxford: Clarendon Press, 1983.

Moorehead, Alan. *The Fatal Impact: An Account of the Invasion of the South Pacific, 1767–1840*. Harmondsworth: Penguin, 1968.

Morgan, D. J. *The Official History of Colonial Development*. 5 vols. London: Macmillan, 1980.

Morgenthau, Ruth Schachter. *Political Parties in French-Speaking West Africa*. Oxford: Clarendon Press, 1964.

Morison, Samuel Eliot. *The Oxford History of the American People*. New York: Oxford University Press, 1965.

Morris, James. *Heaven's Command: An Imperial Progress*. Harmondsworth: Penguin, 1979.

Morris, Jan. *Stones of Empire: The Buildings of the Raj*. Oxford: Oxford University Press, 1983.

Morris-Jones, W. H., and Georges Fischer, eds. *Decolonisation and After: The British and French Experience*. London: F. Cass, 1980.

Morrison, Donald G., Robert C. Mitchell, and John N. Paden. *Black Africa: A Comparative Handbook*. 2d ed. New York: Paragon; Irvington Publishers, 1989.

Mortimer, Robert A. *The Third World Coalition in International Politics*. 2d ed. Boulder: Westview Press, 1984.

Mudimbe, V. Y. *The Idea of Africa*. Bloomington: Indiana University Press, 1994.

Mulford, David. *Zambia: The Politics of Independence, 1957–1964*. London: Oxford University Press, 1967.

Multatuli (pseud.) [Edward Douwes Dekker]. *Max Havelaar, or the Coffee Auctions of the Dutch Trading Company*. Edited by Roy Edwards. Leyden: Sijthoff, 1967.

Murdoch, William W. *The Poverty of Nations: The Political Economy of Hunger and Population*. Baltimore: Johns Hopkins University Press, 1980.

Murphy, Philip. *Party Politics and Decolonization: The Conservative Party and British Colonial Policy in Tropical Africa, 1951–1964*. New York: Oxford University Press, 1995.

Murphy, Robert D. *Diplomat Among Warriors*. Garden City: Doubleday, 1964.

Murray, A. Victor. *The School in the Bush*. London: Longmans, Green, 1929.

Murray, Martin J. *The Development of Capitalism in Colonial Indochina (1870–1940)*. Berkeley: University of California Press, 1980.

Mutibwa, Phares. *The Malagasy and the Europeans*. Atlantic Highlands: Humanities Press, 1974.

Mutiso, Gideon-Cyrus, and S. W. Rohio, eds. *Readings in African Political Thought*. London: Heinemann, 1975.

Myers, Ramon H., and Mark Peattie, eds. *The Japanese Colonial Empire, 1895–1945*. Princeton: Princeton University Press, 1984.

Naipaul, V. S. *A House for Mr. Biswas*. London: Deutsch, 1964.

Nanda, Bal Ram. *Gandhi: Pan-Islamism, Imperialism, and Nationalism in India*. Bombay: Oxford University Press, 1989.

Nandy, Ashis. *The Intimate Enemy: Loss and Recovery of Self under Colonialism*. Delhi: Oxford University Press, 1983.

Naroun, Amar. *Ferhat Abbas, Ou les Chemins de la Souveraineté*. Paris: Denoel, 1961.

Nash, Gary B. *Red, White, and Black: The Peoples of Early America*. 2d ed. Englewood Cliffs: Prentice-Hall, 1982.

Needham, Joseph. *The Grand Titration: Science and Society in East and West*. Toronto: University of Toronto Press, 1969.

Nehru, Jawaharlal. *The Discovery of India*. 4th ed. London: Meridian Books, 1960.

——. *India's Foreign Policy: Selected Speeches, September 1946 to April 1961*. Delhi: Government of India, Ministry of Information and Broadcasting, 1961.

——. *Toward Freedom: The Autobiography of Jawaharlal Nehru*. Boston: Beacon Press, 1958.

——. *Nehru, The First Sixty Years*. Edited by Dorothy Norman. New York: John Day, 1965.

Neill, Stephen. *Colonialism and Christian Missions*. New York: McGraw-Hill, 1966.

Newitt, Malyn. *Portugal in Africa: The Last Hundred Years*. London: Hurst, 1981.

Newman, Peter C. *Company of Adventurers: The Story of the Hudson's Bay Company*. Vol. 1. Harmondsworth: Penguin, 1985.

Nigeria, Western Region. *Proposals for an Education Policy*. Ibadan: Government Printer, 1952.

Nkrumah, Kwame. *Ghana: The Autobiography of Kwame Nkrumah*. London: Nelson & Sons, 1957.

——. *I Speak of Freedom: A Statement of African Ideology*. New York: Praeger, 1961.

——. *Neo-Colonialism, the Last Stage of Imperialism*. London: Nelson, 1965.

Nonini, Donald. *British Colonial Rule and the Resistance of the Malay Peasantry, 1900–1957*. New Haven: Yale University Southeast Asian Studies, 1992.

North, Douglass C. *Institutions, Institutional Change, and Economic Performance*. Cambridge: Cambridge University Press, 1990.

——, and Robert P. Thomas. *The Rise of the Western World: A New Economic History*. Cambridge: Cambridge University Press, 1973.

Nyerere, Julius K. *Freedom and Unity; Uhuru na Umoja: A Selection from Writings and Speeches, 1962–65*. London: Oxford University Press, 1967.

Nzemeke, Alexander. *British Imperialism and African Response: The Niger Valley, 1851–1905*. Paderborn: Schoningh, 1982.

O'Brien, Patrick. "European Economic Development: The Contribution of the Periphery." *Economic History Review*, 2d ser., 35 (1982): 1–18.

O'Donnell, J. Dean. *Lavigerie in Tunisia: The Interplay of Imperialist and Missionary*. Athens: University of Georgia Press, 1979.

Ohadike, Don C. *The Ekumeku Movement: Western Igbo Resistance to the British Conquest of Nigeria, 1883–1914*. Athens: Ohio University Press, 1991.

O'Hanlon, Rosalind, and David Washbrook. "After Orientalism: Culture, Criticism, and Politics in the Third World." *Comparative Studies in Society and History* 34:1 (January 1992): 141–67.

Oliver, Roland. *The Missionary Factor in East Africa*. London: Longmans, Green, 1952.

——, and Anthony Atmore. *The African Middle Ages, 1400–1800*. Cambridge: Cambridge University Press, 1981.

Ollenburger, Jane C., and Helen Moore. *A Sociology of Women: The Intersection of Patriarchy, Capitalism, and Colonization*. Englewood Cliffs: Prentice-Hall, 1991.

Olusanya, Gabriel O. *The West African Students' Union and the Politics of Decolonisation, 1925–1948*. Ibadan: Daystar Press, 1982.

O'Phelan Godoy, Scarlett. *Rebellions and Revolts in Eighteenth-Century Peru and Upper Peru*. Koln: Bohlau, 1985.

Ortiz, Roxanne D. *Indians of the Americas: Human Rights and Self-Determination*. London: Praeger, 1984.

Orwell, George. *Burmese Days*. London: V. Golancz, 1935.

Osborne, Milton E. *The French Presence in Cochinchina and Cambodia; Rule and Response (1859–1905)*. Ithaca: Cornell University Press, 1969.

Osterhammel, Jurgen. *Colonialism: A Theoretical Overview*. Translated by Shelley Frisch. Princeton: Markus Wiener, 1997.

Osuntokun, Akinjide. *Nigeria in the First World War*. Atlantic Highlands: Humanities Press, 1979.

Owen, E. R. J., and Robert Sutcliffe, eds. *Studies in the Theory of Imperialism*. London: Longman, 1972.

Pagden, Anthony. *Lords of All the World: Ideologies of Empire in Spain, Britain, and France, c. 1500–c. 1800*. New Haven: Yale University Press, 1995.

Pakenham, Thomas. *The Scramble for Africa, 1876–1912*. New York: Random House, 1991.

Palmer, R. R. *The Age of the Democratic Revolution: A Political History of Europe and America, 1760–1800*. Princeton: Princeton University Press, 1959.

Pandey, B. N., ed. *The Indian Nationalist Movement, 1885–1947: Select Documents*. New York: St. Martin's Press, 1979.

Panikkar, K. M. *Asia and Western Dominance*. 2d ed. London: George Allen & Unwin, 1959.

Parker, Geoffrey. *The Military Revolution: Military Innovation and the Rise of the West, 1500–1800*. Cambridge: Cambridge University Press, 1988.

Parker, Joseph I. *Directory of World Missions*. New York: International Missionary Council, 1938.

Parry, J. H. *The Discovery of the Sea*. Berkeley: University of California Press, 1981.

——. *The Establishment of the European Hegemony: 1415–1715*. 3d ed., rev. New York: Harper & Row, 1966.

——. *The Spanish Seaborne Empire*. New York: A. Knopf, 1966.

Patterson, Orlando. *The Sociology of Slavery: An Analysis of the Origins, Development, and Structure of Negro Slave Society in Jamaica*. London: MacGibbon & Kee, 1967.

Pearce, R. D. *The Turning Point in Africa: British Colonial Policy, 1938–48*. London: F. Cass, 1982.

Pearce, Roy H. *The Savages of America: A Study of the Indian and the Idea of Civilization*. Baltimore: Johns Hopkins University Press, 1953.

Pearson, M. N. *The Portuguese in India*. Cambridge: Cambridge University Press, 1987.

Peattie, Mark R. *Nan'yo: The Rise and Fall of the Japanese in Micronesia, 1885–1945*. Honolulu: University of Hawaii Press, 1988.

Peires, J. B. *The Dead Will Arise: Nongqawuse and the Great Xhosa Cattle-Killing Movement of 1856–7*. Bloomington: Indiana University Press, 1989.

Penders, C. L. M., ed. *Indonesia: Selected Documents on Colonialism and Nationalism, 1830–1942*. St. Lucia: University of Queensland Press, 1977.

Perham, Margery. *The Colonial Reckoning: The End of Imperial Rule in Africa in the Light of British Experience*. London: Collins, 1961.

——. *Native Administration in Nigeria*. London: Oxford University Press, 1937.

Perkins, Edwin J. *The Economy of Colonial America*. New York: Columbia University Press, 1980.

Perkins, Kenneth. *Qaids, Captains, and Colons*. New York: Africana, 1981.

Perrin, Noel. *Giving up the Gun: Japan's Reversion to the Sword, 1543–1879*. Boulder: Shambhala, 1980.

Persell, Stuart M. *The French Colonial Lobby, 1889–1938*. Stanford: Hoover Institution Press, 1983.

Phelan, John L. *The Millennial Kingdom of the Franciscans in the New World*. 2d rev. ed. Berkeley: University of California Press, 1970.

——. *The People and the King: The Communero Revolution in Colombia, 1781*. Madison: University of Wisconsin Press, 1978.

Phillips, J. R. S. *The Medieval Expansion of Europe*. 2d ed. Oxford: Oxford University Press, 1998.

Pim, Alan. *Colonial Agricultural Production: The Contribution Made by Native Peasants and by Foreign Enterprise*. London: Oxford University Press, 1946.

Pires, Tomé. *The Suma Oriental of Tomé Pires*. Series 2, Vols. 89, 90. London: Hakluyt Society, 1944.

Pitman, Emma. *Central Africa, Japan, and Fiji: A Story of Missionary Enterprise, Trials, and Triumphs*. London: Hodder & Stoughton, 1882.

Plaatje, Sol T. 1916. Reprint, *Native Life in South Africa*. Johannesburg: Ravan Press, 1982.

Plamenatz, John. *On Alien Rule and Self-Government*. London: Longmans, 1960.

Platt, D. C. M., and Guido diTella, eds. *Argentina, Australia, and Canada: Studies in Comparative Development, 1880–1965*. London: Macmillan, 1985.

Poggi, Gianfranco. *The Development of the Modern State: A Sociological Introduction*. Stanford: Stanford University Press, 1978.

Polanyi, Karl. *The Great Transformation: The Political and Economic Origins of Our Time*. Boston: Beacon Press, 1957.

Polo, Marco. *Travels of Marco Polo*. 5th ed. Edinburgh: Oliver & Boyd, 1847.

Porch, Douglas. *The Conquest of Morocco*. New York: Knopf, 1983.

494

Porter, Andrew N. *European Imperialism, 1860–1914*. Basingstoke: Macmillan, 1994.

———, ed. *Atlas of British Overseas Expansion*. New York: Simon & Schuster, 1991.

———, ed., *The Nineteenth Century* (*The Oxford History of the British Empire*, Vol. 3). Oxford: Oxford University Press, 1999.

———, and A. J. Stockwell. *British Imperial Policy and Decolonization, 1938–64*. Basingstoke: Macmillan, 1987.

Porter, Bernard. *Britain, Europe, and the World, 1850–1986: Delusions of Grandeur*. 2d ed. London: Allen & Unwin, 1987.

Porter, Bruce D. *War and the Rise of the State: The Military Foundation of Modern Politics*. New York: Free Press, 1994.

Postma, Johannes. *The Dutch in the Atlantic Slave Trade, 1600–1815*. Cambridge: Cambridge University Press, 1990.

Prakash, Gyan. "Can the 'Subaltern' Ride? A Reply to O'Hanlon and Washbrook." *Comparative Studies in Society and History* 34:1 (January 1992): 168–84.

———. "Writing Post-Orientalist Histories of the Third World: Perspectives from Indian Historiography." *Comparative Studies in Society and History* 32:2 (April 1990): 383–408.

———, ed. *After Colonialism: Imperial Histories and Postcolonial Displacements*. Princeton: Princeton University Press, 1995.

Prakash, Om. *The Dutch East India Company and the Economy of Bengal, 1630–1720*. Princeton: Princeton University Press, 1985.

Pratt, John W., and Richard J. Zeckhauser. *Principals and Agents*. Boston: Harvard Business School Press, 1985.

Pratt, Mary Louise. *Imperial Eyes: Travel Writing and Transculturation*. London: Routledge, 1992.

Prescott, J. R. V. *Political Frontiers and Boundaries*. London: Allen & Unwin, 1987.

Price, A. Grenfell. *The Western Invasions of the Pacific and Its Continents: A Study of Moving Frontiers and Changing Landscapes, 1513–1958*. Oxford: Clarendon Press, 1963.

Price, Richard. *The Guiana Maroons: A Historical and Bibliographical Introduction*. Baltimore: Johns Hopkins University Press, 1976.

———, ed. *Maroon Societies: Rebel Slave Communities in the Americas*. 2d ed. Baltimore: Johns Hopkins University Press, 1979.

Priestley, Herbert I. *The Coming of the White Man, 1492–1848*. New York: Macmillan, 1929.

Prucha, Francis P. *The Great Father: The United States Government and the American Indians*. Lincoln: University of Nebraska Press, 1984.

Prunier, Gerard. *The Rwanda Crisis: History of a Genocide*. New York: Columbia University Press, 1995.

Przeworski, Adam, and Henry Teune. *The Logic of Comparative Social Enquiry*. New York: Wiley-Interscience, 1970.

Puckrein, Gary A. *Little England: Plantation Society and Anglo-Barbadian Politics, 1627–1700*. New York: New York University Press, 1984.

Rafael, Vicente. *Contracting Colonialism: Translation and Christian Conversion in Tagalog Society under Early Spanish Rule*. Ithaca: Cornell University Press, 1988.

Ragin, Charles C. *The Comparative Method: Moving Beyond Qualitative and Quantitative Strategies.* Berkeley: University of California Press, 1987.

Raleigh, (Sir) Walter. 1595. Reprint, *The Discoverie of the Large and Bewtiful Empire of Guiana.* Edited by V. T. Harlow. London: Argonaut Press, 1928.

Ralston, David B. *Importing the European Army: The Introduction of European Military Techniques and Institutions into the Extra-European World, 1600–1914.* Chicago: University of Chicago Press, 1990.

Ranger, Terence O. "Connections between 'Primary Resistance' Movements and Modern Mass Nationalism in East and Central Africa; Parts I and II." *Journal of African History* 9:3/4 (1968): 437–53, 631–41.

———. *The Invention of Tribalism in Zimbabwe.* Harare: Mambo Press, 1985.

———. *Peasant Consciousness and Guerrilla War in Zimbabwe.* London: James Currey, 1985.

———. *Revolt in Southern Rhodesia, 1896–7.* London: Heinemann, 1967.

———, and John Weller. *Themes in the Christian History of Central Africa.* Berkeley: University of California Press, 1975.

Ratcliffe, B. J., and Howard Elphinstone. *The New English-Swahili Phrase Book.* 1932. Reprint, Nairobi: Stationery & Office Supplies, 1966.

Ray, Rajat K., ed. *Entrepreneurship and Industry in India, 1800–1947.* Delhi: Oxford University Press, 1992.

Raychaudhuri, Tapan, and Irfan Habib, eds. *The Cambridge Economic History of India.* Vol. 2. Cambridge: Cambridge University Press, 1983.

Reid, Anthony. *Southeast Asia in the Age of Commerce, 1450–1680.* Vol. 1: *The Lands Below the Winds.* New Haven: Yale University Press, 1988.

———, ed. *Southeast Asia in the Early Modern Era: Trade, Power, and Belief.* Ithaca: Cornell University Press, 1993.

Rich, Paul B. *Race and Empire in British Politics.* Cambridge: Cambridge University Press, 1986.

Ricklefs, M. C. *A History of Modern Indonesia.* Bloomington: Indiana University Press, 1981.

Rippy, J. Fred. *British Investments in Latin America, 1822–1949.* Minneapolis: University of Minnesota Press, 1959.

Robb, Peter. "The British Cabinet and Indian Reform, 1917–1919." *Journal of Imperial and Commonwealth History* 4:3 (1976): 318–34.

———. *The Government of India and Reform: Policies toward Politics and the Constitution, 1916–1921.* Oxford: Oxford University Press, 1976.

Roberts, Andrew D., ed. *The Colonial Moment in Africa: Essays on the Movement of Minds and Materials, 1900–1940.* Cambridge: Cambridge University Press, 1990.

Roberts, Frederick (Lord). *Forty-One Years in India.* London: Macmillan, 1898.

Roberts, Richard L. *Warriors, Merchants, and Slaves: The State and the Economy in the Middle Niger Valley, 1700–1914.* Stanford: Stanford University Press, 1987.

Roberts, Stephen H. *The History of French Colonial Policy (1870–1925).* London: P. S. King & Son, 1929.

Robinson, Ronald, and John Gallagher, with Alice Denny. *Africa and the Victorians: The Official Mind of Imperialism.* New York: St. Martin's Press, 1961.

Rodinson, Maxime. *The Arabs*. Translated by Arthur Goldhammer. Chicago: University of Chicago Press, 1981.

Rodney, Walter. *How Europe Underdeveloped Africa*. London and Dar es Salaam: Bogle L'Ouverture and Tanzania Publishing House, 1972.

Roesdahl, Else. *The Vikings*. London: Penguin, 1992.

Ronen, Dov. *The Quest for Self-Determination*. New Haven: Yale University Press, 1979.

Rosberg, Carl, Jr., and John Nottingham. *The Myth of "Mau Mau": Nationalism in Kenya*. Stanford and New York: Hoover Institution and Praeger, 1966.

Rosen, Stephen J., and James R. Kurth, eds. *Testing Theories of Economic Imperialism*. Lexington: Lexington Books, 1974.

Rosenberg, Nathan, and L. E. Birdzell, Jr. *How the West Grew Rich: The Economic Transformation of the Industrial World*. New York: Basic Books, 1986.

Ross, Andrew. *John Philip (1775–1851): Missions, Race, and Politics in South Africa*. Aberdeen: Aberdeen University Press, 1986.

Rotberg, Robert I. *Christian Missionaries and the Creation of Northern Rhodesia, 1880–1924*. Princeton: Princeton University Press, 1965.

——. *The Rise of Nationalism in Central Africa*. Cambridge: Harvard University Press, 1965.

——, and Ali Mazrui, eds. *Protest and Power in Black Africa*. New York: Oxford University Press, 1970.

Rout, Leslie. *The African Experience in Spanish America*. Cambridge: Cambridge University Press, 1976.

Rowley, Henry. *Africa Unveiled*. London: Society for Promoting Christian Knowledge, 1876.

Royal Institute of International Affairs. *The Colonial Problem*. New York: Oxford University Press, 1937.

——. *The Problem of International Investment*. London: Oxford University Press, 1937.

Rubenson, Sven. *The Survival of Ethiopian Independence*. London: Heinemann Educational Books, 1976.

Rudin, Harry R. *Germans in the Cameroons, 1884–1914: A Case Study in Modern Imperialism*. New Haven: Yale University Press, 1938.

Rudolph, Lloyd I., and Suzanne H. Rudolph. *The Modernity of Tradition: Political Development in India*. Chicago: University of Chicago Press, 1967.

Ruedy, John. *Modern Algeria: The Origins and Development of a Nation*. Bloomington: Indiana University Press, 1992.

Runciman, Stephen. *The White Rajahs: A History of Sarawak from 1841 to 1946*. Cambridge: Cambridge University Press, 1960.

Ryckmans, Pierre. *Dominer Pour Servir*. Brussels: L'Edition Universelle, 1948.

Sahagún, Bernardino de. *The War of Conquest: How it Was Waged Here in Mexico; The Aztecs' Own Story as Given to Bernardino de Sahagún*. Translated by Arthur J. O. Anderson and Charles E. Dibble. Salt Lake City: University of Utah Press, 1978.

Sahlins, Marshall. *Islands of History*. Chicago: University of Chicago Press, 1985.

Said, Edward W. *Culture and Imperialism*. New York: Vintage Books, 1994.

——. *Orientalism*. New York: Random House, 1978.

Sale, Kirkpatrick. *The Conquest of Paradise: Christopher Columbus and the Columbian Legacy*. New York: A. Knopf, 1990.

Samkange, Stanlake. *The Origin of African Nationalism in Zimbabwe*. Harare: Harare Publishing House, 1985.

——. *On Trial for my Country: A Novel of Zimbabwe*. Oxford: Heinemann, 1966.

——. *Origins of Rhodesia*. London: Heinemann, 1968.

Sanderson, Lilian P., and Neville Sanderson. *Education, Religion, and Politics in Southern Sudan, 1899–1964*. London: Ithaca Press, 1981.

Sandhu, Kernial S. *Indians in Malaya: Some Aspects of Their Immigration and Settlement (1786–1957)*. London: Cambridge University Press, 1969.

Sariola, Sakari. *Power and Resistance: The Colonial Heritage in Latin America*. Ithaca: Cornell University Press, 1972.

Sarraut, Albert. *La Mise en Valeur des Colonies Françaises*. Paris: Payot, 1923.

Sartori, Giovanni. "Concept Misformation in Comparative Politics." *American Political Science Review* 64:4 (December 1970): 1033–53.

Scammell, G. V. *The First Imperial Age: European Overseas Expansion, c. 1400–1715*. London: Unwin Hyman, 1989.

——. *The World Encompassed: The First European Maritime Adventures, c. 800–1650*. Berkeley: University of California Press, 1981.

Schirokauer, Conrad. *Modern China and Japan: A Brief History*. New York: Harcourt Brace Jovanovich, 1978.

Schumpeter, Joseph A. 1919. Reprint, *Imperialism and Social Classes*. Translated by Heinz Norden. New York: A. M. Kelly, 1951.

Schurz, William L. *The Manila Galleon*. New York: E. P. Dutton, 1939.

Schwaller, John F. *Origins of Church Wealth in Mexico: Ecclesiastical Revenues and Church Finances, 1523–1600*. Albuquerque: University of New Mexico Press, 1985.

Schwartz, Stuart B. *Sugar Plantations in the Formation of Brazilian Society: Bahia, 1550–1835*. Cambridge: Cambridge University Press, 1985.

Scott, Andrew M. *The Revolution in Statecraft: Intervention in an Age of Interdependence*. Durham: Duke University Press, 1982.

Scott, James C. *The Moral Economy of the Peasant: Rebellion and Subsistence in Southeast Asia*. New Haven: Yale University Press, 1976.

——. *Weapons of the Weak: Everyday Forms of Peasant Resistance*. New Haven: Yale University Press, 1985.

Seed, Patricia. *Ceremonies of Possession in Europe's Conquest of the New World*. Cambridge: Cambridge University Press, 1995.

Semmel, Bernard. *Imperialism and Social Reform: English Social-Imperial Thought, 1895–1914*. Garden City: Doubleday, 1968.

Seton-Watson, Hugh. *Nations and States: An Enquiry into the Origins of Nations and the Politics of Nationalism*. Boulder: Westview Press, 1977.

Shannon, Thomas R. *An Introduction to the World-System Perspective*. Boulder: Westview, 1989.

Shepperson, George, and Thomas Price. *Independent African: John Chilembwe and the Origins, Setting, and Significance of the Nyasaland Native Rising of 1915*. Edinburgh: Edinburgh University Press, 1958.

Sherman, William L. *Forced Native Labor in Sixteenth-Century Central America*. Lincoln: University of Nebraska Press, 1979.

Sherwig, John W. *Guineas and Gunpowder: British Foreign Aid in the Wars with France, 1793–1815*. Cambridge: Harvard University Press, 1969.

Shiels, W. Eugene, S.J. *King and Church: The Rise and Fall of the Patronato Real*. Chicago: Loyola University Press, 1961.

Shils, Edward. "The Intellectuals in the Political Development of the New States." *World Politics* 12:3 (April 1960): 329–68.

Sigmund, Paul E., Jr. *The Ideologies of the Developing Nations*. New York: Praeger, 1963.

Simpson, Lesley B. *The Encomienda in New Spain: The Beginning of Spanish Mexico*. Rev. ed. Berkeley: University of California Press, 1982.

Sinclair, Keith. *A History of New Zealand*. Rev. ed. Harmondsworth: Penguin, 1969.

Singer, Marshall. *Weak States in a World of Powers: The Dynamics of International Relationships*. New York: Free Press, 1972.

Sisson, Richard, and Stanley Wolpert, eds. *Congress and Indian Nationalism: The Pre-Independence Phase*. Berkeley: University of California Press, 1988.

Sithole, Ndabaningi. *African Nationalism*. 2d ed. London: Oxford University Press, 1969.

Sjahrir, Soetan. *Out of Exile*. Translated by Charles Wolf, Jr. New York: John Day, 1949.

Sklar, Richard L. *Nigerian Political Parties: Power in an Emergent African Nation*. Princeton: Princeton University Press, 1963.

Skocpol, Theda. *States and Social Revolutions: A Comparative Analysis of France, Russia, and China*. Cambridge: Cambridge University Press, 1979.

Small, Melvin, and J. D. Singer, eds. *Resort to Arms: International and Civil Wars, 1816–1980*. Beverly Hills: Sage, 1982.

Smith, Adam. 1776. Reprint, *An Enquiry into the Nature and Causes of the Wealth of Nations*. New York: Random House, 1937.

Smith, Alan K. *Creating a World Economy: Merchant Capital, Colonialism, and World Trade, 1400–1825*. Boulder: Westview Press, 1991.

Smith, Anthony. *Theories of Nationalism*. 2d ed. New York: Holmes & Meier, 1983.

Smith, Daniel R. *The Influence of the Fabian Colonial Bureau on the Independence Movement in Tanganyika*. Athens: Ohio University Press, 1985.

Smith, M. G. *The Plural Society in the British West Indies*. Berkeley: University of California Press, 1965.

Smith, Ralph B. *Viet-Nam and the West*. London: Heinemann, 1968.

Smith, Tony. *The French Stake in Algeria, 1945–1962*. Ithaca: Cornell University Press, 1978.

——, ed. *The End of the European Empire: Decolonization after World War II*. Lexington: D. C. Heath, 1975.

Smith, William E. *We Must Run While They Walk: A Portrait of Africa's Julius Nyerere*. New York: Random House, 1971.

Snyder, Louis. *Varieties of Nationalism*. New York: Holt, Rinehart, & Winston, 1976.

Sorum, Paul C. *Intellectuals and Decolonization in France*. Chapel Hill: University of North Carolina Press, 1977.

Spalding, Karen. *Huarochiri: An Andean Society under Inca and Spanish Rule*. Stanford: Stanford University Press, 1984.

Spear, Percival. *A History of India*. Vol. 2, rev. ed. Harmondsworth: Penguin, 1973.

Stahl, Kathleen. *British and Soviet Colonial Systems*. London: Faber & Faber, 1951.

Stanley, Henry M. *The Autobiography of Henry Morton Stanley*. Boston: Houghton Mifflin, 1909.

Stannard, David E. *American Holocaust: The Conquest of the New World*. New York: Oxford University Press, 1992.

Stavrianos, L. S. *Global Rift: The Third World Comes of Age*. New York: William Morrow, 1981.

Stedman, John G. *Narrative of a Five Years' Expedition Against the Revolted Negroes of Suriname*. Edited by Richard and Sally Price. Baltimore: Johns Hopkins University Press, 1988.

Stedman, Stephen J. *Peacemaking in Civil War: International Mediation in Zimbabwe, 1974–1980*. Boulder: Lynne Rienner, 1991.

Steensgaard, Niels. *The Asian Trade Revolution of the Seventeenth Century: The East India Companies and the Decline of the Caravan Trade*. Chicago: University of Chicago Press, 1974.

Stein, Stanley J., and Barbara Stein. *The Colonial Heritage of Latin America: Essays on Economic Dependence in Perspective*. New York: Oxford University Press, 1970.

Steinberg, David J., ed. *In Search of Southeast Asia: A Modern History*. New York: Praeger, 1971.

Stengers, Jean. *Combien le Congo a-t-il Coûté à la Belgique?* Brussels: Academie Royale des Sciences Coloniales, 1957.

Stern, Steve J. *Peru's Indian Peoples and the Challenge of Spanish Conquest: Huamanga to 1640*. Madison: University of Wisconsin Press, 1982.

——, ed. *Resistance, Rebellion, and Consciousness in the Andean Peasant World, 18th to 20th Centuries*. Madison: University of Wisconsin Press, 1987.

Stock, Eugene. *The History of the Church Missionary Society*. London: C.M.S., 1899.

Stocking, George W., Jr., ed. *Colonial Situations: Essays on the Contextualization of Ethnographic Knowledge*. Madison: University of Wisconsin Press, 1991.

Stoecker, Helmuth, ed. *German Imperialism in Africa: From the Beginnings Until the Second World War*. Atlantic Highlands: Humanities Press, 1986.

Strang, David. "From Dependency to Sovereignty: An Event History Analysis of Decolonization, 1870–1987." *American Sociological Review* 55 (December 1990): 846–60.

——. "Global Patterns of Decolonization, 1500–1987." *International Studies Quarterly* 35:4 (December 1991): 429–54.

Sundkler, Bengt. *Bantu Prophets in South Africa*. 2d ed. London: Oxford University Press, 1961.

Susa, Nasim. *The Capitulatory Regime of Turkey, Its History, Origins, and Nature*. Baltimore: Johns Hopkins University Press, 1933.

Sutherland, Heather. *The Making of a Bureaucratic Elite: The Colonial Transformation of the Javanese Priyayi*. Singapore: Heinemann, 1979.

Swainson, Nicola. *The Development of Corporate Capitalism in Kenya, 1918–1977*. Berkeley: University of California Press, 1980.

Swan, Maureen. *Gandhi: The South African Experience*. Johannesburg: Ravan Press, 1985.

Symonds, Richard. *Oxford and Empire: The Last Lost Cause?* London: Macmillan, 1986.

Tarling, Nicholas. *Imperial Britain in South-East Asia*. Kuala Lumpur: Oxford University Press, 1975.

Taylor, A. J. P. *The Struggle for Mastery in Europe, 1848–1918*. Oxford: Clarendon Press, 1954.

Taylor, Alistair M. *Indonesian Independence and the United Nations*. Westport: Greenwood Press, 1975.

Taylor, William B. *Magistrates of the Sacred: Parish Priests and Indian Parishioners in Eighteenth-Century Mexico*. Stanford: Stanford University Press, 1996.

Teichova, Alice, et al., eds. *Multinational Enterprise in Historical Perspective*. New York: Cambridge University Press, 1986.

Temu, A. J. *British Protestant Missions*. London: Longman, 1972.

Teng, Ssu-yu, and John Fairbank. *China's Response to the West: A Documentary Survey, 1839–1923*. Cambridge: Harvard University Press, 1979.

Tetlock, Philip E., and Aaron Belkin, eds. *Counterfactual Thought Experiments in World Politics: Logical, Methodological, and Psychological Perspectives*. Princeton: Princeton University Press, 1996.

Tevoedjre, Albert. *L'Afrique Revoltée*. Paris: Présence Africaine, 1958.

Thomas, Hugh. *The Suez Affair*. Rev. ed. London: Weidenfeld & Nicolson, 1986.

Thomas, P. D. G. *British Politics and the Stamp Act Crisis: The First Phase of the American Revolution, 1763–1767*. Oxford: Clarendon Press, 1975.

Thompson, Leonard. *Survival in Two Worlds: Moshoeshoe of Lesotho, 1786–1868*. Oxford: Oxford University Press, 1975.

Thornton, A. P. *The Imperial Idea and Its Enemies: A Study in British Power*. 2d ed. London: Macmillan, 1985.

Thrupp, Sylvia L., ed. *Millennial Dreams in Action: Studies in Revolutionary Religious Movements*. New York: Schocken Books, 1970.

Thuku, Harry (with Kenneth King). *The Autobiography of Harry Thuku*. Nairobi: Oxford University Press, 1970.

Tilly, Charles. *Big Structures, Large Processes, Huge Comparisons*. New York: Russell Sage Foundation, 1984.

——. *Coercion, Capital, and European States, AD 990–1992*. Rev. ed. Cambridge, Mass: Basil Blackwell, 1992.

——, ed. *The Formation of National States in Western Europe*. Princeton: Princeton University Press, 1975.

Tinker, Hugh. *A New System of Slavery: The Export of Indian Labour Overseas, 1830–1920*. London: Oxford University Press, 1974.

——, ed., with A. Griffin. *Burma, The Struggle for Independence, 1944–1948: Documents from Official and Private Sources*. 2 vols. London: HMSO, 1983–84.

Todorov, Tzvetan. *The Conquest of America: The Question of the Other*. Translated by Richard Howard. New York: Harper & Row, 1984.

Tomich, Dale W. *Slavery in the Circuit of Sugar: Martinique and the World Economy, 1830–1948*. Baltimore: Johns Hopkins University Press, 1990.

Tomlinson, B. R. *The Indian National Congress and the Raj, 1929–1942: The Penultimate Phase*. London: Macmillan, 1976.

——. *The Political Economy of the Raj, 1914–1947: The Economics of Decolonization in India*. London: Macmillan, 1979.

Toussaint, Auguste. *Histoire de l'Ocean Indien*. Paris: Presses Universitaires de France, 1981.

Toynbee, Arnold J. *The World and the West*. New York: Oxford University Press, 1953.

Tracy, James D., ed. *The Rise of Merchant Empires: Long-Distance Trade in the Early Modern World, 1350–1750*. Cambridge: Cambridge University Press, 1990.

——, ed. *The Political Economy of Merchant Empires: State Power and World Trade, 1350–1750*. Cambridge: Cambridge University Press, 1991.

Triska, Jan, ed. *Dominant Powers and Subordinate States: The United States in Latin America and the Soviet Union in Eastern Europe*. Durham: Duke University Press, 1986.

Tucker, Robert, and David Hendrickson. *The Fall of the First British Empire: Origins of the American War of Independence*. Baltimore: Johns Hopkins University Press, 1982.

Turner, Frederick W. *Beyond Geography: The Western Spirit Against the Wilderness*. New York: Viking Press, 1980.

Urquhart, Brian. *Decolonization and World Peace*. Austin: University of Texas Press, 1989.

Utley, Robert M., and Wilcomb Washburn. *Indian Wars*. Boston: Houghton Mifflin, 1987.

Vail, Leroy, ed. *The Creation of Tribalism in Southern Africa*. Berkeley: University of California Press, 1991.

Van der Kraan, Alfons. *Lombok: Conquest, Colonization, and Underdevelopment, 1870–1940*. Singapore: Heinemann, 1980.

Vassall-Adams, Guy. *Rwanda: An Agenda for International Action*. Oxford: Oxfam, 1994.

Vaughn, Alden T. *New England Frontier: Puritans and Indians, 1620–1675*. Rev. ed. New York: Norton, 1979.

Véliz, Claudio. *The Centralist Tradition of Latin America*. Princeton: Princeton University Press, 1980.

Vella, Walter F. *The Impact of the West on Government in Thailand*. Berkeley: University of California Press, 1955.

Verrier, Anthony. *The Road to Zimbabwe, 1890–1980*. London: Jonathan Cape, 1986.

Von Laue, Theodore H. *The World Revolution of Westernization: The Twentieth Century in Global Perspective*. New York: Oxford University Press, 1987.

Wachtel, Nathan. *The Vision of the Vanquished: The Spanish Conquest of Peru Through Indian Eyes, 1530–1570*. Translated by Ben and Sian Reynolds. New York: Barnes & Noble, 1977.

Wagner, Henry R. *The Life and Writings of Bartolomé de Las Casas*. Albuquerque: University of New Mexico Press, 1967.

Waldman, Carl, and Alan Wexler. *Who Was Who in World Exploration*. New York: Facts on File, 1992.

Wallerstein, Immanuel. *Africa: The Politics of Independence*. New York: Vintage Books, 1961.

——. *The Capitalist World-Economy*. Cambridge: Cambridge University Press, 1979.

——. *The Modern World-System: Capitalist Agriculture and the Origins of the European World-Economy in the Sixteenth Century*. New York: Academic Press, 1976.

——. *The Modern World-System II: Mercantilism and the Consolidation of the European World-Economy, 1600–1750*. New York: Academic Press, 1980.

——, ed. *Social Change: The Colonial Situation*. New York: Wiley & Sons, 1966.

Ward, Barbara. *Five Ideas that Change the World*. New York: W. W. Norton, 1961.

Warren, Bill. *Imperialism: Pioneer of Capitalism*. Edited by John Sender. London: NLB, 1980.

Wasserstein, Bernard. *The British in Palestine: The Mandatory Government and the Arab-Jewish Conflict, 1917–1929*. London: Royal Historical Society, 1978.

Watt, W. Montgomery. *The Influence of Islam on Medieval Europe*. Edinburgh: Edinburgh University Press, 1972.

Watts, David. *The West Indies: Patterns of Development, Culture, and Environmental Change since 1492*. Cambridge: Cambridge University Press, 1987.

Webster, J. B. "The Bible and the Plough." *Journal of the Historical Society of Nigeria* 2:4 (December 1963): 418–34.

Weinstein, Brian. *Eboue*. New York: Oxford University Press, 1972.

Weiskel, Timothy C. *French Colonial Rule and the Baule Peoples: Resistance and Collaboration, 1889–1911*. Oxford: Clarendon Press, 1980.

Welch, Claude E., Jr. *Anatomy of Rebellion*. Albany: State University Press of New York, 1980.

Wesseling, H. L. *Divide and Rule: The Partition of Africa, 1880–1914*. Translated by Arnold J. Pomerans. Westport: Praeger, 1996.

——, ed. *Expansion and Reaction: Essays on European Expansion and Reaction in Asia and Africa*. Leiden: Leiden University Press, 1978.

Wesson, Robert G. *The Imperial Order*. Berkeley: University of California Press, 1967.

Whelan, Frederick C. *Edmund Burke and India: Political Morality and Empire*. Pittsburgh: University of Pittsburgh Press, 1996.

Whitaker, Arthur P. *The United States and the Independence of Latin America, 1800–1830*. Baltimore: Johns Hopkins University Press, 1941.

White, Dorothy S. *Black Africa and de Gaulle: From the French Empire to Independence*. University Park: Pennsylvania State University Press, 1979.

Wickberg, Edgar. *The Chinese in Philippine Life, 1850–1898*. New Haven: Yale University Press, 1965.

Wilford, John N. *The Mapmakers*. New York: Random House, 1981.

Wilkinson, John C. *Arabia's Frontiers: The Story of Britain's Boundary Drawing in the Desert*. New York: I. B. Tauris, 1991.

Williams, Eric. *Capitalism and Slavery*. London: Andre Deutsch, 1964.

Williams, Robert A., Jr. *The American Indian in Western Legal Thought: The Discourse of Conquest*. New York: Oxford University Press, 1990.

Wills, John E., Jr. *Pepper, Guns, and Parleys: The Dutch East India Company and China, 1622–1681*. Cambridge: Harvard University Press, 1974.

Wilmsen, Edwin N. *Land Filled with Flies: A Political Economy of the Kalahari.* Chicago: University of Chicago Press, 1989.

Wilson, James Q. *Bureaucracy.* New York: Basic Books, 1989.

Winius, George. *The Fatal History of Portuguese Ceylon.* Cambridge: Harvard University Press, 1971.

Winks, Robin. *British Imperialism: Gold, God, Glory.* New York: Holt, Rinehart and Winston, 1963.

Withey, Lynne. *Voyages of Discovery: Captain Cook and the Exploration of the Pacific.* New York: Morrow, 1987.

Wolf, Eric R. *Europe and the People Without History.* Berkeley: University of California Press, 1982.

——. *Peasant Wars of the Twentieth Century.* New York: Harper & Row, 1969.

Wolpert, Stanley A. *India.* Berkeley: University of California Press, 1991.

Woolman, David S. *Rebels in the Rif: Abd el Krim and the Rif Rebellion.* Stanford: Stanford University Press, 1968.

Worster, Donald, ed. *The Ends of the Earth: Perspectives on Modern Environmental History.* Cambridge: Cambridge University Press, 1988.

Wortman, Miles L. *Government and Society in Central America, 1680–1840.* New York: Columbia University Press, 1982.

Wright, Harrison M., ed. *The "New Imperialism": Analysis of Late Nineteenth-Century Expansion.* 2d ed. Lexington: D. C. Heath, 1976.

Wright, Quincy. *Mandates Under the League of Nations.* Chicago: University of Chicago Press, 1930.

Wylie, Diana S. "Critics of Colonial Policy in Kenya." M.Litt. thesis, University of Edinburgh, 1985.

Yapp, M. E. *The Making of the Modern Near East, 1792–1923.* London: Longman, 1987.

Yates, P. Lamartine. *Forty Years of World Trade.* New York: Macmillan, 1959.

Young, Crawford. *The African Colonial State in Comparative Perspective.* New Haven: Yale University Press, 1994.

——. *Politics in the Congo: Decolonization and Independence.* Princeton: Princeton University Press, 1965.

——. *The Politics of Cultural Pluralism.* Madison: University of Wisconsin Press, 1976.

Young, Robert. *White Mythologies: Writing History and the West.* London: Routledge, 1990.

Zartman, I. William. *The Politics of Trade Negotiations Between Africa and the European Economic Community.* Princeton: Princeton University Press, 1971.

Zimmerman, Arthur F. *Francisco de Toledo, Fifth Viceroy of Peru, 1569–1581.* Caldwell, Idaho: Caxton, 1938.

Zolberg, Aristide. "Origins of the Modern World System: A Missing Link." *World Politics* 33:2 (January 1987): 253–81.

Zuccarelli, François. *La Vie Politique Senegalaise: 1789–1940.* Paris: CHEAM, 1987.

Zurara, Gomes Eanes de. *Conquests and Discoveries of Henry the Navigator: Being the Chronicles of Azurara.* London: George Allen & Unwin, 1936.

INDEX

Abbas, Ferhat, 154
Abbasid caliphate, 202, 203
Abd al-Qadir, 154
Abd el Krim, 126
Abdul-Hafiz (sultan of Morocco), 82–83
Abyssinia. *See* Ethiopia
Adowa, Battle of, 85, 257
Afghanistan, 10, 11, 255
Africa: and European empires, 10, 11, 48, *88,*
  89, 91; and colonialism's impact, 16; and
  European influence, 22, 394; and phase 3,
  23, 81, 83, 84, 91, 98, 99, 106, 231; and theory of imperialism, 28; and trade, 48, 58,
  60, 180; and race relations, 55, 286; and
  Britain, 80, 139, 222; and commodities,
  97, 113; and private profit institutions,
  102; and missionaries, 103, 198, 231, 237,
  238; and phase 4, 114; and invention of
  tradition, 120; and pan-African ideology,
  128, 131, 369; and colonized, 129, 130, 364;
  and decolonization, 138, 140, 141, 142; and
  economics, 164–65; and international
  demonstration effect, 168, 169, 170, 172;
  and interstate competition, 210, 211; and
  Portugal, 213, 233; and Germany, 223; and
  exit option, 304; and education, 334, 335;
  and authoritarian government, 367. *See
  also* East Africa; North Africa; South
  Africa; Southwest Africa; West Africa
Afrikaners. *See* Boers (Afrikaners)
Albuquerque, Afonso d', 246, 247, 248
Alexander VI (pope), 52, 232
Algeciras Conference (1906), 88, 378
Algeria: and postwar crises, 41, 351; and
  phase 3, 81, 92; and France, 83, 127, 128,
  152–57, 216, 267, 284, 350, 365, 376, 377,
  388–89; and commodities, 102; and colonized, 126, 129; and decolonization, 141;

and violence, 152–57, 159; and international demonstration effects, 168, 169,
  358; and religious institutions, 234; and
  indigenous resistance, 258, 259, 273; and
  exit option, 304; and World War I, 349;
  and democracy versus authoritarian
  rule, 367
Al-Idrisi, Abu, 189
All-African People's Conference, 169
American Duties (Sugar) Act (1764), 64
Amerindians: and phase 1, 53, 54, 91; and
  phase 2, 72, 74; and phase 3, 85, 91; and
  Spain, 214; and religious institutions, 221,
  231, 232; and resistance, 257; and individuals' roles, 272; and exit option, 304
Amritsar massacre, 110, 128, 129, 155, 351,
  354, 357
Andrade, José Bonifacio de, 330, 331
Anglo-Boer War, 93
Anglo-Burmese War, 25, 81–82, 179
Angola: and Portugal, 72, 84, 148, 170, 214;
  and decolonization, 142, 147; and violence, 148, 159; and resistance, 257, 273;
  and democracy versus authoritarian
  rule, 367
Arab-speaking world: and maritime capacity, 29, 177–78, 181; geographic features
  of, 32, 184–85; and interstate systems, 35,
  213; and phase 1, 176; and trade, 180, 181,
  203; and western Europe, 183, 202–3, 205;
  and Islam, 199; and sectors, 202–3, 205,
  225, 242, 244–45, 247; and Malacca, 243,
  245, 246; and resistance, 257; and Ottoman Turks, 346, 349
Arciniegas, Germain, 191
Argentina, 65, 67, 91, 353
Asia: and country names, 16; and European
  influence, 22, 394; and phase 3, 23, 81,

DATE DUE

			Printed in USA

HIGHSMITH #45230